PEARSON
Phonics
LEVEL B

ELWELL • MURRAY • KUCIA

PEARSON

Acknowledgments appear on pages 260–261, which constitute an extension of this copyright page.

ISBN-13: 978-1-4284-3100-
ISBN-10: 1-4284-3100-
14 1

Contents

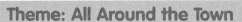

UNIT 2

Short Vowels
Theme: At Work, At Play

UNIT 3

Long Vowels
Theme: On Wings and Wheels

Compounds, Words with le, Hard and Soft c and g, Blends, Digraphs, Y as a Vowel, R-Controlled Vowels

Theme: The World Outside

Contractions, Endings, Suffixes

Theme: Blasting Off

Vowel Pairs, Vowel Digraphs, Diphthongs

Theme: Dinosaur Days

Prefixes, Synonyms, Antonyms, Homonyms

Theme: Make It, Bake It

UNIT 1

Initial, Medial, and Final Consonants

THEME: ALL AROUND THE TOWN

CONTENTS

Student Performance Objectives

In Unit 1, children will review the twenty-one consonants and their sounds within the context of the theme "All Around the Town." As children review consonant letter-sound associations, they will be able to

▶ Associate each of the consonants with the sound it stands for in the initial, medial, and final positions

▶ Distinguish among the consonant sounds in any position

Assessment Options

In Unit 1, assess children's ability to read and write words with initial, medial, and final consonants. Use the Unit Pretest and Posttest for formal assessment. For ongoing informal assessment you may wish to use children's work on the Review pages, Take-Home Books, and Unit Checkups. You may also want to encourage children to evaluate their own work and to participate in setting goals for their own learning.

ESL/ELL To ensure that reading direction lines and identifying picture clues by their English names are not factors in children's ability to complete the Unit 1 Pretest and Posttest successfully, read the directions aloud to the group, model the task, and say each of the items aloud as children move from item to item in the tests. For additional support for English language learners, see page 5j.

FORMAL ASSESSMENT

Use the Unit 1 Pretest on pages 5e–5f to help assess a child's knowledge at the beginning of the unit and to plan instruction.

ESL/ELL Before administering the Pretest, bring to class pictures of the items shown on pages 5e–5f. Have children name them to ensure that they know the words. Ask children to identify the initial, middle, and final sounds of each picture name.

Use the Unit 1 Posttest on pages 5g–5h to help assess mastery of unit objectives and to plan for reteaching, if necessary.

ESL/ELL Assess children's ability to interpret directions. If necessary, read them aloud and model how the pages are to be completed.

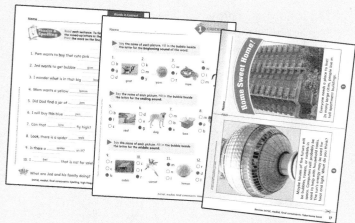

INFORMAL ASSESSMENT

Use the Review pages, Unit Checkup, and Take-Home Books in the student book to provide an effective means of evaluating children's performance.

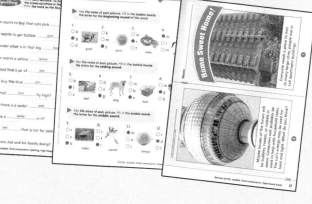

Unit 1 Skills	Review pages	Checkups	Take-Home Books
Initial consonants	15–16	19–20	17–18
Medial consonants	15–16	19–20	17–18
Final consonants	15–16	19–20	17–18

STUDENT PROGRESS CHECKLIST

Use the checklist on page 5i to record children's progress. You may want to cut the sections apart to place each child's checklist in his or her portfolio.

PORTFOLIO ASSESSMENT

This logo appears throughout the teaching plans. It signals opportunities for collecting a student's work for individual portfolios. You may also want to include the Pretest and Posttest, the Review pages, the Unit Checkup, Phonics & Spelling, and Phonics & Writing pages.

PHONEMIC AWARENESS AND PHONICS ASSESSMENT

Use PAPA to obtain an itemized analysis of children's decoding skills.

PAPA Skills	MCP Phonics Lessons in Unit 1
Beginning consonant sounds	Lessons 1, 3, 5
Ending consonant sounds	Lessons 2, 3, 5
Deleting sounds	Lessons 1–4

Pretest and Posttest

DIRECTIONS

To help you assess children's progress in learning Unit 1 skills, tests are available on pages 5e–5h.

Administer the Pretest before children begin the unit. The results of the Pretest will help you identify each child's strengths and needs in advance, allowing you to structure lesson plans to meet individual needs. Administer the Posttest to assess children's overall mastery of skills taught in the unit and to identify specific areas that will require reteaching.

ESL/ELL Take note that the objective of both the Unit 1 Pretest and Posttest is identification of initial, medial, and final consonant sounds, not vocabulary recognition, with which children may be unfamiliar. To ensure that vocabulary comprehension does not interfere with sound recognition, name each of the items aloud as children move from item to item in the tests.

PERFORMANCE ASSESSMENT PROFILE

The following chart will help you identify specific skills as they appear on the tests and will enable you to identify and record specific information about an individual's or the class's performance on the tests.

Depending on the results of each test, refer to the Reteaching column for lesson-plan pages where you can find activities that will be useful for meeting individual needs or for daily phonics practice.

Answer Keys

Unit 1 Pretest, page 5e (BLM 1)

1. w	9. n
2. r	10. d
3. f	11. x
4. c	12. t
5. s	13. m
6. b	14. p
7. d	15. s
8. m	16. g

Unit 1 Pretest, page 5f (BLM 2)

17. m	23. v
18. b	24. l
19. t	25. p, g
20. d	26. t, n
21. g	27. m, p
22. n	28. f, n

Unit 1 Posttest, page 5g (BLM 3)

1. w	9. n
2. r	10. d
3. f	11. x
4. c	12. t
5. s	13. m
6. b	14. p
7. d	15. l
8. m	16. g

Unit 1 Posttest, page 5h (BLM 4)

17. m	23. r
18. b	24. l
19. t	25. h, t
20. d	26. p, n
21. g	27. p, t
22. x	28. l, g

Performance Assessment Profile

Skill	Pretest Questions	Posttest Questions	Reteaching	
			Focus on All Learners	**Daily Phonics Practice**
Initial consonants	1–8, 25–28	1–8, 25–28	7–8, 11–12, 15–18	244
Medial consonants	17–24	17–24	13–18	245
Final consonants	9–16, 25–28	9–16, 25–28	9–12, 15–18	244–245

Student Progress Checklist

Make as many copies as needed to use for a class list. For individual portfolio use, cut apart each child's section.
As indicated by the code, color in boxes next to skills satisfactorily assessed and insert an *X* by those requiring reteaching. Marked boxes can later be colored in to indicate mastery.

Student Progress Checklist

Code: ■ Satisfactory   ☒ Needs Reteaching

Student: _____ _____ Pretest Score: _____ Posttest Score:_____	Skills ☐ Initial Consonants ☐ Medial Consonants ☐ Final Consonants	Comments / Learning Goals
Student: _____ _____ Pretest Score: _____ Posttest Score:_____	Skills ☐ Initial Consonants ☐ Medial Consonants ☐ Final Consonants	Comments / Learning Goals
Student: _____ _____ Pretest Score: _____ Posttest Score:_____	Skills ☐ Initial Consonants ☐ Medial Consonants ☐ Final Consonants	Comments / Learning Goals
Student: _____ _____ Pretest Score: _____ Posttest Score:_____	Skills ☐ Initial Consonants ☐ Medial Consonants ☐ Final Consonants	Comments / Learning Goals

BLM 5 Unit 1 Checklist

Throughout Unit 1 there are opportunities to assess English language learners' ability to read and write words with initial, medial, and final consonants. Some of your English language learners may require additional assessment strategies to meet their language needs. Take note of pronunciation difficulties as they occur but assess performance based on children's ability to distinguish specific sounds when pronounced by a native speaker.

Lesson 1, pages 7–8 Some children may be learning the Roman alphabet for the first time, so discriminate form from size between uppercase and lowercase letters.

Lesson 2, pages 9–10 In Spanish, the consonants *p, g,* and *f* are not used in the final position. Practice *soap, map, cup; bug, bag, log;* and *leaf, beef, elf.*

Lesson 3, pages 11–12 Assess each English language learner's discrimination of initial and final consonants by reviewing answers to items 25–28 of the Pretest on pages 5e–5f.

Lesson 4, pages 13–14 Since words in many Asian languages are monosyllabic, prolonging the medial consonant sound may lead children to say each word as two. With children, practice saying and writing words such as *hammer, kitten,* and *balloon.*

Phonics Games, Activities, and Technology

The following collection of ideas offers a variety of opportunities to reinforce phonics skills while actively engaging children. The games, activities, and technology suggestions can easily be adapted to meet the needs of your group of learners. They vary in approach so as to consider children's different learning styles.

MAKING A SOUND MATCH

Provide partners with a set of consonant letter cards and a set of picture cards whose names begin with consonant sounds. One child can select letter cards and present them to his or her partner. The partner must match each letter card to a picture whose name begins with the letter sound.

BEGINNING, MIDDLE, AND END

Have groups of three children sit side by side. Each child will need scrap paper and a crayon. Pronounce one of these words and ask children to listen for the beginning, middle, and end sounds: *robot, ladder, kitten, dragon, peanut, wagon, cabin, mitten.* Have the child in the first seat write the letter that stands for the beginning sound, the child in the second seat write the letter that stands for the middle sound, and the child in the third seat write the letter that stands for the ending sound. Ask children to change seats after several words.

CITY SIGHTS AND SOUNDS

Draw an outline of a cityscape on mural paper. Help children attach picture cards whose names begin and end with different consonant sounds—for example, door, car, bus, and so on. Have children take turns leading a tour of the city by pointing out a picture, naming it, and identifying the letters that stand for its beginning and ending sounds.

ESL/ELL This activity may be difficult for English language learners who are unfamiliar with a city setting. Substitute a tour of the classroom, pointing out *door, desk, pen, rug, book, shelf,* and so on.

"GUESS MY PICTURE" GAME

Display a number of picture cards whose names have different beginning and ending consonant sounds. Welcome children to this "art gallery," and tell them that you have a favorite picture and that you'd like them to guess which one. Give children a series of both sound and descriptive clues and have them identify the mystery card. For example, for the picture of a fan you might say: *Use me to stay cool when it is hot. I begin with the same sound as fork. I end with the same sound as lion. What am I?* Once children understand the clue structure, invite volunteers to select a picture and make up sound and meaning clues for others to guess its name.

ESL/ELL You can simplify this activity by choosing picture cards recycled from recent lessons and limiting the verbal cues to short, one- or two-sentence descriptions.

PIZZA DELIVERY

Designate five or six children as the pizza shop delivery crew. Give the other children consonant letter cards, for example *B* and *R*, and explain that they are Ms. B or Mr. R. Place a stack of picture cards in a cardboard box labeled "pizza oven." Ask the delivery crew to remove the picture cards from the oven and deliver them to the customers whose letter names stand for the sound heard at the beginning of each picture name. Rotate jobs so that children are both customers and members of the delivery crew.

CONSONANT BINGO

To reinforce initial consonant sounds, provide children with blank game boards and markers for covering letters. Choose up to 16 consonants and write them on the board. Have children fill their boards by randomly writing these consonants in the spaces. To play, call out a word beginning with one of these consonants and have children repeat it, emphasizing the beginning sound. They can cover the letter whose sound is heard at the beginning of the word. Continue until someone has bingo! The game can also be played to reinforce medial and final consonant sounds.

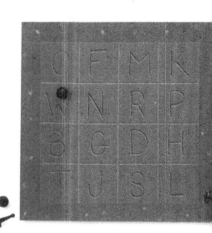

CONSONANT DOMINOES

Have partners use Blackline Master 7 on page 5p to play a game of "consonant dominoes." Before playing, review the picture names under the dominoes with children and then have children cut out the dominoes. Have partners combine their sets and turn all the pictures face down. Each player selects five dominoes. The first player displays a domino. The other player continues the chain by matching a picture whose name begins with the same sound. If the player does not have a domino that matches, he or she must continue to select from the face-down dominoes until a match is made. The game continues until one player is out of dominoes.

Variations: Children can match picture names with the same ending sounds. To make the game even more challenging, children can match the ending sound of one word with the beginning sound of another word. When playing this version, children may wish to make additional domino cards with pictures of their own choice.

ESL/ELL Consonant Dominoes (page 5n), **All Around the Town**, and **Roll a Word** (page 5o) may confuse English language learners who match like objects rather than pictures whose names begin with the same sound. Model each game several times and have teams play together, each with a role commensurate to their ability.

TO MARKET, TO MARKET

Give each child crayons and drawing paper as well as a "shopping list" with five consonants. Have children draw items whose names begin with each letter sound that they might buy in neighborhood stores. Children can cut out their pictures and place them in small shopping bags to share with others.

Variations: Instead of drawing the pictures, give children discarded magazines and scissors and suggest that they cut out the pictures. To further extend the activity, organize children into small groups once they have filled their orders. Have them place their bags and lists in two separate piles on the table. Each child can then select a list and find the bag that contains the filled order.

ALL AROUND THE TOWN

Draw a spiral game board with 15 to 20 spaces on a large piece of tagboard and help children decorate the board with pictures of places in their community. Duplicate a copy of Blackline Master 7. Have children cut out the dominoes and then cut each in half to separate the two pictures. Then, have them randomly place the pictures in the spaces on the game board. Have them take turns using a number cube to move a marker along the game board. As a player lands on a picture, its name must be said and the letter that stands for the initial or final sound identified. Play continues until everyone reaches home.

RHYMING PICTURE CHAINS

Provide children with strips of construction paper, crayons, and paste. To make a rhyming picture chain, have them draw a picture on a strip and print the letter that stands for the word's initial sound next to the picture. The strip can be pasted to form one link in the chain. Have them continue the chain with other labeled pictures of rhyming words. Some words that yield long chains include: *cat, pan, hill, sack, sail, cake, ball, car, pen, pig, sock, hop, bug,* and *sub.*

ROLL A WORD

Cover the faces of a number cube with masking tape. Write six consonants you wish to reinforce on the cube. Children can take turns rolling the cube, identifying the letter that shows, and giving words that begin with the sound the letter represents.

Variations: The same game can be played to reinforce medial or final consonant sounds. For an even more challenging version, use two cubes and have children simultaneously roll letters for both the beginning and ending sound of a word.

The following software products reinforce children's understanding of consonants and other phonics skills.

Stickybear's Reading Fun Park
Children practice phonics through four games that build sight vocabularies, phonics, and memory. As they travel through the park, children also practice critical reading skills including high-frequency words divided into specific categories.

** Optimum Resource, Inc.
   18 Hunter Road
   Hilton Head Island, SC 29926
   (843) 689-8000
   www.stickybear.com

Reader Rabbit's® I Can Read! with Phonics™
Reader Rabbit guides students in learning solid reading skills through engaging activities that build phonemic awareness ar afford practice in identifying consonant blends, short and long vowel sounds, digraphs, and rhyme patterns.

** Riverdeep The Learning Company
   500 Redwood Blvd.
   Novato, CA 94947
   (800) 825-4420
   www.learningcompanyschool.com

Name_____

Consonant Dominoes

robot	dog
pig	ball
lemon	rug
net	seal
goat	map
tail	gum
wig	sun
bun	rat
top	bag
web	nut
pot	ram
coat	balloon
boat	team
doll	bug
deer	bat
leg	mitten
mail	suit
mitt	bed

Home Connections

The Home Connections features of this program are intended to involve families in their children's learning and application of phonics skills. Three effective opportunities to make connections between home and school include the following.

- HOME LETTER
- HOME NOTES
- TAKE-HOME BOOKS

HOME LETTER

A letter is available to be sent home at the beginning of Unit 1. This letter informs family members that children will be learning about consonant letters and the sounds they represent at the beginning, the middle, and the end of words within the context of the unit theme, "All Around the Town." The featured activity suggests taking a neighborhood walk, looking for examples of words on signs, reading these words, and identifying letters that stand for the beginning and end sounds heard in the words. In addition to promoting interaction between child and family members, this activity also reinforces the concept that words are everywhere in a child's environment. The letter, which is available in both English and Spanish, also suggests community-theme books that family members can look for in a local library and enjoy reading together.

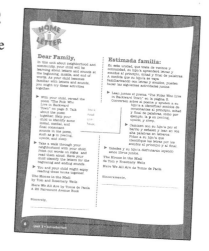

HOME NOTES

Whenever the Home logo appears within the student book, a phonics activity is suggested to be done at home. The activities are simple to do, requiring little or no preparation or special materials, and are meant to reinforce the targeted phonics skill.

Home Notes in Spanish are also available for both teachers and parents to download and use from our website, www.PlaidPhonics.com.

TAKE-HOME BOOKS

Within the student book are many Take-Home Books that can be cut out and assembled. The story language in each book reinforces the targeted phonics skill. The books can be taken home and shared with family members. In Unit 1, one Take-Home Book is available, focusing on different beginning and final consonant sounds as well as the unit theme, "All Around the Town."

Initial, Medial, and Final Consonants

Skill Focus

Assess Prior Knowledge

To assess children's prior knowledge of initial, medial, and final consonants, use the pretest on pages 5e–5f.

Unit Focus

Build Background

- Write the theme "All Around the Town" on the board. Read it aloud and have children find it on page 5. Discuss what the phrase might mean.

- Explain that "The Folk Who Live in Backward Town" is a poem about a silly town. Read the poem aloud as children follow along.

- Invite children to repeat some of the silly things that people in the poem do. Suggest they look at the illustration to find other examples of silly things. Ask children to explain whether this is a place in which they might like to live.

Introduce Consonants

- Remind children that the alphabet is made up of twenty-six letters—twenty-one consonants and five vowels. As children slowly recite the alphabet, write on the board all the consonants. *(b, c, d, f, g, h, j, k, l, m, n, p, q, r, s, t, v, w, x, y, z)*

- Read the poem again. Write the words *live, inside, hats, go,* and *apple* on the board. Point to and pronounce each word, emphasizing the consonants in each word. Explain to children that they will be learning more about consonants that are at the beginning, middle, or end of a word.

Critical Thinking Read the poem again and encourage children to think about why the town is named "Backward Town." Children may suggest that the people in the town do everything opposite to the way things are usually done.

Read Aloud

The Folk Who Live In Backward Town

by Mary Ann Hoberman

The folk who live in Backward Town
Are inside out and upside down.
They wear their hats inside their heads
And go to sleep beneath their beds.
They only eat the apple peeling
And take their walks across the ceiling.

TALK About It Why is the town named "Backward Town"?

THEME FOCUS

TWO TOWNS

Invite children to look again at the picture on page 5. Ask them to discuss ways that this town is different than their town or neighborhood and ways it may be the same.

HOME TOWNS

Encourage children to describe the city, village, or township where they live. To help children respond, ask questions such as *What is the name of the town or place where you live? What kinds of buildings are there? What else—besides buildings—can you see there?*

MODEL OF A TOWN

Draw an outline of the roads of your school neighborhood on mural paper. Lay it flat on a table and invite children to create a three-dimensional model of the community. Provide markers, cardboard boxes, and construction paper. Children can draw rivers and railroad tracks and construct buildings such as the courthouse, library, and stores. Help them think of large open areas they might want to include such as ball fields or parking lots.

Dear Family,

In this unit about neighborhood and community, your child will be learning about letters and sounds at the beginning, middle, and end of words. As your child becomes familiar with letters and sounds, you might try these activities together.

► With your child, reread the poem "The Folk Who Live in Backward Town" on page 5. Talk about the poem together. Help your child to identify some initial, medial, and final consonant sounds in the poem, such as **p** in peeling, upside, and sleep.

bank
road
car
house

► Take a walk through your neighborhood with your child. Point out words on signs and read them aloud. Have your child identify the letters for the beginning and ending sounds.

► You and your child might enjoy reading these books together.

The House in the Mail
by Tom and Rosemary Wells

Here We All Are by Tomie de Paola
A 26 Fairmount Avenue Book

Sincerely,

_____

Estimada familia:

En esta unidad, que trata de vecinos y comunidad, su hijo/a aprenderá letras y sonidos al principio, mitad y final de palabras. A medida que su hijo/a se vaya familiarizando con letras y sonidos, pueden hacer las siguientes actividades juntos.

► Lean juntos el poema "The Folks Who Live in Backward Town" en la página 5. Conversen sobre el poema y ayuden a su hijo/a a identificar sonidos de consonantes al principio, mitad y final de palabras, como por ejemplo, la **p** en peeling, upside, y sleep.

► Caminen con su hijo/a por el barrio y señalen y lean en voz alta palabras en letreros. Pídan a su hijo/a que identifique las letras por los sonidos al principio y al final.

► Ustedes y su hijo/a disfrutarán leyendo estos libros juntos.

The House in the Mail
de Tom y Rosemary Wells

Here We All Are de Tomie de Paola

Sinceramente,

_____

BULLETIN BOARD

Decorate a bulletin board with an outline of a town scene. As the unit progresses, encourage children to cut out shapes of buildings, vehicles, animals, people, plants, and toys and attach them to the board, creating a "Consonant Town." Have children label each cutout and underline the consonants in the names.

HOME CONNECTIONS

• The Home Letter on page 6 introduces family members to the phonics skills children will be studying in this unit. Children can take the page home and complete the activities with family members.

• Encourage children to look for the library books recommended on page 6 and to ask family members to share a book with them.

LEARNING CENTER ACTIVITIES

WRITING CENTER

Invite children to adapt the unit poem to write one about their town. Explain that their poems do not have to rhyme and that they can be silly or realistic. Display a writing framework in the center as a guide.

The Folk Who Live in _____
The folk who live in _____
Are _____ and _____.
They wear _____.
And go to sleep_____.
They only eat _____.
And take their walks _____.

SCIENCE CENTER

Invite children to write and present weather reports. Introduce the activity by playing a video recording of a local TV weather report. In the science center, have children keep a log of weather conditions in your area for a week. At the end of the week, invite interested class members to present weather reports describing such conditions as temperatures, amount of precipitation, and windiness. If possible, videotape the reports.

SOCIAL STUDIES CENTER

Gather business cards and brochures from the local Chamber of Commerce and various businesses, organizations, travel agencies, and tourist sites in your area. Encourage children to add to the collection. Provide shoe boxes in the social studies center. Invite children to divide the pamphlets into different categories that might include stores, restaurants, repair shops, and sightseeing locations. Other children might choose to re-sort the information into different categories.

Initial Consonants

Skill Focus

Children will

★ identify initial consonant sounds.

★ associate the consonant with the sound it represents.

★ identify and spell picture names that begin with consonants.

ESL/ELL Some children may be learning the Roman alphabet for the first time, so discriminate form from size between uppercase and lowercase letters.

Teach

Phonemic Awareness: Phoneme Categorization Say the word *moon*, elongating and emphasizing the beginning /m/ sound. Ask children what consonant sound they hear at the beginning of *moon*. (*m*) Then, say the word *noon*, again emphasizing the initial consonant sound. Ask what sound they hear. (*n*) Read these groups of words to children. Ask them to identify the words that begin with the same consonant sound.

- bell   bottom   ring
- funny   money   fan

Sound to Symbol Display Phonics Picture Card 22. Have children name the picture. (*lion*) Ask what sound they hear. (/l/) Write *Lion, lion* on the board and underline the *L* and *l*. Remind children that the letter *l* stands for the sound they hear at the beginning of *lion*. Repeat the activity, using Picture Cards 15 (*goose*) and 28 (*pillow*).

Practice and Apply

Sound to Symbol Have children identify the pictures on page 7. Explain that they are to write both the uppercase and lowercase letter of the beginning sound. Read the directions on page 8, and go over the names of the pictures on page 8. Remind children to write only the lowercase letter to finish the word.

Reading Use *The Trip*, MCP Phonics and Reading Consonant and Vowel Skills Library, Level B, to reinforce initial consonant sounds.

Name _____

▶ **Say** the name of each picture. **Print** the capital and lowercase letters for its beginning sound.

1. hand	2. fish	3. box	4. wagon
Hh	Ff	Bb	Ww
5. goat	6. kite	7. dinosaur	8. pillow
Gg	Kk	Dd	Pp
9. moon	10. zebra	11. robot	12. volcano
Mm	Zz	Rr	Vv
13. sock	14. lamp	15. car	16. ten
Ss	Ll	Cc	Tt

©Pearson Education, Inc./Modern Curriculum Press/Pearson Learning Group. All rights reserved. Copying strictly prohibited.

Initial consonants   **7**

FOCUS ON ALL LEARNERS

ESL/ELL ENGLISH LANGUAGE LEARNERS

Practice identifying and writing initial consonants by completing page 7.

- Explain that *capital* and *small* mean "uppercase" and "lowercase" respectively.
- Model the activity by completing items 1–4 aloud with the group.
- Ask children to complete items 5–16 in pairs. Review responses aloud.

AUDITORY/VISUAL LEARNERS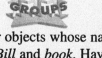

Point to different pairs of children and/or objects whose names begin with the same consonant, such as *Bill* and *book*. Have children say the names aloud. Then, ask them to find a third matching person or item for each pair. Write each set of words on the board. Have volunteers circle the matching initial consonants.

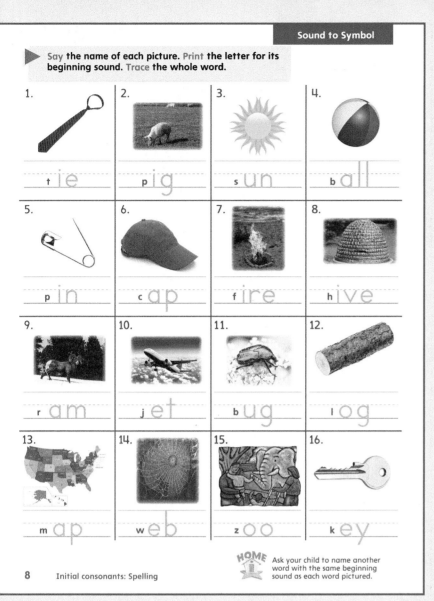

Say the name of each picture. **Print** the letter for its beginning sound. **Trace** the whole word.

1. t ie
2. p ig
3. s un
4. b all
5. p in
6. c ap
7. f ire
8. h ive
9. r am
10. j et
11. b ug
12. l og
13. m ap
14. w eb
15. z oo
16. k ey

HOME Ask your child to name another word with the same beginning sound as each word pictured.

8   Initial consonants: Spelling

CURRICULUM CONNECTIONS

SPELLING

Pretest Unit 1 spelling words by using the following words and dictation sentences.

1. **gum**   I bought a pack of **gum**.
2. **web**   He saw a spider spin its **web**.
3. **jam**   My mom makes **jam** from peaches.
4. **pen**   Should I use a pencil or a **pen**?
5. **box**   The surprise came in a big **box**.
6. **pig**   She raised her **pig** on the farm.

WRITING

List children's favorite place names on the board and discuss their initial sounds. Then,  encourage children to write their own list of places, underlining the letters that stand for the initial sounds.

MATHEMATICS

Print the consonants across the board. Add a column for vowels. Have children write their first and last names under the correct consonant. Tabulate the number of names for each consonant.

TECHNOLOGY   **AstroWord**   Consonant Sounds and Letters

Integrating Phonics and Reading

Guided Reading
Help children list animals they have read about or seen at the zoo. Display the cover, read aloud the title, and ask children where they think the animals might go.
First Reading Ask children which beginning consonant letters appear in the story.
Second Reading List the letters *h, g, y, s, z, r,* and *t* on the board. Have children find and pronounce words in the story that begin with these letters and list them under the letter.
Comprehension
Ask children the following questions:
• Why did the animals decide to go on a trip? *Inference/Reflective Analysis*
• Where did the animals' trip end? Why were they happy now? *Reflective Analysis/Personal Response*
ESL/ELL **English Language Learners**
Tell children that the word *ho-hum* shows boredom and the word *yikes* shows surprise. Have them read these words expressively.

AUDITORY/KINESTHETIC LEARNERS   PARTNERS

Materials: art paper
Invite children to draw an object that begins with a consonant sound. Then, have them exchange papers with a partner. The partner names three or more objects that begin with that letter.

CHALLENGE

Give each pair of children a list of frequently used initial consonants. Suggest that they go on a scavenger hunt around the classroom to find and write the name of an object that begins with each of the consonants.

EXTRA SUPPORT/INTERVENTION

Materials: Phonics Picture Cards: Consonants (1–44); index cards; marker
Make letter cards for the initial sounds of the picture names. As you hold up each picture and say its name, have volunteers choose the matching letter card and name the initial consonant. See Daily Phonics Practice, page 244.

Final Consonants

Skill Focus

Children will

★ identify final consonant sounds.

★ associate the consonant with the sound it represents.

★ identify and spell picture names that end with consonants.

ESL/ELL In Spanish, the consonants *p, g,* and *f* are not used in the final position. Practice *soap, map, cup; bug, bag, log;* and *leaf, beef, elf.*

Teach

Phonemic Awareness: Phoneme Segmentation Say the word *leg*, separating each sound: /l/ /e/ /g/. Emphasize the final *g*. Ask children what consonant sound they hear at the end of the word. (*g*) Have children repeat the word, stretching the final *g*. Repeat the activity, using the words *red* and *green*.

Phonemic Awareness: Phoneme Categorization Read these groups of words to children. Ask them to identify the words that end with the same consonant sound.

* **queen**   **tiger**   **lemon**

* **bell**   **nail**   **web**

Sound to Symbol Hold up Phonics Picture Card 35 (*soap*). Invite children to say the name of the picture. Write *soap* on the board. Ask a volunteer to identify the final consonant sound. (*p*) Underline *p*. Then, write *cat, Tim,* and *cub* on the board. Have volunteers say each word, identify the final consonant sound, and underline the letter that stands for that sound.

Practice and Apply

Sound to Symbol Have children identify the pictures on pages 9 and 10. Remind children to say the name of the picture to themselves, stretching the sounds, before they write the final consonant on the line. Encourage them to trace the entire word on page 10.

Reading Use *When We Are Big*, MCP Phonics and Reading Consonant and Vowel Skills Library, Level B, to reinforce final consonant sounds.

Name_____

➤ Say the name of each picture. Print the letter for its ending sound.

1. soap	2. box	3. ram	4. bat
p	x	m	t

5. seal	6. jeep	7. pen	8. book
l	p	n	k

9. star	10. glass	11. bib	12. bug
r	s	b	g

13. gum	14. log	15. nail	16. bag
m	g	l	g

Final consonants   **9**

FOCUS ON ALL LEARNERS

ESL/ELL ENGLISH LANGUAGE LEARNERS

Reinforce the recognition of final consonants with English language learners.

* Say the words *cap, top,* and *lip* and invite children to say the ending sound and letter for these words.

* Write *cap, top,* and *lip* on the board. Point to each word and model the final sound slowly for English language learners whose native language does not include this sound. Have them repeat the words.

* Invite volunteers to go to the board, circle the letter that stands for the ending sound in each word, and name the letter aloud.

* Repeat the activity, using other pairs of words: *pen, sun; box, fix; car, door;* and so on.

AUDITORY/KINESTHETIC LEARNERS

Invite children to stand and say *yes* when they hear a pair of words that end with the same sound. Use pairs such as *sell, hill; glass, bus; hid, hope; book, lick; bag, wig; nail, gum; lid, bed; star, leaf; cut, hat; rub, tube; sat, mess.*

► Say the name of each picture. Print the letter for its ending sound. Trace the whole word.

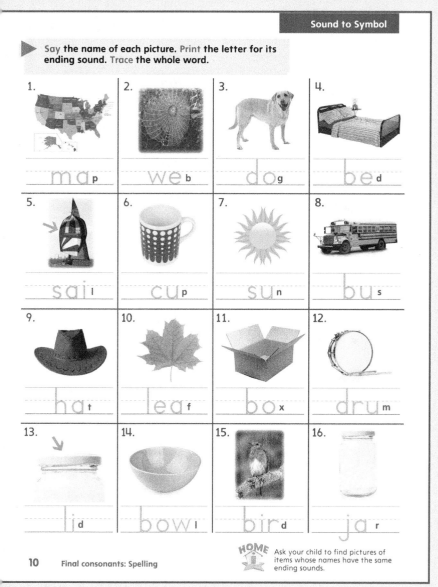

1. ma p
2. we b
3. do g
4. be d
5. sai l
6. cu p
7. su n
8. bu s
9. ha t
10. lea f
11. bo x
12. dru m
13. li d
14. bow l
15. bir d
16. ja r

HOME Ask your child to find pictures of items whose names have the same ending sounds.

10   Final consonants: Spelling

CURRICULUM CONNECTIONS

SPELLING

Write the spelling words *pen, jam, box, gum, pig,* and *web* on the board. Ask children to close their eyes. Erase one word. Define the missing word and have children spell the word on their papers. Repeat for each word. Distribute copies of the spelling list that children can use for home study.

SOCIAL STUDIES

Materials: map of the United States

Work with children to list state names that end with a consonant. Have children pronounce each name. Discuss which state names end with consonants that do not sound the way children might expect, such as Illinois, Arkansas, or Utah.

WRITING

Invite children to use one picture name each from pages 9 and 10 to write two sentences about their community. Review children's sentences for correct spelling of ending consonant sounds.

TECHNOLOGY   **AstroWord** Consonant Sounds and Letters

VISUAL LEARNERS   INDIVIDUAL

Have children choose a picture name from page 10 and write a sentence that includes that word and at least one other word that ends with the same sound. Encourage children to illustrate their sentences.

CHALLENGE

Invite children to work in pairs to make a list of words with as many different ending consonants as possible. After partners have completed their list, they can compare their list with the list of another pair of children and add more words.

EXTRA SUPPORT/INTERVENTION

Display familiar objects that end in the same consonant sound: *book, clock; pencil, bell; paper, ruler; pen, pin;* and so on. Have children name the objects and identify the final consonant for each pair of words. Encourage them to name another word with the same ending sound. See Daily Phonics Practice, pages 244–245.

Integrating Phonics and Reading

Guided Reading
Call attention to the cover of the book. Have children describe the picture. Ask them why they think the girl and boy each has on a different hat.

First Reading Ask children what some of the things are that the boy and girl can be.

Second Reading Encourage children to find words with the following final consonants: *g, t, d, n, p, k, l, s,* and *x*.

Comprehension
After reading, ask the following questions:
• Why does the last sentence say, "We will have to wait and see"? *Inference/Draw Conclusions*
• Which of the things in the story might you like to be? *Reflective Analysis/Personal Response*

ESL/ELL English Language Learners
Read the title with children. Ask them what they think the title means. Be sure they recognize that *we* refers to the girl and boy on the cover and that *big* means "grown up."

Initial and Final Consonants

Skill Focus

Children will

★ recognize initial and final consonant sounds.

★ associate the consonant with the sound it represents.

★ identify and spell picture names that begin and end with consonants.

ESL/ELL Assess each English language learner's discrimination of initial and final consonants by reviewing answers to items 25–28 of the Pretest on pages 5e–5f.

Teach

Phonemic Awareness: Phoneme Substitution Say the word *lap* and *cap*, emphasizing the final sound. Ask children how the two words are the same. (*They both end with* p, *and they rhyme.*) Say *lap* and *cap* again, this time emphasizing the initial sound. Ask children how the words are different. (*They begin with different consonants.*) Ask children what will happen if the *l* in *lap* is changed to a *t*. (*The word becomes* tap.)

Sound to Symbol Write the words *fin* and *fig*, one under the other, on the board. Ask children how the words are the same. (*They both begin with* /f/.) Have a volunteer underline the letter that stands for /f/. Next, write *big* under *fig* on the board. Ask how *fig* and *big* are the same. (*They both end with* /g/.) Have a volunteer underline the *g*. Erase the *g* in *big*. Invite a volunteer to go to the board and write a consonant that will make a different word. (*bin, bit, bid*) Then, have children replace the *b* to make more words.

Practice and Apply

Blend Phonemes Read the directions on page 11. Be sure children understand that they are to make the change to each previous word, not to *cat*. Remind children to say each new word, blending the sounds. Go over the pictures on page 12 before children write the initial and final consonants.

Reading You may wish to use *Let's Go Marching!*, MCP Phonics and Reading Consonant and Vowel Skills Library, Level B, to review initial and final consonants with children.

Name_____

▶ Read **each sentence.** Then, **change the** letters to make new words. **Write** the words on the lines.

cat

1. Change the **c** in **cat** to **m**.   mat

2. Change the **t** to **p**.   map

3. Change the **m** to **l**.   lap

4. Change the **p** to **d**.   lad

5. Change the **l** to **m**.   mad

6. Change the **d** to **n**.   man

7. Change the **m** to **r**.   ran

8. Change the **n** to **t**.   rat

Initial and final consonants   **11**

FOCUS ON ALL LEARNERS

ESL/ELL ENGLISH LANGUAGE LEARNERS

Assist children in completing the exercise on page 11.

• Say the activity directions aloud, modeling with actions.

• Work closely with children while completing number 1 (*cat* to *mat*). You may wish to draw a sketch of each new word on the chalkboard as children work through the page to ensure that children know the meanings of the words they are making.

• Have children work through each item individually. Review each answer aloud before continuing to the next item.

• Review the entire chain of words.

AUDITORY LEARNERS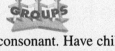

Play Consonant I-Spy. Say a consonant. Have children name objects or people in the classroom that begin or end with that consonant. For example, if you say *t*, children might say *I spy the tape* or *I spy Pat*.

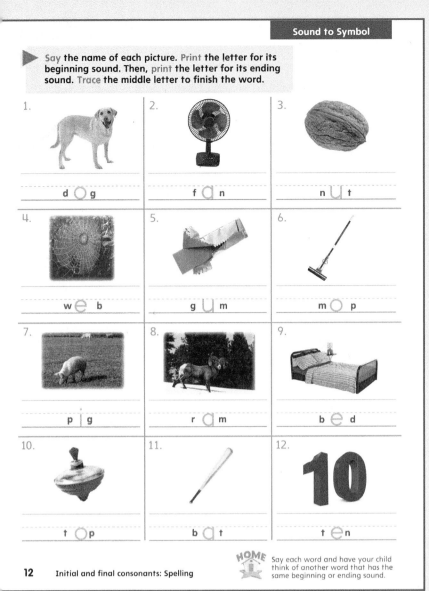

► Say the name of each picture. Print the letter for its beginning sound. Then, print the letter for its ending sound. Trace the middle letter to finish the word.

1. d ◯ g

2. f ◯ n

3. n ∪ t

4. w ⊖ b

5. g ∪ m

6. m ◯ p

7. p | g

8. r ◯ m

9. b ⊖ d

10. t ◯ p

11. b ◯ t

12. t ⊖ n

12   Initial and final consonants: Spelling

HOME
Say each word and have your child think of another word that has the same beginning or ending sound.

CURRICULUM CONNECTIONS

SPELLING

On the board, list the medial vowel between two blank lines for each of the spelling words *jam, pen, web, pig, box,* and *gum.* Say one of the words and have a volunteer write the initial and ending consonants in the correct set of blanks to spell the word. Have children say each word and finger-trace its letters on their desks.

WRITING

Have children write riddles about animals they have seen in their town. Ask them to use the beginning or final consonant as one of the clues for each riddle. For example: *This is an animal you can ride. It begins with* h. (horse)

ART/SCIENCE

Materials: mural paper; markers or paints

Ask children to draw a mural showing and labeling animals of their community, including those found in the wild, in zoos, and in homes. Later, have children point out the initial and final consonants in the animal names.

TECHNOLOGY   **AstroWord** Consonant Sounds and Letters

VISUAL/KINESTHETIC LEARNERS   GROUPS

Materials: index cards, marker

Make and display a set of alphabet letter cards. Say a short vowel word that begins and ends with single consonants, such as *big.* Have one child stand and hold the *i* card as volunteers find the beginning and ending letters and stand in the correct positions to spell the word. Have children suggest words of their own to continue the activity.

CHALLENGE

Have children print the letters of their first and last names vertically down their papers and circle the consonants. Challenge them to write one word that begins and one that ends with each of the consonants.

EXTRA SUPPORT/INTERVENTION

On the board, write a three-letter word, such as *can.* Read the word and have children list new words below it by changing the initial consonant. Then, next to each of the words in the list, have children change the ending consonant to make more new words. See Daily Phonics Practice, pages 244–245.

Integrating Phonics and Reading

Guided Reading

Invite children to look at the pictures in the book. Have them predict what the story will be about.

First Reading Ask children to describe some of the things that the marchers see.

Second Reading Choose a consonant and ask children to identify things the marchers saw that begin or end with that consonant.

Comprehension

After reading, ask the following questions:

• Where are the children marching? *Recall/Draw Conclusions*

• If you could march with the children in the story, what would you like to see? *Reflective Analysis/Personal Response*

ESL/ELL **English Language Learners**

Write the word *marching* on the board. Say the word and have children repeat it. Form a line with children and have them march around the room. Discuss occasions for marching.

Medial Consonants

Skill Focus

Children will

★ identify medial consonant sounds.

★ associate the consonant with the sound it represents.

★ identify and spell picture names with medial consonants.

ESL/ELL Since words in many Asian languages are monosyllabic, prolonging the medial consonant sound may lead children to say each word as two. With children, practice saying and writing words such as *hammer*, *kitten*, and *balloon*.

Teach

Phonemic Awareness: Phoneme Isolation
Say the word *parrot*, drawing out each sound. Then, repeat the word naturally. Ask children what consonant sound they hear in the middle of the word. (/r/) Then, have children say the word, stretching the *r* sound.

Sound to Symbol Say the word *label* and write it on the board. Ask children what sound they hear in the middle of the word. (/b/) Underline the letter *b* and explain that the letter *b* stands for the middle consonant sound. Then, write the word *butter*. Ask children what sound they hear in the middle of the word. (/t/) Underline both *t*'s and explain that the double consonant stands for one sound. Write *pillow* on the board. Have a volunteer say the word, identify the middle sound, and underline the letters that stand for the sound. Repeat the activity with the words *lemon*, *tulip*, and *runner*.

Practice and Apply

Blend Phonemes Read the directions on page 13. Help children name the pictures. Remind children that if a picture name is spelled with a double consonant, they need to write only one consonant. With children, say the names of the pictures on page 14, blending the sounds. Then, have children write the letter that makes the middle consonant sound. You may wish to remind children to complete the additional directions at the bottom of the page.

Reading Use *Wilma's Wagon*, MCP Phonics and Reading Consonant and Vowel Skills Library, Level B, to reinforce medial consonant sounds.

Name _____

▶ Say the name of each picture. Print the letter for its middle sound.

1. ladder	2. robot	3. balloon	4. mitten
d	b	l	t
5. butter	6. ruler	7. kitten	8. wagon
t	l	t	g
9. zipper	10. camel	11. hammer	12. carrot
p	m	m	r
13. button	14. pillow	15. letter	16. tiger
t	l	t	g

Medial consonants   **13**

FOCUS ON ALL LEARNERS

ESL/ELL ENGLISH LANGUAGE LEARNERS

Help English language learners identify single and double medial consonants.

- Write *robot*, *ruler*, and *wagon*, on the board. Say each word and have children repeat it. Ask volunteers to name and with colored chalk circle the medial consonant. Then, have them find and complete these items on page 13.

- Write *ladder*, *balloon*, and *mitten* on the board, saying each word as you write it. Explain that some words have two of the same consonants that stand for one sound. Ask volunteers to name and with colored chalk circle the middle consonants in each word. Now, have them find and complete these items on the page.

- Say the picture names for the remaining items on page 13, and have children work individually to complete the page.

VISUAL LEARNERS

Materials: Phonics Picture Cards: balloon (1), camel (4), ladder (21), ribbon (31), seven (34), tiger (36)

Display and name the pictures one at a time. Draw three boxes on the board. Have volunteers fill in the consonants that stand for each word's beginning, middle, and ending sounds.

▶ Say the name of each picture. Print the letter for its middle sound.
Trace the whole word.

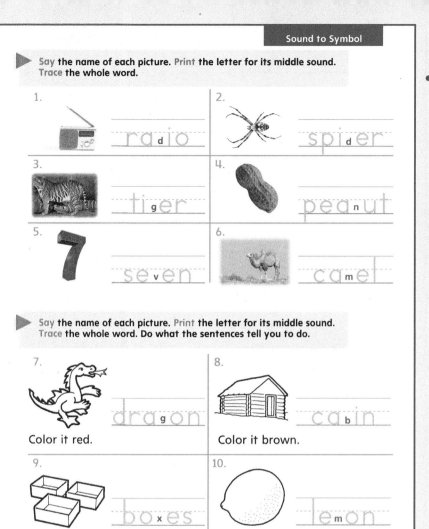

1. ra__d__io

2. spi__d__er

3. ti__g__er

4. pea__n__ut

5. se__v__en

6. ca__m__el

▶ Say the name of each picture. Print the letter for its middle sound.
Trace the whole word. Do what the sentences tell you to do.

7. dra__g__on
Color it red.

8. ca__b__in
Color it brown.

9. bo__x__es
Color them blue.

10. le__m__on
Color it yellow.

14 Medial consonants: Spelling

HOME Ask your child to find three pairs of words on this page with the same middle sounds.

CURRICULUM CONNECTIONS

SPELLING
Be sure each two children have a copy of the spelling words *box, gum, jam, pen, pig,* and *web.* Have partners take turns asking each other to spell the words orally and on paper. When both partners have finished, they can check their written work together.

WRITING

Invite children to write "what if" stories about their neighborhood, using at least one word with a medial consonant in the titles. Children may get ideas from pages 13 and 14, such as "What If a Robot Came to Our Town" or "What If I Saw a Tiger in a Hot-Air Balloon." Encourage children to illustrate their stories.

TECHNOLOGY **AstroWord** Consonant Sounds and Letters

KINESTHETIC LEARNERS GROUPS
For each of the following word groups, write the consonant on the board and have children "rub their middles" (pat their tummies) each time they hear that letter's sound in the middle of a word you say: *(l) lion, lollipop, ball; (n) night, moon, peanut; (d) pudding, desk, ladder; (g) wagon, giggle, gone; (f) fib, jiffy, safer.*

CHALLENGE
Invite children to make two-word crisscross puzzles with clues for words on pages 13 and 14 that have matching medial letter sounds.

EXTRA SUPPORT/INTERVENTION
Ask children to touch the tops of their heads in the middle when they hear a pair of words with matching medial consonant sounds. Use word pairs such as *carrot, narrow; dragon, tiger; lemon, liver; button, kitten; spider, robot; boxes, fixes.* See Daily Phonics Practice, page 245.

Integrating Phonics and Reading

Guided Reading
Have children read the title and look at the illustration on the cover. Ask them to predict what kind of a problem Wilma will have with her wagon.

First Reading Ask children to explain what problem Wilma had with her wagon.

Second Reading Ask children to identify the word in the story that has a double consonant.

Comprehension
After reading, ask the following questions:
• Why did the girls keep telling the wagon to wait? *Inference/Cause and Effect*
• Why did Wilma's wagon finally stop? *Inference/Using Picture Clues*

ESL/ELL English Language Learners
Write *Wilma's Wagon* on the board, using a different color of chalk for the apostrophe. Explain that when an apostrophe comes after a person's name, it means that the person owns or has something. In this case, Wilma has a wagon.

14

Phonics and Spelling / Phonics and Writing

Initial, Medial, and Final Consonants

Skill Focus

Children will

★ spell and write words with initial, medial, and final consonants.

★ write a description of an event using words with initial, medial, and final consonants.

★ recognize and read high-frequency words.

Teach

Phonemic Awareness **Phoneme Isolation**
Review that consonant sounds can come at the beginning, middle, or end of a word. Say the word *rubber*. Invite children to repeat the word and to identify where they hear the *b* sound. (*middle*) Repeat the activity with the words *bigger* and *scrub*.

Sound to Symbol Say and write the words *Sammy, Mother,* and *Pam* on the board. Have children say each word slowly and clearly. Invite volunteers to underline the letters in each word that stand for /m/.

Practice and Apply

Phonics and Spelling Remind children that the letters in the words in the boxes on page 15 are in the wrong order. Model the second item for them by reading the sentence aloud. Explain that the letters *ugm* can form the word *gum* or *mug*, but only the word *gum* makes sense in the sentence. As they complete the page, encourage children to say the entire sentence before they spell the answer.

Children will also have the opportunity to read the following high-frequency words: *wants, buy, what, find, this, look,* and *there.*

Critical Thinking Discuss Talk About It. Children should recognize that the family is buying things in a store.

Writing Before children begin page 16, have them brainstorm a list of events. Write them on the board. Discuss details about each event. Then, invite children to write about the event.

Reading You may wish to use *Night Animals,* MCP Phonics and Reading Consonant and Vowel Skills Library, Level B, to review initial, medial, and final consonants.

15

Name_____

Phonics & Spelling Read **each sentence. To finish the sentence, use the mixed-up letters in the box to make a word. Print the word on the line.**

1. Pam wants to buy that cute pink _____pig_____ .   **gpi**

2. Jed wants to get bubble _____gum_____ .   **ugm**

3. I wonder what is in that big _____box_____ .   **oxb**

4. Mom wants a yellow _____lemon_____ .   **elmno**

5. Did Dad find a jar of _____jam_____ yet?   **maj**

6. I will buy this blue _____pen_____ .   **pne**

7. Can that _____kite_____ fly high?   **ekit**

8. Look, there is a spider _____web_____ !   **bwe**

9. Is there a _____spider_____ in it?   **edrips**

10. I _____bet_____ that is not for sale!   **ebt**

©Pearson Education, Inc./Modern Curriculum Press/Pearson Learning Group. All rights reserved. Copying strictly prohibited.

TALK About It What are Jed and his family doing?

Initial, medial, final consonants: Spelling, high-frequency words, critical thinking   **15**

FOCUS ON ALL LEARNERS

ESL/ELL ENGLISH LANGUAGE LEARNERS

Reinforce awareness of consonant position and spelling by having English language learners unscramble jumbled words.

• Say the word *lemon* and invite a volunteer to name the consonant sound in the middle of the word. Then, ask another volunteer to name the sound at the beginning and end of the word. Continue with words from page 15.

• Write *elmno* on the board. Point to the scrambled word and say that these are the letters in *lemon.* Continue with words from this exercise until children are able to work in pairs to complete the page.

KINESTHETIC LEARNERS GROUPS

Place three chairs in a row at the front of the room—the first chair for beginning sounds, the second for middle sounds, and the third for final sounds. As you say consonants and words, have volunteers sit in the correct chair. Letters and words might include *g, gum; b, web; m, jam; p, pen; x, box; g, pig; m, hammer.*

Phonics & Writing

When you **describe an event**, you name the thing that happened and tell where it took place. Then, you write about the things that happened in the order they took place.

▶ **Think** about something that happened in your neighborhood, school, or community, such as a parade or a fair. **Use** sentences to tell about it. Then, **tell** how you felt about the things that happened. The words in the box may help you.

bird	man	spider	car	kitten
duck	bus	ball	log	box
dog	book	web	bug	zoo

Name the event you are telling about.

Tell where things took place.

Name things that happened in the order they took place.

CURRICULUM CONNECTIONS

SPELLING
Posttest
You can use the following words and sentences to assess the Unit 1 spelling words at this time.
1. **pen**   Which animal is in the **pen**?
2. **pig**   It is a baby **pig**.
3. **box**   Can I take it home in a **box**?
4. **jar**   I can feed it peanut butter from a **jar**.
5. **web**   Look at the fancy spider **web**.
6. **gum**   May I have a piece of **gum**?

MATH
Have children illustrate the items listed in the sentences on page 15 and put price tags of less than five cents on them. Then, have small groups set up a "store" and tell them that they have 13 cents to spend. Ask them what they would choose to buy with their money. Help them write math sentences that describe their purchases. Model the way to calculate how much change they would receive.

 **AstroWord** Consonant Sounds and Letters

AUDITORY LEARNERS

Materials: Phonics Picture Cards: Initial, Medial, and Final Consonants (1–44)

As you show each picture card, ask children to name the consonant sound for a certain position in each picture name, such as *the beginning sound of* dinosaur; *the ending sound of* soap; *the middle sound of* zipper.

CHALLENGE

Have children work in pairs to list words that have double consonants. Beside each word, list one word that begins with that consonant and one that ends with it.

EXTRA SUPPORT/INTERVENTION

List *delom, romot, ldaas,* and *vitsi* on the board. Point to the first group and say these are the letters that spell *model*. Beside *delom*, write _o_e_. Have children fill in the remaining letters by identifying the beginning, middle, and ending sound. Repeat with *romot* (motor), *ldaas* (salad), *vitsi* (visit). See Daily Phonics Practice, pages 244–245.

Integrating Phonics and Reading

Guided Reading
Have children name animals that come out at night. Then, read the title of the story and explain that it is about animals that come out at night.
First Reading Ask children to name the night animals in the story.
Second Reading Have children find words with the initial consonant of *b*, the medial consonant of *x*, and the final consonant of *t*.

Comprehension
After reading, ask the following questions:
• What other animals are in the story besides bats, owls, mice, and foxes? *Recall/Use Picture Clues*
• Why does the girl say "But I don't"? *Inference/Make Judgments*
ESL/ELL English Language Learners
Since English language learners may find the title challenging to read, write it on the board, pointing to and elongating each word as you say it aloud.

Review Initial, Medial, and Final Consonants

Skill Focus

Children will

★ read initial, medial, and final consonants in the context of a nonfiction narrative.

★ review selected high-frequency words in the context of a narrative.

★ reread for fluency.

Teach

Build Background

• Remind children that the theme of this unit is "All Around the Town." Invite children to name some of the words they have learned that can be used in a story about towns.

• Write the word *house* on the board. Explain that people around the world live in many different kinds of houses.

Phonemic Awareness: Phoneme Isolation Write the word *homes* on the board. Say the word, stretching it so that all consonant sounds are evident. Have children repeat the word in the same manner. Then, have them say the word naturally. Point to the initial (*h*), medial (*m*), and final (*s*) consonants and ask children to identify the sound of each. Have children underline the letter that stands for each sound.

Practice and Apply

Read the Book Demonstrate how to tear out and fold the pages to put together the Take-Home Book. Suggest that children look through the book and study the pictures. Ask what they think the book will be about. Then, read the story together.

Sound to Symbol Reread the story aloud or have volunteers read it. Write the words *yurts* and *sampans* on the board and help children to use their knowledge of consonants to sound them out.

Review High-Frequency Words Write the words *what* and *find* on the board. Have children spell the words and then say them, blending the sounds. Encourage children to make up sentences containing the high-frequency words.

Reread for Fluency Have children reread the book to increase their fluency and comprehension. Remind them to take the book home to share with their families.

17

Name _____

Home Sweet Home!

Everyone needs a place to live! In many large cities, people live in tall apartment buildings.

①

FOLD

Maybe houses of the future will be bubbles, towers, or rockets in space. Computers will probably be used to help with household tasks. The sun's energy may be used for heat and light. What do you think?

④

Review initial, medial, final consonants: Take-home book   **17**

FOCUS ON ALL LEARNERS

ESL/ELL ENGLISH LANGUAGE LEARNERS

Have English language learners practice reading words in the context of a narrative while reviewing consonant positions.

• Give children specific tasks to perform within the narrative: circling in red words that relate to kinds of houses, underlining in blue names of places, circling in green words containing the sound of *t*, and so on.

• Have children underline in pencil words they do not recognize. Review the problem words before, during, and after they read the narrative.

AUDITORY LEARNERS *INDIVIDUAL*

Materials: audiocassette tape, tape player

Record the text of *Home Sweet Home!* and have children follow along as they listen to it. Then, have them read the story to a partner.

VISUAL/AUDITORY LEARNERS *GROUPS*

Choose five words from the story. Write them on the board, leaving a blank for a missing consonant letter. Give children a simple definition and have them fill in the blank. For example: *ci_ies, Many people live here.*

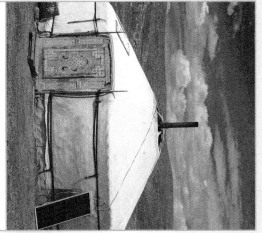

② Some people take their homes from place to place. In Asia, many herders travel with their goats and sheep to find food for them. The herders carry their homes, called *yurts*, with them.

------FOLD------

③ A houseboat is a home that stays in the water all year long. Some people in the United States, Europe, and many parts of Asia live on houseboats. In China these boats are known as *sampans*.

- - - - - ✂ - - - - -

18 Review initial, medial, final consonants: Take-home book

CURRICULUM CONNECTIONS

ART

Materials: magazines, scissors, glue, crayons, large paper

Have children work in groups to make a collage titled "Home Sweet Home." Children can cut out pictures from magazines or draw pictures that show homes or items commonly found in homes. Then, they should arrange them on a large sheet of paper and glue them. Display the collages in the classroom or in the corridor.

SOCIAL STUDIES

With children, reread "Home Sweet Home!" and discuss the homes presented in the book. Have children think about the advantages or benefits of living in each of the homes. Draw a three-column chart on tagboard and help children list the benefits of living in each home. After children have listed as many benefits of each home as they can think of, ask them to write a few sentences telling which home they would prefer to live in and why.

LANGUAGE ARTS

Invite children to write *Home is* on a sheet of paper. Then, have them complete the sentence any way they would like.

AstroWord Consonant Sounds and Letters

KINESTHETIC LEARNERS

Say a consonant and an action word to each child. Have children identify whether the consonant is at the beginning, in the middle, or at the end of the word. If the answer is correct, the child performs the action. Use *j, jump; p, hop; k, walk; n, running;* and so on.

CHALLENGE

Assign a consonant letter to each child. Have children make a three-page booklet. On the first page, they should list all the words they can think of that begin with their consonant. On the second page, they should list words that have that consonant in the middle. On the final page, they should list words that end in the consonant. Children can make a cover for their book with the title, "The Book of ___."

EXTRA SUPPORT/INTERVENTION

After reading the story aloud, invite children to retell the story in their own words. Then, encourage them to take turns reading it aloud. See Daily Phonics Practice, pages 244–245.

Unit Checkup

Review Initial, Medial, and Final Consonants

Skill Focus

Children will

★ review initial, medial, and final consonants.

★ complete sentences with words that contain initial, medial, or final consonants.

Teach

Phonemic Awareness: Phoneme Isolation
Say the words *top, letter,* and *pot,* enunciating the *t* carefully. Repeat the words, one at a time, asking children to say the word and to tell where they hear the *t* sound. Review that consonant sounds can be found at the beginning, middle, or end of a word.

Sound to Symbol
Materials: Phonics Picture Cards: Initial, Medial, and Final Consonants (1, 4, 6, 21, 24, 28, 31, 34, 36, 40, 44)

Display one of the picture cards or a visual (for instance, a *wagon*). Invite a volunteer to name the object. Then, ask children to identify the beginning, middle, and ending sounds of the word. Say which letters stand for each sound, and create a riddle about the object: *You can pull me or ride in me. I am a wagon.* Encourage volunteers to make their own riddles about other objects you name.

Practice and Apply

Assess Skills Help children identify the pictures on page 19. Be sure they understand that the page has three sets of directions. For page 20, assist children in recognizing that these are riddles. The word they write in the blank is the answer to the riddle.

Name _____

▶ Say the name of each picture. Fill in the bubble beside the letter for the **beginning sound** of the word.

1.
○ b
● g
○ d
goat

2.
○ k
○ m
● y
yarn

3.
○ w
● r
○ t
rope

4.
● w
○ l
○ m
worm

▶ Say the name of each picture. Fill in the bubble beside the letter for the **ending sound**.

5.
○ b
● l
○ s
seal

6.
○ d
○ x
● g
dog

7.
○ m
○ b
● x
box

8.
○ m
● p
○ b
map

▶ Say the name of each picture. Fill in the bubble beside the letter for the **middle sound**.

9.
○ r
○ c
● b
cabin

10.
○ c
○ t
● r
carrot

11.
● m
○ n
○ l
lemon

12.
○ r
● d
○ l
ladder

Initial, medial, final consonants: Assessment   **19**

FOCUS ON ALL LEARNERS

ESL/ELL ENGLISH LANGUAGE LEARNERS

Materials: paper

• On the board, draw a three-column chart. Label the columns *beginning, middle, end.* Have children make columns on their papers.

• Say a letter and a word: *b, cabin.* Model writing *cabin* in the column labeled *middle.*

• Continue, using words from pages 19 and 20. Check lists for accuracy.

• Have children complete pages 19 and 20.

VISUAL/KINESTHETIC LEARNERS

Materials: index cards, markers

Have children make and place consonant letter cards beside classroom objects in the order they hear the sounds in the object names. For example, *m* and *p* would be placed to the left and right of a map.

▶ Circle **the word that answers the riddle.**
Print **it on the line.**

1. I rhyme with **ham.** I am _____jam_____.

    (jam)
    car
    farm

2. I rhyme with **drum.** I am _____gum_____.

    gas
    gull
    (gum)

3. A spider spins me. I am a _____web_____.

    (web)
    well
    wet

4. I say "oink." I am a _____pig_____.

    big
    (pig)
    fig

5. I come after six. I am _____seven_____.

    (seven)
    tiger
    robot

6. I rhyme with **fox.** I am a _____box_____.

    bag
    (box)
    bell

7. You can write with me. I am a _____pen_____.

    pet
    peg
    (pen)

8. You can ride in me. I am a _____wagon_____.

    cabin
    (wagon)
    lemon

20   Initial, medial, final consonants: Assessment

HOME With your child, take turns making up riddles using the words on this page.

STUDENT PROGRESS ASSESSMENT

You may wish to review the observational notes you made as children worked through the activities in the unit. These notes will help you evaluate the progress children made with initial, medial, and final consonants.

PORTFOLIO ASSESSMENT

Review the materials children have collected in their portfolios. Conduct interviews with children to discuss their written work and their progress since the beginning of this unit. As you review children's work, evaluate how well they use phonics skills.

DAILY PHONICS PRACTICE

For children who need additional practice with initial, medial, and final consonants, see Daily Phonics Practice, pages 244–245.

PHONICS POSTTEST

To assess children's mastery of initial, medial, and final consonants, use the posttest on pages 5g–5h.

AUDITORY LEARNERS

Say these pairs of words and ask children to tell how they are alike in terms of shared beginning, ending, or medial sounds: *yarn, yell; box, six; rope, cap; goat, get; rabbit, cabin; seal, soap; carrot, robot.*

CHALLENGE

Ask pairs of children to create their own riddle tests and exchange them with classmates to solve. Have them write clues and provide two answer choices. Children might write riddles for these words: *car, farm, gull, gas, well, wet, big, fig, tiger, robot, bag, bell, peg, pet, cabin, lemon.*

EXTRA SUPPORT/INTERVENTION

Materials: Phonics Picture Cards: Initial, Medial, and Final Consonants (1–44)

Have children sort the picture cards into sets of picture names with the same beginning, medial, or ending sound. See Daily Phonics Practice, pages 244–245.

Teacher Notes

Short Vowels

THEME: AT WORK, AT PLAY

CONTENTS

Student Performance Objectives

In Unit 2, children will review and extend their understanding of short vowels and the sounds they stand for within the context of the theme "At Work, At Play." As children apply the concept that consonant and vowel sounds can be blended together to form words, they will be able to

▶ Associate the vowels, *a, e, i, o* and *u* with the short sounds they stand for

▶ Identify rhyming elements containing the short vowel sounds

▶ Distinguish among the short vowel sounds

▶ Apply the short vowel rule as an aid to decoding words presented in isolation and in context

▶ Learn and read high-frequency words in context

Assessment Options

In Unit 2, assess children's ability to read and write words with short vowel sounds. Use the Unit Pretest and Posttest for formal assessment. For ongoing informal assessment you may wish to use children's work on the Review pages, Take-Home Books, and Unit Checkups. You may also want to encourage children to evaluate their own work and to participate in setting goals for their own learning.

ESL/ELL Short vowel sounds may be especially problematic for English language learners. Note pronunciation difficulties, but assess based upon children's ability to distinguish short vowel sounds when pronounced by a native speaker. For additional support for English language learners, see page 21j.

FORMAL ASSESSMENT

Use the Unit 2 Pretest on pages 21e–21f to help assess a child's knowledge at the beginning of the unit and to plan instruction.

ESL/ELL Before administering the Pretest, gather in a paper bag a variety of items (or pictures of them) that match the visuals on pages 21e–21f. Have volunteers select an item and then name it. Ask other children in the group to identify the vowel sound.

Use the Unit 2 Posttest on pages 21g–21h to help assess mastery of unit objectives and to plan for reteaching, if necessary.

ESL/ELL Some children may have difficulty with direction. Read the directions aloud and model how to complete the worksheets.

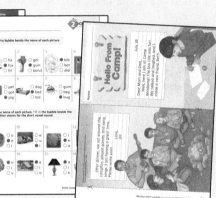

INFORMAL ASSESSMENT

Use the Review pages, Unit Checkup, and Take-Home Books in the student book to provide an effective means of evaluating children's performance.

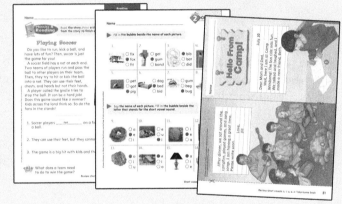

Unit 2 Skills	Review pages	Checkups	Take-Home Books
Short vowel *a*	37–38, 49–50	53–54	51–52
Short vowel *i*	37–38, 49–50	53–54	51–52
Short vowel *u*	37–38, 49–50	53–54	51–52
Short vowel *o*	49–50	53–54	51–52
Short vowel *e*	49–50	53–54	51–52

STUDENT PROGRESS CHECKLIST

Use the checklist on page 21i to record children's progress. You may want to cut the sections apart to place each child's checklist in his or her portfolio.

PORTFOLIO ASSESSMENT

This logo appears throughout the teaching plans. It signals opportunities for collecting a student's work for individual portfolios. You may also want to include the Pretest and Posttest, the Review pages, the Unit Checkup, Phonics & Reading, Phonics & Writing, and Phonics & Spelling.

PHONEMIC AWARENESS AND PHONICS ASSESSMENT

Use PAPA to obtain an itemized analysis of children's decoding skills.

PAPA Skills	MCP Phonics Lessons in Unit 2
Short vowels	Lessons 8–22

Pretest and Posttest

DIRECTIONS

To help you assess children's progress in learning Unit 2 skills, tests are available on pages 21e–21h.

Administer the Pretest before children begin the unit. The results of the Pretest will help you identify each child's strengths and needs in advance, allowing you to structure lesson plans to meet individual needs. Administer the Posttest to assess children's overall mastery of skills taught in the unit and to identify specific areas that will require reteaching.

ESL/ELL Note that the objective of both the Unit 2 Pretest and Posttest is identification of short vowel sounds and writing the letters that stand for them. To ensure that vocabulary comprehension does not interfere with sound recognition, preview visuals in advance of the tests. Then, name each of the items aloud as children move from item to item in the tests.

To assess the high-frequency words for Unit 2, have a child read orally each word on the Pretest and the Posttest as you point to it. Then, have the child check each word read.

PERFORMANCE ASSESSMENT PROFILE

The following chart will help you identify specific skills as they appear on the tests and will enable you to identify and record specific information about an individual's or the class's performance on the tests.

Depending on the results of each test, refer to the Reteaching column for lesson-plan pages where you can find activities that will be useful for meeting individual needs or for daily phonics practice.

Answer Keys

Unit 2 Pretest, page 21e (BLM 8)
1. i	9. u
2. a	10. e
3. o	11. a
4. e	12. i
5. u	13. o
6. o	14. o
7. u	15. i
8. a	16. e

Unit 2 Pretest, page 21f (BLM 9)
17. fun	22. fish
18. tent	23. bed
19. sun	24. bag
20. swim	25. camp
21. rock	

Unit 2 Posttest, page 21g (BLM 10)
1. a	9. o
2. u	10. e
3. a	11. u
4. i	12. i
5. a	13. e
6. a	14. a
7. i	15. i
8. u	16. o

Unit 2 Posttest, page 21h (BLM 11)
17. plan	21. pond
18. fun	22. run
19. Ten	23. best
20. hill	24. dog

Performance Assessment Profile

Skill	Pretest Questions	Posttest Questions	Reteaching Focus on All Learners	Daily Phonics Practice
Short vowel *a*	2, 8, 11, 24, 25	1, 3, 5, 6, 14, 17	23–26, 37–38, 49–52	245–246
Short vowel *i*	1, 12, 15, 20, 22	4, 7, 12, 15, 20	27–30, 37–38, 49–52	245–246
Short vowel *u*	5, 7, 9, 17, 19	2, 8, 11, 18, 22	31–34, 37–38, 49–52	246
Short vowel *o*	3, 6, 13, 14, 21	9, 16, 21, 24	39–42, 49–52	246
Short vowel *e*	4, 10, 16, 18, 23	10, 13, 19, 23	43–46, 49–52	246

Student Progress Checklist

Make as many copies as needed to use for a class list. For individual portfolio use, cut apart each child's section. As indicated by the code, color in boxes next to skills satisfactorily assessed and insert an *X* by those requiring reteaching. Marked boxes can later be colored in to indicate mastery.

Student Progress Checklist

Code: ■ Satisfactory   ☒ Needs Reteaching

Student:	Skills	High-Frequency Words		Comments / Learning Goals
Pretest Score: _____ Posttest Score: _____	☐ Short *a* ☐ Short *i* ☐ Short *u* ☐ Short *o* ☐ Short *e*	☐ does ☐ other ☐ would ☐ under ☐ about ☐ then	☐ care ☐ sure ☐ our ☐ where ☐ because ☐ good	
Student: _____	Skills	High-Frequency Words		Comments / Learning Goals
Pretest Score: _____ Posttest Score: _____	☐ Short *a* ☐ Short *i* ☐ Short *u* ☐ Short *o* ☐ Short *e*	☐ does ☐ other ☐ would ☐ under ☐ about ☐ then	☐ care ☐ sure ☐ our ☐ where ☐ because ☐ good	
Student: _____	Skills	High-Frequency Words		Comments / Learning Goals
Pretest Score: _____ Posttest Score: _____	☐ Short *a* ☐ Short *i* ☐ Short *u* ☐ Short *o* ☐ Short *e*	☐ does ☐ other ☐ would ☐ under ☐ about ☐ then	☐ care ☐ sure ☐ our ☐ where ☐ because ☐ good	
Student: _____	Skills	High-Frequency Words		Comments / Learning Goals
Pretest Score: _____ Posttest Score: _____	☐ Short *a* ☐ Short *i* ☐ Short *u* ☐ Short *o* ☐ Short *e*	☐ does ☐ other ☐ would ☐ under ☐ about ☐ then	☐ care ☐ sure ☐ our ☐ where ☐ because ☐ good	

BLM 12 Unit 2 Checklist

Throughout Unit 2 there are opportunities to assess English language learners' ability to read and write words with short vowel sounds. Short vowel sounds may be especially problematic for English language learners. The home languages spoken by English language learners vary from five pure vowel sounds in Spanish to 35 syllabic vowels in Cantonese. English language learners will need many opportunities to listen to English vowel sounds before being expected to produce them without error. Take note of pronunciation difficulties as they occur but assess progress based on children's ability to distinguish short vowel sounds when pronounced by a native speaker.

Lesson 8, pages 23–24 Korean and Russian speakers may pronounce /ya/ after certain consonants, making the *ca* of *camp* sound like the *kya* series in *brickyard*.

Lesson 10, pages 27–28 Speakers of languages other than English may pronounce short *i* like the long *e* in *see* or *meat*. Practice *mitt, meat, lips, leaps, six, seeks*.

Lesson 12, pages 31–32 Speakers of Spanish, Tagalog, or some Asian languages may pronounce short *u* like the *o* in *hot* or the *a* in *father*.

Lesson 16, pages 39–40 Speakers of Spanish, Tagalog, and some Asian languages may pronounce in the same way the sounds of short *o*, short *a*, and short *u*. Practice *hot, hat, hut; lock, lack, luck*.

Lesson 18, pages 43–44 Since no vowel sound similar to short *e* exists in Korean, offer additional practice with *pen, net, leg, bed, red, belt,* and *tent*.

Lesson 21, pages 49–50 For children challenged by differentiating and pronouncing clearly the five short vowels, practice word groups such as *bat, bet, bit, bob, but,* and *pat, pet, pit, pot, pup*.

Lesson 22, pages 51–52 Overnight camping may be unfamiliar to children of other cultures. Guide children to verbalize some of the activities and hobbies they have participated in that could be offered at camp.

Phonics Games, Activities, and Technology

The following collection of ideas offers a variety of opportunities to reinforce phonics skills while actively engaging children. The games, activities, and technology suggestions can easily be adapted to meet the needs of your group of learners. They vary in approach so as to consider children's different learning styles.

RHYMING FUN

Using words related to the "At Work, At Play" theme, ask children to respond to these questions with rhyming words: What rhymes with *fun? mitt? tent? cap? top? ball?*

BEGINNING, MIDDLE, AND ENDING SOUNDS

Provide children with a three-column chart labeled with the words *Beginning*, *Middle*, and *End*. Then, say a short vowel word that contains three letters, such as *bag, hen, bib, lid, bus, jug, box, dog, bed,* or *ham*. Have children pronounce the word after you, listening for the letter sounds. Then, direct them to write the letter that stands for the beginning sound in the first column, the vowel sound in the middle column, and the final consonant sound in the last column. Repeat with other words.

Beginning	Middle	End
b	a	g
h	e	n

Variation: This chart can also be used to practice identification of the location of a specific sound within a word. Ask such questions as *Where is the /e/ in eggs?* and have children place a marker in the correct column on the chart.

ESL/ELL This activity can have English language learners work as members of a group. More—not fewer—choices may increase children's ability to participate.

HOPSCOTCH GAME

> Jump to the first letter in *ant*.
>
> Jump to the letter that stands for the middle sound in *six*.
>
> Jump to *u* if you can give me a word that has the short *u* sound.
>
> Jump to the middle letter in *dog*.

This variation of the hopscotch game works best with a small group. Draw a game grid on the sidewalk or on the classroom floor using chalk or masking tape. In each of the grid squares, write a vowel letter. Then, give directions like the example at left and have children jump to the spot you've identified. Once children understand the structure of the clues, they can make up their own clues. Have them refer to the short vowel Wo: created for help in thinking up words for clues.

ESL/ELL Simplify this game by focusing on individual tasks. Change the floor game grid to a game board and use stickers to identify the "jumps." Introduce the short vowels *a* and *i* separately from *u, o,* and *e*.

WORD WHEELS

Make a word wheel of a paper plate and a tagboard circle. Write a phonogram on the left side of the plate and next to it cut out a notch from the edge. Write consonants that represent initial sounds around the outside of the tagboard circle. Fasten the wheels together with a brad. As children turn the bottom wheel, have them read the words that are formed.

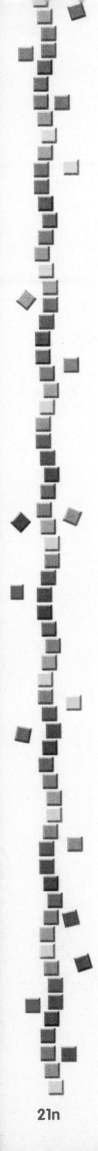

SPELL IT OUT

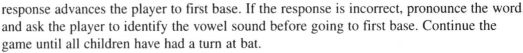

Provide partners with a set of letter cards and a set of picture cards whose names have short vowel sounds. Have children work together to say the picture name and then use the letter cards to spell out the word.

SHORT VOWEL BASEBALL

Set up a baseball diamond, using chairs for the bases and home plate. Have the first batter come to the plate. Display a short vowel word card and ask the batter to read the word aloud. A correct response advances the player to first base. If the response is incorrect, pronounce the word and ask the player to identify the vowel sound before going to first base. Continue the game until all children have had a turn at bat.

Variations: A simpler version of this game can be played with short vowel picture cards. Batters name the picture and identify the short vowel sound in the picture name.

SHORT VOWEL BINGO

Provide children with blank game boards, five different colors of crayons, and markers for covering the squares. Have children fill the board by randomly writing the vowels *a, e, i, o,* and *u* in the spaces. To make the game easier to play, suggest that they use a different color to write each vowel. To play, say a word containing a short vowel sound and have children repeat it. Have them cover the letter whose vowel sound is heard in the word. Play until someone has bingo!

Variations: Instead of writing letters, children can fill the spaces with short vowel words that you wish them to practice. In this case, children will cover each word as you pronounce it.

COOKIE JAR GAME

Partners can play this game to reinforce short vowel phonograms. Draw two large cookie jars on tagboard. Give partners plastic chips or other counters, the cookie jars, a set of consonant cards, and several phonogram cards. After turning the consonant cards face down, have children select a phonogram card and place it face up so both can see it. Then, have them take turns selecting consonant cards and placing them next to the phonogram card to try to form a word. If a player makes a word, he or she can place a chip in the cookie jar. The game continues until no more words can be made.

THREE-RING CIRCUS GAME

This is a game the whole class can play simultaneously. Draw three large circles on the chalkboard. In the first circle, print five or six consonants. In the middle circle, print the vowels you wish to review. In the last circle, print five or six consonants that often appear at the end of words. To play the game, have children form three-letter words by using the letters in the circles. Once children have compiled their lists, suggest they compare them with those of a partner.

Variation: This game can be played with teams of children working together to write words that are each worth one point. It can also be played with children working cooperatively with a partner to form the words.

WORD FLIP BOOKS

Make flip books that feature a short vowel phonogram. As the letter
pages are flipped, each new word that is formed is read. Make
phonogram books representing each of the short vowels.

ROLL-A-VOWEL

Cover the faces of a number cube with masking tape. Write *a, e, i, o,* and *u* on five of the
cube faces, leaving the sixth face blank. Children can take turns rolling the cube and
identifying the letter that shows. Then, have them say a word containing the letter's short
vowel sound. If the blank face shows, children can choose the vowel they wish to use.

SLIDES AND ROPES

Use Blackline Master 14 to make a short vowel version of this board game. Make a master
copy by writing short vowel words on each of the spaces. Then, distribute copies of the
game to pairs of children. Have them take turns using a number cube to move a marker
along the numbered squares. As they land on a square, they must read the word aloud. If
players land on a square at the bottom of a rope, they climb up to the square at the top of
the rope. If they land on a square at the top of a slide, they must move their marker down
the slide to its bottom. Play continues until both players reach the playground.

ESL/ELL This game may be complex if children are unfamiliar with games of this nature.
White out the numbered boxes on the game board. Draw a house in box 1 and label the
roof *Home.* Pair English language learners and native speakers to model the game.

Blend, blend, blend these sounds.
Listen to what I say:
/h/-/a/-/n/-/d/
This game is fun to play!

"BLENDING GAME" SONG

Sing the verse shown to the tune of "Row Your Boat" to
focus on blending sounds to form a short vowel word. Repeat
the sounds and ask a volunteer to identify the word. Then,
repeat the song with other sets of sounds that form short
vowel words.

TECHNOLOGY

The following software products reinforce children's
understanding of short vowels and other phonics skills.

**Reader Rabbit's® Learn to Read with
Phonics™**
Includes two programs designed to help
readers increase their skills. This program
systematically combines three activity
components: word recognition, phonics, and
progressively challenging stories. A wide
range of ability levels are supported and
enhanced in over 100 carefully designed
lessons.

** Riverdeep The Learning Company
   500 Redwood Blvd.
   Novato, CA, 94947
   (800) 825-4420
   www.learningcompanyschool.com

Reading Who? Reading You!
Children learn letter and sound
correspondence for 250 words through
activities such as "The Word Truck," which
allows them to create original phrases and
sentences. New sounds and words are
presented by real children through video
clips.

** Sunburst Technology
   1900 South Batavia Ave.
   Geneva, IL 60134
   (800) 321-7511
   www.sunburst.com

Name _____

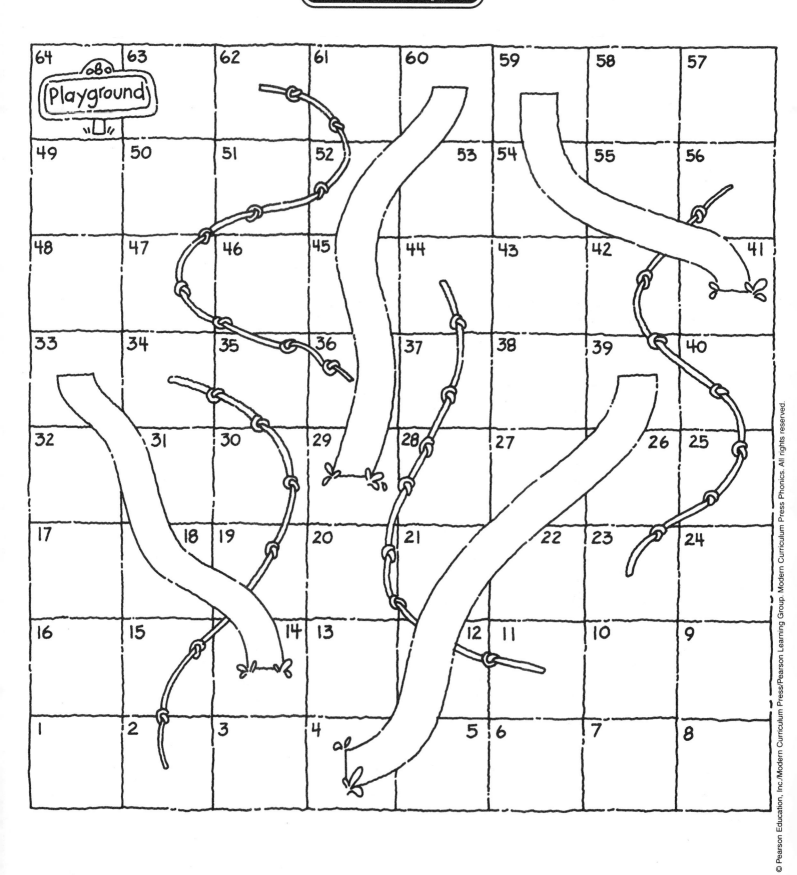

Slides and Ropes

64	63	62	61	60	59	58	57
Playground							
49	50	51	52		53	54	55	56
48	47	46	45	44	43	42	41
33	34	35	36	37	38	39	40
32	31	30	29	28	27	26	25
17	18	19	20	21	22	23	24
16	15	14	13	12	11	10	9
1	2	3	4	5	6	7	8

Home Connections

The Home Connections features of this program are intended to involve families in their children's learning and application of phonics skills. Three effective opportunities to make connections between home and school include the following.

- **HOME LETTER**
- **HOME NOTES**
- **TAKE-HOME BOOKS**

HOME LETTER

A letter is available to be sent home at the beginning of Unit 2. This letter informs family members that children will be learning to read and write words with short vowel sounds within the context of the unit theme, "At Work, At Play." Two activities designed to reinforce short vowel sounds are suggested to parents. Each activity allows children to hear and see words with short vowel sounds. Both activities promote interaction between child and family members while supporting the child's learning to read and write words with short vowel sounds. The letter, which is available in both English and Spanish, also suggests books relating to the unit theme that family members can look for in a local library and enjoy reading together.

HOME NOTES

Whenever the Home logo appears within the student book, a phonics activity is suggested to be done at home. The activities are simple to do, requiring little or no preparation or special materials, and are meant to reinforce the targeted phonics skill.

Home Notes in Spanish are also available for both teachers and parents to download and use from our website, www.PlaidPhonics.com.

TAKE-HOME BOOKS

Within the student book are many Take-Home Books that can be cut out and assembled. The story language in each book reinforces the targeted phonics skill. The books can be taken home and shared with family members. In Unit 2, one Take-Home Book is available, focusing on the five different short vowel sounds as well as the unit theme, "At Work, At Play."

Short Vowels

<blockquote>
Skill Focus

Assess Prior Knowledge
To assess children's prior knowledge of short vowels, use the pretest on pages 21e–21f.
</blockquote>

Unit Focus

▶ Build Background

- Write the theme "At Work, At Play" on the board. Read the theme aloud and ask children for examples of how they work and play.

- Call attention to the picture on page 21. Have children identify how the people in the photo are having fun.

- Read the title and the text aloud as children follow along. After reading, discuss whether they have ever been to a place like Central Park.

▶ Introduce Vowels

- Write the vowels *a, e, i, o,* and *u* on the board. Remind children that the alphabet is made up of twenty-one consonants and five vowels. Explain that in this unit they will be learning about short vowel sounds.

- Read "Fun in the Park" again. Then, read the words *animals, Central, big, lots,* and *fun* slowly, elongating the short vowel sound in each word: *aaanimals, Ceeentral, biiig, looots, fuuun.* Explain that each of these words is an example of a word with a short vowel sound.

Critical Thinking Ask children to imagine that they are in Central Park. Discuss what they would do if they were there. Encourage them to give reasons for their choices.

Read Aloud

Fun in the Park

New York is a big city. People work hard. They also have fun. Many people go to Central Park to have fun. The park is in the middle of the city.

Kids play baseball in the park. Some people sail boats, ride bikes, or jog. Families go to the park to have a picnic or visit the zoo.

In the winter, many families skate on one of two ice-skating rinks. Others go sledding or play in the snow.

TALK about it What would you like to do in Central Park? Why?

Unit 2 • Introduction
Critical Thinking

21

THEME FOCUS

- -

WORK AT SCHOOL

Have children discuss ways in which they can help out in the classroom. Then, work with children to make a list of classroom "jobs." Post the list and invite children to sign up for jobs on a weekly or bimonthly basis.

PLAY AT SCHOOL

Encourage children to think of several activities that can be enjoyed on the school grounds at this time of year. Choose a few that children can play as a large group or as rotating small groups. Help children plan and hold a "Fun at School Day."

FUN ALL YEAR

Write the names of the months on chart paper, grouping them according to seasons. Add the names of the seasons to the chart. Discuss outdoor activities appropriate to each season according to where you live. Then, refer children to the chart and have them name the vowels in the names of the months and in the seasons. Suggest that they see if they can find sounds similar to the vowels in *have, Central, big, lots,* and *fun.*

Dear Family,

In this unit "At Work, At Play," your child will be learning to read and write words with short vowel sounds. The names of many things we do for work and fun contain short vowel sounds such as sit, hop, run, bend, clap. As your child explores the short vowel sounds, you might like to try these activities together.

Estimada familia:

En esta unidad, titulada "Trabajando, jugando" ("At Work, At Play"), su hijo/a aprenderá a leer y escribir palabras con sonidos breves. Los nombres de muchas actividades que realizamos cuando trabajamos o jugamos contienen vocales con sonidos breves, como por ejemplo, sit (sentarse), hop (saltar), run (correr), bend (inclinarse), clap (aplaudir). A medida que su hijo/a se vaya familiarizando con las vocales de sonido breve, pueden hacer las siguientes actividades juntos.

a clap   e bend   i skip   o hop   u run

▶ Reread the selection on page 21 with your child. Talk about life in a city. Help your child to find the words that contain a short vowel sound.

▶ Play a riddle game with your child. Think up a riddle whose answer is a short vowel word; for example: I am what you do with a song. What am I? (sing)

You and your child might enjoy reading these books together.

Busy, Busy City Street
by Cari Meister

The Great Ball Game
by Joseph Bruchac

Sincerely,

▶ Lean con su hijo/a la selección en la página 21. Hablen sobre la vida en una ciudad. Ayuden a su hijo/a a hallar las palabras que contienen una vocal con sonido breve.

▶ Jueguen con su hijo/a a las adivinanzas. Inventen una adivinanza cuya respuesta tenga una palabra con sonido breve; como por ejemplo, I am what you do with a song. What am I? (sing)

Ustedes y su hijo/a disfrutarán leyendo estos libros juntos.

Busy, Busy City Street
de Cari Meister

The Great Ball Game
de Joseph Bruchac

Sinceramente,

(22)
Unit 2 • Introduction

- The Home Letter on page 22 is intended to familiarize family members with examples of short vowel words children will focus on in Unit 2. Have children tear out the page and take it home.

- Encourage children to complete the activities with family members. Suggest that they look in the library for the books and read them with a family member.

LEARNING CENTER ACTIVITIES

WRITING CENTER

Have each child write a numbered "how to" list for playing a favorite outdoor game or activity. Children may enjoy displaying their lists with construction paper cutouts of items related to the activities. Some children might use small rebus pictures of game equipment as part of their instructions. Check children's writing for correct spelling of single consonant sounds.

SCIENCE CENTER

Provide a globe and flashlight in the Science Center. Explain that the globe represents Earth and the flashlight acts as the sun. In a dimmed area, have children work as scientists to experiment with the way sunlight strikes the rotating Earth to make day and night. A supply of library books about the planets and the measurement of time can help children with explanations.

SOCIAL STUDIES CENTER

Provide state road maps and/or travel brochures for local, state, and national tourist sites. Encourage children to plan imaginary vacations, listing a path of five to ten cities or attractions they would like to visit.

BULLETIN BOARD

Make a bulletin board titled "At Work, At Play." Find in magazines and newspapers pictures of people engaged in activities with short vowel sounds. You might use a picture of a dancer, a singer, a doctor, a golfer, and so on. Have children help you label the pictures (dancer, singer, doctor, golfer). Invite children to bring in additional pictures.

Short Vowel a

Skill Focus

Children will

★ recognize the sound of short vowel *a*.

★ identify picture names and words that contain the short *a* sound.

★ identify rhyming short *a* words.

ESL/ELL Korean and Russian speakers may pronounce /ya/ after certain consonant sounds, making the *ca* of *camp* sound like the *kya* series in *brickyard*.

Teach

Phonemic Awareness: Phoneme Identity
Say the word *Dan* twice, elongating the short *a* sound (*Daaan*). Then, say the word naturally and have children repeat it. Explain that the sound heard in the middle of the word is short *a*. Say the following groups of words and invite children to clap each time they hear a word with the short *a* sound.

- man   mitt   rap
- sat   Dan   Tom

Rhyme Say the words *Dan* and *man*, and emphasize the short *a* sound. Have children repeat the words. Ask them what they notice about the sound of the words. (*They both have the short a sound and rhyme.*) Then, say these groups of words. Invite volunteers to tell you which words in each group rhyme.

- tap   rat   map (*tap, map*)
- can   cat   hat (*hat, cat*)

Practice and Apply

Sound to Symbol Read the rhyme at the top of page 23 aloud as children follow along. Invite children to repeat the rhyme with you. Encourage volunteers to print the words with short *a* on the board and underline the letter that makes the short *a* sound.

Read the rule at the top of page 23. Then, have children say the picture names on the page. You may wish to complete the first item on page 24 with children to be sure they understand the directions.

Reading Use *That Cat!*, MCP Phonics and Reading Consonant and Vowel Skills Library, Level B, to provide additional practice in reading words with the sound of short vowel *a*.

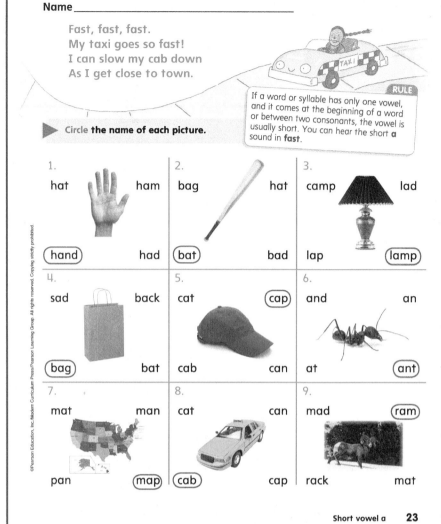

Name _____

Fast, fast, fast.
My taxi goes so fast!
I can slow my cab down
As I get close to town.

▶ Circle **the name of each picture.**

RULE
If a word or syllable has only one vowel, and it comes at the beginning of a word or between two consonants, the vowel is usually short. You can hear the short **a** sound in **fast**.

1.		2.		3.	
hat	ham	bag	hat	camp	lad
(hand)	had	(bat)	bad	lap	(lamp)

4.		5.		6.	
sad	back	cat	(cap)	and	an
(bag)	bat	cab	can	at	(ant)

7.		8.		9.	
mat	man	cat	can	mad	(ram)
pan	(map)	(cab)	cap	rack	mat

Short vowel a   **23**

FOCUS ON ALL LEARNERS

ESL/ELL ENGLISH LANGUAGE LEARNERS

Materials: toy car

Read the directions on page 23 aloud and ask children to explain the activity in their own words. Call out a number from 1 to 9; have a volunteer name the corresponding picture clue. As needed, model item 1 with children. Have them complete the activity; review the answers together aloud.

AUDITORY LEARNERS

As you say the following short *a* words, invite children to respond with as many rhyming words as they can think of for each one: *rack, lad, clam, cat, plan, stand, tap, mash, bag*. When their answers do not rhyme, help children hear the difference between the words.

KINESTHETIC LEARNERS

Materials: yarn, construction paper, glue

Have each child print a short *a* word in large letters on construction paper and glue lengths of yarn to the paper to form the letters. When the glue has dried, suggest children trade papers with one another, close their eyes, name the letters, and pronounce the words as they trace them with their fingers.

▶ **Draw** a line through three words that rhyme in each box. Lines can go across, up and down, or on a diagonal.

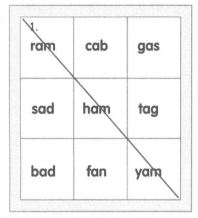

1.

ram	cab	gas
sad	ham	tag
bad	fan	yam

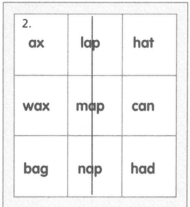

2.

ax	lap	hat
wax	map	can
bag	nap	had

3.

dad	tap	pal
~~bat~~	~~sat~~	~~cat~~
mat	pan	cap

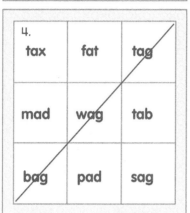

4.

tax	fat	tag
mad	wag	tab
bag	pad	sag

24 Short vowel a: Phonograms

 HOME Help your child think of another word to add to each group of rhyming words.

CURRICULUM CONNECTIONS

SPELLING

Pretest the following words as children begin the lessons on short *a* and short *i*.

1. **cab** You must pay to ride in a **cab**.
2. **ram** A male goat is called a **ram**.
3. **ax** Use an **ax** to chop firewood.
4. **wig** Did she wear a **wig** in the play?
5. **lips** He pressed his **lips** together.
6. **dish** Put the food in that **dish**.

WRITING

Using the rhyme on page 23, have children write sentences about a race, using short *a* words.

MATHEMATICS

Write $2 + 3 + 5 = 10$ on the board. Write the word *add* and note the initial /a/. Then, write $j + a + m = $. Read this "addition" problem by sounds: /j/ + /a/ + /m/ *equals jam*. Complete the equation with the word *jam*. Write similar equations and have others complete them.

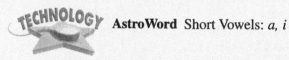 **TECHNOLOGY** **AstroWord** Short Vowels: *a, i*

VISUAL LEARNERS PARTNERS

Materials: Phonics Word Cards, Set 1: Short *a* words (1–33); paper bag

Place the word cards in a bag. Children can each choose a card, use the short *a* sound to orally read one of the words, and use it in a sentence. The partner can do the same for the other word on the card.

CHALLENGE

Invite children to make a list of short *a* words that do not appear on pages 23 and 24, but might rhyme with them. Have them sort their list by the ending sounds.

EXTRA SUPPORT/INTERVENTION

Materials: Phonics Picture Cards: apple (45), ax (46), bag (47), cap (48), cat (49), ham (50), hat (52), flag (136), glass (138)

Have children say the picture names and name the consonant that follows the short *a* sound in each word. See Daily Phonics Practice, pages 245–246.

Integrating Phonics and Reading

Guided Reading
Draw children's attention to the cover of the book and ask them what they think the book will be about.
First Reading Ask children to find the cat in each picture and explain what it is doing.
Second Reading Encourage children to identify the short *a* words, such as *bad, cat, dad, sad, that, Matt, Sam.*
Comprehension
After reading, ask children the following questions:
• Why doesn't Matt see the cat? *Recall/ Sequence*
• How does Matt feel at the end of the story? *Reflective Analysis/ Inference*
ESL/ELL **English Language Learners**
Point out the exclamation point and explain that it is used to express strong feeling. Read *That Cat!* with feeling and ask children why they think there is an exclamation point.

Short Vowel a

Skill Focus

Children will

★ recognize the sound of short vowel *a*.

★ understand that *a* stands for /a/.

★ identify words with the short sound of *a* that rhyme.

★ read and write short *a* words in context.

★ recognize and read high-frequency words.

Teach

Phonological Awareness: Rhyme Say the words *nap* and *tap*, elongating the short *a* sound (*naaap, taaap*). Remind children that the sound they hear in the middle of the word is the short *a* sound. Say *nap* and *tap* again. Ask: *How else are these words alike?* (*They rhyme.*) Next, say these words: *tap, tip, cap.* Have volunteers identify the words that rhyme.

Sound to Symbol Write *Pam* on the board. Say the word and invite a volunteer to underline the letter that stands for the short *a* sound. Then, write the name *Sam* below *Pam.* Ask children how the two names are alike. (*They both have the sound of short* a, *and rhyme.*) Have a volunteer underline the letter that stands for the short *a* sound.

Words in Context: Decodable Words Write the words *cat* and *pat* and the sentence below on the board. Have children select the word that completes the sentence.

• **My pet is a _____.** (*cat*)

Practice and Apply

Sound to Symbol Read the directions to the activity on page 25. Encourage children to say the names of the children in the picture after each rhyming word.

Writing Read the directions on page 26. Remind children to reread the sentence with the word they circled to be sure it makes sense. Children will have an opportunity to read the following high-frequency words: *my, likes, she, does, have, always, that.*

Critical Thinking In discussing Talk About It, children might suggest that Pat likes Sam because she licks Sam's hand and sits on his lap.

Reading You may wish to use *The Best Birthday Mole Ever Had,* MCP Phonics and Reading Consonant and Vowel Skills Library, Level B, to reinforce the short *a* sound.

Name _____

▶ Find **words** in the box that **rhyme** with each child's name. **Print** the rhyming words above or below each child's picture.

cat	ham	dad	fan	jam	van	hat	bad
sad	pan	yam	mat	can	bat	had	ram

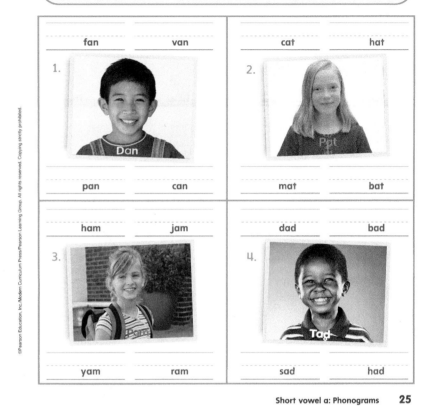

1. fan   van / Dan / pan   can

2. cat   hat / Pat / mat   bat

3. ham   jam / Pam / yam   ram

4. dad   bad / Tad / sad   had

Short vowel a: Phonograms   **25**

FOCUS ON ALL LEARNERS

ESL/ELL ENGLISH LANGUAGE LEARNERS

Verify children's understanding of rhyming words. Then, read directions aloud for the activity on page 25, and help them read the names of the children. Complete item 1 with children. Encourage them to finish items 2 through 4 in pairs.

VISUAL LEARNERS

Materials: Phonics Word Cards, Set 1: *ant* (3), *ax* (5), *band* (6), *fast* (8), *camp* (11), *map* (13), *nap* (15), *gas* (16), *quack* (22), *sand* (26), *tan* (30)

Display the word cards and say a clue for one of the words, such as *This is a group of musicians.* Ask a volunteer to find the answer (*band*), pick up the card, and read it. Have that child give the next clue.

AUDITORY LEARNERS

On the board, write *ra* followed by a blank (*ra_*), and pronounce it. Invite children to quickly think of short *a* words that begin with *ra*. Possible responses might include *rag, ram, ramp, ran, rang,* and *ran.* You may wish to repeat this exercise using *ha_, sa_, la_,* or *pa_.*

Circle the word that will finish each sentence. Print it on the line.

1. I am Sam, and my cat is ___Pat___ .   camp (Pat) cart

2. Pat likes milk and ___cat___ food.   class sat (cat)

3. She eats a lot, but she is not ___fat___ .   van (fat) lamp

4. She likes to lick my ___hand___ .   (hand) gas band

5. Pat likes to sit on my ___lap___ .   (lap) ham Sam

6. Pat does not like to have a ___bath___ .   gap (bath) rack

7. She runs away as ___fast___ as she can.   (fast) class bat

8. I ___can___ always find her.   (can) past fast

9. She takes a nap on a ___mat___ .   mast (mat) fat

10. She takes a ___nap___ on Dad's lap.   ran sat (nap)

11. I ___am___ happy that Pat is my cat.   can (am) as

TALK about it Do you think Pat likes Sam? Why or why not?

HOME Help your child think of words that rhyme with the answers he or she used in the sentences.

26   Short vowel a: High-frequency words, critical thinking

CURRICULUM CONNECTIONS

SPELLING

Give each partner three index cards. One child prints the short *a* spelling words (*cab, ram, ax*) on the cards and the other child prints the short *i* words (*wig, lips, dish*). They then cut apart the letters, trade pieces, and respell the words. Distribute copies of the short *a* and *i* spelling words for children to refer to for practice.

WRITING

Write the title "Imagine That Cat" on chart paper and encourage children to imagine a cat that is the silliest, most talented, or most special in some other way. Record their ideas. Then, have them copy the title on their papers and write a description using phrases from the chart.

PORTFOLIO

HEALTH

Ask children to discuss their feelings such as *happy, sad,* or *mad.* Ask children to name ways they can share good feelings they have? How can they help someone who is feeling bad?

TECHNOLOGY **AstroWord** Short Vowels: *a, i*

KINESTHETIC LEARNERS *PARTNERS*

Have two sets of partners come to the board. Secretly hand one person from each pair a paper showing the short *a* name of a picture that both children should draw on the board. (Ideas can come from the pupil pages.) Children try to be the first to guess what their partner is drawing.

CHALLENGE

Have children find five words that contain a short *a* sound in a story or book they are reading. Ask them to write a clue to each word's meaning and work in a group to guess and spell each other's words.

EXTRA SUPPORT/INTERVENTION

Materials: construction paper, scissors, marker

Write *ap* on a paper square and cut two slits in front of it. Write the letters *c, g, l, m, n, r, s, t,* and *z* on a paper strip. Thread it through the slits. Have children read the resulting words *cap, gap,* and so on. Repeat with other initial letter-phonogram groups. See Daily Phonics Practice, pages 245–246.

Integrating Phonics and Reading

Guided Reading

Direct attention to the cover of *The Best Birthday Mole Ever Had,* and ask children what the story will be about. You may also wish to use the English Language Learners activity below.

First Reading Ask children why Mole's friends came to his house.

Second Reading Invite children to identify the short *a* words in the story, such as *plan, happy, rabbit, thank.*

Comprehension

After reading, ask children the following questions:

• Why did Mole have a problem? *Recall/Cause and Effect*

• Were you satisfied with the way Mole solved his problem? Why or why not? *Reflective Analysis/Personal Response*

ESL/ELL English Language Learners

Have children share what they know about birthday customs before they read the story.

Short Vowel i

Skill Focus

Children will

★ recognize the sound of short vowel *i*.

★ understand that *i* stands for /i/.

★ identify words with the short sound of *i* that rhyme.

ESL/ELL Speakers of languages other than English may pronounce short *i* like the long *e* in *see* or *meat*. Practice *mitt, meat, lips, leaps, six, seeks*.

Teach

Phonemic Awareness: Phoneme Segmentation Hold up a pin. Explain that you have a /p/ /i/ /n/ in your hand, isolating the sound of each letter. Have children repeat the sounds and encourage them to say the word naturally. Point to your lip and repeat the above procedure, saying /l/ /i/ /p/. Tell children that the sound they hear in the middle of *pin* and *lip* is the short *i* sound.

Rhyme Say the words *pig* and *wig* slowly. Ask children how they are alike. (*They have the short* i *sound and rhyme.*) Have children suggest another rhyming word. (*big, dig, fig, rig*)

Practice and Apply

Sound to Symbol Read aloud the rhyme at the top of page 27. Write the words *will* and *sit* from the rhyme on the board. Say the words slowly and have children repeat them. Discuss how the words are the same. (*They both have the short* i *sound.*) Have volunteers underline the letter *i*. Explain that the letter *i* stands for the sound of short *i* in those words. Encourage children to find other words with the short *i* sound in the rhyme and to tell which letter stands for the sound. You may wish to point out that *visit* has two short *i* sounds.

Review the rule at the top of the page with children. Then, have volunteers identify each of the pictures on page 27 before they complete the activity. Suggest that children repeat the name of the picture to themselves as they circle the correct word.

Rhyme With children, read the directions for page 28. Use the words in the first ball to review words that rhyme. (*rip, tip*) Then, ask children to complete the page independently. Remind children that a telling sentence begins with a capital letter and ends with a period.

Reading You may wish to use *Dinner by Five*, MCP Phonics and Reading Consonant and Vowel Skills Library, Level B, to provide practice in reading words with the short vowel *i* sound.

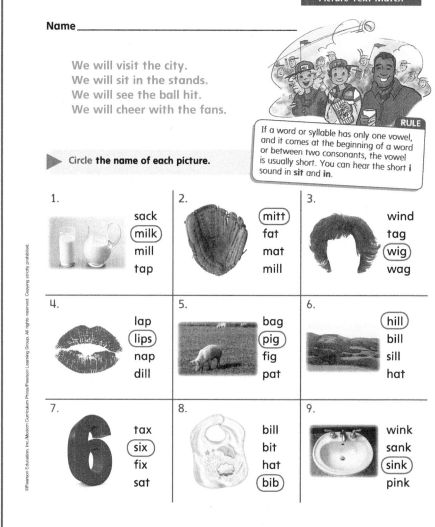

Name _____

We will visit the city.
We will sit in the stands.
We will see the ball hit.
We will cheer with the fans.

RULE
If a word or syllable has only one vowel, and it comes at the beginning of a word or between two consonants, the vowel is usually short. You can hear the short *i* sound in *sit* and *in*.

▶ Circle **the name of each picture.**

1. sack / (milk) / mill / tap
2. (mitt) / fat / mat / mill
3. wind / tag / (wig) / wag
4. lap / (lips) / nap / dill
5. bag / (pig) / fig / pat
6. (hill) / bill / sill / hat
7. tax / (six) / fix / sat
8. bill / bit / hat / (bib)
9. wink / sank / (sink) / pink

Short vowel i   **27**

FOCUS ON ALL LEARNERS

ESL/ELL ENGLISH LANGUAGE LEARNERS

Before reading the rhyme on page 27, ask volunteers to read aloud words in the rhyme that contain short vowel *i*. Then, have them underline the words. Read the entire rhyme aloud and then read one line at a time. Have children repeat. Finally, ask volunteers to read one line each.

AUDITORY LEARNERS GROUPS

Materials: Phonics Picture Cards: Short Vowels (45–84)

Display a combination of short *i* and other picture cards one at a time. Children should name each picture and cheer if it contains the short *i* sound.

KINESTHETIC LEARNERS INDIVIDUAL

Materials: 11 1-in. paper squares per child

Ask children to print the letters *i, b, c, d, g, k, l, l, n, p,* and *t* on their squares. Have them use the letters to spell short *i* words. Ask them to list the words they form.

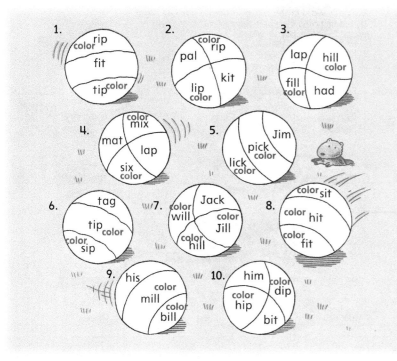

Phonograms/Rhyme

Color the parts of each ball with rhyming words the same color.

Use some of the rhyming words to write a sentence.

28   Short vowel i

CURRICULUM CONNECTIONS

SPELLING
Use a soft foam ball to practice the spelling words *cab, ram, ax, wig, lips,* and *dish.* Have children stand in a circle. Say the words one at a time. As children toss the ball from person to person, they say the next letter of the word.

WRITING
Have children think of things they would like to do. On the board, write the sentence starter *I wish I could _____.* Have children copy and finish it, adding other sentences. Have children read their ideas, noting the short *i* words they used.

HEALTH
Write *Drink milk!* on the board and discuss the importance of milk in children's diets. Explain that milk helps build strong teeth and bones as children grow. Library books about nutrition can help provide information about milk.

TECHNOLOGY AstroWord Short Vowels: *a, i*

VISUAL LEARNERS
Materials: sentence strips
Write the following sentences on strips: *Kim will win the gift; Jim will fix the pin; Bill will spill the milk; Lin will lift the lid.* Have children read the sentences, cut the words apart, and rearrange them into new sentences.

CHALLENGE
Materials: Phonics Word Cards, Set 1: Short *i* words (34–59)
Play charades by placing the word cards in a bag and having each child choose a card. Children can take turns acting out one of the two words on their cards as others guess the short *i* answer and spell it.

EXTRA SUPPORT/INTERVENTION
Materials: art paper, crayons
Have children fold their papers into fourths. In one box, ask them to write and illustrate the phrase *six sticks.* Have them draw six of other short *i* items in the remaining boxes and label each picture. See Daily Phonics Practice, pages 245–246.

Integrating Phonics and Reading
Guided Reading
Have children look at the title and the illustrations. Ask them what they think the story will be about.
First Reading Ask children to explain what Mike and Kim are doing in each picture.
Second Reading Encourage children to identify the short *i* words in the story, such as *Kim, dinner, will, fix, bit, this, mix, in,* and *kids.*
Comprehension
After reading, ask children the following questions:
• Why did Mike and Kim decide to make dinner? *Recall/Cause and Effect*
• What might have happened if Dad did not help the children clean up? *Reflective Analysis/Inference*
ESL/ELL English Language Learners
Invite children to share what they know about preparing meals. Ask them if there are some foods they like to help prepare.

28

Short Vowel i

Skill Focus

Children will

★ recognize the sound of short vowel *i*.

★ understand that *i* stands for /i/.

★ identify and spell picture names that contain the short sound of *i*.

★ complete riddles with words that have the short sound of *i*.

Teach

Phonemic Awareness: Phoneme Isolation
Encourage children to listen carefully as you say these three words, elongating the short *i* medial sound.

- **rip   sit   fill**

Have children repeat the words and then ask them to say aloud the sound they hear in the middle of each word. (/i/) Remind them that this is the sound of short vowel *i*.

Sound to Symbol Write the words *pig, pin,* and *ring* on the board. Have children pronounce each word as you point to it. Ask them to identify the sound that they hear in the middle of each word. (*short i*) Invite volunteers to underline the letter in each word that stands for the short *i* sound.

On the board, draw three columns titled *Beginning, Middle,* and *End* to isolate the short *i* sound. As you say the following words, invite volunteers to come to the board and print an *i* in the correct column: *fit, in, it, miss, lit.*

Words in Context: Decodable Words Write this riddle and the two word choices on the board.

- **It is big and steep. What is it? (hill, hand)**

Invite a volunteer to supply the correct answer and explain why it is correct. (*hill, because a hill is big and steep, and a hand is not*)

Practice and Apply

Sound to Symbol Remind children to say the name of each picture to themselves as they write the answers on page 29.

Writing Remind children to use both the riddle and the picture to help them find the correct answers from each item on page 30.

Reading You may wish to use *Three Little Kittens*, MCP Phonics and Reading Consonant and Vowel Skills Library, Level B, to reinforce the sound of short vowel *i* sound.

Name _____

▶ **Print** the word in the box that names each picture. In the last box, **draw** a picture of a short vowel word. **Print** the picture name.

1.	2.	3.	4.
six	wig	lid	hill
5.	6.	7.	8.
bib	pig	sink	pin
9.	10.	11.	12.
lips	swim	ring	

Short vowel i: Spelling   **29**

FOCUS ON ALL LEARNERS

ESL/ELL ENGLISH LANGUAGE LEARNERS

Ask volunteers to name aloud each picture on page 30. Then, exaggerate each sound for the first item as children record their answers. Continue in this manner as necessary. Pair children to say and write each answer. Review answers and have volunteers write them on the board.

AUDITORY LEARNERS

Ask a volunteer to think of a short *i* word, such as *wing*, and say it aloud. Have children take turns saying a rhyming word, such as *bring*. When someone cannot think of another rhyme or a word is repeated, start again with a new word.

KINESTHETIC LEARNERS

Materials: Phonics Word Cards, Set 1: Short *i* words (34–59)

Divide word cards among group members, but put the last card down on the table. Children can play "word dominoes" by taking turns adding cards to make connected paths of rhyming words. They can start new paths when none of their cards rhyme with those in the paths on the table.

▶ Circle **the word that answers each riddle. Print** it on the line.

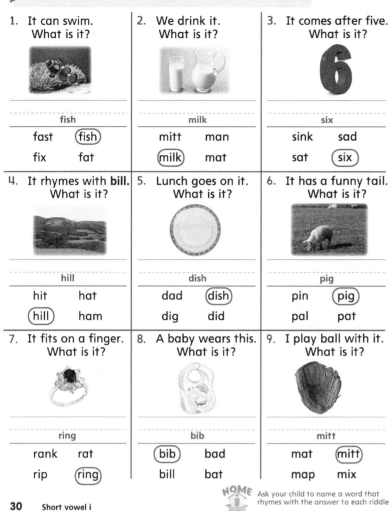

1. It can swim.
   What is it?

   fish

   fast   (fish)

   fix   fat

2. We drink it.
   What is it?

   milk

   mitt   man

   (milk)   mat

3. It comes after five.
   What is it?

   six

   sink   sad

   sat   (six)

4. It rhymes with **bill.**
   What is it?

   hill

   hit   hat

   (hill)   ham

5. Lunch goes on it.
   What is it?

   dish

   dad   (dish)

   dig   did

6. It has a funny tail.
   What is it?

   pig

   pin   (pig)

   pal   pat

7. It fits on a finger.
   What is it?

   ring

   rank   rat

   rip   (ring)

8. A baby wears this.
   What is it?

   bib

   (bib)   bad

   bill   bat

9. I play ball with it.
   What is it?

   mitt

   mat   (mitt)

   map   mix

 Ask your child to name a word that rhymes with the answer to each riddle.

30   Short vowel i

CURRICULUM CONNECTIONS

SPELLING

You may wish to posttest the short *a* and *i* spelling words at this point.

1. **dish**   I placed my **dish** in the sink.
2. **wig**   A **wig** can be a good disguise.
3. **ram**   That **ram** won first prize at the fair.
4. **cab**   We took a **cab** to the city park.
5. **lips**   We use our **lips** to form short vowel sounds.
6. **ax**   An **ax** is used to chop wood.

WRITING

Prompt a discussion about things children do for fun after school, both indoors and outside. Summarize the suggestions on chart paper and note short *i* words as they occur. Ask children to write at least two sentences each about the activity on the list that sounds like the most fun to them.

TECHNOLOGY   **AstroWord**   Short Vowels: *a, i*

VISUAL LEARNERS *PARTNERS*

Have children work in pairs to list the answer words on page 29 according to letter patterns in the words. For example: c-v-c (*six, wig*); c-v-cc (*hill, lips*).

CHALLENGE

Ask children to write sentences using three out of the four words in each of the sets of answer words on page 30.

EXTRA SUPPORT/INTERVENTION

Materials: ten index cards per child

Have partners each write ten short *i* words from pages 29–30 on index cards. Then, ask them to combine their cards and practice reading them together. **See Daily Phonics Practice, pages 245–246.**

Integrating Phonics and Reading

Guided Reading

Read the title of the book and have children look at the cover. Invite them to tell what they think the story will be about. You may also wish to use the activity for English Language Learners below.

First Reading Ask children to explain what the kittens are doing in each picture.

Second Reading Help children identify the words in the story that contain the short *i* sound.

Comprehension

After reading, ask children the following questions:

• Why were the kittens trying on mittens? *Recall/Cause and Effect*

• How do you think the kittens felt at the end of the story? *Reflective Analysis/Inference*

ESL/ELL **English Language Learners**

Review the short *i* sound in *kittens*. Then, ask children to find on the cover a picture of some things that rhyme with *kittens*.

Short Vowel u

Skill Focus

Children will

★ recognize the sound of short vowel *u*.

★ understand that *u* stands for /u/.

★ identify and spell picture names that contain the sound of short *u*.

ESL/ELL Speakers of Spanish, Tagalog, or some Asian languages may pronounce short *u* like the *o* in *hot* or the *a* in *father*.

Teach

Phonemic Awareness: Phoneme Identity
Say the word cut, elongating the medial short *u* sound (*cuuut*). Then, say the word naturally encouraging children to say it after you. Explain that the sound they hear in the middle of *cut* is the short *u* sound. Next, say groups of three words. Invite children to clap each time they hear the sound of short vowel *u*.

- cute   rub   cut
- dump   damp   luck

Sound to Symbol Ask children to complete this sentence:

- **The meal after breakfast is _____.** *(lunch)*

Write *lunch* on the board. Ask children what sound they hear in the middle of lunch. (*short vowel u*) Underline *u*. Then, write *sun* and *jump* on the board. Invite children to say the words and have volunteers underline the letter that stands for the short *u* sound.

Practice and Apply

Sound to Symbol Read the rhyme with children. Encourage them to identify the remaining words that have the /u/ sound. (*bunch, run, fun*) Have volunteers print the words on the board and underline the letter in each word that stands for short *u*.

Read the rule on page 31 aloud. Remind children to say each word before they circle the correct answer. Be sure children understand that they are also to write the vowel on the line.

Writing On page 32, say each picture name with children before they write the word.

Reading You may wish to use *The Lucky Duck*, MCP Phonics and Reading Consonant and Vowel Skills Library, Level B, to provide practice in reading words with the short *u* sound.

Name _____

I will jump, you will run.
We will play in the morning sun.
What great fun, thanks a bunch!
Now it is time to have some lunch!

▶ Circle **the name of each picture.**
Print **the vowel you hear in the word you circled.**

RULE
If a word or syllable has only one vowel, and it comes at the beginning of a word or between two consonants, the vowel is usually short. You can hear the short **u** sound in **run** and **lunch**.

1.	2.	3.
cap (cup)	gas gull	Dick (duck)
kit — u	(gum) — u	dad — u
4.	5.	6.
can cup	as bun	bag tip
(cap) — a	(bus) — u	(bug) — u
7.	8.	9.
not (nut)	(sun) sum	tab but
nap — u	dim — u	(bat) — a

Short vowel u   **31**

FOCUS ON ALL LEARNERS

ESL/ELL ENGLISH LANGUAGE LEARNERS

Use pictures or real objects to prepare English language learners to distinguish between words containing short vowel sounds.

- Place in a bag the items that make up the activity on page 31. Tell children that the items you will describe are on the page.
- Describe the item orally to the group without calling it by name.
- Have children take turns guessing the item's identity. Show children the items one at a time, to verify responses.
- Read aloud the directions for page 31. Ask a volunteer to model item 1. Have children complete items 2–9 individually before reviewing answers.

AUDITORY LEARNERS

Divide the class into Speakers and Writers. Volunteers give clues to short *u* words from pages 31–32, such as *I am a bird. What am I?* First, Writers write the answer. Then, they hold up the word *duck* as the Speakers say it. Trade roles for some of the riddles.

▶ **Say** the name of each picture. **Print** the name on the line.

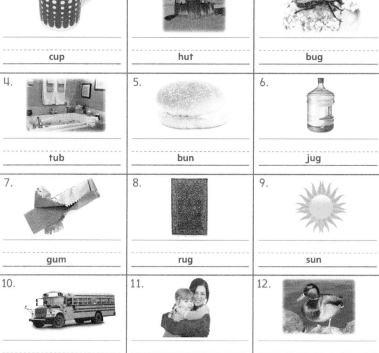

1. cup
2. hut
3. bug
4. tub
5. bun
6. jug
7. gum
8. rug
9. sun
10. bus
11. hug
12. duck

 HOME Have your child make up silly sentences with rhyming words from the page. Include other rhyming words.

32 Short vowel u: Spelling

CURRICULUM CONNECTIONS

SPELLING

Use the following words and sample sentences to pretest the spelling list for short *u, o,* and *e.*

1. **bun** Please pass me a sandwich **bun**.
2. **nut** An acorn is a kind of **nut**.
3. **ox** An **ox** can pull a heavy load.
4. **doll** She is starting a **doll** collection.
5. **net** Hit the volleyball over the **net**.
6. **leg** Can you stand on one **leg**?

WRITING

Compile a word list based on the word sun, such as *sunny, suntan, sunshine.* Refer children to the rhyme on page 31. Invite them to write sentences about having fun in the sun. Review their writing for correctness.

SCIENCE

Have them name familiar bugs or insects. Provide insect information and tell children to write three facts about insects or bugs.

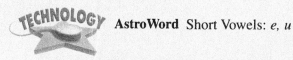 **TECHNOLOGY** **AstroWord** Short Vowels: *e, u*

VISUAL LEARNERS PARTNERS

Materials: 12 index cards for each set of partners

Post a list of the words *hut, cut, tub, rub, sun, run, hug, rug, pup, cup, duck, luck.* Have children write the words on their cards and lay them out upside down. Partners can take turns turning over two cards at a time and keeping the pair if the words rhyme.

CHALLENGE

Invite children to make a list of rhyming short *u* words and use as many as they can in an original poem about having "fun in the sun."

EXTRA SUPPORT/INTERVENTION

Materials: chart paper, markers

Draw a large dump truck on paper. Ask children to fill the truck with as many short *u* words as they can over the next few days. Ask children to practice reading their "truckload" of words aloud. See Daily Phonics Practice, page 246.

Integrating Phonics and Reading

Guided Reading
With children, read the title and look at the book cover. Ask them why the duck looks happy. You may also wish to use the English Language Learners activity.
First Reading Invite children to tell about the duck's problem at the beginning of the story.
Second Reading With children, reread the story and identify words that have the short *u* sound.

Comprehension
After reading, ask children the following questions:
• Why did the truck get stuck? *Inference/Access Prior Knowledge*
• Why do you think the duck is lucky? *Reflective Analysis/Personal Response*
ESL/ELL **English Language Learners**
Have children share what they know about ducks. Discuss where ducks live and what they like to do.

Short Vowel u

Skill Focus

Children will

★ recognize the sound of short vowel *u*.

★ understand that *u* stands for /u/.

★ identify and spell picture names that contain the short sound of *u*.

★ write words that contain the short sound of *u* to complete sentences.

★ Recognize and read high-frequency words.

Teach

Phonemic Awareness: Phoneme Substitution Say the word *bug*, emphasizing the medial *u* sound (*buuug*). Have children repeat *bug*. Then, ask children to replace the *b* with a *t* to make a word that means to pull (*tug*). Review that the middle sound in both *bug* and *tug* is the sound of short *u*.

Sound to Symbol Write the words *cub*, *tub*, and *rub* on the board. Read the words slowly and have children repeat them. Discuss how the words are the same. (*They each have a short* u *sound, end in* ub, *and rhyme.*) Invite volunteers to underline the letter that makes the short *u* sound in each word.

On the board, draw three columns titled *Beginning*, *Middle*, and *End* to isolate the /u/ sound. As you say the following words, invite volunteers to come to the board and print *u* in the correct column: *duck, up, run, us, Russ*.

Practice and Apply

Sound to Symbol Have children read aloud the word choices on page 33. Demonstrate how to fill in the puzzle by completing 2 Across and 1 Down orally.

Writing Remind children to say all three choices for each sentence on page 34 before they write the answer. Children will have an opportunity to read the following high-frequency words: *today, then, saw, was,* and *little*.

Critical Thinking In discussing Talk About It, children should recognize that for safety reasons they should remain in their seats on the bus.

Reading You may wish to use *Three Little Pigs and One Big Pig*, MCP Phonics and Reading Consonant and Vowel Skills Library, Level B, to reinforce the short *u* sound.

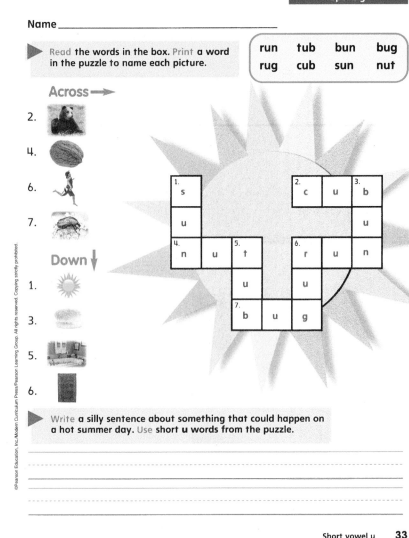

Name_____

▶ Read the words in the box. Print a word in the puzzle to name each picture.

| run | tub | bun | bug |
| rug | cub | sun | nut |

Across →

2.
4.
6.
7.

Down ↓

1.
3.
5.
6.

▶ Write a silly sentence about something that could happen on a hot summer day. Use **short u** words from the puzzle.

Short vowel u   **33**

FOCUS ON ALL LEARNERS

ESL/ELL ENGLISH LANGUAGE LEARNERS

With children, review the puzzle list on page 33 aloud as you emphasize the short *u* sound. As a group, read the directions. Assist children who are not familiar with crosswords by modeling on the chalkboard. Using an overhead transparency, complete the puzzle together.

VISUAL LEARNERS

Have each child write a sentence on paper, leaving a blank where a short *u* word from page 33 or 34 would go. For example: *I (just) saw the bus.* Children pass their papers to the next person who fills in a short *u* word that makes sense and adds a new missing-word sentence.

AUDITORY/KINESTHETIC LEARNERS

Ask children to raise their arms above their heads in U shapes when they hear the short *u* sound in words you pronounce from the following list: *cap, bus, sip, lid, bump, gas, add, plum, if, up, doll, dill, nap, hunt, sun, elf.*

▶ Circle the word that will finish the sentence.
Print it on the line.

1. Today there was a fuss on the _____ bus _____.
   run
   (bus)
   must

2. A _____ bug _____ jumped on Gus.
   us
   (bug)
   hug

3. Gus jumped _____ up _____.
   run
   cup
   (up)

4. Then, it jumped on _____ Russ _____.
   bus
   hug
   (Russ)

5. I saw the bug _____ jump _____ on the window.
   just
   (jump)
   rust

6. It was _____ just _____ a little bug.
   (just)
   cup
   up

7. It liked to _____ run _____ up and down the window.
   rug
   (run)
   cup

8. The bug _____ must _____ like to ride on the bus.
   run
   us
   (must)

TALK What would you do if you were on the bus?

HOME Ask your child to say and spell the words he or she did not write in the sentences.

34 Short vowel u: High-frequency words, critical thinking

CURRICULUM CONNECTIONS

SPELLING

Tell children to use the spelling words *bun* and *nut* and other short *u* words to spell the answers to these riddles as you read them. (Provide copies of the last half of the unit spelling list for children to keep as a study aid.)

1. It is another word for insect. (*bug*)
2. It has a hard shell. (*nut*)
3. It's made from wheat. (*bun*)
4. It's a young bear. (*cub*)
5. It's one way to get into a pool. (*jump*)

WRITING

On chart paper begin a story titled "The Funniest Bus Trip Ever" as follows: *We were in luck. It was a sunny day and the bus was on time. When we got on, we saw a puppy in the driver's seat.* Have children write or tell the rest of the story.

TECHNOLOGY **AstroWord** Short Vowels: *e, u*

AUDITORY/VISUAL LEARNERS *INDIVIDUAL*

Materials: Phonics Word Cards, Set 1: Short *u* words (60–63, 66–82); writing paper

Give one word card to each child. Have children fold their papers into two columns, write one of their words at the top of each column, and list as many rhyming words as possible for each word.

CHALLENGE

Have children work together to list short *u* animal names and find facts about each one. Examples are *seagull, puppy, duck, bug, cub, bunny.*

EXTRA SUPPORT/INTERVENTION

Materials: index cards, marker

Make cards for the words *fuss, cuff, buzz, duck, jump, must, hunt, suds,* and *nuts.* Point out that each word ends with two consonants. Invite children to divide the cards into words ending with one consonant sound and words ending with two sounds. See Daily Phonics Practice, page 246.

Integrating Phonics and Reading

Guided Reading
Invite volunteers to retell the traditional story *The Three Little Pigs.* Then, tell them that the story they are going to read is actually about four pigs.

First Reading Ask children to describe the big pig.

Second Reading Have children find words in the story that have the short *u* sound. You may wish to add them to your Word Wall.

Comprehension
After reading, ask the following questions:
• How are the little pigs different from the big pig? *Recall/Compare and Contrast*
• Do you think the wolf got a surprise? Why or why not? *Reflective Analysis/Personal Response*

ESL/ELL English Language Learners
Invite students to tell what they know about pigs. Suggest that they look at the cover of the book for ideas.

High-Frequency Words

Skill Focus

Children will

★ recognize and write the high-frequency words *does, about, our, other, then, where.*

★ use the high-frequency words to complete sentences.

★ begin to recognize irregular spelling patterns.

Teach

Analyze Words Write the words *does, about, our, other, then,* and *where* on the board. Slowly point to each letter as you read each word aloud.

- Invite children to make and use letter cards to spell each word.

- Repeat each word by stretching each sound. Encourage children to point to each letter in the word as they hear its sound.

- Help children associate the sounds they hear in each word with a familiar word.

- Have children say each word, blending the sounds.

- You may wish to make a Word Wall so that children can use the high-frequency words they learn to find similar spelling patterns and phonemic elements in new words.

Read Words in Context Write the following sentences on the board. Invite volunteers to underline the high-frequency words. Then, help children read the sentences.

- **Where does that black pen belong?**
- **Put it with our other pens.**
- **Then, we can write about the class trip.**

Practice and Apply

Writing Words Direct children to page 35. Read the directions aloud and remind children to reread each sentence with the word they selected. On page 36, be sure children recognize that the words can go across or down. Instruct children to say the words before they write them, using the strategies they have learned to associate sounds and letters. Children can work with a partner to complete Checking Up.

Reading You may wish to use *Where Does the Rabbit Hop?*, MCP Phonics and Reading Library, High Frequency Word Collection, Level B, to provide practice in reading high-frequency words.

Name_____

▶ Read the words in the box. Write a word to finish each sentence.

does	about
our	other
Then	Where

1. What ____does____ an ant eat?

2. ____Where____ can we find the facts?

3. We can look in this book ____about____ ants.

4. It tells about ____other____ bugs, too.

5. ____Then____, we can go out and see some ants.

6. We can take ____our____ book with us.

FOCUS ON ALL LEARNERS

ESL/ELL ENGLISH LANGUAGE LEARNERS

Materials: index cards, markers

Place two sets of high-frequency word cards face down on a table. Have children choose two cards, say the words, and spell them. Encourage them to use words that match in a sentence.

AUDITORY LEARNERS

Materials: high-frequency word cards

Make up six sentences, each containing one high-frequency word. Read the sentences aloud and have children hold up the correct card when they hear the high-frequency word.

KINESTHETIC LEARNERS

Materials: writing paper, yarn, glue

Have children print in large letters one high-frequency word on their paper. Then, have them trace the letters with glue and outline them with yarn. When the glue has dried, have partners exchange cards, use their fingers to trace the letters, and say the word.

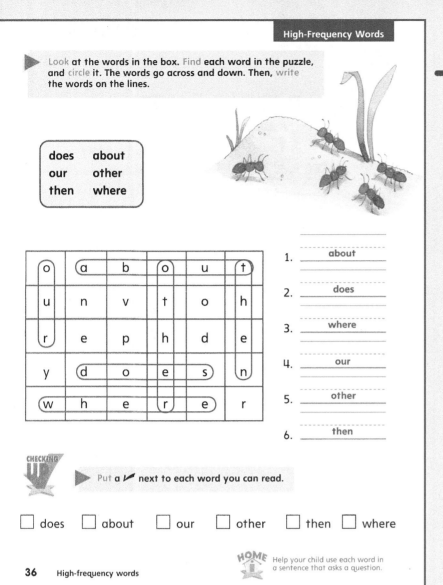

Look at the words in the box. Find **each word** in the puzzle, and circle it. The words go across and down. Then, write the words on the lines.

does	about
our	other
then	where

o	a	b	o	u	t
u	n	v	t	o	h
r	e	p	h	d	e
y	d	o	e	s	n
w	h	e	r	e	r

1. _____ about _____

2. _____ does _____

3. _____ where _____

4. _____ our _____

5. _____ other _____

6. _____ then _____

Put a ✔ next to each word you can read.

☐ does ☐ about ☐ our ☐ other ☐ then ☐ where

HOME Help your child use each word in a sentence that asks a question.

CURRICULUM CONNECTIONS

SCIENCE

Have children share what they know about ants. You may wish to have children visit the library to learn more about ants. Remind children that some ants bite, so they should always keep a safe distance from them. Suggest that children make up sentences about ants, using some of the high-frequency words.

ART

Invite children to make a poster about keeping safe around ants and other bugs. Make an anthill bulletin board to display children's posters.

WRITING

On the board, write *The ants go marching _____*. Brainstorm ideas with children and list them on the board. Ask children to copy and complete the sentences and add additional sentences.

PORTFOLIO

VISUAL LEARNERS GROUPS

Materials: writing paper

Have children write the high-frequency words on paper and cut the letters apart. Write the high-frequency words on the board, leaving out one or two letters in each word. Have children choose the letter cards that will complete the word. Have volunteers go to the board, hold up the correct card(s), and spell the word.

CHALLENGE

Have children create one sentence that uses five or six of the high-frequency words. Remind them that the sentence must make sense. (*Possible answer: Then, where does our other friend live?*)

EXTRA SUPPORT/INTERVENTION

Materials: high-frequency word cards

Have children use the high-frequency word cards at the back of their books to practice recognizing the words with a partner.

Integrating Phonics and Reading

Guided Reading
Read the title aloud. Ask children what they think the story will be about. You may also wish to use the English Language Learners activity below.

First Reading Suggest that children use the illustrations to explain where the rabbit hops.
Second Reading Invite children to find examples of the high-frequency words *where* and *does*.

Comprehension
After reading, ask children the following questions:
• What is the green place in the big city where the rabbit hops? *Inference/Draw Conclusions*
• Would you like to go where the rabbit hops? Why or why not? *Reflective Analysis/ Personal Response*

ESL/ELL English Language Learners
Provide children practice with answering questions that begin with *where*. For example, ask: *Where do you sit?* or *Where is the office?*

Phonics and Reading / Phonics and Writing

Short Vowels a, i, u

Skill Focus

Children will

★ read words that contain the sounds of short vowel *a, i,* and *u.*

★ write short *a, i,* and *u* words to finish sentences.

★ build words with short vowel phonograms *at, ip, ing,* and *ut.*

Teach

Phonemic Awareness: Phoneme Identity
Say the following words and invite children to clap each time they hear a word with the targeted sound.

- short *a*:   did   dad   cat
- short *i*:   lip   lit   ran
- short *u*:   at   nut   rub

Sound to Symbol Write the word *cat* on the board. Have a volunteer say the word and ask children which vowel sound they hear. (*short a*) Then, ask children to think of words that rhyme with *cat.* Invite volunteers to erase the beginning consonant, and write another beginning letter to make a new word. Repeat this exercise using *lit* and *rub.*

Words in Context Write these sentences on the board.

- **Soccer is fun.**
- **Players hit or kick the ball.**
- **The fans cheer.**

Use three different colors of chalk to have volunteers underline the words with the short sounds of *a, i,* and *u.*

Practice and Apply

Writing Help children to read the story aloud on page 37. Remind them to say their word choice in the sentence to be sure that it makes sense.

Critical Thinking In discussing the Talk About It question, children should recognize that a team has to work together.

Building Words Remind children that on page 38 not every letter will make a real word. Encourage them to try each letter with the phonogram before they write their answers.

Reading You may wish to use *Night and Day,* MCP Phonics and Reading Consonant and Vowel Skills Library, Level B, to reinforce reading words with short vowels *a, i,* and *u.*

37

Name_____

 Phonics & Reading

Read the story. Print a short a, i, or u word from the story to finish each sentence.

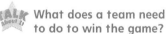 Playing Soccer

Do you like to run, kick a ball, and have lots of fun? Then, soccer is just the game for you!

A soccer field has a net at each end. Two teams of players run and pass the ball to other players on their team. Then, they try to hit or kick the ball into a net. They can use their feet, chests, and heads but not their hands.

A player called the goalie tries to stop the ball. It can be a hard job! Does this game sound like a winner? Kids across the land think so. So do the fans in the stands!

1. Soccer players ____run____ on a field and ____kick____ a ball.

2. They can use their feet, but they cannot use their ____hands____.

3. The game is a big hit with kids and their ____fans____.

 What does a team need to do to win the game?

Review short vowels a, i, u: Critical thinking   **37**

FOCUS ON ALL LEARNERS

ESL/ELL ENGLISH LANGUAGE LEARNERS

Talk about sports that use balls before reading Playing Soccer and completing page 37. With children, read the selection, having them read aloud one sentence at a time. Check comprehension. Then, distribute highlighter markers and ask children to mark words with the short *a* sound. Exchange colors and mark words with the short *i* sound, then the short *u* sound.

AUDITORY LEARNERS GROUPS

Have children sit in a circle. Tell them to clap when they hear a short *a* word, raise their hands for a short *i* word, and pat their heads for a short *u* word. Begin with these words: *fill, fuzz, mix, gas, ham, quit, jump, stand, lift, up, suds, kit, act, six, pump, sit.*

KINESTHETIC LEARNERS GROUPS

Play "baseball" with children. Divide class into two teams. Designate four bases in the room. Say a word to the "batter," who identifies the vowel sound. If the batter is correct, he or she moves to first base. The next batter takes a turn, and the "runners" move on with each correct answer. An incorrect answer is an out.

Building Words

Phonics & Writing

Use a letter tile to make a word with **at, ip, ing** or **ut**. Write each real word on the lines.

c s z m r

at

1. cat
2. sat
3. mat
4. rat

c s r z n

ip

5. sip
6. rip
7. zip
8. nip

w s r n k

ing

9. wing
10. sing
11. ring
12. king

r n c v b

ut

13. rut
14. nut
15. cut
16. but

 HOME Ask your child to choose two words from each group and use them in a silly sentence.

CURRICULUM CONNECTIONS

SPELLING

Say the letters *n-u-t*. Have children name the spelling word *nut*. Repeat the activity with the words *cab, ram, ax, wig, lips, dish,* and *bun*. Have children suggest a word that rhymes with each one.

WRITING

Have children reread the story on page 37. Invite them to write about their favorite sport. It may be a sport they play or one that they watch. As they write, review each child's use of short *a, i,* and *u* words.

MATHEMATICS

Take a poll to find out what ball games are the children's favorites. Tally the results and help children make a bar graph on posterboard. Discuss the results, including the most favorite and least favorite game.

 **TECHNOLOGY** **AstroWord** Short Vowels: *a, i*; Short Vowels: *e, u*

VISUAL LEARNERS *INDIVIDUAL*

Invite children to write a coded message with two or more short *a, i,* and *u* words, leaving out the vowels. Children can challenge classmates to "crack the code."

CHALLENGE

Invite children to write three-sentence clues for a sport that uses a ball. Suggest that they begin with the most difficult clue, leaving the easiest clue for last. For example: *You kick a ball. You try to get a goal. The ball is white and black.*

EXTRA SUPPORT/INTERVENTION

Have class form two equal teams leading to the *board*. Write the word *sat* twice on the *board*, for each team. When you say, *Go*, the first person in each line goes to the *board*, erases one of the letters, and forms a new word. Continue with other short vowel *a, i,* or *u* words.

Integrating Phonics and Reading

Guided Reading
Have children read the title and look at the cover of the story. Ask them what each side of the cover represents and what clues they used to help them know.
First Reading Invite children to explain what the sun is doing in each picture.
Second Reading Make three columns on the board labeled /a/, /i/, /u/. Have children write words from the story in the appropriate column.

Comprehension
After reading, ask children the following questions:
• What happens when the sun takes a nap? *Inference/Cause and Effect*
• Do you agree that the sun should take a nap? Why or why not? *Reflective Analysis/ Personal Response*

ESL/ELL **English Language Learners**
Have children discuss what they think of when they hear the word *day* and the word *night*.

Short vowel o

Skill Focus

Children will

★ recognize the short sound of o.

★ understand that o stands for /o/.

★ identify and spell picture names that contain the short sound of o.

ESL/ELL Speakers of Spanish, Tagalog, and some Asian languages may pronounce in the same way the sounds of short o, short a, and short u. Practice *hot, hat, hut; lock, lack, luck*.

Teach

Phonological Awareness: Rhyme Say the word *job*, elongating the short *o* sound (*jooob*). Repeat *job* naturally and then have children say *job* in both ways. Explain that the /o/ they hear in the middle of *job* is the sound of short vowel *o*. Next, say groups of three words and ask children to choose the two short *o* words that rhyme.

- job   sob   rub
- Dan   Ron   Don

Sound to Symbol Write the word *top* on the board. Read it slowly, blending the individual phonemes before saying it naturally. Underline the *o* in *top* and explain that the /o/ in *top* is the short vowel sound of *o*.

Note: In some regions of the United States, the *o* sound in words such as *dog, log, lost*, and off may be pronounced differently from other short *o* words.

Practice and Apply

Sound to Symbol Direct children to the picture at the top of page 39. Ask what they see coming out of the pan. (*popcorn*) Explain that the kernels of corn pop. Ask children what sound they hear in *pop*. (*short o*) Write the word *pop* on the board and underline *o*. Then, read the rhyme with children. Have them identify the short *o* words and print them on the board, underlining the letter that stands for the short *o* sound in each word.

Review the picture names on page 39 with children. For item 10, tell children that the boy in the picture is named Tom. Encourage children to complete page 40 independently.

Writing You may wish to review the spellings of *-ox, -ock*, and *-oll* before children write the names of the pictures on page 39.

Reading You may wish to use *"POP" Pops the Popcorn*, MCP Phonics and Reading Consonant and Vowel Skills Library, Level B, to provide practice in reading short *o* words.

Name _____

Put it in the pot,
Shake it 'til it's hot.
Pop! Pop! Pop!
See the popcorn hop!

▶ Say the name of each picture. Print the name on the line.

RULE
If a word or syllable has only one vowel, and it comes at the beginning of a word or between two consonants, the vowel is usually short. You can hear the short *o* sound in **pop** and **hot**.

1.	2.	3.	4.
box	mop	pot	pop
5.	6.	7.	8.
hot	doll	lock	top
9.	10.	11.	12.
rock	Tom	sock	fox

Short vowel o: Spelling   **39**

FOCUS ON ALL LEARNERS

ESL/ELL ENGLISH LANGUAGE LEARNERS

Confirm English language learners' ability to pronounce short *o*.

- Have children crouch down in an unobstructed area of the room (the "popper").
- Say some of the words from page 39 aloud. Tell children to pop like popcorn each time they hear a word with a short *o*.
- Read directions for the activity on page 39 aloud; ask children to work with a partner to write the picture names for each item. Review answers as a group.
- With children, read the directions for page 40. Have them complete the page independently, whenever possible.

VISUAL LEARNERS

Materials: Phonics Word Cards, Set 1: Short *o* words (83–95)

Display one side of each card on the chalkboard ledge or on a table. Dictate a sentence, saying *blank* in place of a short *o* word such as, *I "blank" my soccer shoes, but then I found them.* Have a volunteer find a word that makes sense (*lost*) and repeat the sentence, this time using the word.

Circle **the name of each picture.**

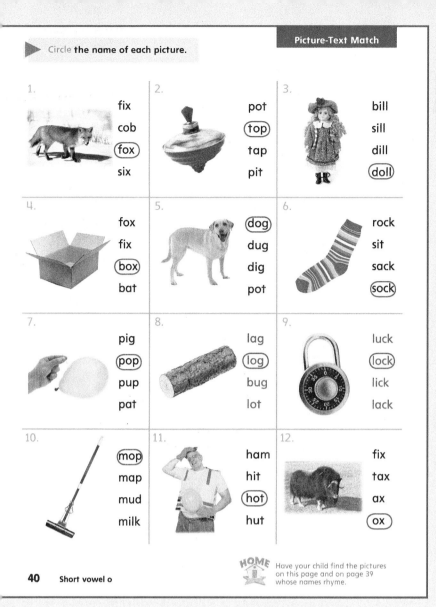

1.
fix
cob
(fox)
six

2.
pot
(top)
tap
pit

3.
bill
sill
dill
(doll)

4.
fox
fix
(box)
bat

5.
(dog)
dug
dig
pot

6.
rock
sit
sack
(sock)

7.
pig
(pop)
pup
pat

8.
lag
(log)
bug
lot

9.
luck
(lock)
lick
lack

10.
(mop)
map
mud
milk

11.
ham
hit
(hot)
hut

12.
fix
tax
ax
(ox)

HOME Have your child find the pictures on this page and on page 39 whose names rhyme.

CURRICULUM CONNECTIONS

SPELLING
Make two sets of large cards for the letters *b, d, e, g, l, n, o, t, u,* and *x.* Give each child one card. Call out each of the spelling words: *leg, ox, nut, net, doll,* and *bun.* Children should spell each word by holding up the correct letter cards in the right order and announcing the letters.

WRITING
With children, generate lists of rhyming short *o* words. Begin with words from pages 39 and 40. List the words on chart paper and have children write two-line poems using the words. They can then illustrate and share their poems with classmates.

PORTFOLIO

MATHEMATICS
Prepare popcorn in your classroom with a hot-air popper. Have children think of ways to use math to study the results. They might measure the original amount of kernels and compare it to the popcorn. Children might weigh the kernels and popcorn and compare their results.

TECHNOLOGY **AstroWord** Short Vowels: *i, o*

AUDITORY/VISUAL LEARNERS **INDIVIDUAL**
Materials: large sheets of art paper

Have children fold their paper into four columns and label the columns *-ob, -ock, -op,* and *-ot.* Tell children to add consonants to the beginning of each word part to make four word lists and to illustrate one word from each list.

CHALLENGE
Invite children to write a recipe for popping popcorn, including ingredients and numbered steps. Children may enjoy demonstrating their recipes as commercials for ingredients they are including.

EXTRA SUPPORT/INTERVENTION
Materials: Phonics Picture Cards: Short Vowels (45–75); a soup pot

Put the pictures in the pot. Children can take turns removing one, saying its name, and stacking it on a pile with other pictures having the same short vowel sound. See Daily Phonics Practice, page 246.

Integrating Phonics and Reading

Guided Reading
Read the title of the story aloud and tell children to look at the pictures. Ask children if they have ever made popcorn. Tell them the story is about two boys who make popcorn.
First Reading Ask children what happened to cause the problem in the story.
Second Reading After children reread, ask them to find words with the short *o* sound.

Comprehension
After reading, ask children the following questions:
• What does Bob do when the corn begins to pop? What is the result of Bob's action? *Recall/Cause and Effect*
• Will the boys be able to eat all the popcorn? What could they do with it? *Reflective Analysis/Predict*

ESL/ELL **English Language Learners**
Help children to tell what they know about growing corn and making popcorn.

Short Vowel o

Skill Focus

Children will

★ recognize the short sound of o.

★ understand that o stands for /o/.

★ identify and spell picture names that contain the short sound of o.

★ apply what they have learned by reading and writing.

★ recognize and read high-frequency words.

Teach

Phonemic Awareness: Phoneme Isolation
Encourage children to listen carefully as you say the words *not, pop, off.* Elongate the short o sound. Have children repeat the words, emphasizing the /o/ sound. Remind them that the vowel sound they hear is the sound of short o.

Sound to Symbol Write the words *frog, on,* and *sock* on the board. Ask children what vowel sound they hear in each word. (*short o*) Print the sentences below on the board. Have volunteers draw boxes around the short o words.

- **The frog jumped off the log.**
- **Tom put a lock on the box.**
- **Bob saw a dog in the fog.**

On the board, make three columns and title them *Beginning, Middle,* and *End.* Have volunteers write the letter o in the appropriate column as you say each of the following words: *off, Bob, lock, on, ox.*

Words in Context: Decodable Words Write *A _____ can spin fast. (sock, top)* sentence on the board. Invite a volunteer to read the sentence aloud. Ask children which word makes sense. (*top*)

Practice and Apply

Sound to Symbol With children, say the words in the word box before they write the names of the pictures on page 41.

Words in Context For page 42, be sure children understand that the correct answer choice is the sentence that describes the picture. After children fill in the circle for their answer choice, remind them to circle all the short o words in every sentence on the page. Children will have an opportunity to read the following high-frequency words: *under, has, see,* and *holding.*

Reading You may wish to use *Grandpa, Grandma, and the Tractor,* MCP Phonics and Reading Consonant and Vowel Skills Library, Level B, to reinforce the short o sound.

41

Name _____

▶ Help the frog hop to the pond. Look at each picture. Write the name of each picture on the line.

| top | dog | box | sock | pot |
| lock | rock | log | fox | |

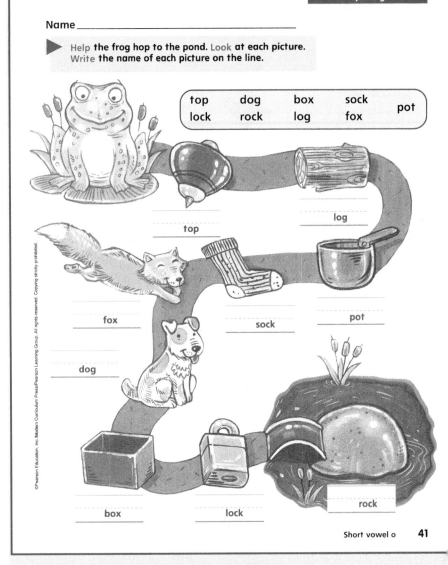

top

log

fox

sock

pot

dog

box

lock

rock

Short vowel o   **41**

FOCUS ON ALL LEARNERS

ESL/ELL ENGLISH LANGUAGE LEARNERS

Adapt the game on page 41 by attaching pictures of the c-v-c pattern words you choose to the "game board" you create on the floor. Have children play the game as a group, and then complete the page in their books.

VISUAL LEARNERS GROUPS

Materials: Phonics Picture Cards: Short Vowels (45–75); red paper

Children can make "stop signs" from red paper and hold them up each time you display a picture with a short o name.

KINESTHETIC LEARNERS GROUPS

Materials: objects with short o or short u names, such as a box, doll, top, mop, rock, lock, sock, pot, cup, nut, toy bug, fuzz, bun, jump rope, toy bus, and gum

Invite children to sort the items into two groups according to their vowel sounds.

▶ Fill in the bubble beside the sentence that tells about the picture. Then draw a circle around each short **o** word in the sentences.

1.
- ○ The (fox) is (not) in the (log).
- ● The (fox) is in the (log).
- ○ The (fox) is (on) the (log).
- ○ The (fox) is under the (log).

2.
- ● (Rob) (lost) his (sock).
- ○ (Rob) sat (on) a big (rock).
- ○ (Rob) is (on) the big (log).
- ○ (Rob) has a big (rock) in his hand.

3.
- ○ The (dog) ran over the (box).
- ○ The (mop) is (not) in the (box).
- ○ I will (hop) (on) the (log).
- ● See the (doll) in the (box).

4.
- ○ I (got) the (mop) for (Don).
- ● Jill has the small (top).
- ○ The small (top) is (on) the (mop).
- ○ The (top) is in (Bob's) hand.

5.
- ○ The (hot) (pot) is (on) the table.
- ○ (Dot) is (not) holding a (hot) (pot).
- ● (Dot) is holding a (hot) (pot).
- ○ The (pot) Dad is holding is (not) (hot).

42   Short vowel o: High-frequency words

HOME Ask your child to read a sentence that is not pictured and draw a picture for it.

CURRICULUM CONNECTIONS

SPELLING

Have each partner scramble the words *bun*, *nut*, *ox*, *doll*, *net*, and *leg* and write them on paper. They then can trade papers and unscramble the words.

WRITING

Invite children to think of "big" words that begin with short *o*, such as *octagon*, an eight-sided shape. On a chart, list children's ideas that may include *octopus*, *operation*, *operator*, *ostrich*, *opposite*, *optical*, *object*, *October*, *olive*, *omelet*, *Ontario*, and *opera*. Distribute large sheets of art paper (rounded off to look like O's). Have partners choose one of the words, and then define and illustrate it.

SOCIAL STUDIES

Talk about some of the jobs people do that make it possible for other people to have fun. List children's ideas, such as hot-dog vendor, lifeguard, doll maker, ballplayer, and popcorn seller at movies. Have them draw and label pictures of one of the jobs.

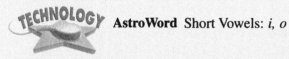 **TECHNOLOGY**   **AstroWord** Short Vowels: *i*, *o*

AUDITORY/KINESTHETIC LEARNERS *INDIVIDUAL*

Materials: one pipe cleaner per child

Invite children to bend their pipe cleaners into O's. Dictate short *o* words and ask children to finger-spell them on their desks, tracing over their *o*'s for that letter. Have volunteers take turns spelling the words on the board at the same time. Sample words: *box, dock, cot, got, lost, mop, off, on, rob, top, socks.*

CHALLENGE

Materials: Phonics Word Cards, Set 1: Short *o* words (83–95)

Have children draw two word cards at random and compose an oral sentence using two words from the cards. They can then draw a third card and add to the sentence, including a word from the new card.

EXTRA SUPPORT/INTERVENTION

Read the following word pairs and have children make the OK sign with their fingers when both words contain short *o*: dog, frog; job, rock; box, tag; pop, drop; not, nut; hop, hot. See Daily Phonics Practice, page 246.

Integrating Phonics and Reading

Guided Reading

Ask children what they know about farm life. Have children read the title and look at the cover. Then, ask them to identify each person and thing mentioned in the title.

First Reading Have children use the illustrations to explain some of the jobs of the tractor.

Second Reading Have children find words in the story that have the short *o* sound, such as *got*, *job*, and *not*.

Comprehension

After reading, ask children the following questions:

- What kinds of jobs did the tractor do each season? *Recall/Sequence*
- At the end of the story, how do you think the tractor's new job made Grandpa feel? *Reflective Analysis/Personal Response*

ESL/ELL English Language Learners

Ask children if they know what a tractor is. Discuss what a tractor is used for.

Lesson 18

Pages 43–44

Short Vowel e

Skill Focus

Children will

★ recognize the short sound of e.

★ understand that e stands for /e/.

★ identify and spell picture names that contain the short sound of e.

★ apply what they have learned by reading and writing.

ESL/ELL Since no vowel sound similar to short e exists in Korean, offer additional practice with *pen, net, leg, bed, red, belt,* and *tent.*

➤ Teach

Phonemic Awareness: Phoneme Identity
Say the word *pet*, emphasizing and elongating the short e sound (*peeet*). Have children repeat the word in the same manner. Then, say the word naturally and have children repeat it. Explain that the sound they hear in the middle of *pet* is the sound of short vowel *e*. Next, say the groups of three words. Encourage children to raise their hand when they hear a word with the sound of short vowel *e*.

- let   bell   bat
- fence   feet   Jen

Sound to Symbol Write the words *desk, hen,* and *belt* on the board. Pronounce the words with children. Ask them to tell how the three words are alike. (*They all have the /e/ sound, which is the short e sound.*) Underline the e in desk. Explain that the letter e stands for the short e sound. Have volunteers underline the letter that stands for the short e sound in *hen* and *belt*.

On the board, make three columns and title them *Beginning, Middle,* and *End.* Say these words aloud: *wet, best, Jen, Fred, end.* Have children write the letter e in the column where they hear the short e sound.

➤ Practice and Apply

Sound to Symbol Read the rhyme at the top of page 43 with children. Have them identify words with the sound of short e. Then, read the rule for short e. You may wish to mention that the word *friend* has the short e sound, but it does not follow the rule.

Help children identify the pictures. On page 44, tell children to color the pictures, following the directions at the bottom of the page.

Reading You may wish to use *Red and I Visit the Vet,* MCP Phonics and Reading Consonant and Vowel Skills Library, Level B, to provide practice in reading short e words.

Name _____

I like to spend a sunny day
Getting shells at the bay,
Or playing with my friend,
Hoping today will not end!

➤ Say the name of each picture. Print the name on the line.

RULE
If a word or syllable has only one vowel, and it comes at the beginning of a word or between two consonants, the vowel is usually short. You can hear the short e sound in **spend** and **shells.**

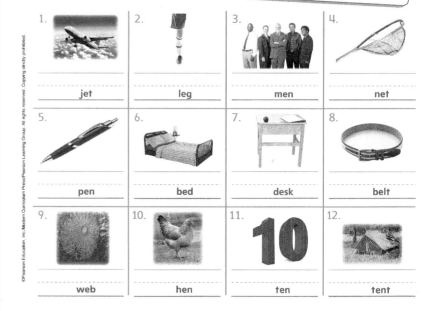

1. jet	2. leg	3. men	4. net
5. pen	6. bed	7. desk	8. belt
9. web	10. hen	11. ten	12. tent

Short e: Spelling   **43**

FOCUS ON ALL LEARNERS

 ESL/ELL ENGLISH LANGUAGE LEARNERS
Tell children that short e often comes between two consonant sounds. Then, have them identify the beginning, middle, and end sounds in item 1 on page 43 (*jet*). Working in pairs, have children complete the page. Write answers on the chalkboard and correct them as a group.

AUDITORY/VISUAL LEARNERS *GROUPS*
Write the words *jet, leg, men, bed, best, sell,* and *dent* on the board as column heads. For each word, in turn, have children say rhyming words. Ask volunteers to list the answers.

AUDITORY/KINESTHETIC LEARNERS *PARTNERS*
Give partners ten minutes to search the room for objects with names containing the short e sound. Examples might include pens, desk, pencil, pet, pegs, checkers, deck of cards, set of word cards, shelf, bell, and ten. When the time is up, have children name their discoveries.

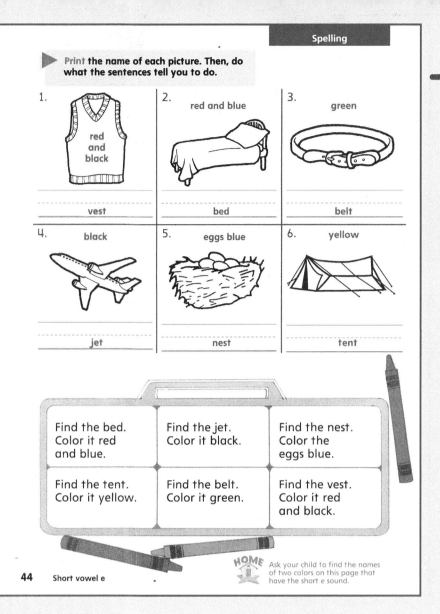

▶ **Print** the name of each picture. Then, do what the sentences tell you to do.

1. red and black — vest

2. red and blue — bed

3. green — belt

4. black — jet

5. eggs blue — nest

6. yellow — tent

Find the bed. Color it red and blue.

Find the jet. Color it black.

Find the nest. Color the eggs blue.

Find the tent. Color it yellow.

Find the belt. Color it green.

Find the vest. Color it red and black.

 Ask your child to find the names of two colors on this page that have the short e sound.

44 Short vowel e

SPELLING

Have children fold writing paper into six parts and write one word in each part as you dictate *net, leg, bun, nut, ox,* and *doll.* With children, recite and review their words. Then, tell them to add as many rhyming words as they can.

WRITING

Ask children to write about a friend. They might tell how they became friends, and what they do together. List short *e* words from their writing for children to read.

SCIENCE

Plan a trip to the library to discover ways of learning about seashells. The librarian might demonstrate finding information in encyclopedias, books, and magazines. Bring some sources to the classroom where children can read and share information.

TECHNOLOGY **AstroWord** Short Vowels: *e, u*

VISUAL LEARNERS **GROUPS**

Materials: Phonics Word Cards, Set 1: Short *e* words (96–117)

As children read the cards, have them think of ways they can sort some of the words into different categories. Cards might be sorted according to number of letters, rhyming sets, matching initial letters, or groups such as objects (nouns) and action words (verbs).

CHALLENGE

Ask children to use short *e* words to design word puzzles in which the *e*'s all line up vertically. Have them draw letter boxes for answers and write clues. Make copies or overhead transparencies for classmates to solve.

EXTRA SUPPORT/INTERVENTION

Materials: brown and yellow construction paper; a shoe box

Attach a brown wishing-well shape to the box. Invite children to write short *e* words on yellow paper "coins" and drop them in the wishing well. Later, read and check the coins together. See Daily Phonics Practice, page 246.

Integrating Phonics and Reading

Guided Reading

Read the title of the story and have children look at the pictures. Ask children what a vet does. You may also wish to use the activity under English Language Learners below.

First Reading Have children use the pictures to explain what the vet is doing.

Second Reading Invite children to identify words that have the short *e* sound, such as *Red, vet, Dr. Chen, questions, help, wet, chest, check, get, pet,* and *checkup.*

Comprehension

After reading, ask children the following questions:

• Why does Red wag his tail? *Recall/Cause and Effect*

• Do you think the girl loves her dog? How do you know? *Reflective Analysis/Inference*

ESL/ELL English Language Learners

Discuss who *Red, I,* and *Vet* refer to in the title. Be sure children understand that the story is being told from the girl's point of view.

Short Vowel e

Skill Focus

Children will

★ recognize the sound of short vowel e.

★ understand that e stands for /e/.

★ read and write words that contain the short sound of e to complete sentences.

★ recognize and read high-frequency words.

Teach

Phonemic Awareness: Phoneme Segmentation Hold up a pen. Explain that you are holding a /p/ /e/ /n/, isolating the sound of each letter. Have children say the word slowly and then naturally. Remind them that the sound they hear in the middle of the word is the sound of short vowel e.

Sound to Symbol Say the word *Jeff*, stretching each sound: *JJJeeefff*. Write *Jeff* on the board. Invite a volunteer to underline the letter that stands for the sound of short vowel e. Repeat the process with the words *Pepper* and *help*.

Words in Context: Decodable Words Write these words on the board: *nest, let, sell*. Then, write this sentence:

• **A home for a bird is a _____.**

Have children choose the word that correctly completes the sentence.

Practice and Apply

Sound to Symbol Have children write the name of the pictures at the top of page 46. At the bottom of the page, remind children to read each sentence, and write *yes* or *no* to tell whether the statement is correct.

Writing Read the directions on page 45. Remind children to reread each sentence with the word they selected to see if it makes sense before writing it on the line. Children will have an opportunity to read the following high-frequency words: *would, care, sure, good,* and *when*.

Critical Thinking Discuss Talk About It. Have children find the sentences that tell why Jeff would be a good pet owner.

Reading You may wish to use *Dee and Me*, MCP Phonics and Reading Consonant and Vowel Skills Library, Level B, to reinforce the short e sound.

45

Name _____

▶ Fill in the bubble below the word that will finish each sentence. Print the word on the line.

	Sentence	men	Jeff	jet
1.	My name is _____ Jeff _____.	○	●	○

| 2. | I want to get a _____ pet _____. | bet ○ | pet ● | yet ○ |

| 3. | I would like a pet dog _____ best _____. | rest ○ | west ○ | best ● |

| 4. | I will _____ help _____ take care of my pet. | help ● | bell ○ | nest ○ |

| 5. | I can take it to the _____ vet _____. | vet ● | bet ○ | set ○ |

| 6. | I will make sure it is _____ fed _____. | get ○ | fed ● | bed ○ |

| 7. | It will need a good _____ bed _____. | bed ● | nest ○ | best ○ |

| 8. | I will _____ let _____ it in and out. | jet ○ | test ○ | let ● |

| 9. | I can dry it when it's _____ wet _____. | net ○ | wet ● | set ○ |

| 10. | I will _____ pet _____ it if I get it. | sled ○ | pet ● | west ○ |

| 11. | I might name my pet _____ Pepper _____. | Pepper ● | fed ○ | set ○ |

| 12. | I will _____ tell _____ Ned about my pet. | sell ○ | tell ● | fell ○ |

 Why would Jeff make a good pet owner?

Short vowel e: High-frequency words, critical thinking   **45**

FOCUS ON ALL LEARNERS

ESL/ELL ENGLISH LANGUAGE LEARNERS

Pair children to take turns reading the sentences on page 46 and answering the questions. Have them complete the top of the page individually to check each child's comprehension of words that contain short vowel sounds.

VISUAL LEARNERS GROUPS

Materials: index cards cut in half, markers

Give each child a card with *e* printed on it and several blank cards. Have each child make their own consonant cards to spell a word with short *e*. Have children read their words and use them in sentences. Repeat the game.

AUDITORY/KINESTHETIC LEARNERS

Play a version of "May I?" Have children line up and take two steps forward when they hear a short *e* word and one step backward when the word does not have short *e*. Use words such as *bed, yes, hut, can, jet, tent, eggs, pill, tell, ask*.

▶ **Print the name of each picture on the line.**

1.	2.	3.	4.	5.
hat	_six_	_sun_	_top_	_jet_

▶ **Print yes or no on the line to answer each statement.**

6. You can sit in a tent. _yes_

7. A hen can lay eggs. _yes_

8. A cat has six legs. _no_

9. A big bus can jump up and down. _no_

10. You can go fast in a jet. _yes_

11. An ant is as big as an ox. _no_

12. Six is less than ten. _yes_

13. You can rest in a bed. _yes_

14. You have ten fingers and ten toes. _yes_

 HOME Ask your child to circle and read the short e words in each sentence.

46 Short vowel e: Spelling

CURRICULUM CONNECTIONS

SPELLING

You can posttest the short *u*, *o*, and *e* spelling words below at this time.

1. **doll** I gave my cousin a new **doll.**
2. **leg** The dog's **leg** is hurt.
3. **nut** I heard the **nut** crack open.
4. **net** I caught this fish in my **net**.
5. **ox** Have you ever seen an **ox**?
6. **bun** I spread mustard on the **bun**.

WRITING

Have each child fold a sheet of art paper in half like a book. On each "page," have children write and illustrate a pet care suggestion. Have children point out the short *e* words they used.

MATHEMATICS

Have children make a pictograph titled "Favorite Pets." On paper squares, have them draw pictures of their choice. Label the graph.

TECHNOLOGY **AstroWord** Short Vowels: *e, u*

AUDITORY LEARNERS GROUPS

Materials: Phonics Picture Cards: 76–84

Display the pictures one at a time. Point to individual children to spell the words, one letter per person.

CHALLENGE

Send children on a word hunt to a story they are reading. Have them hunt for *e* words and list ones in which they discover the short *e* sound.

EXTRA SUPPORT/INTERVENTION

Materials: Phonics Word Cards, Set 1: Short *e* words (96–117)

Work with children to sort the cards into words they can read and ones they need help with. Sort the unknown words by matching word endings. Help children read them by sounding out letters and rhyming the words. See Daily Phonics Practice, page 246.

Integrating Phonics and Reading

Guided Reading

Have children read the title and look at the illustrations. Tell them the book is about a girl and her older sister. Ask what the story may be about.

First Reading Ask children to listen for the sentence that is repeated throughout the story.

Second Reading Have children find words that have the short *e* sound, such as *bed, help, dress, mess, then,* and *pet.*

Comprehension

Ask children the following questions:

• Why does Dee often need help? *Inference/ Access Prior Knowledge*

• Why is Dee's big sister frowning at the end of the story? *Reflective Analysis/Draw Conclusions*

ESL/ELL **English Language Learners**

Discuss with children how younger children act when they are around their older brothers and sisters.

High-Frequency Words

Skill Focus

Children will

★ recognize and write the high-frequency words *would, care, because, under, sure, good.*

★ use the high-frequency words to complete sentences.

★ begin to recognize irregular spelling patterns.

Teach

Analyze Words Write the words *would, care, because, under, sure,* and *good* on the board. As you point to each word, pronounce it slowly and clearly, stretching out the sounds.

- With lined index cards, have children make letter cards. Children use their letter cards to spell each word.

- As volunteers go to the board and point to each of the words, repeat the word with children, stretching the sounds. Invite children to point to each letter in the word as they hear the sound.

- Help children associate the sounds they hear in each word with a familiar word.

- If you have a class Word Wall, add these words so that children can find similar spelling patterns and phonemic elements in new words.

Read Words in Context Write the following sentences on the board. Invite volunteers to underline the high-frequency words. Then, help children read the sentences.

- **Mom is <u>sure</u> that the ball is <u>under</u> my bed.**
- **I <u>would</u> like to find it <u>because</u> I want to play a game.**
- **I will take <u>good</u> <u>care</u> of it next time.**

Practice and Apply

Write Words Read the directions on page 47 with children. Use the high-frequency words to discuss the illustration. On page 48, be sure that children understand how to do a crossword puzzle. Children can work with a partner to complete Checking Up.

Reading You may wish to use *A Stew for Egor's Mom,* MCP Phonics and Reading Library, High Frequency Word Collection, Level B, to provide practice in reading high-frequency words.

Name _____

▶ Read the words in the box. Write a word to finish each sentence.

Would	care
because	under
sure	good

1. Hide-and-seek is a _____ **good** _____ game to play.

2. I am _____ **sure** _____ that I will find you.

3. I will find you _____ **because** _____ I will look everywhere!

4. I see Jan hiding _____ **under** _____ the bush.

5. Sam does not _____ **care** _____ that I see him by the shed.

6. _____ **Would** _____ you like to play again? Now find me!

High-frequency words   **47**

FOCUS ON ALL LEARNERS

ESL/ELL ENGLISH LANGUAGE LEARNERS

Write the high-frequency words on the board. Then, create a question using each word, and invite a child to answer the question using that word. For example, ask *"Would you like to eat lunch?"* A possible response is *"Yes, I would like to eat lunch."*

AUDITORY LEARNERS

Materials: high-frequency word cards

Hold up a high-frequency word card and have a volunteer say the word and create a sentence for that word. Continue until all children have had a turn.

KINESTHETIC LEARNERS

Materials: high-frequency word cards

Using the high-frequency word cards for this lesson at the back of their book, have children select one card. In turn, have each child display his or her card, say the word, and use it in a sentence.

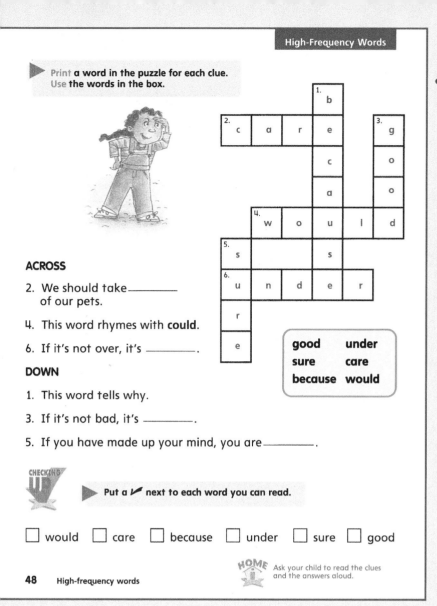

Print a word in the puzzle for each clue.
Use the words in the box.

Crossword puzzle filled in:
- 1. b
- 2. c a r e
- 3. g o o d
- 4. w o u l d
- 5. s ... s
- 6. u n d e r / r / e

ACROSS

2. We should take _____ of our pets.

4. This word rhymes with **could**.

6. If it's not over, it's _____.

DOWN

1. This word tells why.

3. If it's not bad, it's _____.

5. If you have made up your mind, you are _____.

good	under
sure	care
because	would

Put a ✔ next to each word you can read.

☐ would ☐ care ☐ because ☐ under ☐ sure ☐ good

48 High-frequency words

HOME Ask your child to read the clues and the answers aloud.

CURRICULUM CONNECTIONS

WRITING

Invite children to write about their favorite game. It can be something they play indoors or outdoors. Suggest that they tell what the game is, whom they play it with, when they play it, and why they like it. Encourage them to use the high-frequency words as they write about the game.

ART

Have children choose one of the high-frequency words to illustrate. Suggest they write the word at the top of their paper and then draw a scene that "shows" the word. For example, for the word *care*, they might draw a mother caring for a baby. For *under*, they might draw a picture of a cat sleeping under a table.

VISUAL LEARNERS PARTNERS

Materials: paper for sentence strips, scissors

Give each child a sentence strip. Have him or her write a sentence on the strip, using a high-frequency word. Next, instruct each child to cut apart the strip, word by word. Then, have them exchange strips with partners and try to reconstruct the sentences.

CHALLENGE

Invite children to make up silly questions and answers. The question should contain a high-frequency word and the answer should begin with *because*. For example, "Why does a goose make <u>sure</u> it looks both ways before crossing the street?" A possible answer is *"<u>because</u> it does not want to be a silly goose."*

EXTRA SUPPORT/INTERVENTION

Write each high-frequency word on the board, inserting a line in place of one of the letters. Say the complete word and have a volunteer go to the board, write the missing letter, and use the word in a sentence.

Integrating Phonics and Reading

Guided Reading
Have children read the title and look at the illustration. Invite a volunteer to explain what a stew is.

First Reading Ask children to name the ingredients in Egor's stew.

Second Reading Have volunteers find the word *would* in the story and read those sentences.

Comprehension
After reading, ask children the following questions:
- Why does Egor's mom ask what he put in the stew? *Inference/Access Prior Knowledge*
- Would you want to eat Egor's stew? Why or why not? What would you put in a stew? *Reflective Analysis/Personal Response*

ESL/ELL English Language Learners
Review the use of the apostrophe in the title. Remind children that the apostrophe means that *Mom* belongs to *Egor*.

Phonics and Spelling / Phonics and Writing

Short Vowels a, i, u, o, e

Skill Focus

Children will

★ spell words with short vowel sounds.

★ write a postcard, using words with short vowel sounds.

ESL/ELL For children challenged by differentiating and pronouncing clearly the five short vowels, practice word groups such as *bat, bet, bit, bob, but* and *pat, pet, pit, pot, pup.*

Teach

Phonemic Awareness: Phoneme Identity
Review the five short vowel sounds by saying the following groups of words. Invite children to stand each time they hear a word with the targeted sound.

• short *a*:	bet	bat	cab
• short *i*:	tin	ten	sit
• short *u*:	mutt	mitt	hut
• short *o*:	pond	hot	pig
• short *e*:	dip	peg	pet

Sound to Symbol Review the spelling of the short vowel sounds. List on the board these words: *ax, dish, sun, box, leg.* Read the words aloud, one at a time, and have children identify the short vowel sound. Have volunteers go to the board and underline the letter that stands for the short vowel sound. Ask other children to print a rhyming word for each word on the board. (*Possible answers: tax, wish, run, fox, peg*)

Practice and Apply

Sound to Symbol Suggest that children say each word to themselves on page 49 and identify the vowel sound they hear. As they identify each sound, they can print the word on the correct banner.

Writing Before children begin writing on page 50, discuss the purpose of the postcard. Have children write complete sentences that include some of the words in the word box. Remind them to begin each sentence with a capital letter.

Reading You may wish to use *The Case of the Furry Thing*, MCP Phonics and Reading Consonant and Vowel Skills Library, Level B, to reinforce the short vowel sounds.

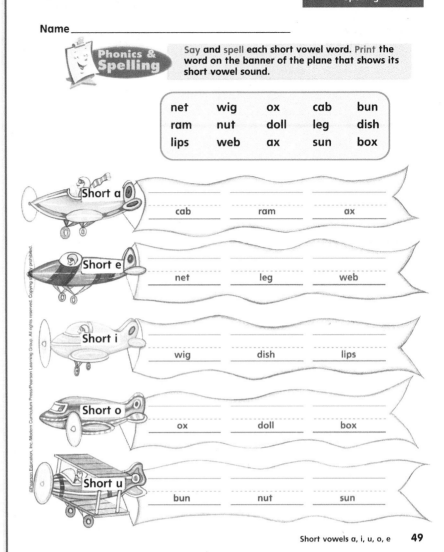

Spelling

Name_____

Phonics & Spelling — Say and spell each short vowel word. Print the word on the banner of the plane that shows its short vowel sound.

net	wig	ox	cab	bun
ram	nut	doll	leg	dish
lips	web	ax	sun	box

Short a cab   ram   ax

Short e net   leg   web

Short i wig   dish   lips

Short o ox   doll   box

Short u bun   nut   sun

Short vowels a, i, u, o, e   **49**

FOCUS ON ALL LEARNERS

ESL/ELL ENGLISH LANGUAGE LEARNERS
Review the short vowel words in the word box on page 50. Have each child create an oral sentence containing some of these words. Encourage them to write the sentence as they complete the postcard activity on this page. Allow children who need additional support to brainstorm ideas aloud with you before writing.

AUDITORY/VISUAL LEARNERS
Materials: drawing paper, crayons
Partners can play a game in which each player thinks of a short vowel word to draw and has his or her partner guess and spell the word based on the picture.

KINESTHETIC LEARNERS
Materials: large index cards or art paper, markers
Make large letter cards for the consonants *n, t, g, w, d, s, h, p, x, c, l, l, b* and for the vowels. Give each child at least one letter card. As you say the following words, have children come forward with the letters to spell each word: *net, leg, web, wig, dish, pig, cab, ox, doll, ax, box, bun, nut, sun.*

Phonics & Writing

A **postcard** is a way of sending a short message to a friend while you are away on vacation. It uses words that tell the friend that you are having fun.

▶ Use **some** of the words in the box to write a postcard telling a friend about the fun you had at the beach.

dig	fun	swim	hot	camp
run	net	doll	sand	pet

Tell what you did.

TO:
My Friend
2 Blue Lane
Yourtown, USA
12345

Sign your name.

HOME Ask your child to name the words on the postcard that have short vowel sounds.

50 Short vowels a, i, u, o, e

CURRICULUM CONNECTIONS

SPELLING

Cumulative Posttest Assess mastery of the Unit 2 spelling list by dictating the following words. You may wish to test only half of the words at one session.

1. **cab** We took a **cab** to the airport.
2. **wig** Mom has a red **wig**.
3. **doll** The **doll** is dressed in jeans.
4. **bun** This is the last hot-dog **bun**.
5. **net** Did you hit the **net** with the ball?
6. **lips** My **lips** are very dry.
7. **ox** The **ox** is back in the barn.
8. **ram** Was there a **ram** at the farm?
9. **nut** Crack the **nut** carefully.
10. **ax** Dad needs to sharpen the **ax**.
11. **leg** The cut on her **leg** has healed.
12. **dish** I ate a large **dish** of ice cream.

ART

Materials: white art paper

Invite children to design their own travel brochures for a beach vacation. Display samples from local travel agencies. Have children draw pictures and write about their vacation sites, which can be real or fictional.

TECHNOLOGY **AstroWord** Short Vowels: *a, i*; Short Vowels: *i, o*; Short Vowels: *e, u*

Integrating Phonics and Reading

Guided Reading
As children look at the cover of the book, ask them what they think of when they see the words *the Case of* and a magnifying glass.
First Reading Ask children who the main character is and what he does.
Second Reading Make five columns on the board and have children write short vowel words from the story in the appropriate columns.

Comprehension
Ask children the following questions.
• Why does Peg call Casey? *Recall/Make Inferences*
• What does Casey mean when he says, "And now I really smell!"? *Inference/Draw Conclusions*

ESL/ELL English Language Learners
Write the word *skunk* on the board and say it aloud. Invite children to tell what they know about skunks.

AUDITORY/VISUAL LEARNERS **GROUPS**

Invite children to write short vowel "hink-pinks" (pairs of one-syllable rhyming words that answer riddles). You might also introduce them to a "hinky-pinky" (a pair of two-syllable rhyming words). For example: *What kind of rabbit tells jokes?* (a funny bunny)

CHALLENGE

Have children print the letters of the words *FUN IN THE SUN* vertically on their papers. Ask children to think of a short vowel word that contains each of the letters and add letters before, after, or around the original letters to spell the words.

EXTRA SUPPORT/INTERVENTION

Materials: Phonics Picture Cards: Short Vowels (45–84)

Ask each child to select a picture for each short vowel sound. Have partners lay all their cards face down, turn them over two at a time, and keep the cards if the vowel sounds match. See Daily Phonics Practice, pages 245–246.

Take-Home Book

Review Short Vowels

Skill Focus

Children will

★ read short *a, e, i, o,* and *u* words in the context of a letter.

★ review selected high-frequency words in the context of a letter.

★ reread for fluency.

ESL/ELL Overnight camping may be unfamiliar to children of other cultures. Guide children to verbalize some of the activities and hobbies they have participated in that could be offered at camp.

Teach
Build Background

• Remind children of this unit's theme, "At Work, At Play." Ask children to name some words they learned that might describe their work and play.

• Write the word *camp* on the board. Explain that there are two basic kinds of camps: day camps and overnight camps. Tell children that they will be reading about an overnight camp.

Phonemic Awareness: Phoneme Substitution Draw attention to the word *camp* on the board. Have children say the word and identify the vowel sound they hear. (*short a*) Then, have children replace the *c* at the beginning of the word with other consonant sounds. (*cramp, champ, damp, lamp, ramp, stamp*) Follow the same procedure with the words *fun, went, pond,* and *hill.*

Practice and Apply

Using the Pages Demonstrate how to put together the Take-Home Books. Invite children to look through the book and talk about the pictures. Point out that this story is in the form of a letter. Then, help children read the story. Discuss what Jill wanted to tell her parents.

Sound to Symbol After children have read the story, suggest that they go back and identify some words that contain short vowel sounds.

Review High-Frequency Words Write *about, then,* and *our* on the board. Have children say each word and spell it. Then, have children find these high-frequency words in the Take-Home Book.

Reread for Fluency Have children reread the book to increase their fluency and comprehension. Remind children to take their books home to read and share with their family.

51

Name _____

Hello From Camp!

July 10

Dear Mom and Dad,

Well, here I am at Camp Windsong! The bus ride was fun. We talked and laughed, and I made a new friend, Beth.

— FOLD —

After dinner, we sat around the campfire, played games, and sang songs. I am having a great time. Please write soon.

Love,
Jill

Review short vowels a, i, u, o, e: Take-home book   **51**

FOCUS ON ALL LEARNERS

ESL/ELL ENGLISH LANGUAGE LEARNERS

Discuss the story with children to verify their comprehension of vocabulary and pronunciation of short vowels. Invite volunteers to read a passage aloud. Encourage children to offer an oral summary of the book.

AUDITORY/KINESTHETIC LEARNERS

Have children sit around a "campfire" and play the game of short vowel tag. Whoever is "it" walks around the outside of the circle, naming a vowel. The child tags someone who has to supply a word with that sound. If the tagged child answers correctly, he or she becomes "it."

KINESTHETIC/VISUAL LEARNERS

Materials: construction paper, scissors

Invite children to think of an object with a short vowel sound. The object should be something they can draw. For example, children might choose an apple or a bell. Have them draw a picture of the object, print the word in the object, and then cut it out.

As soon as we got here, we went up the hill and set up our tents. Then, we hiked around the pond. I saw a box turtle about to dive into the water.

- - - - - - - FOLD - - - - - - -

Next, we learned about Native Americans who lived here many years ago. We used sign language and made dolls from corn husks.

52   Review short vowels a, i, u, o, e: Take-home book

CURRICULUM CONNECTIONS

WRITING

Have children work in small groups to create daily activities for a camp. Have children name their camp and each day's activities in the order they would occur. Each child should be responsible for describing one day's activities. Remind them to include meals. When they are finished, they can put their group's work together in a folder and share it with the rest of the class.

MUSIC

Explain that most camps have a time for sing-a-longs, a time when the campers get together and sing songs that almost everyone knows. Often the songs are silly. Have children work in groups to plan some songs for a sing-a-long. Then, have the groups sing them for the class.

ART

Invite children to pretend that they are at camp. They are to draw a picture of themselves doing their favorite camp activity. After they have finished their picture, they should write a caption for it.

TECHNOLOGY **AstroWord** Short Vowels: *a, i*; Short Vowels: *i, o*; Short Vowels: *e, u*

AUDITORY LEARNERS GROUPS

Have children play "I went to camp," using words with short vowels. The first child says, "I went to camp and brought an apple." The second child says, "I went to camp and brought an apple and a bat." The game continues alphabetically with each child, in turn, remembering what the previous children brought.

CHALLENGE

Materials: Phonics Word Cards, Set 1: Short Vowels (1–117)

Challenge children to write a poem, using several of the short vowel words on the word cards. The topic can be any aspect of going to camp.

EXTRA SUPPORT/INTERVENTION

Invite children to reread "Hello from Camp!" with partners. Encourage them to use the pictures and context clues to help them decode difficult words. See Daily Phonics Practice, pages 245–246.

Unit Checkup

Review Short Vowels

Skill Focus

Children will

★ review the short sounds of *a, e, i, o,* and *u.*

★ identify and spell picture names that contain short vowel sounds.

★ write words that contain short vowel sounds to complete sentences.

★ review high-frequency words.

Teach

Phonemic Awareness: Phoneme Isolation
Say the word *send* slowly, isolating the short *e* sound. Ask children what sound they hear. (*short e*) Have a volunteer suggest another word with the short *e* sound. Repeat the same process with the words *log, run, sick, pan.*

Sound to Symbol Draw a five-column chart on the board with these headings: *short a, short e, short i, short o, short u.* Say words with short vowels and have children tell you which vowel sound they hear. Then, invite volunteers to write the words in the appropriate columns. You may wish to use these words: *web, rug, sink, nest, cot, bed, fox, pig, ham, tub, had, fun, hop, hid,* and *map.*

Practice and Apply

Sound to Symbol Read the directions on page 53 and have children identify the pictures. At the bottom of the page, remind them to say each word to themselves before they identify the short vowel sound.

Writing For page 54, remind children to reread the sentence with the word they chose to make sure it makes sense in the sentence.

High-Frequency Words Remind children to place a check mark only before those words they can read. You may wish to assess children's progress individually, as needed.

UNIT 2 CHECKUP

Name _____

▶ Fill in the bubble beside the name of each picture.

1.	2.	3.	4.
○ fix ● fox ○ fit	○ get ● gum ○ band	● bib ○ bat ○ did	● flag ○ flip ○ flop

5.	6.	7.	8.
○ pet ○ got ● pig	○ dog ● bed ○ bid	○ gum ○ beg ● bug	○ ball ○ band ● bell

▶ Say the name of each picture. Fill in the bubble beside the letter that stands for the short vowel sound.

9. nest	10. fish	11. web	12. rug
○ a ● e ○ i	○ e ○ u ● i	○ i ● e ○ a	○ o ● u ○ e

13. rock	14. tent	15. lamp	16. ham
● o ○ i ○ u	● e ○ i ○ o	● a ○ i ○ e	● a ○ e ○ i

Short vowels: Assessment   **53**

FOCUS ON ALL LEARNERS

- - - - - - - - - - - - - - - - - -

ESL/ELL ENGLISH LANGUAGE LEARNERS

Have children complete the top of page 54 in pairs. Verify accuracy, then ask them to complete the page individually. Explain and pantomime the meaning of unfamiliar words.

AUDITORY LEARNERS GROUPS

Materials: Phonics Picture Cards: Short Vowels (45–84); five paper bags

Label the bags for the short vowel sounds. Invite children to sort the picture cards into the appropriate bags. When children have finished, have them say aloud the cards in each bag.

KINESTHETIC LEARNERS GROUPS

Materials: Phonics Word Cards, Set 1: Short Vowel words (1–117); chairs set up for musical chairs, one less chair than players

Hand volunteers sets of word cards to read. For each set, all cards except the last one should represent the same short vowel. Players circle the chairs until they hear a word with a different vowel sound. The person left standing can read the next set of words.

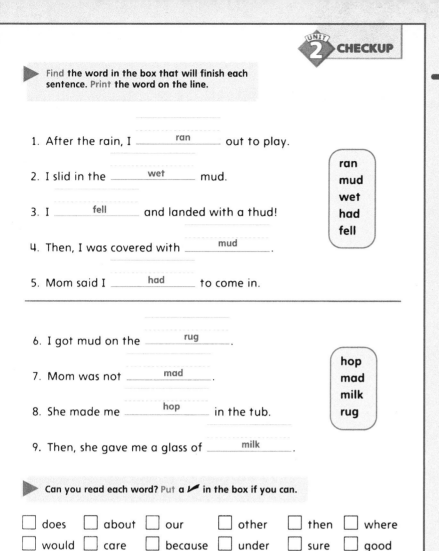

Find the word in the box that will finish each sentence. Print the word on the line.

1. After the rain, I _____ran_____ out to play.

2. I slid in the _____wet_____ mud.

3. I _____fell_____ and landed with a thud!

4. Then, I was covered with _____mud_____.

5. Mom said I _____had_____ to come in.

| ran |
| mud |
| wet |
| had |
| fell |

6. I got mud on the _____rug_____.

7. Mom was not _____mad_____.

8. She made me _____hop_____ in the tub.

9. Then, she gave me a glass of _____milk_____.

| hop |
| mad |
| milk |
| rug |

Can you read each word? Put a ✔ in the box if you can.

☐ does ☐ about ☐ our ☐ other ☐ then ☐ where
☐ would ☐ care ☐ because ☐ under ☐ sure ☐ good

54 Short vowel and high-frequency words: Assessment

ASSESS UNDERSTANDING OF UNIT SKILLS

STUDENT PROGRESS ASSESSMENT

You may wish to review any observational notes you made as children worked through the activities in this unit. These notes will help you evaluate children's progress with short vowel words.

PORTFOLIO ASSESSMENT

Review the collected materials in children's portfolios. You may wish to interview children to discuss their written work and progress since the beginning of this unit. As you review children's work, evaluate their success in using phonics skills.

DAILY PHONICS PRACTICE

For children who need additional practice with short vowels, quick reviews are provided. See Daily Phonics Practice on pages 245–246.

PHONICS POSTTEST

To assess children's mastery of short vowels and high-frequency words, use the posttest Blackline Masters, 10 and 11 on pages 21g–21h.

VISUAL LEARNERS

Have several children come to the board at one time. Name a specific short vowel sound and have each child write a word with that sound. Ask children to use their words in sentences. Classmates can check the spellings and tell whether the sentences make sense.

CHALLENGE

Tell children that the word *thud* is an example of onomatopoeia, or a word whose name echoes the sound of the object or action named. Have children make a list of onomatopoeic words that contain short vowels, such as *crack, snap,* and *pop.* Children may enjoy drawing cartoons using the words.

EXTRA SUPPORT/INTERVENTION

Materials: writing paper

Have pairs of children write short vowel words on paper, using a blank line in place of the vowel. For example, a child might write *b_g.* The partner then fills in the blank. Point out that often more than one vowel may be correct: *bag, beg, big, bog, bug.* Have partners alternate roles. See Daily Phonics Practice, pages 245–246.

Teacher Notes

UNIT 3

Long Vowels
THEME: ON WINGS AND WHEELS

CONTENTS

Student Performance Objectives

In Unit 3, children will review and extend their understanding of long vowels and the sounds they stand for within the context of the theme "On Wings and Wheels." As children apply the concept that consonant and vowel sounds can be blended together to form words, they will be able to

▶ Associate the vowels *a, e, i, o* and *u* with the long sounds they stand for

▶ Identify rhyming elements containing the long vowel sounds

▶ Distinguish among the short and long vowel sounds

▶ Apply the long vowel rule as an aid in decoding and in using words in context

▶ Learn and read high-frequency words in context

Assessment Options

In Unit 3, assess children's ability to read and write words with long vowel sounds. Use the Unit Pretest and Posttest for formal assessment. For ongoing informal assessment you may wish to use children's work on the Review pages, Take-Home Books, and Unit Checkups. You may also want to encourage children to evaluate their own work and to participate in setting goals for their own learning.

ESL/ELL Long vowel sounds may be especially problematic for English language learners. Note pronunciation difficulties but assess progress based on children's ability to distinguish long vowel sounds when pronounced by a native speaker.

FORMAL ASSESSMENT

Use the Unit 3 Pretest on pages 55e–55f to help assess a child's knowledge at the beginning of the unit and to plan instruction.

ESL/ELL Before administering the Pretest on pages 55e–55f, preview the visuals so that children become familiar with the picture names.

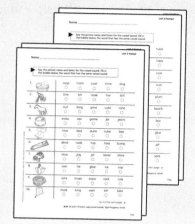

Use the Unit 3 Posttest on pages 55g–55h to help assess mastery of unit objectives and to plan for reteaching, if necessary.

ESL/ELL Some children may understand a concept but have difficulty comprehending direction lines. Read the directions aloud to the group and model how the Pretest is to be completed.

INFORMAL ASSESSMENT

Use the Review pages, Unit Checkup, and Take-Home Books in the student book to provide an effective means of evaluating children's performance.

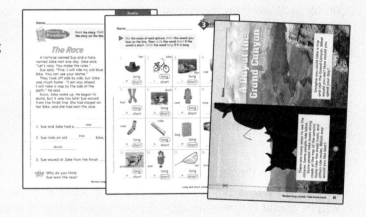

Unit 3 Skills	Review pages	Checkups	Take-Home Books
Long vowel *a*	65–68, 71–72, 75–76, 79–80	83–84	81–82
Long vowel *i*	65–68, 71–72, 75–76, 79–80	83–84	81–82
Long vowel *u*	65–68, 71–72, 75–76, 79–80	83–84	81–82
Long vowel *o*	71–72, 75–76, 79–80	83–84	81–82
Long vowel *e*	75–76, 79–80	83–84	81–82

STUDENT PROGRESS CHECKLIST

Use the checklist on page 55i to record children's progress. You may want to cut the sections apart to place each child's checklist in his or her portfolio.

PORTFOLIO ASSESSMENT

This logo appears throughout the teaching plans. It signals opportunities for collecting a student's work for individual portfolios. You may also want to include the Pretest and Posttest, the Review pages, the Unit Checkup, Phonics & Reading, Phonics & Writing, and Phonics & Spelling pages.

PHONEMIC AWARENESS AND PHONICS ASSESSMENT

Use PAPA to obtain an itemized analysis of children's decoding skills.

PAPA Skills	MCP Phonics Lessons in Unit 3
Long vowels	Lessons 23–35

Pretest and Posttest

DIRECTIONS

To help you assess children's progress in learning Unit 3 skills, tests are available on pages 55e–55h.

Administer the Pretest before children begin the unit. The results of the Pretest will help you identify each child's strengths and needs in advance, allowing you to structure lesson plans to meet individual needs. Administer the Posttest to assess children's overall mastery of skills taught in the unit and to identify specific areas that will require reteaching.

ESL/ELL The objectives of both the Unit 3 Pretest and Posttest are to read and write words with long vowel sounds. English language learners may require additional assessment strategies to meet their special language needs. Long vowel sounds may be especially problematic for English language learners. Note pronunciation difficulties but assess progress based on children's ability to distinguish long vowel sounds when pronounced by a native speaker.

To assess the high-frequency words for Unit 3, have a child read orally each word on the Pretest and Posttest as you point to it. Then, have the child check each word read.

PERFORMANCE ASSESSMENT PROFILE

The following chart will help you identify specific skills as they appear on the tests and will enable you to identify and record specific information about an individual's or the class's performance on the tests.

Depending on the results of each test, refer to the Reteaching column for lesson-plan pages where you can find activities that will be useful for meeting individual needs or for daily phonics practice.

Answer Keys

Unit 3 Pretest, page 55e (BLM 15)

1. (soap) coat	6. (tube) rude
2. (bike) line	7. (jeep) bead
3. (mule) cute	8. (cape) rain
4. (cake) game	9. (hose) snow
5. (feet) bee	10. (kite) bike

Unit 3 Pretest, page 55f (BLM 16)

11. June	15. hike
12. lake	16. jeep
13. boat	17. three
14. trail	18. like

Unit 3 Posttest, page 55g (BLM 17)

1. (tree) jeans	6. (hay) plate
2. (cane) tape	7. (boat) stove
3. (robe) toad	8. (flute) glue
4. (cube) mule	9. (pie) hive
5. (hive) tie	10. (bee) seal

Unit 3 Posttest, page 55h (BLM 18)

11. ride	15. see
12. blue	16. make
13. blow	17. raced
14. rain	18. time

Performance Assessment Profile

Skill	Pretest Questions	Posttest Questions	Reteaching Focus on All Learners	Daily Phonics Practice
Long vowel *a*	4, 8, 12, 14	2, 6, 14, 16, 17	57–58, 65–68, 71–72, 75–76, 79–82	247
Long vowel *i*	2, 10, 15, 18	5, 9, 11, 18	59–60, 65–68, 71–72, 75–76, 79–82	247
Long vowel *u*	3, 6, 11	4, 8, 12	63–68, 71–72, 75–76, 79–82	247–248
Long vowel *o*	1, 9, 13, 18	3, 7, 13	69–72, 75–76, 79–82,	247–248
Long vowel *e*	5, 7, 16, 17	1, 10, 15	73–76, 79–82	248

Student Progress Checklist

Make as many copies as needed to use for a class list. For individual portfolio use, cut apart each child's section. As indicated by the code, color in boxes next to skills satisfactorily assessed and insert an *X* by those requiring reteaching. Marked boxes can later be colored in to indicate mastery.

Student Progress Checklist

Code: ■ Satisfactory   ☒ Needs Reteaching

Student: _____ _____ Pretest Score: _____ Posttest Score: _____	**Skills** □ Long *a* □ Long *i* □ Long *u* □ Long *o* □ Long *e*	**High-Frequency Words** □ could □ said □ song □ girl □ these □ over □ people □ very □ come □ boy □ one □ something	**Comments / Learning Goals**
Student: _____ _____ Pretest Score: _____ Posttest Score: _____	**Skills** □ Long *a* □ Long *i* □ Long *u* □ Long *o* □ Long *e*	**High-Frequency Words** □ could □ said □ song □ girl □ these □ over □ people □ very □ come □ boy □ one □ something	**Comments / Learning Goals**
Student: _____ _____ Pretest Score: _____ Posttest Score: _____	**Skills** □ Long *a* □ Long *i* □ Long *u* □ Long *o* □ Long *e*	**High-Frequency Words** □ could □ said □ song □ girl □ these □ over □ people □ very □ come □ boy □ one □ something	**Comments / Learning Goals**
Student: _____ _____ Pretest Score: _____ Posttest Score: _____	**Skills** □ Long *a* □ Long *i* □ Long *u* □ Long *o* □ Long *e*	**High-Frequency Words** □ could □ said □ song □ girl □ these □ over □ people □ very □ come □ boy □ one □ something	**Comments / Learning Goals**

BLM 19 Unit 3 Checklist

Throughout Unit 3 there are opportunities to assess English language learners' ability to read and write words with long vowel sounds. English language learners may find that some sounds in especially Vietnamese, Khmer, Hmong, and Spanish conflict with certain long vowel sounds in English. Have children practice saying the picture clues aloud; reinforce with reading and spelling opportunities throughout the unit.

Lesson 24, pages 57–58 Speakers of languages other than English may confuse long *a* with short *e*. Native speakers of Spanish may write *e* instead of long *a* in words.

Lesson 25, pages 59–60 Speakers of Asian languages and of Spanish may clip the long *i* from *i_e* words and pronounce it like short *a*; practice *mine, man; bike, back; flight, flat.*

Lesson 27, pages 63–64 Speakers of Cantonese or Vietnamese may pronounce a "round" *u*. Spanish speakers may have trouble with /yu/ as in *music* or *cube* (saying *moosic* or *coob*).

Lesson 29, pages 67–68 Many languages do not discriminate between long and short vowel sounds. Provide opportunities for speakers of other languages to hear and say words that contain long vowel sounds.

Lesson 30, pages 69–70 Speakers of Asian languages may confuse long *o* with the sound of *aw* in *awful*; practice *low, law; so, saw;* and so forth.

Lesson 32, pages 73–74 Speakers of languages other than English may pronounce long *e* and short *i* in a similar manner. Practice *feet, fit; Pete, pit.*

Phonics Games, Activities, and Technology

The following collection of ideas offers a variety of opportunities to reinforce phonics skills while actively engaging children. The games, activities, and technology suggestions can easily be adapted to meet the needs of your group of learners. They vary in approach so as to consider children's different learning styles.

LONG VOWEL MYSTERY WORDS

Give partners some sentence strips, two markers, and a pair of scissors. Direct each child to write a mystery word on a sentence strip, leaving space between letters. Then, he or she cuts the word to make separate letter cards. Each child mixes up the letters and places them on the table for his or her partner to see. Children then try to rearrange the letters to form and then read their partner's word.

Hint: This game becomes very challenging when played with words containing more than four letters. If a child is stumped, you may wish to suggest that the partner give a clue.

ESL/ELL Simplify this activity by having children select words from the Unit 3 Word List, found on pages 55k–55l.

PRESTO-CHANGO

Write these short vowel words on the board: *pin, pan, rid, ton, hid, rid, red, led, not, cut, cot, got, man, tap, plan, van, bit, fin, mop, hop, rob, us, cub,* and *tub.* Have a volunteer use a ruler to select a word, tap it, read it, and then add a vowel to transform it into a word with a long vowel sound. After the child reads this new word, he or she gives the ruler to another child.

ESL/ELL Help focus English language learners on pronouncing new words. Clarify to add the letter *e.* Model changing *pin* to *pine, pan* to *pane,* and so on.

ALL ABOARD

Arrange rows of chairs with an aisle in the center to simulate a bus or train. Then, distribute "boarding passes" that have a vowel written on each. To board the vehicle, children must display their passes and state a word that contains the long vowel sound that corresponds to the letter on their pass.

Variations: Vary the game by writing long vowel words or phonograms on the boarding passes. In the first case, children read the words. In the second, children give a word that contains the long vowel phonogram.

HOT POTATO

To review a specific long vowel sound, write the sound on paper and tape it to a ball or block. Then, have children sit in a circle and pass the object around as music plays. When the music stops, the child holding the "hot potato" must give a word containing this long vowel sound. To make the game more challenging, suggest that children spell the word as well.

LONG VOWEL SKITS

Divide the class into small groups. Then, give each group five or six long vowel words. After groups read the words, challenge each group to create a skit using its assigned words. Tell children that their skits can be humorous if they wish, but all of the long vowel words must be used at least once.

Variation: Before each group presents its skit, have the group write its words on a sheet of chart paper. Then, as each word is used in the skit, have children in the audience raise their hands to signal a volunteer to check it off.

WORD-SHAPE PUZZLES

Write the word *tube* on the chalkboard and show children how a word-shape puzzle can be created by drawing letter boxes, as shown at left. Partner children and give each pair a set of five or six long-vowel word cards and a word-shape puzzle for the word. (If two words have the same shape, suggest children write a brief clue for the word as well.) Have children exchange puzzles and word cards with another pair and solve the puzzles.

GRANDMOTHER'S TRUNK

This traditional game, played by a small group or the entire class, can be modified for long vowel sounds. Identify the vowel sound you wish to target. The first player says, "In my grandmother's trunk I packed a (object whose name contains the vowel sound)." Subsequent players list everything already contained in the trunk, and then add one more item. If a child has difficulty recalling a previously named item, the player who initially packed the item can give a clue. Continue the game until the list gets too long for anyone to remember, or until every player has had a turn.

ESL/ELL Modify the activity having children discriminate meaningful words to add to the list. They can also number responses given to help them recall previous items.

AWAY WE GO TIC-TAC-TOE

Each pair of players will need a nine-square-grid playing board and two sets of vowel playing cards. The playing cards can feature vowels and forms of transportation in place of X's and O's. The playing cards for long *a* could depict a train, for long *i* a bike, for long *u* a mule, for long *o* a boat, and for long *e* a jeep. Each player chooses one set of long vowel cards. Players take turns saying a word that contains the long vowel sound represented on their cards. If correct, a card may be placed on the game grid. Players continue taking turns until one wins or until the board is filled.

Variations: Instead of playing with picture cards, children can use cards with long vowel phonograms. To make a move in this version, a player must say and spell a word that ends with the phonogram. Then, the card can be placed on the tic-tac-toe grid.

ESL/ELL Laminate the cards, then have children print the name of each picture clue in dry-erase marker. Children can pair related cards.

LONG VOWEL BEAN TOSS

To play this small-group game, each group will need a six-cup muffin tin or half of a cardboard egg carton. Have children write the five vowel letters on small slips of paper and place them in the cups. One cup will be free. Give each player five lima beans and have players mark them with their initials. Players take turns tossing their beans into the cups. If successful, they give a word that contains the long vowel sound associated with the letter in the cup. The game continues until each player has a bean in each of the five cups. If a player's bean lands in the free cup, he or she may place the bean in any of the vowel cups.

WORD SORTS

Give partners two bags and a set of word cards that contains words with both long vowel and short vowel sounds. Have children label the bags "long vowel words" and "short vowel words." Children can take turns reading the words aloud and then placing them in the correct bag based on the vowel sound.

Variations: Ask children to choose other sorts, such as word length or rhyming elements.

RACETRACK GAME

Use Blackline Master 21 to make a game board featuring words with long vowels. Make a master copy by writing the following long vowel phonograms in the spaces: *-ay, -une, -oat, -ike, -ule, -eat, -ame, -one, -ide, -ean, -ose, -eed, -ail, -ow, -ube, -ime, -eal, -ie, -ue, -ake.* Then, make copies to distribute to pairs of children. They can take turns using a number cube to move a small car or other marker along the racetrack. As a player lands on a phonogram, an initial consonant must be supplied to create a word. Play continues until both players have successfully crossed the finish line.

TECHNOLOGY

The following software products reinforce children's understanding of long vowels and other phonics skills.

Reader Rabbit's® Reading 2
Engaging activities afford children a playful way to develop an essential foundation to reading. Four activities with four levels of difficulty provide practice in identifying consonant blends, short and long vowel sounds, and digraphs.

** Riverdeep The Learning Company
500 Redwood Blvd.
Novato, CA 94947
(800) 825-4420
www.learningcompanyschool.com

Reading Blaster™ Ages 7–8
Through a fun adventure to Islandia, students will learn beginning and ending sounds, short and long vowels, compound words, contractions, syllables, prefixes and suffixes, and many other basic reading skills.

** Sunburst Technology
1900 South Batavia Ave.
Geneva, IL 60134
(800) 321-7511
www.sunburst.com

Magic Letter Factory
Four activities invite beginning readers to learn letters and their sounds. Children make words by filling in blanks, create wacky sentences by combining nouns and verbs, and watch video clips to reinforce letter and word recognition.

** Educational Activities, Inc.
1937 Grand Avenue
Baldwin, NY 11510
(800) 645-3739

Name_____

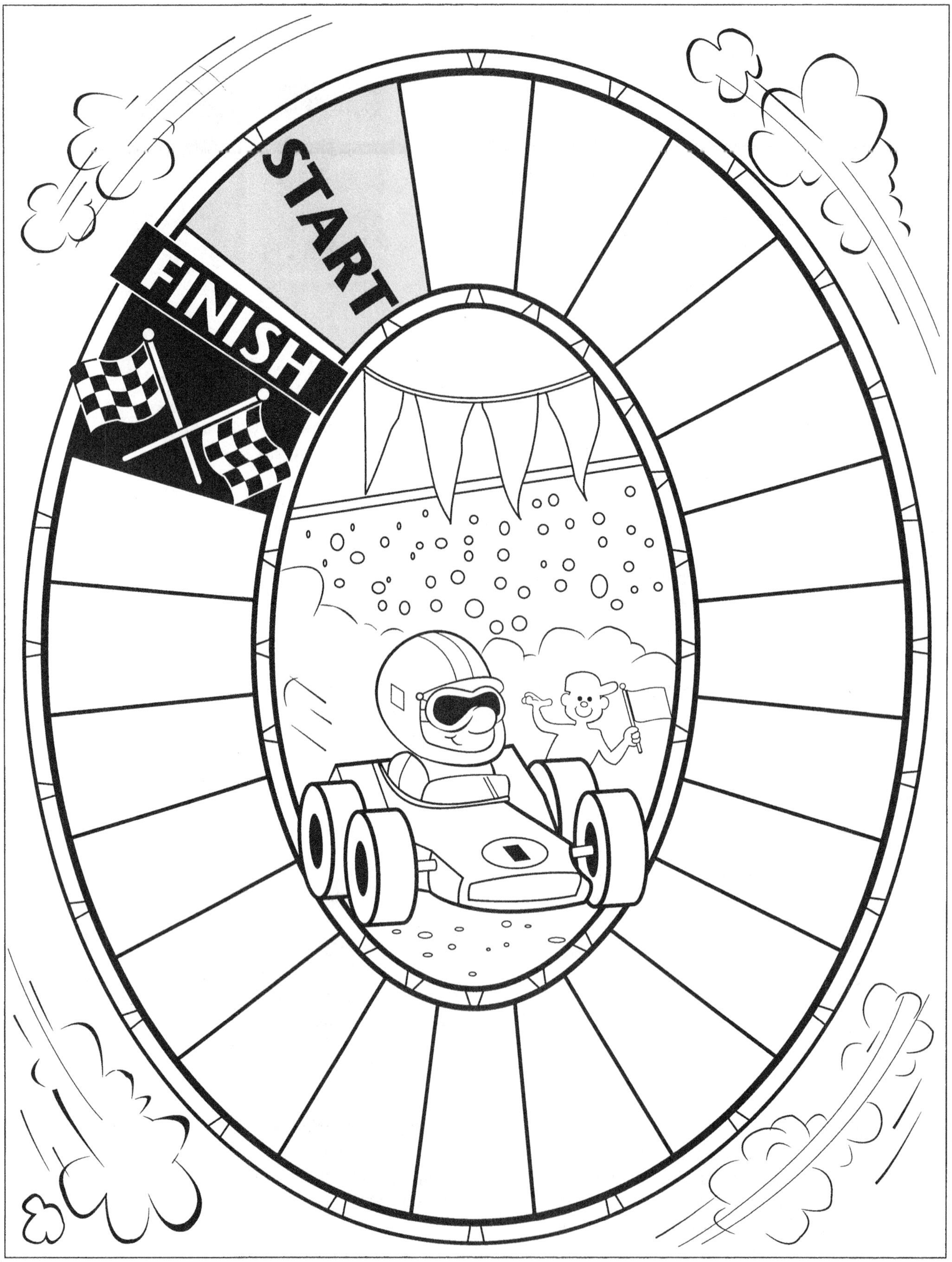

START

FINISH

BLM 21 Unit 3 Activity

Home Connections

The Home Connections features of this program are intended to involve families in their children's learning and application of phonics skills. Three effective opportunities to make connections between home and school include the following.

- **HOME LETTER**
- **HOME NOTES**
- **TAKE-HOME BOOKS**

HOME LETTER

A letter is available to be sent home at the beginning of Unit 3. This letter informs family members that children will be learning to read and write words with long vowel sounds within the context of the unit theme, "On Wings and Wheels." Two activities designed to reinforce long vowel sounds are suggested to parents. The first activity invites family members to look for words with long vowel sounds while reading a travel brochure or an advertisement together. In the second activity, children are asked to write and illustrate a story about a trip they'd like to take. Family members then talk about the story, pointing out words with long vowel sounds. Both activities promote interaction between child and family members while supporting the child's learning to read and write words with long vowel sounds. The letter, which is available in both English and Spanish, also suggests transportation-theme books that family members can look for in a local library and enjoy reading together.

HOME NOTES

Whenever the Home logo appears within the student book, a phonics activity is suggested to be done at home. The activities are simple to do, requiring little or no preparation or special materials, and are meant to reinforce the targeted phonics skill.

Home Notes in Spanish are also available for both teachers and parents to download and use from our website, www.PlaidPhonics.com.

TAKE-HOME BOOKS

Within the student book are many Take-Home Books that can cut out and assembled. The story language in each book reinforces the targeted phonics skills. The books can be taken home and shared with family members. In Unit 3, one Take-Home Book is available, focusing on the five long vowel sounds as well as the theme, "On Wings and Wheels."

Long Vowels

Skill Focus

Assess Prior Knowledge
To assess prior knowledge of long vowels, use the pretest on pages 55e and 55f (Blackline Masters 16 and 17).

Unit Focus

Build Background

• Ask children if they have ever flown in a plane. Invite volunteers to share their experiences.

• Write the theme "On Wings and Wheels" on the board. Ask them what they think the theme means. Then, draw attention to the illustration and discuss it.

• Read the text aloud as children follow along. Ask why the plane becomes "just a speck against the sky."

Introduce Long Vowels

• Ask children to name the vowels. Write *a, e, i, o,* and *u* on the board as they name each one. Have volunteers review the short sound of each vowel.

• Read "Taking Off" again. Write the words *taking, wheels, higher,* and *rises* on the board. Point to each word and say it, emphasizing the long vowel sound: *taaaking, wheeels, hiiigher,* and *riiises.* Explain that these are words with long vowel sounds and that children will be learning more about these sounds in this unit.

Critical Thinking

• Have children brainstorm ways to travel to faraway places. Discuss the advantages and the disadvantages of each.

Read Aloud

Taking Off

Mary McB. Green

The airplane taxis down the field
It lifts its wheels above the ground,
It skims above the trees,
It rises higher and higher
Away up toward the sun,
It's just a speck against the sky
—And now it's gone!

TALK About It How would you travel to faraway places?

Unit 3 • Introduction
Critical Thinking
55

THEME FOCUS

FROM PLACE TO PLACE

Ask children where the airplane in the poem may be going. Invite children to tell about the ways they have traveled from place to place. Point out that any way we have for getting from place to place is called transportation.

WINGS, WHEELS, AND WATER

Ask children what forms of transportation they think of when they hear "On Wings and Wheels." Write the headings *Wings, Wheels,* and *Water* on chart paper, leaving space for a fourth column. On the chart, list the types of transportation children suggest. Use the last column to list things that do not fall into one of the three categories.

VEHICLES OF THE FUTURE

Ask children to collect items that might serve as construction materials for building "vehicles of the future." Supplies might include cardboard tubes, shoe boxes, milk cartons, wheels from old toys, buttons, paper clips, wooden or plastic parts from building sets, glue, and tape. Invite children to use their imaginations to design new modes of transportation.

Dear Family,

As we explore different ways of traveling and places to visit, your child will be learning long vowel sounds in words such as boat, jeep, bike, plane, and mule. Here are some activities you and your child can do together to practice long vowel sounds.

▶ Read a travel article, advertisement, or brochure about a place you would like to visit. Help your child find words with long vowel sounds.

▶ Ask your child to write about a trip he or she would like to take. Talk about the story, and then take turns pointing to all the words with long vowel sounds.

▶ You and your child might enjoy reading these books together.

Axle Annie by Robin Pulver
Iron Horses by Verla Kay

Sincerely,

_____

Estimada familia:

A medida que exploremos las diferentes formas de viajar y los lugares a visitar, su hijo/a aprenderá las vocales de sonidos largos en inglés, tales como boat (barco), jeep (yip), bike (bicicleta), plane (avión) y mule (mula). Aquí tienen algunas actividades que pueden hacer juntos para practicar las vocales de sonidos largos.

▶ Lean un artículo, un anuncio o un volante de viajes acerca de un lugar que les gustaría visitar. Ayuden a su hijo/a a encontrar palabras con vocales de sonidos largos.

▶ Pídanle a su hijo/a que escriba acerca de un viaje que le gustaría dar. Hablen acerca de lo que escribió y tomen turno para señalar todas las palabras que contienen vocales de sonidos largos.

▶ Ustedes y su hijo/a disfrutarán leyendo estos libros juntos.

Axle Annie de Robin Pulver
Iron Horses de Verla Kay

Sinceramente,

_____

BULLETIN BOARD

Ask children to draw pictures of various ways to travel by land, sea, and air. Display pictures on a bulletin board entitled "Getting Around." For a variation, have children draw or cut out pictures of people whose jobs involve transportation. Have children write a sentence caption describing each of their pictures.

HOME CONNECTIONS

- The Home Letter on page 56 will help acquaint families with the phonics skills children will study in this unit. Remind children to take the page home and work on the activities with family members.

- Suggest that children look for the pictured books at the library. Encourage them to read them with family members.

LEARNING CENTER ACTIVITIES

WRITING CENTER

Display a copy of the class's transportation chart in the Writing Center. Invite children to choose three forms of transportation from the chart and write a sentence about each. You may wish to suggest that children use one of the following formats:

I like to _____ because _____.
I don't like to _____ because _____.

SCIENCE CENTER

Tell children that in order for things to move, they need energy from fuel. For example, a car runs on gas, a bike runs on leg motion, and a body runs on food. Recall the kinds of travel mentioned in the poem. Challenge children to think of how each form of transportation gets its energy. Have each visitor to the science center draw a picture of one example. These might include a jet being refueled and a mule eating grain.

MATH CENTER

Place small cardboard cutouts of a tennis shoe, a skate, a bike, a car, an airplane, and a rocket in the math center. Children should arrange and trace the cutouts across a sheet of paper in order from slowest to fastest or fastest to slowest forms of transportation.

Long Vowel a

Skill Focus

Children will

★ recognize the sound of long vowel *a*.

★ identify that *a_e*, *ai*, and *ay* stand for /ā/.

★ apply what they have learned by reading and writing long *a* words in context.

★ recognize and read high-frequency words.

ESL/ELL Speakers of languages other than English may confuse long *a* with short *e*. Native speakers of Spanish may write *e* instead of long *a* in words.

Teach

Phonemic Awareness: Phoneme Identity
Say *cave*, emphasizing the long *a* sound (*caaave*). Repeat the word normally, and have children say *cave*. Remind them that the sound they hear in the middle is the sound of long vowel *a*. Then, say each group of words below. Have children raise their hands when they hear a word with the long *a* sound.

- **day   save   sign**
- **hail   need   gate**

Words in Context: Decodable Words Write the sentence and the words that follow it on the board. Have children read the sentence, choose the correct word, and explain their choice.

- **Her _____ is Jane. (*same, name*)**

Children will have an opportunity to read the following high-frequency words: *go, outside, over, inside, children, piece, nice, we, could, come, with,* and *any.*

Practice and Apply

Sound to Symbol With children, read the rhyme on page 57. Have them identify the long *a* words, print them on the board, and underline the letters that make up the long *a* sound.

Read aloud the rule on page 57. As they complete the pages, remind children to read the entire sentence to make sure that their word choice makes sense.

Critical Thinking Discuss Talk About It. Children might suggest activities such as playing ball or tag.

Reading You may wish to use *Save That Trash*, MCP Phonics and Reading Consonant and Vowel Skills Library, Level B, to provide practice in reading the long *a* sound.

57

Name _____

I made a small, gray boat today.
I shaped it from some clay.
Let's take it to the clear, blue bay
And watch it sail away.

▶ Find **the word that will finish each sentence. Print it on the line.**

RULE
If a syllable or one-syllable word has two vowels, the first vowel usually stands for the long sound, and the second vowel is silent as in **made**, **bay**, and **sail**. The letters **a_e, ai,** and **ay** can stand for the long **a** sound.

1. Jane made a _____ face _____ when she saw the rain.

2. She wanted the rain to go _____ away _____.

3. She had planned to _____ play _____ outside.

4. Then, Jake _____ came _____ over.

5. Jake and Jane played _____ games _____ inside.

away
face
games
came
play

6. The children had to _____ wait _____ for the rain to stop.

7. Jane's mom baked a _____ cake _____.

8. Jane and Jake _____ ate _____ a piece.

rain
ate
wait
cake

9. At last, the _____ rain _____ stopped.

TALK About It What could Jane and Jake do outside?

Long vowel a: High-frequency words, critical thinking   **57**

FOCUS ON ALL LEARNERS

ESL/ELL ENGLISH LANGUAGE LEARNERS
Pronounce the sound of long *a* for children. Then, read the rhyme on page 57 aloud. Ask children to listen for the sounds of long *a*. Reread it, and have children stretch their arms out like wings on a plane each time they hear a word with the long *a* sound.

AUDITORY LEARNERS **PARTNERS**
Invite children to make sentence chains. Have one child start a sentence using one or more long *a* words. The partner adds at least one more long *a* word to the sentence. Then, the first child tries to add another long *a* word and so on. A sample chain might be *Nate has a snake; Nate has a snake named James; Nate has a snake named James that plays in the rain.*

KINESTHETIC LEARNERS **GROUPS**
Invite children to participate in a treasure hunt. The treasure is long *a* words. Give them time to look for objects with long *a* names or for classmates' names that contain the long *a* sound. Compile the words on a chart.

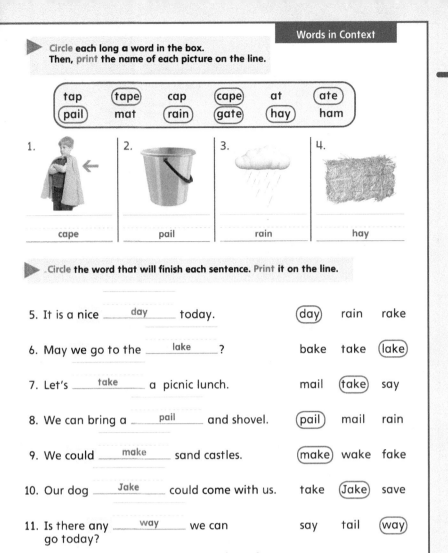

▶ Circle each long **a** word in the box.
Then, print the name of each picture on the line.

tap	(tape)	cap	(cape)	at	(ate)
(pail)	mat	(rain)	(gate)	(hay)	ham

1.

cape

2.

pail

3.

rain

4.

hay

▶ Circle the word that will finish each sentence. Print it on the line.

5. It is a nice ___day___ today.   (day)   rain   rake

6. May we go to the ___lake___?   bake   take   (lake)

7. Let's ___take___ a picnic lunch.   mail   (take)   say

8. We can bring a ___pail___ and shovel.   (pail)   mail   rain

9. We could ___make___ sand castles.   (make)   wake   fake

10. Our dog ___Jake___ could come with us.   take   (Jake)   save

11. Is there any ___way___ we can
    go today?   say   tail   (way)

58   Long vowel a: Sound to symbol,
high-frequency words

 With your child, take turns writing long *a* words by changing the *m* in *make* and the *d* in *day*.

CURRICULUM CONNECTIONS

SPELLING

Pretest the following words as children begin the long *a* and long *i* lessons.

1. **cape**   The superhero wore a **cape**.
2. **mail**   Please see if the **mail** is here.
3. **hay**   My horse eats **hay**.
4. **dime**   I need change for a **dime**.
5. **nine**   It is **nine** days until our trip.
6. **tie**   We gave our uncle a new **tie**.

WRITING

Have children copy and complete the sentence below and then add details with two more sentences. Have children use some long *a* words from pages 57 and 58. *When it rains, I like to _____.*

SCIENCE

Discuss with children how they feel about rainy days. Talk about and display pictures of the earth's water cycle. Have children make and label posters that illustrate the water cycle.

 **AstroWord** Long Vowels: *a, i*

Integrating Phonics and Reading

Guided Reading
Have children read the title and look at the illustrations. Ask them what they think the book will be about. You may also wish to use the activity in the English Language Learners section below.
First Reading Ask children to identify some things they can make.
Second Reading Suggest children identify some of the long *a* words in the story.
Comprehension
After reading, ask children the following questions:
• What is the first step in each project? Why? *Recall/Make Inferences*
• Which project would be the most fun to make? Why? *Reflective Analysis/Personal Response*
ESL/ELL **English Language Learners**
Point out the illustration on the cover. Have children identify some of the objects. Ask them why someone might want to save trash.

VISUAL LEARNERS GROUPS

Materials: Phonics Word Cards, Set 1: Short *a* and Long *a* words (1–33, 118–142); paper bag

Place the word cards in the bag. Have children take turns choosing a card, reading both sides, and identifying the words as long *a* or short *a*. Invite children to sort the cards into long *a* and short *a* piles.

CHALLENGE

Invite children to make a list of long *a* words, including words from the lesson and others they know. Then, have them use the words to make a comic strip about a rainy day or a trip to a lake.

EXTRA SUPPORT/INTERVENTION

Materials: cutouts of raindrops

Have children write long *a* words on the raindrops. Ask them to attach the raindrops to a bulletin board or the chalkboard. Invite pairs of children to work together, taking turns pointing to words and reading them. See Daily Phonics Practice, page 247.

Long Vowel i

Skill Focus

Children will

★ recognize the sound of long vowel *i*.

★ identify that *i_e* and *ie* often stand for /ī/.

★ apply what they have learned by reading and writing long *i* words in context.

★ recognize and read high-frequency words.

ESL/ELL Speakers of Asian languages and of Spanish may clip the long *i* from *i_e* words and pronounce long *i* like short *a*; practice *mine, man; bike, back;* and *flight, flat.*

Teach

Phonological Awareness: Rhyme Say *bike, like,* and *hike,* being sure to pronounce the long *i* in each word clearly. Have children repeat the words. Ask them how the words are the same. (*They rhyme.*) Point out that the vowel sound they hear in each of the rhyming words is long *i*. Then, say groups of three words. Have volunteers identify which two words rhyme.

- **light   bite   book**
- **may   tie   lie**

Practice and Apply

Sound to Symbol Read the rhyme on page 59. Have children identify the long *i* words and write them on the board as you reread the rhyme. Tell children that *y* and *igh*, in addition to *i_e* and *ie*, can also spell the long *i* sound. Ask volunteers to underline the letters that stand for the long *i* sound in each word.

Read the rule at the top of page 59. Help children identify the pictures on pages 59 and 60.

Writing Read the directions on page 60. Remind children to reread each sentence with the word they circled to see if it makes sense. Children will have an opportunity to read the following high-frequency words: *very, behind, anywhere, things, here,* and *one.*

Reading You may wish to use *Six Fine Fish,* MCP Phonics and Reading Consonant and Vowel Skills Library, Level B, to provide practice in reading the long *i* sound.

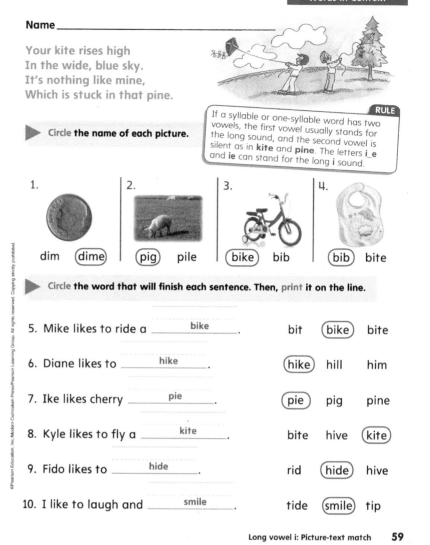

Name _____

Your kite rises high
In the wide, blue sky.
It's nothing like mine,
Which is stuck in that pine.

▶ Circle **the name of each picture.**

RULE
If a syllable or one-syllable word has two vowels, the first vowel usually stands for the long sound, and the second vowel is silent as in **kite** and **pine.** The letters **i_e** and **ie** can stand for the long **i** sound.

1. dim   (dime)
2. (pig)   pile
3. (bike)   bib
4. (bib)   bite

▶ Circle **the word that will finish each sentence. Then, print it on the line.**

5. Mike likes to ride a _____bike_____.   bit   (bike)   bite

6. Diane likes to _____hike_____.   (hike)   hill   him

7. Ike likes cherry _____pie_____.   (pie)   pig   pine

8. Kyle likes to fly a _____kite_____.   bite   hive   (kite)

9. Fido likes to _____hide_____.   rid   (hide)   hive

10. I like to laugh and _____smile_____.   tide   (smile)   tip

Long vowel i: Picture-text match   **59**

FOCUS ON ALL LEARNERS

ESL/ELL **ENGLISH LANGUAGE LEARNERS**

Practice writing long *i* words in context by completing the activity on page 59. Ask a volunteer to read the directions aloud. Have children complete items 5 through 10 individually as you monitor efforts.

AUDITORY LEARNERS

Gather children in a circle and have them name as many rhyming words as they can for *kite, ride, nine, dime, tie,* and *hive.* Pass a dime as each child names a rhyming word. See how many dimes they can "earn" before they run out of rhymes for each word.

KINESTHETIC LEARNERS

Materials: Phonics Word Cards, Set 1: Short *i* and Long *i* words (34–59, 143–157); two shoe boxes

Place two shoe boxes with mail-slot cutouts on a table. Label one mailbox *Short i Words* and the other *Long i Words.* Stack the word cards next to the boxes. Invite partners to take turns playing "mail carrier" by reading and putting each card into the appropriate mailbox.

▶ Circle the word that will finish each sentence. Print it on the line.

1. A turtle can ___hide___ inside its shell.   dime   time   (hide)

2. ___Mice___ can hide in a nest very well.   (Mice)   tile   pie

3. My dog can hide behind our ___bikes___ .   likes   (bikes)   dives

4. A bee can hide in its ___hive___ .   (hive)   time   kite

5. A spider can hide anywhere it ___likes___ .   pine   mine   (likes)

6. I ___like___ to hide things here and there.   (like)   mile   dime

7. No one can find ___Mike___ at bedtime.   dime   (Mike)   tries

▶ Circle each long i word in the box.
Print the name of each picture on the line.

| dim | (dime) | pin | (pine) | rid | (ride) |
| (mine) | (tie) | sit | (kite) | (nine) | (line) |

8. [image: tie] — tie

9. [image: 9] — nine

10. [image: person riding horse] — ride

11. [image: kite] — kite

60 Long vowel i: Sound to symbol, high-frequency words

HOME Ask your child to think of a word that rhymes with each of the picture names above.

CURRICULUM CONNECTIONS

SPELLING

You may wish to use these sentences to posttest the long *a* and long *i* spelling words.

1. **dime**   Two nickels equals a **dime**.
2. **mail**   I received a letter in the **mail**.
3. **hay**   **Hay** is made from dry grass.
4. **tie**   Please **tie** a string on the kite.
5. **nine**   Our team scored **nine** goals.
6. **cape**   My woolen **cape** keeps me warm.

SOCIAL STUDIES

Materials: large sheets of construction paper

Talk about types of transportation children have seen recently. Have each child choose one to draw and cut out. Invite children to list, on their cutouts, uses for that type of transportation.

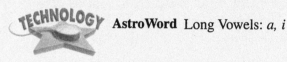 **TECHNOLOGY** **AstroWord** Long Vowels: *a, i*

VISUAL LEARNERS GROUPS

Display a list of short *i* words that can become long *i* words by adding a final *e*. These include *bit, hid, dim, rid, slim, fin, pin, shin, spin, rip, grip,* and *strip*. Have volunteers rewrite each word adding *e*. Practice reading the word pairs together.

CHALLENGE

Ask children to think of short *i* and long *i* pairs such as *dim* and *dime, kit* and *kite, pin* and *pine*, or invite them to use the list from the previous activity. Challenge them to use both words in a single sentence. For example: *I could not see the shiny dime in the dim light.*

EXTRA SUPPORT/INTERVENTION

Materials: mural paper, yarn, paper bow-tie shapes

Draw and cut a large kite shape from the mural paper. On it write *Tie Long i on the Kite in Flight* and attach a length of yarn to it. Have children write long *i* words on the bow-tie shapes and tie or tape them to the tail of the kite. See Daily Phonics Practice, page 247.

Integrating Phonics and Reading

Guided Reading
Encourage children to find pictures of the six fine fish on the cover. Ask if they have ever seen any of them.
First Reading Invite children to name the six fish.
Second Reading Have children find words in the story with the long *i* sound.
Comprehension
After reading, ask children the following questions:
• Which fish would you not want to meet while you are swimming? Why? *Reflective Analysis/ Make Judgments*
• Which fish do you think is most interesting? Why? *Reflective Analysis/Personal Response*
ESL/ELL **English Language Learners**
Children may have difficulty pronouncing the title. Read the title of the story and have children repeat it several times.

High-Frequency Words

Skill Focus

Children will

★ recognize and write the high-frequency words *could, come, over, one, very, these.*

★ use the high-frequency words to complete sentences.

★ begin to recognize irregular spelling patterns.

▶ Teach

Analyze Words Write the words *could, come, over, one, very,* and *these* on the board. Read the word slowly as you point to each letter.

- Have children make and use letter cards to spell each word.

- Repeat each word, stretching the sounds. Have children point to each letter in the word as they hear its sound.

- Help children associate the sounds they hear in each word with a familiar word.

- Have the children say each word, blending the sounds.

- Add the words to the class Word Wall so that children can use the words to find similar spelling patterns and phonemic elements in new words.

Read Words in Context Write the following sentences on the board. Then, invite volunteers to read the sentences and underline the high-frequency words.

- **Please come over the hill to my house.**
- **We could stay very warm by the fireplace.**
- **One of my friends gave me these mittens.**

▶ Practice and Apply

Write Words Have children turn to page 61. Read the directions aloud as children follow along. Suggest that they say each word before writing it in the sentence, using the strategies they have learned to associate sounds with letters and blend words. On page 62, remind children that the shape of the boxes should help them put the letters in the correct order to make a word.

Reading You may wish to use *Hunt for Clues*, MCP Phonics and Reading Library, High Frequency Word Collection, Level B, to provide practice in reading high-frequency words.

Name _____

▶ Read the words in the box. Write a word to finish each sentence.

could
over
very
come
One
these

1. _____One_____ day, Mom and I drove to Lake Baker.

2. We asked Jane to _____come_____ with us.

3. Mom told Jane she _____could_____ bring her dog Ike.

4. We went _____over_____ a bridge to get to the lake.

5. The lake was _____very_____ blue.

6. We drew _____these_____ pictures of our day.

FOCUS ON ALL LEARNERS

ESL/ELL ENGLISH LANGUAGE LEARNERS

Some children whose first language is not English may have difficulty pronouncing /v/ and /th/. Write the high-frequency words on the board. Have children repeat them. Keep returning to *very* and *these* for those children who have difficulty. Suggest they work with a partner and say aloud the sentences on page 61.

AUDITORY LEARNERS

Materials: high-frequency word cards

Have children remove the high-frequency words for this lesson from the back of their book. Then, invite a volunteer to choose a card and give a simple clue such as, "I begin with *o* and end with *r*." The remainder of the group answers *over* and spells the word aloud.

VISUAL LEARNERS

Materials: white paper

Have children make letter cards to spell each high-frequency word. Then, have them scramble the letters for each word and exchange places with their partner. Partners unscramble the words, then say and spell each word.

▶ Unscramble the letters to write the words. The shapes will help you print the words.

1. vero
| o | v | e | r |

2. ervy
| v | e | r | y |

3. ldcou
| c | o | u | l | d |

4. ethse
| t | h | e | s | e |

5. moce
| c | o | m | e |

6. neo
| o | n | e |

CHECKING UP

▶ Put a ✔ next to each word you can read.

☐ come ☐ very ☐ one ☐ these ☐ could ☐ over

 HOME Help your child make up a sentence for each high-frequency word, such as *These books are heavy.*

CURRICULUM CONNECTIONS

SOCIAL STUDIES

Use a map of the United States to point out the five Great Lakes to children. Pinpoint your state on the map and help determine the general direction of the Great Lakes from your location. Discuss the importance of lakes. Encourage children to use one of the high-frequency words to make up a sentence about a lake.

SCIENCE

Provide children with nature books and magazines relating to animals that live in or near lakes, such as sunfish, frogs, muskrats, beavers, and birds. Make a large lake on blue paper and have children draw some of the animals they might find there and add them to the "lake."

WRITING

Have children pretend that they are the narrator of the story on page 59. Encourage them to write an invitation to Jane to go to the lake. Remind them to use high-frequency words in their invitation.

PORTFOLIO

KINESTHETIC/VISUAL LEARNERS GROUPS

Materials: brown and green construction paper, scissors

Cut out a brown tree trunk and six green strips of paper as follows: one strip for a high-frequency word with three letters, two strips for each five-letter word, and three strips for each four-letter word. Working in groups of six, each child prints a high-frequency word on the appropriate strip. When children finish, have them make a "fir" tree by arranging the strips on the tree trunk so that the largest strips are on the bottom and the smallest on top.

CHALLENGE

Using the high-frequency words have children make a Word Search puzzle. Model making a grid by writing the answers in first. Then, have them add the other letters. Have them exchange puzzles with a partner.

EXTRA SUPPORT/INTERVENTION

Write the high-frequency words on the board. Ask children to name the word that rhymes with *would, Rover, berry, some, done, please.*

Integrating Phonics and Reading

Guided Reading

With children read the title and look at the illustrations. Ask what the story will be about.

First Reading Ask children what problem Mary Sue has.

Second Reading Have children find the high-frequency word *could* and read aloud the sentences that contain the word.

Comprehension

After reading, ask children the following questions:

• In what places did True Blue find clues? *Recall/Sequence*

• Do you think True Blue was really looking for clues? Explain. *Reflective Analysis/Making Judgments*

ESL/ELL English Language Learners

Write the words *True Blue* on the board. Explain that True Blue is the name of the dog in the story. Tell children that the phrase *true blue* is used to describe a real or faithful friend.

Long Vowel u

Skill Focus

Children will

★ recognize the sound of long vowel *u*.

★ identify that *u_e, ui,* and *ue* often stand for /ū/.

★ distinguish between short *u* and long *u* sounds.

★ recognize and read high-frequency words.

ESL/ELL Speakers of Cantonese or Vietnamese may pronounce a "round" *u*. Spanish speakers may have trouble with /yu/ as in *music* or *cube* (saying moosic or coob).

▶ Teach

Phonemic Awareness: Phoneme Substitution Say *blue*, elongating the long sound of *u*. Repeat the word normally and ask children to say it. Have them isolate the long *u* sound. Invite them to replace the initial *bl* with *cl* (*clue*), *gl* (*glue*), and *S* (*Sue*).

Sound to Symbol Explain that long *u* has two slightly different sounds. Use the words *mule* and *blue* to demonstrate the /oo/ and /yu/ sounds. Write *cube, tune,* and *rule* on the board. Invite volunteers to say each word and ask children what sound they hear. (*long o*)

▶ Practice and Apply

Words in Context Read the rhyme aloud on page 63 and have children clap each time they hear the long *u* sound. Then, talk about the rule and read the directions with children. Explain to children that they should first say whether the sentence is correct or incorrect by circling *yes* or *no* before they find and write the word with the long *u* sound.

Children will have an opportunity to read the following high-frequency words: *you, together,* and *song*.

Sound to Symbol For page 64, remind children to say each word to decide whether the sound is long *u* or short *u*.

Reading You may wish to use *Blue Sue,* MCP Phonics and Reading Consonant and Vowel Skills Library, Level B, to provide practice in reading long *u* words.

63

Name _____

Sue's old blue truck has bells.
It plays some jolly tunes.
Sue loves the way it sounds,
But not its smelly fumes!

Circle **yes** or **no** **to answer each sentence.** Then circle **the long u word in each sentence.** Print **it on the line.**

RULE
If a syllable or one-syllable word has two vowels, the first vowel usually stands for the long sound, and the second vowel is silent as in **Sue, blue,** and **fumes.** The letters **u_e, ui,** and **ue** can stand for the long **u** sound.

1. A red vase is (blue.) — blue — yes (no)

2. We can get toothpaste in a (tube.) — tube — (yes) no

3. A baby lion is a (cube.) — cube — yes (no)

4. A (mule) has nine tails. — mule — yes (no)

5. You stick things together with (glue.) — glue — (yes) no

6. We can eat a (suit.) — suit — yes (no)

7. A (rule) is a pet that can sing. — rule — yes (no)

8. We play a song with a (flute.) — flute — (yes) no

9. We can hum a (tune.) — tune — (yes) no

Long vowel u: High-frequency words **63**

FOCUS ON ALL LEARNERS

ESL/ELL ENGLISH LANGUAGE LEARNERS

Read the directions aloud for the sorting activity on page 64; ask a volunteer to explain the task. Monitor progress as children complete the activity individually. Review answers by having volunteers contribute to lists on an overhead transparency.

AUDITORY LEARNERS

Materials: Phonics Picture Cards: Short and Long *u* (61–69, 103–107)

Place the picture cards face down in a pile. Invite volunteers to choose a card, identify the vowel sound as long *u* or short *u*, and describe the picture without naming it. Ask other children to guess the name of the picture based on the description.

KINESTHETIC LEARNERS

Materials: Phonics Word Cards, Set 1: Long *u* words (158–164)

Give children one card each and have them locate partners with a rhyming word or a word with the same spelling pattern for one of their words. Have them write word pairs on the board.

Read the words in the box. Print the short **u** words in the ducks' pond. Print the long **u** words in the mule's pen.

bug	jump	suit	tune	bump	tube
dug	glue	nut	rule	music	hum
	luck	jug	blue	flute	

short

bug

jump

bump

dug

nut

hum

luck

jug

long

suit

tune

tube

glue

rule

music

blue

flute

64 Long and short vowel u

HOME Ask your child to suggest three short *u* words and three long *u* words to add to the lists.

CURRICULUM CONNECTIONS

SPELLING

Use the following words and sample sentences to pretest the spelling list for long *u, o,* and *e.*

1. **rule** Did you follow the **rule**?
2. **use** I can **use** this tool safely.
3. **coat** I shopped for a new **coat**.
4. **note** Write a **note** to your mom.
5. **heel** There is a blister on my **heel**.
6. **bead** I broke a **bead** on my necklace.

WRITING

Ask children to think about recent trips they have taken. Discuss rules they must follow on a trip, such as wearing seat belts. Then, have children write sets of "Safe Traveling Rules."

PORTFOLIO

MUSIC

Invite an instrumental music teacher to visit your class and explain how the flute is played. Ask the musician to play a few familiar tunes and have children identify them.

TECHNOLOGY **AstroWord** Long Vowels: *e, u*

Integrating Phonics and Reading

Guided Reading
Invite children to read the title and look at the illustrations. Ask what they think the story will be about.
First Reading Encourage children to explain why Sue is called *blue.*
Second Reading Write *Blue Sue* on the board. Invite children to add other long *u* words from the story to the list.

Comprehension
After reading, ask children the following questions:
• Did Sue, Bud, and everything else turn blue? How do you know? *Recall/Draw Conclusions*
• What would you think if things around you turned blue? *Reflective Analysis/Personal Response*

ESL/ELL **English Language Learners**
Read the title to children. Ask how the words *blue* and *Sue* are the same. (*Both words make the long* u *sound and rhyme.*)

VISUAL LEARNERS *INDIVIDUAL*

Have children write *blue* and *tune* as column headings on their papers. Ask them to find other long *u* words on pages 63 and 64 and write each in the column with the matching pattern. (*ue* or *u*-consonant-*e*). Invite them to find the long *u* words with a different pattern. (*suit, music*)

CHALLENGE

Ask children to make a list of long *u* words that rhyme. Have them use these words to write new lyrics for a tune they already know.

EXTRA SUPPORT/INTERVENTION

Materials: chart paper, markers

Invite children to create a Word Wall of long *u* words. Draw brick shapes on chart paper. Have children fill in the bricks on the chart with long *u* words. After they complete this lesson, review the words on the wall by asking children to use each one in a sentence. See Daily Phonics Practice, pages 247–248.

Pages 65–66

Review Long and Short Vowels a, i, u

Skill Focus

Children will

★ review the long sound of *a*, *i*, and *u*.

★ discriminate between the long sound and the short sound of *a*, *i*, and *u*.

★ write words that contain the long sound of *a*, *i*, and *u* to complete sentences.

★ recognize and read high-frequency words.

Teach

Phonemic Awareness: Phoneme Isolation
Say *bit* and *bite*, elongating the medial vowel sound. Remind children that *bit* has the short *i* sound while *bite* has the long *i* sound. Repeat the procedure, using *cut*, *cute*, and *cap*, *cape*.

Sound to Symbol Write these word pairs on the board: *rain, ran; rid, ride; tube, tub*. Point to and say each pair aloud. Ask a volunteer to say and point to the words with the short *u* sound, and underline the letter that stands for that sound. (*tub, u*) Next, ask how *tube* is different from *tub*. (*Tube ends in* e *and contains the long sound of* u.) Remind children that when a word contains the vowel-consonant-*e* pattern, the first vowel is usually long and the *e* is silent. Invite volunteers to identify the vowel sounds in the remaining pairs, and tell how the words are different.

Words in Context: Decodable Words Write this sentence on the board.

- **He can play a tune on his _____.** (*music, flute*)

Have children choose the correct word and explain why it is correct.

Practice and Apply

Sound to Symbol As children complete page 65, remind them to look at the vowel pattern and say each word before they mark the answer.

Writing Tell children to try each word choice in the blanks on page 66 before they write their answer. Children will have the opportunity to read the following high-frequency words: *his, her*, and *too*.

Critical Thinking In response to Talk About It, children may say that it is a band or other kind of musical group.

Reading You may wish to use *Erik and the Three Goats*, MCP Phonics and Reading Consonant and Vowel Skills Library, Level B, to reinforce the long and short vowels *a*, *i*, and *u*.

Name _____

▶ Read **each** word. If the word has a long vowel, fill in the bubble in front of long. If the word has a short vowel, fill in the bubble in front of short.

1. late — ● long ○ short	2. June — ● long ○ short	3. mule — ● long ○ short
4. man — ○ long ● short	5. tube — ● long ○ short	6. ride — ● long ○ short
7. rain — ● long ○ short	8. pick — ○ long ● short	9. six — ○ long ● short
10. use — ● long ○ short	11. cute — ● long ○ short	12. cap — ○ long ● short
13. bat — ○ long ● short	14. time — ● long ○ short	15. fun — ○ long ● short
16. bake — ● long ○ short	17. lick — ○ long ● short	18. us — ○ long ● short
19. map — ○ long ● short	20. wide — ● long ○ short	21. gate — ● long ○ short
22. wipe — ● long ○ short	23. pie — ● long ○ short	24. tune — ● long ○ short

Review long and short vowels a, i, u **65**

FOCUS ON ALL LEARNERS

ESL/ELL ENGLISH LANGUAGE LEARNERS
Discuss musical instruments whose names contain the sound of long *u*: *tuba, ukulele, bugle*, and *flute*. Bring to class these instruments or pictures of these instruments. Encourage children to talk about their own experiences with musical instruments. Assign page 66 as pair work. Monitor progress and equal participation. Review answers aloud.

AUDITORY/VISUAL LEARNERS
Materials: audiocassette tape, cassette player

Print these words on the board: *bike, pie, kite, play, ate, tail, rain, lake, mule, tune, blue*. Ask children to work together to create a silly story using as many of the words as possible. Have them tape the story and play it later.

VISUAL LEARNERS
Materials: Phonics Word Cards, Set 1: Long *a*, *i*, *u* words (118–164)

Mix the cards in a stack. Have each child read five cards in a row as you flash them.

Circle the word that will finish each sentence.
Print it on the line.

Words in Context

1. We _____like_____ to play music.   ride (like) hike

2. It is a nice _____way_____ to spend a day.   pay side (way)

3. June likes to play her _____flute_____.   (flute) suit time

4. Jay can play his _____tuba_____.   bake (tuba) tub

5. Mike _____plays_____ tunes on his bugle.   side skit (plays)

6. _____Sue_____ plays a bugle, too.   (Sue) suit like

7. _____I_____ like to play my drum.   It (I) Ice

8. We all sing _____tunes_____.   (tunes) times tiles

9. We can play _____music_____ in a parade.   (music) suit fan

10. Will our uniforms come on _____time_____? tip cub (time)

11. We play at football _____games_____, too!   gum (games) gate

 What kind of group do the children belong to?

 Ask your child to group the words he or she wrote according to the vowel sounds.

66   Review long vowels a, i, u: High-frequency words, critical thinking

---

CURRICULUM CONNECTIONS

SPELLING
Write the incomplete spelling words *b_ad, n_te, _se, c_at, h_el,* and *r_le* on the board. Ask the questions below and have children fill in the vowels to complete the answers.
1. What is a direction to follow? (*rule*)
2. What is something you wear? (*coat*)
3. What is something you write? (*note*)
4. What is part of your foot? (*heel*)
5. What can be put on a string? (*bead*)
6. What is an action word? (*use*)

WRITING
Display these incomplete phrases: *_ce cream and c_ke; fun and g_mes; a t_ne on a fl_te; r_in or sh_ne; w_it and see.* Have children use *a, i,* or *u* to finish the words in the phrases and then write sentences with the sayings.

TECHNOLOGY **AstroWord** Long Vowels: *a, i;* Long Vowels: *e, u*

KINESTHETIC LEARNERS **GROUPS**
Materials: nine 12" × 12" cardboard squares, button

Print these words on the squares: *cake, cane, pail, bike, pie, time, mule, cute, tube.* Tape them on the floor in a hopscotch pattern. Each player tosses the button onto a card, hops through the pattern avoiding that square, and reads all the other words.

CHALLENGE
Invite children to use long *a, i,* and *u* words to create two- and three-word crossword puzzles with clues for classmates to solve.

EXTRA SUPPORT/INTERVENTION
Materials: Phonics Picture Cards: Long *a, i, u* (85–107); three paper grocery bags

Write *long a, long i,* and *long u* on the three paper bags. Have children sort the picture cards whose names contain these sounds into the appropriate bags. See Daily Phonics Practice, pages 247–248.

Integrating Phonics and Reading

Guided Reading
Have children look at the illustrations to find out who the characters are.

First Reading Ask children what Erik's problem is.

Second Reading Make six columns on the board with the headings long *a, i, u* and short *a, i, u.* Invite children to write words from the story in the appropriate columns.

Comprehension
After reading, ask children the following questions.
- Why did Erik, the rabbit, and the fox at first laugh at the bees? *Inference/Draw Conclusions*
- Why did the goats leave the grain when the bees came? *Inference/Accessing Prior Knowledge*

ESL/ELL **English Language Learners**
Direct children's attention to the title and illustration on the cover. Ask them to share what they know about goats.

Phonics and Reading / Phonics and Writing

Long Vowels a, i, u

Skill Focus

Children will

★ read words that contain the long sound of *a*, *i*, and *u*.

★ write long *a*, *i*, and *u* words to finish sentences.

★ build words, using word ladders.

ESL/ELL Many languages do not discriminate between long and short vowel sounds. Provide opportunities for speakers of other languages to hear and say words that contain long vowel sounds.

▶ Teach

Phonemic Awareness: Phoneme Identity
Review the long vowel sounds of *a*, *i*, and *u* by saying the following words. Invite children to raise their hand when they hear a word with the targeted sound.

- **long a:** date   cat   paid
- **long i:** bin   time   dried
- **long u:** cute   blue   cut

Sound to Symbol Write *late* on the board. Have children say the word. Ask them what vowel sound they hear. (*long* a) Invite a volunteer to go to the board and change the *l* to another consonant to make a new long *a* word. (*gate, hate, Kate, date, mate, Nate, rate*) Using *die*, ask children to make rhymes (*lie, pie, tie*) and then to change the *i* to make a new word. (*doe, due*)

Words in Context On the board write and read this sentence: *Jake will use a bike for the race.* Have children underline the words with the long sound of *a* (*Jake, race*), *i* (*bike*), and *u* (*use*).

▶ Practice and Apply

Writing With children, read the story on page 67. Encourage them to reread the story and to try their answers in the sentences.

Critical Thinking Discuss Talk About It. Children should recognize that Sue won because she kept on trying.

Building Words With children, complete the example on page 68. Guide children to understand that only one letter can be changed in each word and that each change must result in a real word.

Reading You may wish to use *The Lion Roars*, MCP Phonics and Reading Consonant and Vowel Skills Library, Level B, to reinforce the long vowels *a* and *i*.

67

Name_____

 **Phonics & Reading**   Read the story. Print a long a, i, or u word from the story on the line to finish each sentence.

The Race

A tortoise named Sue and a hare named Jake met one day. Jake said, "Let's race. You make the rules."

Sue said, "Fine. I will ride my old blue bike. You can use your skates."

They took off side by side, but Jake was much faster. "I am way ahead. I will take a nap by the side of the path," he said.

Soon, Jake woke up. He began to skate, but it was too late! Sue waved from the finish line. She had stayed on her bike, and she had won the race.

1. Sue and Jake had a ___**race**___.

2. Sue rode an old ___**blue**___ bike, and Jake used ___**skates**___.

3. Sue waved at Jake from the finish ___**line**___.

TALK About It Why do you think Sue won the race?

Review long vowels a, i, u: Critical thinking   **67**

FOCUS ON ALL LEARNERS

ESL/ELL ENGLISH LANGUAGE LEARNERS
Materials: crayons

Reread *The Race* aloud to children. Then, have children read the story aloud chorally. Give children a specific task for each vowel sound, such as underlining in blue words that contain the sound of long *u*.

AUDITORY LEARNERS GROUPS

Invite children to pretend that they are in charge of prizes for Sue the Tortoise. Each prize must have the long *a*, *i*, or *u* sound. One child begins by naming a "prize," and then each child repeats the prize name and adds another one to the list.

KINESTHETIC LEARNERS GROUPS
Materials: index cards

Each child should write *a*, *i*, or *u* on each of the index cards. Read the story on page 67 aloud. Have children hold up the appropriate card when they hear a word with that long vowel sound.

Use long **a**, **i**, and **u** words to finish each word ladder. Change only one letter in each word.

1. Begin with **cute**.
   End with **tune**.

   cute

   cu_be_

   tube

   tune

2. Go from **five** to **lone**.

   five

   fine

   line

   lone

3. Go from **base** to **hike**.

   base

   bake

   bike

   hike

4. Go from **June** to **cave**.

   June

   Jane

   cane

   cave

HOME Have your child make up a sentence for each word in one word ladder, such as *A kitten is soft and cute.*

68   Review long a, i, u

CURRICULUM CONNECTIONS

SPELLING
Materials: 4 index cards per child, scissors

Have partners print the spelling words *cape, dime, hay,* and *rule* on their cards. Have children cut their cards between two letters. Children can have their partners reassemble the words and take turns spelling them orally.

SOCIAL STUDIES
Materials: world map

Explain that the story on page 67 is based on a fable, a story that teaches a lesson. Tell children that a man named Aesop, who lived in Greece more than 2,500 years ago, created many fables. Help children to locate Greece on a map. Point out that Greece is on the continent of Europe.

MATHEMATICS
Materials: world map

Use the scale of miles to help children determine how many air miles it is from your community to Greece.

TECHNOLOGY   AstroWord Long Vowels: *a, i*; Long Vowels: *e, u*

VISUAL LEARNERS   INDIVIDUAL
Materials: Phonics Word Cards, Set 1: Long *a, i, u* words (118–164)

Give each child word cards with two different vowel sounds. Invite children to use at least two words from the cards to write two sentences about Sue, Jake, or a race. Have volunteers share their sentences.

CHALLENGE
The story of Sue and Jake is based on the fable "The Tortoise and the Hare." Have children change the characters or setting and write their own fable based on the story. When they have finished, encourage children to underline long *a, i,* and *u* words.

EXTRA SUPPORT/INTERVENTION
Materials: Phonics Word Cards, Set 1: Long *a, i, u* words (118–164), game spinner

Divide the spinner into sections for long *a, i,* and *u*. Children can take turns spinning for a vowel sound, reading a word card for that sound, and using the word in a sentence. See Daily Phonics Practice, pages 247–248.

Integrating Phonics and Reading

Guided Reading
Have children read the title and look at the cover illustration. Ask them to explain whether they think this story is going to be about a real lion. You may also wish to use the activity under English Language Learners below.

First Reading Ask children what Matt is supposed to say in the play.

Second Reading Have children work in pairs to list the long *a* and *u* words in the story.

Comprehension
After reading, ask children the following questions.
- What were the things that happened when Matt tried to roar on stage? *Recall/Sequence*
- Why do you think Matt was unable to roar at first? *Reflective Analysis/Personal Response*

ESL/ELL English Language Learners
Remind children what a play is. Ask children to tell about plays they have seen.

Long Vowel o

Children will

★ recognize the sound of long vowel o.

★ understand that o_e, ow, oe, and oa often stand for /ō/.

★ apply what they have learned by reading and writing long o words in context.

★ recognize and read high-frequency words.

ESL/ELL Speakers of Asian languages may confuse long o with the sound of aw in awful; practice low, law; so, saw; and so forth.

Teach

Phonemic Awareness: Phoneme Isolation
Say *goat, close, flown,* emphasizing the medial vowel sound. Repeat each word. Then, ask children to say the vowel sound that they hear in each word. Tell them that this sound is long vowel o.

Rhyme Say *goat, coat,* and *boat.* Ask how the words are the same. (*All have the long o sound, and they rhyme.*)

Sound to Symbol Write *boat, hope,* and *rows* on the board. Invite volunteers to say each word aloud. Then, point to each word and ask children what vowel sound they hear. (*long o*)

Practice and Apply

Sound to Symbol Read the rhyme on page 69, encouraging children to listen for words with long o. Ask volunteers to name each long o word, write it on the board, and circle the letters that make the long o sound.

Writing On page 69, remind children to say the word in the sentence to be sure it makes sense. Children will have an opportunity to read the following high-frequency words: *into, along, something, said, boy, finally,* and *began.*

Have children identify the pictures on page 70. Before they complete the bottom of the page, be sure they understand that they are to write a rhyming word in the blank.

Critical Thinking Discuss Talk About It. Children may suggest that dogs like to eat bones, bury them, or dig them up.

Reading You may wish to use *Sparky's Bone,* MCP Phonics and Reading Consonant and Vowel Skills Library, Level B, to provide practice in reading long o words.

Name _____

I know a silly mole
In a yellow overcoat.
He rows down the coast
In a little silver boat.

I hope to go with Mole
To places near and far.
If we can't go by boat,
Then we'll go by car.

RULE
If a syllable or one-syllable word has two vowels, the first vowel usually stands for the long sound, and the second vowel is silent as in **mole** and **boat**. The letters **o_e, ow, oe,** and **oa** can all stand for the long **o** sound.

▶ Find **the word in the box that will finish each sentence.** Print **it on the line.**

1. Rover poked his _____ nose _____ into his bowl.

2. He hoped to find a _____ bone _____.

3. There was no bone in his _____ bowl _____.

4. Then, along came his _____ owner _____, Joe.

5. Something was in the pocket of Joe's _____ coat _____.

6. Joe said, "I have something to _____ show _____ you."

7. Oh, boy! It was a bone for _____ Rover _____

| coat |
| owner |
| Rover |
| show |
| bowl |
| bone |
| nose |

TALK about it What do dogs like to do with bones?

Long vowel o: High-frequency words, critical thinking   **69**

FOCUS ON ALL LEARNERS

ESL/ELL **ENGLISH LANGUAGE LEARNERS**
Talk about dogs with the children. Ensure that children understand the concept of dogs as pets. Point out that Rover is a very common name for a pet dog. Then, read the activity directions on page 69. Ask children to read aloud the word list. Correct mispronunciations through modeling. Have children complete the activity in pairs.

AUDITORY LEARNERS
Have children take turns naming words that rhyme with *goat, coast, nose, row, road, rope,* and *pole.* Accept all rhyming words including those that are spelled differently, such as *row* and *go; nose* and *blows.*

KINESTHETIC LEARNERS
Play "long vowel o musical chairs." As children walk around the chairs (with one less chair than the number of children), call out a series of words. When they hear a word with the long o sound, children sit in the chairs. The player left standing is out, and a chair is removed. You might start with the words *make, bat, wig, know.*

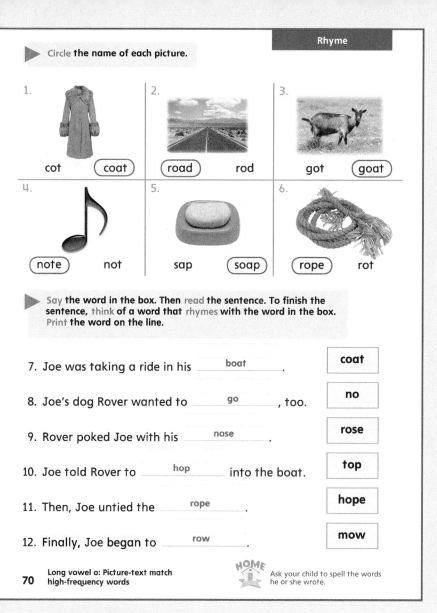

Circle **the name of each picture.**

1. cot (coat)
2. (road) rod
3. got (goat)
4. (note) not
5. sap (soap)
6. (rope) rot

Say **the word in the box. Then** read **the sentence. To finish the sentence,** think **of a word that** rhymes **with the word in the box.** Print **the word on the line.**

7. Joe was taking a ride in his ___boat___ . | **coat**

8. Joe's dog Rover wanted to ___go___ , too. | **no**

9. Rover poked Joe with his ___nose___ . | **rose**

10. Joe told Rover to ___hop___ into the boat. | **top**

11. Then, Joe untied the ___rope___ . | **hope**

12. Finally, Joe began to ___row___ . | **mow**

70 Long vowel o: Picture-text match
high-frequency words

HOME
Ask your child to spell the words he or she wrote.

CURRICULUM CONNECTIONS

SPELLING
Have children write the long *o* spelling words *coat* and *note* on their papers and make lists of other long *o* words that contain the same spelling patterns. Remind children that the vowel patterns should match (*oa* and *o*-consonant-*e*) but the words will not all end the same or rhyme.

WRITING
Ask children to think about a place they have gone that they would like to go back to with a friend. Have them write invitations to their friends, asking them to take a trip to the locations with them. After they finish, have children point out any long *o* words they used.

PORTFOLIO

SOCIAL STUDIES
Materials: mural paper; crayons, or markers

Invite children to make a mural showing many kinds of boats, including steamboats, rowboats, tugboats, freighters, and ocean liners. Ask them to label each boat and add a sentence explaining what the boat carries or what service it performs.

TECHNOLOGY  **AstroWord** Long Vowels: *i, o*

VISUAL LEARNERS INDIVIDUAL
On the board, print scrambled long *o* words such as *epor* (rope), *atgo* (goat), *onse* (nose), *odat* (toad), *enob* (bone). Invite children to unscramble the words on paper. Remind them to think of common long *o* spelling patterns.

CHALLENGE
Invite children to create a code using numbers to represent letters (*A* = 1, *B* = 2, for example). Then, have them use long *o* words to write a secret message with the numbers. Have them exchange messages with a partner. (Remind them to include the code!)

EXTRA SUPPORT/INTERVENTION
Materials: chart paper, markers

Draw a large boat on chart paper and ask children to write long *o* words in the boat. Before children leave for the day, have the group read the words aloud. See Daily Phonics Practice, pages 247–248.

Integrating Phonics and Reading

Guided Reading
Have children read the title and look at the illustration to tell what they think the story will be about. You may also wish to use the activity in English Language Learners below.
First Reading Ask children to explain what Sparky's problem was.
Second Reading Encourage children to find words with the short *o* sound in the story.

Comprehension
After reading, ask children the following questions:
• Why did Sparky think someone stole her bone? *Inference/Cause and Effect*
• What really happened to Sparky's bone? *Reflective Analysis/Draw Conclusions*

ESL/ELL English Language Learners
Point out the apostrophe in *Sparky's.* Remind children that the apostrophe means that Sparky owns or has something—in this case, a bone.

Review Long Vowels
a, i, u, o

Skill Focus

Children will

★ review the long vowel sounds of *a*, *i*, *u*, and *o*.

★ identify and spell picture names that contain the long sounds of *a*, *i*, *u*, and *o*.

★ use rhyming words to complete sentences.

★ discriminate between long and short vowel sounds.

★ recognize and read high-frequency words.

Teach

Phonemic Awareness: Phoneme Identity
Ask children to listen for the long *u* sound in *blue cube*. Repeat *blue cube*, separating each sound. Remind them that the sound they hear is long *u*. To review long *a*, *i*, and *o*, say these phrases, one at a time, separating each sound. Have children identify the targeted sound.

- **play games   nice bike   phone code**

Rhyme Read aloud the words below. Ask children to suggest rhymes.

- play (*bay, clay, day, hay, lay, may*)
- bike (*hike, Ike, like, Mike*)
- phone (*bone, cone, lone, tone, zone*)

Words in Context: Decodable Words Write on the board: *That _____ tree is tall. (pin, pine)* Have a volunteer read the sentence and word choices aloud and then supply the answer (*pine*).

Practice and Apply

Sound to Symbol Help children identify the pictures on page 71 before they write the picture names.

Writing For page 72, suggest that children try each word choice. Children will have the opportunity to read the following high-frequency words: *they, every.*

Critical Thinking Discuss Talk About It. Children may say that Tim and June did many interesting things. Encourage them to list the things they did.

Reading You may wish to use *Blast Off!*, MCP Phonics and Reading Consonant and Vowel Skills Library, Level B, to reinforce the long vowels *a*, *i*, *u*, and *o*.

Name _____

▶ Print **the name of each picture on the line.**

1.	2.	3.
soap	tail	kite

4.	5.	6.
road	tube	dive

▶ **What would you pack if you were taking a trip?** Choose a word from the word box that rhymes and print it on the line.

7. Very nice! Pack some toy _____mice_____ .

8. Oh, my! Don't forget your _____tie_____ .

9. How cute! Take your bathing _____suit_____ .

10. For goodness' sake! Bring a little _____rake_____ .

> tie
> mice
> suit
> rake

Review long vowels a, i, u, o: Rhyme   **71**

FOCUS ON ALL LEARNERS

ESL/ELL ENGLISH LANGUAGE LEARNERS

Children may experience difficulty spelling the picture names on page 71. Review the letter patterns for the long vowel sounds to help them. Then, pair children and have them say each picture name aloud before they print it on the lines.

AUDITORY LEARNERS

Draw a circle on the board and print these letters around it: *l, m, s, t, b*. Have children take turns going around the circle and naming long *a* words that begin with each letter. Continue the game, using the long *i*, *u*, and *o* sounds.

KINESTHETIC LEARNERS

Materials: blank game spinner

Divide the spinner into sections for long *a*, *i*, *u*, and *o*. Invite children to take turns spinning for a vowel, saying a word with that sound, and then using the word in a sentence.

▶ Fill in the bubble in front of the word that will finish each sentence. Print the word on the line.

1. Tim had a nice ___time___ outside. ○ Tim ● time

2. He ___rode___ his bike. ● rode ○ rod

3. He flew his ___kite___ with June. ● kite ○ kit

4. He played ___hide___ and seek. ○ hid ● hide

5. Then, ___Tim___ and June came inside. ● Tim ○ time

6. They ___made___ some cookies. ○ mad ● made

7. They ___ate___ every bite. ● ate ○ at

8. "Let's make ice ___cubes___," said June. ● cubes ○ cub

9. "We can ___use___ grape juice." ○ us ● use

10. Next, Tim made a paper ___plane___. ○ plan ● plane

11. June made a paper ___hat___. ○ hate ● hat

12. Tim said, "I ___hope___ you had fun." ● hope ○ hop

 Do you think Tim and June had fun? Why or why not?

HOME Have your child read the sentences and identify each word with a long vowel sound such as *nice* and *bike*.

72 Review long vowels a, i, u, o: High-frequency words, critical thinking

---

CURRICULUM CONNECTIONS

SPELLING

On the board draw six sets of blank lines corresponding to the number of letters in *rule, use, coat, note, heel,* and *bead*. Have children guess letters and fill in correctly guessed letters until the spelling words are completed.

WRITING

Write these sentence starters on the board. Children are to copy them and write a long *a, i, o,* or *u* word to complete each one.
1. I hope I can make _____.
2. I can play a _____.
3. I like to use _____.

MATHEMATICS

Brainstorm a list of things children like to do, and call attention to words on the list with long *a, i, o,* and *u* sounds. Have children vote for their two favorite activities from the list. Tally the choices. Compare the results.

 **AstroWord** Long Vowels: *a, i*;
Long Vowels: *i, o*;
Long Vowels: *e, u*

VISUAL LEARNERS GROUPS

Materials: Phonics Picture Cards: Long Vowels (four cards for each of the long vowel *a, i, u,* and *o* sounds)

Place the cards face down in four rows. Invite children to take turns turning over two cards at a time and naming the pictures. When the cards have the same vowel sound, the player keeps them.

CHALLENGE

Challenge children to make a list of five long vowel words with *a, i, o,* or *u*. Then, have children write a riddle for each word. Invite them to exchange their riddles with partners.

EXTRA SUPPORT/INTERVENTION

Dictate the words *mad, at, us, pin,* and *hop* as children write them on sheets of paper. Have children add *e* to the end of each word, read the new words, and use them in sentences. See Daily Phonics Practice, pages 247–248.

Integrating Phonics and Reading

Guided Reading
Read the title and have children look at the pictures. Ask them what this story will be about.

First Reading Have children use the pictures to explain what is happening aboard the shuttle.

Second Reading Make a chart with four columns, one for long *a, i, u,* and *o*. Invite children to write long vowel words from the story on the chart.

Comprehension
After reading, ask the following questions:
• What does Earth look like from space? Explain. *Recall/Access Prior Knowledge*
• Would you like to take a ride in the space shuttle? Why or why not? *Reflective Analysis/ Personal Response*

ESL/ELL English Language Learners
Review with children the meaning of the exclamation point. Remind them that it shows excitement or strong feeling. Ask why an exclamation point is used after *blast off*.

Long Vowel e

Skill Focus

Children will

★ recognize the sound of long vowel *e*.

★ understand that *ee* and *ea* often stand for /ē/.

★ apply what they have learned by reading and writing long *e* words in context.

ESL/ELL Speakers of languages other than English may pronounce long *e* and short *i* in a similar manner. Practice *feet, fit; Pete, pit*.

Teach

Phonemic Awareness: Phoneme Identity
Say *need*, elongating the long *e* (*neeed*). Then, repeat it naturally. Have children repeat the word. Review that the vowel sound in *need* is long *e*. Next, say groups of three words. Have children raise their hand when they hear a word that has the sound of long vowel *e*.

- **bead   seen   met**
- **hot   heat   meet**

Sound to Symbol Ask children what color grass is. (*green*) Write *green* on the board and underline *ee*. Explain that these letters stand for the long *e* sound. Then, write *seal* on the board. Explain that this word also has the long *e* sound, but it is spelled *ea*. Next, make two columns on the board—one marked *ee*, the other, *ea*. Read the rhyme on page 73 and have children identify the long *e* words. Invite volunteers to write each word in the correct column. Point out that the word *he* also has the long *e* sound, but it is spelled with an *e* alone at the end of the word.

Words in Context Write this sentence on the board and have children choose the correct word.

- **The horn _____. (beeps, beams)**

Practice and Apply

Sound to Symbol Help children identify the pictures on page 73. For items 7 through 11, remind them to underline the letters in the words they circled before writing them on the lines. Remind them that the words in the puzzle on page 74 can go across or up and down.

Writing Be sure students know that the answers to the sentences on page 74 can be found in the word box for the puzzle.

Reading You may wish to use *Pete's Bad Day*, MCP Phonics and Reading Consonant and Vowel Skills Library, Level B, to provide practice in reading long *e* words.

73

Name_____

Meet Neal the Seal
Who moves on wheels.
He drives a green jeep
And makes the horn beep.

RULE If a syllable or one-syllable word has two vowels, the first vowel usually stands for the long sound, and the second vowel is silent. You can hear the long *e* sound in *seal* and *jeep*. The letters *ea* and *ee* can stand for the long *e* sound.

▶ Circle **the name of each picture.**

| 1. set **(seal)** seed | 2. feel fell **(feet)** | 3. jays **(jeans)** jeeps |
| 4. bet **(bee)** beat | 5. beets beds **(beads)** | 6. jet **(jeep)** Jean |

▶ Circle **the word that will finish each sentence.** Underline **the letters in the word that stand for the long e sound.** Then print **the word on the line.**

7. Seals live in the ___sea___.   seat **(sea)** set

8. They ___eat___ fish.   neat **(eat)** feet

9. We can teach ___seals___ tricks.   east **(seals)** beets

10. Have you ___seen___ a seal show?   set free **(seen)**

11. We will see one next ___week___.   **(week)** met beak

Long vowel e: Picture-text match   **73**

FOCUS ON ALL LEARNERS

ESL/ELL ENGLISH LANGUAGE LEARNERS
On page 73, have children use paper strips to cover the word lists to the right of items 1 through 6. Identify the visuals as a group. Then, complete the items together. Have children work with partners to complete the page.

AUDITORY LEARNERS
Ask children to imagine going on a trip in a jeep. Their job is to think of items with long *e* in their names to take with them. Begin by saying *I'm going in my jeep, and I'm taking beans.* Have each child repeat the previous items on the list and add one more long *e* item.

KINESTHETIC LEARNERS
Materials: green construction paper, marker, glue
Give each child (or have them make) two beanstalks—one that has *ee* printed on the stem and one that has *ea*. Distribute to each child cutout leaves on which you have written *beat, beet, meat, meet, seat, seed, bead, bean, heel,* and *keep*. Ask children to read the words and glue them onto the correct beanstalk.

▶ Circle **the long e words in the puzzle.**

k	f	s	r	j
s	e	e	n	e
a	e	a	o	a
s	t	t	p	n
p	e	a	b	s

jeans
feet
pea
seat
seen

▶ Write **the word from the box that will finish each sentence.**

1. I wore my new blue _____jeans_____ to the zoo.

2. I sat on a _____seat_____ that had gum on it.

3. I spilled ____pea____ soup on my jeans.

4. Mud from my _____feet_____ splashed on them.

5. I've never ____seen____ such a big mess.

 Help your child make up a new story using the long e words in the word box.

74 Long vowel e: Words in context

CURRICULUM CONNECTIONS

SPELLING

On the board, write the spelling words *rule, use, coat, note, heel,* and *bead.* Have children write the words in sentences.

WRITING

On the board, write the title "My Week with Neal the Seal." Invite children to use several long *e* words, to write a description of a week with a seal. Stories might describe a realistic setting, or an adventure with an imaginary character. Brainstorm several sentences, such as *I spent a week at the zoo.* or *Neal and I drove in his jeep to the beach.*

SCIENCE

Invite children to look at and discuss picture books about seals. Ask volunteers to tell something they have learned about seals. Summarize key points on the board as you go along.

TECHNOLOGY **AstroWord** Long Vowels: *e, u*

VISUAL LEARNERS GROUPS

Write the following short *e* words on the chalkboard, leaving space under each one: *fed, set, bet.* Have children say the words aloud. Ask volunteers to change each word into a long *e* word by adding a vowel. Have them write each new long *e* word under the original word. Possible answers: *feed, seat, beet,* and *beat.*

CHALLENGE

Invite children to write five sentences about seals that contain long *e* words. Encourage them to illustrate their sentences.

EXTRA SUPPORT/INTERVENTION

Materials: small slips of paper

Ask each child to choose a long *e* word from page 73 or 74 and write it on a slip of paper. Then, collect the words and have children take turns choosing a word, spelling it aloud, and calling on someone to pronounce it. See Daily Phonics Practice, page 248.

Integrating Phonics and Reading

Guided Reading
Encourage children to look at the title and the illustration and tell what they think the story will be about.
First Reading Ask children what Pete does each time something goes wrong.
Second Reading Write Pete on the board. Invite volunteers to list other words from the story that have the long *e* sound.
Comprehension
After reading, ask the following questions:
• What things went wrong for Pete? *Recall/ Sequencing*
• Do you agree with what Pete did at the end of the story? Why or why not? *Reflective Analysis/Personal Response*
ESL/ELL **English Language Learners**
Help children to explain what the phrase *bad day* means.

Review Long and Short Vowels

Skill Focus

Children will

★ identify and distinguish between long and short vowel sounds.

★ identify and write rhyming words.

★ replace vowels to write new words.

Teach

Phonemic Awareness: Phoneme Isolation
Say *met* and *meat*, isolating and elongating the medial vowel sound. Remind children that the word *met* has the short *e* sound, and the word *meat* has the long *e* sound. Then, repeat the activity using *cot, coat; kit, kite; bat, bait; cub, cube*. Invite children to repeat the words and identify the short and long vowel sounds.

Rhyme Repeat the words you used above, and ask children to provide rhyming words for each.

Sound to Symbol Write these word pairs on the board: *sock, soak; rack, rake; bite, bit; cap, cape; us, use*. Pronounce words with children. Then, have volunteers go to the board, say a word, identify the vowel sound, and draw a line under the letter or letters that stand for the sound.

Phoneme Substitution Write the word *wide* on the board. Ask children to change the *i* to another vowel to make a new word. (*wade*) Repeat the process with the word *map*. (*mop*)

Practice and Apply

Sound to Symbol With children, identify the pictures on page 75. Remind children to say each word before they identify and write the vowel sound.

Writing On page 76, be sure children understand that they are to change only the first vowel in each word to make new words.

Reading You may wish to use *Summer at Cove Lake*, MCP Phonics and Reading Consonant and Vowel Skills Library, Level B, to reinforce the long and short vowel sounds.

Name_____

▶ Say the name of each picture. Print the vowel you hear on the first line. If the vowel is short, print an **S** on the second line. If the vowel is long, print an **L** on the second line.

1. sock	2. cup	3. rake	4. bike
o S	u S	a L	i L

5. leaf	6. bed	7. lamp	8. tube
e L	e S	a S	u L

9. coat	10. fish	11. pie	12. kite
o L	i S	i L	i L

▶ Finish the rhyming words.

13. hat   mat   sat

14. went   d ent   r ent

15. fun   r un   b un

16. gate   ate   d ate

17. like   b ike   h ike

18. goat   c oat   b oat

FOCUS ON ALL LEARNERS

- - - - - - - - - - - - - - - - - - - -

ESL/ELL ENGLISH LANGUAGE LEARNERS
Some English language learners may find it too complex to identify both answers at the top of page 75. Have children identify and print each vowel first. Then, have them go back and indicate whether the vowel is short or long.

AUDITORY LEARNERS
Ask children to listen to pairs of words, clapping their hands if the vowel sounds are the same and stamping their feet if they are different. Use words such as *mat, lamp* (clap); *late, cape* (clap); *hop, hope* (stamp); *fun, blue* (stamp); *tent, jet* (clap).

KINESTHETIC/VISUAL LEARNERS
Write the words *flute, feed, cape, rub, toad, belt, rope, bike, mop, coat, hat,* and *fish* on slips of paper and fold them. Have children take turns choosing a word and pantomiming it as the rest of the class tries to guess the word. Remind children to use gestures, not words, when pantomiming.

▶ Change the first vowel in each word to another vowel. Write the new word.

1. boat __beat__ 5. sod __sad__ 9. red __rid/rod__

2. oar __ear__ 6. hop __hip__ 10. ran __run__

3. cone __cane__ 7. wide __wade__ 11. bake __bike__

4. nip __nap__ 8. tame __time__ 12. map __mop__

▶ Find a word in the box that rhymes with each word. Print it on the line.

13. time __dime__

14. cube __tube__

15. rub __cub__

16. need __feed__

17. tape __cape__

18. bat __hat__

19. clue __blue__

| tube |
| cub |
| blue |
| cape |
| dime |
| hat |
| feed |

20. seat __heat__

21. fin __tin__

22. hope __rope__

23. bet __get__

24. rob __cob__

25. toad __road__

26. fine __mine__

| tin |
| road |
| cob |
| mine |
| rope |
| get |
| heat |

HOME Ask your child to read the rhyming words and tell whether each pair has a long or short vowel sound.

76 Review long and short vowels: Rhyme

CURRICULUM CONNECTIONS

SPELLING

You may posttest these long vowel spelling words using the sample sentences below.

1. **note** I am writing a thank-you **note**.
2. **rule** Did you break the **rule**?
3. **heel** I have a splinter in my **heel**.
4. **use** You can **use** my scissors.
5. **bead** This **bead** matches your shirt.
6. **coat** May I leave my **coat** at home?

WRITING

Invite children to write hink-pink rhymes (pairs of one-syllable rhyming words). Model examples, such as *air hair, clean bean, fat cat,* and *fish dish*. Have children share their rhymes with classmates.

TECHNOLOGY **AstroWord** Short Vowels: *a, i;*
Short Vowels: *i, o;*
Short Vowels: *e, u;*
Long Vowels: *a, i;*
Long Vowels: *i, o;*
Long Vowels: *e, u*

VISUAL LEARNERS GROUPS

Materials: Phonics Word Cards, Set 1: Short and Long Vowel words (1–196)

Give each child one of the ten groups of word cards to read and make rhyming pairs from. Have children read their rhymes aloud. Rotate the word cards to other children as time allows.

CHALLENGE

Have children make word chains. Write a word on the board and have them add, change, or drop a letter to make a new word. For each new word, have children tell whether the vowel is long or short. A sample chain might be *boat, coat, cat, can, cane, came, tame, tale*.

EXTRA SUPPORT/INTERVENTION

Write these words on the board: *tin, poke, get, boat, fine, rub, cube, time, need, hop, beat, nap, cake*. Have children erase the consonant at the beginning of each word and use another consonant to make a rhyming word. See Daily Phonics Practice, pages 247–248.

Integrating Phonics and Reading

Guided Reading

Invite children to look at the illustrations in the book. Discuss what the story might be about.

First Reading Ask children to tell about some of the things Rose did.

Second Reading Have children work in pairs to find and list ten words, one for each long and short vowel sound.

Comprehension

After reading, ask children the following questions:

• Why did Rose write many letters? *Inference/ Draw Conclusions*

• If you could go to Cove Lake with Rose, what would you like to do? *Reflective Analysis/ Personal Response*

ESL/ELL English Language Learners

Be sure children recognize that the story is in the form of letters. Explain that *P.S.* is used to add a thought after the letter is finished.

High-Frequency Words

Skill Focus

Children will

★ recognize and write the high-frequency words *song, boy, said, girl, something, people.*

★ use the high-frequency words to complete sentences.

★ begin to recognize irregular spelling patterns.

Teach

Analyze Words Write the words *song, boy, said, girl, something,* and *people* on the board. Point to the letters in each word as you read the words aloud.

• Have children remove the high-frequency word cards for this lesson from their book. Say each word again, stretching each sound. Suggest that children point to each letter in the word as they hear it.

• Help children associate the sounds in each word with a familiar word.

• Then, have children say each word, blending the sounds as they say it.

• Add these words to the class Word Wall. Children can use the words they learn to find similar spelling patterns and phonemic elements in new words.

Read Words in Context Write the following sentences on the board. Invite volunteers to underline the high-frequency words. Then, help children read the sentences.

  • **People were looking at something.**
  • **A girl and boy stood on the stage.**
  • **The children said a poem and sang a song.**

Practice and Apply

Writing Words With children read the directions on page 77. Have them read the words in the word box aloud. Suggest that they try each word in the sentence before they write the answer. On page 78, be sure children understand that the shape of the boxes is an additional clue to the word. Have children work with partners to complete Checking Up.

Reading You may wish to use *Ice Fishing,* MCP Phonics and Reading Library, High Frequency Word Collection, Level B, to provide practice in reading high-frequency words.

Name _____

▶ Read the words in the box. Write a word to finish each sentence.

song	boy
said	girl
something	people

1. We met many _____ people _____ at the bus stop.

2. Steve _____ said _____ , "We will have to wait."

3. "Let us do _____ something _____ until the bus comes," I said.

4. One _____ girl _____ read to us from her book.

5. One _____ boy _____ sang to us.

6. Then, we all sang a _____ song _____ .

High-frequency words: Words in context   **77**

FOCUS ON ALL LEARNERS

ESL/ELL ENGLISH LANGUAGE LEARNERS

Materials: high-frequency word cards

Have partners place the high-frequency word cards face down on their desks to play a matching game. The first child turns over one of his or her cards and says the word. The partner turns over one of his or her own cards, says the word, and determines whether it matches. If it matches, the child keeps both cards.

AUDITORY/KINESTHETIC LEARNERS GROUPS

Materials: high-frequency word cards, lightweight ball

Display the high-frequency word cards. Begin the game by throwing the ball in the air and calling out one of the high-frequency words. The person who catches the ball takes the appropriate card, says the word, spells it, and uses it in a sentence about the classroom. If the child cannot create a sentence, a volunteer can make up a sentence. Play continues with the person who created the sentence throwing the ball.

Unscramble the letters to write the words. The shapes will help you print the words.

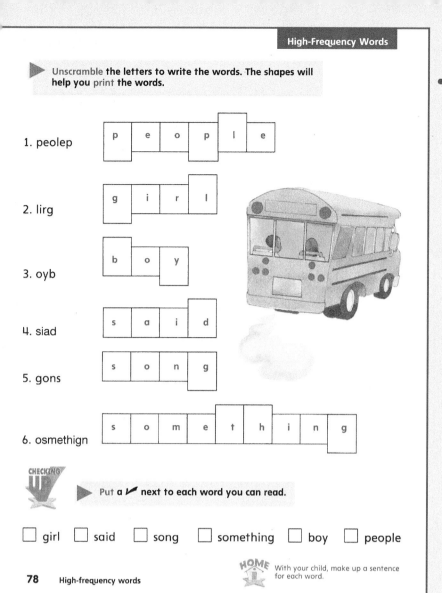

1. peolep   p e o p l e

2. lirg   g i r l

3. oyb   b o y

4. siad   s a i d

5. gons   s o n g

6. osmethign   s o m e t h i n g

CHECKING UP

Put a ✔ next to each word you can read.

☐ girl   ☐ said   ☐ song   ☐ something   ☐ boy   ☐ people

78   High-frequency words

 With your child, make up a sentence for each word.

CURRICULUM CONNECTIONS

MATHEMATICS

Discuss the various ways that children get to school each day: walk, ride a bike, take a bus, ride in a car, take the subway. Talk about why different means of transportation to school are necessary. Then, make a chart, using some high-frequency words, that summarizes how many children use each method of transportation.

WRITING

Invite children to choose one of the sentences from page 77 and use it as a story starter. Have them write the sentence at the top of their papers and then write the rest of their story. Encourage them to make their story different than the one in the book. When they have finished, suggest that they go back and see whether they used any of the high-frequency words.

VISUAL LEARNERS *INDIVIDUAL*

Have children write and illustrate a sentence for each of the following pairs of words: *song, boy; said, girl; something, people.*

CHALLENGE

Have children list the words in alphabetical, or *a-b-c*, order, leaving space between each word. Then, have them write two more words that belong between each word on their list. They can check their work by exchanging papers with partners.

EXTRA SUPPORT/INTERVENTION

Write the high-frequency words on the board. Then, play "Categories." For example, say a list of girls' names and then ask "What category am I?" Children should answer *girl*. For *said*, you might say "talk, answer, state, chat."

Integrating Phonics and Reading

Guided Reading

Ask children whether they have ever gone fishing. Invite them to share their experiences. Tell them that they are going to read about a special kind of fishing.

First Reading Ask children where people go ice fishing.

Second Reading Have children find some high-frequency words they have learned. You might point out that *once* is slightly different from *one*.

Comprehension

After reading, ask the following questions:
• What is one way ice fishing is the same as regular fishing? *Recall/Compare*
• What is one way ice fishing is different from regular fishing? *Recall/Contrast*

ESL/ELL English Language Learners

Help children read the title of the book by suggesting they look for clues in the pictures.

Long Vowels a, i, u, o, e

Skill Focus

Children will

★ spell words with long vowel sounds.

★ write a description, using words with long vowel sounds.

Teach

Phonemic Awareness: Phoneme Categorization Review the five long vowel sounds. Say the following groups of words and ask children to raise their right hand each time they hear a word with a long vowel sound.

- long *a*:   date   pail   pal
- long *i*:   tin   nice   tie
- long *u*:   fuse   fuss   suit
- long *o*:   bat   goat   toes
- long *e*:   beam   red   seed

Sound to Symbol Review the spelling of the long vowel sounds. List the following words on the board: *mail, nine, tube, coat, heel.* Read each word aloud, and have children repeat it. Point to each word and ask children what vowel sound they hear. Then, have volunteers go to the board and underline the letters that stand for the long vowel sound. Ask children to suggest a word that rhymes with each word in the list. (*Possible answers: sail, dine, cube, boat, feel*)

Practice and Apply

Sound to Symbol Before children begin page 79, suggest that they pronounce each word in the word box. You might encourage them to underline the letters that stand for the long vowel sound.

Writing For page 80, discuss places children have visited and suggest they describe aloud something about the places. You may wish to list some of the details on the board, drawing attention to descriptive words. Remind them to try to use some of the words in the box as they write their description.

Reading You may wish to use *The Doctor Has the Flu*, MCP Phonics and Reading Consonant and Vowel Skills Library, Level B, to review long vowel words in context.

Name_____

 **Phonics & Spelling**   Say and spell each long vowel word. Print the word in the box that shows its long vowel sound.

use	heel	hay	nine	note
coat	tube	dime	rule	bead
cape	tie	seen	mail	row

Long a	hay	cape	mail
Long i	nine	dime	tie
Long o	note	coat	row
Long u	use	tube	rule
Long e	heel	bead	seen

Review long vowels   **79**

FOCUS ON ALL LEARNERS

- - - - - - - - - - - - - - - - - - -

ESL/ELL ENGLISH LANGUAGE LEARNERS

Before children write a description of a place on page 80, brainstorm ideas aloud with them, and write some words that may be useful to them on the board. Bring in travel pictures from magazines and ask directed questions to cue children and guide their writing, such as "What do you do at this place?"

KINESTHETIC LEARNERS

Invite children to go on a long-vowel scavenger hunt. Divide the class into five teams, one for each vowel, and have each team look in the classroom for objects whose names have the group's long vowel sound. Ask each group to share its discoveries.

AUDITORY/VISUAL LEARNERS

Materials: index cards, crayon

Have children make letter cards for *a, e, i, o,* and *u.* As you say the following words, ask them to hold up the card that has that long vowel sound: *play, tail, bean, goes, toes, rule, low, tape, cute, eat, kite, way, bite, cube, cake, hive, coat, feet, bike, goat, hike, tube, take, see, blow, fine.*

Phonics & Writing

When you **describe a place**, you tell how it looks. You may tell about colors, shapes, things you see, and sounds. You may say how a place feels such as *hot* or *cold*.

▶ Think about a place you have visited. It can be a place in your town, or faraway. Use sentences to describe this place. Tell how you felt when you visited this place. Some of the words in the word box may help you.

blue	boat	hay	hole	seat
mail	jeans	hope	train	row
bike	ride	use	time	rain

Name the place in the first sentence.

Use colorful words to tell how the place looks.

HOME Help your child think of a title for his or her story.

80   Review long vowels

CURRICULUM CONNECTIONS

SPELLING

Cumulative Posttest Assess mastery of Unit 3 spelling words by using the following words and dictation sentences.

1. **bead**   I have a red **bead** on my necklace.
2. **note**   Mom wrote a **note** to my teacher.
3. **rule**   Talk quietly is a **rule** in our class.
4. **nine**   My sister is **nine** years old.
5. **mail**   I got a letter in the **mail** today.
6. **use**   I like to **use** a pencil.
7. **coat**   I need a warmer **coat**.
8. **dime**   This candy stick costs one **dime**.
9. **hay**   The farmer fed **hay** to the mule.
10. **tie**   My dad wore a colorful **tie**.
11. **heel**   I told my dog to **heel**.
12. **cape**   My grandmother wears a red **cape**.

SOCIAL STUDIES

Materials: world map, colored pushpins

Attach the map to a bulletin board. Have children share their writing from page 80. Then, ask each child to tell where each place is located and pinpoint those places on the map.

TECHNOLOGY   **AstroWord** Long Vowels: *a, i*;
Long Vowels: *i, o*;
Long Vowels: *e, u*

AUDITORY LEARNERS   GROUPS

Play a long vowel version of "I Spy." Begin by saying I spy something whose name has a long *u* sound. (ruler) Whoever guesses the classroom object continues the game by choosing another object whose name has a certain long vowel sound.

CHALLENGE

Materials: lined index cards

Divide the lined side of each card in half. Then, ask children to send postcards home from the places they wrote about on page 80. Have them draw pictures of the sites on the blank side, and write the messages and addresses on the lined side.

EXTRA SUPPORT/INTERVENTION

Materials: colored chalk

Write these words on the board in chalk and have children take turns replacing the vowels whose name they hear with a different color chalk and the silent vowels with yet another color: *blue, mail, bike, boat, jeans, ride, hope,* and so on. See Daily Phonics Practice, pages 247–248.

Integrating Phonics and Reading

Guided Reading
With children, read the title and look at the cover. Encourage them to tell what they know about doctors and what is different about this title.
First Reading Encourage children to explain why this is a silly story.
Second Reading Have children find the words with long vowel sounds and list them on the board.
Comprehension
After reading, ask the following questions:
• What are some of the things the children did to help the doctor? *Recall/Sequence*
• How would this story change if the doctor and children switched roles? *Reflective Analysis/Personal Response*
ESL/ELL English Language Learners
Help children understand that the doctor in the story is also the children's father. Discuss different roles people have.

Take-Home Book

Review Long Vowels

Skill Focus

Children will

★ read long *a, e, i, o,* and *u* words in the context of a nonfiction narrative.

★ review selected high-frequency words in the context of a narrative.

★ reread for fluency.

➤ Teach

Build Background

• Review with children the theme of the unit, "On Wings and Wheels." Ask children to name some of the things that fly and the things that have wheels in this unit. (*airplane, boat, kite, truck, car, bicycle, skates, car, jeep, bus*) Then, have them name some words they learned that they might use to describe ways to travel.

• Write the word *canyon* on the board and say it. Ask children if any of them have ever seen a canyon. Explain that this story will tell facts about the Grand Canyon.

Phonemic Awareness: Phonemic Substitution Write *place* on the board. Explain that the Grand Canyon is a special place. Have children say *place* and identify the vowel sound they hear. (*long a*) Then, have children replace the *pl* at the beginning of *place* with other consonant sounds. (*face, grace, lace, pace, race*)

➤ Practice and Apply

Using the Pages Help children put together the books. Encourage them to look at the pictures. Read the story aloud with children. Then, discuss what they learned about the Grand Canyon.

Sound to Symbol Encourage children to go back and identify some words that contain long vowel sounds. Make five columns on the board, one for each long vowel sound, and invite volunteers to write the words in the appropriate columns.

Review High-Frequency Words Write the words *could, very,* and *people* on the board. Have children say each word, spell it, and use it in a context sentence.

Reread for Fluency Have children reread the book to increase their fluency and comprehension. Remind children to take their books home and share them with family members.

81

Imagine you could take a trip and visit the Grand Canyon. What would you see? How would you spend your day?

There are many ways to see the canyon. Some people ride bikes. Some people take buses along roads at the top of the canyon. Some hike the steep trails, and others ride mules. Which way would you like best?

Name _____

A Day at the Grand Canyon

Review long vowels: Take-home book   **81**

FOCUS ON ALL LEARNERS

ESL/ELL ENGLISH LANGUAGE LEARNERS

Ask children to look through the story "A Day at the Grand Canyon" for familiar words that contain long vowel sounds. Make a list on the board of all the words they find.

AUDITORY/VISUAL LEARNERS INDIVIDUAL

Materials: audiotape, cassette player

Have a volunteer reread and record the story, and encourage children to take turns listening to the tape. When they feel ready, suggest that other children make their own recording of the story.

AUDITORY/KINESTHETIC LEARNERS GROUPS

Reread the story aloud and invite children to raise their hand each time they hear a long vowel sound.

You would see that the canyon is very wide and deep. In some places, it is up to 18 miles wide and more than a mile deep.

2

You would see walls of rock rise from below. The rock has stripes of color. It looks like a rainbow with many shades of red and brown.

3

CURRICULUM CONNECTIONS

SOCIAL STUDIES

Materials: map of the United States

Display the map and help children find the Grand Canyon and the Colorado River. Then, have them locate where they live and tell how they would travel to the Grand Canyon.

WRITING

Have children plan "dream" family vacations. Ask them to decide where they want to go, what they want to do there, and how they would travel there. Encourage them to illustrate their stories. When they have finished writing their stories, suggest that they circle words with long vowels.

ART

Materials: mural paper, crayons

Invite children to create a mural that shows people in your community using various types of transportation. Children might show people in cars, buses, trains, trucks, and so on. When the mural is completed, display it so that other classes might also enjoy it.

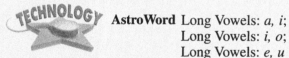 **AstroWord** Long Vowels: *a, i;*
Long Vowels: *i, o;*
Long Vowels: *e, u*

VISUAL/KINESTHETIC LEARNERS

Materials: Phonics Word Cards, Set 1: *day* (125), *take* (139), *way* (142), *bike* (143), *hike* (147), *like* (149), *mile* (152), *ride* (155), *mule* (166), *deep* (182), *see* (191)

Give children the word cards and have them find and match each word in the story.

CHALLENGE

Encourage children to draw on experiences with family trips or field trips to create their own book about traveling to a place. Have them draw pictures and write captions about the trip.

EXTRA SUPPORT/INTERVENTION

Reread the story to children. Then, invite them to read it aloud with you. Discuss words children have difficulty with. See Daily Phonics Practice, pages 247–248.

Unit Checkup

Review Long and Short Vowels

Skill Focus

Children will

★ review the long and short sounds of *a, e, i, o,* and *u.*

★ identify and spell picture names that contain long or short vowel sounds.

★ write words that contain long or short vowel sounds to complete sentences.

★ review high-frequency words.

Teach

Phonemic Awareness: Phoneme Isolation
Say the words *bit* and *bite*, isolating and elongating the medial vowel sound. Ask children what vowel sound they hear in each word. (*bit,* short i; *bite,* long i) Repeat the process with these word pairs: *net, neat; cot, coat; can, cane; cut, cute.*

Sound to Symbol Make two columns on the board. Head the first column *Long Vowels* and the second column *Short Vowels.* Then, as you say these words, invite volunteers to write them in the appropriate column and underline the letter or letters that stand for the long or short vowel sound: *tell, bean, play, dog, eat, like, lot, bite, goat, top, nose, cap, hat, bus, suit, let, gate, time, rule.*

Words in Context: Decodable Words Write this sentence on the board.

- A story can be called a _____. (tale, sail)

Read the sentence aloud and have children select the correct word. (*tale*) Invite a volunteer to explain the choice.

Practice and Apply

Sound to Symbol Read the directions on page 83. Help children identify the pictures. Remind children to write the vowel in the space provided before they circle *long* or *short.*

Writing Read the directions on page 84. Remind children to say their word choice in the sentence before they write it.

High-Frequency Words Pair children to read the words at the bottom of page 84 and place a check mark before the words they know.

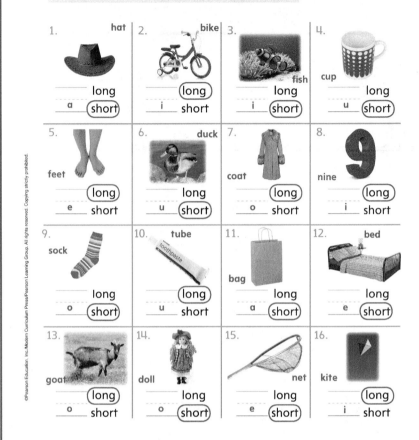

Name _____

UNIT 3 CHECKUP

Say the name of each picture. Print the vowel you hear on the line. Then circle the word short if the vowel is short. Circle the word long if it is long.

1. hat — a / (short) — long
2. bike — i / (long) / short
3. fish — i / (short) — long
4. cup — u / (short) — long
5. feet — e / (long) / short
6. duck — u / (short) / long
7. coat — o / (long) / short
8. nine — i / (long) / short
9. sock — o / (short) / long
10. tube — u / (long) / short
11. bag — a / (short) / long
12. bed — e / (short) / long
13. goat — o / (long) / short
14. doll — o / (short) / long
15. net — e / (short) / long
16. kite — i / (long) / short

Long and short vowels: Assessment   **83**

FOCUS ON ALL LEARNERS

ESL/ELL ENGLISH LANGUAGE LEARNERS
With children, read the directions aloud. Then, have them complete page 84 on their own. Circulate to identify and correct areas of difficulty. Have small groups read the story aloud to review answers.

VISUAL LEARNERS GROUPS

Materials: Phonics Picture Cards: Short Vowels and Long Vowels (45–120)

Mix the cards together and have children sort the pictures into two groups, one for short vowel sounds and one for long vowel sounds.

KINESTHETIC LEARNERS GROUPS

Materials: one-inch tagboard squares, markers

Make alphabet letter cards from the squares. Have children make additional ones as needed to spell the short vowel words *tub, cap, net, kit, got, cut, hug, us,* and *at.* Then, have them add another vowel card to each word to change them into long vowel words. (*tube, cape, neat, kite, goat, cute, huge, use, eat*)

> Fill in the bubble in front of the word that will finish each sentence.

UNIT 3 CHECKUP

1. I have a ___ named Wags. ○ fog ● dog ○ day

2. Wags is a very ___ dog. ● cute ○ cut ○ cat

3. He ___ food by the bags. ● eats ○ ears ○ east

4. His tummy is ___ and sags. ○ bite ● big ○ kite

5. His long ears flap ___ flags. ● like ○ lime ○ lit

6. We like to ___ walks in the park. ● take ○ tack ○ tail

7. I ___ him to go one way. ○ fell ● tell ○ bean

8. He always ___ the other way. ○ toes ○ got ● goes

9. A dog like Wags is a ___ of fun. ● lot ○ lock ○ low

> Can you read each word? Put a ✔ in the box if you can.

☐ could ☐ come ☐ over ☐ song
☐ one ☐ very ☐ these ☐ said
☐ boy ☐ people ☐ girl ☐ something

84   Long and short vowels and high-frequency words: Assessment

ASSESS UNDERSTANDING OF UNIT SKILLS

STUDENT PROGRESS ASSESSMENT

You may wish to review the observational notes you made as children worked through the activities in the unit. These notes will help you evaluate the progress children made with long vowel sounds.

PORTFOLIO ASSESSMENT

Review the materials children have collected in their portfolios. Conduct interviews with children to discuss their written work and their progress since the beginning of this unit. As you review children's work, evaluate how well they use phonics skills.

DAILY PHONICS PRACTICE

For children who need additional practice with long vowels, quick reviews are provided. See Daily Phonics Practice on pages 247–248.

PHONICS POSTTEST

To assess children's mastery of long vowels and high-frequency words, use the posttest Blackline Masters 17 and 18 on pages 55g–55h.

AUDITORY LEARNERS GROUPS

Say these words and ask children to tell what vowel sound they hear in each one: *yell, mail, bean, toes, use, coat, dog, cute, big, like, play, cap, take, lot, go, run, net, doll, goat, tube, feet, hen.*

CHALLENGE

Invite each child to write about a dog they have or would like to have. Encourage them to tell what they do with their dog and to describe the dog's personality. You might ask questions such as *Does the dog do funny things? How does it get into trouble? What tricks have you taught the dog?*

EXTRA SUPPORT/INTERVENTION

Materials: Phonics Word Cards, Set 1: Short and long vowel words (1–196)

Give each child one short vowel and one long vowel word card. Provide time for children to review their word cards. Then, ask them to say one of the words on their cards and to say a rhyming word. If the child cannot think of a rhyming word, a volunteer may suggest one. Have children take turns until they have used all four of their words. **See Daily Phonics Practice, pages 247–248.**

84

Teacher Notes

UNIT 4

Compounds, Words with le , Hard and Soft c and g, Blends, Digraphs, Y as a Vowel, R-Controlled Vowels

THEME: THE WORLD OUTSIDE

CONTENTS

Student Performance Objectives

In Unit 4, children will be introduced to compound words, the le ending, hard and soft g and c, consonant blends and digraphs, r-controlled vowels, and y as a vowel within the context of the theme "The World Outside." As children apply the concept that consonant and vowel sounds can be blended together to form words, they will be able to

▶ Identify and decode compound and other two-syllable words

▶ Recognize the hard and soft sounds of c and g

▶ Distinguish the sounds of consonant blends and digraphs

▶ Recognize the sounds of r-controlled vowels

▶ Apply these skills in decoding and in using words in context

Assessment Options

In Unit 4, assess children's ability to read and write two-syllable and compound words and words with hard and soft consonant sounds, blends, digraphs, and *r*-controlled vowel sounds. Use the Unit Pretest and Posttest for formal assessment. For ongoing informal assessment, you may wish to use children's work on the Review pages, Take-Home Books, and Unit Checkups. You may also want to encourage children to evaluate their own work and to participate in setting goals for their own learning.

ESL/ELL Some of your English language learners may require additional assessment strategies to meet their special language needs.

FORMAL ASSESSMENT

Use the Unit 4 Pretest on pages 85e–85f to help assess a child's knowledge at the beginning of the unit and to plan instruction.

ESL/ELL Before administering the Pretest, preview the visuals on page 85e so children are familiar with the picture names. Some children may understand a concept but have difficulty comprehending directions. Read them aloud to the group and model how to complete the test.

Use the Unit 4 Posttest on pages 85g–85h to help assess mastery of unit objectives and to plan for reteaching, if necessary.

INFORMAL ASSESSMENT

Use the Review pages, Unit Checkup, and Take-Home Books in the student book to provide an effective means of evaluating children's performance.

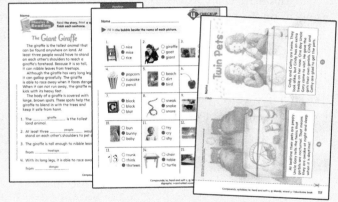

Unit 4 Skills	Review pages	Checkups	Take-Home Books
Compound words	99–100, 115–116	141–142	117–118
Two-syllable words	99–100, 115–116	141–142	117–118
Words ending with *le*	99–100, 115–116	141–142	117–118
Hard and soft *c* and *g*	99–100, 115–116	141–142	117–118
Consonant blends	109–110, 115–116	141–142	117–118
y as a vowel	115–116	141–142	117–118
Consonant digraphs	129–130, 137–138	141–142	139–140
r-controlled vowels	137–138	141–142	139–140

STUDENT PROGRESS CHECKLIST

Use the checklist on page 85i to record children's progress. You may want to cut the sections apart to place each child's checklist in his or her portfolio.

PORTFOLIO ASSESSMENT

This logo appears throughout the teaching plans. It signals opportunities for collecting children's work for individual portfolios. You may also want to include the Pretest and Posttest, the Review, and the Unit Checkup pages.

PHONEMIC AWARENESS AND PHONICS ASSESSMENT

Use PAPA to obtain an itemized analysis of children's decoding skills.

PAPA Skills	MCP Phonics Lessons in Unit 4
Deleting sounds	Lesson 43
Letter sounds	Lessons 39–42
Consonant blends	Lessons 43–48
Consonant digraphs	Lessons 53–57
Long vowels	Lessons 49, 50
r-controlled vowels	Lessons 58–61

Pretest and Posttest

DIRECTIONS

To help you assess children's progress in learning Unit 4 skills, tests are available on pages 85e–85h. Administer the Pretest before children begin the unit. The results of the Pretest will help you identify each child's strengths and needs in advance, allowing you to structure lesson plans to meet individual needs. Administer the Posttest to assess children's overall mastery of skills taught in the unit and to identify specific areas that will require reteaching.

ESL/ELL To ensure that vocabulary recognition is not a distraction, have English language learners practice saying the picture clues aloud. Reinforce with frequent sight recognition, reading, and spelling opportunities throughout the unit.

To assess the high-frequency words for Unit 4, have a child read orally each word on the Pretest and Posttest as you point to it. Then, have the child check each word read.

PERFORMANCE ASSESSMENT PROFILE

The following chart will help you identify specific skills as they appear on the tests and enable you to identify and record specific information about an individual's or the class's performance on the tests.

Depending on the result of each test, refer to the Reteaching column for lesson-plan pages where you can find activities that will be useful for meeting individual needs or for daily phonics practice.

Answer Keys

Unit 4 Pretest, page 85e (BLM 22)
1. whale
2. truck
3. hammer
4. giraffe
5. gift
6. knot
7. turtle
8. pencil
9. popcorn
10. shell
11. girl
12. fly
13. sled
14. baby
15. wreath
16. strawberry

Unit 4 Pretest, page 85f (BLM 23)
17. block
18. cone
19. barn
20. pebble
21. puppy
22. mailbox
23. wheat

Unit 4 Posttest, page 85g (BLM 24)
1. grapes
2. apple
3. corn
4. teeth
5. wheel
6. cry
7. club
8. circus
9. slide
10. letter
11. chain
12. backpack
13. star
14. giant
15. ring
16. tiger

Unit 4 Posttest, page 85h (BLM 25)
17. belt
18. nurse
19. gate
20. bunny
21. wren
22. mailbox
23. bottle

Performance Assessment Profile

Skill	Pretest Questions	Posttest Questions	Reteaching Focus on All Learners	Daily Phonics Practice
Compound words	9, 16, 22	12, 22	87–88, 99–100, 115–118	248–249
Two-syllable words	3, 4, 7, 8, 9, 14, 20–22	2, 10, 12, 14, 16, 20, 23	89–90, 99–100, 115–118	249
Ending le	7, 20	2, 23	91–92, 99–100, 115–118	249–250
Hard and soft c and g	4, 5, 8, 9, 11, 18	1, 3, 6, 7, 8, 12, 14, 15, 16, 19	93–96, 99–100	250
Consonant blends	2, 5, 12, 13, 16, 17	1, 6, 7, 9, 13, 15, 17	101–110, 115–118	250–251
y as a vowel	12, 14, 16, 21	6, 20	111–118	251
Consonant digraphs	1, 2, 6, 10, 15, 17, 23	4, 5, 11, 12, 21	119–126, 129–130, 137–142	251–252
r-controlled vowels	3, 4, 7, 9, 11, 19	3, 8, 10, 13, 16, 18	131–142	252–253

Student Progress Checklist

Make as many copies as needed to use for a class list. For individual portfolio use, cut apart each child's section. As indicated by the code, color in boxes next to skills satisfactorily assessed and insert an *X* by those requiring reteaching. Marked boxes can later be colored in to indicate mastery.

Student Progress Checklist

Code: ■ Satisfactory   ☒ Needs Reteaching

Student: _____ _____ Pretest Score: _____ Posttest Score: _____	**Skills** ☐ Compound and Two-Syllable Words ☐ Ending words with *le* ☐ Hard and Soft *c* and *g* ☐ Consonant Blends ☐ *y* as a Vowel ☐ Consonant Digraphs ☐ *r*-Controlled Vowels	**High-Frequency Words** ☐ only ☐ laugh ☐ own ☐ even ☐ their ☐ might ☐ your ☐ two ☐ believe ☐ once ☐ bought ☐ new	**Comments / Learning Goals**
Student: _____ _____ Pretest Score: _____ Posttest Score: _____	**Skills** ☐ Compound and Two-Syllable Words ☐ Ending words with *le* ☐ Hard and Soft *c* and *g* ☐ Consonant Blends ☐ *y* as a Vowel ☐ Consonant Digraphs ☐ *r*-Controlled Vowels	**High-Frequency Words** ☐ only ☐ laugh ☐ own ☐ even ☐ their ☐ might ☐ your ☐ two ☐ believe ☐ once ☐ bought ☐ new	**Comments / Learning Goals**
Student: _____ _____ Pretest Score: _____ Posttest Score: _____	**Skills** ☐ Compound and Two-Syllable Words ☐ Ending words with *le* ☐ Hard and Soft *c* and *g* ☐ Consonant Blends ☐ *y* as a Vowel ☐ Consonant Digraphs ☐ *r*-Controlled Vowels	**High-Frequency Words** ☐ only ☐ laugh ☐ own ☐ even ☐ their ☐ might ☐ your ☐ two ☐ believe ☐ once ☐ bought ☐ new	**Comments / Learning Goals**

BLM 26 Unit 4 Checklist

Throughout Unit 4 there are opportunities to assess English language learners' abilities to read and write two-syllable and compound words and words with hard and soft consonant sounds, blends, digraphs, and *r*-controlled vowel sounds. Take note of difficulties with pronunciations, but assess children based on their ability to distinguish specific sounds when pronounced by a native speaker.

Lesson 38, pages 87–88 Speakers of Hmong, Vietnamese, Cantonese, or Spanish may need additional practice with compound words, since few words in their native language are formed in this manner.

Lesson 40, pages 91–92 Speakers of Korean, Hmong, Vietnamese, Khmer, or Cantonese may have difficulty producing the *l* sound in *le* versus a final *er*. Practice: *little, litter; bottle, bother; people, peeper.*

Lessons 41–42, pages 93–96 Korean, Khmer, Hmong, and Vietnamese speakers may confuse the hard *c* with an initial hard *g*. Check pronunciation with minimal pairs such as *cold, gold; cap, gap;* and *clue, glue.* Tagalog, Korean, Hmong, Khmer, or Vietnamese speakers may have difficulty differentiating /j/ or soft *g* and the sound of *sh* or *ch*. Verify that children produce correctly the initial sounds of *giant, shy,* and *child.*

Lessons 45–47, pages 101–106 Native speakers of Vietnamese, Hmong, Korean, Khmer, and Cantonese may confuse *r* blends and *l* blends. Have children practice pronouncing *glow, grow; braid, blade; fright, flight.* Spanish-speaking children may pronounce a short *e* before *sl* words since Spanish lacks initial *s* blends. Verify that English language learners do not separate the two consonants with an intervening *schwa* sound (where *blow* might sound like *below*). Khmer, Hmong, Cantonese, Korean, and Vietnamese do not contain initial *s* blends. Russian speakers might pronounce a voiced *z* sound in some blends.

Lesson 48, pages 107–108 Cantonese, Khmer, or Korean speakers will be unfamiliar with most final blends except *ng*. Tagalog or Spanish speakers may "clip" the blend, pronouncing only the first consonant of each.

Lesson 49, pages 109–110 Speakers of Asian languages including Korean and Tagalog may have difficulty making the sounds of consonant blends. Provide opportunities to practice words with blends.

Lesson 50, pages 111–112 Spanish speakers should have little difficulty with the long *e* sound of *y*, since *y* can have a similar sound in Spanish. For other English language learners treat the different sounds as two different sounds for one letter: *bunny, sorry, sunny; shy, fry, why.*

Lesson 52, pages 115–116 Many Asian languages are monosyllabic, so native speakers of those languages may pronounce two-syllable words in English as separate words.

Lesson 54, pages 119–120 Speakers of Vietnamese, Khmer, Korean, or Hmong may confuse *ch* with *sh* or initial *j*. Offer additional listening and speaking practice.

Lesson 56, pages 123–124 Most English language learners will be familiar with voiced and unvoiced sounds and silent letters. Practice *kn* orally with native speakers of Chinese, Vietnamese, and Spanish.

Lesson 57, pages 125–126 Some English language learners may experience difficulty if they do not differentiate /r/ and /l/. Spanish and Tagalog speakers who trill initial *r* may need additional practice.

Lessons 60–62, pages 131–136 Speakers of Hmong or Vietnamese may clip the *r* and pronounce a sound similar to short *o*. Practice and reinforce the sound of *ar* in isolation with these children. Among Hmong, Vietnamese, and Khmer speakers, *ar* and *or* might sound alike. Practice auditory discrimination and distinct pronunciation with word pairs such as *born, barn; tore, tar; for, far;* and so on. In Spanish, *ir, er,* and *ur* do not stand for a sound similar to the English sound, and each letter stands for a distinct sound. Spanish speakers may pronounce *bird* as *beard.*

Lesson 63, pages 137–138 In Spanish, *ar, or, ir, er,* and *ur* each stands for a distinct sound. Practice with *part, hard; first, third; under, her; corn, torn; purse, burn.*

Phonics Games, Activities, and Technology

The following collection of ideas offers a variety of opportunities to reinforce phonics skills while actively engaging children. The games, activities, and technology suggestions can easily be adapted to meet the needs of your group of learners. They vary in approach so as to consider children's different learning styles.

COMPOUND CONCENTRATION

Have pairs of children write these words on index cards to make a deck for "compound concentration": *pea, nut, sea, weed, oat, meal, my, self, back, pack, pop, corn, class, mate, sail, boat, neck, tie, cup, cake, dragon, fly, sun, glasses, skate, board, button, hole, horse, shoe.* Have children mix up the words and place them face down. To play, children take turns turning over two cards to make a match. When a compound word is formed, have each child use it in a sentence that illustrates its meaning.

ESL/ELL To help familiarize English language learners with compound words, cut and paste magazine pictures illustrating the compound words onto sheets of tagboard. Write the words beneath the pictures. Have children practice saying the words as you point out the individual smaller words.

CREATE PUNIDDLES

Explain to children that a puniddle is a word puzzle in which two pictures are combined to suggest a word with a separate meaning. To illustrate this puzzle form, draw puniddle equations for *starfish* and *toenail* on the board, and have children guess the compound words. Working with partners, have children create their own puniddles to share with the group. Possible words to depict include *rainbow, firecracker, pineapple, snowsuit, treetop,* and *dragonfly.*

SPOTLIGHT ON WORDS

Place around the room pictures whose names are compounds or whose names contain blends, digraphs, *r*-controlled vowels, or *y* as a vowel. Have children form teams of two or three, and give each team a list of picture names and a flashlight. At your signal, team members read the words on the list and go in search of the corresponding pictures. To indicate that they've found the picture, children shine the light on it. When the hunt is over, have each team match its words and pictures for the group.

SPIN A SOUND

To play this small-group game, draw a large circle on a piece of tagboard. Divide the circle into seven parts and write a digraph in each section. To make a spinner, partially fill a liter soda bottle with sand to weight it and place it in the center of the circle. After a child spins, have him or her give a word that contains the digraph indicated by the bottle. Continue the game until everyone has had several turns to spin a sound.

Variation: To modify the game, write consonant blends or *r*-controlled vowel combinations in each space of the circle.

ESL/ELL To enable English language learners to independently produce and pronounce new words that contain digraphs, create word lists, charts, or posters of familiar words that contain digraphs and post in the classroom. Allow children of similar ability levels to use the word lists to help them name words that contain the digraph indicated by the bottle.

CLIMB JACK'S BEANSTALK

Using a green marker or paint, draw a tall beanstalk with many large leaves on mural paper and place it on the floor or wall. On the leaves, place cards with words that you wish children to review. Have children take turns "climbing" the beanstalk by reading the words.

Variation: Instead of using word cards, place cards containing consonant blends or digraphs on the leaves. To climb the stalk, children should point to each card and give a word that contains the blend or digraph.

MISTRESS MARY'S GARDEN

Divide a bulletin board into different "garden patches"; for example: a compound word patch, a two-syllable word patch, a soft *c* patch, and so on. Give children paper cupcake cups or small paper plates and have them write words that belong in each patch. Help children attach these word flowers to paper stems and leaves to create a word garden of the different words and sounds in this unit.

BLEND BINGO

Each pair of players will need a nine-square-grid playing board. Write these blends on the chalkboard and have children select nine of them to write on their grid: *sp, fl, gr, sn, cl, gl, pl, cr, dr, pr, br, fr, bl*. Then, say words containing these blends. If the blend appears on the game board, have children cover it with a marker. The game continues until someone has bingo!

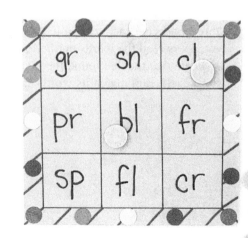

Variations: Instead of playing with blends, use digraphs, *r*-controlled vowel combinations, or words containing phonetic elements covered in the unit that you wish to reinforce.

HINK PINKS

Explain to children that a hink pink is a riddle in which the answer is a pair of rhyming words. Share these examples and have children write the rhyming words, which end with *y* as a vowel. Encourage children working with partners to make up their own hink pinks to share with a small group. They can continue to focus on words ending with *y* as a vowel, or they can target words that contain consonant blends, digraphs, or *r*-controlled vowels.

ESL/ELL Create the riddles for English language learners and supply either the adjective or the noun. Have children suggest responses to replace the missing word, instead of having them create the rhyme and the riddle.

> What do you call a beautiful cat?
> (a pretty kitty)
>
> What do you call a thin horse?
> (a bony pony)
>
> What do you call a silly rabbit?
> (a funny bunny)

WORDS IN BLOOM

Distribute copies of Blackline Master 28 to small groups. Using the following letter-distribution chart, children write these 62 letters on small paper circles approximately 1 inch in diameter. Then, children place the letters in a bag.

A = 5 E = 6 I = 5 M = 3 Q = 1 U = 2 Y = 1

B = 2 F = 2 J = 1 N = 4 R = 3 V = 1 Z = 1

C = 2 G = 2 K = 1 O = 5 S = 2 W = 2

D = 2 H = 2 L = 2 P = 2 T = 2 X = 1

To play the game, players take turns selecting one letter per turn from the bag and placing it on their game board. In any turn, a player may reject a letter by replacing it in the bag rather than putting it on the game board, remove a letter from the game board by replacing it in the bag, or move a letter from one space to another on the game board. Each of these actions counts as a turn, and play then passes to the next player. The object of the game is to make words of three or more letters on the board. Words can go in any direction on the game board as long as the letters connect. The first player to form four words wins the game.

Variation: To emphasize a specific phonetic element, have children write blends, digraphs, or *r*-controlled vowel combinations on letter chips and add them to the bag.

TECHNOLOGY

The following software products reinforce children's understanding of the phonics skills in this unit.

Reader Rabbit's® I Can Read! with Phonics™
Included in this software are *Interactive Reading Journey 2* and *Reader Rabbit 2*. Children continue to develop phonemic awareness as they explore 15 lands along the Reading Road with Sam the Lion, Reader Rabbit, and friends. Along the way, they learn phonics, reading comprehension, vocabulary, multisyllable words, consonant blends, and consonant digraphs. With Reader Rabbit 2, children are offered four activities, each with four levels of difficulty.

** Riverdeep The Learning Company
500 Redwood Blvd.
Novato, CA 94947
(800) 825-4420
www.learningcompanyschool.com

JumpStart 2nd Grade™
Second grade skills are learned through a program feature that adjusts to children's level of skill, so they can learn at their own pace. Included are phonics and reading skills such as basic grammar, spelling, vocabulary, writing, reading, sentence structure, complex vowels, and consonant blends.

** Sunburst Technology
1900 South Batavia Ave.
Geneva, IL 60134
(800) 321-7511
www.sunburst.com

Name _____

Words in Bloom

Home Connections

The Home Connections features of this program are intended to involve families in their children's learning and application of phonics skills. Three effective opportunities to make connections between home and school include the following.

- **HOME LETTER**
- **HOME NOTES**
- **TAKE-HOME BOOKS**

HOME LETTER

A letter is available to be sent home at the beginning of Unit 4. This letter informs family members that children will be learning to read and write compound words, words with consonant blends and digraphs, words that end in *le*, words with *r*-controlled vowels, and words containing *y* as a vowel. Two activities are suggested to parents. The first activity involves rereading of the selection on page 85 and asking children to find words with consonant blends. The second activity has family members help their child create a list of fruits and vegetables and circling the words that contain *r*-controlled vowels. Both activities support the child's learning to read and write words with various phonics elements. The letter, available in both English and Spanish, suggests books relating to the theme of "The World Outside" that family members can look for in a local library and enjoy reading together.

HOME NOTES

Whenever the Home logo appears within the student book, a phonics activity is suggested to be done at home. These activities require little or no preparation or special materials, and are meant to reinforce the targeted phonics skill.

Home Notes in Spanish are also available for both teachers and parents to download and use from our website, www.PlaidPhonics.com.

TAKE-HOME BOOKS

Within the student book are Take-Home Books that can be cut out and assembled. The story language in each book reinforces the targeted phonics skills. The books can then be taken home and shared with family members. In Unit 4, two Take-Home Books are available, focusing on several of the phonics elements in this unit as well as the unit theme "The World Outside."

Compounds, Words with le, Hard and Soft c and g, Blends, y as a Vowel, Digraphs, r-Controlled Vowels

Skill Focus

Assess Prior Knowledge

To assess children's prior knowledge of compounds, consonant blends and digraphs, r-controlled vowels, and other skills presented in this unit, use the pretest on pages 85e–85f.

Unit Focus

Build Background

- Write the theme "The World Outside" on the board. Ask children what the theme means to them. Then, draw children's attention to the picture on page 85. Tell them they are going to read about a tree that may be the oldest living thing on Earth.

- With children, read the text aloud. Ask them how scientists know the age of the bristlecone pine tree. (*from the number of rings*) Point out California on a map so that children can see where the trees grow.

Introduce the Unit Skills

- Write the word *bristlecone* on the board. Draw a vertical line between *bristle* and *cone*. Explain that *bristlecone* is a compound word because it is made up of two smaller words. Then, have children find another compound word in the article. (*rainfall*)

- Write the words *count* and *piece* on the board. Explain that the *c* in *count* is a hard sound, like the sound of *k*. The *c* in *piece* is a soft *c* like the sound of *s*. Ask children to find another example of a hard *c* and a soft *c*. (*cold, places*)

- Tell children in this unit that they will be learning about and reading compound words, words with hard *c* and soft *c*, and words with other sounds.

Critical Thinking When discussing the Talk About It question, children should recognize that the tree rings can show whether the weather was dry or wet over a long period of time.

Read Aloud

Earth's Oldest Living Thing

How old is old? Bristlecone pine trees may be the oldest living things on earth. The oldest known bristlecone is almost 5,000 years old.

How do people know how old bristlecone pines are? Scientists study a piece of a tree and count the rings. There is one ring for every year the tree is alive. A thin ring means the year was dry. A thick ring shows good rainfall.

The oldest bristlecone pine trees are found in California. Their secret to a long life is to grow very slowly.

TALK about it How could the tree rings tell a story about weather over a long time?

Unit 4: Introduction
Critical Thinking **85**

THEME FOCUS

- - - - - - - - - - - - - - - - - - - -

CLASSROOM GARDENING

As the unit progresses, help children bring a little of the outside world into the classroom. Have children plant bean or grass seeds in cups or jars of soil, put their plants in a sunny window, and water them as needed. Guide them in setting up logs to record their plants' progress, day-to-day or week-to-week.

NATURAL TREATS

Provide various vegetables and fruits for children to sample as you study the phonics elements in the names of the foods. List the foods on a chart titled "Nature's Menu" and encourage children to find examples of concepts from the unit in the words. Possible foods might include strawberries, blueberry or corn muffins, apples, cider, lettuce, carrots, cucumbers, celery, oranges, tangerines, grapes, broccoli, and sunflower seeds.

NATIVE TREES

Bring in pictures of trees that are native to your area and encourage children to do the same. Work with children to identify and label the pictures of trees.

Dear Family,

In this unit "The World Outside," your child will learn about compound words (scarecrow), words ending in **le** (candle), hard and soft **c** and **g** (camp, city, go, giant) consonant blends (grapes, plants), digraphs (peach, shell, wheat), **y** as a vowel (baby, try), and r-controlled vowels (barn, fern, bird, corn, fur).

As your child becomes familiar with these words and sounds, you might try these activities together.

▶ With your child, read the selection on page 85. Then, ask your child to find the words with consonant blends such as tree and grow.

▶ Help your child plant a lima bean in a paper cup. Talk about what seeds need to grow. Then, have your child make a list of fruits and vegetables that he or she would like to grow in a garden and circle the words with r-controlled vowels.

▶ You and your child might enjoy reading these books together.

The Pumpkin Patch
by Elizabeth King

A Farm of Her Own
by Natalie Kinsey-Warnock

Sincerely,

_____

Estimada familia:

En esta unidad, titulada "El mundo a nuestro alrededor" ("The World Outside"), su hijo/a aprenderá palabras compuestas (scarecrow/ espantapájaros), palabras que terminan en **le** (candle/vela), la **c** y la **g** suave y dura (camp/ campamento, city/ciudad, go/ir, giant/gigante), combinaciones de consonantes (grapes/uvas, plants/plantas), **digramas** (peach/pera, shell/ concha, wheat/trigo), **y** como una vocal (baby/bebé, try/tratar) y combinaciones de vocales **y** r (barn/granero, fern/helecho, bird/pájaro, corn/maíz, fur/pelambre). A medida que su hijo/a se vaya familiarizando con estas palabras y sonidos, pueden hacer las siguientes actividades juntos.

▶ Lean con su hijo/a la selección en la página 85. Después, ayuden a su hijo/a a hallar las palabras con combinaciones de consonantes, como tree (árbol) y grow (crecer).

▶ Si es posible, ayuden a su hijo/a a sembrar una planta de frijoles, por ejemplo habas, en un vaso de papel. Conversen sobre lo que necesitan las semillas para crecer. Luego, pidan a su hijo/a que haga una lista de las frutas y vegetales que le gustaría sembrar en un huerto y, entonces, encierren en un círculo las palabras con combinaciones de vocales y r.

▶ Ustedes y su hijo/a disfrutarán leyendo estos libros juntos.

The Pumpkin Patch de Elizabeth King

A Farm of Her Own de Natalie Kinsey-Warnock

Sinceramente,

_____

HOME CONNECTIONS

- The Home Letter on page 86 will introduce family members to the phonics skills children will be studying in this unit. Children can tear out the page and take it home.
- Encourage children to complete the activities with a family member. Suggest that children look in the library for the books cited so that they can read them with their families.

LEARNING CENTER ACTIVITIES

WRITING CENTER

Display pictures of outdoor scenes in the form of photographs, posters, or children's drawings. Provide these sentence starters and invite children to write paragraphs using any of the openings. Encourage children to illustrate their paragraphs and to share them with the class while sitting in a special "author's chair."

The best thing about going outside is _____.

Once I grew _____.

When I go outside, I like to _____.

I would like to plant _____.

SCIENCE CENTER

Set up a bird feeder outside classroom windows and have children observe the different birds that come to eat the food. Provide field guides or charts of bird pictures so children can discover the names of their bird visitors. Binoculars can also add interest to the project.

SOCIAL STUDIES CENTER

Display pictures of farms and farm crops, along with books that tell about farm life. Post a KWL chart about farming, on which children can list things they already know, what they want to know, and then new ideas that they learn. If possible, invite a farmer to speak to the class about the work he or she does. Before the visitor comes, have children use the *W* column of the chart to make a list of questions they wish to ask him or her about farming.

BULLETIN BOARD

Display a bulletin-board background of "The World Outside"—an outdoor setting, such as a garden, field, or park. Invite children to add labeled cutouts of items related to nature. The names of the items should represent consonant blends and digraphs, vowel-*r* combinations, and other phonics skills covered in the unit.

Compound Words

Skill Focus

Children will

★ identify compound words.

★ form a compound word from two words.

★ write compound words to finish sentences.

ESL/ELL Speakers of Hmong, Vietnamese, Cantonese, or Spanish may need additional practice with compound words, since few words in their native language are formed in this manner.

Teach

Introduce Compound Words Write *pancake* and *sandbox* on the board. Point to each word as you say them and have children repeat them after you. Explain that *pancake* and *sandbox* are compound words because they are made up of two separate words. Draw a vertical line to separate the two smaller words each word contains.

Say the following sentence: *I picked some blueberries.* Repeat the sentence and ask children which word might be a compound word—a longer word made up of two shorter words. (*blueberries*) Write *blueberries* on the board. Then, use two different colors of chalk to circle each of the words, *blue* and *berries*.

Practice and Apply

Sound to Symbol Read the rhyme at the top of page 87. Encourage children to listen for the compound words and then identify them. (*grapevines, beanstalks, watermelons, noonday, sunflowers, everyone*) Write each of the compound words on the board. Invite volunteers to go to the board, say a compound word, and circle the two smaller words that it contains.

Writing Have children read the rule for a compound word on page 87. Then, invite volunteers to restate it in their own words. Read the directions for the activity. Remind children that the compound word has to be a real word. Point out that the two words that make up the compound word may be in any position within the item. For page 88, explain that the pictures are clues to the correct answer.

Reading Use *A Rainbow Somewhere*, MCP Phonics and Reading Word Study Skills Library, Level B, to provide practice in recognizing compound words.

Name_____

In the garden where the grapevines grow,
Beanstalks sprout in the very first row.
Watermelons ripen in the noonday sun,
And sunflowers tower over everyone.

▶ Say the words in each box. Put two words together to make new words. Print the new words on the lines.

> **RULE**
> A **compound word** is made up of two or more words joined together to make a new word. **Granddad** is made from the words **grand** and **dad**.

1.	pea weed	2.	meal oat
	sea nut		my self
	peanut		oatmeal
	seaweed		myself

3.	cup rain	4.	be rail
	coat cake		road may
	cupcake		maybe
	raincoat		railroad

5.	base class	6.	pack corn
	mate ball		back pop
	baseball		backpack
	classmate		popcorn

Compound Words   87

FOCUS ON ALL LEARNERS

ESL/ELL ENGLISH LANGUAGE LEARNERS

Have English language learners complete page 88 independently to assess their progress with compound words. Then, ask them to read the sentences aloud to a partner. Monitor pronunciation and check answers. Expand the activity to include other compound words: "If a *mailbox* is a *box* for *mail*, what would you call a *box* for *shoes*?"

VISUAL LEARNERS

Materials: index cards, marker, drawing paper

Make and distribute cards for compound words, such as *starfish, haircut, pigpen, sunglasses, skateboard, dragonfly,* and *buttercup.* Invite children to draw rebus equations for the words. Some illustrations will be logical (*hair + cut = haircut*), and others may be silly (*dragon + fly = dragonfly*).

Look at the picture. Read the two words below it. Put them together to make one new word that names the picture. Print the new word on the line to finish the sentence.

1. mail + box   A box for mail is a _____mailbox_____.

2. rain + coat   A coat for rain is a _____raincoat_____.

3. back + pack   A pack for your back is a _____backpack_____.

4. sail + boat   A boat with a sail is a _____sailboat_____.

5. pop + corn   Corn that pops is _____popcorn_____.

6. sand + box   A box full of sand is a _____sandbox_____.

7. cup + cake   A cake the size of a cup is a _____cupcake_____.

88 Compound words

HOME Help your child think of other compound words and draw pictures of each one.

CURRICULUM CONNECTIONS

SPELLING
You may wish to pretest the following spelling words, representing Lessons 36–42, at this time.
1. **peanut**   This **peanut** is very salty.
2. **ribbon**   Tie a red **ribbon** on the gift.
3. **apple**   The **apple** tasted tart.
4. **ice**   Did you get **ice** for the drinks?
5. **cake**   I will bake the **cake** today.
6. **gym**   Is **gym** your favorite class?
7. **goat**   A **goat** is fun to raise.

WRITING
Write the words *popcorn, peanuts, seaweed,* and *oatmeal* on the board. Have each child write about one of the words by answering these questions.
- Is it a plant or a plant product?
- Where can you find it?
- How is it useful?

TECHNOLOGY **AstroWord** Compound Words

KINESTHETIC LEARNERS GROUPS
Materials: index cards, marker

Give each child an index card listing part of a compound word such as *foot, ball, cup, cake, back, pack, watch, dog, sand, box, any,* and *time.* Have children find partners with whom they can form compound words. List the words.

CHALLENGE
Provide several of the following "word starters" and see how many compound words children can make with each one: *foot, black, horse, home, rain, wind, flash, down,* and *water.* (Dictionaries may help.)

EXTRA SUPPORT/INTERVENTION
Have each child fold a sheet of paper into fourths and write the words *sun, grand, air,* and *snow* in the spaces. Then, have them add to each word to make a compound word, which they can illustrate. See Daily Phonics Practice, pages 248–249.

Integrating Phonics and Reading

Guided Reading
Display the cover and read the title. Invite children to predict what the girl might be looking for.
First Reading Have children use the story to identify the rainbow activities completed by Jenny and Grandpa.
Second Reading Have children find the compound words in the story and identify the two smaller words in each one.

Comprehension
Ask children these questions:
- Why do you think Jenny wanted to see a rainbow? *Reflective Analysis/Personal Opinion*
- Do you think Jenny preferred to play indoors or outside? Explain. *Reflective Analysis/ Draw Conclusions*

ESL/ELL **English Language Learners**
Verify that children understand the meaning of rainbow. Use colored chalk to draw a rainbow on the board.

One- and Two-Syllable Words

Skill Focus

Children will

★ identify the number of vowel sounds in words.

★ read and write one- and two-syllable words in context.

★ recognize and read a high-frequency word.

Teach

Phonological Awareness: Identify Syllables Ask children to listen for the vowel sounds in each word as you say the words *five, ten,* and *fifteen.* Then, invite them to clap the rhythm of the words with you. Explain that they are clapping for each vowel sound in the word, and that this number tells how many syllables a word has.

Say the words *six, sixty, thirteen,* and *three.* Repeat the words and ask children to raise their hands when they hear the words with one vowel sound. *(six, three)* Then, say the words again and have children raise their hands when they hear the words with two vowel sounds. *(sixty, thirteen)*

Sound to Symbol Write *pencil* on the board. Ask children how many vowel sounds they hear. *(two)* Circle each vowel. Explain that *pencil* has two vowel sounds and two syllables. Then, write the words *pens* and *yellow* on the board. Have volunteers identify the vowel sounds and the number of syllables in each word.

Practice and Apply

Phonological Awareness: Syllables Read the rhyme on page 89. Invite children to raise their hand when they hear a word with two syllables.

Sound to Symbol Read the rule on page 89. Have children say the words *them* and *carrots* so that they can hear the vowel sounds in each. Read the directions and have a volunteer restate them.

Writing Read the words in the box on page 90. Remind children to say the entire sentence before they write their answer. Children will have the opportunity to read the high-frequency word *only.*

Critical Thinking Discuss Talk About It. Encourage children who have kittens to give examples of how kittens can act like babies.

Reading Use *Tiger's Tummy Ache,* MCP Phonics and Reading Word Study Skills Library, Level B, to give children practice in reading two-syllable words.

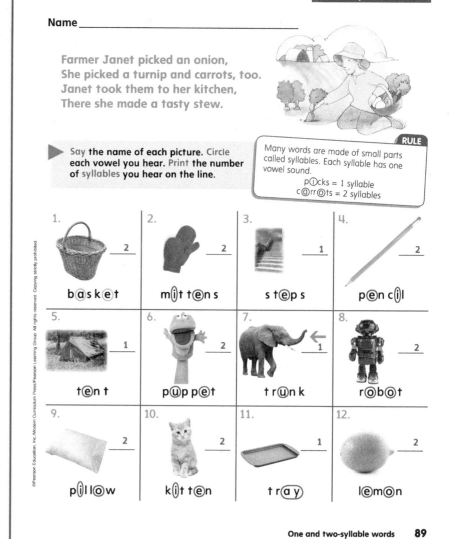

FOCUS ON ALL LEARNERS

ESL/ELL ENGLISH LANGUAGE LEARNERS

Review examples of two-syllable words before children begin page 89.

• Have children name picture clues 1–12 aloud. Then, complete the activity orally as a group.

• Read aloud the story on page 90 as English language learners listen with closed books. Use gestures and illustrations to enhance meaning. Read again, one sentence at a time. Have children say the two-syllable words.

• Read directions aloud; pair children to complete the story in writing. Check their work by having them read the sentences aloud.

• Have children circle and name the vowel sounds in each syllable.

AUDITORY/VISUAL LEARNERS

Play "I Spy." Ask a volunteer to choose an object in the classroom that has two syllables in its name and give a clue to its identity. For example, *I spy something blue.* The child who guesses correctly (perhaps some paper or a jacket) goes next. Print the answer words on the board and have children "look and listen" for the syllables.

▶ Find the word in the box that names each picture.
Print it on the line to finish the sentence.

| ribbon | basket | button | pillow |
| kitten | boxes | seven | baby |

1. Molly got a tiny _____kitten_____ named Popcorn.

2. She tied a blue _____ribbon_____ on Popcorn.

3. Popcorn was only _____seven_____ weeks old.

4. She had a nose like a _____button_____.

5 She liked to play inside _____boxes_____.

6. Molly made a bed for Popcorn in a _____basket_____.

7. She put a _____pillow_____ in the bed to make it soft.

8. Popcorn was like a little _____baby_____.

TALK *about it* What makes Popcorn like a baby?

HOME Say one- and two-syllable words and have your child identify the number of syllables in each word.

90 Two-syllable words: High-frequency words, critical thinking

---

CURRICULUM CONNECTIONS

SPELLING

Have children spell orally or write the list words that complete these phrases: birthday (*cake*); (*gym*) class; (*ice*) cream; (*peanut*) butter; (*apple*) pie; baby (*goat*); blue (*ribbon*). (You may wish to distribute copies of the first portion of the unit spelling list at this time.)

WRITING

Invite a parent to visit the classroom with a kitten, puppy, or bunny. Allow time for small groups of children to observe the animal, being careful not to scare it or handle it too much. Ask children to write about the animal and draw illustrations of it. Afterward, compile a list of two-syllable words they used.

PORTFOLIO

SCIENCE

Materials: heavy cream, baby food jars, crackers, plastic knives

Have children make butter by shaking a tablespoon or two of heavy cream in the jars until it separates into butter and whey. Invite them to spread the butter on crackers. Make lists of one- and two-syllable words that describe what they used or did.

AUDITORY/KINESTHETIC LEARNERS **GROUPS**

Invite children to name plants, fruits, flowers, or vegetables with names made up of two or more syllables, such as *carrot, apple, lemon, daisy, lily, lettuce, spinach,* and *orange.* Have the class repeat each word and clap out its rhythm of syllables.

CHALLENGE

Invite children to make a list of ten two-syllable words they know. Then, have them draw lines separating the syllables. Ask them to check their syllabication by using dictionaries.

EXTRA SUPPORT/INTERVENTION

Materials: five index cards per child

Have each child write five two-syllable words from pages 89 and 90 on their cards. Children should combine their cards with a partner's and practice reading and clapping all ten words. After a short time, children might switch cards with classmates. See Daily Phonics Practice, page 249.

Integrating Phonics and Reading

Guided Reading
Have children read the title and look at the illustration on the cover. Ask them why Tiger might have a tummy ache.
First Reading Ask children what Tiger wanted to do with Rabbit.
Second Reading Have children find an example of at least one two-syllable word on each page of the story.
Comprehension
Ask children these questions:

• Why did Tiger get a tummy ache? *Inference/ Cause and Effect*
• Was it a good idea for Rabbit to tell Tiger about the rice cakes? Why or why not? *Reflective Analysis/Make Judgments*

ESL/ELL English Language Learners
Write the title on the board, saying each word. Point out that *tiger* and *tummy* are two-syllable words. Have children repeat them. Pantomime the meaning of *tummy ache* if necessary.

Lesson 40   Pages 91–92

Words Ending in le

Skill Focus

Children will

★ identify the sound of *le* at the end of a word.

★ read and write *le* words in context.

★ recognize and read high-frequency words.

ESL/ELL Speakers of Korean, Hmong, Vietnamese, Khmer, or Cantonese may have difficulty producing the *l* sound in *le* versus a final *er*. Practice: *little, litter; bottle, bother; people, peeper.*

Teach

Phonological Awareness: Syllable Categorization Say the words *little, purple,* and *turtle,* emphasizing the final syllable. Then, ask children to tell you what is the same in the sound of these three words. (*the ending sound of* le) After children recognize that the ending sounds are the same, ask them to identify the words that end with the same sound as *little* in the following groups.

- **puddle   paddle   boat**
- **wiggle   wig   whistle**
- **jump   jiggle   eagle**

Sound to Symbol Write *paddle* and *wiggle* on the board. Have volunteers say the words, and then identify the final sound in each word. Then, ask them to circle the letters that make the final sound in each word. (*le*)

Practice and Apply

Sound to Symbol Read the rhyme on page 91. Ask children to find the words that end with the same sound as *little.* (*table, pickle*) Have them tell what letters stand for that sound. (*le*)

Read the directions on page 91. Help children identify the pictures before they write the picture names.

Writing After reading the directions on page 92, remind children to use the words in the boxes to finish the sentences. Children will have the opportunity to read the high-frequency words *around, laugh, own, house, scare, might,* and *even.*

Critical Thinking Discuss Talk About It. Children should identify that the turtles in the first story live in a pond, and the turtles in the second story live at the zoo.

Reading Use *The Apple Farm,* MCP Phonics and Reading Super Skills Library 1, Level B, to reinforce reading words ending in *le.*

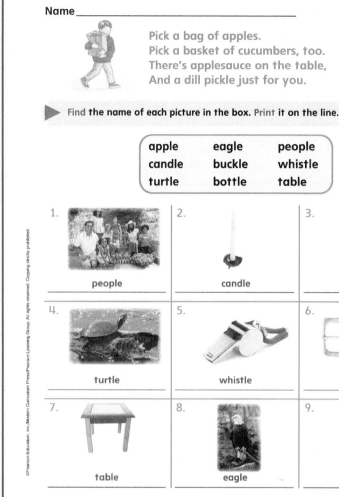

Picture-Text Match

Name _____

Pick a bag of apples.
Pick a basket of cucumbers, too.
There's applesauce on the table,
And a dill pickle just for you.

▶ Find the name of each picture in the box. Print it on the line.

apple	eagle	people
candle	buckle	whistle
turtle	bottle	table

1. people
2. candle
3. apple
4. turtle
5. whistle
6. buckle
7. table
8. eagle
9. bottle

Words ending in le   **91**

FOCUS ON ALL LEARNERS

ESL/ELL ENGLISH LANGUAGE LEARNERS

Assess English language learners' abilities to recognize, pronounce, and spell final *le* in familiar words.

- English language learners, like many English-speaking children, will mistakenly write *el* instead of *le* in familiar words. Say the rhyme on page 91 clearly; then, have groups of children repeat it. Ask volunteers to say the rhyme alone.

- Model saying the words in the word box on page 91. Encourage volunteers to name each picture clue; then, ask the group to match the word in the box to the picture. Complete items 1–4 together.

- Point out to children that double medial consonants stand for one sound (*apple, bottle*), that *t* stands for no sound in *stle* (*whistle*), and that *ck* stands for *k* (*buckle*).

VISUAL/KINESTHETIC LEARNERS INDIVIDUAL

Materials: construction paper, crayons

In an activity center titled "Gobble, Gobble!" have children trace one hand to serve as a turkey outline—the thumb as the head and fingers as the feathers. Invite children to print a word ending with *le* on each feather (starting with *gobble*) and then color the turkeys as they wish.

91

▶ Find **the word that will finish each sentence.**
Print **it on the line.**

1. A _____turtle_____ uses its own shell for a house.

2. It can swim in a pond or a _____puddle_____.

3. It can _____paddle_____ around in the water.

4. It climbs on _____pebbles_____ and rocks.

5. An _____eagle_____ might fly over and scare it.

6. Sometimes, _____people_____ may scare it, too.

7. Then, the turtle can _____huddle_____ safely
in its shell.

> pebbles
> eagle
> people
> turtle
> huddle
> puddle
> paddle

_____

1. My _____uncle_____ took me to the zoo.

2. Many _____people_____ watched the turtles.

3. We saw _____little_____ turtles hatching
from their eggs.

4. They were not even as big as a small,
green _____pickle_____.

5. As they came out of their shells, they
began to _____wiggle_____.

6. The zookeeper placed them on a _____table_____.

7. I started to laugh and _____giggle_____
when they tried to huddle together.

> giggle
> table
> little
> wiggle
> pickle
> people
> uncle

 **Where do the turtles
in the stories live?**

HOME Help your child make up sentences
using some of the words in the boxes.

92 Words ending in le: High-frequency words, critical thinking

---

CURRICULUM CONNECTIONS

SPELLING
Have children stand one behind the other in line(s). Dictate the spelling words *peanut, ribbon, apple, ice, cake, gym,* and *goat* one at a time. Each child can gently trace the words with one finger on the back of the next person. The first person in each line should spell one word aloud and then move to the back of the line.

WRITING
Ask children to write about what makes them giggle or about a time they had the "giggles" and couldn't stop. Some children may enjoy expressing themselves in poetry form.

SCIENCE
Materials: cucumber, pickle, apple, applesauce

Ask children how the four foods are related. (*Pickles are made from cucumbers, and applesauce from apples.*) Bring in recipes and talk about the processes that change cucumbers into pickles and apples into applesauce. Make homemade applesauce if space and time permits.

AUDITORY LEARNERS GROUPS
Say the following words and have children wiggle each time they hear a word that ends with the same sound that *wiggle* ends with: *tickle, popcorn, whistle, pickle, uncle, aunt, paddle, bottle, hamburger, eagle, pebble, river, people,* and *giggle.*

CHALLENGE
On the board, write the title "The Little Purple People." Invite children to write four-line rhymes about these imaginary creatures, beginning each line with the phrase *The little purple people.*

EXTRA SUPPORT/INTERVENTION
Materials: purple crayons, drawing paper

Write the following phrases on the chalkboard: *purple table, purple pickle, purple candle, purple turtle, purple bottle,* and *purple apple.* Have children choose one or more of the phrases to illustrate. Encourage them to write silly sentences using the phrases. See Daily Phonics Practice, pages 249–250.

Integrating Phonics and Reading

Guided Reading
Have children read the title and look at the cover illustration. Invite children to discuss times they may have picked apples.
First Reading Ask children what color apples the family in the story picks.
Second Reading Have children find as many instances as they can of the base word *apple* in both text and pictures.

Comprehension
After reading, ask children the following questions:

• Why does the girl say, "We need all the apples"? ***Recall/Drawing Conclusions***

• If you had picked the apples, what would you do with them? ***Reflective Analysis/Personal Response***

ESL/ELL English Language Learners
Hold up an apple or a picture of an apple. Invite volunteers to tell about various ways of preparing apples and foods made from apples.

Hard and Soft c

Skill Focus

Children will

★ identify the hard and soft sounds of *c* in words.

★ apply the rule for the soft *c* sound.

★ read and write hard and soft *c* words in context.

★ recognize and read high-frequency words.

ESL/ELL Korean, Khmer, Hmong, and Vietnamese speakers may confuse the hard *c* with an initial hard *g*. Check pronunciation with minimal pairs such as *cold, gold; cap, gap;* and *clue, glue.*

▶ Teach

Phonemic Awareness: Phoneme Identity
Say the following words: *cone, city, cup.* Repeat the words, stressing the initial consonant sound. Invite children to clap when they hear words that begin with the same sound as *kitten.* (*cone, cup*) Then, say *ceiling, celery, come.* Ask children to stand when they hear words that begin with the same sound as *sister.* (*ceiling, celery*)

Sound to Symbol Write the words *cone* and *cup* on the board. Say them aloud and underline the initial *c.* Explain that the /k/ sound is the hard sound of *c.* Then, write *ceiling* and *celery* on the board, saying them and circling the initial *c.* Explain that the /s/ sound is the soft sound of *c.*

▶ Practice and Apply

Sound to Symbol Read the rhyme aloud. As children follow along, have them identify words with the hard sound of *c* (*cute, carrots*) and the soft sound of *c.* (*Spice, Lucy's, mice, nice, slice*)

Read the rule and the directions on page 93. Be sure children understand how to indicate the difference between a hard and soft *c.*

Writing For page 94, model item 1 by reading the word choices and then reading the sentence, trying out each possible answer. Children will have the opportunity to read the high-frequency words *watch, first,* and *their.*

Critical Thinking As you discuss Talk About It, elicit from children that Cindy and Vince probably enjoy racing because they are able to run fast, and they have smiling faces.

Reading Use *The City Cat and the Country Cat,* MCP Phonics and Reading Super Skills Library 1, Level B, to reinforce the difference between hard and soft *c.*

Name _____

Sugar and Spice are Lucy's pet mice.
They are cute and very nice.
Sugar nibbles a slice of cheese,
Spice snacks on carrots and on peas.

▶ Say the name of each picture. If it has a soft **c** sound, circle the picture. If it has a hard **c** sound, draw a line under it.

RULE
When **c** is followed by **e, i,** or **y,** it usually has a soft sound. You can hear the soft **c** sound in **mice.**

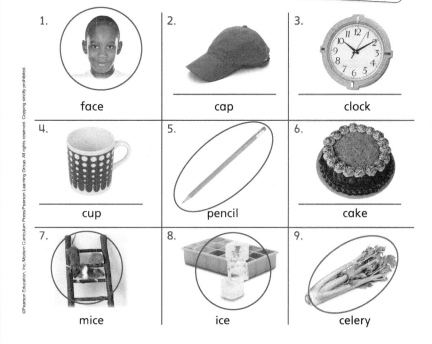

1. face	2. cap	3. clock
4. cup	5. pencil	6. cake
7. mice	8. ice	9. celery

Hard and soft c   **93**

FOCUS ON ALL LEARNERS

ESL/ELL ENGLISH LANGUAGE LEARNERS

Have English language learners practice the two sounds of *c* by reading aloud the rhyme on page 93 to a partner and completing page 93.

• Say the rhyme aloud and have children repeat as a group. Have children practice saying the rhyme aloud to a more English-proficient partner.

• On their worksheets, ask children to underline the words with soft *c* and draw a box around words with hard *c.* Model items 1–3 for the group and correct together. As you do, ask children to explain why the picture clues they circled have the soft *c* sound.

AUDITORY/KINESTHETIC LEARNERS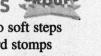

Play a "May I?" game. Have children take two soft steps forward if they hear a soft *c* word and two hard stomps backward if they hear a hard *c* word. If they hear neither, they should stay put. Use words such as *nice, ice, mice, cup, cap, hit, place, fence, can, help, come, cave,* and *cereal.*

Words in Context

► Circle the word that will finish each sentence. Print it on the line.

1. Cindy and Vince __can__ run fast.
   - (can) cage
   - cape came

2. They will run in a __race__ at school.
   - mice (race)
   - nice next

3. The kids __come__ to watch.
   - cap cane
   - (come) cat

4. Cindy hopes to win first __place__ .
   - nice rice
   - (place) slice

5. The __laces__ of their shoes are tied.
   - rice nice
   - (laces) price

6. They race past the __fence__ .
   - next nice
   - (fence) can

7. It's a tie. They win __nice__ prizes.
   - mice cereal
   - (nice) price

8. The __class__ cheers for them.
   - clue cats
   - case (class)

9. Cindy and Vince have smiling __faces__ .
   - lace (faces)
   - race space

10. The kids get ice-cream __cones__ .
    - (cones) cape
    - mice nice

 Do Cindy and Vince enjoy racing? How do you know?

 Help your child group all the hard *c* words and all the soft *c* words.

94   Hard and soft c: High-frequency words, critical thinking

CURRICULUM CONNECTIONS

SPELLING

Have children write sentences for the spelling words *ice, cake, gym, goat, peanut, ribbon,* and *apple,* inserting blank spaces in place of the words. When children have finished, remove the spelling list and have them fill in the words.

WRITING

Read Beatrix Potter's *The Tale of Peter Rabbit* to children. Discuss the trouble that Peter got into by going under the fence. Then, write these words on the board: *celery, mice, fence, nice, come,* and *can.* Invite children to create stories about three mice that go under a fence and into a garden.

MATH

Ask children to talk about what they do at certain hours of different days. Use a manipulative clock to model the times. On chart paper, list children's responses and the times of day. Circle any words with *c* in them and have children distinguish between hard and soft *c* sounds.

 AstroWord Consonant Sounds and Letters

AUDITORY/VISUAL LEARNERS

Draw two ice cubes as column heads on chart paper. Write *ice* inside the first one and *cube* inside the second. Have children name and write soft and hard *c* words under the headings with the matching sounds. Provide space to list suggested words in which the same sounds are spelled by *s, k,* or *ck.*

CHALLENGE

Materials: index cards

Have partners make word cards, leaving out the letters that spell /k/ or /s/, such as __atch (catch), tra__e (trace), __one (cone), ri__e (rice), __astle (castle), __ir__u__ (circus). Partners can trade cards with another pair of classmates and try to determine each other's words.

EXTRA SUPPORT/INTERVENTION

Materials: Phonics Word Cards, Set 2: Soft *c* words (7–13)

Lay the word cards out on a table. Say sentences that are each missing one of the words. Have children find the words that make sense and repeat the sentences, using the words. Repeat with words on the other side of each card. See Daily Phonics Practice, page 250.

Integrating Phonics and Reading

Guided Reading

Have children read the title and look at the illustrations. Have them predict what the story will be about.

First Reading Encourage children to retell the story, using the illustrations.

Second Reading Make a chart on the board with one column for hard *c* and one for soft *c*. Invite children to use words from the story to fill the columns.

Comprehension

After reading, ask children the following questions:
- Why did the two cats have a problem? *Inference/Cause and Effect*
- How did the City Cat and the Country Cat solve their problem? *Inference/Using Picture Clues*

ESL/ELL English Language Learners

Some children may not have experienced the city or country. Reread the story drawing attention to the vocabulary that belongs to each.

Hard and Soft g

Skill Focus

Children will

★ identify the hard and soft sounds of *g* in words.

★ apply the rule for the soft *g* sound.

★ write words with the hard and soft *g* sounds.

ESL/ELL Tagalog, Korean, Hmong, Khmer, or Vietnamese speakers may have difficulty differentiating /j/ or soft *g* and the sound of *sh* or *ch*. Verify that children produce correctly the initial sounds of *giant*, *shy*, and *child*.

Teach

Phonemic Awareness: Phoneme Isolation
Say the words *goat* and *game*, emphasizing the initial /g/. Have students repeat the words. Explain that the beginning sound /g/ is the hard *g* sound. Then, say the words *giraffe* and *gym*. Ask children what sound they hear at the beginning of the words. (/j/) Explain that /j/ is the soft *g* sound.

Sound to Symbol Write *goat, giraffe, game,* and *gym* on the board. Point to each word as children say them aloud. Remind children that /g/ is the hard *g* sound. Have volunteers identify the words with the hard *g* sound and circle the letter that makes the sound. (*goat, game;* g) Review that /j/ is the soft *g* sound. Have volunteers identify the words with the soft *g* sound and underline the letter that makes the sound. (*giraffe, gym;* g)

Practice and Apply

Sound to Symbol Read the rhyme on page 95. Make two columns on the board, one labeled hard *g*, and the other soft *g*. Have children write words from the rhyme in the appropriate column. (*hard g: gaze, bigger; soft g: gentle, giraffes, giants*)

Read the rule on page 95. Have children explain how the rule applies to the words in the rhyme. You may wish to point out that *bigger* does not follow the rule. Go over the directions and have children identify the pictures before they do the activity.

Writing On page 96, have volunteers read the words in the box, and then have children read them together. Remind children to say each word to themselves and to look at the word to see if it follows the soft *g* pattern before they write it in the soft *g* or hard *g* column.

Reading Use *I Got a Goldfish,* MCP Phonics and Reading Super Skills Library 1, Level B, to provide practice in reading hard and soft *g.*

95

Name _____

Gentle giraffes,
Gaze through the trees.
Bigger than giants,
They nibble the leaves.

▶ Say the name of each picture. If the name has a soft g sound, circle the picture. If it has a hard g sound, draw a line under it.

RULE
When *g* is followed by **e, i,** or **y,** it usually has a soft sound. You can hear the soft *g* sound in **giraffe.**

1. game
2. gym
3. goat
4. page
5. giant
6. gum
7. dragon
8. egg
9. giraffe

Hard and soft g   **95**

FOCUS ON ALL LEARNERS

ESL/ELL ENGLISH LANGUAGE LEARNERS

Confirm that English language learners can recognize and correctly pronounce words with soft *g.*

• Read aloud the rule for soft *g* on page 95 and apply the rule to the words in this lesson. Model pronunciation and spelling of each lesson word. Remind children that *y* can be a vowel as in *gym* and *fudgy.*

• Write on the board several words from the box on page 96. Say the words, one at a time. Ask children to identify which sound of *g* each word contains.

• Invite volunteers to suggest other words that contain the soft sound of *g.* Encourage children to use the word list.

VISUAL LEARNERS *INDIVIDUAL*

Invite children to be "word detectives." Tell them to find ten words containing *g* in a story they are reading and list them according to the soft *g* or hard *g* sound. You might also ask them to find five words with *j* and compare that consonant sound to the soft *g* words.

The letter **g** can make a hard or a soft sound. **Read** the words in the box. **Listen** for the sounds of **g**. **Print** the words under **Soft g Words** or **Hard g Words**.

gift	gem	age	dog	cage	large	good	gum
huge	gave	goat	stage	wag	page	wage	gold
gym	gate	giant	gentle	egg	game	giraffe	give

Soft g Words	Hard g Words
gem	gift
age	dog
cage	good
large	gum
huge	gave
stage	goat
page	wag
wage	gold
gym	gate
giant	egg
gentle	game
giraffe	give

 HOME Say a word from the box. Ask your child to spell it and tell if the word has a soft or hard g sound.

96 Hard and soft g

CURRICULUM CONNECTIONS

SPELLING

In groups of three, one child dictates a list of the spelling words *goat, gym, cake, ice, apple, ribbon,* and *peanut.* The other two children write alternate letters of each word as the first child watches and says *Try again!* if an incorrect letter is used. Children can take turns saying the words and spelling them.

WRITING

Write the word *giant* in the middle of a word web on chart paper. Add words to the web that describe children's impressions of giants. *Are they large or small? huge or tiny? Are they gentle? What are they known for in stories? Are giants real?* Invite children to use words from the web to write sentences about giants and to attach them to a "giant-sized" picture of a giant that children can draw together.

TECHNOLOGY **AstroWord** Consonant Sounds and Letters

VISUAL/KINESTHETIC LEARNERS GROUPS

Materials: paper bag, index cards, marker

Make hard *g* and soft *g* cards with such words as *gas, gate, goat, rug, wig, giraffe, giant, gym, bridge,* and *cage,* and put them in the bag. Invite volunteers to draw two cards and make up sentences using both words. Classmates can identify the hard and soft *g* words in the sentences.

CHALLENGE

Have children use soft *g* words to write tongue twisters. Have children illustrate their tongue twisters and teach the class to say it as fast as they can.

EXTRA SUPPORT/INTERVENTION

Materials: index cards; black, red, and green markers

Write hard *g* and soft *g* words on the cards in black, but print the vowels *e, i,* and *y* in green and *a, o,* and *u* in red. Have children apply the rule on page 95 to help read each word. See Daily Phonics Practice, page 250.

Integrating Phonics and Reading

Guided Reading

Have children read the title and then look through the story to find animals that begin with *g.* You might also wish to use the English Language Learners' activity below.

First Reading Have children use the pictures to explain why the girl got more pets.

Second Reading Make two columns on the board. Have children write hard *g* words in one column and soft *g* words in the other.

Comprehension

After reading, ask children the following questions:

• Why did the girl get a goldfish? *Recall/Cause*

• Which do you think was the best pet for the girl? Why? *Reflective Analysis/Evaluate*

ESL/ELL **English Language Learners**

Ask children to name each animal as you point to it in the story. Then, ask them to tell if the animal would be a good pet. Encourage English language learners to tell why or why not.

High-Frequency Words

Skill Focus

Children will

★ recognize and read the high-frequency words *only, own, their, laugh, even,* and *might.*

★ use high-frequency words to complete sentences.

Teach

Analyze Words Write the words *only, own, their, laugh, even,* and *might* on the board. Point to each word and read it aloud. Have children repeat each word after you.

• Then, say each word slowly as you point to the letters in the word. Encourage children to listen for the consonant and vowel sounds. Have children repeat each word, blending the sounds.

• Point out any irregular spellings in words, such as the *gh* /f/ in *laugh,* and the *igh* /ī/ sound in *might.*

• Help children associate the sounds they hear in each word with a familiar word.

• You may wish to add these words to a class Word Wall so that children can use the words they learn to find similar spelling patterns and phonemic elements in new words.

Read Words in Context Write the following sentences on the board. Invite volunteers to read the sentences and underline the high-frequency words. Then, have children read the sentences together.

• **Jim and Kate's kitten makes me laugh.**
• **The kitten is their only pet, and it is very silly.**
• **I hope to have my own kitten someday.**
• **I might like a kitten even better than my fish.**

Practice and Apply

Write Words Read the directions on page 97. Be sure children understand what to do. For page 98, review how to do a crossword puzzle before they write their answers. Also, encourage them to use strategies they have learned to associate sounds with letters and blend words to help them read.

Reading You may wish to use *The Case of the Furry Thing,* MCP Phonics and Reading Library, High Frequency Word Collection, Level B, to have children practice reading some of the high-frequency words.

Name _____

▶ Complete **each sentence with one of the words in the box.** Write **the word on the line. One word is used more than once.**

only	laugh	own
even	their	might

1. Jill and Sam took _____their_____ little sister Bea to the fair.

2. Sam was the _____only_____ one who wanted to milk a cow.

3. Jill said the petting zoo _____might_____ be fun for Bea.

4. Bea liked the piglets _____even_____ better than the lambs.

5. The silly clowns made them all _____laugh_____.

6. Jill got some popcorn to share, but Sam wanted his _____own_____ box of popcorn.

7. Bea asked Jill and Sam when they _____might_____ come back to the fair.

Words in context   **97**

FOCUS ON ALL LEARNERS

ESL/ELL ENGLISH LANGUAGE LEARNERS

Materials: high-frequency word cards

English language learners may experience difficulty pronouncing the high-frequency words and completing the crossword puzzle on page 98.

• Have children remove the word cards from the back of their book. Then, have pairs practice pronouncing the words. Model each word as needed. Recognize that some children may have difficulty pronouncing the long *o* sound in *only* and *own,* the final *f* sound in *laugh,* and the *v* in *even.*

• On the board, copy the grid shown on page 98. Model the meaning of *across* and *down.*

• With children, complete the puzzle, asking volunteers to read and answer the clues.

• Then, have partners work together to complete the puzzle in their books.

AUDITORY/VISUAL LEARNERS   GROUPS

Write the high-frequency words on the board. Ask children to name the high-frequency word that rhymes with each of the following words as you say each word aloud: *hair, night, lonely, Steven, calf, bone, sight, staff, loan, dare, light, phone, pair.*

▶ Read the words in the box. Write the word that goes with each clue in the puzzle.

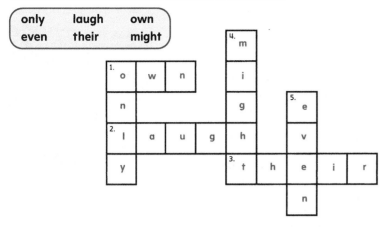

| | only | laugh | own |
| | even | their | might |

Puzzle grid (Across/Down):

```
4.
m
1.
o w n      i
n          g
2.         5.
l a u g h  e
y          h  v
3.
t h e i r
n
```

Across
1. When something belongs to you, you _____ it.
2. You do this when you hear a funny joke. _____
3. If a book belongs to Sue and Moe, it is _____ book.

Down
1. If there is no one but you, then you are the _____ one.
4. *Maybe* means you _____ be able to go to a friend's house.
5. This word means the opposite of odd. _____

▶ Write a sentence using one of the words on this page.

_____

_____

HOME With your child, make flash cards for the words in this lesson, and have him or her use each word in a sentence.

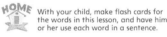

CURRICULUM CONNECTIONS

WRITING
Invite children to talk about fairs. If your community or school puts on a fair, focus on that fair. Ask children to name some of the things they can do at fairs. Then, have children write at least three sentences about a fair. Encourage them to include as many high-frequency words as they can. Check for children's spelling of high-frequency words.

ART
If children could be in charge of a fair for the school, what would they have at the fair? Invite children to draw a picture of a fair they would like to see.

VISUAL LEARNERS INDIVIDUAL
List the high-frequency words on the board. Then, have children scramble the letters in the high-frequency words and write clues to identify each word. Children should exchange their papers and unscramble the words, using the clues.

CHALLENGE
Have children brainstorm a list of words that rhyme with some of the high-frequency words. Then, have them write sentences, using a high-frequency word and at least one rhyming word. Example: *Terry and Wade forgot their bus fare.*

EXTRA SUPPORT/INTERVENTION
Materials: 2 sets of high-frequency word cards

Place the high-frequency word cards face down. Have a child turn over two cards, saying each word aloud. If the cards match, the child removes them and takes another turn. If they do not match, the child turns the cards over again, and another child takes a turn.

Integrating Phonics and Reading

Guided Reading
Display the book cover and point out the magnifying glass. Ask children to predict what the story might be about.

First Reading Ask children about the cause-effect situations in this story.

Second Reading Have children find the word *laugh* and read the sentence aloud. Then, have them make up a sentence about the story, using the word *laugh*.

Comprehension
Ask children these questions:

• How does Casey Moon know that the furry thing was a skunk? *Inference/Using Prior Knowledge*

• Why do you think Casey always looks, listens, and smells? *Reflective Analysis/ Personal Response*

ESL/ELL English Language Learners
Discuss with children what the word *case* means in the story. Invite children to role-play being "on a case."

Phonics and Reading / Phonics and Writing

Compound Words, Two-Syllable Words, Hard and Soft c and g, and le

Skill Focus

Children will

★ read and write compound words, two-syllable words, words with hard and soft *c* and *g*, and words with *le* in context.

★ build words with *c*, *g*, or *le*.

Teach

Phonemic Awareness: Phoneme Isolation
Read this sentence to children: *The gentle giraffe walked in a complete circle as he ate the green grass.* Have children identify the words with hard *g* (*green, grass*); soft *g* (*gentle, giraffe*); hard *c* (*complete*); soft *c* (*circle*); and *le* (*gentle, circle*).

Sound to Symbol Write these words on the board: *giant, gallop, covered, race, able,* and *forehead.* Read the words and have volunteers identify the words with the hard sounds of *c* and *g*, the soft sounds of *c* and *g*, and the words that end with the *le* sound. Have them circle the letters that stand for each sound. Then, have a volunteer underline the compound word and tell which two words it contains. (*forehead; fore, head*) Finally, ask students which words have more than one syllable. (*giant, gallop, covered, able, forehead*)

Read Words in Context Write these sentences on the board.

* **Cindy saw Carlos at the game.**
* **The game was in the little gym.**
* **After the game, they walked across the schoolyard.**

Have children read the sentences and use different colors of chalk to circle words with hard or soft *c* and *g*, *le*, and compound words.

Practice and Apply

Phonics and Reading After children have read the story, have them identify words with the targeted sounds.

Phonics and Writing With children, complete the first item on page 100 to be sure they understand how to build words.

Reading Use *A Rainbow Somewhere,* MCP Phonics and Reading Word Study Skills Library, Level B, to provide practice in reading compound words.

99

Name_____

 **Phonics & Reading** Read **the story.** Print **a word from the story to** finish each sentence.

The Giant Giraffe

The giraffe is the tallest animal that can be found anywhere on land. At least three people would have to stand on each other's shoulders to reach a giraffe's forehead. Because it is so tall, it can nibble leaves from treetops.

Although the giraffe has very long legs, it can gallop gracefully. The giraffe is able to race away when it faces danger. When it can not run away, the giraffe will kick with its heavy feet.

The body of a giraffe is covered with large, brown spots. These spots help the giraffe to blend in with the trees and keep it safe from harm.

1. The _____giraffe_____ is the tallest land animal.

2. At least three _____people_____ would have to stand on each other's shoulders to pet a giraffe.

3. The giraffe is tall enough to nibble leaves from _____treetops_____.

4. With its long legs, it is able to race away from _____danger_____.

Compounds; syllables; le; sounds of c, g   **99**

FOCUS ON ALL LEARNERS

ESL/ELL **ENGLISH LANGUAGE LEARNERS**
Materials: chart paper, markers, highlighters
Review target vocabulary from the story before asking English language learners to read "The Giant Giraffe."

* Encourage children to work in small groups to scan the story and highlight words they know that contain hard or soft *c* or *g*, *le*, compound words, or two-syllable words.

* Print four column headings on chart paper. Have groups write their highlighted words under the correct headings. In a different color, have volunteers supply other words that fit each category.

* Read the story aloud. Have children practice reading in small groups or into a cassette recorder for later replay.

VISUAL LEARNERS *INDIVIDUAL*

Ask children to create a color code for identifying words in the story on page 99 that are examples of the phonics skills children are learning. Children might circle compound words in blue, *le* words in purple, soft *g* words in orange, and hard *g* words in green, for example.

Phonics & Writing

Use **words with le, c, and g** to finish each word ladder. **Change** only one letter in each word.

1. Begin with **gave**.
   End with **come**.

   gave

   ga**m**e

   came

   come

2. Begin with **tangle**.
   End with **jiggle**.

   tangle

   tingle

   jingle

   jiggle

3. Begin with **page**.
   End with **rice**.

   page

   rage

   race

   rice

4. Begin with **cage**.
   End with **wigs**.

   cage

   wage

   wags

   wigs

 Work with your child to make a word ladder beginning with *come* and ending with *long*.

100 Compounds; syllables; words with le; sounds of c, g

CURRICULUM CONNECTIONS

SPELLING

You may now wish to posttest the spelling words studied so far in this unit.

1. **peanut** The elephant ate a **peanut**.
2. **apple**   I gave my teacher an **apple**.
3. **ice**   There is **ice** on the sidewalk.
4. **gym**   I think we have **gym** today.
5. **goat**   This **goat** does not eat paper.
6. **ribbon** I won a **ribbon** at the fair.
7. **cake**   I will make a **cake** today.

WRITING

Review with children some of the facts they learned about the giraffe. Then, tell them they are going to write a silly story about a make-believe giraffe. Write these opening sentences on the board and read them aloud: *Ginny the Giraffe was lost. She looked at the houses all around her. She was taller than most of them!* Discuss possible things Ginny the Giraffe might do. Then, have children finish the story and draw a picture to illustrate it.

TECHNOLOGY **AstroWord** Compound Words; Consonant Sounds and Letters

Integrating Phonics and Reading

Guided Reading
Have children read the title and look at the pictures. Invite them to tell about some things that they like to do on rainy days.
First Reading Encourage children to use the pictures to explain some of the things that Grandpa and Jenny did.
Second Reading Have children list the compound words and then think of other compound words that begin with *rain, grand,* and *some*.

Comprehension
After reading ask these questions:
• Why did Grandpa keep telling Jenny that they would not see a rainbow yet? *Inference/Accessing Prior Knowledge*
• Have you ever seen a rainbow? If so, describe what you saw. *Reflective Analysis/Personal Response*
ESL/ELL English Language Learners
Help children understand words in the story that show time is passing. *(today, soon, now)*

AUDITORY/KINESTHETIC LEARNERS GROUPS

As you call out these words, have children tap out the syllables and tell whether they hear one or two syllables in each word: *mitten, sailboat, seven, six, ribbon, tape, puppy, pillow, kids, baby, mother, lemon, robot, trunk.*

CHALLENGE

Materials: tape measure

Explain that some giraffes grow to 18 feet, which is 216 inches. Invite children to measure the height in inches of one another, round the heights, and then determine which children's heights would add up most closely to 216 inches.

EXTRA SUPPORT/INTERVENTION

Read the story on page 99 to children as they follow along. Then, read the incomplete sentences at the bottom of the page, having children fill in the missing words orally. Then, ask them to write their answers. See *Daily Phonics Practice*, pages 248–250.

Blends with r

Skill Focus

Children will

★ define *consonant blend*.

★ identify blends with *r* and the sounds they stand for.

★ read and write words with initial *r* blends.

ESL/ELL Native speakers of Vietnamese, Hmong, Korean, Khmer, and Cantonese may confuse *r* blends and *l* blends. Have children practice pronouncing *glow, grow; braid, blade; fright, flight*.

Teach

Phonological Awareness: Blending Onsets and Rimes Say the word *frog*, emphasizing the initial *fr: ffffrrrrog*. Repeat the word and ask children if they hear one or two sounds at the beginning. (*two*) Explain that *fr* is a consonant blend—two sounds that blend together but each sound is heard.

Sound to Symbol Write the word *frog* on the board. Circle the *fr* and explain it is called an *r* blend. Then, write the words *trick, brick, crib, drum, gray,* and *price* and tell children that these, too, are *r* blends. Invite volunteers to circle the blend in each word.

Practice and Apply

Sound to Symbol Read the rhyme at the top of page 101. Have children identify the *r*-blend words and write them on the board: *frogs, bullfrogs, green, tree,* and *brown*. Invite volunteers to go to the board, say the word, identify the *r* blend, and circle it. (*gr, tr, br*) Ask children to suggest other *r*-blend words. (*Possible responses: friend, grow, train, bring*)

Read the rule on page 101. Help children identify the pictures. Remind them that the names of the pictures will be used to answer the riddles. On page 102, suggest that they read all the choices under each picture before they circle their answer. Remind them that at the bottom of the page they need both to circle the blend and to write it.

Reading You may want to use *At the Track,* MCP Phonics and Reading Super Skills Library 1, Level B, to reinforce recognizing and reading words with *r* blends.

Name_____

Green frogs, tree frogs,
There are so many kinds.
Brown frogs, bullfrogs,
We can't make up our minds.

▶ **Say** the name of each picture. **Print** its beginning blend on the line. **Trace** the whole word.

RULE

A **consonant blend** is two or more consonants that come together in a word. Their sounds blend together, but each sound is heard. You can hear **r** blends in **green, tree,** and **frogs.**

1. g r **apes**

2. f r **og**

3. t r **ee**

4. t r **ain**

▶ **Use** the words above to answer the riddles.

5. I can jump and hop.
   You find me in a pond.
   I eat bugs.

   I am a ___**frog**___ .

6. I am green.
   You can find me in a park.
   Birds live in me.

   I am a ___**tree**___ .

7. I can be small or big.
   I make a good toy.
   I run on a track.

   I am a ___**train**___ .

8. We grow on vines.
   We come in bunches.
   We are good to eat.

   We are ___**grapes**___ .

Blends with r: Picture-text match   **101**

FOCUS ON ALL LEARNERS

ESL/ELL **ENGLISH LANGUAGE LEARNERS**

Have English language learners begin to work on pages 101–102 to assess their progress and comprehension of lesson content.

• Print *gr, fr, tr, br, cr, pr,* and *dr* on the board and draw a large circle around each. Allow sufficient room within each circle to add *r*-blend words.

• Have children look at pages 101 and 102 and name a picture clue or word for each initial *r* blend. Ask them to write their words on the board in the correct circles.

• Have children complete items 1 through 4 on page 101 and items 1 through 8 on page 102 in small groups or individually. Review answers together and reinforce through questioning that English language learners grasp concepts before completing the pages.

AUDITORY/KINESTHETIC LEARNERS

Write the blends *br, cr, dr, fr, gr, pr,* and *tr* spaced apart across the width of the board. Have each child slide an eraser across the ledge and name a word that begins with the *r* blend that the eraser lands closest to. Children in their seats should help decide if the answer is correct.

Circle the word that names the picture.

1.	2.	3.	4.
(grapes)	trim	trade	drive
grass	(truck)	trap	(drum)
grade	train	(tree)	drink

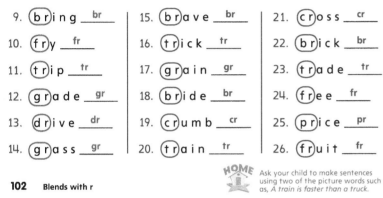

5.	6.	7.	8.
from	(train)	(dress)	gray
frost	truck	drapes	(grass)
(fruit)	trick	drum	grab

Find the blend in each word. Circle it. Print it on the line.

9. (br)i n g ___br___
10. (fr)y ___fr___
11. (tr)i p ___tr___
12. (gr)a d e ___gr___
13. (dr)i v e ___dr___
14. (gr)a s s ___gr___

15. (br)a v e ___br___
16. (tr)i c k ___tr___
17. (gr)a i n ___gr___
18. (br)i d e ___br___
19. (cr)u m b ___cr___
20. (tr)a i n ___tr___

21. (cr)o s s ___cr___
22. (br)i c k ___br___
23. (tr)a d e ___tr___
24. (fr)e e ___fr___
25. (pr)i c e ___pr___
26. (fr)u i t ___fr___

 Ask your child to make sentences using two of the picture words such as, *A train is faster than a truck.*

102 Blends with r

CURRICULUM CONNECTIONS

SPELLING

Pretest the *r-* and *l*-blend spelling words below. Use the sample sentences to help children understand the meanings of the words.

1. **drum** A **drum** is fun to play.
2. **frog** I can hear a **frog** in the pond.
3. **tree** 'This **tree** gives a lot of shade.
4. **cloud** The **cloud** passed by slowly.
5. **globe** Find our country on the **globe**.
6. **block** The top **block** fell off the stack.

SCIENCE

Ask children to return to pages 101 and 102 to find *r*-blend items that are part of "The World Outside." Ask: *Which ones are natural or living objects and which are made by people?* Encourage children to add pictures of the objects from nature to the unit bulletin board.

 AstroWord Consonant Blends and Digraphs

AUDITORY/VISUAL LEARNERS *GROUPS*

Draw seven large empty ice-cream cones on the chalkboard and print one of the following in each one: *br, cr, dr, fr, gr, pr, tr*. Invite volunteers to name a word that begins with each blend. Ask each child to draw a scoop of ice cream on the correct cone and print the word inside it.

CHALLENGE

Materials: Phonics Word Cards, Set 1: *r* Blends (197–210)

Challenge children to sort the *r-* blend word cards into different categories. Suggest that they sort them into such groups as specific blends, ending sounds, and names of objects and action words.

EXTRA SUPPORT/INTERVENTION

On the board, print these letter + word combinations: *c + rib; d + rag; p + ride; t + rim; f + risky; g + rain*. Show children how to add the letter *c* to *rib* to make a new word with a beginning blend. Have volunteers complete the rest and use each new word in a sentence. See Daily Phonics Practice, pages 250–251.

Integrating Phonics and Reading

Guided Reading

Invite children to read the title and look at the picture. Ask them what they think this story will be about. You might also use the activity under English Language Learners.

First Reading Ask children what both Brad and Fred like to do.

Second Reading Help children make a list of *r*-blend words and categorize them according to the blend.

Comprehension

After reading, ask children the following questions:

- What happens each time either Brad or Fred goes ahead? *Recall/Sequence*
- Why do Brad and Fred say "We can't beat each other"? *Inference/Draw Conclusions*

ESL/ELL English Language Learners

Help children understand the meaning of the phrase *to brag* by reading Brad's and Fred's lines in a boastful way.

Blends with l

Skill Focus

Children will

★ identify blends with *l* and the sounds they stand for.

★ read words with initial *l* blends.

★ write words with *l* blends to complete sentences.

ESL/ELL Spanish-speaking children may pronounce a short *e* before *sl* words since Spanish lacks initial *s* blends. Verify that English language learners do not separate the two consonants with an intervening *schwa* sound (where *blow* might sound like *below*).

Teach

Phonological Awareness: Blending Onsets and Rimes Say the word *blow*, emphasizing and blending the initial *bl* sound: *bbbbllllow*. Repeat the word naturally, and then have children say it. Ask children what sound they hear at the beginning of the word. Explain that the sounds of *b* and *l* are blended together into the *bl* blend.

Sound to Symbol Write the word *blow* on the board, say it aloud, and underline the initial *bl*. Then, write the words *close, plan, slim, fleet,* and *glad* on the board. Ask children what letter these words have in common. (*l*) Invite volunteers to go to the board, read the word, identify the initial blend, and circle the letters that stand for the sound.

Practice and Apply

Sound to Symbol Read the rhyme at the top of page 103. Have children identify the words with *l* blends. (*blows, clouds, sleet, sledding*)

With children, say the names of the pictures on pages 103 and 104. Stress the initial blends. Then, read the directions to the activities.

Writing Remind children to try each word choice in the sentence before they write their answers to finish the sentences on page 103. Have children say the words in the box at the bottom of page 104 before they complete the sentences.

Reading Use *Planting a Garden*, MCP Phonics and Reading Super Skills Library 1, Level B, to give children practice in reading *l* blends in context.

103

Name _____

The wind blows the clouds.
Sleet turns to snow.
Winter's here again,
And sledding we will go!

▶ **Say** the name of each picture. **Print** its beginning blend on the line.

1. plants — pl	2. slippers — sl	3. glass — gl
4. block — bl	5. flat — fl	6. cloud — cl

▶ **Circle** the word that will finish each sentence. **Print** it on the line.

7. Snow covers the ground like a white ____cloud____.   (cloud)   clap

8. The wind ____blows____ the snow around.   blue   (blows)

9. It covers the trees and ____plants____, too.   (plants)   plays

10. I like to ____play____ in the snow.   (play)   plants

11. I am ____glad____ that it is wintertime.   (glad)   glass

Blends with l: Words in context   **103**

FOCUS ON ALL LEARNERS

ESL/ELL ENGLISH LANGUAGE LEARNERS

Enable children to successfully complete the sentences on pages 103 and 104.

• For children who need support in spelling and sight recognition, print consonant blends on a chart: *bl, fl, gl, cl,* and *pl*.

• Work individually with children on *l* blends that pose problems in pronunciation or recognition.

• Help children practice identifying the word choices to complete the sentences on their pages. Have children identify target words, read them aloud in isolation, and then read each choice again in the context of the sentence.

AUDITORY/VISUAL LEARNERS

Help children compose sentences using several *l*-blend words in each one. Write the sentences on a chart or the board. Practice reading them and have volunteers identify the words with *l* blends. Examples: *Slim Sal slurps sloppy soup,* and *Flossie's flags fly fine.*

▶ Print **the word on the line that answers each riddle. The pictures will help you.**

1. Sometimes I ring.
   Sometimes I chime.
   I tick-tock all the time.

   clock

2. High up on a pole I go.
   I flap when breezes begin to blow.

   flag

3. I hold the food you eat.
   Find me under rice or meat.

   plate

4. I make things stick for you. I stick to you, too.

   glue

▶ Find **a word in the box to finish each sentence. Print it on the line.**

5. I have a new magnifying _____glass_____.

6. When I hold it _____close_____ to things, they get bigger.

7. A blade of _____grass_____ looks like a stem.

8. _____Blocks_____ of wood are really full of holes.

9. A _____fly_____ looks like a big black monster!

10. A toy _____plane_____ looks like a real plane.

| Blocks |
| grass |
| fly |
| plane |
| close |
| glass |

104 Blends with l

HOME Ask your child to name other words that begin with cl, fl, pl, and bl, such as *flower* or *cloud*.

CURRICULUM CONNECTIONS

SPELLING

You can posttest the *r*- and *l*-blend words using these sentences.

1. **cloud** There wasn't a **cloud** in the sky.
2. **drum** Burt plays a **drum** in the band.
3. **globe** A **globe** is a model of the earth.
4. **tree** A bird is nesting in that **tree**.
5. **block** Meg lives on the same **block** as I do.
6. **frog** A **frog** can croak loudly.

WRITING

Record children's thoughts about snow on a web titled "When It Snows." Include such categories as *How it feels; What the wind does; What I do;* and *What happens to plants.* Circle any *l*-blend words in the web. Have children use the web ideas to write snow stories.

TECHNOLOGY **AstroWord** Consonant Blends and Digraphs

VISUAL/KINESTHETIC LEARNERS INDIVIDUAL

Materials: drawing paper

Print the following words on the chalkboard: *glue, sleep, blanket, plant, blue, fly, plate.* Ask children to work independently to draw scenes that picture all of the items. Have them label their pictures with the words and circle the *l* blends.

CHALLENGE

Print the following words on the board: *fly, plane, blows, cloud, glad.* Challenge children to write stories that contain all the words. Stories might begin *I had always wanted to fly a plane.*

EXTRA SUPPORT/INTERVENTION

Materials: common objects whose names have *l* and *r* blends, such as blocks, glass, grass, clock, plate, flag, glue, grape, truck, and fruit

Have children sort the objects into groups of *l* or *r* blends. Write the names of the items in a two-column chart. See Daily Phonics Practice, pages 250–251.

Integrating Phonics and Reading

Guided Reading

Ask children about plants or gardens they might have had. Discuss the care of a plant or garden.

First Reading Using the pictures and text, have children point out the steps the girls followed to start the garden.

Second Reading Write the words *flat, flower, glad, plant, planting,* and *plum* on the board. Have children find each word in the story and read the sentence aloud.

Comprehension

Ask children these questions:

• What did the girls say they wanted in their garden? *Recall/Sequence*

• Why were the girls surprised when their plant grew? *Inference/Using Picture Clues*

ESL/ELL English Language Learners

Draw attention to the question mark at the end of each sentence. Explain that this mark shows that a question is asked.

Blends with s

Skill Focus

Children will

★ identify blends with *s* and the sounds they stand for.

★ read words with initial *s* blends.

★ write words with *s* blends to complete sentences.

ESL/ELL Khmer, Hmong, Cantonese, Korean, and Vietnamese do not contain initial *s* blends. Russian speakers might pronounce a voiced *z* sound in some blends.

Teach

Phonemic Awareness: Phoneme Identity

Say the word *snake*, emphasizing the initial *sn* blend: *sssssnnnnake*. Have children repeat the word, listening to the beginning sounds. Tell them that you are going to say two words and they are to identify the word that begins with the same sounds as *snake: snail, slip.* (*snail*) Explain that both *snake* and *snail* begin with *sn*, an *s* blend.

Sound to Symbol
Review the definition of a consonant blend. Then, explain that there are several *s* blends. Write these words on the board and say them aloud: *sneaky, slid, steps, squid,* and *straw.* Circle the *s* blend in each word. Point out to children that sometimes a blend can consist of three letters as in *straw* and *squid.* Then, write *scale, star, space, scrub, string, small, swamp,* and *square* on the board. Invite volunteers to circle the blends in these words.

Practice and Apply

Sound to Symbol
Next, read the rhyme on page 105 aloud and have children repeat it chorally. Have volunteers identify the *s*-blend words, write them on the board, and circle the initial *s* blend. (*squiggle, snake, slimy, snail, slide, slippery, slow*)

Read the rule on page 105. Have several children repeat the rule in their own words. Then, read the directions. Be sure children can identify the pictures on both pages.

Writing
Read the words in the box on page 106. Suggest that children read the entire sentence before they decide on their answer. Remind them to reread the sentence after they write their answer to make sure it makes sense.

Reading
You may wish to use *Sally's Spaceship,* MCP Phonics and Reading Super Skills Library 1, Level B, to reinforce reading words with initial *s* blends.

Name_____

Said Squiggle Snake to Slimy Snail,
"Let's slide on the slippery trail."
Said Slimy Snail to Squiggle Snake,
"Slow down, for goodness' sake!"

▶ Say **the name of each picture. Find its beginning blend in the box. Print it on the line.**

RULE
Remember that in a **consonant blend** the sounds of the consonants blend together, and each sound is heard. You can hear **s** blends in **slide, snake,** and **squiggle.**

| sc | st | sp | sn | squ | scr | str | sl | sm | sw |

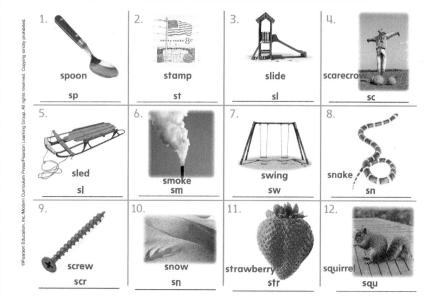

1. spoon — sp
2. stamp — st
3. slide — sl
4. scarecrow — sc
5. sled — sl
6. smoke — sm
7. swing — sw
8. snake — sn
9. screw — scr
10. snow — sn
11. strawberry — str
12. squirrel — squ

Blends with s   **105**

FOCUS ON ALL LEARNERS

ESL/ELL ENGLISH LANGUAGE LEARNERS

Reinforce English language learners' ability to say words with initial *s* blends.

Materials: index cards with blends *sc, st, sp, sn, squ, scr, str, sl, sm, sw*

• Invite volunteers to name the pictures on page 105. Whenever needed, model the picture names, and have children repeat them after you.

• Ask children to select the index card representing the blend they hear at the beginning of each clue. Then, have them say the blend and the picture name to be sure they correspond.

• Finally, have children write the blend below the picture.

AUDITORY LEARNERS

Ask each set of partners to choose an *s* blend and use it to make up a tongue twister. For example: *Sneaky snakes snicker at snack time.* Have them repeat the sayings to other pairs who should identify the blend and say the twister quickly five times.

Words in Context

▶ Find a word in the box to finish each sentence. Print it on the line.

1. Did you ever _____stop_____ to think about snakes?

2. Snakes have long, _____slim_____ bodies.

3. Snakes can move both fast and _____slow_____.

4. _____Snakes_____ have no arms or legs.

5. They still have the _____skill_____ to move.

6. Some snakes can even _____swim_____.

7. Their _____skin_____ looks slimy, but it's dry.

8. Snakes _____scare_____ some people, but not me.

scare
slim
skin
stop
skill
Snakes
swim
slow

▶ Circle the name of each picture.

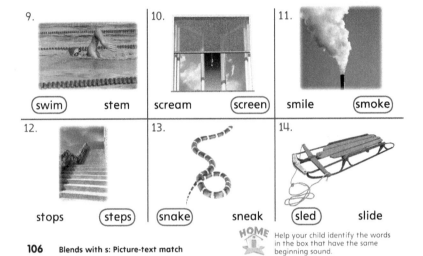

9.	10.	11.
(swim) stem	scream (screen)	smile (smoke)
12.	13.	14.
stops (steps)	(snake) sneak	(sled) slide

 HOME Help your child identify the words in the box that have the same beginning sound.

106 Blends with s: Picture-text match

CURRICULUM CONNECTIONS

SPELLING

You can use the following pretest for children's next set of phonics spelling words.

1. **stamp** Put a **stamp** on the letter.
2. **sled** My new **sled** goes fast.
3. **plant** My **plant** is starting to grow.
4. **belt** You can loosen your **belt**.
5. **sky** The **sky** is getting cloudy.
6. **baby** Is the **baby** crying?

SCIENCE

Write questions about garter snakes on chart paper: *Where can you find garter snakes? Are they harmful? What do they eat?* Ask each child to find one fact about garter snakes, or any snake. Children can record their ideas on round cutouts and connect the pieces in a long snake display.

 **TECHNOLOGY** **AstroWord** Consonant Blends and Digraphs

---

VISUAL/KINESTHETIC LEARNERS GROUPS

Materials: index cards, marker

On the cards, write scrambled *s*-blend words, such as *diles* (slide) and *recas* (scare). Place the cards face down. Have each child choose a card, unscramble the word, and print it on the board. Tell them to find the *s*-blend letters first.

CHALLENGE

Have children write secret sentences with two or more *s*-blend words, using blanks in place of the blends. For example: *I won't _ _ im in there.* (swim) *Did you see the _ _ ake?* (snake) Children can ask partners to decode the messages.

EXTRA SUPPORT/INTERVENTION

Materials: index cards, marker

Write words with *s* blends on cards. (Use pairs of matching blends such as *swim* and *swell*.) Place cards face down and have children take turns turning over two at a time. If the cards have matching blends, children keep the pair. See Daily Phonics Practice, pages 250–251.

Integrating Phonics and Reading

Guided Reading
Have children read the title and look at the illustration. Ask them what they think the girl is sitting in.

First Reading Remind children that Mom thought of several problems and Sally came up with a solution to those problems. Review the problems and their solutions with children, listing them on the board.

Second Reading Encourage children to find words with *s* blends and use them in new sentences.

Comprehension
Ask children these questions:
• What steps did Sally take to get her spaceship ready? *Recall/Sequence*
• Could you see the stars as Sally did? Explain. *Reflective Analysis/Personal Response*

ESL/ELL **English Language Learners**
Have children identify the *s* blend in the title. Review that the apostrophe shows ownership. Ask children to tell who owns what.

Final Blends

Skill Focus

Children will

★ identify final blends in words.

★ read and write words with final blends.

ESL/ELL Cantonese, Khmer, or Korean speakers will be unfamiliar with most final blends except *ng*. Tagalog or Spanish speakers may "clip" the blend, pronouncing only the first consonant of each.

Teach

Phonemic Awareness: Phomene Categorization Say the words *rang* and *sing*, emphasizing the ending blend. Ask children how the words are alike. (*They have the same ending sound.*) Then, say the following word groups and have children identify the two words in each group that end the same: *raft, fast, gift; sell, felt, belt; tank, think, ring.*

Sound to Symbol Write the words *rang, raft, gift,* and *belt* on the board. Pronounce each word, stressing the final blend in each. Explain that the final sound children hear in each word is a consonant blend because it is made up of two sounds that blend together but each sound is heard. Circle the blend in each word.

Then, write these words on the board: *jump, swing, last.* Have children say the words and identify the letters that form the final blends. Encourage them to name words that rhyme with each of the words. Write them on the board and have children circle the final blends. (*Possible responses: lump, hump, bump; ring, sing, thing; fast, mast, cast*)

Practice and Apply

Sound to Symbol Read the rhyme on page 107 and have children identify all the words that have final blends and list them on the board. Then, read the directions for page 107. Be sure children understand that they are to circle the answer to the riddle and write it on the line. Before children complete page 108, be sure that they can identify each picture. You may want to point out that the word *plants* ends with a three-letter blend.

Reading Children may enjoy reading *That Pig Can't Do a Thing,* MCP Phonics and Reading Super Skills Library 1, Level B, to provide practice in reading and recognizing final blends.

Name_____

A skunk is just outside my tent.
I think I'd best not scare it.
For if it sprays me with its scent,
All week long, I'll wear it.

> **RULE**
> Remember that in a **consonant blend** the sounds of the consonants blend together, and each sound is heard. You can hear blends at the end of **swing** and **trunk**.

▶ Circle **the word that answers each riddle.** Print **it on the line.**

1. All mail needs these. What are they?
   (stamps)   stumps
   stamps

2. We can ride on it. What is it?
   string   (swing)
   swing

3. An elephant has one. What is it?
   skunk   (trunk)
   trunk

4. We can eat it. What is it?
   (toast)   list
   toast

5. It hides your face. What is it?
   task   (mask)
   mask

6. We can sleep in it. What is it?
   (tent)   plant
   tent

7. We have two of these. What are they?
   lands   (hands)
   hands

8. Fish swim in it. What is it?
   (tank)   wink
   tank

9. It can float. What is it?
   (raft)   left
   raft

Final blends 107

FOCUS ON ALL LEARNERS

ESL/ELL ENGLISH LANGUAGE LEARNERS

Materials: bingo markers, index cards

Adapt the activity on page 108 to develop English language learners' comprehension of final blends.

- Play a game of bingo by calling out the name of a picture clue and having children cover it with a marker. Have children say the final blend they hear and repeat the word.

- Vary and reinforce with final blend cards. Display cards one at a time; have children cover the correct picture clues with markers.

- Have English language learners complete page 108 with a more English-proficient partner. Encourage children to correct their own papers as you review responses with the group.

AUDITORY LEARNERS

Say these words and ask children to name words that have the same ending blends and rhyme with the given words: *trunk* (bunk, skunk); *dust* (must, just, rust); *stamp* (damp, camp, ramp, clamp); *ring* (swing, sting, king); *land* (hand, band, stand, sand).

▶ **Find** the word in the box that names each picture. **Print** it on the line.

milk	skunk	tent	belt	trunk	plants
nest	ring	stamp	raft	desk	mask

1. plants
2. nest
3. skunk
4. desk
5. stamp
6. tent
7. trunk
8. raft
9. milk
10. belt
11. ring
12. mask

HOME Ask your child to name other words that end with *ng*, *sk*, and *mp*, such as *sing* and *camp*.

CURRICULUM CONNECTIONS

SPELLING

Write these incomplete words on the board and have children fill in the blanks with *s* blends or final blends to form the spelling words *stamp, sled, plant, belt, baby,* and *sky:* __a__, __ed, pla__, be__, __y, and *bab__*.

WRITING

Have children make lists of places where plants are found in and around the school. Ask them to each draw one of the plants and write its name (if known) and location. Have them arrange and glue the pictures into a "Plants Near Our School" collage. Find any words in the collage with final blends.

TECHNOLOGY  **AstroWord** Consonant Blends and Digraphs

VISUAL/KINESTHETIC LEARNERS

Materials: index cards, marker

Print these letter combinations and final blends on separate index cards: *ba-, bri-, bla-, ra-, be-, ri-, -nd, -st, -ft, -lt, -mp, -ng, -nk, -sk.* Give one to each child. Invite children to find partners to make as many words as they can in ten minutes. Have them keep lists of words they make.

CHALLENGE

Have children write riddles similar to the ones on page 107 for the words in the box on page 108. Allow time for children to share their riddles with classmates.

EXTRA SUPPORT/INTERVENTION

Materials: construction paper, scissors, marker

Write a final blend such as *sk* on a sheet of paper and cut out a slit in front of the letters. Pull a strip of paper showing initial consonants and vowel sounds (for example: *ma, tu,* and *de*) through the slit. Have children pronounce the words. See Daily Phonics Practice, pages 250–251.

Integrating Phonics and Reading

Guided Reading

Have children read the title and look at the illustrations in the story. Ask them to tell what they think this story will be about.

First Reading Ask children what the girl wanted her pig to do.

Second Reading Head four columns on the board with the final blends *nk, nt, mp, ng.* Have children identify words with final blends from the story and write them in the correct column.

Comprehension

After reading, ask children the following questions:

• Why does the pig begin to sing? *Inference/ Draw Conclusions*

• How else could the pig have become a ham? *Reflective Analysis/Understand Humor*

ESL/ELL **English Language Learners**

Explain the two meanings of *ham* to children. Help children to see that the sentence *That's how my pig became a ham* is a play on words.

Phonics and Reading / Phonics and Writing

Consonant Blends

Skill Focus

Children will

★ read words with initial and final blends.

★ write words with blends to finish sentences.

★ build words using consonant blends.

ESL/ELL Speakers of Asian languages including Korean and Tagalog may have difficulty making the sounds of consonant blends. Provide opportunities to practice words with blends.

▶ Teach

Phonemic Awareness: Phoneme Categorization Hold up Phonics Picture Cards *bread* (121), *bridge* (122), and *dress* (126). Have children name each picture. Ask them which two pictures begin with the same consonant blend. (*bread, bridge*) Then, hold up Phonics Picture Cards *spring* (148), *stamp* (149), and *swing* (152). Invite volunteers to name the pictures and tell which two pictures end with the same consonant blend. (*spring, swing*)

Sound to Symbol Write the word *stamp* on the board. Have children say the word aloud. Explain that *stamp* has two consonant blends. Have volunteers go to the board and circle the initial blend (*st*) and then circle the final blend. (*mp*)

Read Words in Context Write the following sentence on the board and read it.

• **Scott plants flowers in the spring.**

Have volunteers identify the words with initial blends (*Scott, plants, flowers, spring*) and final blends (*plant, spring*) and circle each blend.

▶ Practice and Apply

Phonics and Reading After children have read the story, encourage them to identify the words with initial and final blends.

Critical Thinking Discuss Talk About It. Be sure children recognize that Europe did not have sunflowers before the explorers brought them back.

Phonics and Writing For page 110, remind children that each step of the ladder must contain a real word. Then, complete the first item with them to ensure their success.

Reading Use *The River Grows*, MCP Phonics and Reading Super Skills Library 1, Level B, to reinforce reading initial blends.

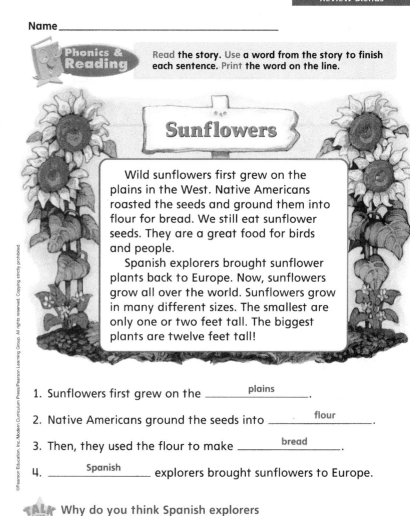

Review Blends

Name_____

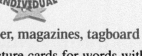 Read **the story. Use a word from the story to finish each sentence. Print** the word on the line.

Sunflowers

Wild sunflowers first grew on the plains in the West. Native Americans roasted the seeds and ground them into flour for bread. We still eat sunflower seeds. They are a great food for birds and people.

Spanish explorers brought sunflower plants back to Europe. Now, sunflowers grow all over the world. Sunflowers grow in many different sizes. The smallest are only one or two feet tall. The biggest plants are twelve feet tall!

1. Sunflowers first grew on the _____plains_____.

2. Native Americans ground the seeds into _____flour_____.

3. Then, they used the flour to make _____bread_____.

4. _____Spanish_____ explorers brought sunflowers to Europe.

TALK Why do you think Spanish explorers brought sunflowers back to Europe?

Review r, l, s blends: Reading; critical thinking   **109**

FOCUS ON ALL LEARNERS

ESL/ELL ENGLISH LANGUAGE LEARNERS

Have children locate target vocabulary on page 109 before reading the selection aloud.

• Print a consonant blend on the board or display a blend card.

• Ask children to scan the story and identify as many words as they can using that blend. Confirm clear pronunciations.

• Ask children to take turns reading the story aloud in groups of three and to complete items 1 through 4 that follow. Verify answers aloud.

VISUAL LEARNERS   INDIVIDUAL

Materials: drawing paper, magazines, tagboard squares, glue

Invite children to make picture cards for words with initial or final blends. They can cut pictures from magazines or draw their own to glue on tagboard squares. Have children print the words on the backs of the cards.

Phonics & Writing

Use beginning or ending blends to finish each word ladder. Change only one letter at a time.

1. Go from harp to band.

harp
hard
hand
band

2. Go from song to silk.

song

sing

sink

silk

3. Go from clips to glass.

clips

claps

class

glass

4. Go from spell to stall.

spell

smell

small

stall

HOME Using one of the words he or she formed, work with your child to make a word ladder of four words.

110   Review blends

CURRICULUM CONNECTIONS

SPELLING

Have children write the following sentences and fill in the missing spelling words. Be sure each child has a list of the spelling words.

1. Will you help me (*plant*) a tree?
2. It is time to feed the (*baby*).
3. This (*stamp*) will not stick.
4. I need a (*belt*) for my jeans.
5. The (*sled*) reached the bottom of the hill.
6. There was a rainbow in the (*sky*).

SOCIAL STUDIES

Have children locate Spain on a world map and discuss the routes Spanish explorers may have taken from Europe to parts of the Americas.

HEALTH/SOCIAL STUDIES

Talk about the foods we need to eat to stay healthy. Discuss the diet Native Americans might have enjoyed, including sunflower seeds, vegetables, deer and buffalo meat, fruits, and fish.

 **TECHNOLOGY**   **AstroWord** Consonant Blends and Digraphs

AUDITORY/KINESTHETIC LEARNERS   GROUPS

Materials: mural paper, wide marker

Draw a large hopscotch pattern on mural paper and write an *r, l,* or *s* blend on each section of the pattern. Have children take turns jumping the hopscotch pattern and saying a blend word for each square they choose to hop to.

CHALLENGE

Invite interested children to read more about Native Americans and their diets. Have them look in encyclopedias or nonfiction books. Invite children to report on what they learned.

EXTRA SUPPORT/INTERVENTION

Materials: blank game spinner

Print some initial and final blends on a blank game spinner. Have children take turns spinning and naming a word that begins or ends with the blend. List the words. See Daily Phonics Practice, pages 250–251.

Integrating Phonics and Reading

Guided Reading
Display the cover of the book and encourage children to tell what they already know about rivers.
First Reading Using the text and the photos, ask children to trace the growth of the river. Talk about how the size of the river changes as the book progresses.
Second Reading Invite children to find a word with an initial or final blend and have them read the sentence. Suggest they create their own sentence with the word.

Comprehension
Ask children these questions:
• How does the river get to the sea? *Recall/ Sequence*
• Which picture of the river is your favorite? Explain. *Reflective Analysis/Personal Response*

ESL/ELL **English Language Learners**
List nouns from the story such as *snow, water, river, trees, grass,* and *sea* on the board. Invite volunteers to pronounce the words after you.

Vowel Sounds of y

Skill Focus

Children will

★ identify the different vowel sounds of *y*.

★ read words that end with *y*.

★ read sentences with words that end with the vowel sounds of *y*.

ESL/ELL Spanish speakers should have little difficulty with the long *e* sound of *y* since *y* can have a similar sound in Spanish. For other English language learners, treat the different sounds as two different sounds for one letter: *bunny, sorry, sunny; shy, fry, why.*

Teach

Phonemic Awareness: Phoneme Isolation
Say the word *baby,* emphasizing the final sound: *babeeee.* Have children repeat the word, first elongating it, and then naturally. Ask children what vowel sound they hear at the end of the word. (*long e*) Then, say the word *cry,* stressing the final sound: *criiii.* Have children repeat the word in the same manner, and then naturally. Ask children what vowel sound they hear in *cry.* (*long i*)

Sound to Symbol Write *baby* and *cry* on the board. Ask how both words are the same. (*They end with* y.) Explain that although both words end with *y,* the *y* stands for a different vowel sound in each word.

Practice and Apply

Sound to Symbol Read the rhyme at the top of page 111. Have children repeat the rhyme together. Then, make two columns on the board, one labeled *long e,* the other labeled *long i.* Invite children to write the words that end with *y* in the rhyme under the appropriate column. (*long e: baby, ready, tiny; long i: try, fly*) Explain that if *y* is at the end of a word with two or more syllables, it generally has a long *e* sound. If *y* is the only vowel at the end of a one-syllable word, it usually has a long *i* sound.

Read the rule at the top of page 111 and 112. Have volunteers review which sound is apt to be at the end of a one-syllable word and which at the end of a two-syllable word. Then, read the directions to each section on pages 111 and 112. You may wish to do the first item under each section to be sure children understand.

Reading Use *The Night Sky,* MCP Phonics and Reading Super Skills Library 1, Level B, to provide children with practice in reading words that end with *y.*

Name _____

Baby bird, are you ready?
Baby bird, can you try?
Spread your tiny wings,
For now it is time to fly!

▶ Circle **each word in which y has a long e sound.**

> **RULE**
> Sometimes **y** can stand for the vowel sound of long **e** or long **i**. You can hear the long **e** sound in **baby**.

1. (baby)   2. cry   3. (happy)   4. why
5. try   6. (every)   7. (hurry)   8. (tiny)
9. (Molly)   10. (sandy)   11. shy   12. (puppy)
13. (penny)   14. (Freddy)   15. (funny)   16. (bunny)

▶ Circle **the words in the sentences in which y has a long e sound.**

17. Ty and (Molly) were helping take care of (baby) (Freddy.)

18. They heard (Freddy) cry in his crib.

19. They went to help in a (hurry.)

20. They had to try (everything) to make him (happy.)

21. Ty read him a (funny) book about fish that fly.

22. (Molly) gave him her (bunny) to play with.

23. Ty made (very) (silly) faces.

24. (Finally) (Freddy) was (happy.)

Vowel sounds of y: Words in context   **111**

FOCUS ON ALL LEARNERS

ESL/ELL **ENGLISH LANGUAGE LEARNERS**
Ask English language learners to demonstrate comprehension of lesson content by completing several activities in pairs or on their own.

• Read and confirm each set of directions when assigned.

• Have children independently complete the following tasks: items 1–16, page 111, and items 1–30 on page 112 to check for understanding.

• Working in pairs, have children read aloud the sentences on pages 111 and 112 and complete the exercises.

KINESTHETIC LEARNERS

Materials: Phonics Word Cards, Set 1: Vowel *y* words (237–245); two shoe boxes

Cut slots in the boxes and label one *Long* i *Sound* and the other *Long* e *Sound.* Stack the word cards nearby and invite children to be "mail carriers" and put the cards into the appropriate "mailboxes."

Circle **each word with a y that sounds like long i.**

> **RULE**
> When **y** is the only vowel at the end of a one-syllable word, **y** usually has the long **i** sound. You can hear the long **i** sound in *try*.

1. (try)   2. Freddy   3. (sly)   4. buggy   5. funny

6. bunny   7. (dry)   8. silly   9. rocky   10. (my)

11. (Ty)   12. windy   13. (by)   14. (sky)   15. sunny

16. sleepy   17. (fly)   18. happy   19. muddy   20. (cry)

21. sneaky   22. lucky   23. (shy)   24. puppy   25. Molly

26. (why)   27. jolly   28. baby   29. (fry)   30. very

Circle **each word with y that sounds like long i in the sentences.**

31. (Why) do onions make us (cry) when we are happy ?

32. (Why) is the (sky) blue on a sunny day ?

33. (Why) do bats (fly) at night ?

34. (Why) is a desert (dry) and a swamp muddy ?

35. (Why) can a bird (fly) but not a puppy ?

36. (Why) do we look silly if we (try) to (fly) ?

37. (Why) is a fox sneaky and (sly) ?

38. (Why) is a bunny (shy) ?

39. (Why) does a rainy (sky) make you sleepy ?

40. Do you ever wonder (why) ?

HOME Ask your child to use three of the circled words on this page in a sentence.

112   Vowel sounds of y: Words in context

CURRICULUM CONNECTIONS

SPELLING

Write these scrambled words on the chalkboard and have children unscramble them to write their spelling words: *1. yks* (sky) *2. abby* (baby) *3. sdel* (sled) *4. tnalp* (plant) *5. mpats* (stamp) *6. telb* (belt).

HEALTH

Invite children to talk about babies and baby care. Invite a child-care professional, such as a pediatric nurse or a day-care provider, to speak to the class about caring for babies. Before the professional comes to class, have children think of questions they want to ask and record them on chart paper.

WRITING

After completing page 112, discuss with children things they "wonder why" about. Write their questions on chart paper. Have each child choose one question and write it on paper. Encourage children to take their questions home and discuss them with family members. Have them record possible answers and discuss them in class.

VISUAL LEARNERS

Materials: chart paper, markers

On a chart, draw a cherry tree with large red cherries. Add a background of blue sky. Then, have children write words with the long *i* sound spelled *y* in the sky area and words with the long *e* sound spelled *y* in the cherries.

CHALLENGE

Invite children to each choose one *Why* question on page 112 to answer. If children do not know the answers, encourage them to make up something silly or fanciful. Have them write out their answers and share them with the class.

EXTRA SUPPORT/INTERVENTION

Materials: drawing paper; crayons or markers

Have children make entries for a *y*-as-a-vowel "pictionary." Ask each child to choose a word to write and illustrate. Gather the pages together and have children share their pictures and words. See Daily Phonics Practice, page 251.

Integrating Phonics and Reading

Guided Reading

Read the title and talk about what children see when they look at the night sky. You may wish to use the activity below under English Language Learners.

First Reading Have children use the illustrations to tell the story of the seven sisters and the boy.

Second Reading Have children find the words in which *y* stands for long *i*. Have them find other long *i* words and compare the spelling.

Comprehension

Ask children these questions:

• Why did people make up stories about the stars? *Inference/Draw Conclusions*

• What do the pictures on pages 4 and 5 look like to you? *Reflective Analysis/Personal Response*

ESL/ELL English Language Learners

Read the title with children. Ask them what vowel sound they hear in *night* and *sky*. Then, ask how the words are different.

Vowel Sounds of y

Skill Focus

Children will

★ distinguish between the different vowel sounds of *y*.

★ read words that end with *y*.

★ write words that end with *y* to complete sentences.

Teach

Phonemic Awareness: Phoneme Isolation
Say the following phrase and ask children to tell you in what part of each word they hear the long *e* sound: *Silly Billy.* (*at the end of each word*) Then, say *try to fly.* Ask children which words have the long *i* sound. (*try, fly*) Ask them in what part of each word is the long *i* sound. (*at the end*)

Sound to Symbol Write *Silly Billy* and *try to fly* on the board. Have volunteers read the words and circle the *y*'s that are vowels. Ask children what vowel sound the *y* stands for in each word. Then, write these sentences on the board. Invite children to draw a line under words in which *y* has a long *i* sound and to circle words in which *y* has a long *e* sound.

- **Jenny rides her pony.**
- **The sky is sunny and blue.**
- **The fly buzzed around the jelly.**

Tell children that sometimes *y* makes the long *e* sound as in *Jenny, pony, sunny,* and *jelly;* and sometimes *y* makes the long *i* sound as in *sky* and *fly.*

Practice and Apply

Sound to Symbol Read the directions at the top of page 113. You may want to have children underline the phrase *long i* and circle the phrase *long e* in the directions to remind themselves of what to do. Before children begin page 114, have them name each of the pictures. Then, read the directions and have several children repeat the directions in their own words.

Writing For page 113, be sure children understand that they can find the words that finish the sentences in the paw prints. Remind them to read the entire sentence after they write their answer.

Reading Use *Pick Up Nick!,* MCP Phonics and Reading Super Skills Library 1, Level B, to review and reinforce the different vowel sounds of *y.*

113

Name _____

▶ Read the word in each paw print. If the **y** stands for a long **i** sound, draw a line under the word. If it stands for a long **e** sound, circle the word.

<u>cry</u>   (bunny)   (sorry)   **my**   (Yuppy)

<u>try</u>   <u>why</u>   <u>shy</u>   (sunny)   (any)

▶ Find a word from the top of the page to finish each sentence. Print it on the line.

1. ____Yuppy____ the puppy was digging a hole

2. Suddenly he heard a ____cry____ from inside.

3. A very angry ____bunny____ popped out of the hole.

4. "Why are you digging up ____my____ happy home?"

5. Yuppy yapped, "Oh, my! I'm very ____sorry____."

6. "I'll ____try____ to help you fix it!"

Vowel sounds of y: Words in context   **113**

FOCUS ON ALL LEARNERS

ESL/ELL ENGLISH LANGUAGE LEARNERS

Reinforce English language learners' recognition and pronunciation of the vowel sounds of *y.*

- Review the rule for the vowel sounds of *y: If a word that ends with* y *has two or more syllables, the* y *usually stands for the long* e *sound. If a word that ends with* y *has only one syllable, the* y *usually stands for the long* i *sound.* Have volunteers repeat the rule.

- Ask children to complete pages 113 and 114 in pairs, asking for help from you if they need it.

- To review, correct the pages together, asking volunteers to read aloud the sentences and words.

AUDITORY/VISUAL LEARNERS

Draw a donkey and a fly on the board. Read the words *cry, fifty, puppy, sly, happy, lady, sky, shy.* Have children call out the name of the animal (*donkey* or *fly*) whose ending sound matches that of each word. As children respond, write each word near the appropriate animal.

► Say the name of each picture. Circle each word that has the same sound of y as the picture name.

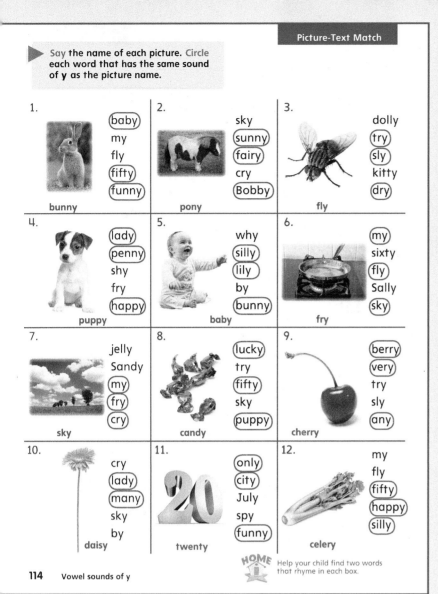

1. baby / my / fly / (fifty) / (funny)
bunny

2. sky / (sunny) / (fairy) / cry / (Bobby)
pony

3. dolly / (try) / (sly) / kitty / (dry)
fly

4. (lady) / (penny) / shy / fry / (happy)
puppy

5. why / (silly) / (lily) / by / (bunny)
baby

6. (my) / sixty / (fly) / Sally / (sky)
fry

7. jelly / Sandy / (my) / (fry) / (cry)
sky

8. (lucky) / try / (fifty) / sky / (puppy)
candy

9. (berry) / (very) / try / sly / (any)
cherry

10. cry / (lady) / (many) / sky / by
daisy

11. (only) / (city) / July / spy / (funny)
twenty

12. my / fly / (fifty) / (happy) / (silly)
celery

114   Vowel sounds of y

Help your child find two words that rhyme in each box.

CURRICULUM CONNECTIONS

SPELLING
You may wish to posttest the following spelling words at this time.

1. **baby** — Did you feed the **baby**?
2. **belt** — Fasten your seat **belt**.
3. **sky** — The **sky** was full of shooting stars.
4. **plant** — **Plant** the seeds close together.
5. **stamp** — This **stamp** is from Mexico.
6. **sled** — Use this rope to pull the **sled**.

MATH
Ask children to count by tens. Then, make a class list of number words that end in *y*, such as *twenty, thirty, forty, fifty, sixty, seventy, eighty,* and *ninety.* Have children use manipulatives (number cubes, for example) to illustrate each number.

KINESTHETIC LEARNERS GROUPS

Materials: 2 paper bags, index cards, marker

Prepare twelve to eighteen cards with words with the targeted sounds. Mark one paper bag *y=long i,* the other *y=long e.* Children should take turns choosing a card, saying the word aloud, and placing it in the appropriate paper bag.

CHALLENGE

Invite children to compose sentences using as many words from pages 113 and 114 in each one as they can. For example: *My very happy puppy found many bones.*

EXTRA SUPPORT/INTERVENTION

Materials: Phonics Word Cards, Set 1: Vowel *y* words (237–245)

Have children sort the word cards into two piles—one for *y* that sounds like long *e* and one for *y* that sounds like long *i.* Then, help them read each set aloud. See Daily Phonics Practice, page 251.

Integrating Phonics and Reading

Guided Reading
Have children read the title and look at the picture. Ask children who they think Nick might be.
First Reading Ask children who Nick is and what he likes to do.
Second Reading Have children find the words that end with *y* and explain which vowel rule applies. Be sure they recognize that when *a* and *y* come together in a word, the letters make the sound of long *a,* as in *okay* and *day.*

Comprehension
After reading, ask children the following questions:
• Why do you think the girl does not try to make Nick stop crying at first? *Inference/Using Picture Clues*
• Why do you think Nick finally stops crying? *Reflective Analysis/Personal Response*
ESL/ELL English Language Learners
Introduce the words *sure* and *okay* in context and encourage children to suggest words from their first language that have a similar meaning.

Compounds, Syllables, le, Hard and Soft c and g, Blends, y as a Vowel

Skill Focus

Children will

★ spell and write compounds, two-syllable words, words with hard and soft *g*, words with blends, and words in which *y* is a vowel.

★ build words that have the vowel sound of *y*.

ESL/ELL Many Asian languages are monosyllabic, so native speakers of those languages may pronounce two-syllable words in English as separate words.

Teach

Review Phonics Skills Review the following with children:

- A *compound word* is made up of two or more words joined together to make one new word. Ask children to spell a compound word that begins with *grand*.

- A *syllable* has one vowel sound. Ask children how many syllables are in *run, donkey*.

- When *c* or *g* is followed by *e, i,* or *y*, it usually has a soft sound. Have children spell examples of hard and soft *c* or *g* words, such as *race, cone, page,* and *game*.

- In a *consonant blend*, two or more sounds blend together and each sound is heard. Have children identify the blends in *brake, thing,* and *clap*.

- Sometimes *y* stands for a vowel. Ask children to identify the vowel sound of *y* in *fly, baby*.

Practice and Apply

Phonics and Spelling Read the directions on page 115. Have volunteers name each picture before children spell the words.

Phonics and Writing Explain that children are to make words from the word tiles on page 116. Point out that not every consonant blend will form a real word. Remind children to write two sentences, using some of the words they formed.

Reading You may wish to use *Pick Up Nick!*, MCP Phonics and Reading Super Skills Library 1, Level B, to review words that end in *le* and consonant blends.

Name _____

 **Phonics & Spelling**

Say the name of each picture. Find the word in the box and spell it. Then, print the word on the line.

ribbon	gym	globe	baby
stamp	peanut	apple	sky
plant	belt	ice	frog

1. apple
2. belt
3. ice
4. baby
5. plant
6. ribbon
7. globe
8. peanut
9. stamp
10. gym
11. frog
12. sky

Compounds; syllables; le; hard and soft c, g; blends; vowel y   **115**

FOCUS ON ALL LEARNERS

ESL/ELL ENGLISH LANGUAGE LEARNERS

Review orally with English language learners words that contain the targeted skills.

- On page 115, invite children to name each picture clue, one at a time. Ask them to point to, or otherwise identify, the word in the word list to match.

- Ask children to suggest other words as examples of the same structure. For example, for item 1, *apple*, you might ask: *What other words can you think of that end in the same sound or letters as* apple? Write answer choices on the board, as needed.

- Repeat for compound words, hard and soft *c* and *g*, blends, and *y* as a vowel. Model correct pronunciation and guide children to select a variety of answer choices.

AUDITORY/VISUAL LEARNERS

Materials: chart paper, glue, magazines

Divide the class into several groups. Have each group find pictures of words that begin or end with a blend and glue them on chart paper. Ask group members to display their collections and name the pictures.

Phonics & Writing

Use a **letter tile** to make a word with **y**.
Write **the words you made on the lines.**

| cr | dr | tr | br | fr | | sl | sn | sh | sk | sp |

  y

1. _____ cry
2. _____ dry
3. _____ try
4. _____ fry

 y

5. _____ sly
6. _____ shy
7. _____ sky
8. _____ spy

▶ Write **two sentences using some of the words you made.**

_____

_____

_____

_____

HOME Have your child write two more sentences using some of the other words he or she made.

CURRICULUM CONNECTIONS

SPELLING

Cumulative Posttest Assess mastery of the first half of the Unit 4 spelling list by using the following words and sentences.

1. **baby**   I can hear a **baby** crying.
2. **sky**   There is an airplane in the **sky**.
3. **peanut**   A **peanut** grows on a plant.
4. **apple**   That **apple** is shiny and red!
5. **frog**   Can the **frog** swim?
6. **globe**   A **globe** is a kind of map.
7. **plant**   We **plant** flowers in the spring.
8. **tree**   I read under the **tree**.
9. **gym**   We played kickball in **gym**.
10. **ice**   I need more **ice** in my drink.

READING

Read a version of the fable "The Ant and the Grasshopper" to the class. Talk about the lessons the story teaches.

TECHNOLOGY **AstroWord** Compounds Words; Consonant Blends and Digraphs

KINESTHETIC/AUDITORY LEARNERS GROUPS

Ask children to jump forward two jumps like a grasshopper if you say a compound word. If you say a two-syllable (not compound) word, they should jump two hops back. Use words such as: *turtle, wiggle, puddle, bedroom, whiskers, airplane,* and *baseball.*

CHALLENGE

Invite children to use the words in the box on page 115 to write a silly story. Encourage children to illustrate their stories and share them with the class.

EXTRA SUPPORT/INTERVENTION

Write each spelling word lightly in pencil on paper for each child. As you call out each word, have children locate the word and trace it, saying each letter. Then, have them write each word on their own. See Daily Phonics Practice, pages 248–251.

Integrating Phonics and Reading

Guided Reading

Point out the crying baby on the cover. Ask children what are some ways to quiet a baby's crying.

First Reading Have children use the pictures and text in the story to tell what problem the family in the story has.

Second Reading Have children find words that begin or end with blends and ask children to think of another word that has the same blend.

Comprehension

After reading, ask these questions:

• Why does everyone want the baby to stop crying? *Inference/Draw Conclusions*

• How do you think the girl felt when the baby stopped crying? *Reflective Analysis/Personal Response*

ESL/ELL English Language Learners

Review that an exclamation point expresses strong feeling. Tell children that this mark is found only at the end of a sentence. Have children take turns reading the title with expression.

Take-Home Book

Review Compounds, Syllables, Words with le, Hard and Soft c and g, Blends, y as a Vowel

Skill Focus

Children will

★ read compound words, two-syllable words, words that end with *le*, words with hard and soft *c* and *g*, words with blends, words with *y* as a vowel.

★ review selected high-frequency words in the context of a story.

★ reread for fluency.

Teach

Build Background

- Remind children that the theme of this unit is "The World Outside." Ask children to tell about some of the things they have learned about in this unit.

- Write the word *gerbil* on the board. Say it aloud and have children share what they know about gerbils. Explain that they will be reading about twins who receive gerbils as pets.

Phonemic Awareness: Phoneme Isolation
Write *gerbil* on the board and have children say it aloud. Ask them to name the sound they hear at the beginning of the word. (*soft* g) Invite a volunteer to explain the rule for words with soft *g*. (*When* g *is followed by* i, e, *or* y, *the sound of* g *is usually soft.*) Then, ask children to identify the syllables in *gerbil* and to explain how they know. (*two syllables because there are two vowel sounds*)

Practice and Apply

Read the Book Help children put their books together. Then, suggest that they look through the pictures. Read the story together. Discuss what they learned about gerbils.

Sound to Symbol Have volunteers read the story aloud. Invite children to find at least one example of compounds (*bedtime*), two-syllable words (*visit*), *le* (*freckle*), hard and soft *c* and *g* (*Cathy, Cindy; Gary, gerbils*), blends (*black*), and *y* as a vowel (*peppy, why*).

Review High-Frequency Words Write the words *their, own,* and *even* on the board. Have children spell each word and then say it, blending the sounds.

Reread for Fluency Have children reread the book to increase their fluency and comprehension. Remind them to take the book home to share with their families.

117

Name _____

Twin Pets

Cindy and Cathy are twins. They look alike, but Cindy has an extra freckle on her nose. One day Uncle Gary came to visit. He gave the girls their own gerbils. Cindy and Cathy are glad to get the pets.

1

At bedtime their pets are peppy. Uncle Gary tells the twins that gerbils are *nocturnal.* That means they are awake at night and sleep when it is daytime!

4

Compounds; syllables; le; hard and soft c, g; blends; vowel y: Take-home book   **117**

FOCUS ON ALL LEARNERS

ESL/ELL ENGLISH LANGUAGE LEARNERS
Analyze which skills to target with English language learners and use the Take-Home Book to reinforce them.

- Encourage English language learners to read the story aloud to more English-proficient partners. Identify and pronounce problem sounds.

- Expand vocabulary by asking volunteers to explain story words.

- Verify comprehension by asking content questions. For example, you might ask, *Are the two gerbils exactly alike?*

- Have children practice writing by first orally summarizing the story in one or two sentences and then writing their summary.

AUDITORY/VISUAL LEARNERS

Materials: audiocassette tape, cassette player

Prerecord the story for children and have them listen to it as they look at the pictures in their books. (You might set up a learning center where children can record themselves reading the story.)

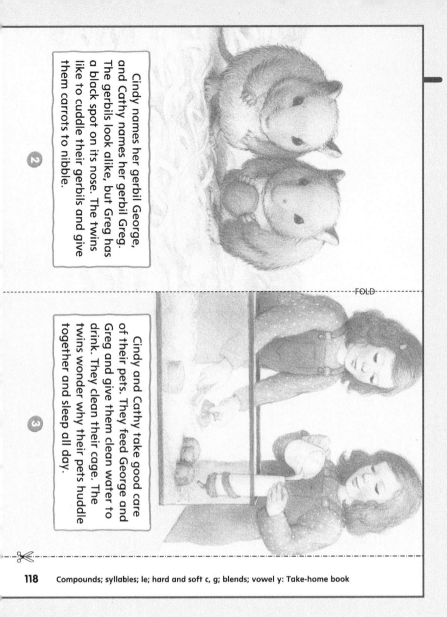

Cindy names her gerbil George, and Cathy names her gerbil Greg. The gerbils look alike, but Greg has a black spot on its nose. The twins like to cuddle their gerbils and give them carrots to nibble.

- FOLD - - - - - - - - - - - - - - -

Cindy and Cathy take good care of their pets. They feed George and Greg and give them clean water to drink. They clean their cage. The twins wonder why their pets huddle together and sleep all day.

✂ -

118   Compounds; syllables; le; hard and soft c, g; blends; vowel y: Take-home book

CURRICULUM CONNECTIONS

SOCIAL STUDIES

Materials: world map

Explain that there are more than one hundred kinds of gerbils, but the most common is the Mongolian gerbil. This gerbil lives in parts of China and Russia. Pet gerbils are descendants of these gerbils. In 1954, a Japanese laboratory sent the first gerbils to the United States. Use a map to locate China, Russia, and Japan. Have children trace a possible route on a map from Japan to the United States.

WRITING

Discuss what children learned from the story about taking care of gerbils. Invite them to write two or three sentences that summarize how to take care of a gerbil.

MATHEMATICS

Have children complete this sentence:

- **My favorite pet is a _____.**

Tally children's responses and then show children how to make a simple bar graph with the data. The horizontal axis should identify the pets, and the vertical axis should show the number who chose that pet.

 **AstroWord** Compounds Words; Consonant Blends and Digraphs

AUDITORY LEARNERS

Slowly reread the Take-Home Book *Twin Pets* and ask children to raise their hand when they hear a word with exactly two syllables.

CHALLENGE

Encourage children to work in pairs to expand on the first page of the story by writing a paragraph about what happens when Uncle Gary arrives with the gerbils. Children might consider what Uncle Gary says to the girls, how the girls react when they see the gerbils, or how the gerbils react in their new home.

EXTRA SUPPORT/INTERVENTION

As children preview *Twin Pets*, have them find and read aloud words they recognize. Then, have them point to words they are unfamiliar with and practice them together. Use context clues to help them learn new words. See Daily Phonics Practice, pages 248–251.

Consonant Digraphs sh, th, wh, ch

Skill Focus

Children will

★ define a consonant digraph.

★ read and write words with digraphs *sh, th, wh,* and *ch* in context.

★ recognize and read high-frequency words.

ESL/ELL Speakers of Vietnamese, Khmer, Korean, or Hmong may confuse *ch* with *sh* or initial *j*. Offer additional listening and speaking practice.

Teach

Phonemic Awareness: Phoneme Identity

Say these sentences and ask children what sound they hear at the beginning of each word.

- **Charles chases chipmunks.**
- **Shona shears sheep.**
- **Thor thanks Thelma.**
- **Which whale whistled?**

Sound to Symbol Write *chipmunks* on the board and say the word aloud. Underline *ch* and say /ch/. Explain that *ch* is a consonant digraph because *ch* makes only one sound. Write *sheep, thanks,* and *whale* on the board. Have children pronounce each word. Underline *sh, th,* and *wh* and explain that these are also consonant digraphs. Then, write *teeth.* Ask a volunteer to say the word and circle the digraph. (*th*) Explain that digraphs can also come at the end of a word.

Practice and Apply

Sound to Symbol Read the rhyme at the top of page 119. Have children raise their hand when they hear words with consonant digraphs.

Read the rule for a consonant digraph on page 119. Then, read the directions. Explain that there are more than two correct answers for each item at the bottom of page 119.

Writing Read the directions on page 120. Remind children to both fill in the bubble and to write the word on the line that completes the sentence. Children will have the opportunity to read the high-frequency words *decided, everything,* and *choose.*

Critical Thinking In discussing Talk About It, encourage children to name a particular type of store, rather than the mall in general.

Reading Use *Dragon's Lunch,* MCP Phonics and Reading Super Skills Library 1, Level B, to practice reading words with consonant digraphs.

Name _____

Shiny, wet shells on the shore,
More shells down the beach,
There's such a lot to choose from!
Why don't we pick one of each?

▶ Circle **the word that will finish each sentence. Print it on the line.**

RULE
A **consonant digraph** is two consonants that together stand for one sound. You can hear consonant digraphs in **shells, choose, the,** and **why.**

1. I go to the zoo to see the ____chimp____ .   chop   (chimp)   check

2. It smiles to show its ____teeth____ .   then   (teeth)   these

3. They are big and ____white____ .   which   what   (white)

4. It eats bananas by the ____bunch____ .   (bunch)   reach   much

5. Once, I saw it eat a ____peach____ .   that   ship   (peach)

6. At times it eats from its ____dish____ .   wish   (dish)   swish

7. Then, it naps in the ____shade____ .   fresh   shut   (shade)

▶ Find **two words from the list above that begin with ch, wh, th, and sh. Print them on the lines beside the correct consonant digraph.**

8. **ch**	chop	9. **th**	then
	chimp/check		these/that
10. **wh**	which	11. **sh**	ship
	what/white		shut/shade

Consonant digraphs sh, th, wh, ch   **119**

FOCUS ON ALL LEARNERS

ESL/ELL ENGLISH LANGUAGE LEARNERS

Practice pronunciation of digraphs while teaching spelling and recognition of lesson vocabulary.

- Assess English language learners' ability to hear the differences among target and similar sounds with a "Same or Different" activity. Use word pairs, such as *this, dish; three, thread; ten, them,* and so on.

- Discuss the rule on page 119; offer examples and invite children to supply additional words containing each digraph.

- Say the rhyme; have children repeat. Ask them to find and underline target words on their own; have volunteers identify and children pronounce the words together to confirm.

KINESTHETIC/AUDITORY LEARNERS

Materials: one index card per child, marker

Write *th, sh, wh,* or *ch* on each card. Invite children to stand up with their cards when they hear words with their digraphs. Read the words *that, while, chip, wish, rich, white, shiny, these, cheese, fresh, wheat, thimble, crush, chip, teeth, wheel.*

▶ Fill in the bubble beside the word that will finish each sentence. Print it on the line.

1. Chip and I didn't know _____where_____ to go.
   - ● where
   - ○ what

2. We decided to go to the mall to _____shop_____.
   - ○ chop
   - ● shop

3. They sell everything _____there_____.
   - ○ this
   - ● there

4. There was so _____much_____ to choose from.
   - ○ catch
   - ● much

5. I couldn't decide _____what_____ I wanted most.
   - ● what
   - ○ who

6. Then, I saw some model _____ship_____ kits.
   - ○ shirt
   - ● ship

7. _____That_____ was what I wanted most.
   - ○ When
   - ● That

8. I _____chose_____ a clipper ship to make.
   - ● chose
   - ○ chair

9. _____Chip_____ chose a spaceship kit.
   - ○ Choose
   - ● Chip

10. _____Then_____, we had lunch.
    - ● Then
    - ○ That

 Where do you think Chip bought his model kit?

 Say one of the words in the list. Have your child name the other words that begin with the same sound.

120 Consonant digraphs sh, th, wh, ch: High-frequency words, critical thinking

CURRICULUM CONNECTIONS

SPELLING
Pretest the following spelling words. Use the sentences as samples.
1. **shoe** Is this the left **shoe**?
2. **thorn** A **thorn** is very sharp.
3. **wheel** Turn the **wheel** three times.
4. **chair** I like this rocking **chair**.
5. **knock** Did you **knock** on the door?
6. **write** Can you **write** a story?

WRITING
Ask children to share their experiences watching animals at a zoo. Have them write descriptions of unusual animals they have seen. Confer with children about their spelling of words with consonant digraphs.

SCIENCE
Provide books in which children can read about different kinds of seashells and the animals who live in them. Display shell samples if possible.

TECHNOLOGY **AstroWord** Consonant Blends and Digraphs

VISUAL LEARNERS GROUPS
Materials: coat hangers, string, construction paper, tape
Invite children to make mobiles with *sh, th, wh,* and *ch* words. On construction paper squares, have them write words with digraphs and then illustrate them on the back. Tape string to each card and tie the cards to the hangers.

CHALLENGE
Invite pairs of children to play "ping-pong digraphs." Have children take turns naming a word that begins or ends with a certain digraph until one of the players can't think of a new word.

EXTRA SUPPORT/INTERVENTION
Materials: Phonics Word Cards, Set 1: Consonant Digraph words (246–256)
Have children sort and read first one side of the cards and then the other. Words might be sorted by matching digraphs or by initial or final digraphs. See Daily Phonics Practice, pages 251–252.

Integrating Phonics and Reading

Guided Reading
Have children read the title and look at the cover. Ask them what they think Dragon might like for lunch.
First Reading Have children review the things Dragon ate.
Second Reading Write the words *fish, lunch, sandwich, teeth,* and *toothbrush* on the board. Have children say each word, circle the consonant digraph, and find the word in the story.

Comprehension
Ask children these questions:
- What happened each time Dragon finished eating something? Why do you think this happened? *Recall/Sequence/Personal Response*
  Were you surprised by what Dragon did at the end? Explain. *Reflective Analysis/Personal Response*

ESL/ELL **English Language Learners**
Point out the two apostrophes on the cover. Explain that the first apostrophe tells that the lunch belongs to Dragon. The other apostrophe is used for the shortened form of *let us.*

Consonant Digraphs
sh, th, wh, ch, ck

Skill Focus

Children will

★ identify the consonant digraph *ck*.

★ distinguish among the digraphs *sh, th, wh, ch,* and *ck*.

★ read and write words with consonant digraphs.

Teach

Phonemic Awareness: Phoneme Isolation
Say this tongue twister: *How much wood would a woodchuck chuck if a woodchuck could chuck wood?* Repeat and invite children to raise their hand each time they hear hard *c,* or /k/.

Sound to Symbol Write *woodchuck* and *chuck* on the board. Say each word and underline *ch*. Remind children that *ch* is a consonant digraph. Ask a volunteer to review the definition of a consonant digraph. (*two consonants that together stand for one sound*) Say the words again. Ask children what two consonants in each word stand for /k/. (*ck*) Explain that *ck* is a consonant digraph. Then, write these pairs of words on the board: *duck, lick; rich, chop; shell, wish; what, when; thing, them.* Have volunteers go to the board, read a pair of words, and underline the digraphs in each one.

Practice and Apply

Sound to Symbol With children, say the picture names on page 121. Suggest children repeat the names to themselves as they circle the correct consonant digraph.

Writing Read the directions on page 122. Help children find the hidden pictures, if necessary. Remind them that after they write the words on the lines, they should circle the consonant digraph in each one. Tell them that they may write the words in any order.

Reading Use *How the Chick Tricked the Fox,* MCP Phonics and Reading Super Skills Library 1, Level B, to reinforce reading words with consonant digraphs.

Name _____

▶ **Say** the name of each picture. **Circle** the consonant digraph you hear.

#	Picture	Digraphs
1.	shoe	th, (sh), ck, ch, wh
2.	thirteen	(th), sh, ck, ch, wh
3.	clock	th, sh, (ck), ch, wh
4.	cherry	th, sh, ck, (ch), wh
5.	whale	th, sh, ck, ch, (wh)
6.	thumb	(th), sh, ck, ch, wh
7.	shell	th, (sh), ck, ch, wh
8.	duck	th, sh, (ck), ch, wh
9.	chair	th, sh, ck, (ch), wh
10.	truck	th, sh, (ck), ch, wh
11.	wheat	th, sh, ck, ch, (wh)
12.	ship	th, (sh), ck, ch, wh
13.	thorn	(th), sh, ck, ch, wh
14.	cheese	th, sh, ck, (ch), wh
15.	thimble	(th), sh, ck, ch, wh
16.	wheel	th, sh, ck, ch, (wh)

Consonant digraphs sh, th, wh, ch, ck   **121**

FOCUS ON ALL LEARNERS

ESL/ELL **ENGLISH LANGUAGE LEARNERS**
Provide practice for English language learners to write words that contain consonant digraphs.

Materials: Phonics Picture Cards (154–169)

• Display picture cards face up in a grid. Invite children to sort the cards into piles according to their beginning digraph sounds.

• After reviewing the picture cards, have children complete the activity on page 121, in pairs or individually.

• Modify the hidden picture activity on page 122 by having children first circle the digraphs and then read the words. If necessary, assist children as they look for the hidden pictures.

KINESTHETIC LEARNERS GROUPS

Materials: modeling clay

Invite each child to make a clay model of one object whose name contains a consonant digraph. Gather the items on a table and ask children, during learning center times, to sort the items into five categories: *sh, th, ch, wh,* and *ck*. Children can get ideas for the objects from the pictures on their pages.

Read the words in the box and circle the hidden pictures.
Write the words on the lines. Circle the consonant digraph
in each word.

| whale | wheel | thumb | clock | truck | duck |
| fish | peach | chair | thimble | shell | shoe |

1. w(h)ale
2. du(ck)
3. (sh)ell
4. tru(ck)
5. (th)imble
6. clo(ck)
7. (ch)air
8. (th)umb
9. pea(ch)
10. w(h)eel
11. fi(sh)
12. (sh)oe

Answers may be written in any order.

 HOME Have your child find the words with
the same consonant digraphs.

122   Review digraphs sh, th, wh, ch, ck

CURRICULUM CONNECTIONS

SPELLING

Copy and distribute to children the words *shoe,
thorn, wheel, chair, knock,* and *write* from the
unit spelling list. Have children recite and spell
the words orally together, circle the consonant
digraphs, and take the words home to practice.

ART

Extend the hidden-picture theme to include the
use of words themselves as part of a scene. Have
children choose a word with a consonant digraph,
such as *whale* or *truck,* and incorporate the letters
into the drawing. The word *whale* might be printed
in capital letters to form the outline of a whale.
The letters of *truck* can be written in the shape of
the body of a truck or inside one of the wheels.

TECHNOLOGY **AstroWord** Consonant Blends
and Digraphs

AUDITORY/VISUAL LEARNERS *INDIVIDUAL*

Print *cat* on the chalkboard. Show children how this word becomes
chat by adding an *h.* List the following words: *case, heat, he, hair, hem,
hat, hen, hop, tank, sell,* and *hip.* Invite children to change each one to
form a word that begins with one of the digraphs *sh, ch, wh,* and *th.*

CHALLENGE

Invite children to draw hidden pictures that use words containing
consonant digraphs. Suggest that they choose four items that can be
easily drawn and hide them in an illustration of a jungle. Have children
share their drawings with several partners.

EXTRA SUPPORT/INTERVENTION

Materials: two index cards per child

Have children write *ch* on one card and *ck* on the other. As you recite a
list of words, have them hold up the card that shows which digraph
each word contains. Use the words *cheese, truck, lick, lunch, back,
each, much, sick, luck, crack, crunch, clock, inch, pinch, pick, reach,
rack,* and *ranch.* See Daily Phonics Practice, pages 251–252.

Integrating Phonics and Reading

Guided Reading

Have children read the title and
look at the illustration. Discuss the
possible significance of the colors
that the illustrator chose.

First Reading Have children use the story and
illustrations to point out the fox's three wishes.
Second Reading Make five columns on the
board, labeled *sh, th, wh, ch,* and *ck.* Invite
children to write words from the story in the
appropriate column and use each in a sentence.

Comprehension

After reading, ask the following questions:
• How did the chick trick the fox? *Recall/
Summarize*
• Why do you think the chick was able to trick the
fox? *Reflective Analysis/Personal Response*
ESL/ELL **English Language Learners**
Some children may need help understanding
the concept behind the chick's trick—explain
the difference between making a wish and
making a wish come true.

Consonant Digraph kn

Skill Focus

Children will

★ identify the consonant digraph *kn*.

★ read and write words with the digraph *kn* in context.

ESL/ELL Most English language learners will be familiar with voiced and unvoiced sounds and silent letters. Practice *kn* orally with native speakers of Chinese, Vietnamese, and Spanish.

Teach

Phonological Awareness: Rhyme Say the word *nap*. Ask children what sound they hear at the beginning of the word. (/n/) Tell children you are going to say several words and they are to say rhyming words that begin with /n/: *wife (knife); grow (know); sock (knock); bit (knit).*

Sound to Symbol Explain that /n/ heard at the beginning of the rhyming words they identified is actually a consonant digraph. Have a volunteer review the definition of a consonant digraph. Then, write *knife, know, knock,* and *knit* on the board. Circle *kn* in each word and again tell children that *kn* is a consonant digraph. Say the words and ask children which letter is silent. (*k*)

Practice and Apply

Sound to Symbol Read the rhyme on page 123. Have children repeat the rhyme. Invite volunteers to identify words that have the *kn* digraph, write them on the board, circle the digraph, and spell the word aloud.

Read the rule and the directions to the first activity on page 123. Have children look at each picture and then say its name. Ask what digraph each picture name begins with. Be sure children understand that each item has two answers.

Writing Remind children that the answers to the riddles at the bottom of page 123 can be found in the word box. For page 124, explain that they should first circle the answer and then say it in the sentence. You may want to do item 9 orally to be sure children recognize they are to write rhyming words that begin with *kn*.

Reading Use *Flip's Trick,* MCP Phonics and Reading Super Skills Library 1, Level B, to provide children with practice in reading words with consonant digraph *kn*.

Picture-Text Match

Name _____

We garden for hours.
We know how to plant seeds.
We kneel to plant flowers.
We kneel to pull weeds.

▶ Read **each sentence.** Find **the picture it tells about.** Write **the sentence letter under the picture.**

> **RULE**
> You can hear the consonant digraph *kn* in *kneel* and *knees.*

1.
knot   a

   a. John has a knot in the rope.
   b. I know what is in the box.
   c. Joan turned the knob.

knob   c

2.
knocks   c

   a. Theo will knock down the pile.
   b. Mom cut it with a knife.
   c. She knocks on the door.

knife   b

3.
knight   a

   a. The knight wore armor.
   b. Tad's knee needs a patch.
   c. Grandma likes to knit.

knit   c

▶ Find **a word in the box that answers each riddle.** Print **it on the line.**

4. Something that can cut   _____knife_____

5. Someone who wore armor   _____knight_____

6. Something you can tie   _____knot_____

> knife
> knot
> knight

Consonant digraph kn   **123**

FOCUS ON ALL LEARNERS

ESL/ELL ENGLISH LANGUAGE LEARNERS

Use pages 123–124 to affirm English language learners' progress with recognition and spelling of *kn* words.

- Have children read the directions for page 123 to the group; invite a volunteer to explain them in his or her own words. Have children complete items on the page individually.

- Pair children to complete the sentences at the top of page 124, then model items 9 through 11 orally and on the board. Encourage children to complete the page independently, whenever possible.

- Check work together to assess children's understanding of concepts.

KINESTHETIC LEARNERS

Materials: 15 one-inch paper squares for each two children

On their squares, have each set of partners print the letters *k, k, n, n, e, e, o, w, n, t, b, i, f, g, h.* Invite children to form digraph *kn* words with the letters and keep a list of the words they make. Possible answers might include *knee, know, knot, knob, knife,* and *knight.*

▶ Circle the word that will finish each sentence.
Print it on the line.

1. I _____know_____ how to do many things. (know) knot

2. I can spread butter with a ____knife____. knot (knife)

3. I can touch my ____knees____ to my chin. (knees) knew

4. I can tie ____knots____. (knots) knits

5. I can turn the ____knob____ of a door. knee (knob)

6. I can read about ____knights____. know (knights)

7. I can ____knit____ a sweater. (knit) knife

8. I've ____known____ how to do these knit (known)
   things for a long time.

▶ Think of a word that begins with **kn** and rhymes with
each word. Print the word on the line.

9.	snow	10.	block	11.	wife
	know		knock		knife
12.	blew	13.	see	14.	hot
	knew		knee		knot
15.	own	16.	sit	17.	sob
	known		knit		knob

Ask your child to make up sentences
using the *kn* words on the page.

124 Consonant digraph kn

CURRICULUM CONNECTIONS

SPELLING

Print the following incomplete spelling words on the board and have children write them on paper filling in the correct consonant digraphs: __eel, __ite, __orn, __air, __oe, __o__. Ask volunteers to then complete the words *wheel, write, thorn, chair, shoe,* and *knock* on the board as classmates check the spellings.

WRITING

Invite children to choose specific skills or activities that they know how to do and to write about them. Their topics might include sports, hobbies, and musical abilities. Children can detail what they know and how they learned it.

HEALTH

Reread the rhyme on page 123 and talk about how the people in the illustration are kneeling to do work. Discuss knees and how we use them. Ask questions such as: *Why do football and basketball players wear pads over their knees? What do knees enable us to do with our bodies?*

TECHNOLOGY **AstroWord** Consonant Blends and Digraphs

AUDITORY/VISUAL LEARNERS GROUPS

Materials: Phonics Word Cards, Set 2: *kn* words (208–215)

Have volunteers take turns choosing a word card at random and giving a clue for one word on the card. Clues can be sentences with the *kn* word missing or word meanings. Display the word cards after the answers are guessed.

CHALLENGE

Ask children to spell the initial *kn* words that sound the same as *no, new, not,* and *night. (know, knew, knot, knight)* Have children use the homophone pairs in sentences that show they know the meaning of each word.

EXTRA SUPPORT/INTERVENTION

Pantomime the meaning of *knock, kneel,* and *knit.* When children guess correctly, have a volunteer write the word on the board, underlining *kn.* Then, write the different verb forms of *know (know, knows, knew, known).* Work as a group to compose sentences for each form. See Daily Phonics Practice, pages 251–252.

Integrating Phonics and Reading

Guided Reading
Have children read the title and look at the cover. Encourage them to identify Flip and predict what tricks Flip can do.
First Reading Ask children to explain what Flip's favorite trick is.
Second Reading Have children find and read aloud sentences with the words *know* and *knows.*
Comprehension
Ask children these questions:
• Do you think Flip can do a million tricks? Explain. *Reflective Analysis/Personal Response*
• What makes Flip's Trick a funny story? *Reflective Analysis/Make Judgments*
ESL/ELL **English Language Learners**
Focus on the text on page 9, *So much for being nice.* Encourage children to talk about how Tim feels, and ask them to think of another way Tim could say what he means.

Consonant Digraph wr

Skill Focus

Children will

★ identify the consonant digraph *wr.*

★ read and write words with the digraph *wr* in context.

★ recognize and read a high-frequency word.

ESL/ELL Some English language learners may experience difficulty if they do not differentiate /r/ and /l/. Spanish and Tagalog speakers who trill initial *r* may need additional practice.

Teach

Phonemic Awareness: Phoneme Categorization Say the following three words and ask children which words begin with the same sound: *wrist, when, wrong. (wrist, wrong)* Then, ask children to identify the sound they hear at the beginning of those words. *(/r/)*

Sound to Symbol Write the words *wrist* and *wrong* on the board. Point to each word as you say it aloud. Explain that each word begins with the consonant digraph *wr.* Ask what sound the digraph stands for. *(/r/)* Have volunteers circle the digraph. Ask which letter of the digraph is silent. *(the first letter, w)* Then, ask what other digraph has a silent first letter. *(kn)*

Practice and Apply

Sound to Symbol Read the rhyme on page 125 as children follow along. Then, have a volunteer read it aloud. Tell children to raise their hand each time they recognize a word that begins with the consonant digraph *wr. (wren, wreath, wren's, wrong)*

Read the rule at the top of the page. Invite volunteers to tell the definition of a digraph. Then, have children read the words in the box, identifying the digraph.

Writing Read the directions on page 125 and have a volunteer restate them. Complete item 1 as a group before children work on the remainder of the sentences. Children will have the opportunity to read the high-frequency word *your.* For page 126, remind children that the answers to the riddles can be found in the word box at the top of the page.

Reading Use *Wrong Way Robot,* MCP Phonics and Reading Super Skills Library 1, Level B, to help children practice reading the digraph *wr.*

Name _____

A busy wren high on a wreath,
Sang to children playing beneath.
They tried to copy the wren's song.
They sang the tune, but got it wrong.

▶ Find the word in the box that will finish each sentence. Print it on the line.

RULE
You can hear the consonant digraph **wr** in **wriggles** and **wren.**

wren	wreck	wrap	wrestle	write
wrist	wrench	wrecker	wrong	wriggle

1. To move around is to _____wriggle_____.

2. The opposite of **right** is _____wrong_____.

3. A small bird is a _____wren_____.

4. A thing that is ruined is a _____wreck_____.

5. To hide a gift in paper is to _____wrap_____ it.

6. When you put a story on paper, you _____write_____.

7. Your _____wrist_____ holds your hand to your arm.

8. A truck that clears away wrecks is a _____wrecker_____.

9. A kind of tool is a _____wrench_____.

10. One way to fight is to _____wrestle_____.

Consonant digraph wr: High-frequency words   **125**

FOCUS ON ALL LEARNERS

ESL/ELL **ENGLISH LANGUAGE LEARNERS**

Have English language learners practice writing and using digraphs in context.

• Read the activity directions aloud; ask children to complete items 1 through 5 on page 125 with a partner, and then complete the page independently.

• Have children read their sentences aloud to their partners and check their work as you informally evaluate pronunciation.

• On page 126, rephrase riddles as questions, such as *Which word names a useful tool that can fix things?* Have children complete the page to confirm understanding of lesson vocabulary. Review together.

KINESTHETIC LEARNERS

Materials: index cards, marker

Play charades with *wr* words. Write these words on cards and have volunteers choose one to pantomime for the class: *wrinkle, write, wreck, wrestle, wriggle, wrong,* and *wren.* Suggest that they use partners when it would be helpful.

▶ Find a word in the box that answers each riddle. Print it on the line.

wren	wrecker	wriggle	wrong	wrist
wrench	wreath	writer	wristwatch	wrinkle

1. I am a useful tool.
   I can fix things.
   What am I?

   _____wrench_____

2. I am the opposite of **right**.
   I rhyme with **song**.
   What am I?

   _____wrong_____

3. I can fly.
   I like to sing.
   What am I?

   _____wren_____

4. I am round and pretty.
   You can hang me up.
   What am I?

   _____wreath_____

5. I am next to a hand.
   I can twist and bend.
   What am I?

   _____wrist_____

6. I tell time.
   People wear me on their wrist.
   What am I?

   _____wristwatch_____

7. I am a big truck.
   I tow things away.
   What am I?

   _____wrecker_____

8. I write stories. They can be
   real or make-believe.
   What am I?

   _____writer_____

9. I am a fold in a dress.
   I am a crease in a face.
   What am I?

   _____wrinkle_____

10. I am another word for **squirm**.
    I rhyme with **giggle**.
    What am I?

    _____wriggle_____

HOME Ask your child to write sentences for two of the words on this page.

CURRICULUM CONNECTIONS

SPELLING

Have children write the spelling word that is something you do with a pencil (*write*); something you wear (*shoe*); something to sit on (*chair*); something round (*wheel*); something sharp (*thorn*); and a sound (*knock*).

SOCIAL STUDIES

Invite a writer or reporter from a local newspaper to speak to the class about his or her job. Read an article by the writer beforehand, if possible. Also, have children list questions they would like to ask, such as *What do you like to write about? Do you use a typewriter or a computer? What does it mean to "wrap up" a story?* Circle any *wr* words in the list.

TECHNOLOGY **AstroWord** Consonant Blends and Digraphs

AUDITORY/VISUAL LEARNERS GROUPS

Materials: newspapers, scissors, glue

Instruct children to hunt through newspapers for words beginning with *r* and *wr* and to cut out and glue five of the words on paper. Have children take turns writing one of their words on the board without the initial letter(s). Classmates can say the word using /r/ and show how to spell the initial sound.

CHALLENGE

Have children use clues like the ones on pages 125 and 126 to make two-word crossword puzzles for digraph *wr* words. Duplicate completed puzzles for classmates to solve.

EXTRA SUPPORT/INTERVENTION

Materials: Phonics Word Cards, Set 2: *wr* words (216–222); red crayons

Have each child choose one word card and write both words from the card on paper, tracing the *wr* digraphs in red. Have children read the words, trade cards with each other, and repeat the activity. See Daily Phonics Practice, pages 251–252.

Integrating Phonics and Reading

Guided Reading
Have children read the chapter titles and preview the illustrations. Ask them what the book might be about.
First Reading Using the book, encourage children to tell about some of the problems Katy has with her robot.
Second Reading Have children write the word *wrong,* circling the initial digraph. Ask children to find other words in the story that begin with /r/ and to identify how /r/ is spelled.
Comprehension
Ask children these questions:
• What happened when Katy took Plato to school? *Recall/Cause and Effect*
• What title would you have chosen for this story? Explain your answer. *Reflective Analysis/Personal Response*
ESL/ELL English Language Learners
Write the title on the board with the arrow around *wrong way.* Review what an arrow like this means on a street sign. Then, ask children what the title might mean.

High-Frequency Words

Skill Focus

Children will

★ recognize and read the high-frequency words *your, believe, bought, two, once, new.*

★ use high-frequency words to complete sentences.

Teach

Analyze Words Write these words on the board: *your, believe, bought, two, once, new.*

- Point to each word and read it aloud. Then, have children repeat each word after you.

- Slowly say each word again, pointing to the letters. Encourage children to listen for the consonant and vowel sounds in the word. Have children again say each word, blending the sounds.

- Help children associate the sounds they hear in the word with a more familiar word. You may wish to put these words on a class Word Wall so that children can use words they learn to find similar spelling patterns and phonemic elements in new words.

Read Words in Context Write the following sentences on the board. Invite volunteers to read the sentences and underline the high-frequency words. Then, have children read the sentences together.

- **I believe you bought two plants.**
- **Begin a new garden with your plants.**
- **Once you plant them, watch them grow.**

Practice and Apply

Write Words Read the directions on page 127. Remind children to read the sentence with their word choice in place to be sure that the sentence makes sense. Then, read the directions for page 128. Make sure children understand how the shapes of the letters can help them. Also suggest that they use strategies they have learned to associate sounds with letters and blend words to help them read. Encourage them to work with a partner to complete Checking Up.

Reading You may wish to use *Shell Shopping,* MCP Phonics and Reading Library, High Frequency Word Collection, Level B, to help children practice recognizing and reading high-frequency words in the context of a story.

Name _____

▶ Complete each sentence with one of the words in the box. Write the word on the line.

your	two	believe
once	bought	new

1. Many people ____believe____ that animals have feelings.

2. When ____your____ dog is happy, it will wag its tail.

3. Dolphins seem to enjoy learning ____new____ tricks.

4. Many pet birds are ____bought____ and sold in pairs.

5. Having ____two____ parakeets will keep them from being lonely.

6. A gorilla ____once____ cared lovingly for a kitten.

7. How do ____your____ pets show their feelings?

High-frequency words   **127**

FOCUS ON ALL LEARNERS

ESL/ELL ENGLISH LANGUAGE LEARNERS

Materials: high-frequency word cards

Confirm that English language learners can recognize and pronounce the high-frequency words.

- Hold up the cards, one at a time, and pronounce each word slowly. Have children repeat the words and use them in sentences.

- Review the names of the animals on page 127. Use pictures or drawings, whenever necessary, to help children understand the animals named.

- Then, have children work in pairs to read aloud and complete the sentences on page 127.

KINESTHETIC/AUDITORY LEARNERS

Materials: construction paper, yarn, glue

Assign one high-frequency word to each child. Have children print their words in large letters on construction paper. Then, have them glue pieces of yarn on the letters. Encourage children to trace the words as they say each word aloud. Next, have children make up sentences that include high-frequency words.

► Unscramble the letters to write the words. The word shapes will help you print the words.

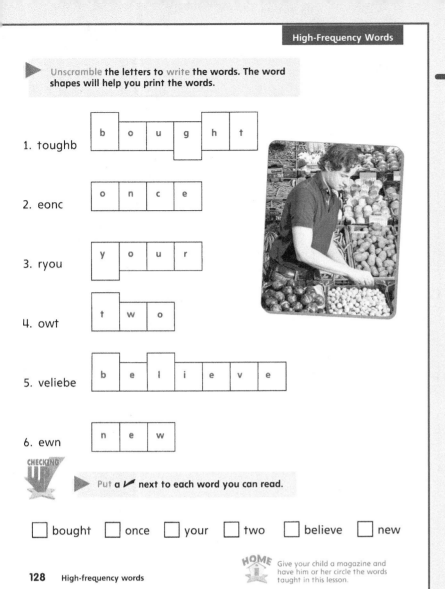

1. toughb b o u g h t

2. eonc o n c e

3. ryou y o u r

4. owt t w o

5. veliebe b e l i e v e

6. ewn n e w

CHECKING

► Put a ✔ next to each word you can read.

☐ bought ☐ once ☐ your ☐ two ☐ believe ☐ new

128 High-frequency words

HOME
Give your child a magazine and have him or her circle the words taught in this lesson.

128

CURRICULUM CONNECTIONS

LANGUAGE ARTS

Challenge children to find two high-frequency words whose letters can be rearranged to form new words. Explain that all of the letters in the original words must be used to make the new word. After children have discovered the words, have them write one sentence for each pair of words. (*The word pairs are* once *and* cone *and* two *and* tow.)

HEALTH

Discuss the different ways in which people show their feelings. For example, you might ask children how someone might act who feels the following way: *happy, sad, shy, excited, nervous.*

VISUAL LEARNERS *INDIVIDUAL*

Have children choose three of the high-frequency words and write a sentence for each one. Then, have them rewrite the sentences, omitting the high-frequency words. Have children exchange papers and see if they can finish the sentence with the correct word.

CHALLENGE

Have children work in pairs to make a crossword puzzle using as many of the high-frequency words as possible. Explain that they should start by putting the words together in patterns that work for a puzzle. Then, they should write the meanings. When they have finished, each pair can make a new copy of their puzzle and challenge others to fill it in.

EXTRA SUPPORT/INTERVENTION

Write the high-frequency words on the board. Point to each one and have children say it. Then, have children make up clues for each word. For example, for *two*, someone might say, "I'm thinking of a word that means more than one." Classmates can guess the answer.

Integrating Phonics and Reading

Guided Reading
Have children read the title and look at the illustration. Invite them to give reasons why people go shopping.
First Reading Have children tell why the hermit crab went shopping.
Second Reading Have children find and read the sentence that explains what Hermit Crab needed and the sentence that tells what Hermit Crab did after she walked out of her old shell.
Comprehension
After reading, ask children the following questions:
• Why did Hermit Crab have problems finding a new shell? *Recall/Summarize*
• Which kind of shell did Hermit Crab choose? Why do you think she chose it? *Reflective Analysis/Picture Clues, Compare*
ESL/ELL English Language Learners
Clarify for children that the pronoun *she* refers to Hermit Crab and the pronoun *it* refers to the shell.

Phonics and Reading / Phonics and Writing

Review Consonant Digraphs

Skill Focus

Children will

★ read words with consonant digraphs *sh, th, wh, ch, ck, kn,* and *wr* in context.

★ write words with consonant digraphs to finish sentences about a story.

★ build words with consonant digraphs.

Teach

Phonemic Awareness: Phoneme Categorization Display the following Phonics Picture Cards: *whale* (157), *wheel* (159), and *fish* (163). Have volunteers name each picture. Ask children which picture names begin with the same sound. (*whale, wheel*) Remind children that the beginning sound is a consonant digraph. Invite a volunteer to explain what a consonant digraph is.

Sound to Symbol Write *whale* on the board. Ask a volunteer to read the word and underline the digraph. Then, write the following words: *shoe, thing, chip, knife, wrist,* and *back.* Point to each word and have children say it aloud. Invite volunteers to go to the board, say the word, identify the consonant digraph, and underline it.

Practice and Apply

Phonics and Reading Read the story on page 129 aloud. Have children identify words with consonant digraphs. Then, have them complete the sentences.

Critical Thinking Discuss Talk About It. Children should note that the story tells them that a chipmunk wriggles its nose as it turns a nut over and over with its paws.

Phonics and Writing For page 130, remind children that the consonant digraph they write must make a real word. Tell them there is an extra digraph in each box that does not form a word.

Reading Use *Rush, Rush, Rush,* MCP Phonics and Reading Super Skills Library 1, Level B, to review reading words with consonant digraphs in context.

Name _____

 Read **the story.** Use **a word from the story to finish each sentence.** Print **the word on the line.**

Chipmunks

Chipmunks have brown fur with black-and-white stripes. These colors help the chipmunk blend in with trees and bushes. You might not even see or hear them unless they move, and they can move fast.

The chipmunk is known to build its den or home under rocks or bushes. This is where it stores nuts and seeds. This food will keep the chipmunk from going hungry during the winter.

Chipmunks are fun to watch. You may have seen one wriggle its nose as it turns a nut over and over with its paws. Chipmunks carry nuts and other food in their cheek pouches. A chipmunk with bulging cheeks is really cute!

1. This story is about _____chipmunks_____ .

2. Chipmunks build their dens under rocks or _____bushes_____ .

3. Their fur has black-and- _____white_____ stripes.

4. The chipmunk can _____wriggle_____ its nose.

 Why might a chipmunk be fun to watch?

Review digraphs: Critical thinking   **129**

FOCUS ON ALL LEARNERS

ESL/ELL ENGLISH LANGUAGE LEARNERS

Materials: books about woodland creatures

Practice lesson objectives by having English language learners read the story and complete page 129.

• Read the story in small groups. Ask children to summarize in their own words what they read. Prompt as needed.

• Discuss the Talk About It question in their groups.

• Have children complete items 1 through 4 with partners; have them read the completed sentences to one another.

• With English language learners who need additional support, review the story one-on-one.

AUDITORY/VISUAL LEARNERS

Materials: bingo cards with sixteen spaces, markers

Have children write *wh, th, sh,* and *ch* four times each on their cards. Say the words: *thumb, wheel, dish, chipmunk, thirty, pouch, white, bush, shell, chase, wheat, mother, whiskers, shy, peach, thorn.* Have children mark each digraph heard. Start again when a child marks four in a row and yells *bingo!*

Phonics & Writing

Use a digraph tile to finish each of the words below. Write the digraphs on the lines.

wh	ck	ch	kn

1. __ch__ irp
2. __wh__ ale
3. __kn__ ot

th	sh	wr	ck

4. flo __ck__
5. tee __th__
6. swi __sh__

wr	th	ch	kn

7. __kn__ ees
8. __wr__ ench
9. __th__ umb

ck	sh	wh	ch

10. bun __ch__
11. clo __ck__
12. fi __sh__

▶ Write sentences for two of the words you made.

_____

_____

130   Review digraphs

HOME Work with your child to make a word ladder beginning or ending with any of the words he or she made.

CURRICULUM CONNECTIONS

SPELLING
You may wish to posttest the following words, using the sample sentences as needed.
1. **thorn**   The **thorn** tore my jeans.
2. **chair**   We need an extra **chair**.
3. **write**   Did you **write** to your cousin?
4. **wheel**   The **wheel** on my bike is wobbling.
5. **shoe**   Please help me find my left **shoe**.
6. **knock**   Did you **knock** on the door?

SCIENCE
With children, make an animal chart with headings such as *Name of Animal, What It Eats, What Sound It Makes, Where It Sleeps,* and *How It Acts.* Use information about chipmunks from page 129. Add other animals children know well such as hamsters, horses, and birds.

TECHNOLOGY   **AstroWord** Consonant Blends and Digraphs

AUDITORY/KINESTHETIC LEARNERS   GROUPS
Materials: egg carton, paper clips

Write the following digraphs two times each inside the bottom half of an egg carton: *kn, wr, sh, th, wh, ch.* Have children take turns dropping a paper clip into the carton. Then, they say a word that has the digraph where the clip landed and use the word in a sentence.

CHALLENGE
Talk with children about chipmunks. Discuss favorite cartoon chipmunks they have seen. Invite them to create a cartoon chipmunk of their own. Have them draw the picture, name the animal, and write down some things the chipmunk might say.

EXTRA SUPPORT/INTERVENTION
Read the story on page 129 with children. Have children circle words with consonant digraphs and read the words and the sentences containing them. See Daily Phonics Practice, pages 251–252.

Integrating Phonics and Reading

Guided Reading
Have children read the title and look at the picture. Ask them why this family might be rushing.
First Reading Ask children to explain why the family was rushing.
Second Reading Invite children to find picture names in the story that include consonant digraphs.

Comprehension
After reading, ask children the following questions:
• What were some of the things the family did to get ready for Grandmother? *Recall/Summarize*
• How do you think the children felt about all of the rushing? *Reflective Analysis/Personal Response*

ESL/ELL English Language Learners
Invite children to find illustrations in the story that contain consonant digraphs. List the words on the board and and have children circle the digraphs.

Sound of ar

Skill Focus

Children will

★ identify the sound of *ar* in words.

★ read and write *ar* words in context.

★ write rhyming words with the sound of *ar*.

★ recognize and read high-frequency words.

ESL/ELL Speakers of Hmong or Vietnamese may clip the *r* and pronounce a sound similar to short *o*. Practice and reinforce the sound of *ar* in isolation with these children.

Teach

Phonological Awareness: Rhyme Tell children that you are going to say three words and they are to tell you how the words are alike: *cart, dart, part.* (*The three words rhyme.*) Ask children to suggest another word that rhymes with the three words. (*start, mart, chart, tart*)

Sound to Symbol Write *cart, dart,* and *part* on the board. Point to each word and have children read it aloud. Circle the letters *ar* in each word. Explain that the *r* after the *a* gives the vowel a different sound that is neither a short nor a long *a*.

Read Words in Sentences Write this sentence on the board.

   • **Marty parks his car by the barn.**

Invite a volunteer to read the sentence aloud and then circle the letters *ar* in the appropriate words.

Practice and Apply

Sound to Symbol Read the rhyme on page 131. Then, have children read it together. Invite volunteers to name the words that have the same sound of *ar* as in *cart.* (*hard, start, largest, tart*)

Blend Phonemes Read the rule on page 131. Have volunteers restate it in their own words. Then, invite children to say the words in the boxes on pages 131-132, blending together the phonemes. Children will have the opportunity to read the high-frequency words *two* and *believe.*

Writing For both pages, remind children to read the entire sentence with their answer choice to make sure it makes sense. For the bottom of page 132, explain that there may be more than three rhyming words for items 10 and 11.

Reading You may wish to use *The Not-So-Scary Scarecrow,* MCP Phonics and Reading Super Skills Library 2, Level B, to reinforce the sound of *ar.*

Name _____

So many strawberries to pick,
It's hard to know where to start!
Let's pick the largest ones
And bake them in a tart.

▶ Find **the word in the box that will finish each sentence.** Print it on the line.

> **RULE**
> An **r** after a vowel makes the vowel sound different from the usual short or long sound. You can hear the **ar** sound in **hard, start,** and **largest.**

apart	star	hard	part	car
hardly	start	large	jars	

1. I picked out a new model _____car_____ kit.

2. I got two _____jars_____ of paint, too.

3. I could hardly wait to _____start_____ on it.

4. I used glue so the car wouldn't fall _____apart_____.

5. There were small parts and _____large_____ parts.

6. The tires were _____hard_____ to fit, but I did it.

7. I stuck _____star_____ stickers on the sides.

8. I could _____hardly_____ believe it when it was done.

9. The best _____part_____ was showing it to my friends.

Words with ar: High-frequency words   **131**

FOCUS ON ALL LEARNERS

ESL/ELL ENGLISH LANGUAGE LEARNERS

Practice rhyming words that contain the target sound of *ar.*

• Have children read the words in the boxes on page 132.

• Review the rule for *ar* on page 131. Say the sound of *ar* for children. Point out the difference between this sound and the long and short sounds of *a.*

• Invite volunteers to suggest words that contain the sound of *ar* and rhyme with the words in the boxes. Write them on the board. Model pronunciation and have children repeat.

• With children, read aloud each sentence on page 132. Ask children to raise their hand when they know the rhyming word that will complete the blank. Then, have them reread the sentences with the answer they chose to see if it makes sense.

AUDITORY/VISUAL LEARNERS

Materials: index cards, marker

Write scrambled *ar* words on index cards. Words might include *rtas* (star), *arj* (jar), *trast* (start), and *drac* (card). Stack the cards face down. Invite volunteers to pick cards, unscramble the words, print them on the board, and read them.

▶ Finish **each sentence. Use a word that** rhymes **with the word beside the sentence. Print** it on the line.

1. A shark is a very ____smart____ animal.

2. It lives in the deep, ____dark____ part of the ocean.

3. It can grow to be very ____large____ .

4. A shark's teeth are very ____sharp____ .

5. It has no problem tearing food ____apart____ .

6. I live ____far____ from the ocean.

7. I like to visit the animal ____park____ .

8. It is not far from my house by ____car____ .

9. I can watch the sharks there free from ____harm____ .

part
bark
barge
carp
start
car
lark
tar
farm

▶ Print **three rhyming words under each word.**

10. mark	11. start	12. hard
bark	part	card
dark/hark	cart/tart	yard
park/lark	dart/art	lard

Ask your child to list words that rhyme with *car*.

CURRICULUM CONNECTIONS

SPELLING

You may choose to pretest the following set of spelling words at this point.

1. **car** I wish we had a red **car**.
2. **fork** I need a **fork** to eat my dinner.
3. **girl** A **girl** and a boy came to the door.
4. **her** Did you see **her** new puppy?
5. **nurse** A **nurse** took care of me.
6. **under** Did you find a bug **under** the rock?

SCIENCE

With children, construct a concept web listing facts about sharks. Read a non-fiction selection aloud from which children can gather information. Provide library books about sharks. If possible, show a video about these interesting animals.

 **TECHNOLOGY** **AstroWord** *r*-Controlled Vowels

AUDITORY/KINESTHETIC LEARNERS GROUPS

Have children stand in a circle. As you say words, have them reach far into the air with their hands when they hear a word that has the *ar* sound. Use words such as *start, cart, from, dark, large, swim, tall, part, hardly, curly, jars,* and *stars.*

CHALLENGE

Have children make a list of synonyms for these *ar* words: *car, hard, harm, smart, start, bark;* and then create a list of antonyms for these words: *dark, hard, harm, smart.*

EXTRA SUPPORT/INTERVENTION

Materials: Phonics Word Cards, Set 2: *ar* words (21–31)

Invite children to choose a word card, pronounce both words on the card, and tell what they mean. Have them list words they cannot define and encourage them to find them in the dictionary. See Daily Phonics Practice, pages 252–253.

Integrating Phonics and Reading

Guided Reading
Have children read the title and look at the picture. Ask them to predict why this scarecrow is "Not-So-Scary."

First Reading Using the pictures and text in the book, invite children to explain why the scarecrow was "Not-So-Scary." **Second Reading** Invite children to list the words that have the same sound of *ar* as in *cart.*

Comprehension
After reading, ask children the following questions:

• Why did Mark make a scarecrow? *Inference/ Cause and Effect*
• Why do you think Mark's scarecrow did not scare the crows? *Reflective Analysis/Personal Response*

ESL/ELL **English Language Learners**
Invite volunteers to identify the compound word in the story title (*scarecrow*) and tell the two words that form it. Then, have them find another compound word in the story. (*backyard*)

Sound of or

Skill Focus

Children will

★ identify the sound of *or* in words.

★ read and write words with *or* and *ar*.

ESL/ELL Among Hmong, Vietnamese, and Khmer speakers, *ar* and *or* might sound alike. Practice auditory discrimination and distinct pronunciation with word pairs such as *born, barn; tore, tar; for, far;* and so on.

Teach

Phonological Awareness: Rhyme Say the following three words and ask children how the words are alike: *core, store, more.* (*The words rhyme.*) Then, say the words *corn, torn, born.* Ask children how these words are alike. (*They rhyme.*) Have children suggest another word that rhymes with *corn, torn,* and *born.* (*horn, worn*)

Sound to Symbol Write *store, core, born,* and *torn* on the board. Point to each word and say it aloud, emphasizing the sound of *or.* Have children repeat each word. Then, circle the letters *or* in each word. Explain that the *r* after the *o* makes the *o* sound different than short or long *o.*

Practice and Apply

Sound to Symbol Read the rhyme on page 133. Have children repeat it chorally. Invite volunteers to identify words with the sound of *or,* write the words on the board, and circle *or* in each word. (*corn, form, more*)

Read the rule on page 133. Have volunteers repeat it. Then, read the directions. Caution children that they are not writing the word that appears next to the riddle but a word that rhymes with it. You might want to do item 1 together. Before children complete page 134, you may want them to practice the difference between *or* and *ar* by having them pronounce these word pairs: *for, far; store, star; cord, card.* Then, demonstrate how to trace the maze to find the *ar* and *or* words.

Reading You may wish to use *A Stew for Egor's Mom,* MCP Phonics and Reading Super Skills Library 2, Level B, to help children recognize and read words with the sound of *or.*

Name _____

Corn is such a tasty treat
In any form you please.
It is much more fun to eat
Than broccoli or peas.

RULE
An **r** after a vowel makes the vowel sound different from the usual short or long sound. You can hear the **or** sound in **corn** and **more.**

▶ Read **each riddle.** Answer **it with a word** that **rhymes** with the word beside the riddle. Print it on the line.

1. Something we can pop and eat	_corn_	**horn**
2. Something on a unicorn	_horn_	**born**
3. Something we eat with	_fork_	**cork**
4. Something with rain, wind, and thunder	_storm_	**form**
5. Something we can play or watch	_sport_	**port**
6. Something sharp on a rose	_thorn_	**born**
7. Something beside the sea	_shore_	**tore**
8. Something to close up a bottle	_cork_	**pork**
9. Something that gives us light	_torch_	**porch**

Words with or: Words in context   **133**

FOCUS ON ALL LEARNERS

ESL/ELL ENGLISH LANGUAGE LEARNERS

Practice with English language learners words containing the sounds of *or* and *ar.*

• Model pronunciation of the words in the colored boxes on page 133, and encourage children to think of rhyming words.

• Pair children and have them take turns reading a sentence and thinking of a rhyming word to complete the sentence.

• Adapt the maze activity on page 134 by preparing a worksheet with words from the maze for children to use in sentences. Informally, assess each child's ability to discriminate *ar* from *or.* Then, navigate the maze together as a group.

AUDITORY/VISUAL LEARNERS

Give pairs of children two lists—one with the words *horn, store, fort, pork,* and one with the words *bark, jar, arm, hard.* Have one child read the *or* list, one word at a time, while the other child names words that rhyme. Then, have children reverse roles for the other list.

Help the horse get to the barn. Find the words in the maze with **ar** and **or**. Follow them to get to the barn. Write each word on the line beside the puzzle.

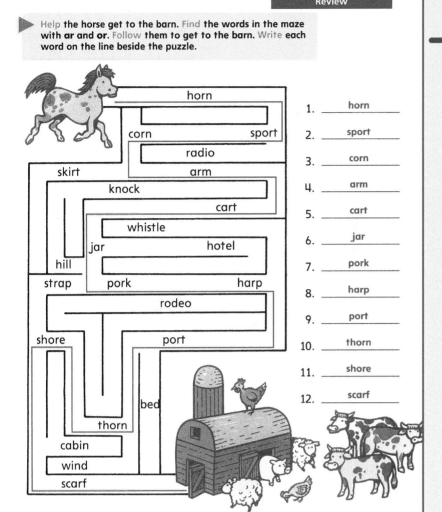

1. _____ horn
2. _____ sport
3. _____ corn
4. _____ arm
5. _____ cart
6. _____ jar
7. _____ pork
8. _____ harp
9. _____ port
10. _____ thorn
11. _____ shore
12. _____ scarf

HOME Have your child separate the words in the list into two groups: *ar* words and *or* words.

CURRICULUM CONNECTIONS

SPELLING

Make copies of the final portion of the unit spelling list for children to keep in their notebooks or take home to study. You may wish to provide new copies of the entire list at this time. Have children circle the vowel-*r* combination in each new word and practice spelling the words with a partner.

MATH

Materials: mural paper, markers

Ask children to draw items that might be found in an *ar/or* store, such as a jar, toy cars, horses, horns, a star, a scarf, and corn. Have them put tags showing prices less than a dollar on each item. Invite children to write word problems for the items. Compile the problems on a duplicated sheet for all children to solve.

TECHNOLOGY **AstroWord** *r*-Controlled Vowels

AUDITORY/KINESTHETIC LEARNERS GROUPS

Materials: beanbag or foam ball

Have children sit in a circle and pass around the beanbag as you chant the rhyme *Round and round the circle I go. Stop and tell me what you know.* When you stop, the player holding the bag names an *or* or *ar* word.

CHALLENGE

Write these words on the board: *fork, store, core, form, star, jar, dart, park,* and *lark*. Challenge children to look up their meanings in a dictionary. Then, have them write sentences demonstrating two different meanings for each word.

EXTRA SUPPORT/INTERVENTION

Materials: Phonics Word Cards, Set 2: *ar* and *or* words (21–40)

Ask each child to choose a card, read the words, and place the card in an *ar* or *or* pile. Then, have them sort the cards by other characteristics, such as number of letters, or words that name animals, places, and things. See Daily Phonics Practice, pages 252–253.

Integrating Phonics and Reading

Guided Reading

After reading the title and looking at the cover, ask children if they notice anything strange about what is in the pot.

First Reading Have children explain what is strange about Egor's stew.

Second Reading Make three columns on the board: *short o; long o; or*. Have children find words in the story and write them in the correct column.

Comprehension

Ask these questions:

• Why does Egor keep adding more things to the stew? *Inference/Draw Conclusions*

• What do you think Egor's mom will do with the stew? *Reflective Analysis/Personal Response*

ESL/ELL **English Language Learners**

Help children to identify that a stew does not include some of the ingredients Egor added. Reread and invite volunteers to add other real ingredients a stew can have.

Sound of ir, er, ur

Skill Focus

Children will

★ identify the sound of *ir*, *er*, and *ur* in words.

★ read and write words with *ir*, *er*, and *ur*.

★ write words with the sound of *ir*, *er*, and *ur* to finish sentences.

ESL/ELL In Spanish, *ir*, *er*, and *ur* do not stand for a sound similar to the English sound, and each letter stands for a distinct sound. Spanish speakers may pronounce *bird* as *beard*.

Teach

Phonemic Awareness: Phoneme Isolation

Say the words *bird*, *germ*, and *fur*, emphasizing the medial vowel-*r* sound. Repeat the words naturally one at a time and have children say them after you. Ask children what sound they hear in the middle of each word. (/er/)

Sound to Symbol Write *bird*, *germ*, and *fur* on the board. Point to each one and have children say it aloud. Circle the *ir* in *bird*, the *er* in *germ*, and the *ur* in *fur*. Explain that the *r* makes the vowels *i*, *e*, and *u* sound different than their short or long sound. Write *first*, *third*, *term*, *nurse*, *girl*, *burn*, *herd*, *churn*, and *never* on the board. Encourage volunteers to come to the board, say the words, and circle the vowel plus *r* in each word.

Practice and Apply

Sound to Symbol Read the rhyme aloud. Then, have volunteers take turns reading it. Ask children to identify the words with *ir*, *er*, or *ur*. (*bird, fir, turn, chirp, never, ever*) Point out the word *never*. Explain that the sound of *er* often comes at the end of a two-syllable word.

Invite a volunteer to read the rule on page 135. Have other children restate it in their own words. Read the directions and help children identify the picture names on pages 135 and 136. Remind children that they need to circle more than one answer for items 1 through 3 on page 135.

Writing Read the directions for items 7–12 on page 136. Have volunteers read the word choices before children write their answers.

Reading Use *Miss Muffet and the Spider*, MCP Phonics and Reading Super Skills Library 2, Level B, to reinforce reading words with the sound of *ir*, *er*, and *ur*.

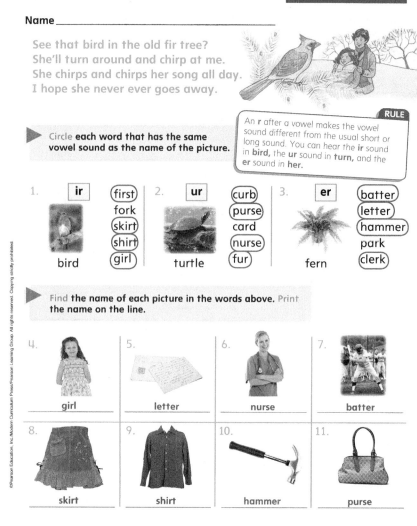

Name_____

See that bird in the old fir tree?
She'll turn around and chirp at me.
She chirps and chirps her song all day.
I hope she never ever goes away.

RULE
An **r** after a vowel makes the vowel sound different from the usual short or long sound. You can hear the **ir** sound in **bird**, the **ur** sound in **turn**, and the **er** sound in **her**.

▶ Circle **each word that has the same vowel sound as the name of the picture.**

1. **ir** — first, fork, (skirt), (shirt), (girl)
   bird

2. **ur** — (curb), (purse), card, (nurse), (fur)
   turtle

3. **er** — (batter), (letter), (hammer), park, (clerk)
   fern

▶ Find **the name of each picture in the words above.** Print **the name on the line.**

4. girl
5. letter
6. nurse
7. batter
8. skirt
9. shirt
10. hammer
11. purse

Words with ir, er, ur: Picture-text match   **135**

FOCUS ON ALL LEARNERS

ESL/ELL ENGLISH LANGUAGE LEARNERS

Continue practicing spelling of target words by having children complete activities on pages 135 and 136.

- Ask children to complete items 1 through 6 on page 136 with partners.

- As a follow-up, have individuals complete items 4 through 11 on page 135.

- Review answers aloud and monitor consistent pronunciation of r-controlled *i*, *e*, and *u*.

- In another session with books closed, name each picture clue on page 135 and have children write the words as you say them.

AUDITORY/VISUAL LEARNERS

Read aloud the following sentences: *Mom put the card in her purse; Does this shirt go with that skirt?; Did you water the big green fern?; The girls formed a large circle.* Have children identify words with the *ir*, *er*, and *ur* sound. Write them on the board by spelling pattern.

Picture-Text Match

▶ Underline the name of the picture. Circle the box that has the same vowel with r.

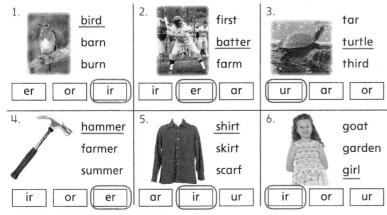

1. <u>bird</u> / barn / burn
   er | or | (ir)

2. first / batter / farm
   ir | (er) | ar

3. tar / turtle / third
   (ur) | ar | or

4. hammer / farmer / summer
   ir | or | (er)

5. shirt / skirt / scarf
   ar | (ir) | ur

6. goat / garden / <u>girl</u>
   (ir) | or | ur

▶ Circle the word that will finish the sentence. Print it on the line.

7. Dogs have ____fur____ and bark.   far (fur)

8. Birds have feathers and ____chirp____.   cheat (chirp)

9. Kittens ____curl____ up when they nap.   (curl) car

10. Fish have fins and swim in the ____river____. (river) hurt

11. Worms wiggle and live in ____dirt____.   burn (dirt)

12. Have you ____ever____ wondered why?   other (ever)

HOME ▶ Help your child list the words on the page that contain *ir*, *er*, or *ur*.

136 Words with ir, er, ur: Words in context

CURRICULUM CONNECTIONS

SPELLING

You may wish to posttest the *r*-controlled spelling words at this time.

1. **nurse**   I went to the school **nurse**.
2. **fork**   I eat using a spoon or **fork**.
3. **under**   My kitten hides **under** my bed.
4. **car**   I will wash our **car** today.
5. **her**   **Her** name is Mary.
6. **girl**   Which **girl** is your sister?

WRITING

Reread the rhyme on page 135. Ask children why the bird is chirping. *Is it happy? Is it talking to other birds? What if the bird could talk?* Have them draw pictures of the bird and, in speech balloons, write what the bird might be saying, using some *ir*, *er*, and *ur* words.

TECHNOLOGY   **AstroWord** *r*-Controlled Vowels

AUDITORY/KINESTHETIC LEARNERS   GROUPS

Play "Mother, May I?" Tell children if they hear a word with the *ir*, *er*, *ur* sound, they must take two steps forward. If the sound isn't present, they take one step backward. Use words such as: *nurse, horse, dirt, curl, river, burn, hot, farm, garden, chirp, fur, batter, letter, girl, got,* and *purse*.

CHALLENGE

Invite children to talk about any mystery series they know of from books or television. Have them write titles for imaginary mysteries, using words with *er*, *ir*, or *ur*, such as *The Case of the Chirping Bird* or *The Batter Who Never Made It to First*.

LEARNERS WHO NEED EXTRA SUPPORT

Materials: Phonics Word Cards, Set 2: *ir, er, ur* words (41–60)

Have children choose cards, pronounce the words on them, and sort out words they cannot read or define. Practice the unfamiliar words together and model a sentence with each. See Daily Phonics Practice, pages 252–253.

Integrating Phonics and Reading

Guided Reading

Encourage children to predict how this story may be different from the original nursery rhyme.

First Reading Have children tell what Miss Muffet's problem was at the beginning and end of the story.

Second Reading On the board, draw and label three spider webs *ir*, *er*, and *ur*. Invite children to list words from the story in the appropriate web.

Comprehension

Ask children these questions:

• What excuses did the characters use to avoid helping Miss Muffet? *Recall/Sequence*

• What do you think Miss Muffet will do now that the giant is sitting on her tire? *Inference/Assess Prior Knowledge*

ESL/ELL English Language Learners

Familiarize non-native speakers with the tales alluded to in the story to help them appreciate the humor in the story.

136

Phonics and Spelling / Phonics and Writing

Review Consonant Digraphs and r-Controlled Vowels

Skill Focus

Children will

★ spell and write words with consonant digraphs and *r*-controlled vowels.

★ write a news story using words with consonant digraphs and *r*-controlled vowels.

ESL/ELL In Spanish, *ar, or, ir, er,* and *ur* each stands for a distinct sound. Practice with *part, hard; first, third; under, her; corn, torn; purse, burn.*

Teach

Phonics and Spelling Review the following with children:

• A consonant digraph is two consonants that together stand for one sound.

• When a vowel is followed by *r*, the vowel is neither short nor long.

Then, write the following words in a list on the board: *why, star, turtle, each, this, burn, wrist, which, bush, write, knock, fork, clerk.* Invite volunteers to go to the board, choose a word, say it, underline consonant digraphs, and circle *r*-controlled vowels.

Practice and Apply

Phonics and Spelling Before children begin the activity on page 137, have them together read aloud the words in the box. Be sure they understand the directions. Suggest they say each word to themselves as they write in the box.

Phonics and Writing Write the five *W*'s of news reporting on the board: *Who, What, When, Where, Why* (or *How*). Explain why each word is important to a news story. Tell children that each news story begins with a headline that should make the reader want to read the story. Before children write their story, discuss the prompt and go over the words in the box on page 138. Remind children that after they have written their story, they should check that they have included the five *W*'s.

Reading Use *A Fox Lives Here,* MCP Phonics and Reading Super Skills Library 2, Level B, to review consonant digraphs and *r*-controlled vowels.

Spelling

Name _____

Phonics & Spelling Say and spell each word in the box below. Then, print the word on the line where it belongs.

shoe	beach	truck	wheel	car	girl
write	thorn	why	chair	wrong	nurse
knit	fork	knock	wish	bath	block

sh
1. shoe
2. wish

th
3. thorn
4. bath

wh
5. why
6. wheel

ch
7. beach
8. chair

ck
9. block
10. truck

kn
11. knit
12. knock

ir, ur
13. girl
14. nurse

wr
15. write
16. wrong

ar, or
17. car
18. fork

Digraphs, r-controlled vowels   **137**

FOCUS ON ALL LEARNERS

ESL/ELL **ENGLISH LANGUAGE LEARNERS**

Encourage English language learners to complete the activity on page 137 independently, after you model directions aloud for the group.

• Review the words in the colored box with children to correct any misconceptions before they begin. Model directions and monitor.

• Invite groups of three to go to the board and print the answers to items 1 through 6, 7 through 12, and 13 through 18.

• Have children correct their papers, confirming answers and pronunciation, when necessary.

AUDITORY LEARNERS

Divide the class into two spelling bee teams. Dictate words from the unit spelling list and from page 137. Have children from each team take turns spelling them aloud. Award points for correctly spelled words.

Phonics & Writing

A **news story** tells a story about an event that just happened. It should tell *who* or *what* the event is about, *when* and *where* it happened, and *why* or *how* it happened. The *headline* gives the reader clues about the event.

▶ **Pretend** someone you know just won a prize for growing the largest pumpkin in town. **Write** a news story about it. **Use** some of the words in the box.

dirt	water	when	each	know
this	brother	write	where	little
show	start	rocks	large	yard

Begin with a headline.

Tell *who* or *what* the story is about.

Tell *when*, *where*, *why*, or *how* it happened.

138 Words with sh, th, wh, ch, ck, kn, wr; r-controlled vowels

HOME

Ask your child to circle the words in the news story he or she wrote, with digraphs and r-controlled vowels.

CURRICULUM CONNECTIONS

SPELLING
Cumulative Posttest
You might wish to use the following words and sentences to posttest the spelling list for Unit 4.

1. **chair**   This **chair** is broken.
2. **her**   Hang **her** coat on a hook.
3. **belt**   I need a **belt** for my costume.
4. **shoe**   You need a new lace for your **shoe**.
5. **car**   My mom repaired the **car**.
6. **drum**   Can you hear the **drum** playing?
7. **stamp**   Are you a **stamp** collector?
8. **thorn**   The lion had a **thorn** in its paw.
9. **wheel**   A **wheel** for a truck is large.
10. **girl**   That **girl** is on our team.
11. **ribbon**   Tie a **ribbon** on his gift.
12. **knock**   The dog may **knock** over that vase.
13. **nurse**   I asked the **nurse** for help.
14. **write**   Can you **write** in cursive?
15. **block**   Ride around the **block** quickly.

TECHNOLOGY   **AstroWord** Consonant Blends and Digraphs; *r*-Controlled Vowels

VISUAL/KINESTHETIC LEARNERS

 GROUPS

Materials: mural paper, orange and green markers, beanbag

On mural paper, draw outlines of pumpkins. Inside each pumpkin, write a spelling word and put a point value next to it. Tape the paper to the floor and have children take turns tossing a beanbag at the words. Children score points by reading the words in the pumpkins.

CHALLENGES

Have partners read their news stories about the largest pumpkin in town to each other. Ask them to take notes on each other's stories and then retell the stories in their own words.

EXTRA SUPPORT/INTERVENTION

Duplicate practice papers on which the spelling list has been printed in large letters. Invite children to finger-trace each word, say the letters, and then finger-trace the words on a blank surface. **See Daily Phonics Practice, pages 251–253.**

Integrating Phonics and Reading

Guided Reading
Explain to children the climate of the Arctic and point out its location on a globe. Help them imagine what life for an arctic fox may be like.

First Reading Have children recreate the life of an arctic fox as described in the story.

Second Reading On the board, make five columns for each *r*-controlled vowel. Have them find these words in the story and write them in the correct column.

Comprehension
Ask children these questions:
• What will each pup do when it goes out on its own? *Recall/Make Judgments*
• Why does the fur of the arctic fox change color? *Inference/Assess Prior Knowledge*

ESL/ELL **English Language Learners**
Some children may not know the meaning of the word *den*. Explain that animals such as foxes and bears often make their home or dens under rocks or in underground tunnels.

Take-Home Book

Review Consonant Digraphs and r-Controlled Vowels

Skill Focus

Children will

★ read words with consonant digraphs and *r*-controlled vowels in the context of a nonfiction story.

★ review selected high-frequency words in the context of a story.

★ reread for fluency.

Teach
Build Background

• Remind children that the unit theme is "The World Outside." Ask children to name some of the animals and plants they have read about in this unit.

• Write the words *wolf* and *wolves* on the board. Explain that the word *wolves* is the plural form of *wolf*. Tell children that they will be reading about the gray wolf, an *endangered* animal. Explain that *endangered* means that there are very few gray wolves that still live.

Phonemic Awareness: Phoneme Categorization Write these words on the board and say them aloud as you point to each: *wolf, together, pack*. Ask children which word does not contain a consonant digraph. (*wolf*) Have children identify the digraphs in the other two words. (*th, ck*) Then, write the words *gray, together, members*. Have children identify the word that does not have an *r*-controlled vowel. (*gray*) Ask volunteers to underline the *r*-controlled vowels in the other two words. (*er*)

Practice and Apply

Read the Book Help children make the Take-Home book. Encourage them to preview the book. Then, read the story and discuss what children learned about wolves.

Sound to Symbol Have volunteers read the book aloud. Help children find examples of words that have consonant digraphs or *r*-controlled vowels. Write the words on the board.

Review High-Frequency Words Write *their, might, even* on the board. Have children spell each word and say it, blending the sounds.

Reread for Fluency Have children reread the book to increase their fluency and comprehension. Remind them to take the book home to share with their family.

Name _____

The Gray Wolf

Gray wolves are known to be among the smartest animals. They live in packs or families. They are loyal to members of their own pack. They eat and play together. They even all help care for their young.

1

FOLD

The gray wolf is *endangered*. This means that very few of them are alive. Soon, there might be no more gray wolves anywhere. We can save the gray wolf by choosing to share the earth with wild animals.

4

Review digraphs, r-controlled vowels: Take-home book **139**

FOCUS ON ALL LEARNERS

ESL/ELL ENGLISH LANGUAGE LEARNERS

Use the Take-Home Book as an opportunity for English language learners to gain additional practice with digraphs and *r*-controlled vowels.

• Read the story aloud for children. Then, read it again, this time encouraging children to take turns reading the story aloud. Introduce and explain unfamiliar terms. Point out words that contain consonant digraphs and *r*-controlled vowels.

• Build vocabulary awareness and sequencing by printing on chart paper five sentences from the story out of sequence. Then, have them write the sentences in order.

• Verify comprehension of the story by asking content-related questions.

VISUAL/KINESTHETIC LEARNERS

Materials: index cards, markers

Invite children to make word cards for story words with vowel-*r* combinations and then sort the words into the different *r*-controlled vowel sounds (*ar; or; ur, ir, er*). Have them read aloud each group of words and use each word in a sentence.

The howl of the gray wolf can be heard at any time of day or night. Wolves howl to call the pack together before or after a hunt. They howl to find one another, or to warn other packs to stay away.

2

--------FOLD--------

Wolves are meat eaters. They hunt either alone or with the pack. When an animal is caught, the pack eats its fill. Then, animals such as the fox or coyote, get the leftovers so there is no waste.

3

CURRICULUM CONNECTIONS

READING

Tell children the story of "The Three Little Pigs" or "Little Red Riding Hood" or have a volunteer tell one or both stories. Have children explain how these stories are the same and different from "The Gray Wolf." Ask children to explain how they can tell when a story is real and when it is make-believe.

SCIENCE

Have interested children find out more about endangered animals. You might encourage children to visit the library or use an age-appropriate encyclopedia or on-line resources to find out what other animals are endangered. Have children try to discover what endangers the animals. Suggest they report their findings to the rest of the class.

ART

Invite children to imagine that they have been asked to draw some different pictures to go along with the story "The Gray Wolf." Have children jot down ideas for pictures for each page of the story. Then, encourage them to turn one of their ideas into an illustration.

 **AstroWord** Consonant Blends and Digraphs; r-Controlled Vowels

AUDITORY LEARNERS GROUPS

Read "The Gray Wolf" aloud to children, having them raise their hands when they hear a word with an *r*-controlled vowel. Pause to have them repeat each of these words.

CHALLENGE

Challenge children to make as many words of three letters or more as they can from the letters in *endangered*. They can use a letter more than once in a word only if it appears in *endangered* more than once. When they have finished their list, have them underline words that contain *ar* or *er*.

EXTRA SUPPORT/INTERVENTION

Have children work with a partner to take turns reading the story, one page at a time, to each other. As they finish each page, have them write two sentences that tell what they learned. See Daily Phonics Practice, pages 251–253.

Unit Checkup

Review Compounds, Words with le, Hard and Soft c and g, Blends, y as a Vowel, Digraphs, r-Controlled Vowels

Skill Focus

Children will

★ read and write compound words, words that end with *le*, words with hard and soft *c* and *g*, blends, *y* as a vowel, consonant digraphs, and *r*-controlled vowels.

★ review high-frequency words.

Teach

Phonological Awareness: Review Skills
Say these words, one at a time, asking children to repeat the sound they hear at the beginning of each word: *blue* (/bl/); *circus* (/s/); *goat* (/g/); *shoe* (/sh/) *thing* (/th/); *giraffe* (/j/). Then, say these words and ask children to repeat the sound they hear at the end of the word: *middle* (/el/); *sick* (/k/) *farmer* (/er/); *rich* (/ch/).

Sound to Symbol Write these sentences on the board, one at a time. Invite children to read the sentence and identify words that are examples of the phonics skills in this unit.

- **Should I buy the green shirt, the black turtleneck, or that nice scarf?**
- **When did you see a shy giraffe and a baby goat?**

Practice and Apply

Assess Skills Read the directions to page 141. Then, invite volunteers to name each picture, one at a time. Remind children to fill in only one bubble beside each picture. Be sure children can recognize and read the word *vegetables* on page 142. Have children chorally say the words in the box and then encourage individuals to repeat them before children finish the sentences independently.

Assess High-Frequency Words Pair children to check each other's reading of the high-frequency words. Encourage individuals to ask for help if they have difficulty reading any of the high-frequency words. Make note of those words that are difficult for a child.

Name _____

▶ Fill in **the bubble beside the name of each picture.**

1.		2.		3.	
	○ nice ● mice ○ rice		○ giraffe ○ goat ● giant		○ turn ○ train ● turkey

4.		5.		6.	
	● popcorn ○ cupcake ○ pencil		○ beach ○ dirt ● bird		○ clock ● cherry ○ check

7.		8.		9.	
	● block ○ black ○ blot		○ sneak ● snake ○ snore		● skunk ○ skate ○ skill

10.		11.		12.	
	○ bun ● bunny ○ baby		○ try ● cry ○ shy		● ship ○ shop ○ shell

13.		14.		15.	
	○ trunk ○ think ● thirteen		○ chair ● table ○ turtle		○ wrap ● write ○ wriggle

Compounds; le; hard and soft c, g; blends; vowel y; **141**
digraphs; r-controlled vowels: Assessment

FOCUS ON ALL LEARNERS

ESL/ELL ENGLISH LANGUAGE LEARNERS

Ask English language learners to complete the pages independently.

- Review directions aloud with the group for both pages.
- Monitor children as they complete the pages.
- Once all children have finished, ask volunteers to write the answers to the first activity (page 141) on the board.
- Have children review their sentences for page 142 aloud in small groups; monitor pronunciation and check their work.

AUDITORY LEARNERS

Materials: Phonics Word Cards, Set 1: Consonant Blend words (197–236), Consonant Digraph words (246–256); Set 2: Consonant Digraph words (208–222)

As you read the word cards at random, have children identify the consonant blend or digraph they hear in each one.

▶ **Find the word in the box that will finish each sentence. Print it on the line.**

knife	garden	Maybe
peppers	who	corn
celery	fresh	glad

1. Many kinds of vegetables grow in a _____garden_____.

2. The _____celery_____ is green and leafy.

3. We need a _____knife_____ to cut the stalks.

4. Both red and green _____peppers_____ taste good in a salad.

5. _____Maybe_____ I can eat one of the peppers right now.

6. Let's go pick some sweet yellow _____corn_____.

7. Vegetables taste best when they are _____fresh_____.

8. I'm _____glad_____ it's almost time to eat.

9. Now _____who_____ will cook them for us?

▶ **Can you read each word? Put a ✔ in the box if you can.**

☐ only ☐ own ☐ their ☐ laugh ☐ even ☐ might

☐ your ☐ two ☐ believe ☐ once ☐ bought ☐ new

142 Compounds; le; hard and soft c, g; blends; vowel y; digraphs; r-controlled vowels: Assessment

 HOME
Ask your child to make up new sentences containing some of the words from the box.

ASSESS UNDERSTANDING OF UNIT SKILLS

STUDENT PROGRESS ASSESSMENT

You may wish to review the observational notes you made as children worked through the activities in the unit. These notes will help you evaluate the progress children have made with the various parts of this unit.

PORTFOLIO ASSESSMENT

Review the written materials children have collected in their portfolios. Conduct interviews with children to discuss their work and progress since the beginning of this unit. As you review children's work, evaluate how well they use phonics skills.

DAILY PHONICS PRACTICE

For children who need additional practice with the skills in this unit, see Daily Phonics Practice, pages 248–253.

PHONICS POSTTEST

To assess children's mastery of skills in this unit, use the posttest on pages 85g–85h.

VISUAL/KINESTHETIC LEARNERS   INDIVIDUAL

Materials: drawing paper; markers or crayons (optional)

Write the following words on the board: *mice, turkey, bird, grapes, snake, skunk, bunny, try, ship, knapsack, table, wrapper, jar, corn,* and *peach.* Invite children to draw scenes that contain as many of these items as possible. Have children trade drawings with partners and list the objects they find in each other's pictures.

CHALLENGES

Encourage children to write recipes for healthy vegetable salads using some of the words found on page 142. Remind children to include a list of ingredients and then directions written in logical order using complete sentences.

EXTRA SUPPORT/INTERVENTION

Before children complete page 142, invite volunteers to read each of the sentences in turn without the missing words. Provide pronunciation help as needed. Review the words in the box by having children point to and repeat each word after you. See Daily Phonics Practice, pages 248–253.

Teacher Notes

UNIT 5

Contractions, Endings, Suffixes

THEME: BLASTING OFF

CONTENTS

TEACHING PLANS

Student Performance Objectives

In Unit 5, children will be introduced to contractions, word endings, and suffixes within the context of the theme "Blasting Off!" As children progress through this unit, they will be able to

▶ Identify and distinguish among contracted forms in which the words *not, is, have, am, are, will,* and *us* are shortened

▶ Add the endings *-s* and *-es* to change singular nouns into plural nouns

▶ Add the inflected endings *-ed* and *-ing* to base words, including words ending in a single consonant and words ending in silent *e*

▶ Add the suffixes *-ful, -less, -ness* and *-ly* to base words

▶ Add the comparative forms *-er* and *-est* to base words, including words ending in *y*

▶ Add the ending *-es* to words ending in *y* to form the plural

▶ Apply these skills in decoding and in using words in context

Assessment Options

In Unit 5, assess children's ability to read and write contractions and words with plural endings, inflectional endings, and suffixes. Use the Unit Pretest and Posttest for formal assessment. For ongoing informal assessment, you may wish to use children's work on the Review pages, Take-Home Books, and Unit Checkups. You may also want to encourage children to evaluate their own work and to participate in setting goals for their own learning.

ESL/ELL Note pronunciation difficulties as they occur, but assess performance based upon children's ability to distinguish specific sounds when pronounced by a native speaker. For additional support for English language learners, see page 143j.

FORMAL ASSESSMENT

Use the Unit 5 Pretest on pages 143e–143f to help assess a child's knowledge at the beginning of the unit and to plan instruction.

ESL/ELL Before the Pretest, preview visuals on page 143e so children are familiar with picture names. Point out that many show more than one item, indicating that children are to make them plural. Give examples to show what "more than one" means.

Use the Unit 5 Posttest on pages 143g–143h to help assess mastery of unit objectives and to plan for reteaching, if necessary.

ESL/ELL Have children read the direction lines. To confirm understanding of the tasks, have them restate in their own words what they are to do.

INFORMAL ASSESSMENT

Use the Review pages, Unit Checkup, and Take-Home Book in the student book to provide an effective means of evaluating children's performance.

Unit 5 Skills	Review pages	Checkups	Take-Home Books
Contractions	150–152 173–174	177–178	175–176
Plural endings	161–162, 173–174	177–178	175–176
Inflected endings	161–162, 173–174	177–178	175–176
Suffixes	166, 173–174	177–178	175–176

STUDENT PROGRESS CHECKLIST

Use the checklist on page 143i to record children's progress. You may want to cut the sections apart to place each child's checklist in his or her portfolio.

PORTFOLIO ASSESSMENT

This logo appears throughout the teaching plans. It signals opportunities for collecting children's work for individual portfolios. You may also want to include the Pretest and Posttest, the Review pages, the Unit Checkup, Phonics & Reading, Phonics & Spelling, and Phonics & Writing pages.

PHONEMIC AWARENESS AND PHONICS ASSESSMENT

Use PAPA to obtain an itemized analysis of children's decoding skills.

PAPA Skills	MCP Phonics Lessons in Unit 5
Vowel digraphs	Lessons 89–93, 100

Pretest and Posttest

DIRECTIONS

To help you assess children's progress in learning Unit 5 skills, tests are available on pages 143e–143h.

Administer the Pretest before children begin the unit. The results of the Pretest will help you identify each child's strengths and needs in advance, allowing you to structure lesson plans to meet individual needs. Administer the Posttest to assess children's overall mastery of skills taught in the unit and to identify specific areas that will require reteaching.

ESL/ELL Note that the objective of both the Unit 5 Pretest and Posttest are to assess reading and writing contractions and words with plural and inflectional endings, and suffixes. To ensure that the amount of text on each page does not interfere with the objectives, reinforce print readiness through frequent sight recognition, reading, and spelling opportunities throughout the unit.

PERFORMANCE ASSESSMENT PROFILE

The following chart will help you identify specific skills as they appear on the tests and enable you to identify and record specific information about an individual's or the class's performance on the tests.

Depending on the results of each test, refer to the Reteaching column for lesson-plan pages where you can find activities that will be useful for meeting individual needs or for daily phonics practice.

Answer Keys

Unit 5 Pretest, page 143e (BLM 29)

1. couldn't	9. daisies	17. fastest
2. he's	10. boxes	18. dipped
3. you've	11. bricks	19. helping
4. let's	12. dishes	20. saving
5. can't	13. planning	21. careless
6. you're	14. kindness	22. sillier
7. I'll	15. wished	23. slower
8. won't	16. quietly	24. waves

Unit 5 Pretest, page 143f (BLM 30)

25. Let's	31. hoped
26. I'll	32. cloudiest
27. peaches	33. hiding
28. cherries	34. brightest
29. handful	35. lovely
30. watching	36. darkness

Unit 5 Posttest, page 143g (BLM 31)

1. don't	9. brushes	17. funniest
2. aren't	10. stars	18. baked
3. let's	11. babies	19. walking
4. they've	12. glasses	20. skillful
5. she'll	13. harmless	21. hoped
6. we're	14. skipping	22. darkness
7. I'm	15. earlier	23. highly
8. that's	16. dreamed	24. taller

Unit 5 Posttest, page 143h (BLM 32)

25. nearest	29. stories	33. larger
26. It's	30. harmful	34. mainly
27. patches	31. learned	35. moons
28. believed	32. They're	36. wasn't

Performance Assessment Profile

Skill	Pretest Questions	Posttest Questions	Reteaching	
			Focus on All Learners	**Daily Phonics Practice**
Contractions	1–8, 25, 26	1–8, 26, 32, 36	145–152, 173–176	253
Plural endings	9–12, 24, 27, 28	9–12, 27, 29, 35	153–154, 161–162, 170–176	253–254
Inflected endings	13, 15, 18, 19, 20, 30, 31, 33	14, 16, 18, 19, 21, 28, 31	155–162, 173–176	254
Suffixes	14, 16, 17, 21, 22, 23, 29, 32, 34, 35, 36	13, 15, 17, 20, 22, 23, 24, 25, 30, 33, 34	163–176	254–255

Name _____

▶ Print the contraction that means the same as each pair of words.

1. could not	2. he is	3. you have	4. let us
_____	_____	_____	_____
5. can not	6. you are	7. I will	8. will not
_____	_____	_____	_____

▶ Add an ending to make each word mean more than one.
Print the new word on the line.

9.	10. 	11. 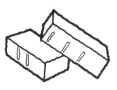	12.
daisy	box	brick	dish
_____	_____	_____	_____

▶ Add the ending to each base word.
Print the new word on the line.

13. plan + ing	14. kind + ness	15. wish + ed	16. quiet + ly
_____	_____	_____	_____
17. fast + est	18. dip + ed	19. help + ing	20. save + ing
_____	_____	_____	_____
21. care + less	22. silly + er	23. slow + er	24. wave + s
_____	_____	_____	_____

Go to the next page. ➔

BLM 29 Unit 5 Pretest: Contractions, plural endings, inflected endings, suffixes

Name _____

> ▶ Fill in the bubble under the word that will finish each sentence.

	It's	Let's	We're
25. _____ look at the moon tonight.	○	○	○

	I've	It's	I'll
26. _____ meet you on the roof.	○	○	○

	peaches	peach	peachs
27. Can you bring _____ for a snack?	○	○	○

	cherry	cherries	cherrys
28. I'll bring a bag of _____.	○	○	○

	hand	hands	handful
29. I'll put in a _____ of nuts.	○	○	○

	watching	watcher	watched
30. Do you like _____ the stars?	○	○	○

	hopped	hoped	hopping
31. I _____ that we would see Mars.	○	○	○

	cloudier	cloudy	cloudiest
32. This is the _____ night we've had.	○	○	○

	hide	highest	hiding
33. The moon is _____ behind a cloud.	○	○	○

	brighter	brightest	bright
34. The sun is the _____ star in the sky!	○	○	○

	love	loveless	lovely
35. What a _____ night.	○	○	○

	darkness	darker	dark
36. The stars twinkle in the _____.	○	○	○

Possible score on Unit 5 Pretest is 36. Number correct _____

BLM 30 Unit 5 Pretest: Contractions, plural endings, inflected endings, suffixes

Name _____

▶ Print the contraction that means the same as each pair of words.

1. do not	2. are not	3. let us	4. they have
_____	_____	_____	_____
5. she will	6. we are	7. I am	8. that is
_____	_____	_____	_____

▶ Add an ending to make each word mean more than one.

9. brush	10. star	11. baby	12. glass
_____	_____	_____	_____

▶ Add the ending to each base word.
Print the new word on the line.

13. harm + less

_____

14. skip + ing

_____

15. early + er

_____

16. dream + ed

_____

17. funny + est

_____

18. bake + ed

_____

19. walk + ing

_____

20. skill + ful

_____

21. hop + ed

_____

22. dark + ness

_____

23. high + ly

_____

24. tall + er

_____

Go to the next page. →

Name _____

> Fill in the bubble under the word that will finish each sentence.

	nearly	nearest	nearer
25. The planet Mars is our _____ neighbor.	○	○	○

	It's	I'm	I've
26. _____ easy to see Mars in the night sky.	○	○	○

	patch	patche	patches
27. It has dark and light _____ like the moon.	○	○	○

	believe	believing	believed
28. Once people _____ that there was life on Mars.	○	○	○

	stories	story	storys
29. People told _____ about creatures on Mars.	○	○	○

	harm	harmful	harming
30. Some thought these creatures would be _____.	○	○	○

	learning	learned	learn
31. Today scientists have _____ a lot about Mars.	○	○	○

	They've	They'll	They're
32. _____ sure that there is no life on Mars.	○	○	○

	larger	largest	large
33. Jupiter is much _____ than Mars.	○	○	○

	main	mains	mainly
34. This planet is _____ made up of gas.	○	○	○

	moonless	moons	moon
35. Jupiter has thirteen _____.	○	○	○

	wasn't	won't	weren't
36. One moon _____ even discovered until 1980.	○	○	○

Possible score on Unit 5 Posttest is 36. Number correct _____

BLM 32 Unit 5 Posttest: Contractions, plural endings, inflected endings, suffixes

Student Progress Checklist

Make as many copies as needed to use for a class list. For individual portfolio use, cut apart each child's section. As indicated by the code, color in boxes next to skills satisfactorily assessed and insert an *X* by those requiring reteaching. Marked boxes can later be colored in to indicate mastery.

Student Progress Checklist

Code: ■ Satisfactory   ☒ Needs Reteaching

Student: _____ _____ Pretest Score: _____ Posttest Score:_____	**Skills** ☐ Contractions ☐ Plural Endings ☐ Inflected Endings ☐ Suffixes	**Comments / Learning Goals**
Student: _____ _____ Pretest Score: _____ Posttest Score:_____	**Skills** ☐ Contractions ☐ Plural Endings ☐ Inflected Endings ☐ Suffixes	**Comments / Learning Goals**
Student: _____ _____ Pretest Score: _____ Posttest Score:_____	**Skills** ☐ Contractions ☐ Plural Endings ☐ Inflected Endings ☐ Suffixes	**Comments / Learning Goals**
Student: _____ _____ Pretest Score: _____ Posttest Score:_____	**Skills** ☐ Contractions ☐ Plural Endings ☐ Inflected Endings ☐ Suffixes	**Comments / Learning Goals**

BLM 33 Unit 5 Checklist

Throughout Unit 5 there are opportunities to assess English language learners' abilities to read and write contractions and words with plural and inflectional endings, and suffixes. Take note of difficulties with pronunciations as they occur, but assess children based on their ability to distinguish specific sounds when pronounced by a native speaker.

Lesson 66, pages 145–146 Spanish speakers may be familiar with contractions (*al, del*) but not with the apostrophe used to show the letters that are left out. Provide many visual examples.

Lesson 67, pages 147–148 English language learners who are accustomed to languages not written with the Roman alphabet may be unfamiliar with the apostrophe as a form of punctuation rather than as representing a sound in spoken language.

Lesson 68, pages 149–150 Children may not be fully aware of the baseline beneath letters of a contracted word and may confuse the apostrophe with a comma. Reinforce written punctuation.

Lesson 69, pages 151–152 Many languages do not form contractions by combining subject plus verb/modal, so provide frequent oral and written modeling.

Lesson 70, pages 153–154 The ability to distinguish between sibilant sounds such as those of *x, z, ss, sh,* or *ch* is highly dependent on the phonetics of the speaker's first language. Children may have difficulty perceiving meaningful differences between certain pairs of these sounds.

Lesson 71, pages 155–156 Many languages other than English do not use inflectional endings to mark verb tenses. Speakers of such languages may need help understanding that these endings tell when the action of the verb takes place.

Lesson 72, pages 157–158 English language learners may not hear the difference between the sound of a final *-n* and that of a final *-ng* and say *runin* instead of *running*. Demonstrate the position of the open mouth as you model each sound.

Lesson 73, pages 159–160 Speakers of languages in which syllables normally end in vowels may find it difficult not to pronounce the silent *e*.

Lesson 74, pages 161–162 Some languages distinguish consonants that are aspirated, or pronounced with a puff of air, from those that are not. Children from those language backgrounds may experience some confusion with the inflectional ending *-ed* in various contexts.

Lesson 75, pages 163–164 Overstressing suffixes when pronouncing words may cause some English language lerners to think one word is actually two.

Lesson 76, pages 165–166 Because of their monosyllabic backgrounds, speakers of Cantonese, Hmong, Vietnamese, Korean, or Khmer may think that two-syllable words are two words.

Lesson 77, pages 167–168 In Spanish, *er* stands for a different sound than in English, so some English language learners may say *late-air* instead of *later*, for example.

Lessons 78–79, pages 169–172 English language learners other than Spanish should consider the different sounds as they do long and short vowel differences—as two sounds for the same letter. English language learners may have little experience in forming plurals of words ending in *y* and making the spelling changes. Point out that the sound of *y* and *ie* is the same.

Lesson 80, pages 173–174 English language learners may forget to prolong the long *i* sound of *y* or to pronounce *ie* as one sound.

Lesson 81, pages 175–176 Spanish speakers may pronounce short *i* as long *e* (*eats* instead of *it's*). Model correct pronunciation.

Phonics Games, Activities, and Technology

The following collection of ideas offers a variety of opportunities to reinforce phonics skills while actively engaging children. The games, activities, and technology suggestions can easily be adapted to meet the needs of your group of learners. They vary in approach so as to consider children's different learning styles.

CONTRACTION TARGET PRACTICE

Draw a large spaceship on a piece of tagboard and divide it into six sections. In each section, print one of these words: *am, not, are, is, will,* and *have.* Give pairs of children a beanbag and have them take turns tossing it at the target. Have children make a contraction with the word they hit and use it in a sentence.

Variation: Divide the spaceship into 12 sections and write a contraction in each section. After each toss, have children pronounce the contraction they hit, use it in a sentence, and identify the two words that make up the contraction.

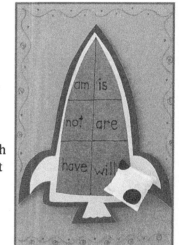

CONTRACTION CONCENTRATION

Have pairs of children write the following on index cards to make a deck to play "contraction concentration": *you'll, you will; we'll, we will; they'll, they will; I'll, I will; she'll, she will; he'll, he will; can't, can not; didn't, did not; weren't, were not; isn't, is not; doesn't, does not; won't, will not; don't, do not; haven't, have not; he's, he is; she's, she is; that's, that is; it's, it is; I'm, I am; we're, we are; they're, they are; they've, they have; we've, we have; let's, let us.* Have children mix up the words and place them face down on a desk. To play, children take turns turning over two cards to make a match. When a match is made, have the child use both the contracted and the uncontracted forms in a sentence.

ESL/ELL Because subject pronouns are not necessary in some native languages, remind English language learners that they must be used in English.

> On the first day of school,
> Our teacher read to us,
> A story about a yellow school bus.
> On the second day of school,
> Our teacher read to us,
> Two stories about foxes,
> And a story about a yellow school bus.

"ON THE FIRST DAY OF SCHOOL"

Help children change the traditional words to "The First Day of Christmas" to create verses of a song containing plurals. Record the words on chart paper and then, have children identify plural words formed by adding *-s* and those formed by adding *-es.* To help them get started, you may wish to present the example.

ESL/ELL Print song sheets of the verses and have children search the printed lyrics for the target words.

OPEN WORD SORTS

Assign children to work in groups of three and give each child ten index cards. Ask each child to look over the Unit 5 pages and write ten different words on the index cards. Have children pool their word cards and read them aloud. Then, have them work together to decide how to sort them. Possible sorts include by base word, by ending, by suffix, singular or plural words, vowel sound, by contraction, by word length, by beginning letter, or by category. After each sort, have children describe the sorting criteria they used.

CREATE-A-SENTENCE GAME

To make this sentence-building game, have a small group cut index cards into strips. Challenge each child to make up several six-word sentences that contain words with the endings *-ed* and *-ing*. Have them print each word on a separate strip. Place the strips in a box and have each child select six words from the box. The object of the game is to form a six-word sentence. On subsequent turns, each child selects one word from the box and then discards a word by putting it back in the box. When a player finally is able to form a six-word sentence, all words are returned to the box and the game begins again.

Variation: To reinforce contractions, plurals, and suffixes by writing the words you wish to target on the word strips and place them in the box.

GOING 'ROUND IN CIRCLES

Have a small group sit in a circle. Display a word card that features a base word to which different suffixes can be added. Have the first child read the word on the card and say another word made up of the base word and the suffix. The word card is then passed on to the next child in the circle, and the procedure continues. Once the card has traveled around the circle, begin again with a new base word card.

LIGHTS, CAMERA, ACTION!

Print these and other words with suffixes on index cards: *sleepless, fearless, helpless, helpful, hopeful, cheerful, careful, softly, gently, swiftly, bravely.* Then, have children take turns selecting a word and acting it out for a small group to guess.

Variation: The same word cards can be distributed around the room. Have children form teams of two or three and give each a card with one of these suffixes: *-less, -ful,* or *-ly.* Have each team hunt for words that end with the suffix they have been given.

HOT, HOTTER, HOTTEST!

Provide groups of three with a set of these word cards: *hot, big, tall, long, short, fat, thin, young, old, hard, soft, loud, high, low, sweet, full, mad.* Have one child select a card and use the word in a sentence; for example: *A match is hot.* The second and third child then give sentences using the comparative and superlative forms; for example: *A candle is hotter* and *The sun is the hottest of all.* Have children take turns selecting cards to begin each round.

Variation: Children can also work in small groups to make illustrated booklets with sets of three comparative adjectives.

MUSICAL ASTEROIDS

Randomly arrange children's chairs in an open area of the classroom and tell children that the chairs are asteroids. On each chair tape a base word card to which a suffix can be added. Play some space theme music and ask children to "fly" around the chairs. Once the music stops, children land on the nearest asteroid. Then, they take turns rising to read the base word taped to the back of their chair and giving another word that is formed by adding a suffix to this base word. When everyone has had a turn, start the music to play the game again.

SPACE-RACE GAME

Distribute copies of Blackline Master 35 to pairs of children to have them play the "space race" game. Each player will need to draw a small spaceship to use as a marker. At the beginning of the game, both markers should be placed on Pluto. Print the following words on small cards and place them face down on the Word Cards asteroid: *book, seal, box, fox, peach, star, bush, sandwich, glass, paintbrush, patch, city, family, pony, baby, berry, story, horse, dress*. Have players take turns selecting a card, reading aloud the word, and then printing the plural form of the word on a piece of paper. They can also use the word in a sentence. For each correct response, a player advances his or her marker to the next planet. Continue the game until both players reach the sun.

Variation: The game can also be played to reinforce forming contractions or adding inflected endings or suffixes. To focus on contractions, write on the word cards two words that can be combined to form a contraction. To advance, children must correctly write the contracted form. To focus on inflected endings or suffixes, write base words on the cards to which endings can be added and have children write the new words.

WORD-ENDINGS LADDERS

Divide the class into small teams. Then, draw eight ladders with five rungs on each ladder and label them with these endings: *-ed, -ing, -ly, -ness, -ful, -less, -er,* and *-est.* Give each team a different ladder. On your signal, have children work together as teams to "climb" the ladders by writing a word with the specified ending upon each rung. Have each team review its ladder with the group by reading the words it has written. In discussing the words, ask children to call attention to any spelling changes made to base words when the ending was added.

CONTRACTION HUNT

Many traditional children's songs include contractions. Print the words to songs such as "She'll Be Coming 'Round the Mountain" and "I've been Working on the Railroad" on chart paper. Review the words with children. Then, have them search the lyrics for contractions, circle any that they find with a colored marker, and then identify the two words that make up the contracted form. Lead them in singing the songs, and ask them to clap or stand whenever they reach a contraction.

TECHNOLOGY

The following software products reinforce children's understanding of a variety of phonics skills.

Reading Blaster™ Ages 6–8
Directed at developing and practicing reading and word usage skills, this software includes seven games. Among the many reading and phonics skills, children will learn to practice identifying compound words and contractions, syllables, vowel sounds. The five skill levels enable children to practice at their ability range.

** Sunburst Technology
    1900 South Batavia Ave.
    Geneva, IL 60134
    (800) 321-7511
    www.sunburst.com

Woobie's World of Phonics
Children learn basics of phonics along with Woobie as he goes to school and learns about sounds and words. Through different games and exercises, children relate word sounds to word meanings, learn about suffixes, prefixes, and other word additions, dig into syllables, and find out about the basics of spelling.

** Arc Media International Inc.
    238 Davenport Rd., #306
    Toronto, ON M5R IJ6, Canada
    www.arcmedia.com

Name _____

Space-Race Game

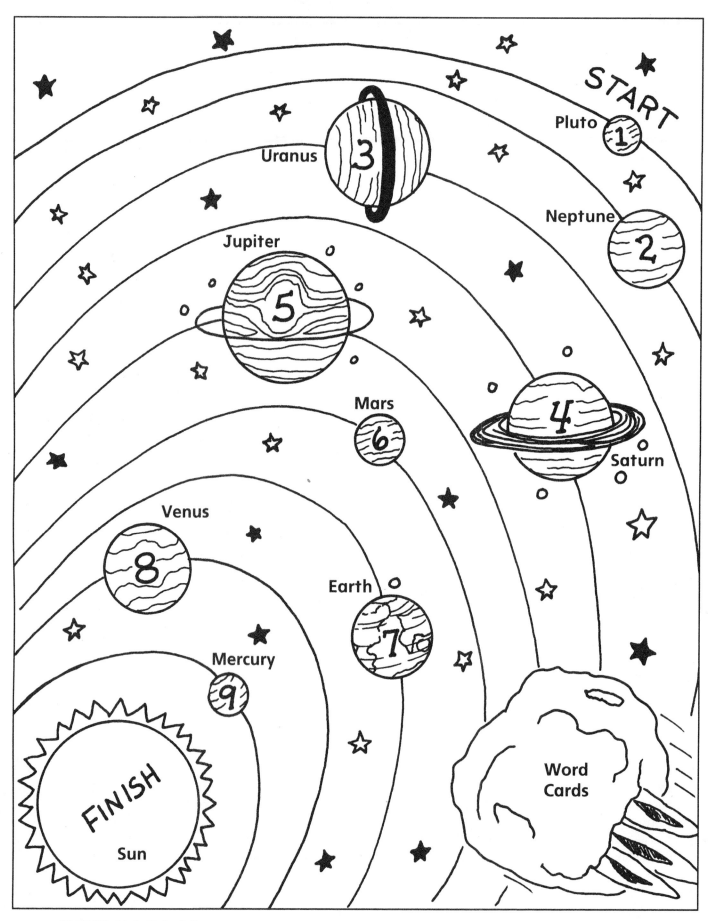

Home Connections

The Home Connections features of this program are intended to involve families in their children's learning and application of phonics skills. Three effective opportunities to make connections between home and school include the following.

- HOME LETTER
- HOME NOTES
- TAKE-HOME BOOKS

HOME LETTER

A letter is available to be sent home at the beginning of Unit 5. This letter informs family members that children will be learning to read and write contractions, words with plural and inflected endings, and words with suffixes within the context of the unit theme, "Blasting Off." Two activities are suggested to parents. In the first activity, children reread the selection on page 143 and identify contractions and words with endings or suffixes. In the second activity, family members look for articles about space to read together. Children are then asked to circle contractions and words with inflected endings or suffixes. Both activities support the child's learning to read and write words with various endings. The letter, available in English and Spanish, suggests space-theme books family members can look for in a local library and enjoy reading together.

HOME NOTES

Whenever the Home logo appears within the student book, a phonics activity is suggested to be done at home. The activities are simple to do, requiring little or no preparation or special materials, and are meant to reinforce the targeted phonics skill.

Home Notes in Spanish are also available for both teachers and parents to download and use from our website, www.PlaidPhonics.com

TAKE-HOME BOOKS

Within the student book are Take-Home Books that can be cut out and assembled. The story language in each book reinforces the targeted phonics skills. The books can be taken home and shared with family members. In Unit 5, one Take-Home Book is available focusing on several of the phonetic elements presented in this unit as well as the unit theme "Blasting Off."

UNIT 5

Pages 143–144

Contractions, Endings, Suffixes

Skill Focus

Assess Prior Knowledge

To assess children's prior knowledge of contractions, endings, and suffixes, use the pretest on pages 143e and 143f.

Unit Focus

Build Background

• Write the theme "Blasting Off" on the board. Then, ask children whether they have ever seen the space shuttle blast off, either in person or on TV. Encourage them to share their experiences.

• Read aloud the selection "Traveling in Space." Remind children that the people who travel on the space shuttle are called astronauts. Three U.S. space shuttles are *Discovery*, *Atlantis*, and *Endeavor*. Discuss the photograph. Then, ask children to explain why seeing Earth from space is valuable.

Introduce Contractions, Endings, and Suffixes

• With children, reread the selection. Write the word *you've* on the board, say it, and point to the apostrophe. Ask children to find another word in the story that has an apostrophe. Explain that these words are called contractions.

• Write the word *loud* on the board. Draw children's attention to the word *loudest* in the second sentence. Explain that *loudest* is a form of *loud*. Then, write *look*, *high*, and *storm* on the board. Invite children to find forms of these words in the story. Tell them that they will be learning about words with endings in this unit.

Critical Thinking

• Have children brainstorm other ways that space travel helps us learn about Earth. You may wish to mention that satellites that tell about weather are sometimes launched from space shuttles.

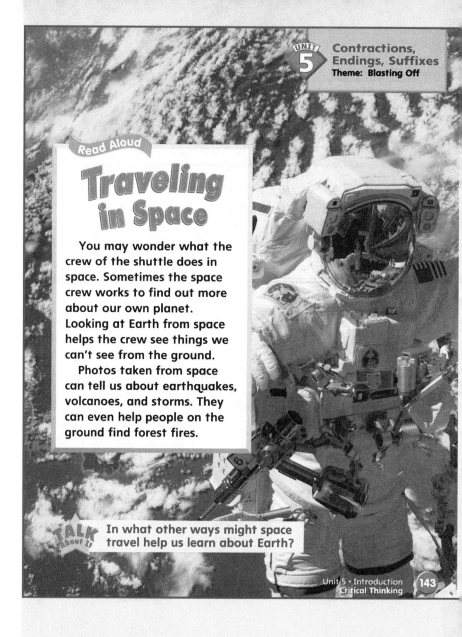

Contractions, Endings, Suffixes
Theme: Blasting Off

Read Aloud

Traveling in Space

You may wonder what the crew of the shuttle does in space. Sometimes the space crew works to find out more about our own planet. Looking at Earth from space helps the crew see things we can't see from the ground.

Photos taken from space can tell us about earthquakes, volcanoes, and storms. They can even help people on the ground find forest fires.

TALK about it In what other ways might space travel help us learn about Earth?

Unit 5 • Introduction
Critical Thinking **143**

THEME FOCUS

- - - - - - - - - - - - - - - - - -

BLAST OFF

Read the selection again. Encourage children to discuss whether they would like to travel in a space shuttle some day. For those who would like to go, what would they like to learn?

SPACE TRAVEL COLLAGE

Have children collect or draw pictures related to astronauts, space travel and exploration, and astronomy. Invite them to assemble a collage on poster board. Ask children to add labels to the collage for words that name or describe objects or actions in the pictures. Encourage them to circle endings on base words as they study those skills in the unit.

COUNTDOWN TO LIFT-OFF

Play all or part of a video recording showing the launch of a spacecraft. Show it once or twice with the sound on. Then, ask children to take turns narrating the countdown sequence in their own ways as you replay the tape with the sound off.

143

Dear Family,

In this unit about space, your child will be learning about contractions, word endings, and suffixes. As your child becomes familiar with these forms, you might like to try these activities together.

▶ Read the selection on page 143 with your child. Talk about space travel with him or her. Together, identify contractions, such as you've and can't, words with endings, such as zooms and looking, and words with suffixes, such as higher and loudest.

▶ With your child, look through newspapers and magazines for articles about space. Read the articles and circle words with contractions, endings, and suffixes.

You and your child might enjoy reading these books together.

Sun, Moon, and Stars
by Mary Hoffman and Jane Ray

Space Busters by Philip Wilkinson

Sincerely,

_____

Estimada familia:

En esta unidad, que trata sobre el espacio, su hijo/a aprenderá contracciones, terminaciones de palabras y sufijos. A medida que su hijo/a se vaya familiarizando con estas formas, pueden hacer las siguientes actividades juntos.

▶ Lean con su hijo/a la selección en la página 143. Hablen sobre los viajes espaciales. Juntos, identifiquen contracciones, como por ejemplo you've y can't, terminaciones de palabras como zooms y looking, y palabras con sufijos, como higher y loudest.

▶ Busquen con su hijo/a artículos sobre el espacio en revistas y periódicos. Lean los artículos y encierren en un círculo las palabras con contracciones, las terminaciones y los sufijos.

Ustedes y su hijo/a disfrutarán leyendo estos libros juntos.

Sun, Moon, and Stars
de Mary Hoffman y Jane Ray

Space Busters de Philip Wilkinson

Sinceramente,

_____

Destination: Mars

Traveling to Mars (isn't) a new idea. (We've) done it for 25 (years) (using) robotic (rovers.) What is new is getting (humans) to land on Mars. Mars is farther than anywhere (humans) have traveled in space to date. The current Space Shuttle (isn't) built to travel this far. NASA is (working) on new (ways) to get us to Mars.

BULLETIN BOARD

A KWL bulletin board entitled "Launching into Space Facts" can help children become aware of contractions and words with endings as they use them to express questions and record facts about space and astronomy. Invite children to add to the three spaceship outlines on the display throughout the unit.

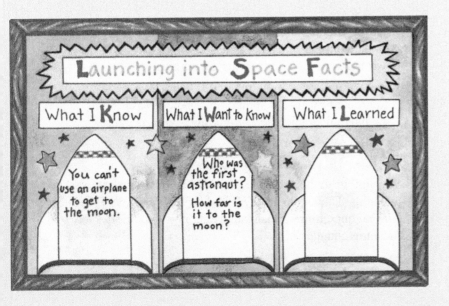

HOME CONNECTIONS

- The Home Letter on page 144 can be used to inform family members about the phonics skills children will be studying in Unit 5. Children can take home the page and complete it with family members.

- Encourage children to look for the books pictured on page 144 in the library so they can read and share them at home.

LEARNING CENTER ACTIVITIES

WRITING CENTER

In the Writing Center, display a picture of an astronaut and invite children to finish this sentence: *I'd be a good astronaut because* _____. Encourage them to add additional sentences to their explanations. Later, help children locate word endings and contractions they used in their writing.

HEALTH CENTER

Tell children that astronauts must exercise to stay in top physical condition. Space explorers have to work out before and during each flight. Display a chart titled "Getting Fit" in the Health Center. Invite children to record the amount of time they spend exercising each day (running, playing sports and games, biking, walking). You might also add a place where children can list the number of push-ups, jumping jacks, sit-ups, rope skips, and other exercises they can do.

SOCIAL STUDIES CENTER

Invite children to apply for a job as an astronaut. Design and duplicate an employment application with spaces for name, address, qualifications, health, and a written answer to a question, such as *What would you like to study as you travel in space?* Take time to "interview" each candidate. Talk about his or her answers and also review the child's progress in using the phonics skills studied thus far.

Contractions with will and not

Skill Focus

Children will

★ recognize that a contraction is a short word made from two other words.

★ identify and write contractions with will and not.

★ recognize and read high-frequency words.

ESL/ELL Spanish speakers may be familiar with contractions (al, del) but not with the apostrophe used to show the letters that are left out. Provide many visual examples.

▶ Teach

Introduce Contractions Read the rhyme on page 145 to children as they follow along. Repeat the rhyme and ask them to name a word that means "I will." (*I'll*)

Write *I will* on the board. Demonstrate how to change *I will* to *I'll* by boxing the *wi* and then replacing those letters with an apostrophe. Explain that *I'll* is a contraction or short form for *I will* and that the apostrophe replaces the missing letters.

Write the words *we will* on the board. Have a volunteer go to the board, erase the *wi* and add the apostrophe to make the contraction *we'll*.

Explain that many contractions are formed from the word *not*. Write *have not* on the board. Box the *o*, then replace the letter with an apostrophe. Then, write and have children say the word *haven't*. Have volunteers form contractions for *you will, she will, does not,* and *do not*.

▶ Practice and Apply

Writing Before children begin page 145, have them read the rule for contractions with *will*. Remind children to capitalize the contraction when it is the first word of the sentence. Then, have children read the rule for contractions with *not* on page 146. You may want to point out two exceptions to the way contractions are usually formed: *can not = can't* and *will not = won't*. While completing the pages, children will have the opportunity to read the following high-frequency words: *down, climb, enough,* and *friends*.

Reading Use *Looking for Angus*, MCP Phonics and Reading Word Study Skills Library, Level B, to provide practice in identifying and understanding contractions in a story.

145

Name_____

I'll build a rocket.
We'll go to the moon.
We'll explore outer space.
You'll be home by noon.

▶ **Print a contraction from the box that means the same as the two words beside each line.**

RULE

A **contraction** is a short way of writing two words. It is formed by putting two words together and leaving out one or more letters. An apostrophe (') is used to show where something is left out. Some contractions are formed with the word **will**.

I will = I'll

| you'll | they'll | she'll |
| we'll | I'll | he'll |

1. I will _____ I'll _____   2. he will _____ he'll
3. we will _____ we'll _____   4. they will _____ they'll
5. she will _____ she'll _____   6. you will _____ you'll

▶ **Print the short form of the two underlined words in each sentence.**

7. <u>I will</u> get in the boat after you.   I'll
8. <u>He will</u> climb aboard next.   He'll
9. <u>She will</u> join us, too.   She'll
10. <u>They will</u> hop in for the ride.   They'll
11. All aboard? Oh, no! <u>We will</u> sink!   We'll

Contractions with will: Words in context   **145**

FOCUS ON ALL LEARNERS

ESL/ELL ENGLISH LANGUAGE LEARNERS

Confirm that English language learners recognize and understand both the uncontracted and contracted forms of *will* and *not*.

- Teach children guidelines for identifying contractions with *will* by reviewing the rule on page 145. Ask a volunteer to read aloud the rule; give examples.
- On the chalkboard, write *I will = I'll*; point out to children that a contraction is simply a shorter way to write the two words *I* and *will*. Both forms are correct.
- Read aloud the words in the box. Work together to choose the contracted forms for items 1–6. Then, have children complete the page independently, providing help as needed.

KINESTHETIC LEARNERS

Say and write the sentence *I'll sit down*. Demonstrate its meaning. Then, substitute *He'll, She'll, They'll,* and *We'll* for *I'll*, having children read each version as they model the meaning changes.

Contractions

Print **a contraction from the box that means the same as the two words beside each line.**

> **RULE**
> Some contractions are formed with the word **not**.
> does not = doesn't

can't	couldn't	weren't	doesn't	don't
didn't	aren't	isn't	won't	haven't

1. are not _____aren't_____
2. do not _____don't_____
3. did not _____didn't_____
4. will not _____won't_____
5. were not _____weren't_____
6. is not _____isn't_____
7. could not _____couldn't_____
8. can not _____can't_____
9. does not _____doesn't_____
10. have not _____haven't_____

Print **two words that mean the same as each underlined word.**

11. Mitten the kitten <u>can't</u> get down from the tree. _____can not_____

12. She <u>isn't</u> brave enough to climb down. _____is not_____

13. She <u>doesn't</u> know what to do. _____does not_____

14. We <u>didn't</u> have any problem getting her down. _____did not_____

15. "<u>Aren't</u> you a lucky kitten to have friends to help?" _____Are not_____

146 Contractions with not: Words in context, high-frequency words

 HOME With your child, take turns forming contractions with the words *will* and *not*.

CURRICULUM CONNECTIONS

SPELLING

You may pretest the contractions from the unit spelling list by using the words and sample sentences below.

1. **I'll**   **I'll** be an astronaut someday.
2. **can't**   I **can't** wait until then.
3. **it's**   **It's** going to be exciting.
4. **we've**   **We've** learned a lot about space.
5. **I'm**   **I'm** going to read these books about it.
6. **they're** **They're** full of great pictures.

WRITING

Reread the rhyme on page 145 and ask children to name the rhyming words. *(moon, noon)* Invite them to think about what the children in the picture might do next, such as exploring the moon or talking on walkie-talkies. Have children work with partners to add two or more lines to the poem. The rhyming word *soon* may be helpful.

PORTFOLIO

VISUAL/AUDITORY LEARNERS GROUPS

Materials: Phonics Picture Cards: cookies (6), bus (62), pie (100); index cards; marker

Prepare three cards saying *will*, *will not*, and *won't*. Invite children to make up sentences about the pictures using these words. For example: *I will eat a lot of cookies* or *I won't take the bus.*

CHALLENGE

Have children write sentences about space travel, using contractions to help express their ideas. Have partners rewrite the sentences, using the full form of the contracted words. Ask children to decide which sentence in a pair sounds better.

EXTRA SUPPORT/INTERVENTION

Materials: Phonics Word Cards, Set 2: Contractions (125–136)

Have partners take turns showing the side of the cards with two words and saying the contraction and then showing the contractions and saying the two words from which each is formed. **See Daily Phonics Practice, page 253.**

Integrating Phonics and Reading

Guided Reading

Read the title and have children look at the picture. Ask children what they think the girl is looking for.
First Reading Ask children to explain why the young girl was upset.
Second Reading Have children find sentences that contain contractions with *will* or *not*. Have children read each sentence and then read it again, changing the contraction to two words.

Comprehension

After reading, ask children the following questions:
- Why couldn't anyone find Angus? *Inference/ Using Picture Clues*
- How did the girl feel at the end of the story? *Reflective Analysis/Personal Response*

ESL/ELL **English Language Learners**

Have children look at the pictures to identify by pointing to some of the places the characters look for Angus.

Contractions with is and have

Skill Focus

Children will

★ identify and write contractions with *is* and *have*.

★ use contractions to complete sentences.

ESL/ELL English language learners who are accustomed to languages not written with the Roman alphabet may be unfamiliar with the apostrophe as a form of punctuation rather than as representing a sound in spoken language.

Teach

Introduce Contractions with *is* and *have* Review that a contraction is a shortened form of two words. Say these sentences.

- **That is my pen on the desk.**
- **That's my pen on the desk.**

Repeat the sentences and ask children to identify the contraction. (*that's*) Then, write *that is* on the board. Demonstrate erasing the *i* and replacing it with an apostrophe to form the contraction. Write *it is* on the board and invite a volunteer to form the contraction. (*it's*) Repeat with *she is.*

Explain that the word *have* can also be used to make contractions. Write the following sentences on the board.

- **I have written in my journal.**
- **I've written in my journal.**

Say the sentences aloud and have a volunteer underline the contraction in the second sentence and circle the words in the first sentence that it represents. Then, write *we have* and *you have* on the board. Have volunteers write the contractions.

Practice and Apply

Writing Go over the rules on pages 147 and 148 with children. Remind them to leave a space between letters for writing an apostrophe. Suggest they repeat the sentences to themselves after they write the contractions.

Critical Thinking Discuss Talk About It. Children may say that since it is a birthday present for Rocky, Jess wants it to be a surprise.

Reading Use *Three Wishes*, MCP Phonics and Reading Word Study Skills Library, Level B, to reinforce children's recognition of contractions with *is* and *have.*

Name_____

▶ Circle **two words in each sentence that can be made into one of the contractions in the box.** Print **the contraction on the line.**

RULE
Some contractions are formed with the word **is.**
he is = he's

| he is = he's | That is = That's | it is = it's |
| she is = she's | It is = It's | |

1. (It is) Rocky's birthday. _____ It's

2. What a surprise (he is) going to get! _____ he's

3. Jess has his gift, but (she is) hiding it. _____ she's

4. Do you think (it is) something Rocky wants? _____ it's

5. What will Rocky get? Look at the picture at the top. (That is) what Rocky wants the most. _____ That's

 Why does Jess hide Rocky's present?

Contractions with is: Critical thinking **147**

FOCUS ON ALL LEARNERS

ESL/ELL ENGLISH LANGUAGE LEARNERS

Provide children with the guidelines for identifying contractions with *is* by reviewing the rule on page 147.

- On the chalkboard, write *he is = he's* to help English language learners understand that the contraction is simply a shorter way to write the two words *he is*. If needed, explain the equal sign (=).

- Ask children to work in pairs. Have one partner read the uncontracted forms in the text box on page 147 and have the other partner read the contracted form.

- Help children find and underline the word *is* in items 1–5 and then circle the two words in each sentence that can be made into one of the contractions in the box.

AUDITORY LEARNERS GROUPS

Write *that's, it's, he's, she's, you've, we've,* and *they've* on the board. Have children make up a progressive story, using the contractions as often as possible. Each person should repeat the previous sentences and add a new one to the story.

Print the contraction that means the same as the underlined words in each sentence.

RULE
Some contractions are formed with the word **have**.
You have = You've
I have = I've
We have = We've
They have = They've

1.
I have made you smile.

_____I've_____ made you smile.

2.
We have shown you tricks.

_____We've_____ shown you tricks.

3.
They have tossed a ball with their noses.

_____They've_____ tossed a ball with their noses.

4.
You have had a good time.

_____You've_____ had a good time.

148 Contractions with have

HOME Write contractions and have your child write the two words that combine to form each one.

CURRICULUM CONNECTIONS

SPELLING
Write the following phrases in a column on the board: *it is; they are; I will; we have; can not; I am.* Ask children to write each phrase followed by its matching contraction spelling word. *(it's, they're, I'll, we've, can't, I'm)* Distribute copies of the contraction portion of the unit spelling list to children for checking and practice.

WRITING
Ask children if they would like to be a person who explores outer space, and if so, why. Have them write sentences that describe their wishes about space exploration, which might include traveling into space or exploring from the earth through telescopes. Encourage children to include *I've, it's, that's,* and other contractions they know as they write.

PORTFOLIO

VISUAL/KINESTHETIC LEARNERS *INDIVIDUAL*
Materials: construction paper, marker, scissors
Cut paper circles in half, using a different zigzag cut for each. Write a contraction on half of each circle and the matching phrase on the other. Children can practice matching the puzzles on their own.

CHALLENGE
Have children think of topics related to space flight or astronomy, including the space shuttle, astronauts, planets, stars, and so on. Then, have them write riddles about a few of these topics, using contractions with *is, have, will,* and *not.*

EXTRA SUPPORT/INTERVENTION
Materials: index cards cut in half, marker
Make cards for *i, t, s, h, e, t, i, s, a,* and an apostrophe. Invite children to use the cards to form contractions with *is* and then their matching phrases. Model how to replace the *i* in *is* with the apostrophe. Make additional cards for *have* contractions if you wish. See Daily Phonics Practice, page 253.

Integrating Phonics and Reading

Guided Reading
Have children read the title. Ask them what they think the man in the story might wish for.
First Reading Ask children what the man thought about wishing for.
Second Reading Invite children to find the contractions in the story and identify the two words that each represents.

Comprehension
After reading, ask children the following questions:
• What were the three wishes? *Recall/Sequence*
• Did the husband and wife have a good idea when they said they should have asked for three more wishes? Why or why not?
Reflective Analysis/Personal Response
ESL/ELL English Language Learners
Invite children to look through the pictures in the story to point to and identify who the characters are. If necessary, explain that the tree is also a character.

Contractions with am, are, and us

Skill Focus

Children will

★ identify and write contractions with *am*, *are*, and *us*.

★ use contractions to complete sentences.

★ review contractions with *is*, *will*, *not*, and *have*.

ESL/ELL Children may not be fully aware of the baseline beneath letters of a contracted word and may confuse the apostrophe with a comma. Reinforce written punctuation.

Teach

Introduce Contractions with *am*, *are*, and *us* Encourage children to listen carefully. Say, *Let's stand*. After children stand say, *Let's sit down*. Explain that you used a contraction in each of the sentences. Ask children to identify it. (*let's*) Write *let's = let us* on the board.

Next, write these sentences on the board.

- **I'm writing on the board.**
- **We're learning about contractions.**

Invite a volunteer to read the first sentence and underline the contraction. (*I'm*) Ask children what two words *I'm* is made from. (*I am*) Write *I'm = I am* on the board. Have a volunteer read the second sentence and circle the contraction. Ask what two words make up *we're*. (*we are*) Write *we're = we are*. Have volunteers read each sentence, substituting the uncontracted form for the contraction.

Practice and Apply

Writing Have children read the rule at the top of page 149. Together, read the directions and be sure children understand them. Remind them to say the entire sentence with both the contracted and uncontracted form. Before children begin page 150, you may wish to quickly review the contractions with *is*, *have*, *will*, and *not*. Invite children to restate the directions in their own words for the top of page 150.

Reading You may wish to use *A Pot of Stone Soup*, MCP Phonics and Reading Word Study Skills Library, Level B, to reinforce and review contractions.

Name _____

▶ Print **two words that mean the same as the underlined word in each sentence.**

> **RULE**
> Contractions can be formed with the words *am*, *are*, or *us*.
> I am = I'm
> we are = we're
> let us = let's

1. <u>Let's</u> have a party.   Let us
2. <u>We'll</u> ask our friends to come.   We will
3. <u>I'm</u> going to pop popcorn.   I am
4. <u>He's</u> going to bring some lemonade.   He is
5. <u>She's</u> going to bring some cupcakes.   She is
6. <u>They're</u> going to bring games.   They are
7. <u>We're</u> going to have fun!   We are

▶ Print **the contraction that means the same as the two words beside the line.**

8. you are — you're		14. she is — she's
9. I am — I'm		15. it is — it's
10. let us — let's		16. they are — they're
11. we are — we're		17. we will — we'll
12. he is — he's		18. they will — they'll
13. I will — I'll		19. he will — he'll

Contractions with am, are, us, is, will   **149**

FOCUS ON ALL LEARNERS

ESL/ELL ENGLISH LANGUAGE LEARNERS

Use the following activity with English language learners to help them practice recognizing contractions and their meanings.

- Point out the box at the top of page 150. Explain that the box contains the contractions for each pair of words in items 1–20.
- Ask children to count how many contractions in the box include the word *I*. (*three*) Confirm that they can distinguish the word *I* from the lowercase letter *l*.
- Complete the first few items together. Then, have English language learners work with more English-proficient partners to complete the activity.

AUDITORY LEARNERS

Have children substitute contractions for *am*, *are*, and *us* phrases as you read the following paragraph: *I am the first astronaut from my school.* (*I'm*) *I am going with someone from another school.* (*I'm*) *We are flying to Mars on Sunday.* (*We're*) *They are not sure if anybody lives on Mars.* (*They're*) *Let us go and see!* (*Let's*)

Print the letter of each contraction next to the words that have the same meaning.

a. we're	b. you'll	c. it's	d. can't	e. I'm
f. he's	g. won't	h. let's	i. don't	j. she's
k. you're	l. isn't	m. he'll	n. we'll	o. I'll
p. I've	q. they'll	r. she'll	s. we've	t. aren't

1. we will __n__   2. we are __a__   3. will not __g__   4. he is __f__

5. you will __b__   6. let us __h__   7. can not __d__   8. it is __c__

9. is not __l__   10. you are __k__   11. they will __q__   12. I am __e__

13. do not __i__   14. I have __p__   15. she will __r__   16. she is __j__

17. he will __m__   18. we have __s__   19. are not __t__   20. I will __o__

Find a word in the box that will finish each sentence. **Print** it on the line.

| Let's |
| I'm |
| It's |
| I'll |
| don't |
| we're |

21. ____Let's____ go skating in the park.

22. ____It's____ time for us to go.

23. I ____don't____ want to be late.

24. ____I'm____ ready to go. Are you?

25. ____I'll____ help you find your skates.

26. I think ____we're____ going to have fun.

HOME With your child, take turns making up a sentence for each contraction.

150 Review contractions: Words in context

CURRICULUM CONNECTIONS

SPELLING

Duplicate the code and sentences below. Have children decode the spelling words that complete the sentences.

1 = '	6 = e	11 = t
2 = I	7 = h	12 = s
3 = w	8 = v	13 = y
4 = c	9 = l	14 = r
5 = a	10 = n	15 = m

1. <u>2-1-15</u> going to read about astronauts. (*I'm*)

2. <u>3-6-1-8-6</u> got books about them. (*We've*)

3. <u>11-7-6-13-1-14-6</u> brave people. (*They're*)

4. <u>2-11-1-12</u> fun to read about astronauts. (*It's*)

5. I <u>4-5-10-1-11</u> wait to grow up. (*can't*)

6. Maybe <u>2-1-9-9</u> be an astronaut, too. (*I'll*)

WRITING

Ask children to each write five questions they would like to ask an astronaut. Encourage them to use contractions. A child might ask *Do you get scared when you're in space?* or *What should I study if I'm planning to be an astronaut?*

KINESTHETIC LEARNERS **GROUPS**

Materials: index cards, markers

Make and distribute cards for *I, we, they, let, s, m, r, e,* and two apostrophes. Ask children to form the contractions *I'm, we're, let's,* and *they're.* Then, dictate sentences, such as *I'm seven* and *We're astronauts.* Have children use the cards to spell the contractions.

CHALLENGE

Challenge children to write poems describing what space travel might be like. Have them use at least three contractions in their verse.

EXTRA SUPPORT/INTERVENTION

Practice using the verb *am* with the pronoun *I.* Then, work with the verb *are* and the pronouns *you, we,* and *they.* Have children compose sentences about themselves using contractions with *am* and *are.* See Daily Phonics Practice, page 253.

Integrating Phonics and Reading

Guided Reading
With children, read the title and look at the illustration. Ask them what is unusual.

First Reading Ask children to explain what problem the two men have at the beginning of the story.

Second Reading Have children identify the contractions and the words they represent. Then, have them find pairs of words that can form contractions.

Comprehension
Ask children the following questions:

- Why doesn't Ned let the woman taste the soup when she wants to? *Inference/Draw Conclusions*

- Is the woman correct when she says the soup tastes like her chicken soup? Why or why not? *Reflective Analysis/Personal Response*

ESL/ELL English Language Learners
Ask children whether they have ever helped make soup. Encourage children to tell what ingredients are found in soup.

Pages 151–152

Phonics and Reading / Phonics and Writing

Review Contractions

Skill Focus

Children will

★ read contractions in the context of a letter.

★ write contractions to finish sentences.

★ build contractions with *not*, *have*, *will*, and *is*.

ESL/ELL Many languages do not form contractions by combining subject plus verb/modal, so provide frequent oral and written modeling.

Teach

Identify Contractions: Say these words aloud: *didn't, won't, have not*. Ask children to explain which word or words do not belong with the others. (*have not, because the others are contractions*) Repeat the procedure with *she's, it is, he's*.

Sound to Symbol Write the words *have not* on the board. Ask children what the contraction is for *have not*. (*haven't*) Invite a volunteer to come to the board and write the contracted form. Do the same with *it is, let us, we are,* and *I am*.

Read Words in Sentences Write these sentences on the board.

- I can't eat lunch yet.
- I'll wait in the office for Jan.

Read the sentences with children. Have volunteers circle the contractions and tell what two words were combined to make each contraction.

Practice and Apply

Phonics and Reading After children read the letter, have them identify the contractions and tell what two words were combined.

Critical Thinking Discuss Talk About It with children. Ask them to think about what they know about computers and then brainstorm ways in which computers might help astronauts.

Phonics and Writing With children, work through the first box on page 152 modeling how to fill in the blanks by making contractions with *not*.

Reading Use *The Family Tree*, MCP Phonics and Reading Word Study Skills Library, Level B, to provide practice in reading contractions.

151

Name_____

 Phonics & Reading — Read the letter. Print a contraction on the line to finish each sentence.

July 10

Dear Mom and Dad,

I can't believe I've been at Space Camp for four days. I'm having so much fun. I don't ever want to leave!

We're being trained like real astronauts. We made models of rockets. Yesterday, we launched them and mine worked! It's hard work. There's so much to remember.

Today, I'll take my place at Mission Control. There, I will use a computer to help our flight crew lift off using the sights and sounds of a real space mission. I can't wait!

Love,
Cara

1. Cara said, "I _____can't_____ believe _____I've_____ been at Space Camp for four days."

2. "_____We're_____ being trained like real astronauts," she said.

3. "_____It's_____ hard work. _____There's_____ so much to remember."

TALK About It How might a computer be used to help astronauts in space?

Review contractions: Critical thinking   **151**

FOCUS ON ALL LEARNERS

ESL/ELL ENGLISH LANGUAGE LEARNERS

Use the activity on page 151 to teach finding contractions in context.

- Have English language learners and more English-proficient children work together in small groups to highlight the contractions in the letter on page 151.

- Invite volunteers to read each of the sentences at the bottom of the page. Working in pairs, have children underline the same sentence in the letter. Assist English language learners by helping them scan for key words.

- Have pairs complete the activity by providing the missing contractions orally, then in writing.

VISUAL/KINESTHETIC LEARNERS

Materials: beanbag, mural paper, marker

Make a nine-square grid on mural paper taped to the floor and write a contraction in each square. Invite children to take turns tossing the beanbag into the grid. Have the player identify the two words that form the contraction on which the beanbag lands.

Phonics & Writing

Use a word tile to make contractions with **not, have, will,** or **is.** Write each contraction on the lines.

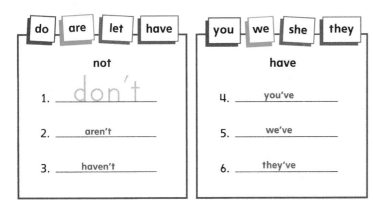

| do | are | let | have |

not

1. don't

2. aren't

3. haven't

| you | we | she | they |

have

4. you've

5. we've

6. they've

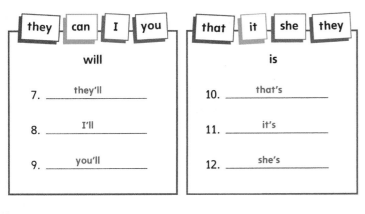

| they | can | I | you |

will

7. they'll

8. I'll

9. you'll

| that | it | she | they |

is

10. that's

11. it's

12. she's

HOME Ask your child to write sentences for the contractions on the page.

CURRICULUM CONNECTIONS

SPELLING

You may wish to use the sample sentences as you posttest the contractions below.

1. **can't**   I **can't** go to school today.
2. **we've**   **We've** got science class in the morning.
3. **they're** **They're** visiting a museum.
4. **I'm**   **I'm** feeling better.
5. **I'll**   Maybe **I'll** go after all.
6. **it's**   **It's** the last day of the week.

SOCIAL STUDIES

Provide nonfiction books, encyclopedia articles, and computer software from which children can gather important dates and events in the history of the United States space program. Build a vertical time line inside an outline of a rocket on a bulletin board. List the earliest events children suggest at the bottom and lead to most recent history near the top.

PORTFOLIO

AUDITORY/VISUAL LEARNERS   GROUPS

Materials: Phonics Picture Cards: horse (18), nurse (27), snowman (146)

Write the contractions *he'll, she'll,* and *it'll* on the board. Ask children to take turns picking up a picture and making a sentence about it by using a contraction. For example: *He'll melt when the sun comes out.*

CHALLENGE

Invite children to imagine that they have just been accepted at Space Camp. Have them write a letter to the director of the camp, explaining whether or not they plan to attend. Suggest that they give three reasons for their choice. Encourage them to use contractions appropriately.

EXTRA SUPPORT/INTERVENTION

Materials: Phonics Word Cards, Set 2: Contractions (125–148)

Distribute the cards among children. Say sentences using the contractions and invite children to hold up their cards when they hear those contractions. **See Daily Phonics Practice, page 253.**

Integrating Phonics and Reading

Guided Reading
Have children look at the illustrations and predict what the story will be about.
First Reading Ask children how the family's problem starts.
Second Reading Have children reread the story, identify the contractions, and tell which words were combined to make each contraction.
Comprehension
After reading, ask children the following questions:
• Why did the tree branch break? *Inference/Cause and Effect*
• If you could join the family in the tree, what would you take with you? *Reflective Analysis/Personal Response*
ESL/ELL English Language Learners
Read the title of the story and have children determine who they think each of the characters is on the cover. Invite volunteers to name each family member, such as *Mother* in English and in their primary language.

Plural Endings -s and -es

Skill Focus

Children will

★ recognize and read words with plural endings.

★ distinguish between the use of -s and -es to form plural nouns.

★ write words with plural endings to complete sentences and lists.

ESL/ELL The ability to distinguish between sibilant sounds such as those of *x, z, ss, sh,* or *ch* is highly dependent on the phonetics of the speaker's first language. Children may have difficulty perceiving meaningful differences between certain pairs of these sounds. Practice word pairs within noted areas of difficulty.

▶ Teach

Introduce Plurals Say the following sentences:

- **I see a dog in the yard.**
- **I see the dogs in the yard.**

Repeat the sentences and then ask children to explain the difference between them. (*The first sentence refers to one dog. The second refers to more than one dog.*) Explain that the word *dog* is singular and the word *dogs* is plural. Write the words *dog* and *dogs* on the board. Underline the *s* and explain that the -*s* makes the word plural.

Then, write these sentences on the board.

- **I have a new brush.**
- **My sister and I have new brushes.**

Have children read the sentences and tell which form of *brush* is singular and which is plural. Point out that the plural form *brushes* ends with -*es*. Have a volunteer underline the ending.

▶ Practice and Apply

Writing Have children read the rhyme on page 153 and identify the plural forms. You may wish to point out that *Mars* is not a plural form although it ends with *s*. Then, read the rules for plurals. Ask children to explain which rule applies to *dog* and to *brush*. Be sure they understand the directions for both pages. Remind them to read the entire item before they write the word.

Reading You may wish to use *Winter's Song,* MCP Phonics and Reading Word Study Skills Library, Level B, to practice reading plural nouns.

Name_____

Sandwiches, books, a snack—
What things shall I pack?
I'll blast off to Mars,
And zoom past the stars!

▶ Circle **the word that will finish each sentence. Print it on the line.**

RULE
When **s** or **es** is added to a word it forms the plural. Plural means "more than one." If a word ends in **x, z, ss, sh,** or **ch,** usually add **es** to make it mean more than one. For other words just add **s.**
one brush	two **brushes**
one sandwich	many **sandwiches**
one book	three **books**

1. At the zoo we saw some
   seal (seals)
   seals _____

2. We like to eat fresh
   peach (peaches)
   peaches _____

3. We have toys in three
   box (boxes)
   boxes _____

4. June will use a
   (brush) brushes
   brush _____

5. Ed's mom gave him a
   (cap) caps
   cap _____

6. Just look at those
   dog (dogs)
   dogs _____

7. Look at those shiny
   star (stars)
   stars _____

8. The box was used for
   mitten (mittens)
   mittens _____

FOCUS ON ALL LEARNERS

ESL/ELL ENGLISH LANGUAGE LEARNERS

Materials: index cards

Confirm that English language learners understand that -*s* or -*es* is used to show that a word refers to more than one.

- On the board, write the words *peach, box,* and *brush,* along with their plural forms. Help children identify the similarities between these three words and others that form plurals with -*es.* Underline the final letters in each word. Pronounce the final sounds of each word clearly, pointing to the underlined letters as you say them. Have children say singular and plural forms.

- Have children work in small groups to complete page 154. Complete Steve's List together and the remaining lists in pairs. Have children write -*s,* and *x, z, ss, sh, ch* + -*es* on index cards as reminders of the plural forms as they complete the lists.

KINESTHETIC/AUDITORY LEARNERS

Reinforce that when -*es* is added to words that end in *x, z, ss, sh,* or *ch,* the new word has an extra syllable. Have children practice saying these words and tapping out the syllables as they do so: *peaches, boxes, foxes, dresses, buzzes, wishes.* Then, try *sandwiches* and *toothbrushes.*

> Read **each shopping list.** Finish **each word** by adding the ending **s** or **es**. Print **the ending** on the line.

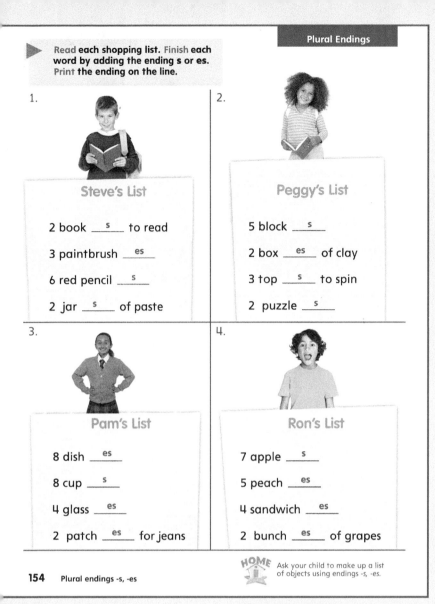

1.

Steve's List

2 book __s__ to read

3 paintbrush __es__

6 red pencil __s__

2 jar __s__ of paste

2.

Peggy's List

5 block __s__

2 box __es__ of clay

3 top __s__ to spin

2 puzzle __s__

3.

Pam's List

8 dish __es__

8 cup __s__

4 glass __es__

2 patch __es__ for jeans

4.

Ron's List

7 apple __s__

5 peach __es__

4 sandwich __es__

2 bunch __es__ of grapes

 Ask your child to make up a list of objects using endings -s, -es.

154 Plural endings -s, -es

CURRICULUM CONNECTIONS

SPELLING

You may use the following to pretest the new set of spelling words.

1. **books**   I have five **books** in my bag.
2. **likes**   She **likes** reading about rockets.
3. **glasses**   I washed the **glasses**.
4. **bushes**   My mom planted two **bushes**.
5. **wanted**   I **wanted** to go to school today.
6. **waiting**   I have been **waiting** an hour.

ART

Materials: white mural paper, stapler, newspaper, string, coat hangers, markers

Have children write plural words of things they would take with them to the planet on two cutout and decorated spaceship shapes. Staple the pieces together, leaving an opening for stuffing the rocket with newspaper. Staple closed and attach to a hanger with string.

TECHNOLOGY   **AstroWord** Base Words and Endings

VISUAL LEARNERS GROUPS

Materials: two large paper bags, index cards, marker

Mark one bag *-s ending* and the other *-es ending*. Make cards with singular nouns whose plurals are formed by adding *-s* or *-es*. Then, have children sort the words into the bags. When they finish, have volunteers draw the cards out and say the singular and plural forms of the words.

CHALLENGE

Ask children to list items they might like to take with them to outer space. Invite them to rewrite the rhyme on page 153 with these lists of objects, and have them illustrate the rhymes.

EXTRA SUPPORT/INTERVENTION

Invite children to take turns choosing a classroom object and saying the singular and plural form of its name, such as *pencil* and *pencils*. Write each singular noun on the board and have children use the rule on page 153 to write the plural forms. **See Daily Phonics Practice, pages 253–254.**

Integrating Phonics and Reading

Guided Reading

Read the title and have children look at the pictures in the story. Have them predict what the title means.

First Reading Ask children to identify some of the songs of winter.

Second Reading Have children find some examples of plural nouns. If children mention verbs that end in *-s* or *-es*, remind them that they are looking for words that name objects.

Comprehension

After reading, ask the following questions:

- What does the title mean? *Inference/Drawing Conclusions*
- Does winter really sing? Explain. *Reflective Analysis/Personal Response*

ESL/ELL English Language Learners

Read the title with children. Point out that the word *Winter's* ends with *-s*, but it is not plural. Remind children that an apostrophe can be used to show ownership.

Inflectional Endings -ing and -ed

Skill Focus

Children will

★ identify the inflectional endings -*ing* and -*ed*.

★ read and write new words by adding -*ing* and -*ed* to base words.

ESL/ELL Many languages other than English do not use inflectional endings to mark verb tenses. Speakers of such languages may need help understanding that these endings tell when the action of the verb takes place.

Teach

Introduce Inflectional Endings -*ing* and -*ed* Say the following three sentences aloud.

• **The astronauts float in space.**
• **They are floating everywhere.**
• **They floated across the cabin.**

Repeat the sentences and ask children to identify the three words that are nearly the same. (*float, floating, floated*) Write the three words on the board. Underline *float* in each of the words. Explain that *float* is a base word and -*ing* and -*ed* are endings. Then, write *drift, drifting,* and *drifted* on the board. Have a volunteer identify and underline the base word.

Practice and Apply

Sound to Symbol Read the rhyme on page 155. Have children identify the words with the -*ing* and -*ed* endings. Invite volunteers to write the words on the board and underline the base word. You may wish to point out that the spelling of the base words *bob* and *try* changes when the ending is added.

Writing Before children begin working on pages 155–156, have them read the rule at the top of the page. Remind them that they will be adding -*ing* to the words on page 155 and -*ed* to the words on page 156.

Reading Use *All About Bats,* MCP Phonics and Reading Word Study Skills Library, Level B, to provide practice in reading words with -*ing* and -*ed* endings.

Name _____

Floating and bobbing,
We drifted in space.
We tried hard to run,
But just stayed in one place.

> **RULE**
>
> A **base word** is a word to which the ending **ing** or **ed** can be added to form a new word.
>
> float + ing = floating
> drift + ed = drifted

▶ Add **ing** to each base word. Print the new word on the line.

1. sleep ____sleeping____   2. jump ____jumping____

3. play ____playing____   4. help ____helping____

5. start ____starting____   6. work ____working____

7. fish ____fishing____   8. turn ____turning____

▶ Add **ing** to the word beside each sentence. Print the new word on the line.

9. We are ____waiting____ for the bus. | wait |

10. Doris and Mark are ____jumping____ rope. | jump |

11. Sam is ____looking____ for the bus. | look |

12. Bart's dog is ____staying____ with him. | stay |

13. Terry is ____holding____ his lunch. | hold |

14. Meg is ____reading____ a book. | read |

15. Now, the bus is ____turning____ our corner! | turn |

Inflectional ending -ing: Words in context   **155**

FOCUS ON ALL LEARNERS

ESL/ELL ENGLISH LANGUAGE LEARNERS

The activities on page 156 provide English language learners with additional practice identifying and manipulating inflectional endings.

• Review the rule for applying inflectional endings by adding the ending -*ed* to the base words on page 155.

• Introduce the meaning of -*ed* to show action that has already taken place by giving clue words such as *yesterday* or *last week.* Some children may find expressing sequence of action confusing. Remember that the focus of this lesson is to help children form new words with inflectional endings.

• Read aloud the directions for both activities on page 156; have children complete items 1–11 in small groups; review aloud together. Then, complete items 12–20 on the chalkboard.

AUDITORY LEARNERS

Materials: Phonics Word Cards, Set 2: -*ed*, -*ing* words (73, 79, 81, 84, 91, 96, 99, 103)

Invite volunteers to read the word on a card and call on classmates to name the base word. Other children can use the base words and inflected forms in sentences.

Add **ed** to each base word. Print the new word on the line. Use the new words to finish the sentences.

1. look	2. want	3. help
looked	wanted	helped

4. leap	5. fix	6. paint
leaped	fixed	painted

7. Jess __helped__ me catch a frog.

8. We __wanted__ a frog for a pet.

9. We __looked__ everywhere for frogs.

10. Suddenly, a frog __leaped__ over a rock.

11. We __fixed__ up a box as a frog home.

Print each base word on the line.

12. locked	13. marched	14. dreamed
lock	march	dream

15. played	16. cleaned	17. passed
play	clean	pass

18. watched	19. wanted	20. missed
watch	want	miss

156 Inflectional ending -ed: Words in context

HOME
With your child, take turns acting out each base word; then add -ed.

CURRICULUM CONNECTIONS

SPELLING

Use each of the spelling words *books, glasses, wanted, likes, bushes,* and *waiting* in an oral sentence. Ask children to trace the spelling word on their desks, reciting the letters together. Distribute copies of the spelling words for children to practice from at home.

SCIENCE

Ask children to jump into the air and then ask why they landed back on the floor. Discuss Earth's gravitational pull that prevents people and objects from floating into space. Explain that astronauts in space are weightless and can float because they are too far away from Earth's gravity—the force that makes things fall towards the ground.

TECHNOLOGY **AstroWord** Base Words and Endings

KINESTHETIC/VISUAL LEARNERS GROUPS

Materials: string and magnet "fishing poles," bowl, fish cutouts, paper clips, marker

On the cutouts, print base words to which -ed and -ing can be added without spelling changes. Invite children to "fish" words from the bowl, read them, add -ed and -ing, and write each set of three words on the board.

CHALLENGE

Ask children to make a list of activities that might be part of an astronaut's day on a space shuttle or in a space station. Have them write paragraphs using these ideas and circling words that end in -s, -es, -ed, and -ing when they finish.

EXTRA SUPPORT/INTERVENTION

After children complete page 155, invite them to role-play the rhyme about floating in space. As you read each phrase, have children demonstrate and describe what is happening. See Daily Phonics Practice, page 254.

Integrating Phonics and Reading

Guided Reading

Invite children to tell what they know about bats. Tell them that they are going to read about bats.
First Reading Ask children to tell something they learned about bats.
Second Reading Have children identify the words with the endings -ing or -ed. Write them on the board and have children circle the base word.

Comprehension

After reading, ask the following questions:
• How can bats be both helpful and harmful? *Recall/Compare and Contrast*
• Would you like to be the person in the picture on page 3? Explain your answer. *Reflective Analysis/Personal Response*
ESL/ELL English Language Learners
On the board, write the word *bat* and say it. Then, ask children what a *bat* is. After children have responded, explain that they are going to be reading about the bats that are animals.

156

Inflectional Endings -ing and -ed (doubling final consonant)

Skill Focus

Children will

★ identify base words that require doubling a final consonant before adding an ending.

★ write words that end with *-ing* and *-ed* to complete sentences.

★ recognize and read high-frequency words.

ESL/ELL English language learners may not hear the difference between the sound of a final *-n* and that of a final *-ng* and say *runin* instead of *running*. Demonstrate the position of the open mouth as you model each sound.

Teach

Introduce Doubling the Final Consonant

On the board, write *plan*. Then, write these sentences. Ask children to identify the base word and the two words formed from the base word. (*planning, planned*)

- I plan to be an astronaut.
- I am planning to be an astronaut.
- Shannon Lucid planned to be an astronaut.

Be sure children recognize that the consonant *n* was doubled before the endings were added. Explain that when a word with a short vowel ends in one consonant, that consonant is usually doubled before adding *-ing* or *-ed*. Write *hop* and *drip* on the board. Have volunteers write new words, adding the endings *-ing* and *-ed*.

Practice and Apply

Writing Read the rules on pages 157–158 with children. Tell them the words such as *walk* and *pick* do not end in one consonant, and so the final consonant is not doubled. As children complete the page, they will have the opportunity to read the high-frequency words *were* and *everywhere*.

Critical Thinking Discuss Talk About It. For page 157, children should use picture clues and text clues to determine that it is summer. For page 158, encourage children's responses to various ways Wags might have gotten muddy.

Reading Use *A Lot Happened Today*, MCP Phonics and Reading Word Study Skills Library, Level B, to reinforce doubling the final consonant before adding *-ing* and *-ed*.

Name _____

▶ Add **ing** to the base word in the box. Print the new word on the line.

> **RULE**
> When a short vowel word ends in a single consonant, usually double the consonant before adding **ing**.
> stop + ing = stopping

1. Maria and Dana were _____planning_____ to go shopping.   **plan**

2. First, they went _____walking_____ in the park.   **walk**

3. Children were _____swinging_____ on the swings.   **swing**

4. A cat was _____napping_____ in the shade.   **nap**

5. People were _____jogging_____ along a path.   **jog**

6. Dana saw two bunnies _____hopping_____ by.   **hop**

7. Maria's ice cream cone was _____dripping_____ .   **drip**

8. They saw a man _____roasting_____ hot dogs.   **roast**

9. His dog was _____begging_____ for one.   **beg**

10. "_____Stopping_____ by the park was fun," said Maria.   **Stop**

11. "Now, let's go _____shopping_____ ," Dana said.   **shop**

TALK About It What time of year is this?

Inflectional ending -ing: High-frequency words, critical thinking   **157**

FOCUS ON ALL LEARNERS

ESL/ELL ENGLISH LANGUAGE LEARNERS

Have children practice adding *-ed* and *-ing* to base words requiring doubling of final consonants.

- Read the rule on page 157; on chart paper, write the base words in the shaded boxes, then write the word with the *-ing* ending. Apply the rule for doubling final consonants by having children hold up one finger if a base word ends in a single consonant or two fingers if the word ends in double consonants.

- Read sentences aloud, followed by the base words. Have volunteers say, then spell the new words before writing them. Read or have volunteers read aloud the completed story.

- Follow this process to complete page 158 for adding *-ed*.

KINESTHETIC LEARNERS **GROUPS**

Materials: index cards, marker

Print words such as *bat, pitch, slip, stop, skip, pack, lock, stack, step, jump, fish, bump,* and *drag* on cards. Invite volunteers to draw cards and pantomime the words for classmates to guess. Then, have children add *-ed* and *-ing* to the words and write them on the board.

RULE

Add **ed** to the word beside each sentence to make it tell about the past. Print the word on the line.

To make a word tell about the past, usually add **ed**. If a short vowel word ends in a single consonant, usually double the consonant before adding **ed**.
I **skip** on my way home.
Yesterday I **skipped**, too.

1. My dog _____wagged_____ his tail when I got home. **wag**

2. He _____jumped_____ up on me with a happy smile. **jump**

3. I _____stepped_____ back because he was muddy. **step**

4. "Wags, you need to be _____scrubbed_____!" **scrub**

5. I _____picked_____ him up and put him in the tub. **pick**

6. I _____rubbed_____ him with soap and rinsed him. **rub**

7. He _____splashed_____ water everywhere! **splash**

8. Then, he _____dripped_____ all over my floor. **drip**

9. I laughed as I _____watched_____ him. **watch**

10. When Wags _____stopped_____, he was clean but the bathroom was a mess! **stop**

11. I _____mopped_____ up the mess. **mop**

12. Then, I _____played_____ with Wags. **play**

TALK How do you think Wags got muddy?

HOME Take turns with your child saying and spelling a word with the -ed ending.

CURRICULUM CONNECTIONS

SPELLING

Have children list their spelling words in four columns according to their endings *(books, likes; glasses, bushes; wanted; waiting)*. Then, invite children to add more words with matching base word and ending patterns to each column. Children can do this activity independently or as a whole class exercise.

LANGUAGE

Read the following sentences and ask children to tell you if the action described in each one takes place in the present or past.

1. Jan hopped on the trampoline. *(past)*
2. A man walked the dog. *(past)*
3. A boy is riding a pony. *(present)*
4. The pony is trotting around the track. *(present)*

 **AstroWord** Base Words and Endings

---

AUDITORY/VISUAL LEARNERS

Write these words on the chalkboard and have children add -*ed* to them and use the resulting words in sentences: *stop, scrub, pat, hop, wag.* Repeat, using -*ing* endings.

CHALLENGE

Using books they are reading, have children find examples of verbs in which the final consonant has been doubled before an ending was added. Invite them to write ten of these verbs and their base words.

EXTRA SUPPORT/INTERVENTION

Materials: Phonics Word Cards, Set 2: -*ed* and -*ing* words (73–104)
Have children find words on the cards in which the final consonant of the base word has been doubled. Ask them to write these inflected forms and their base words on the chalkboard. Test the rules on pages 157 and 158 against the base words. See Daily Phonics Practice, page 254.

Integrating Phonics and Reading

Guided Reading
After reading the title and looking at the pictures in the story, invite children to predict what this story will be about.
First Reading Ask children to explain some of the things that happened.
Second Reading Have children look for words that end with -*ing* and -*ed*. List words in which the final consonant was doubled before the ending was added.
Comprehension
After reading, ask the following questions:
• Why does Jared tell his teacher he needs a new book? *Inference/Cause and Effect*
• Did everything that Jared wrote really happen? Explain. *Reflective Analysis/Make Judgments*
ESL/ELL English Language Learners
Direct children's attention to the picture on the cover. Encourage volunteers to explain the game of baseball and to compare this sport with similar sports in their native countries.

Lesson 73
Pages 159–160

Inflectional Endings -ed and -ing (dropping final e)

Skill Focus

Children will

★ identify base words that require dropping a final e before adding an ending.

★ write words that end with -ed and -ing to complete sentences.

★ spell words that end with -ing and -ed.

ESL/ELL Speakers of languages in which syllables normally end in vowels may find it difficult not to pronounce the silent e.

Teach

Introduce Dropping the Final e Read the poem below and have children raise their hands when they hear a word with an -ed or -ing ending.

> Off we went, we blasted away,
> Looking at the planets today.
> We glided toward the stars,
> Hoping to find life on Mars.

Write the words *blasted, glided, looking,* and *hoping* on the board. Have volunteers identify and write the base words *blast, glide, look,* and *hope.*

Draw children's attention to *glide* and *hope.* Ask how the two words are the same. (*They both end in silent e.*) Demonstrate adding -ed and -ing to glide by erasing the final e and writing the endings. Have a volunteer do the same for *hope.*

Make three columns on the board. Write *skate, rake, tape, race* in the first column. Then, have volunteers write the -ed form in the second column and the -ing form in the final column.

Practice and Apply

Writing Read the rule on page 159. Have children restate the rule in their own words. Then, have them complete the sentences. For page 160, remind them that sometimes they may have to double a consonant or drop the final e before adding an ending.

Reading You may wish to use *Bedtime at Aunt Carmen's,* MCP Phonics and Reading Word Study Skills Library, Level B, to reinforce the spelling of words with the inflectional endings -ed and -ing.

159

Name _____

▶ Circle the word that finishes each sentence. Print it on the line.

> **RULE**
> If a word ends with a silent **e**, drop the **e** before adding **ing** or **ed**.
> I **bake** cookies with my mom.
> We **baked** cookies yesterday.
> We are **baking** cookies today, too.

1. Yesterday, I ____jogged____ to the park. (jogged) jogging

2. Then, I ____walked____ home. (walked) walking

3. Today, I am ____skating____ with friends. (skating) skated

4. We are ____stopping____ for lunch. stopped (stopping)

▶ Read each pair of sentences. Add **ing** or **ed** to the base word. Print the new word on the line.

clean	5. Today, Dad is ____cleaning____ the garage.
	He ____cleaned____ the car yesterday.
save	6. I am ____saving____ my money to buy a bike.
	Last week, I ____saved____ about $3.00.
wag	7. Last night, my dog was happy, so she ____wagged____ her tail. She is ____wagging____ her tail now, too.

Inflectional endings -ing, -ed **159**

FOCUS ON ALL LEARNERS

ESL/ELL ENGLISH LANGUAGE LEARNERS

Model for English language learners how to identify base words with a final e and how to apply the rule on page 159 to add inflectional endings.

• Read and explain the rule on page 159. Be sure children understand that the e is called silent because it is not pronounced aloud.

• Read aloud the answer choices for items 1–4. Have children underline the base words. Then, have children complete the items, one at a time. Invite a volunteer to explain how and why the rule was applied to item 3.

• Help children add -ed and -ing to the words in items 5–7. Then, have them work together to complete the sentences.

AUDITORY LEARNERS GROUPS

Invite children to play "Once upon a time." Each child will add a sentence to a story using a word ending in -ed or -ing. Start the game with a line such as *Once upon a time there was a frog who steered a spaceship.* Write words with -ing and -ed on the chalkboard.

▶ Add **ing** to each base word. Print the new word on the line.

1. ride   _riding_
2. fry   _frying_
3. rub   _rubbing_
4. hide   _hiding_
5. frame   _framing_
6. dig   _digging_
7. take   _taking_
8. jump   _jumping_
9. poke   _poking_
10. ship   _shipping_
11. pack   _packing_
12. quit   _quitting_

▶ Add **ed** to each base word. Print the new word on the line.

13. pin   _pinned_
14. rock   _rocked_
15. chase   _chased_
16. hop   _hopped_
17. march   _marched_
18. bake   _baked_
19. wish   _wished_
20. drop   _dropped_
21. hope   _hoped_
22. quack   _quacked_

160 Inflectional endings -ing, -ed: Spelling

 HOME With your child, take turns choosing a word, adding an ending, and then using the new word in a sentence.

CURRICULUM CONNECTIONS

SPELLING
Make large cards for each of the letters in the words *books, glasses, waiting, wanted, likes,* and *bushes.* Display them in random order. Dictate the words, calling on volunteers to pick up one letter each until the words are spelled.

ART
Materials: white, yellow, and black construction paper; glue; yellow chalk

On black construction paper, have children make torn-paper pictures of spaceships in flight. Stars, comets, and planets might be torn from paper or drawn with chalk.

 **TECHNOLOGY** **AstroWord** Base Words and Endings

VISUAL/KINESTHETIC LEARNERS GROUPS
On the board, print the words *take, chase, hope, time, glide, slope, name,* and other verbs ending in silent *e* that you wish to use. Dictate *-ed* and *-ing* forms of the base words and call on volunteers to erase the silent *e* in the matching base words, spell the new words, and use them in sentences.

CHALLENGE
Materials: audiocassette tape, cassette player

Ask children what they have done recently that was lots of fun. Have them tell about their experiences and record the stories. Ask children to listen to the stories and list words from them that end in *-ed* or *-ing.*

EXTRA SUPPORT/INTERVENTION
Materials: index cards, marker, tape

Make cards for base words ending in silent *e* and several each of *-ed* and *-ing.* Have children tape an ending to each base word, covering the silent *e.* Read the new words together deciding whether they make sense. For example: *taking,* is correct, but not *taked.* See Daily Phonics Practice, page 254.

Integrating Phonics and Reading

Guided Reading
After children read the title and look at the cover, ask what the characters are doing.

First Reading Ask children what problem the girl and Edgar are having.

Second Reading Have children find words with *-ed* and *-ing* endings. Write them on the board. Invite children to identify the base words and explain how the ending was added.

Comprehension
After reading, ask the following questions:

• What happened after Edgar left the bedroom? ***Recall/Sequence***

• Who do you think bumped, poked, and shoved the girl? Explain. ***Reflective Analysis/Personal Response***

ESL/ELL **English Language Learners**
Read the title aloud. Explain that the word *house* is left out of the title. Have children say what the complete title really is: *Bedtime at Aunt Carmen's House.*

Phonics and Reading / Phonics and Writing

Endings -s, -es, -ed, -ing

Skill Focus

Children will

★ read words ending with -s, -es, -ed, and -ing in the context of an article.

★ write words with these endings to finish sentences.

★ build words ending with -s, -es, -ed, and -ing.

ESL/ELL Some languages distinguish consonants that are aspirated, or pronounced with a puff of air, from those that are not. Children from those language backgrounds may experience some confusion with the inflectional ending -ed in various contexts.

Teach

Review Plural and Inflectional Endings
Say the following words: *cats, dishes, played, singing*. Ask children how the words are the same. (*They each contain a base word and an ending.*) Then, ask children to identify the endings. (*-s, -es, -ed, -ing*) Remind children that *-s* and *-es* make words plural and that *-ed* and *-ing* show action.

Sound to Symbol Write *lunch, class, box, buzz,* and *watch* on the board. Have volunteers come to the board and make each word plural. (*lunches, classes, boxes, buzzes, watches*) Then, list these words on the board: *fade, trot, jump*. Review the rules for adding inflectional endings and then have volunteers add *-ed* and *-ing* to each word. (*faded, fading; trotted, trotting; jumped, jumping*)

Practice and Apply

Phonics and Reading After children have read the article, have them identify the words with endings. Remind them that they can fill in the blanks with words from the story.

Critical Thinking Discuss Talk About It. Be sure children understand that without the sun, Earth would be too cold for life.

Phonics and Writing For page 162, explain that they are to add the endings that are given in each box. Remind children that the spelling of the base word may sometimes change. Tell children to write a sentence at the bottom of page 162, using at least one of the words they made.

Reading Use *Never Say Never*, MCP Phonics and Reading Word Study Skills Library, Level B, to review reading words with endings.

Name_____

 **Phonics & Reading**   Read the story. Print a word that ends in **s, es, ed,** or **ing** on the line to finish each sentence.

The Sun: Star of Our Solar System

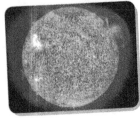

The sun shines on us giving Earth light and heat. Without the sun, Earth would be so cold that no plants and animals would be able to live there. That is why the sun is so important.

The sun is a star. Like other stars, the sun is made of burning gases. From Earth, the sun looks like a glowing yellow ball because of the burning gases. The sun is closer to us than other stars, so it seems larger. Earth and the other planets move around the sun. The sun and the planets are called the solar system.

1. The sun shines on us, _____giving_____ Earth light and heat.

2. Like other stars, the sun is made up of burning _____gases_____.

3. The sun is closer to us than other _____stars_____ , so it seems larger.

4. The sun and the planets are _____called_____ the solar system.

 Would there be life on Earth without the sun? Why or why not?

Review -s, -es, -ed, -ing: Critical thinking   **161**

FOCUS ON ALL LEARNERS

- -

ESL/ELL ENGLISH LANGUAGE LEARNERS
Confirm that English language learners can read words ending with *-s, -es, -ed,* and *-ing*.

• Read the directions on page 161 aloud. Have children work in pairs to complete 1–4.

• Ask one child to read aloud as the partner listens for the sentences that correspond to each item. Some children may find this task easier if they choose a single word from the item and then scan the reading for that word, rather than searching for the entire sentence.

• Have partners write the words to finish each sentence. Review completed sentences aloud as a group.

AUDITORY/VISUAL LEARNERS
Materials: Phonics Picture Cards:
fox (12), girls (13), mittens (24), nuts (65), eggs (80), tray (88), nails (90), grapes (129), slippers (142), skates (143), dishes (162)
Display the picture cards. Have volunteers say and spell the singular and plural forms of each picture. List the words.

Phonics & Writing

Add **the ending to each word inside the box. You may have to change the spelling of a word before adding the ending.**

s or es
1. star ___stars___
2. dish ___dishes___
3. moon ___moons___
4. lunch ___lunches___

ing
5. stop ___stopping___
6. fly ___flying___
7. walk ___walking___
8. shine ___shining___

ed
9. fix ___fixed___
10. step ___stepped___
11. play ___played___
12. save ___saved___

s or es
13. fox ___foxes___
14. jump ___jumps___
15. buzz ___buzzes___
16. watch ___watches___

▶ Write **a sentence using one or more of the words you made.**

_____

_____

_____

 Ask your child to write sentences for three of the other words on the page.

CURRICULUM CONNECTIONS

SPELLING

You may wish to posttest the spelling words below at this time.
1. **waiting** We have been **waiting** for you.
2. **wanted** We **wanted** new skates.
3. **glasses** I forgot my **glasses**.
4. **likes** My sister **likes** to play tennis.
5. **books** I left my **books** at school.
6. **bushes** Can you wait by the **bushes**?

SCIENCE

Materials: poster of the solar system

Display the solar system illustration and have children name the nine planets. List them on the board, from closest to farthest from the sun. Talk about the orbits around the sun that the planets travel in.

 **AstroWord** Base Words and Endings

VISUAL/KINESTHETIC LEARNERS PARTNERS

Materials: 12 pieces of note paper for each pair

Have partners write each -s, -es, -ed, or -ing ending word on a sheet of paper. Ask children to list the words in groups of matching endings, read the words, and circle the base words.

CHALLENGE

Materials: mural paper; markers or paints

Have each child research one of the nine planets. Then, invite the group to work together to create a mural about our solar system. Ask them to label and write a caption for the sun and each of the planets.

EXTRA SUPPORT/INTERVENTION

Before children begin page 161, read the article aloud as children follow along. Then, have volunteers read the sentences at the bottom of the page and find the missing words in the story. **See Daily Phonics Practice, pages 253–254.**

Integrating Phonics and Reading

Guided Reading

Display the cover and read the title of *Never Say Never.* Ask if anyone can guess what the title means.

First Reading Have children tell what Little Bunny's problem was and how he solved it.

Second Reading Have children find and list words with the -ed or -ing ending and their base words.

Comprehension

After reading, ask the following questions:
• Why did Little Bunny think he would never get the carrots? *Recall/Drawing Conclusions*
• What would you have told Little Bunny about getting the carrots? *Reflective Analysis/ Personal Response*

ESL/ELL English Language Learners

Ask children if they can find Little Bunny in the clump of grass on pages 6–7. Then, help them find the word *grass* on page 6. Repeat this procedure for the words *rope* and *loop*.

Suffixes -ful, -less, and -ness

Skill Focus

Children will

★ identify the suffixes *-ful*, *-less*, and *-ness*.

★ form new words by adding suffixes to base words.

★ use words with suffixes to complete sentences.

ESL/ELL Overstressing suffixes when pronouncing words may cause some English language learners to think one word is actually two.

Teach

Introduce Suffixes *-ful*, *-less*, *-ness* Say the following groups of words and have children identify how the words in each group are the same.

- **cheerful, helpful** (*end with* -ful)
- **careless, harmless** (*end with* -less)
- **loudness, darkness,** (*end with* -ness)

Explain that the ending of each word is called a suffix. Tell children that a suffix is added to a base word. Explain that a base word is the root word, or a word without an ending. Write *cheerful, useless,* and *loudness* on the board. Underline the base word and circle the suffix for each word. Explain that *-ful* means "full of," so cheerful means "full of cheer"; *-less* means "without," so *careless* means "without any care"; and *-ness* means "a way of being," so *loudness* means "being loud."

Practice and Apply

Identify Suffixes Read the rhyme on page 163. Have children identify the words with the suffix *-ful*. (*handful, wonderful*) Invite volunteers to write the words on the board, underlining the base word and circling the suffix. Then, read the rhyme on page 164. Have children identify the words with the suffixes *-less* and *-ness*. (*fearless, darkness*) Have them write the words on the board, underlining the base word and circling the suffix.

Writing Have children read the rule on page 163. Then, go over the directions, asking children to restate them in their own words. For page 164, have children read the rule. Then, read the directions. Remind children that they will use some of the words in items 1–8 to complete items 9–15.

Reading Use *Sara's Lovely Songs,* MCP Phonics and Reading Word Study Skills Library, Level B, to practice reading and understanding words with suffixes.

Name _____

A handful of moon dust,
A lunar rock or two—
Visiting the moon must
Be wonderful to do!

▶ Add the ending **ful** to each base word. Print the new word on the line. Use the new words to finish the sentences.

> **RULE**
> You can make a new word by adding the ending **ful** to a base word.
> color + ful = colorful

1. care   __careful__   2. cheer   __cheerful__

3. wonder   __wonderful__   4. hope   __hopeful__

5. Pablo was __hopeful__ that he could have a new scooter.

6. He promised to be __careful__ if he got one.

7. His family looked __cheerful__ when they gave him his gift.

8. It was a scooter! What a __wonderful__ gift!

▶ Draw a box around each base word.

9. u s e |f u l   10. h o p e |f u l

11. r e s t |f u l   12. h a r m |f u l

13. f e a r |f u l   14. h e l p |f u l

15. p l a y |f u l   16. c a r e |f u l

Suffix -ful: Words in context   **163**

FOCUS ON ALL LEARNERS

ESL/ELL ENGLISH LANGUAGE LEARNERS

Have children identify and form words with suffixes *-ful, -less,* and *-ness* on pages 163–164.

- Model each activity by reading directions aloud and completing the first item on each page as a group. Encourage children to complete the first activity on each page with partners. Review answers aloud as a group.

- Read aloud to children the word and sentence prompts for the remaining activities on these pages. Copy onto the chalkboard the first item in each section. Use colored chalk to highlight the physical changes made to each target suffix.

KINESTHETIC LEARNERS

Materials: index cards, marker

Print *-less, -ness,* and *-ful* on the board. On the cards, print base words to which at least one of these suffixes can be added. Divide the class into teams. Players in turn take a card and add a suffix to print a new word on the board. The first team to finish wins.

What's that in the darkness?
A space monster in flight?
I'm almost fearless,
But I'll turn on the light!

RULE

You can add the ending **ness** or **less** to a base word to make a new word.
dark + ness = darkness
fear + less = fearless

▶ Add **less** or **ness** to each base word. Print the new word on the line. Use the new words to finish the sentences.

less		**ness**	
1. use	useless	5. weak	weakness
2. sleep	sleepless	6. dark	darkness
3. harm	harmless	7. loud	loudness
4. fear	fearless	8. sharp	sharpness

9. It is _____ useless _____ to tell me bears are harmless.

10. I am not brave or _____ fearless _____ .

11. If I think about bears when I'm in bed, I'm _____ sleepless _____ .

12. The bear's eyes are glowing in the _____ darkness _____ .

13. The _____ loudness _____ of their snarls worries me.

14. I can almost feel the _____ sharpness _____ of their teeth.

15. I wish that bears were known for _____ weakness _____ .

164 Suffixes -less, -ness: Words in context

 HOME Write base words and suffixes on separate cards and have your child match them.

CURRICULUM CONNECTIONS

SPELLING

The final group of spelling words for this unit can be pretested at this time.

1. **careful**   Be **careful** near the stove.
2. **darkness**   Does **darkness** scare you?
3. **lovely**   It was a **lovely** spring morning.
4. **stories**   We wrote **stories** about space.
5. **funnier**   That joke was **funnier** than the last one.
6. **happiest**   Who is the **happiest** clown?

SCIENCE

Ask children if they agree with the author of the rhyme on page 161 that visiting the moon is a wonderful thing to do. Ask why people might be interested in viewing displays of moon rocks. Share information about igneous, metamorphic, and sedimentary rocks and what they can tell us about Earth's history.

TECHNOLOGY   **AstroWord** Suffixes

AUDITORY/VISUAL LEARNERS   **GROUPS**

Review the suffix meanings. Write these phrases on the board and have children name *-ful, -less,* and *-ness* words that mean the same as the phrases: *being sick* (sickness), *full of thanks* (thankful), *without use* (useless), *full of play* (playful), *without care* (careless).

CHALLENGE

Challenge children to make new words by adding *-ful* and *-less* to the base words *care, cheer, harm, use, hope, help, rest,* and *fear*. Have them use each pair of words in sentences that show the words' opposite meanings.

EXTRA SUPPORT/INTERVENTION

Materials: Phonics Word Cards, Set 2: *-ful, -less,* and *-ness* words (105–118)

Invite each child to choose a card, read the words aloud, and tell their meanings. Have children use each word in several different sentences. See Daily Phonics Practice, pages 254–255.

Integrating Phonics and Reading

Guided Reading
Have children read the title and look at the cover. Ask who the girl in the picture might be.
First Reading Have children use the book to name the songs that Sara sings.
Second Reading Have children find the words *carefully* and *cheerfully* in the story. Explain that each of these words has two suffixes. Ask them to identify the suffix that means "full of."
Comprehension
After reading, ask the following questions:
• Why does Sara want to be a singer when she grows up? *Inference/Cause and Effect*
• What song do you think Sara is singing on page 4? *Reflective Analysis/Personal Response*
ESL/ELL English Language Learners
Talk to children about the meaning of the word *notes* in the story. Explain that the word *note* can mean a short letter to someone or a musical sound. Encourage children to explain the meaning of notes in the story.

Suffixes -ly, -ful, -less, -ness

Skill Focus

Children will

★ identify base words and the suffix *-ly*.

★ form new words by adding the suffix *-ly* to base words.

★ review the suffixes *-ful*, *-less*, and *-ness*.

ESL/ELL Because of their monosyllabic backgrounds, speakers of Cantonese, Hmong, Vietnamese, Korean, or Khmer may think that two-syllable words are two words.

Teach

Introduce the Suffix -ly Say the following words aloud and ask children to identify how the words are the same: *lovely, quickly, softly.* (*Their endings are the same.*)

Write the above words on the board. Review that a suffix is an ending added to a base word. Point to the word *lovely.* Ask children what the base word is. (*love*) Underline *love.* Then, ask what the suffix is. (*-ly*) Circle the suffix. Explain that the suffix *-ly* tells how something happens or is. Repeat the process with *quickly* and *softly.*

Practice and Apply

Identify Suffixes Read the rhyme on page 165 aloud. Then, have children read it chorally. Ask children to identify the words with a suffix. (*slowly, quickly, slowly, nearly*) Have volunteers write each word on the board, underlining the base word and circling the suffix.

Writing Invite a volunteer to read the rule on page 165. Then, read the directions. Have children do items 1 and 9 orally to verify that they know what to do. Page 166 is a review of suffixes. Be sure children understand how to complete the matching activity.

Reading You may wish to use *Sara's Lovely Songs*, MCP Phonics and Reading Word Study Skills Library, Level B, to reinforce the recognition and use of suffixes.

Name _____

Slowly, the sun rises.
Quickly, the sky gets bright.
Slowly, the sun will set again,
When it's nearly night.

▶ Add **the ending ly to each base word.** Print **the new word on the line.**

RULE
Add the ending **ly** to a base word to make a new word.
slow + ly = slowly

1. close   closely
2. swift   swiftly
3. soft   softly
4. brave   bravely
5. loud   loudly
6. slow   slowly
7. love   lovely
8. near   nearly

▶ Circle **each ly ending in the sentences.** Print **the base words on the lines.**

9. Tigers walk soft(ly)   soft

10. Lions roar brave(ly)   brave

11. Monkeys screech loud(ly)   loud

12. Turtles crawl slow(ly)   slow

13. Deer run swift(ly)   swift

14. I watch the animals close(ly) at the zoo.   close

15. The zoo near my house is love(ly)   love

FOCUS ON ALL LEARNERS

ESL/ELL ENGLISH LANGUAGE LEARNERS

Have children match base words to words with the suffixes *-ly, -ful, -less,* and *-ness.*

• On page 166, read aloud the directions and the word *quick,* the first item.

• Tell children you will read some words. They are to listen for a word that sounds like *quick.* Read choices a–e; have children select *quickly.* Explain that *quickly* is the base word *quick* with the suffix *-ly.* Model writing the letter of the answer on the line.

• Follow the process for items 2–6, reviewing correct answers.

• If English language learners become confused by the multistep directions, allow them to just draw lines from the words in the left column to their matching words in the right column.

KINESTHETIC LEARNERS

Materials: index cards, marker, shoe box

Make a boxful of word cards, using base words from pages 165–166. Print *-ly, -ful, -less,* and *-ness* across the board. Each child picks a card and places it in front of each suffix in turn. Classmates should read aloud each word that makes sense and say nothing for a base word that does not form a real word.

▶ Match the base word in the first column with the new word in the second column. Print the letter on the line.

1.

b	quick	a.	slowly
c	sweet	b.	quickly
a	slow	c.	sweetly
d	loud	d.	loudly
e	nice	e.	nicely

2.

d	glad	a.	softly
a	soft	b.	nearly
b	near	c.	lovely
c	love	d.	gladly
e	brave	e.	bravely

3.

c	use	a.	playful
a	play	b.	handful
e	cheer	c.	useful
b	hand	d.	harmful
d	harm	e.	cheerful

4.

d	care	a.	fearless
e	sleeve	b.	helpless
a	fear	c.	endless
c	end	d.	careless
b	help	e.	sleeveless

5.

c	home	a.	sleepless
a	sleep	b.	hopeless
d	use	c.	homeless
e	wire	d.	useless
b	hope	e.	wireless

6.

d	good	a.	softness
c	dark	b.	sadness
e	kind	c.	darkness
b	sad	d.	goodness
a	soft	e.	kindness

HOME With your child, think of other word pairs to add to the boxes.

CURRICULUM CONNECTIONS

SPELLING

Give children copies of the final set of words from the unit spelling list: *careful, darkness, lovely, stories, funnier, happiest.* Before they add the words to their notebooks or take them home, study them together. Have children read each word aloud, point to each letter with a pencil, say it, and then read the word again. Have children identify the base words.

WRITING

Ask children if they have ever seen a sunrise or a sunset. What are some words they might use to describe the appearance of a sunrise or sunset or how they feel when they see one? Have children write about whether they like a sunrise or sunset better and explain why. Encourage them to use words with *-ly, -ful, -ness,* and *-less* suffixes.

PORTFOLIO

TECHNOLOGY **AstroWord** Suffixes

AUDITORY/VISUAL LEARNERS

Materials: Phonics Word Cards, Set 2: *-ful, -less, -ness, -ly* words (105–120)

Start an imaginary space story and have children use words from the cards to add to the tale. You might begin by saying *I thought I was alone in the darkness of space, but.* . . . Write the story sentences on chart paper, highlighting words with suffixes.

CHALLENGE

Tell children that words that tell how something happens, such as *-ly* words, are called adverbs. Have them identify the adverbs and the verbs being described in the sentences on page 165. (*For example,* softly *tells how tigers walk.*)

EXTRA SUPPORT/INTERVENTION

Materials: Phonics Word Cards, Set 2: *-ful, -less, -ness, -ly* words (105–120)

Display the word cards. Define each word by using a phrase such as *Find the word that means "without sleep."* Have children find and read the card for *sleepless.* See Daily Phonics Practice, pages 254–255.

Integrating Phonics and Reading

Guided Reading

Point to the musical notes on the cover. Ask children what they are. Have children suggest why they might be on the cover. You may also wish to use the suggestion in English Language Learners section below.

First Reading Ask children when does Sara sing.

Second Reading Invite children to find all the words with the suffix *-ly.* Have them list the words on the board and underline the base words.

Comprehension

After reading, ask the following questions:

• How does Sara seem to choose the song to sing? *Inference/Generalize*

• Which of Sara's songs is your favorite? Why? *Reflective Analysis/Personal Response*

ESL/ELL **English Language Learners**
Point out the word *lovely* in the title, *Sara's Lovely Songs.* Ask children to identify the suffix. Explain that *lovely* describes Sara's songs.

Suffixes -er and -est

Skill Focus

Children will

★ identify the suffixes -er and -est.

★ form new words by adding -er and -est to base words.

★ recognize that -er is used to compare two things and -est is used to compare more than two things.

★ write words that end with -er or -est to complete sentences.

ESL/ELL In Spanish, er stands for a different sound than er in English, so some English language learners may say late-air instead of later, for example.

Teach

Introduce Suffixes -er and -est Cut three strips of paper of unequal length that can be used to demonstrate the relationship among the words *short, shorter, shortest.* Line the papers up and say the following sentences as you point to each one.

- **This paper strip is short.**
- **This paper strip is shorter.**
- **This paper strip is shortest.**

Have children repeat the words *short, shorter, shortest,* as you point to the appropriate strip. Ask how the words are alike and different. (*They all have the same base word* short, *but they end differently.*)

Write *short, shorter,* and *shortest* on the board. Have volunteers underline the base word short and circle the suffixes. Explain that the suffix -er is used to compare two things and means "more." The suffix -est is used to compare more than two things and means "most."

Practice and Apply

Reading Read the rhyme on page 167 with children. Have them identify the words with suffixes and write them on the board. (*nearer, nearest*) Invite volunteers to go to the board and underline the base word and circle the suffix.

Writing Have a volunteer read the rule on page 167. Then, explain the directions and have children complete the first item together. For page 168, discuss the pictures. Be sure children understand the relationships among the pictures in each item.

Reading Use *The World's Biggest Baby,* MCP Phonics and Reading Word Study Skills Library, Level B, to practice reading words with the suffixes -er and -est.

Suffixes

Name _____

Earth is nearer to our sun
Than planets such as Mars.
But Mercury is the nearest one
To the sun, our nearest star.

▶ Add **the ending er and est to each word. Print the new words on the lines.**

RULE
You can add the ending **er** to a base word to make a new word that tells about two things. Add the ending **est** to tell about more than two things.
bright brighter brightest

	er	**est**
1. near	nearer	nearest
2. long	longer	longest
3. fast	faster	fastest
4. dark	darker	darkest
5. thick	thicker	thickest
6. deep	deeper	deepest
7. soft	softer	softest

▶ Draw **a picture to show the meaning of each word.**

8.	9.	10.
long	longer	longest

FOCUS ON ALL LEARNERS

ESL/ELL ENGLISH LANGUAGE LEARNERS

Read aloud the rule on page 167 and apply it for children as they complete the activity on this page.

- Read the rule and the example; chant the rhyme again.
- With books closed, read directions and item 1 for the group. Use a prop from the previous activity to cue -er and -est endings.
- Write -er on the chalkboard. Tell children that a form of -er is used to tell about two things. Usually, the word *than* also appears in the sentence. Give oral examples such as, *"The ball is nearer to me than to Selma."*

AUDITORY/VISUAL LEARNERS

Materials: Phonics Picture Cards: goose (15), mule (103), fly (137)

Invite children to take turns making statements comparing the animals on the cards by using words with -er and -est. For example: *The fly is the smallest; The mule is bigger than the goose; The fly moves faster than the mule.*

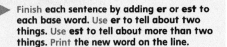

Finish each sentence by adding **er** or **est** to each base word. Use **er** to tell about two things. Use **est** to tell about more than two things. Print the new word on the line.

1. tall   Meg is _____taller_____ than Jay.

2. hard   The rock is _____harder_____ than the soap.

3. fast   The horse is the _____fastest_____ of the three.

4. long   The top fish is the _____longest_____ .

5. cold   Ice is _____colder_____ than water.

6. small   The ant is the _____smallest_____ .

168   Suffixes -er, -est: Words in context

HOME With your child, take turns using *-er* and *-est* words to compare things at home.

CURRICULUM CONNECTIONS

SPELLING

Have partners print the spelling words *careful, darkness, lovely, stories, funnier,* and *happiest* on index cards and then cut apart the letters. Then, as you dictate the words, partners can work together to respell them.

WRITING

Display an illustration of the sun and the planets that shows the position of each planet and its distance from the sun. Encourage children to write a paragraph about the planets, using the suffixes *-er* and *-est* to make comparisons.

SCIENCE

Tell children that the sun and its planets are part of our solar system. Explain that the sun is at the center of our solar system, and each planet moves in its own path around the sun. Show children the order of the planets from the sun. Ask them to consider what the temperature would be like on the planets nearest and farthest from the sun.

TECHNOLOGY   **AstroWord** Base Words and Endings

Integrating Phonics and Reading

Guided Reading
Have children read the title and look at the pictures on the cover. Ask them to predict what the world's biggest baby is.
First Reading Ask children what animal is the world's biggest baby.
Second Reading Have children tell about the comparisons described in the story using the words *bigger* and *biggest*.

Comprehension
After reading, ask the following questions:

• How long is a baby blue whale when it is born? *Recall/Compare*

• Compared to the amount of food you eat, how much food do you think a baby whale eats each day? *Reflective Analysis/Personal Opinion*
ESL/ELL English Language Learners
Point to each picture on the cover and invite volunteers to identify it. Have children repeat the name of each animal after you.

KINESTHETIC LEARNERS   GROUPS

Materials: Phonics Word Cards, Set 2: *-er, -est* words (121–124)

Invite children to act out the meanings of the words on the cards and their base words. For example, children could walk in such a way as to demonstrate the meanings of *slow, slower, slowest;* and *fast, faster, fastest*.

CHALLENGE

Invite children to create "quiz" questions that demonstrate their knowledge of the suffixes *-er* and *-est*. For example, children might write questions such as "Who sits nearer to the window, Carmen or Mark?" or "Which plant on the shelf is tallest?" Children can exchange questions and answer them.

EXTRA SUPPORT/INTERVENTION

Materials: drawing paper; crayons or markers

Invite children to fold the paper in thirds. Then, have them write a base word on the first third, the word with *-er* added on the second third, and the word with *-est* on the third section. Ask children to illustrate the three words. See Daily Phonics Practice, page 255.

y plus -er, -est, -es

Skill Focus

Children will

★ recognize the suffixes *-er*, *-est* and the plural ending *-es*.

★ identify base words that require changing a final *y* to *i* before adding *-er*, *-est*, or *-es*.

★ write words that end with *-er*, *-est*, and *-es* to complete sentences.

ESL/ELL English language learners other than Spanish should consider the different sounds as they do long and short vowel differences—as two sounds for the same letter.

Teach

Introduce Changing the y to i Say the following sentence, emphasizing the words that end with *y*: *The happy baby crawled across the floor.* Ask children to identify the words that end with a long *e* sound. (*happy, baby*)

Write the word *baby* on the board. Ask which letter stands for the long *e* sound. (*y*) Then, ask what is added to most words to make them plural. (*s* or *es*) Explain that *-es* is added to form the plural of a word that ends with a consonant and *y*. Erase the *y* and add *-ies*. Explain that the *y* changes to *i* before the *-es* is added to a word like *baby*. Write *pony* on the board. Invite a volunteer to say, spell, and write the plural form. (*ponies*)

Next, write the word *happy* on the board. Have children form two new words by adding the suffixes *-er* and *-est*. Review with children that the suffixes *-er* and *-est* are added to words to make comparisons. Write *happier* and *happiest*. Point out that the *y* changes to *i* before the suffixes are added. Write *silly* on the board. Invite a volunteer to add the suffixes *-er* and *-est* to *silly*. (*sillier, silliest*) Use the words in sentences to demonstrate their meaning.

Practice and Apply

Writing Read the rule at the top of page 169. Before children complete the sentences, remind them that the suffix *-er* is used to compare two things while *-est* is used to compare more than two. Have a volunteer read the rule on page 170 for forming plurals. Then, do items 1–3 together before children complete the sentences.

Reading Use *Suki and the Case of the Lost Bunnies*, MCP Phonics and Reading Word Study Skills Library, Level B, to reinforce changing *y* to *i* before adding an ending.

169

Name_____

▶ Add **er** and **est** to each word. Print **the new words on the lines.**

RULE
When a word ends in **y** after a consonant, change the **y** to **i** before adding **er** or **est**.
busy + est = busiest

	er	est
1. silly	sillier	silliest
2. happy	happier	happiest
3. windy	windier	windiest
4. fluffy	fluffier	fluffiest

▶ Finish **each sentence by adding er or est to the base word beside each sentence. Print it on the line.**

5. Today was Justin's _____ happiest _____ day of the week.   **happy**

6. He got to the bus stop _____ earlier _____ than he had on the other days.   **early**

7. It was _____ sunnier _____ than it had been all week.   **sunny**

8. He made up the _____ silliest _____ joke he could.   **silly**

9. The other kids said it was the _____ funniest _____ one they had heard.   **funny**

Suffixes -er, -est: Words ending in y, words in context   **169**

FOCUS ON ALL LEARNERS

ESL/ELL ENGLISH LANGUAGE LEARNERS

Expand children's growing confidence with *-er* and *-est*.

- On page 169, read aloud the rule for writing words that end in *y* after a consonant before adding *-er* or *-est*. Model examples on the board.

- Complete the chart for items 1–4; copy it onto the board.

- Add to the chalkboard the five words in the shaded boxes; have children form the *-er* and *-est* forms of both; add to the chart.

- Read items 5–9 aloud. Prompt each sentence to guide children to select the correct ending. Clue children that *-er* often implies "more than something else"; model with items 6 and 7.

AUDITORY/KINESTHETIC LEARNERS

Materials: Phonics Word Cards, Set 2: *-s*, *-es*, *-ies* words (61–72)

Read the words aloud and have children name the base words. Then, write the words on the board, having volunteers erase and add letters where needed to spell the base words.

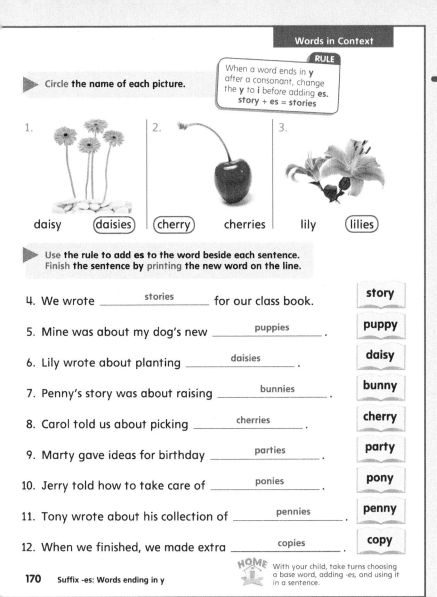

► Circle the name of each picture.

RULE
When a word ends in **y** after a consonant, change the **y** to **i** before adding **es**.
story + es = stories

1. daisy   (daisies)

2. (cherry)   cherries

3. lily   (lilies)

► Use the rule to add **es** to the word beside each sentence. Finish the sentence by printing the new word on the line.

4. We wrote _____ stories _____ for our class book. | story |

5. Mine was about my dog's new _____ puppies _____ . | puppy |

6. Lily wrote about planting _____ daisies _____ . | daisy |

7. Penny's story was about raising _____ bunnies _____ . | bunny |

8. Carol told us about picking _____ cherries _____ . | cherry |

9. Marty gave ideas for birthday _____ parties _____ . | party |

10. Jerry told how to take care of _____ ponies _____ . | pony |

11. Tony wrote about his collection of _____ pennies _____ . | penny |

12. When we finished, we made extra _____ copies _____ . | copy |

170   Suffix -es: Words ending in y

 With your child, take turns choosing a base word, adding -es, and using it in a sentence.

CURRICULUM CONNECTIONS

SPELLING

Invite children to copy the sentences below from the board, changing the underlined base words to the spelling words that make sense.

1. He read us two <u>story</u>. (*stories*)
2. <u>Dark</u> filled the room. (*darkness*)
3. My joke is <u>funny</u> than yours. (*funnier*)
4. The yellow rose is <u>love</u>. (*lovely*)
5. I am very <u>care</u> when I cut things. (*careful*)
6. She is the <u>happy</u> girl out of everyone. (*happiest*)

SCIENCE

Invite children to study newspaper national weather reports to find the hottest, windiest, sunniest, and coldest locations. Have them compare their area with other locations using the *-er* and *-est* words.

 **TECHNOLOGY** **AstroWord** Base Words and Endings

VISUAL LEARNERS *INDIVIDUAL*

Materials: drawing paper; crayons or markers

Invite children to each choose one adjective that ends in *y* such as *silly, happy, windy, early, sunny,* or *funny*. Have them divide their papers into three panels for the base word, the *-er* form, and the *-est* form. Ask them to write the three words and illustrate one row of words.

CHALLENGE

Have children write a comparison of three of their favorite cartoon characters, using words ending with *-er* and *-est*. They can use words that describe the characters' appearance, personality, voices, and actions.

EXTRA SUPPORT/INTERVENTION

Materials: index cards, marker

Make word cards for the answer words used in the sentences on page 169. Read the sentences aloud, leaving out the answers, and have children find the missing word cards. Repeat with the sentences on page 170. See Daily Phonics Practice, pages 253–255.

Integrating Phonics and Reading

Guided Reading

Have children read the title and look at the cover. Ask who they think Suki is and what she does.
First Reading Have children explain what Suki does.
Second Reading Ask children to find *bunnies, families,* and *stories*. Have them spell the words and then spell each base word.

Comprehension

Ask children the following questions:

• Why does Suki decide to help Sam? *Inference/Draw Conclusions*

• Do you agree that sometimes Suki needs a little help? Why or why not? *Reflective Analysis/Personal Response*

ESL/ELL **English Language Learners**
Read the title and have children look at the illustration. Ask them what the girl is holding in her hand. If necessary, explain that it is a magnifying glass and that detectives use one to search for clues.

Suffix -es
(Words Ending in y)

Skill Focus

Children will

★ recognize the plural ending *-es*.

★ form plurals of words ending in *y*.

★ distinguish between the use of singular and plural forms in context.

★ recognize and read high-frequency words.

ESL/ELL English language learners may have little experience in forming plurals of words ending in *y* and making the spelling changes. Point out that the sound of *y* and *ie* is the same.

Teach

Introduce Plurals of Words Ending in *y*
Invite children to tap on their desk one time when they hear a singular word and to tap twice when they hear a plural word as you read these words: *spaceship, captain, families, cities, astronauts, stars.*

Ask a volunteer to review for the class how words that end in a consonant and *y* are made plural. (*change* y *to* i *and add* -es.) Write *family* and *city* on the board and model changing the *y* to *i* and adding *-es* to form *families* and *cities.* Then, write these words on the board: *berry, bunny, story,* and *puppy.* Invite volunteers to go to the board and write the plural form of each word. (*berries, bunnies, stories, puppies*)

Practice and Apply

Writing Read the directions on page 171 with children. Review that words ending in *ss, x, sh, ch,* and *z* form their plurals by adding *-es.* Remind children that for items 7–14 they need to decide whether the word should be singular or plural. For page 172, explain that they should read the entire sentence and spell their answers carefully. Children will have an opportunity to read the high-frequency words *different, usually,* and *grow.*

Critical Thinking In discussing Talk About It, be sure children recognize that although the story is about a farm, the family that visits the farm probably lives in a city.

Reading You may wish to use *Suki and the Case of the Lost Bunnies*, MCP Phonics and Reading Word Study Skills Library, Level B, to reinforce recognition of words that end in *-ies.*

171

Name_____

▶ Add **endings to make the words mean more than one.**

1. bunny	2. city	3. box
bunnies	cities	boxes
4. lily	5. dress	6. pony
lilies	dresses	ponies

▶ Circle **the word that will finish each sentence. Print it on the line. Then,** print **the name of each picture below.**

7. Mary's birthday _____party_____ was fun.   (party) parties

8. Her dad read scary _____stories_____ .   story (stories)

9. We tossed _____pennies_____ into bottles.   penny (pennies)

10. Instead of cake, we ate _____cherry_____ pie.   (cherry) cherries

11. We got little _____candies_____ to take home.   candy (candies)

12.	13.	14.
bunny	lilies	ponies

Suffix -es: Words ending in y   **171**

FOCUS ON ALL LEARNERS

ESL/ELL ENGLISH LANGUAGE LEARNERS

Clarify for English language learners the rule for forming plurals of words that end in *y* after a consonant.

• Point out that the sound of *y* and *ie* can be long *e*. Write in a column on the board items 1, 2, 4, and 6 on page 171, using colored chalk to emphasize the final *y*. Say each word aloud as you write it. Have children repeat it together.

• Repeat the rule for making these words plural. Draw an *X* over the colored *y*. Rewrite the plural form of the word with the *-ies* ending. Say the singular form and then the plural form. Have children repeat the words together and then individually as they feel more comfortable.

AUDITORY/KINESTHETIC LEARNERS GROUPS

Materials: beanbag
Have children pass a beanbag around a circle while you chant *Listen, listen, for my name. Spell the plural to play this game.* When you stop, the player holding the bag must say and spell the plural of a word ending in *y* that you name.

► Change **the y to i and add es** to the word in each box. **Print** the new word to finish the sentence.

1. Farms are not found in ___cities___. | city |

2. Sometimes my friends and our ___families___ visit a farm. | family |

3. Sometimes there are ___daisies___ in the fields. | daisy |

4. ___Lilies___ often grow by the streams. | Lily |

5. We like to ride the ___ponies___. | pony |

6. There are many different animal ___babies___. | baby |

7. It's fun to play with the ___bunnies___. | bunny |

8. We usually see some ___puppies___. | puppy |

9. Apples and ___berries___ grow on farms. | berry |

10. We climb trees to pick ___cherries___. | cherry |

11. I like to write ___stories___ about our trips to the country. | story |

12. I give ___copies___ to my friends to read. | copy |

 Where does the family in the story live?

 Work with your child to write a story using the plural form of some of the words in the boxes above.

172 Suffix -es for words ending in y: High-frequency words, critical thinking

CURRICULUM CONNECTIONS

SPELLING
Use these words and sentences to posttest the last set of spelling words for this unit.
1. **stories**   I like **stories** about monsters.
2. **darkness** I like to hear them in the **darkness** of night.
3. **lovely**   There is often a **lovely** princess.
4. **careful**   I am **careful** to listen to every word.
5. **funnier**   These stories are **funnier** than cartoons.
6. **happiest** Still I am **happiest** when the lights are turned back on.

WRITING
Invite children to briefly retell the plot of the story *101 Dalmatians* and then write stories entitled *101 Bunnies* or *101 Ponies*.

 **AstroWord** Base Words and Endings

VISUAL LEARNERS
Have each group of children make a list of the singular and plural forms of ten items they see in the classroom. Encourage them to use dictionaries to check spellings they are unsure of.

CHALLENGE
On the board, write the words *city, way, story, bluejay, lily, toy, bunny, birthday, penny, boy.* Have volunteers change each word into its plural form, noting whether a vowel or consonant comes before the final *y.* Then, invite children to choose five of the plural words and write them in sentences.

EXTRA SUPPORT/INTERVENTION
Say the following words and ask children to respond as a group and tell if each word is singular or plural. Use *copy, horses, pennies, cherries, candies, lilies, pony, daisy, babies, families, bunny, berries, puppies, boxes.* See Daily Phonics Practice, pages 253–254.

Integrating Phonics and Reading

Guided Reading
Have children look through the story to preview who the characters are.
First Reading Ask children to use the book to tell where Suki looks for the bunnies.
Second Reading Have children find singular and plural words, write them on the board, and underline words ending in *-ies.*

Comprehension
After reading, ask the following questions:
• What does Sam mean when he says his bunnies hop? *Inference/Using Picture Clues*
• Why do you think Suki has a lot of trouble finding Sam's bunnies? *Reflective Analysis/Personal Response*

ESL/ELL English Language Learners
Help children compile a list of words from the story for things found around the house, such as *table, chair, bed, toy box, closet,* and so on. Some children may benefit by saying the object name in their native language.

Phonics and Spelling / Phonics and Writing

Review Contractions, Endings, and Suffixes

Skill Focus

Children will

★ spell and write contractions and words with endings and suffixes.

★ write a log entry using contractions and words with endings and suffixes.

ESL/ELL English language learners may forget to prolong the long *i* sound of *y* or to pronounce *ie* as one sound. If necessary, model words with these sounds.

Teach

Review Contractions, Endings, Suffixes Write these sentences on the board.

- **I don't like apples and cherries.**
- **I am going to be careful.**

Review that a contraction is a short way of writing two words as one. Remind children that the apostrophe replaces one or two letters that are left out. Have children find the contraction and tell which two words form the contraction. (*don't; do not*) Then, have volunteers put a check above the plural words and write the base words. (*apples, cherries; apple, cherry*) Review the rules for forming plurals, helping children to remember that plural means more than one.

Next, have children find the word with an ending (*going*) and the word with a suffix (*careful*). Have volunteers circle the ending and underline the suffix. Encourage children to name another word that ends with *-ing* and another word that has a suffix.

Practice and Apply

Phonics and Spelling Read the directions on page 173. Be sure children understand that they can find the answers in the word list at the top of the page. You may wish to have children read the words aloud before they begin the activity.

Phonics and Writing Before children begin their log entry, brainstorm possible things they might have seen, heard, and touched if they were on the moon. List appropriate words and phrases on the board. Remind children to begin their entry with a date and to use words from the box and the board to help them.

Reading Use *Kids in Tune*, MCP Phonics and Reading Word Study Skills Library, Level B, to review contractions, endings, and suffixes.

Name _____

 **Phonics & Spelling** Print two words from the list next to the matching ending. For the last one, print two contractions.

coldness	going	can't	thoughtful	lovely	funnier
blasted	waiting	darkness	deepest	glasses	bushes
happiest	wanted	slowly	careful	brighter	they're

1. ed   _____wanted_____   _____blasted_____

2. ing   _____waiting_____   _____going_____

3. ly   _____slowly_____   _____lovely_____

4. ful   _____careful_____   _____thoughtful_____

5. es   _____glasses_____   _____bushes_____

6. ness   _____darkness_____   _____coldness_____

7. er   _____funnier_____   _____brighter_____

8. est   _____happiest_____   _____deepest_____

9. contractions   _____can't_____   _____they're_____

Contractions, endings, suffixes   **173**

FOCUS ON ALL LEARNERS

ESL/ELL ENGLISH LANGUAGE LEARNERS

Materials: nine colored pencils

Group the word list on page 173 to help English language learners say and print examples of words with the target endings.

- Point out to children that items 1–9 include the types of words they have been practicing in this unit. Review word endings separately and give examples of each, reviewing appropriate rules, as needed.

- Focus children's attention on item 1 and the ending *-ed*. Have children each select a pencil, color the *-ed*, then color both words in the word list that have the same ending. Continue with the remaining eight items, choosing a different color for each.

- Review items 1–9 aloud; confirm oral responses, then have children spell words aloud as they print them on the lines.

AUDITORY/KINESTHETIC LEARNERS

Have children stand. Dictate words from the unit spelling list or words from pages 173 and 174. As children in turn add one letter to the word being spelled, they sit down. On their next turn, they stand after saying their letters. Continue as time allows.

A **log** is a kind of notebook where you write about things you see around you. Keeping a log can help you remember places you visit and things you do each day.

▶ Imagine you were the first astronaut ever to walk on the moon. **Write** about what it was like to walk on the moon. Tell how the moon looked and felt. Some of the words in the box may help you.

lighter	finest	lovelier	bouncing	darkness
it's	hopped	walking	weightless	wished
wonderful	happiest	hopes	I'll	slowly

Write the date to help you remember when you walked on the moon.

Tell about what you saw, heard, and touched.

Ask your child to write a sentence for each of the words not included in his or her log entry.

174 Contractions, endings, suffixes

CURRICULUM CONNECTIONS

SPELLING

Cumulative Posttest
Assess children's knowledge of the Unit 5 spelling list by posttesting at this point.

1. **I'll**   **I'll** wait here for you.
2. **can't**   I **can't** stay any longer.
3. **it's**   **It's** time for the sun to rise.
4. **we've**   **We've** put everything away.
5. **I'm**   **I'm** still very sleepy.
6. **they're**   **They're** not back yet.
7. **books**   Do you have my **books**?
8. **happiest**   This is the **happiest** feeling.
9. **darkness**   **Darkness** filled the house.
10. **wanted**   I **wanted** to go with you.
11. **likes**   My brother **likes** to ski.
12. **bushes**   Did you trim the **bushes**?
13. **careful**   Be **careful** when you skate.
14. **waiting**   Are you **waiting** for the bus?
15. **lovely**   That is a **lovely** dress.
16. **stories**   I like **stories** about giants.
17. **funnier**   Which riddle is **funnier**?
18. **glasses**   My **glasses** are in the case.

TECHNOLOGY   **AstroWord** Base Words and Endings

VISUAL LEARNERS *INDIVIDUAL*

Write these sentences on the board and have children copy them and unscramble the words in parentheses. 1) *My (sagsels) slip off my nose.* (glasses) 2) *Dan (skeli) going to school.* (likes) 3) *I like to read (skobo).* (books) 4) *She has a (lyevol) smile.* (lovely)

CHALLENGE

Have children use the word list and activity on page 173 as a model to write a new, similar page. Encourage them to work individually to replace the words in the word list with similar words. Then, have them number from 1–9, using the same items as on page 173. Finally, partners should exchange papers and write the answers.

EXTRA SUPPORT/INTERVENTION

On the board, draw connected letter boxes to show the shape or configuration of several spelling words. As you say the spelling words, have volunteers find the matching word shapes and fill in the correct letters. See Daily Phonics Practice, pages 253–255.

Integrating Phonics and Reading

Guided Reading
Explain to children that this book is nonfiction. Then, ask what they think the book will be about, based on the chapter titles and photographs.

First Reading Encourage children to explain what a chorus is and where the children sing.

Second Reading Have children find and write the words *cities, loved, youngest, older, oldest,* and *putting* and their base words.

Comprehension
After reading, ask the following questions:
• How do children audition for the Tampa Bay Children's choir? *Recall/Sequence*
• Would you like to become a member of this choir? Explain. *Reflective Analysis/Personal Response*

ESL/ELL **English Language Learners**
Encourage children to write their own definitions for words such as *duet, solo,* and *chorus* based on details in the text.

Take-Home Book

Review Contractions, Endings, and Suffixes

Skill Focus

Children will

★ read contractions, words with endings, and words with suffixes in the context of a story.

★ review selected high-frequency words in the context of a story.

★ reread for fluency.

ESL/ELL Spanish speakers may pronounce short *i* as long *e* (*eats* instead of *it's*). Model correct pronunciation.

Teach

Build Background

• Recall with children that the theme of this unit is "Blasting Off." Invite children to explain some of the things they have learned about space in this unit.

• Write the word *astronaut* on the board. Tell children that they will read a book about astronauts.

Review Skills Review the meaning of plural, contraction, and suffix. Then, say these words and have children identify the words that are plural: *babies, kitten, toys*; the words with suffixes: *neatness, happily, lady*; and the contractions: *can not, won't, didn't*.

Practice and Apply

Read the Book Demonstrate how to make the Take-Home Books. Suggest that children look through the books and discuss the pictures with them. Then, read the story together. Have children explain what they learned about space travel.

Sound to Symbol Have children find words with suffixes on page 1. (*blasts, soars, swiftly, cloudless, climbs, higher, speeds, darkness, moves, farther, wonderful*) Ask them to find a word that ends with *-less* on page 2. (*weightless*) Then, have them find plural words on page 3. (*astronauts, others, beds*) Finally, have children find two contractions on page 4. (*didn't, wouldn't*)

Review High-Frequency Words Write the word *climbs* on the board. Have children spell the word and then say it, blending the sounds. Have children identify the base word. (*climb*)

Reread for Fluency Have children reread the book to increase their fluency and comprehension. Remind them to take their books home to share with their families.

175

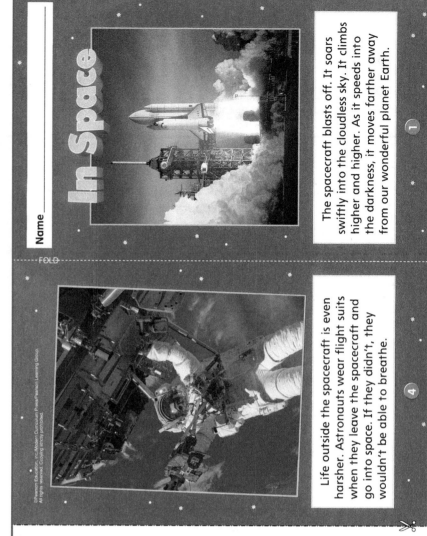

Name _____

In Space

The spacecraft blasts off. It soars swiftly into the cloudless sky. It climbs higher and higher. As it speeds into the darkness, it moves farther away from our wonderful planet Earth.

1

Life outside the spacecraft is even harsher. Astronauts wear flight suits when they leave the spacecraft and go into space. If they didn't, they wouldn't be able to breathe.

4

©Pearson Education, Inc./Modern Curriculum Press/Pearson Learning Group
All rights reserved. Copying strictly prohibited.

Review contractions, endings, suffixes: Take-home book **175**

FOCUS ON ALL LEARNERS

ESL/ELL ENGLISH LANGUAGE LEARNERS

Materials: newspapers or books containing pictures of outer space or space flights

Have children preread the Take-Home Book to identify target phonics skills before reading the narrative for content and pleasure.

• Make a four-column chart on the board with the headings *Contractions* ('), *Plural Endings* (*-s, -es*), *Inflected Endings* (*-ing, -ed*), and *Suffixes* (*-ly, -ful, -ness, -less, -er, -est, -y*) as children make their Take-Home Books.

• Divide the class into four groups, each containing a similar number of children, and ask them to locate and highlight in their Take-Home Books a specific target skill from the chart.

• Ask volunteers to print their findings on the chart under the correct headings. Confirm answers as a class.

AUDITORY/VISUAL LEARNERS

Invite partners to "buddy read" their Take-Home Books. One child reads the first page, the other reads the next, and so on. Encourage children to ask each other for help as they need it.

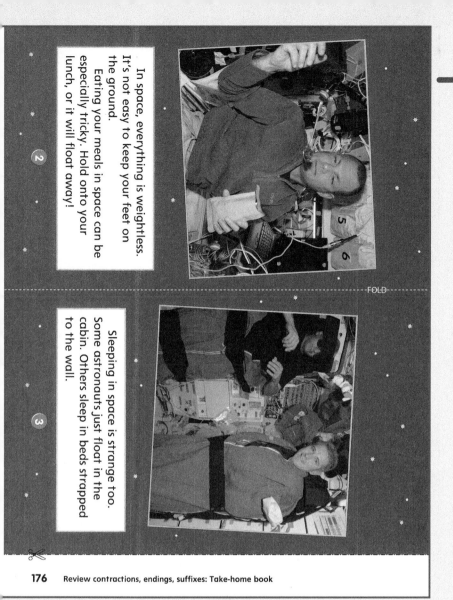

In space, everything is weightless. It's not easy to keep your feet on the ground.

Eating your meals in space can be especially tricky. Hold onto your lunch, or it will float away!

2

Sleeping in space is strange too. Some astronauts just float in the cabin. Others sleep in beds strapped to the wall.

3

---FOLD---

CURRICULUM CONNECTIONS

HEALTH/SCIENCE

Astronauts in space now eat meals very similar to on-Earth menus. Have children plan a day's worth of meals for a space flight. Encourage them to include low-fat foods and fruits and vegetables as they plan their menus.

WRITING

Invite children to create space-related names for the menu items they listed in the previous activity. Examples might include names such as Anti-gravity Grapes and Mashed Potato Clouds.

PORTFOLIO

READING/LANGUAGE ARTS

Explain that this story is told in third person, that is, by a narrator who is not in the story. Have children imagine that they are one of the astronauts. Using the pictures on each page, have them use the first person voice and retell the story in their own words. You might start them off by saying *Our spacecraft is blasting off.*

TECHNOLOGY

AstroWord Base Words and Endings Suffixes

VISUAL LEARNERS

Materials: newspapers, markers

Divide the class into small groups. Have groups hunt through newspaper headlines and articles for contractions or words with the suffixes and endings studied in this unit. Ask students to circle the words they find and list them on paper. Later, compile lists, identify base words, and see which category has the highest total words.

CHALLENGE

Have children locate and read books about famous astronauts, such as Sally Ride, John Glenn, Neil Armstrong, or a more contemporary astronaut to find out why these persons wanted to explore space and how they were able to become astronauts.

EXTRA SUPPORT/INTERVENTION

Have children echo-read *In Space* with you before they read it independently. You might also want to pre-record the text of the book so that children can listen several times as they reread the story. See Daily Phonics Practice, pages 253–255.

Review Contractions, Endings, and Suffixes

Skill Focus

Children will

★ distinguish among base words and words with inflectional endings to identify pictures.

★ read and write contractions and words with endings and suffixes in context.

Teach

Review Skills Write these words on the board and have children read them together: *sailing, picked, hopping, cheerful, fearless, tallest, faster, puppies, peaches, stars, saving, baked, thickness*

Have children identify the base word and the ending or suffix in each word. Then, write these words on the board and ask volunteers to change each one to a contraction: *does not, I am, she is, can not, will not.* Encourage children to use each contraction in an original sentence.

Practice and Apply

Assess Skills Read the directions on page 177. Have children name each picture before they fill in the bubbles. For page 178, read the words in the box with children. Remind them to read the entire sentence with their word choice before they write their answer. Encourage them to check their spelling.

Name_____

▶ Fill in the bubble beside the word that names or describes each picture.

1.
- ○ box
- ○ socks
- ● boxes

2.
- ● fishing
- ○ sleeping
- ○ runs

3.
- ○ glass
- ○ guess
- ● glasses

4.
- ○ puppy
- ○ ponies
- ● puppies

5.
- ● daisy
- ○ daisies
- ○ days

6.
- ○ dish
- ○ ditches
- ● dishes

7.
- ● star
- ○ stars
- ○ start

8.
- ● peaches
- ○ peach
- ○ beach

9.
- ● mailing
- ○ nails
- ○ sailed

10.
- ● baked
- ○ bank
- ○ back

11.
- ● raking
- ○ baking
- ○ jumped

12.
- ○ racing
- ● reading
- ○ walked

Contractions, endings, suffixes: Assessment   **177**

FOCUS ON ALL LEARNERS

ESL/ELL ENGLISH LANGUAGE LEARNERS

Help English language learners understand words in context by telling them a space story and having them summarize it.

• Have children sit on the floor in a circle. Use page 178 as a script. With lights out and in a dramatic voice tell them the story in items 1–12.

• Turn on the lights. Repeat the story, again dramatically. Have children listen to each item as you say it, select the missing word, and write it in the blank.

VISUAL LEARNERS

Materials: index cards, marker

Make word cards for *fast, sail, dark, big, quick, jump, box, lock, pop,* and *rest.* Write *-ful, -ness, -less, -ly, -es, -s, -ing, -ed, -er,* and *-est* on the board. Have children take turns choosing a word and writing a new word on the board by adding one of the endings or suffixes. Classmates can suggest other endings or suffixes for the same base word.

▶ **Find the word in the box that will finish each sentence. Print the word on the line.**

strangest	fearful	waited	happily
quietly	biggest	We're	darkness
longer	couldn't	watched	brightest

1. The spaceship arrived _____quietly_____ .

2. We all _____watched_____ it land.

3. We _____couldn't_____ see much from where we were standing.

4. Then, a blinding light filled the _____darkness_____ .

5. It was the _____brightest_____ light we had ever seen.

6. We _____waited_____ in silence as a figure appeared.

7. He was the _____strangest_____ looking little creature.

8. His ears were long, much _____longer_____ than mine.

9. His eyes were huge, the _____biggest_____ I have seen!

10. We were _____fearful_____ of what he might do.

11. "_____We're_____ looking for pizza," he said.

12. We _____happily_____ gave them all the pizza we could find.

Have your child read the story on this page aloud. Then, ask him or her to give the story a title.

178   Contractions, endings, suffixes: Assessment

ASSESS UNDERSTANDING OF UNIT SKILLS

STUDENT PROGRESS ASSESSMENT

You may want to review the observational notes you made as children worked through the activities in the unit. These can help you evaluate the progress children have made in the unit.

PORTFOLIO ASSESSMENT

Review the written materials children have collected in their portfolios. Conduct interviews with children to discuss their work and progress since the beginning of this unit. As you review children's work, evaluate how well they use phonics skills.

DAILY PHONICS PRACTICE

For children who need additional practice with the skills in this unit, quick reviews are provided in Daily Phonics Practice, pages 253–255.

PHONICS POSTTEST

To assess children's mastery of skills in this unit, use the posttest on pages 143g–143h.

AUDITORY/KINESTHETIC LEARNERS   GROUPS

Have children stand in a circle and listen as you read a list of words. Children should crouch down and then stand up if they hear a base word and step to the right if they hear a word with a suffix or ending. Read words such as: *biggest, long, scariest, gladly, hard, harder, family, families.*

CHALLENGE

Ask children to write new endings for the story told by the sentences on page 178. Have them begin where the action leaves off at the end of sentence 6. Invite writers to confer with one another to correct spelling and offer editing suggestions.

EXTRA SUPPORT/INTERVENTION

Materials: index cards, marker

Make word cards for base words that end in *y*, silent *e*, or short vowel-consonant patterns. Examples can be found on pages 157–160 and 169–172. Have children sort the words according to their patterns and practice adding endings or suffixes to the words. See Daily Phonics Practice, pages 253–255.

Teacher Notes

UNIT 6

Vowel Pairs, Vowel Digraphs, Diphthongs

THEME: DINOSAUR DAYS

Student Performance Objectives

In Unit 6, children will review the long vowel rule as it applies to vowel pairs *ai, ay, ee, ea, oa, oe,* and *ie*; be introduced to the sounds of vowel digraphs *oo, ea, au,* and *aw*; and study the sounds of diphthongs *ou, ow, oi, oy,* and *ew* within the context of the theme "Dinosaur Days." As children apply what they know about vowel combinations, they will be able to

▶ Associate vowel pairs with the sounds each stands for

▶ Distinguish among the vowel pairs

▶ Associate vowel digraphs with the sound each stands for

▶ Distinguish among vowel pairs and vowel digraphs

▶ Associate diphthongs with the sound each stands for

▶ Apply these skills in decoding and in using words in context

Assessment Options

In Unit 6, assess children's ability to read and write words with vowel pairs, vowel digraphs, and diphthongs. Use the Unit Pretest and Posttest for formal assessment. For ongoing assessment, you may wish to use children's work on the Review pages, Take-Home Books, and Unit Checkups. You may also want to encourage children to evaluate their own work and to participate in setting goals for their own learning.

ESL/ELL Some English language learners may require additional assessment strategies to meet their special language needs. Note pronunciation difficulties as they occur, but assess performance based on children's ability to distinguish specific sounds when pronounced by a native speaker.

FORMAL ASSESSMENT

Use the Unit 6 Pretest on pages 179e–179f to help assess a child's knowledge at the beginning of the unit and to plan instruction.

ESL/ELL Before administering the Pretest, preview visuals on page 179e so children are familiar with picture names. Say the name of each picture clue, then sound out the words in the box together. Repeat for children, clearly saying the name of the picture followed by the three answer choices. Children can match the word names to the picture clues. Fill in answer bubbles as a group.

Use the Unit 6 Posttest on pages 179g–179h to help assess mastery of unit objectives and to plan for reteaching, if necessary.

ESL/ELL Help children read the directions by reading them aloud to the group. To confirm understanding of the tasks, have volunteers restate in their own words what they are to do.

INFORMAL ASSESSMENT

Use the Review pages, Unit Checkup, and Take-Home Books in the student book to provide an effective means of evaluating children's performance.

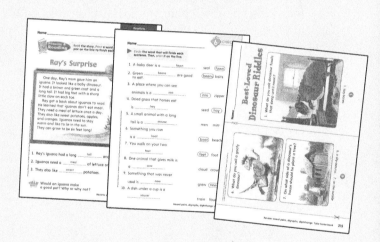

Unit 6 Skills	Review pages	Checkups	Take-Home Books
Vowel pairs	187–188, 213–214	217–218	189–190 215–216
Vowel digraphs	197–198, 199–200, 213–214	217–218	201–202 215–216
Diphthongs	213–214	217–218	215–216

STUDENT PROGRESS CHECKLIST

Use the checklist on page 179i to record children's progress. You may want to cut the sections apart to place each child's checklist in his or her portfolio.

PORTFOLIO ASSESSMENT

This logo appears throughout the teaching plans. It signals opportunities for collecting student's work for individual portfolios. You may also want to include the Pretest and Posttest, the Review pages, the Unit Checkup, Phonics & Reading, and Phonics & Writing pages.

PHONEMIC AWARENESS AND PHONICS ASSESSMENT

Use PAPA to obtain an itemized analysis of children's decoding skills.

PAPA Skills	MCP Phonics Lessons in Unit 6
Deleting sounds	Lessons 89, 92
Vowel pairs	Lessons 84–87, 100
Vowel digraphs	Lessons 89–93, 100
Diphthongs	Lessons 95–100

Pretest and Posttest

DIRECTIONS

To help you assess children's progress in learning Unit 6 skills, tests are available on pages 179e–179h.

Administer the Pretest before children begin the unit. The results of the Pretest will help you identify each child's strengths and needs in advance, allowing you to structure lesson plans to meet individual needs. Administer the Posttest to assess children's overall mastery of skills taught in the unit and to identify specific areas that will require reteaching.

ESL/ELL Note that the objective of both the Unit 6 Pretest and Posttest is reading and writing words with vowel pairs, vowel digraphs, and diphthongs. To ensure that vocabulary recognition is not a distraction, have children practice saying the names of the picture clues aloud. Reinforce with frequent sight word recognition and reading opportunities throughout the unit.

PERFORMANCE ASSESSMENT PROFILE

The following chart will help you identify specific skills as they appear on the tests and enable you to identify and record specific information about an individual's or the class's performance on the tests.

Depending on the results of the tests, refer to the Reteaching column for lesson-plan pages where you can find activities that will be useful for meeting individual needs or for daily phonics practice.

Answer Keys

Unit 6 Pretest, page 179e (BLM 36)

1. (book) good
2. (saw) crawl
3. (tray) spray
4. (house)mouse
5. (cow) towel
6. (bread)steady
7. (toys) enjoy
8. (tie) pie
9. (feet) teeth
10. (stew) blew
11. (feather)ready
12. (coins) foil
13. (flowers)plow
14. (August)haul
15. (soap) boat
16. (zoo) stool

Unit 6 Pretest, page 179f (BLM 37)

17. dead
18. seen
19. found
20. teeth
21. food
22. chewed
23. stood
24. about
25. claws
26. crown
27. new
28. books

Unit 6 Posttest, page 179g (BLM 38)

1. (mouse)about
2. (seat) reach
3. (broom) loose
4. (sweater) thread
5. (oil) boil
6. (straw) hawk
7. (tie) lie
8. (flowers) owl
9. (August)fault
10. (toes) hoe
11. (stew) chew
12. (boy) toys
13. (jeep) seed
14. (hook) book
15. (clown) howl
16. (hay) gray

Unit 6 Posttest, page 179h (BLM 39)

17. paint
18. looked
19. drew
20. spread
21. down
22. draw
23. brown
24. tail
25. stood
26. ready
27. jaws
28. pointed

Performance Assessment Profile

Skill	Pretest Questions	Posttest Questions	Reteaching	
			Focus on All Learners	**Daily Phonics Practice**
Vowel pairs	3, 8, 9, 15, 18, 20	2, 7, 10, 13, 16, 17, 24	181–190, 213–216	255–256
Vowel digraphs	1, 2, 6, 11, 14, 16, 17, 21, 23, 25, 28	3, 4, 6, 9, 14, 18, 20, 22, 25, 26, 27	191–202, 213–216	256–257
Diphthongs	4, 5, 7, 10, 12, 13, 19, 22, 24, 26, 27	1, 5, 8, 11, 12, 15, 19, 21, 23, 28	203–216	257

Name _____

> Say the name of each picture. Fill in the bubble below the word that has the same vowel sound.

1. 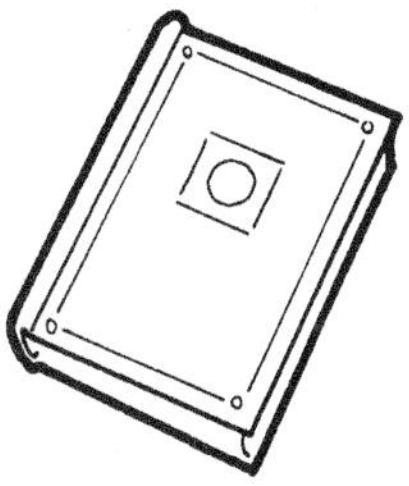
horn good noon
○ ○ ○

2. 
crawl clue chew
○ ○ ○

3.
toe tree spray
○ ○ ○

4. 
crow mouse boil
○ ○ ○

5. 
throw snow towel
○ ○ ○

6. 
steady meat great
○ ○ ○

7. 
bow toe enjoy
○ ○ ○

8. 
toe pie tail
○ ○ ○

9. 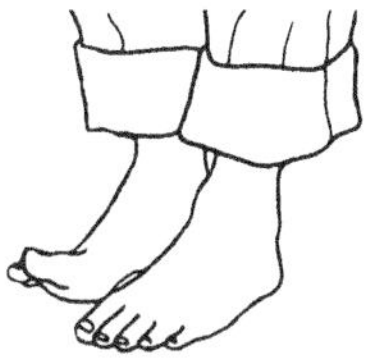
teeth dead few
○ ○ ○

10. 
no sea blew
○ ○ ○

11. 
reach ready leaf
○ ○ ○

12. 
tow floor foil
○ ○ ○

13. 
row plow crew
○ ○ ○

14. 
haul foot faint
○ ○ ○

15. 
boy spoil boat
○ ○ ○

16. 
stool book bone
○ ○ ○

Go to the next page. →

BLM 36 Unit 6 Pretest: Vowel pairs, vowel digraphs, diphthongs

Name _____

> ► Find the word in the box that will finish each sentence.
> Print the word on the line.

found
chewed
claws
new
seen
stood
food
crown
books
dead
about
teeth

17. Dinosaurs have been _____ for millions of years.

18. No one has ever _____ a dinosaur.

19. We learn about dinosaurs from bones _____ in the ground.

20. Dinosaur _____ help us know what they ate.

21. Those with sharp teeth ate meat for their _____ .

22. Those with flat teeth _____ on leaves.

23. Some dinosaurs _____ taller than a house.

24. Other dinosaurs were _____ the size of chickens!

25. Many dinosaurs had long sharp _____ on their feet.

26. Some had a _____ of bones on top of their heads.

27. Scientists learn _____ things about dinosaurs every day.

28. You can read about dinosaurs in _____ and newspapers.

Possible score on Unit 6 Pretest is 28. Number correct _____

BLM 37 Unit 6 Pretest: Vowel pairs, vowel digraphs, diphthongs

Name _____

 Say the name of each picture. Fill in the bubble below the word that has the same vowel sound.

1.
moose   paw   about
○   ○   ○

2.
head   reach   heart
○   ○   ○

3.
bow   good   loose
○   ○   ○

4.
thread   teach   steak
○   ○   ○

5.
boil   bow   out
○   ○   ○

6.
house   hawk   hose
○   ○   ○

7.
foil   tin   lie
○   ○   ○

8.
owl   oil   wood
○   ○   ○

9.
fault   pool   know
○   ○   ○

10.
too   hoe   town
○   ○   ○

11.
cow   pout   chew
○   ○   ○

12.
tail   toys   tow
○   ○   ○

13.
blew   break   seed
○   ○   ○

14.
book   spoon   zoo
○   ○   ○

15.
show   howl   low
○   ○   ○

16.
gray   haul   cloud
○   ○   ○

Go to the next page. →

BLM 38 Unit 6 Posttest: Vowel pairs, vowel digraphs, diphthongs

Name _____

> ► Find the word in the box that will finish each sentence.
> Print the word on the line.

Word Box
down
jaws
ready
paint
tail
draw
looked
stood
spread
drew
brown
pointed

17. We wanted to _____ a dinosaur mural.

18. First, we_____ at dinosaurs in many books.

19. With pencils we _____ sketches of different dinosaurs.

20. Then, we_____ out a sheet of paper on the floor.

21. We got _____ on our hands and knees.

22. We began to _____ the dinosaurs.

23. Then, we painted the dinosaurs gray and _____.

24. We added spikes to one dinosaur's long _____.

25. One huge dinosaur _____ by its nest.

26. She looked as if she were _____ to protect her eggs.

27. Our biggest dinosaur had huge _____ .

28. Its teeth were long and _____ .

Possible score on Unit 6 Posttest is 28. Number correct _____

BLM 39 Unit 6 Posttest: Vowel pairs, vowel digraphs, diphthongs

Student Progress Checklist

Make as many copies as needed to use for a class list. For individual portfolio use, cut apart each child's section. As indicated by the code, color in boxes next to skills satisfactorily assessed and insert an *X* by those requiring reteaching. Marked boxes can later be colored in to indicate mastery.

Student Progress Checklist

Code: ■ Satisfactory   ☒ Needs Reteaching

Student: _____ _____ Pretest Score: _____ Posttest Score: _____	**Skills** ☐ Vowel Pairs ☐ Vowel Digraphs ☐ Diphthongs	**Comments / Learning Goals**
Student: _____ _____ Pretest Score: _____ Posttest Score: _____	**Skills** ☐ Vowel Pairs ☐ Vowel Digraphs ☐ Diphthongs	**Comments / Learning Goals**
Student: _____ _____ Pretest Score: _____ Posttest Score: _____	**Skills** ☐ Vowel Pairs ☐ Vowel Digraphs ☐ Diphthongs	**Comments / Learning Goals**
Student: _____ _____ Pretest Score: _____ Posttest Score: _____	**Skills** ☐ Vowel Pairs ☐ Vowel Digraphs ☐ Diphthongs	**Comments / Learning Goals**

BLM 40 Unit 6 Checklist

Throughout Unit 6 there are opportunities to assess English language learners' ability to read and write words with vowel pairs, vowel digraphs, and diphthongs. Some of your English language learners may require additional assessment strategies to meet their special language needs. Take note of difficulties with pronunciations, but assess children based on their ability to distinguish specific sounds when pronounced by a native speaker.

Lesson 83, pages 181–182 Native speakers of Spanish will likely sound *ai* and *ay* in English as the short, not long, *ai* sound. Reinforce the correct sound as needed.

Lesson 84, pages 183–184 Speakers of Spanish may have difficulty distinguishing the sounds of long *e* and short *i*. Practice with word pairs, such as *cheek, chick; eat, it; neat, nit; seat, sit.*

Lesson 85, pages 185–186 English language learners from backgrounds where each letter stands for one sound may have difficulty understanding that two vowels together can stand for one sound.

Lesson 86, pages 187–188 For those English language learners who have difficulty making long vowel sounds, point out that the sound is the same as the name of the letter in English.

Lesson 87, pages 189–190 Speakers of Spanish may tend to clip vowel sounds in English. They may need additional practice stretching out the vowels to their appropriate lengths.

Lesson 88, pages 191–192 Children who have difficulty pronouncing *oo* vowel digraphs (*book/boot*) may need additional support and oral/listening practice with the long *oo* sound. Exaggeration of the sound with a focus on the lip position may be helpful.

Lesson 89, pages 193–194 Children may have difficulty pronouncing and distinguishing short vowels, including the sound of short *e*. In Tagalog, short *e* sounds like *a* in *say*. No similar sound exists in Korean.

Lesson 90, pages 195–196 Children whose home language is Korean may introduce the sound /ya/ when they anticipate the sound of short *a* after *g* and have difficulty saying words such as *August*.

Lesson 94, pages 203–204 English language learners whose native languages identify one sound per letter may experience difficulty understanding that a vowel plus a consonant can make a separate sound.

Lesson 95, pages 205–206 If you notice oral hesitation among English language learners whose native languages identify one sound per letter, provide additional oral practice.

Lesson 96, pages 207–208 English language learners whose native languages have a separate sound for each vowel may have a tendency to add an additional syllable when pronouncing words.

Lesson 98, pages 211–212 Native Spanish speakers are familiar with diphthongs formed by two vowels, but they are not familiar with diphthongs formed by a vowel and a consonant. Provide practice with words containing these sounds.

Spelling Connections

INTRODUCTION

The Unit Word List is a comprehensive list of spelling words drawn from this unit. The words are grouped by the phonetic elements presented in this unit. To incorporate spelling into your phonics program, use the activity in the Curriculum Connections section of each teaching plan.

ESL/ELL It is recommended that English language learners reach the intermediate fluency level of English proficiency before focusing on spelling.

For English language learners introduce 5–7 words at a time and their meaning through visuals or realia.

The spelling lessons utilize the following approach for each phonetic element.

1. Administer a pretest of the words that have not yet been introduced. Dictation sentences are provided.

2. Provide practice.

3. Reassess. Dictation sentences are provided.

A final review that covers vowel pairs, vowel digraphs, and diphthongs is provided at the end of the unit, on page 213.

DIRECTIONS

Make a copy of Blackline Master 41 for each child. After administering the pretest, give children a copy of the appropriate word list.

Children can work with a partner to practice spelling the words orally and identifying the vowel sound in each word. They can also create letter cards to form the words on the list. You may want to challenge children to make new words by substituting the vowel sounds. Children can write words of their own on My Own Word List (see Blackline Master 41).

Have children store their list words in the envelope in the back of their book. You may want to suggest that students keep a spelling notebook, listing words with similar patterns. Another idea is to build Word Walls with children and display them in the classroom. Each section of the wall could focus on words with a single phonics element. The walls will become a good resource for spelling when children are engaged in writing.

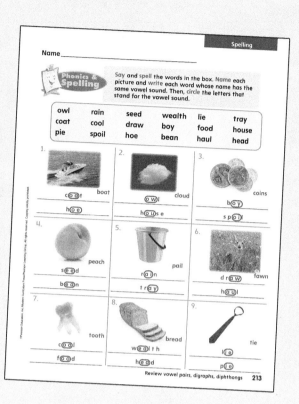

Unit Word List

Vowel Pairs
rain
tray
seed
bean
boat
hoe
pie
tie

Vowel Digraphs
book
head
haul
draw
food

Diphthongs
house
owl
spoil
boy
grew

Name _____

Unit 6 WORD LIST

Vowel Pairs

rain

tray

seed

bean

boat

hoe

pie

tie

Vowel Digraphs

book

head

haul

draw

food

Diphthongs

house

owl

spoil

boy

grew

My Own Word List

BLM 41 Unit 6 Spelling Words

Phonics Games, Activities, and Technology

The following collection of ideas offers a variety of opportunities to reinforce phonics skills while actively engaging children. The games, activities, and technology suggestions can easily be adapted to meet the needs of your group of learners. They vary in approach so as to consider children's different learning styles.

TAPE THE TAIL ON THE DINOSAUR

On tagboard, draw the outline of a large dinosaur minus the tail. Then, cut out a tagboard or construction-paper tail for each child. Write these vowel pairs on the board and have children select one to write on the tail: *ai, ay, ee, ea, ie, oe, oa*. Children can take turns displaying the tails and giving a word that contains the sound their vowel pair stands for. Then, have them tape the tails on the dinosaur.

Variation: To review vowel digraphs, have children select from the following vowel combinations: *oo, ea, au,* and *aw*. To review diphthongs, have them choose from these combinations: *ou, ow, oi, oy,* and *ew*.

ESL/ELL English language learners should be familiar with a wide variety of words that contain digraphs. Simplify by having children use their Unit 6 Word List.

DIPHTHONG TARGET PRACTICE

To review diphthongs, draw a large dinosaur on a piece of tagboard and divide it into five sections. In each section, print one of these words: *loud, howl, choice, enjoy, chew*. Place the dinosaur on the floor. Give pairs of children a beanbag and have them take turns tossing it at the target. Have them read the word in the section they hit, identify its vowel sound, and give another word that contains the same sound.

Variation: To review vowel digraphs, modify the activity by using words such as these: *brook, zoo, feather, pause, crawl*.

DINO EGGS

To review vowel pairs, vowel digraphs, or diphthongs, write the vowels you wish to reinforce on small slips of paper and place them inside plastic eggs. (If eggs are not available, write the vowels on egg-shaped pieces of tagboard.) Place all the eggs in a large nest made from twigs and grass or in a hollow depression in a sand table. Have children take turns selecting an egg, opening it to discover the vowels, and then giving a word that contains the sound that the letters represent. If any children select the vowel combinations *ea* or *oo*, challenge them to give words for each sound these vowels can represent.

WORD FLIP BOOKS

Make flip books that feature phonograms containing vowel pairs, vowel digraphs, or diphthongs. As the pages are flipped, each new word that is formed is read. Flip books are a good way to reinforce words that contain the variant sounds of *oo, ea,* and *ow*.

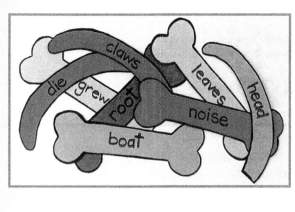

BONE PILE

Give small groups of children a number of dinosaur "bones" cut from tagboard. On each bone, write a word containing a vowel pair, a vowel digraph, or a diphthong. Have children attach a paper clip to each bone and place the bones in a box or bag. Using a fishing pole made by attaching a magnet to a ruler with a string, children take turns fishing in the bone pile. Each time they snag a word, have them read it aloud, isolate the vowel sound, and identify the letters that stand for the sound.

Variation: After all the bones have been removed from the bone pile, have children work together to sort the words into three different piles: those with vowel pairs, those with vowel digraphs, and those with diphthongs.

ESL/ELL English language learners will independently need to pronounce new words that contain vowel pairs, digraphs, and diphthongs. Create word lists or charts of familiar words and post these lists in the classroom.

DINOSAUR TIC-TAC-TOE

Reproduce a nine-square grid and give a copy to each pair of players. Each pair will also need two sets of vowel digraph playing cards. The playing cards feature dinosaur parts in place of *X*'s and *O*'s. The playing card for the digraph *aw* could show a dinosaur jaw, for *ea* a dinosaur head, and for *oo* a dinosaur tooth. Each player chooses one set of vowel digraph cards. Players then take turns saying a word that contains this vowel digraph sound represented on the playing cards. If correct, the card may be placed on the game board. Players continue taking turns until one wins in a tic-tac-toe pattern or until the board is filled.

Variation: Instead of pictures, use phonogram cards that contain diphthongs or vowel pairs. To make a move, players must say and spell a word that ends with the specified phonogram. The card can then be placed on the grid.

VOWEL RUMMY

Give a small group of children 52 index cards. Then, have them look through the unit and write sets of four words with these combinations: *ai, ay, ee, ea, ie, oa, oe, oo, au, aw, ou, oi, oy, ew*. Make sure that children understand that in each set, the letters must stand for the same sound. To play, children shuffle the cards and deal seven cards to each player. The remaining cards go face down in a pile, with the top card placed face up beside this deck. The first player selects either the face-up card or the top card from the deck. The

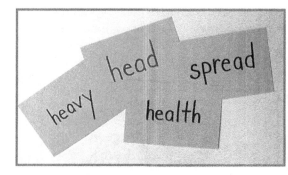

player then discards an unwanted card by placing it on the face-up pile. The next player either takes this card or the top card from the deck. When players have a set of three or four cards with the same vowel sound, they place the set on the table. (If only three cards have been laid down, other players can lay down the fourth matching card.) Continue playing until all the cards are used up.

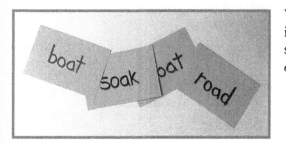

Variation: To make this game even more challenging, include sets of four word cards for each of the different sounds of *oo* (*boot* and *foot*), *ea* (*jeans* and *feather*), and *ow* (*slow* and *howl*).

DINOSAUR DIG

Use Blackline Master 42 to make a game board featuring words containing vowel pairs, vowel digraphs, and diphthongs. Make a master copy by writing the following 24 incomplete words in the spaces: *p__l, d__, t__m, j__p, __ch, t__, b__t, b__, s__p, fl__r, h__k, r__m, sp__n, st__d, dr__m, br__d, p__se, str__, cl__d, t__n, t__, pi__, dr__, st__.* Then, make copies to distribute to pairs of children. They can take turns using a number cube to move a marker along the game board. As a player lands on a space, a vowel pair, vowel digraph, or diphthong must be inserted and the complete word said aloud. Play continues until both players reach the dinosaur fossil.

Variation: To vary the game, write complete words in each space on the game board for children to read and use in a sentence.

ESL/ELL Modify game rules by permitting all participants to suggest words during each player's turn. The player then moves the number of spaces indicated by the roll of the number cube.

WORD SLIDES

Make a dinosaur word slide featuring words with vowel pairs, vowel digraphs, or diphthongs that you wish to reinforce. Individuals or partners can slide the word strip, reading the word that appears in the window.

Variation: Instead of providing the words, give children a blank word strip and have them write their own words. They can then trade slides with a partner and read the words.

SPIN-A-VOWEL DIGRAPH

To play this small-group game, draw a large circle on a piece of tagboard. Then, divide the circle into four parts and write these vowel digraphs in each section: *oo, ea, au, aw.* To make a spinner, partially fill a liter soda bottle with sand to weight it and place it in the center of the circle. After a child spins, have him or her give a word that contains the vowel digraph indicated by the bottle. Continue the game until everyone has had several turns.

Variation: To modify the game, write vowel pairs or diphthongs in each space of the circle. Another alternative is to place cards with words that you wish to review in each section of the circle. After spinning, children can read the words, identify the vowel sound, and give another word that contains the same sound.

TECHNOLOGY

The following software products reinforce children's understanding of vowel pairs, vowel digraphs, and diphthongs.

Reader Rabbit's® Learn to Read with Phonics™
This software combines the activities from Reader Rabbit's® Learn to Read and Reader Rabbit's® Reading 1 to develop phonemic awareness and sight vocabulary. It includes over 100 lessons focused on developing reading and language arts skills for a wide range of ability levels.

** Riverdeep The Learning Company
   500 Redwood Blvd.
   Novato, CA 94947
   (800) 825-4420
   www.learningcompanyschool.com

Magic Letter Factory
Activities invite early readers to learn letters and their corresponding sounds: making words by filling in blanks, creating wacky sentences by combining nouns and verbs, and watching video clips to reinforce letter and word recognition.

** Educational Activities, Inc.
   1937 Grand Avenue
   Baldwin, NY 11510
   (800) 645-3739

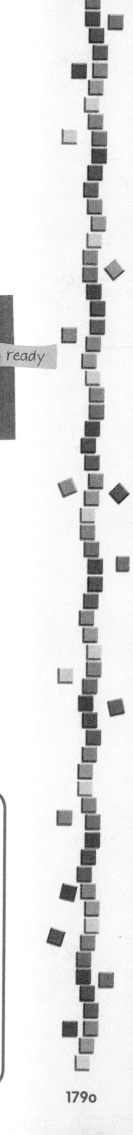

Name _____

Dinosaur Dig

START

Home Connections

The Home Connections features of this program are intended to involve families in their children's learning and application of phonics skills. Three effective opportunities to make connections between home and school include the following.

- **HOME LETTER**
- **HOME NOTES**
- **TAKE-HOME BOOKS**

HOME LETTER

A letter is available to be sent home at the beginning of Unit 6. This letter informs family members that children will be learning to read and write words containing vowel pairs, vowel digraphs, and diphthongs within the context of the unit theme, "Dinosaur Days." The first activity suggests that children reread the selection on page 179 with a family member, and then talk about the size of a dinosaur and what can be learned from examining its footprint or bone. The second activity suggests children make a clay dinosaur and then label its body parts, circling any words that contain vowel pairs, digraphs, or diphthongs. These activities support children's learning of vowel pairs, vowel digraphs, and diphthongs. The letter, available in both English and Spanish, suggests dinosaur-theme books family members can look for in a local library and enjoy reading together.

HOME NOTES

Whenever the Home logo appears within the student book, a phonics activity is suggested to be done at home. The activities are simple to do, requiring little or no preparation or special materials, and are meant to reinforce the targeted phonics skill.

Home Notes in Spanish are also available for both teachers and parents to download and use from our website, www.PlaidPhonics.com.

TAKE-HOME BOOKS

Within the student book are Take-Home Books that can be cut out and assembled. The story language in each book reinforces the targeted phonics skills. The books can be taken home and shared with family members. In Unit 6, three Take-Home Books are available focusing on different vowel sounds presented in this unit as well as the theme, "Dinosaur Days."

Vowel Pairs, Vowel Digraphs, Diphthongs

Skill Focus

Assess Prior Knowledge
To assess children's prior knowledge of vowel pairs, vowel digraphs, and diphthongs, use the pretest on pages 179e–179f.

Unit Focus

Build Background

- Discuss with children what they know about dinosaurs. You might ask questions such as these: *Have you ever seen a dinosaur? When did dinosaurs live? What do dinosaurs look like? What are the names of some dinosaurs?*

- Write the theme "Dinosaur Days" on the board. Ask children what they think the theme means. Be sure that children recognize that dinosaurs no longer exist but that scientists have found their bones and footprints, so they know dinosaurs lived at one time.

- Read the text aloud, emphasizing the humor. Have children discuss the poem. Ask why the author said he hopes he never meets "it." What do children think "it" is?

Introduce Vowel Pairs, Vowel Digraphs, and Diphthongs

- On the board write *see, meet,* and *footprints.* As you reread the poem, point to each word on the board as you say it.

- Have children read each word on the board. Underline *ee, ee,* and *oo* as they say each respective word. Explain that they will be learning more about vowel sounds such as these in this unit.

Critical Thinking

- As you discuss Talk About It, be sure children recognize that scientists can learn new information about dinosaurs by studying their bones, and that new dinosaurs are still being discovered.

Read Aloud

Something Big Has Been Here
by Jack Prelutsky

Something big has been here,
what it was, I do not know,
for I did not see it coming,
and I did not see it go,
but I hope I never meet it,
if I do, I'm in a fix,
for it left behind its footprints,
they are size nine-fifty-six.

TALK About It Why do you think people search for dinosaur bones?

Unit 6 · Introduction
Critical Thinking   179

THEME FOCUS

FUN WITH DINO-FACTS

Ask children to name dinosaurs they know. Invite them to use the names and other information to make a dinosaur facts game. Provide books for research and index cards on which children can write questions and answers. Decide on point values for different questions. Have partners, small groups, or class teams play the game in a memory-matching or question-and-answer format.

A MUSEUM VISIT

Plan a visit to a science or natural history museum where dinosaur bones or models are displayed. Before the trip, make a list of children's questions about dinosaurs. Afterward, have children use what they have learned to answer the questions on a chart or as a class book.

A DINO-DOCUMENTARY

Have small groups of children each gather information about a particular dinosaur. Group members can write scripts and draw pictures or make models of the dinosaurs. Videotape each group of children as they present their information.

HOME LETTER

Dear Family,

In this unit about dinosaurs, your child will learn about vowel pairs, vowel digraphs, and diphthongs. As your child becomes familiar with these forms, you might try these activities together.

▶ Reread the poem "Something Big Has Been Here" on page 179 with your child. Talk about the size of the dinosaur. Discuss what people can learn from examining a footprint or a bone of a dinosaur.

▶ Make a clay model of a dinosaur. Help your child to identify and record its parts. Circle words with vowel pairs, such as tail, teeth, and toes; vowel digraphs such as jaw, foot, and head; and diphthongs such as mouth.

Your child might enjoy reading these books with you. Look for them in your local library.

Eyewitness Readers: Dinosaur Dinners by Lee Davis

Asteroid Impact by Douglas Henderson

Sincerely,

_____

Estimada familia:

En esta unidad, que trata sobre dinosaurios, su hijo/a aprenderá las parejas de vocales, digramas de vocales y diptongos. A medida que su hijo/a se vaya familiarizando con estas formas, pueden hacer las siguientes actividades juntos.

▶ Lean de nuevo con su hijo/a el poema "Something Big Has Been Here" ("Algo grande estuvo aquí") en la página 179. Hablen sobre el tamaño del dinosaurio. Conversen sobre lo que se puede aprender a partir del examen de una huella o de un hueso de dinosaurio.

▶ Hagan un modelo de arcilla de un dinosaurio. Ayuden a su hijo/a a identificar y anotar sus partes. Encierren en un círculo las palabras con parejas de vocales, como tail (cola), teeth (dientes) y toes (pezuñas); digramas de vocales como jaw (mandíbula), foot (pata) y head (cabeza); y diptongos como mouth (boca).

▶ Ustedes y su hijo/a disfrutarán leyendo estos libros juntos. Búsquenlos en su biblioteca local.

Eyewitness Readers: Dinosaur Dinners de Lee Davis

Asteroid Impact de Douglas Henderson

Sinceramente,

_____

head

tail—

BULLETIN BOARD

Construct a "Dinosaur Days" bulletin board around the Dino-Facts game suggested on page 179. Have children add cutouts of their favorite dinosaurs on which they can write vowel pair, vowel digraph, and diphthong words they discover as they work through the unit.

HOME CONNECTIONS

• The Home Letter on page 180 can help involve family members in the phonics skills children will be studying in this unit. Children can take home the letter and complete the activities with family members.

• Encourage children to look for the books suggested on page 180 when they visit the community or school library.

LEARNING CENTER ACTIVITIES

WRITING CENTER

Display a list entitled "Dinosaur Wishes" on chart paper. Encourage children to imagine themselves living the lives of dinosaurs and have them think of wishes a dinosaur might make. Ask them to write their dinosaur wishes on the chart. Encourage them to be funny and creative as well as practical. Wishes might include *I wish I could find shoes big enough for my feet* or *I wish Tyrannosaurus rex wouldn't chase me when I'm trying to eat.*

MATH CENTER

Gather a supply of dinosaur books, fact cards, and science magazine articles. Invite children to find information to make Dinosaur Math Cards. Children should look for and write number-related dinosaur facts. These might include such things as the animal's height, length, weight, age, and speed. For example: *The Brachiosaurus weighed as much as ten elephants* or *Some dinosaurs may have lived to be 100 to 200 years old or more.*

SCIENCE CENTER

Provide materials from nature (sticks, plants, rocks, sand) and other materials (foil, construction paper, straws, cardboard) for children to make habitats for dinosaurs inside cardboard boxes. Also, provide clay from which children can model dinosaurs to put inside the dioramas. Children can use their habitat models and clay dinosaurs as part of their documentary presentations, as explained in the Theme Focus.

Vowel Pairs ai, ay

Skill Focus

Children will

★ use the vowel pair rule to read words containing *ai* and *ay*.

★ write words that contain *ai* and *ay* to answer riddles.

★ recognize and read a high-frequency word.

ESL/ELL Native speakers of Spanish will likely sound *ai* and *ay* in English as the short, not long, *ai* sound. Reinforce the correct sound as needed.

Teach

Phonemic Awareness: Phoneme Categorization Say the following words, emphasizing the vowel sound in each: *rain, may, ran*. Repeat the words and ask children to identify the words that contain the long *a* sound. (*rain, may*)

Sound to Symbol Write the words *rain* and *may* on the board. Point to each one as children say it aloud. Circle *ai* in *rain* and *ay* in *may*. Explain that *ai* and *ay* are vowel pairs in which the first vowel stands for the long sound of *a* and the second vowel is silent. Write *tail* and *stay* on the board. Have volunteers say each word and circle the letters that stand for the long *a* sound.

Practice and Apply

Sound to Symbol Tell children to listen for the sound of long *a* as you read the rhyme aloud. Invite children to reread the rhyme with you. Then, ask volunteers to identify the long *a* words, write them on the board, and circle the letters that stand for the sound. (*claimed, away, day*)

Read the rule on page 181 to children. Invite volunteers to restate the rule in their own words. Then, have children say aloud the picture names. Read the directions and encourage children to complete the page independently.

Writing Suggest that children read the words in the box on page 182 before they try to answer the riddles. Explain that they will use each word only once. Children will have the opportunity to read the high-frequency word *before*.

Reading Use *A Giant-Sized Day*, MCP Phonics and Reading Super Skills Library 2, Level B, to provide children practice in reading words with vowel pairs *ai* and *ay*.

Name_____

Dinosaurs once claimed the land,
And then they died away.
Why, we don't quite understand,
But hope to learn some day.

▶ Find the word in the box that names each picture. Print it on the line.

RULE

In a **vowel pair,** two vowels come together to make one long vowel sound. The first vowel stands for the long sound and the second vowel is silent. You can hear the long **a** sound in **claimed** and **day.**

sail	pay	rain	tail	hay
tray	spray	chain	nail	

1. hay

2. rain

3. tray

4. nail

5. pay

6. tail

7. spray

8. chain

9. sail

Vowel pairs ai, ay **181**

FOCUS ON ALL LEARNERS

ESL/ELL ENGLISH LANGUAGE LEARNERS

Materials: chart paper, colored markers

Confirm that English language learners can identify the meanings of words containing vowel pairs *ai* and *ay* by completing page 182.

• Verify English language learners' understanding of the words *I* and *me* in the riddles. To simplify, pretend the object is speaking in those cases.

• Solve the odd-numbered riddles as a class, asking volunteers to write the answers on the chalkboard. Have children work in pairs or on their own to solve all even-numbered riddles. Ask other volunteers to write the answers on the chalkboard. Have children spell riddles aloud to confirm spellings.

AUDITORY/VISUAL LEARNERS

Have children label two columns on paper as *ay* and *ai*. Tell them that *ay* usually represents long *a* at the end of a base word and *ai* is usually found at the beginning or in the middle of a word. Have children write these words in the correct column as you dictate them: *day, nail, snail, way, clay, sail, stair, train, pay, chain, jail, gray, aid, bait, hair, jay, braid.*

▶ **Find** the word in the box that answers each riddle.
Print the word on the line.

chain	stain	mailbox	hay	pail	rain	tray
play	paint	May	train	gray	sail	day

1. I ride on railroad tracks. _____train_____

2. You put letters in me. _____mailbox_____

3. I am a blend of black and white. _____gray_____

4. If I start, you put on a raincoat. _____rain_____

5. I am the month after April. _____May_____

6. I am made of many links. _____chain_____

7. I am part of a boat. _____sail_____

8. I am an ink spot on a shirt. _____stain_____

9. I am piled in a stack. _____hay_____

10. I am the opposite of work. _____play_____

11. You can carry water in me. _____pail_____

12. I am spread on a wall. _____paint_____

13. You carry food on me. _____tray_____

14. I come **before** night. _____day_____

 With your child, take turns using a word from the box in a sentence.

CURRICULUM CONNECTIONS

SPELLING

You may use the following words and sentences to pretest the spelling words with vowel pairs.

1. **rain** The **rain** helps the flowers grow.
2. **tray** I use a **tray** to carry my lunch in school.
3. **seed** A **seed** grows with water and the sun.
4. **bean** A **bean** is the seed of a plant.
5. **boat** I sail my **boat** on the lake.
6. **hoe** We use a **hoe** in the garden.
7. **pie** I like apple **pie**.
8. **tie** My dad often wears a suit and **tie**.

WRITING

Invite children to reread the rhyme on page 181 with you. Have them brainstorm ideas about why the dinosaurs died away. List their responses on the board. Then, suggest that children choose the idea that they think represents what happened to the dinosaurs. Have them write a paragraph stating their choice and giving their reasons.

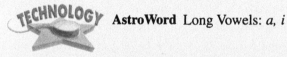 **AstroWord** Long Vowels: *a, i*

Integrating Phonics and Reading

Guided Reading
Have children read the title and look at the illustrations. Then, ask them to predict what this story will be about.
First Reading Ask children to explain what Clad's problem was.
Second Reading Make three columns on the board: *ai, ay,* other long *a* words. Have children find long *a* words in the story and write them in the appropriate column.

Comprehension
Ask children the following questions:
• Why did Clad need to put three skates on each foot? *Inference/Draw Conclusions*
• Why do you think Clad wanted to take a nap when he got to the beach? *Inference/Cause and Effect*

ESL/ELL English Language Learners
On page 4, help children reread and understand that the giant's glass is being compared to a pail. Then, ask them to identify the two objects on page 5 that are being compared.

VISUAL/KINESTHETIC LEARNERS GROUPS

Materials: Phonics Picture Cards: Long Vowels (85–120, 129, 130, 143, 145, 167); mural paper or chalk

Draw a large dinosaur outline on paper (or a chalk outline on the playground). Have children jump into and then out of the "dinosaur" if the picture card you show has a long *a* name.

CHALLENGE

Challenge partners to compile a list of two-syllable words that have the *ai* and *ay* spellings. Examples include *remain, regain, sailing, today, refrain, waited,* and *payment.*

EXTRA SUPPORT/INTERVENTION

Materials: Phonics Word Cards, Set 1: Long *a* words (118–142)

Have children sort the cards into *ai, ay,* and other long *a* spellings. Have them read each group aloud. Encourage them to then sort the cards in other ways, such as action words and names for people or things. See Daily Phonics Practice, pages 255–256.

Vowel Pairs ee, ea

Skill Focus

Children will

★ use the vowel pair rule to read words containing *ee* and *ea*.

★ write words that contain *ee* and *ea* to finish sentences.

★ recognize and read high-frequency words.

ESL/ELL Speakers of Spanish may have difficulty distinguishing the sounds of long *e* and short *i*. Practice with word pairs, such as *cheek, chick; eat, it; neat, nit; seat, sit.*

Teach

Phonemic Awareness: Phoneme Categorization Tell children that the word *leap* contains the long *e* sound. Then, say these pairs of words and have children "leap" from their seats if both words have the long *e* sound: *eager, feet; leaves, street; ten, peach; ribbon, seed; seen, saw; teeth, seed.*

Sound to Symbol Write the words *feet* and *leap* on the board. Say each word aloud and have children repeat it. Ask children to suggest which letters make the long *e* sound in each word. After they respond, circle *ee* in *feet* and *ea* in *leap*.

Write the words *meet, seed, bean,* and *seal* on the board. Invite volunteers to read each word and use it in a sentence. Then, have children identify the vowel sound in each word and the letters that stand for the sound.

Practice and Apply

Blend Phonemes Read the rule and the directions on page 183. As children complete the activity, encourage them to say each picture name, blending the phonemes.

Writing Read the directions on page 184. Have children say each word in the box before they finish the sentences. As they complete the activity, children will have the opportunity to read the high-frequency words *ever, build,* and *often.*

Critical Thinking As you discuss Talk About It, be sure children recognize that the beaver is busy because it works, chewing down trees and building dams.

Reading You may wish to use *An Eagle Flies High*, MCP Phonics and Reading Super Skills Library 2, Level B, to reinforce reading words with vowel pairs *ee* and *ea*.

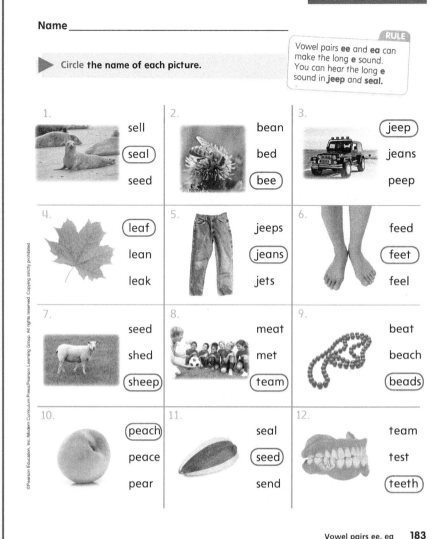

Name _____

► Circle **the name of each picture.**

RULE
Vowel pairs **ee** and **ea** can make the long e sound. You can hear the long e sound in **jeep** and **seal**.

1. sell
   (seal)
   seed

2. bean
   bed
   (bee)

3. (jeep)
   jeans
   peep

4. (leaf)
   lean
   leak

5. jeeps
   (jeans)
   jets

6. feed
   (feet)
   feel

7. seed
   shed
   (sheep)

8. meat
   met
   (team)

9. beat
   beach
   (beads)

10. (peach)
    peace
    pear

11. seal
    (seed)
    send

12. team
    test
    (teeth)

Vowel pairs ee, ea **183**

FOCUS ON ALL LEARNERS

ESL/ELL ENGLISH LANGUAGE LEARNERS
Clarify for English language learners the guidelines for spelling words with the long *e* sound as you introduce the words on page 183.

• Read aloud the rule on page 183. Explain that the words *can make* mean that the vowel pairs do not always make the long *e* sound. Provide examples to familiarize children with words that have the long *e* sound formed by the vowel pairs *ee* and *ea*.

• Read aloud the directions, the picture name, and the three answer choices for each item on the page and invite volunteers to respond.

• Have children complete items 1–6 on page 183 in pairs or small groups and exchange papers to verify responses. Then, encourage children to complete items 7–12 on their own; review aloud.

AUDITORY/VISUAL LEARNERS

Materials: chart paper, marker

Draw a large outline of a pair of jeans with bare feet sticking out. As children name long *e* words, write *ea* words on the jeans, *ee* words on or near the feet, and other long *e* words on another area of the paper.

► Find the word that will finish each sentence. Print it on the line. Circle the vowel pair in each word.

keep	eager	easy	meal
feet	streams	beaver	tree
teeth	leaves	seem	seen

1. Have you ever ___se(e)n___ a beaver?

2. Beavers live in rivers and ___str(ea)ms___.

3. A ___b(ea)ver___ chews down trees.

4. It makes a ___m(ea)l___ of the bark.

5. It uses ___tr(ee)___ branches to build a dam.

6. It ___l(ea)ves___ only the stump behind.

7. A beaver's ___t(ee)th___ have to be strong.

8. Its webbed ___f(ee)t___ help it swim along.

9. It's not ___(ea)sy___ being a beaver.

10. Beavers always ___s(ee)m___ to be working.

11. They ___k(ee)p___ working until all their work is done.

12. That's why busy people are often called
" ___(ea)ger___ beavers."

 TALK Why is the beaver so busy?

 HOME Help your child sort the words according to vowel pairs (ea or ee).

184 Vowel pairs ee, ea: High-frequency words, critical thinking

---

CURRICULUM CONNECTIONS

SPELLING

On the board, write the spelling words *rain, tray, seed, bean, boat, hoe, pie,* and *tie.* Have volunteers give clues to the length and meaning of each word, such as *This word has three letters and is something you eat.* (*pie*) Other children say the answers and spell them.

WRITING

Explain that the term *eager beaver* means someone who can't wait to do something. Have children think about times they have felt like "eager beavers." Invite each child to write two sentences that describe what happened and draw a picture about it.

SCIENCE

Materials: chart paper, markers

Brainstorm a list of animal names with the vowel pairs *ee* or *ea* (*beaver, seal, bee, sheep*). Have each child find three facts about one of the animals and add the facts to a "Long *e* Animals" fact chart.

 **TECHNOLOGY** **AstroWord** Long Vowels: *e, u*

AUDITORY/KINESTHETIC LEARNERS **GROUPS**

Invite children to stand in a circle and have them move like dinosaurs when they hear long *e* words. Tell them to "freeze" when a word does not have the long *e* sound. Use such words as *keep, seem, easy, beaver, stand, seen, meal, chair, eat, teacher, each, teeth, hid, peach, freeze, feet, play.*

CHALLENGE

Have children make a sentence chain with *ee* or *ea* words. For example, one child says *I see a seal;* the second child says *I see a seal playing in the sea;* the third child says *I see a seal playing in the deep blue sea.*

EXTRA SUPPORT/INTERVENTION

Materials: Phonics Word Cards, Set 1: Long *e* words (180–196)

Review the rule for long vowel pairs and help children practice reading the words. Have them find words that they can draw pictures of. Ask them to write and illustrate a sentence using at least two of the words. See Daily Phonics Practice, pages 255–256.

Integrating Phonics and Reading

Guided Reading

Display the book cover and have children share what they already know about eagles and what they would like to learn.

First Reading Have children explain why an eagle lives near a river or the sea.

Second Reading Have children find the words with the vowel pairs *ee* and *ea* in the story and then use them in sentences of their own.

Comprehension

Ask children the following questions:
- How is an eagle able to catch fish without swimming? *Recall/Summarize*
- What are some things an eagle can and cannot do well? *Reflective Analysis/Personal Response*

ESL/ELL English Language Learners

Invite children to locate the homonyms *see* and *sea* in the story. Have them read the sentences where each word is found, and tell what the word means.

Vowel Pairs ie, oe, oa

Skill Focus

Children will

★ use the vowel pair rule to read words containing *ie, oe,* and *oa.*

★ write words that contain *ie, oe,* and *oa* to finish sentences.

★ recognize and read a high-frequency word.

ESL/ELL English language learners from backgrounds where each letter stands for one sound may have difficulty understanding that two vowels together can stand for one sound.

Teach

Phonological Awareness: Rhyme Read the following sentences aloud.

- **Moe the goat had a new fur coat.**
- **He met Joe the toad along the road.**
- **Moe wanted to float in Joe's boat.**
- **Joe croaked but Moe got soaked.**
- **Moe cried as he dried his new coat.**

Reread the sentences and ask children to listen for and name the rhyming words and identify the vowel sounds. (*goat, coat; toad, road; float, boat; Joe, Moe; croaked, soaked, long* o; *cried, dried, long* i)

Sound to Symbol On the board write *Joe, throat,* and *tie* and say them aloud. Have children repeat each word. Circle the *oe* in *Joe* and the *oa* in *throat.* Explain that these vowel pairs stand for the long *o* sound. Remind children that the vowel *o* and the consonant *w* can also stand for the long *o* sound. Next, circle the *ie* in *tie* and explain that *ie* can stand for the long *i* sound.

Practice and Apply

Sound to Symbol Invite children to read the rules on pages 185 and 186. Have them explain how they apply to the sample long *i* and long *o* words.

Blend Phonemes Read the directions to the activities on both pages and have children say the word choices, blending phonemes.

Writing Suggest that children try each answer in the sentences before they write their choice. Children will have the opportunity to read the high-frequency word *some* as they complete page 185.

Critical Thinking Discuss Talk About It. Children should recognize that Joe's friend wanted to buy a red tie.

Reading Use *Frog or Toad?,* MCP Phonics and Reading Super Skills Library 2, Level B, to practice reading words with vowel pairs.

185

Name_____

Circle **the word that will finish each sentence.** Print **it on the line.**

> **RULE**
> The vowel pair **ie** sometimes has the long **i** sound. You can hear the long **i** sound in **tie.** The vowel pair **oe** has the long **o** sound. You can hear the long **o** sound in **toe.**

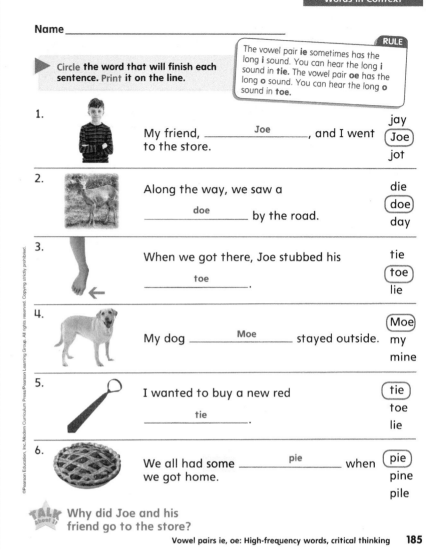

1. My friend, ____Joe____, and I went to the store.
   - jay
   - (Joe)
   - jot

2. Along the way, we saw a ____doe____ by the road.
   - die
   - (doe)
   - day

3. When we got there, Joe stubbed his ____toe____.
   - tie
   - (toe)
   - lie

4. My dog ____Moe____ stayed outside.
   - (Moe)
   - my
   - mine

5. I wanted to buy a new red ____tie____.
   - (tie)
   - toe
   - lie

6. We all had some ____pie____ when we got home.
   - (pie)
   - pine
   - pile

 TALK About It Why did Joe and his friend go to the store?

FOCUS ON ALL LEARNERS

ESL/ELL ENGLISH LANGUAGE LEARNERS

Materials: magazines, construction paper, glue

Reinforce the rule for vowel pairs by writing words in context.

- Read aloud the rule on page 185. Write *tie* and *toe* on the board. Say the words; have children repeat chorally.

- Invite a volunteer to read the first sentence and the answer choices on page 185. Ask another volunteer to choose an answer. Have children complete the activity independently, whenever possible.

- Read aloud the rule on page 186. Recite aloud and write *doe* and *boat* on the board. Ask children if they follow the rule. (*yes*)

- Say aloud the words in the box on page 186; have children repeat them. Use visuals to confirm meanings of unfamiliar words. Label pictures together; have children exchange papers to verify their printing against the word box.

AUDITORY/VISUAL LEARNERS *INDIVIDUAL*

Materials: drawing paper; crayons or markers

Have children design Dinosaur Directory pages by choosing a word from pages 185–186 or from classroom lists and drawing and labeling a dinosaur with the object. Examples might include dinosaurs wearing ties, polishing toenails, or washing with soap.

RULE

The vowel pair **oe** sometimes has the long **o** sound. The vowel pair **oa** has the long **o** sound. You can hear the long **o** sound in **doe** and **boat**.

▶ **Print** the name for each picture on the line below it.

| boat | doe | goat | toe | soap | coat |

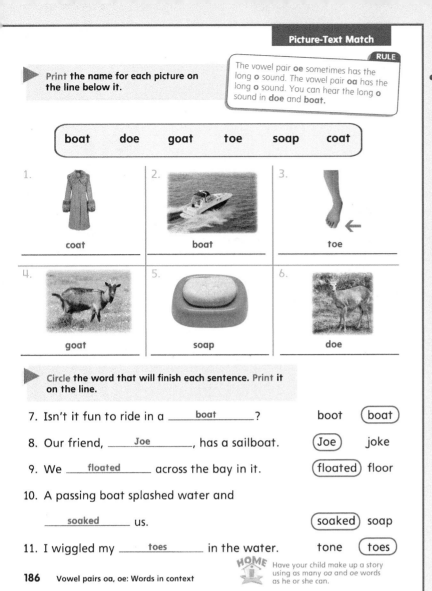

1. coat
2. boat
3. toe
4. goat
5. soap
6. doe

▶ **Circle** the word that will finish each sentence. **Print** it on the line.

7. Isn't it fun to ride in a ___boat___?   boot   (boat)

8. Our friend, ___Joe___, has a sailboat.   (Joe)   joke

9. We ___floated___ across the bay in it.   (floated)   floor

10. A passing boat splashed water and

    ___soaked___ us.   (soaked)   soap

11. I wiggled my ___toes___ in the water.   tone   (toes)

 HOME Have your child make up a story using as many oa and oe words as he or she can.

186   Vowel pairs oa, oe: Words in context

CURRICULUM CONNECTIONS

SPELLING

Ask children to unscramble the following letters to write their spelling words. Remind them that each word is spelled with a vowel pair.

1. ite (*tie*)
2. tabo (*boat*)
3. ipe (*pie*)
4. neab (*bean*)
5. anir (*rain*)
6. yatr (*tray*)
7. edes (*seed*)
8. ohe (*hoe*)

WRITING

Discuss various types of boats, such as sailboats, tugboats, and steamboats. Invite each child to choose a boat he or she would like to ride or work on, write the reasons why, and draw a picture of himself or herself on the boat.

MATH

Tell children they are going to the store with Joe. They have $3.00 to spend. Ask children to choose items with *ie, oa,* or *oe* in their names from pages 185–186 and to write receipts with items and prices totaling $3.00.

TECHNOLOGY **AstroWord** Long Vowels: *i, o*

Integrating Phonics and Reading

Guided Reading
Have children read the title. Ask them if they know which animal on the cover is a frog and which is a toad.

First Reading Have children use the pictures to explain differences between frogs and toads.

Second Reading Ask children how the vowel sounds in *frog* and *toad* are different. Have children find other examples of words with the vowel sound in *toad*.

Comprehension
After reading, ask children the following questions:

• How can you tell a frog from a toad? *Recall/ Summarize*

• Do you think frogs and toads are more alike or more different? Explain. *Reflective Analysis/ Make Judgments*

ESL/ELL **English Language Learners**
Read the title and point out the question mark. Ask children why they think the title ends with a question mark.

VISUAL/KINESTHETIC LEARNERS **GROUPS**

Materials: Phonics Word Cards, Set 1: Long *o* words (165–179)

Ask children to sort out and read the cards containing words with the vowel pairs *oa* and *oe*. Then, invite children to pick up two cards at a time and use the words together in a sentence.

CHALLENGE

Invite children to draw dinosaur-related pictures, hiding five pictures with *oe, oa,* and *ie* names in the drawings. Have them put answer keys on the back and exchange pictures with partners.

EXTRA SUPPORT/INTERVENTION

Materials: index cards, markers

Make cards for the vowel pair words on pages 185–186. Display the cards and have children take turns reading the sentences from the pages as classmates find and read the correct answers from the word cards. See Daily Phonics Practice, pages 255–256.

Lesson 86   Pages 187–188

Phonics and Reading / Phonics and Writing

Review Vowel Pairs

Skill Focus

Children will

★ read words that contain vowel pairs.

★ write words with vowel pairs to complete sentences.

★ build words using vowel pairs.

ESL/ELL For those English language learners who have difficulty making long vowel sounds, point out that the sound is the same as the name of the letter in English.

Teach

Phonemic Awareness: Phoneme Categorization Hold up Phonics Picture Cards tray (88), nails (90), and nose (115). Have children match picture names with the same vowel sound and tell what the vowel sound is. (*tray, nails; long* a) Repeat with lion (22), leaf (120), and jeep (119). (*leaf, jeep; long* e)

Sound to Symbol Write the words *tray, nails, leaf,* and *jeep* on the board. Have children say the words aloud. Then, invite volunteers to go to the board, identify the vowel sound, and underline the letters that stand for that sound. (*tray, nails, long* a; *leaf, jeep, long* e)

Read Words in Sentences Write these sentences on the board.

- **That animal has a tail and a claw on each toe.**
- **It has a green and brown coat.**

Have children read the sentences and circle the words with long vowel sounds. (*tail, each, toe, green, coat*)

Practice and Apply

Phonics and Reading After children have read the story, have them find words containing long vowel pairs.

Critical Thinking When you discuss Talk About It with children, elicit both positive and negative aspects of the iguana.

Reading Use *Who Has a Tail?*, MCP Phonics and Reading Super Skills Library 2, Level B, to review words with vowel pairs.

Phonics and Writing Complete the first item on page 188 together. Remind children that each word they make must be a real word.

187

Reading

Name_____

 Read the story. Print a word with a vowel pair on the line to finish each sentence.

Ray's Surprise

One day, Ray's mom gave him an iguana. It looked like a baby dinosaur. It had a brown and green coat and a long tail. It had big feet with a sharp little claw on each toe.

Ray got a book about iguanas to read. He learned that iguanas don't eat meat. They need a meal of lettuce once a day. They also like sweet potatoes, apples, and oranges. Iguanas need to stay warm and like to lie in the sun. They can grow to be six feet long!

1. Ray's iguana had a long ____tail____ and big ____feet____.

2. Iguanas need a ____meal____ of lettuce once a ____day____.

3. They also like ____sweet____ potatoes.

 TALK About It Would an iguana make a good pet? Why or why not?

Review vowel pairs: Critical thinking   **187**

FOCUS ON ALL LEARNERS

ESL/ELL **ENGLISH LANGUAGE LEARNERS**

Expand English language learners' ability to make the sounds of vowel pairs by relating written vowel pairs to the sounds they make.

- Read aloud *Ray's Surprise* on page 187. Allow children to follow along with their books. Ask questions to verify comprehension.

- Invite a volunteer to read aloud the first paragraph. Encourage other volunteers to name words with vowel pairs and make the long vowel sounds they represent.

- On the board, write and group the words according to their vowel pairs. Then, complete items 1–3 as a group and discuss the Talk About It question.

AUDITORY/VISUAL LEARNERS

Draw four large dinosaur footprint shapes on the board. Print *-ies, -eat, -ay,* and *-oat* in them. Have children use different initial sounds to write rhyming words in, or below, the matching footprints. A word should only be added if the child can define it or use it in a sentence.

Building Words

Phonics & Writing Use **words with vowel pairs** to finish each word ladder. Change **only one letter** at a time.

1. Begin with **beam**.
End with **coat**.

beam
beat
boat
coat

2. Begin with **lean**.
End with **road**.

lean

loan

load

road

3. Begin with **fried**.
End with **trees**.

fried

freed

treed

trees

4. Begin with **dies**.
End with **goes**.

dies

ties

toes

goes

 HOME With your child, make a word ladder of four words, beginning or ending with any word you made.

188 Review vowel pairs: Writing

CURRICULUM CONNECTIONS

SPELLING

The first set of spelling words for this unit may be posttested at this time.

1. **rain**   Summer **rain** is like a cool shower.
2. **tray**   Carry your lunch on that **tray**.
3. **seed**   A flower will grow from this **seed**.
4. **bean**   I planted a **bean** plant in my garden.
5. **boat**   My **boat** can float on the sea.
6. **hoe**   He used a **hoe** to weed the garden.
7. **pie**   We had a pizza **pie** for lunch.
8. **tie**   Please **tie** your shoelace.

SCIENCE

On chart paper, list children's ideas for taking care of an iguana. Have children gather information from pet stores and books to confirm or add to their suggestions.

MATH

Have children compare and contrast iguana and dinosaur characteristics, recording responses in a Venn diagram.

 **TECHNOLOGY** **AstroWord** Long Vowels: *a, i;*
Long Vowels: *i, o;*
Long Vowels: *e, u*

AUDITORY/VISUAL/KINESTHETIC LEARNERS GROUPS

Materials: duplicated 16-box grids, bingo markers

Have children write these words in the grids in any order: *rain, tray, seed, bean, coat, hoe, pie, tie, boat, day, mail, may, cries, float, bead, beet.* Call out the words at random. A child covering four words in a row yells Bingo!, reads the four words, and becomes the next caller.

CHALLENGE

Invite children to find out more about iguanas. They can report what they discover about the animal's native areas, what its natural habitat is, who its enemies are, and why iguanas make good pets.

EXTRA SUPPORT/INTERVENTION

Materials: index cards, four shoe boxes

Attach cards to the "iguana aquariums" (the boxes) that read *ai, ay; ee, ea; oa, oe; ie.* Have children reread the story on page 187, print vowel pair words on cards, and drop them in the correct "aquariums." See *Daily Phonics Practice*, pages 255–256.

Integrating Phonics and Reading

Guided Reading
Have children read the title and look at the cover. Ask them to identify the pictured animal.
First Reading Have children use the text and pictures to name the animals and describe their tails.
Second Reading Write *ai, ay, ee,* and *ea* on the board. Have children find example words in the story, write them on the board, and create original sentences for each one.
Comprehension
Ask children the following questions:
• How can you have the tails in the story? *Inference/Picture Clues*
• Do you agree that the peacock was the best animal for the cover? Explain. *Reflective Analysis/Personal Response*
ESL/ELL **English Language Learners**
Read the title to children. Encourage them to answer the question by finding and reading the sentences in the story that name the animals.

188

Take-Home Book

Review Vowel Pairs

Skill Focus

Children will

★ read words with vowel pairs in the context of a nonfiction story.

★ review selected high-frequency words in the context of a story.

★ reread for fluency.

ESL/ELL Speakers of Spanish may tend to clip vowel sounds in English. They may need additional practice stretching out the vowels to their appropriate lengths.

Teach
Build Background

• Ask children what the theme of this unit is. (*Dinosaur Days*) Encourage them to share what they have learned so far.

• Write the word *fossils* on the board. Explain that fossils are the remains of plants and animals that lived long ago. Ask children what they think scientists might learn from fossils.

Sound to Symbol Write this sentence on the board: *Fossils are the remains of plants and animals.* Have children read it aloud. Underline and say the word *remains*. Ask children what vowel sound they hear in the second syllable. (*long* a) Invite a volunteer to circle the letters that stand for the long *a* sound. (ai)

Practice and Apply

Read the Book Have children tear out and assemble the Take-Home Book. Suggest that they look through the pictures. Then, read the story together. Discuss what new information they learned about dinosaurs.

Sound to Symbol Review the long vowel pairs. Have children find words with long vowel pairs and write them on the board. (*seen, say, layers, away, teeth, needed, remains, died, teams, days, weeks, deep, may, main, painted, tie, each, roamed*)

Review High-Frequency Words Write the words *build* and *ever* on the board. Have children spell the words and say them as they blend the sounds.

Reread for Fluency Have children reread the book to increase their fluency and comprehension. Remind them to take their books home to read with family members.

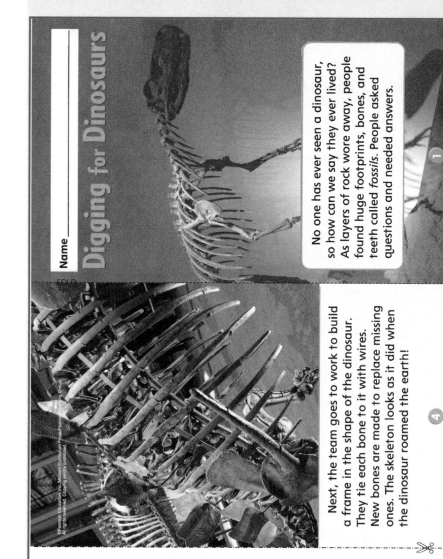

Name _____

Digging for Dinosaurs

FOLD

No one has ever seen a dinosaur, so how can we say they ever lived? As layers of rock wore away, people found huge footprints, bones, and teeth called *fossils*. People asked questions and needed answers.

1

Next, the team goes to work to build a frame in the shape of the dinosaur. They tie each bone to it with wires. New bones are made to replace missing ones. The skeleton looks as it did when the dinosaur roamed the earth!

4

©Pearson Education Inc./Modern Curriculum Press/Pearson Learning Group.
All rights reserved. Copying strictly prohibited.

Review vowel pairs: Take-home book   **189**

FOCUS ON ALL LEARNERS

ESL/ELL ENGLISH LANGUAGE LEARNERS

Materials: index cards, markers

Support English language learners as they review vowel pairs and their corresponding sounds using familiar words in context.

• On index cards, write words from the Take-Home Book, *Digging for Dinosaurs*, that contain vowel pairs. (*seen, say, layers, away, teeth, needed, remains, died, teams, days, weeks, may, deep, main, painted, tie, each, roamed*)

• Read the Take-Home Book aloud to the group. Have children follow along silently as you read.

• Reread the story aloud. Have volunteers find the words on the index cards as they appear in the story and sort them in order of presentation. Encourage children to repeat them.

• Ask volunteers to underline the vowel pair, make the sound it represents, and repeat each word. Monitor pronunciation.

AUDITORY/VISUAL LEARNERS

Before children take their books home, have them "buddy read" with a partner, taking turns reading the pages and helping each other with unfamiliar words.

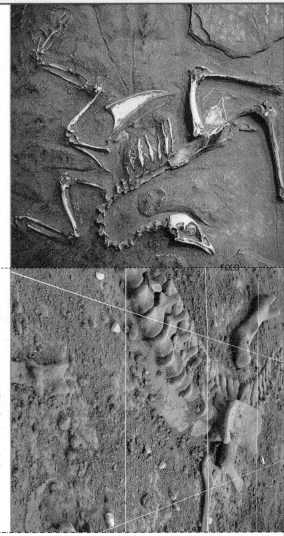

2 Fossils are the remains of plants and animals that died long ago. Teams of workers find fossils all over the world. It can take days, weeks, or years to find the smallest fossil. It is hard work to find the fossils deep in the rock.

FOLD

3 The team may find enough bones to put together the main parts of a dinosaur. Pictures of each bone are taken, so there can be no mix-up. Then, the bones are painted with a kind of glue so they won't fall apart.

190   Review vowel pairs: Take-home book

CURRICULUM CONNECTIONS

SCIENCE

Explain that scientists have recently discovered what they think are two new dinosaurs they call *Supersaurus* and *Ultrasaurus*. Both were herbivores—they ate plants and no meat. *Supersaurus* may have been 100 to 120 feet long and *Ultrasaurus* might have been even larger. Have children find information about which dinosaurs were carnivores (meat eaters) or herbivores (plant eaters).

WRITING

Have children imagine that they meet a dinosaur on their way to school tomorrow. What would they say to the dinosaur? How might the dinosaur respond? Have them draw cartoons of the event with dialogue in speech balloons.

READING

Explain that *nonfiction* books give facts about a certain topic. Ask children if the Take-Home Book is fiction or nonfiction. Have children tell some of the main ideas about dinosaurs covered in this nonfiction book. List responses. Then, chart details that tell more about the main ideas.

 **TECHNOLOGY**   **AstroWord** Long Vowels: *a, i;*
Long Vowels: *i, o;*
Long Vowels: *e, u*

AUDITORY/VISUAL LEARNERS   GROUPS

Have children circle the words in their books that have the vowel pairs they have studied. Read the words together and identify the vowel pairs. Then, have children close their books. Read the book aloud and have children raise their hands when they hear the vowel pair words.

CHALLENGE

Invite children to read the story to small groups in a younger grade. Encourage them to share facts they have learned about dinosaurs.

EXTRA SUPPORT/INTERVENTION

Read *Digging for Dinosaurs* as children follow along. Pause before the following words to have children read them aloud: *seen, say, layers, away, teeth, needed, remains, died, teams, days, weeks, may, deep, team, main, each, painted, tie, roamed.* Then, have children read the book independently or chorally. See Daily Phonics Practice, pages 255–256.

Vowel Digraph oo

Skill Focus

Children will

★ define a vowel digraph.

★ read and write words with the vowel digraph *oo*.

★ recognize the different sounds of the digraph *oo*.

★ recognize and read a high-frequency word.

ESL/ELL Children who have difficulty pronouncing *oo* vowel digraphs (*book/boot*) may need additional support and oral/listening practice with the long *oo* sound. Exaggeration of the sound with a focus on the lip position may be helpful.

Teach

Phonological Awareness: Rhyme Say the pairs of words below and have children stand each time they hear a word pair that rhymes: *spoon, soon; nook, look; good, glad; mood, food; hook, hold.*

Sound to Symbol Write the words *spoon* and *look* on the board and have a volunteer read the words aloud. Ask children if the vowel sound in each word is short or long. (*neither*) Explain that the *oo* in each word is neither short nor long but has its own special sound. The vowel pair *oo* is known as a vowel digraph; a vowel digraph can make a long or short sound, have a sound of its own, or have more than one sound.

Practice and Apply

Sound to Symbol With children, read the rhyme at the top of the page. Have children find words with the digraph *oo* and say them aloud: *tooth, foot, tools, look, nook.* Then, have volunteers go to the board and write the words that sound like *spoon* in one column and *took* in another column.

Read the rule on page 191 and have volunteers restate it in their own words. Then, read the directions. Children will have the opportunity to read the high-frequency word *should*. Then, review the pictures on page 192 with children.

Writing Read the directions at the top of page 192. Remind children to reread the sentence with their answer to make sure it makes sense.

Critical Thinking In discussing Talk About It, children should recognize that taking a bite of food caused the loose tooth to fall out.

Reading Use *Freddy Frog's Note*, MCP Phonics and Reading Super Skills Library 2, Level B, to reinforce the sounds of the digraph *oo*.

191

Name_____

We may learn what was not known,
When finding a dinosaur tooth or foot bone.
With tools, scientists chip rocks and look
All around the world, in every nook.

RULE A vowel digraph is two letters together that stand for one vowel sound. The vowel sound can be long or short, or have a special sound of its own. You can hear the different sounds of the vowel digraph *oo* in **tooth** and **foot**.

▶ Circle **the word that will finish each sentence. Print it on the line.**

1. One of my teeth felt a little _____loose_____ .
   broom
   (loose)

2. I wanted to see the _____tooth_____ .
   tool
   (tooth)

3. I ran to my _____room_____ .
   (room)
   zoo

4. I stood on a _____stool_____ to look in the mirror.
   spoon
   (stool)

5. My tooth should fall out _____soon_____ .
   moon
   (soon)

6. At _____noon_____ it was time for lunch.
   soon
   (noon)

7. I took a bite of _____food_____ with my spoon.
   (food)
   fool

8. Out came my loose tooth on the _____spoon_____ .
   soothe
   (spoon)

9. My friend lost a tooth, _____too_____ .
   (too)
   zoo

TALK About It What made the loose tooth come out?

Vowel digraph oo: High-frequency words, critical thinking   **191**

FOCUS ON ALL LEARNERS

ESL/ELL ENGLISH LANGUAGE LEARNERS

Encourage English language learners to practice using words with vowel digraph *oo* in context.

- Read aloud the rule on page 191. Then, say aloud the word choices for the activity on the same page. Have children repeat aloud after you, chorally. Ask which words rhyme.

- Read aloud the directions; as a class complete items 1–9. Invite volunteers to read completed sentences.

- Have a volunteer read the directions at the top of page 192 to the group; encourage children to complete sentences individually or in pairs; review answers aloud together.

VISUAL/KINESTHETIC LEARNERS GROUPS

Materials: Phonics Word Cards, Set 2: Vowel Digraph *oo* words (149–160)

Have children practice reading the words and then think of ways to sort them into categories. They might group words by *oo* sounds or by nouns and verbs.

▶ Find a word in the box that will finish each sentence. Print it on the line.

cookie	look	good	stood
book	cook	took	hook

1. I was looking for a good ____book____.

2. I took a ____look____ at a cookbook.

3. I ____stood____ in line to pay for the book.

4. Then, I ____took____ my new book home.

5. I decided to ____cook____ something.

6. I took my apron off a ____hook____.

7. I tried a ____cookie____ recipe.

8. The cookies were very ____good____.

▶ Print the missing letters of each picture's name. Print the missing letters for a word that rhymes with it. Trace the whole word.

9.
b ook
sh ook

10.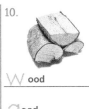
w ood
g ood

11.
h ook
br ook

12.
h ood
st ood

 HOME With your child, make up a rhyme for each pair of words above.

192 Vowel digraph oo: Rhyme

CURRICULUM CONNECTIONS

SPELLING

These words and context sentences can be used to pretest the vowel digraph spelling words.

1. **book** I just read a great **book**.
2. **food** I eat only good **food**.
3. **head** Put a hat on your **head**.
4. **haul** Did they **haul** away the trash?
5. **draw** She likes to **draw** animals.

WRITING

Have children share their experiences with losing baby teeth. Invite children to write about what happens when they lose a tooth.

MATH

Ask children to bring in favorite healthful snack recipes from home. Compile a class list of measurements used in the recipes. Then, write out measurement terms in full and abbreviated forms. Display kitchen utensils and invite children to match them to the words and abbreviations on the list.

TECHNOLOGY **AstroWord** Vowel Digraphs & Diphthongs

Integrating Phonics and Reading

Guided Reading

After children look at the cover, ask if they think Freddy has a problem with the note from his mother.

First Reading Have children tell the things Freddy did and explain why he did them.

Second Reading Have children find the words *soon*, *took*, *bathroom*, and *room* and tell if the digraph *oo* makes the sound heard in *book* or *pool*.

Comprehension

Ask children the following questions:

• Why couldn't Freddy read his mother's note? *Recall/Reflective Analysis*

• What would you have done if you were Freddy? *Reflective Analysis/Personal Response*

ESL/ELL English Language Learners

Read pages 5 and 6 and ask what children think the word *it* means. Point out that readers sometimes must go back a sentence or two to learn what a word means.

AUDITORY/VISUAL LEARNERS GROUPS

Materials: chart paper, marker

Cut out the shapes of a large foot and a large boot from the paper. Label them and say *foot* and *boot*. Invite children to print as many *oo* words as they can think of on the shape that corresponds to the pronunciation of the *oo* sound. Then, read all the words in each group together.

CHALLENGE

Invite children to reread the rhyme on page 191 and imagine they are digging for dinosaur bones. As they brush away the dirt, they find a tooth from an undiscovered dinosaur! Have children write about what happens next.

EXTRA SUPPORT/INTERVENTION

Materials: Phonics Picture Cards: book (3), goose (15), moon (25), broom (123)

Display the pictures and have children say each name as you write them on the board. Ask children to add rhyming words for each one. (book: *cook, look, hook, nook, took;* goose: *loose, moose;* moon: *soon, spoon, loon;* broom: *room, boom*) See Daily Phonics Practice, pages 256–257.

Vowel Digraph ea

Skill Focus

Children will

★ read and write words with the vowel digraph sounds of *ea*.

★ distinguish among the sounds of the digraph *ea*.

ESL/ELL Children may have difficulty pronouncing and distinguishing short vowels, including the sound of short *e*. In Tagalog, short *e* sounds like *a* in *say*. No similar sound exists in Korean.

Teach

Phonemic Awareness: Phoneme Substitution Say the word *head*, emphasizing the short vowel sound: *heeeed*. Have children repeat the word. Ask them what vowel sound they hear. (*short e*) Then, ask them to replace the *h* with the following consonants or blends to form other words with the short *e* sound: *br* (*bread*); *d* (*dead*); *dr* (*dread*); *spr* (*spread*).

Sound to Symbol Write the words *head, bread, dead, dread*, and *spread* on the board. Point to each one as you say it. Have children repeat it. Then, circle the *ea* in *head*. Explain that *ea* is a vowel digraph that often stands for the short *e* sound. Have volunteers go to the board, read the word, and circle the letters that stand for the short *e* sound.

Write *beak* and *break* on the board. Have volunteers say the words. Remind children that *ea* can also stand for the long *e* sound as in *beak*. Explain that sometimes *ea* can also stand for long *a* as in *break*.

Practice and Apply

Sound to Symbol Have a volunteer read the rule on page 193 and explain what it means. Then, read the directions to both pages. Help children identify the pictures on page 194, if necessary. Remind them that not all *ea* words have the sound of short *e*.

Writing You may wish to read the word choices on page 193 with children before they finish the sentences.

Reading Use *Heather's Book,* MCP Phonics and Reading Super Skills Library 2, Level B, to provide children with additional practice reading *ea* words in the context of a story.

Name _____

▶ Find the word in the box that will finish each sentence. Print it on the line.

> **RULE**
> The vowel digraph **ea** can stand for the short **e** sound. You can hear the short **e** sound in **ready**.

ahead	already	breakfast	spread
bread	breath	head	

1. When you wake up, take a deep _____breath_____.

2. It will help clear your _____head_____.

3. Now you are ready for _____breakfast_____.

4. Here is some _____bread_____ to make toast.

5. You can _____spread_____ butter and jam on it.

6. The eggs are _____already_____ made.

7. Go _____ahead_____ and eat.

▶ Circle the correct word to finish each sentence.

8. What is the (feather, (weather,) leather) like today?

9. Will you need to wear a ((sweater,) weather, meadow)?

10. Maybe you will need a (ready, (heavy,) cleanser) coat.

11. Is it cold enough for (bread, thread, (leather)) boots?

12. Cover your ((head,) heavy, breakfast) with a warm hat.

13. Now you are (meadow, heavy, (ready)) to go outside.

FOCUS ON ALL LEARNERS

ESL/ELL ENGLISH LANGUAGE LEARNERS

Familiarize English language learners with common words that contain the vowel digraph *ea* with the sound of short *e*.

- Read aloud the rule on page 193. Read aloud the words in the box. Have children repeat chorally each word after you. Ask if the words all fit the rule. (*yes*) Have children circle the vowel digraph in each word.

- Confirm that English language learners understand the meaning of each word. Use gestures, pantomime, realia, and short phrases to clarify.

- As a group, complete in writing the first activity on page 193. Encourage volunteers to suggest answers aloud. Write answers on the board as children compare them to their papers.

KINESTHETIC LEARNERS INDIVIDUAL

Materials: colored paper, magazines, crayons, glue

Challenge children to make picture collages (or draw pictures) for one of the following topics: dinosaur weather, a dinosaur's breakfast, or a dinosaur's dreams. Have children add titles and captions to their pictures.

▶ Say the name of each picture. Circle the words with the same **ea** sound as the picture's name.

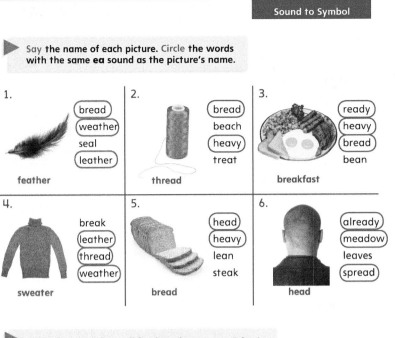

1.
bread
(weather)
seal
(leather)

feather

2.
(bread)
beach
(heavy)
treat

thread

3.
(ready)
(heavy)
(bread)
bean

breakfast

4.
break
(leather)
(thread)
(weather)

sweater

5.
(head)
(heavy)
lean
steak

bread

6.
(already)
(meadow)
leaves
(spread)

head

▶ Circle the word that will finish each sentence. Print it on the line.

7. I have _____read_____ many books about dinosaurs.

ready (read)

8. Dinosaurs were _____dead_____ before people lived.

(dead) head

9. I _____already_____ knew some dinosaurs ate only plants.

(already) steady

10. Many dinosaurs were very _____heavy_____.

(heavy) ahead

194 Vowel digraph ea

HOME With your child, take turns naming words that rhyme with some of the words he or she circled.

CURRICULUM CONNECTIONS

SPELLING

Ask a volunteer to spell *book* on the board. Then, tell others to use the same digraph to spell these words below *book:* cook, stood, brook, shook. Repeat with *food:* zoo, spoon, school, troops; *head:* read, breath, thread, heavy; *haul:* Paul, August, Paula; *draw:* law, lawn, hawk, straw, crawl. Give each child a copy of the spelling words to practice.

WRITING

Ask children to finish one of the sentence starters below to form a main idea and to then add sentences that give more details about the main idea.

I am always ready to _____ .

My favorite breakfast is _____ .

The best kind of weather is _____ .

AstroWord Vowel Digraphs & Diphthongs

AUDITORY/VISUAL LEARNERS

Materials: Phonics Picture Cards: leaf (120) and bread (121)

Display and label each picture. Tell children that you are going to say words that contain *ea* and that they should respond by saying the picture name that has the matching vowel sound: *jeans, sweater, feather, breakfast, wheat, head, beaver, eagle, thread, ready, leather, heavy, weather, beans, beads, spread.*

CHALLENGE

Invite children to make lists of words with the short *e* and long *e* sounds of *ea*. Then, have them write sentences, using at least three words with matching *ea* sounds in each.

EXTRA SUPPORT/INTERVENTION

Materials: index cards, pencils

Have children write the following *ea* words on index cards: *leak, bread, heat, ready, bead, reach, bean, ready, tea, lead, thread, head, jeans, breath, breathe, breakfast, seat, heavy, leaf.* Have them read and sort the cards into different *ea* sounds. See Daily Phonics Practice, pages 256–257.

Integrating Phonics and Reading

Guided Reading

Ask children to look at the title and illustrations, then suggest what Heather's book may be about.

First Reading Ask children when and where the story took place.

Second Reading Write *Heather* on the board. Have children find words that have the same *ea* vowel sound and list the words below *Heather.*

Comprehension

After reading, ask children the following questions:

- After Heather's family reaches their land, what are some of the things they do? *Recall/ Sequence*
- Do you think Heather is happy in her new home? Why or why not? *Reflective Analysis/ Make Judgments*

ESL/ELL English Language Learners

Explain to children that this story takes place over one hundred years ago. Then, help them find words that refer to this time.

Vowel Digraphs au, aw

Skill Focus

Children will

★ read words with the vowel digraphs *au* and *aw*.

★ write words with the digraphs *au* and *aw* to finish sentences.

★ recognize and read high-frequency words.

ESL/ELL Children whose home language is Korean may introduce the sound /ya/ when they anticipate the sound of short *a* after *g* and have difficulty saying words such as *August*.

Teach

Phonemic Awareness: Phoneme Categorization Say the following words, emphasizing the vowel sounds: *lawn, let, cause*. Repeat the words and then ask children to say the two words that have the same vowel sounds. (*lawn, cause*)

Sound to Symbol Write *lawn* and *cause* on the board. Have children say the vowel sound they hear in the middle of the words. Circle the *aw* in *lawn* and the *au* in *cause*. Explain that *aw* and *au* are vowel digraphs that usually make the same sound. Then, write the names *Dawn* and *Paul* on the board. Have volunteers pronounce the words and circle the digraphs in each.

Practice and Apply

Blend Phonemes Read the rule on page 195. Encourage children to say it after you. Then, help children to read the words in the box on page 195 and in the crayons on page 196. Model how to blend phonemes as they sound out unfamiliar words.

Writing As children finish the sentences, circulate through the classroom and offer help in reading the sentences to individuals who need it. Children will have the opportunity to read the high-frequency words *water, after,* and *near.*

Critical Thinking Discuss the Talk About It questions. For page 195, children should recognize that in August the family does many activities that are fun. For page 196, encourage children to name other animals.

Reading Use *Lobster Fishing at Dawn,* MCP Phonics and Reading Super Skills Library 2, Level B, to reinforce reading words with *au* and *aw.*

195

Name _____

▶ Find **the word in the box that will finish each sentence.** Print **it on the line.**

RULE
The vowel digraphs **au** and **aw** usually have the same sound. You can hear the sound of **au** and **aw** in **August** and **paw.**

drawing	straws	
lawn	yawn	August
autumn	haul	Paula
pause	crawls	

1. _____August_____ is a lazy month.

2. We _____pause_____ in our work to relax.

3. _____Paula_____ and I play games in the shade.

4. I water the _____lawn_____ in the evenings.

5. We _____haul_____ the picnic basket to the lake.

6. After swimming, we _____yawn_____ and nap in the sun.

7. We sip lemonade through _____straws_____.

8. My baby brother _____crawls_____ on the grass.

9. Summer's end is _____drawing_____ near.

10. Soon, _____autumn_____ will come, and school will start.

TALK About It Why does this family like August?

Vowel digraphs au, aw: High-frequency words, critical thinking   **195**

FOCUS ON ALL LEARNERS

ESL/ELL ENGLISH LANGUAGE LEARNERS

Present to English language learners words that contain the vowel digraphs *au* and *aw* and the vowel sound they represent.

● Read aloud the rule on page 195 and paraphrase it. Say aloud the words *drawn, sauce,* and *jaw.* Ask children if each word fits the rule. Have children repeat each word.

● Read aloud the words in the box on page 195 and have children repeat them. Confirm that each word follows the rule and suggest that children spell each word.

● Read the directions and model item 1. Then, invite a volunteer to serve as "teacher" to lead the group in completing the activity.

VISUAL/KINESTHETIC LEARNERS

Materials: index cards, container

Write these words on index cards: *yawn, haul, crawl, draw, hawk, faucet, claw, paw.* Have volunteers choose words and pantomime their meanings. Classmates can guess the *aw* or *au* digraph words and print them on the board.

► Find a word in a crayon that will finish each sentence. Print it on the line.

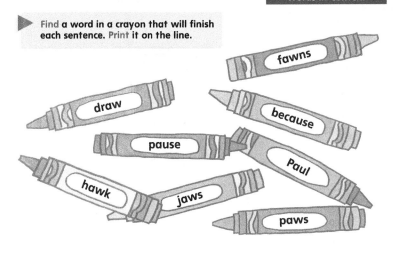

1. After school, _____Paul_____ likes to draw.

2. When he draws, he doesn't _____pause_____.

3. He can _____draw_____ any kind of animal.

4. Paul can make a _____hawk_____ with sharp claws.

5. He can draw a dinosaur with powerful _____jaws_____.

6. He draws dogs with huge _____paws_____.

7. He draws _____fawns_____ hiding near trees.

8. Paul draws so well _____because_____ he practices a lot.

 What other animals might Paul like to draw?

 Have your child write a story using one or more of the words on pages 195–196.

196 Vowel digraphs au, aw: High-frequency words, critical thinking

---

CURRICULUM CONNECTIONS

SPELLING

Write the scrambled spelling words below on the board. As you read each clue, ask a volunteer to point to the set of letters that form the answer and to say the word. All can spell the word orally before it is written.

1. **rawd** Do this with crayons. (*draw*)

2. **ulah** It means to carry. (*haul*)

3. **deha** You have one of these. (*head*)

4. **ofod** You can eat this. (*food*)

5. **kobo** It opens easily. (*book*)

ART

Talk about ways to draw realistic-looking animals. Use animal figurines or classroom pets as models. Conduct a class critique. Ask children which parts of each drawing look the most realistic.

TECHNOLOGY **AstroWord** Vowel Digraphs & Diphthongs

VISUAL/AUDITORY LEARNERS

Have partners create one or more riddles whose answers are *au* and *aw* words. Model this sample: *Make an O with your mouth, and you'll know my name.* (*yawn*) Invite children to ask the class their riddles.

CHALLENGE

Materials: one-inch squares cut from paper or index cards

Have children assemble a crosswordlike pattern of *au* and *aw* words, printing letters they need on the squares. Children can start a new puzzle when they have made as many words with one as they can.

EXTRA SUPPORT/INTERVENTION

Help children define the words *pause* and *fawn*. Show a picture of a fawn and explain that it is a baby deer. Give examples of a pause in music, in speaking, and in action, and have children model examples of their own. See Daily Phonics Practice, pages 256–257.

Integrating Phonics and Reading

Guided Reading

Have children discuss the photograph on the cover. Point out the lobster trap and the net. Explain that the lobster in the picture is commonly found in the cold waters of the North Atlantic Ocean.

First Reading Ask children why lobsters go into the traps.

Second Reading Write the words *dawn* and *haul* on the board. Have children find other words in the story with the same vowel digraphs.

Comprehension

After reading, ask children the following questions:

• What steps do the people take to catch lobsters? *Recall/Sequence*

• Why does each person have a different color marker? *Inference/Draw Conclusions*

ESL/ELL English Language Learners

Reread the book and draw attention to the fishing words (*fish, lobster, raw, bait, anchor, salt water, marker, hook, gaff, claws, trap*).

Review Vowel Digraphs

Skill Focus

Children will

★ read and write words with the vowel digraphs *oo, ea, au,* and *aw.*

★ distinguish among the vowel digraph sounds of *oo, ea, au,* and *aw.*

Teach

Phonemic Awareness: Phoneme Categorization Tell children that you are going to say some groups of words. They are to identify which two words have the same vowel sound and which word has a different vowel sound.

- **look   mood foot**
- **bread head   bead**
- **raw   row   haul**

Sound to Symbol Write the words *look, food, bread, raw,* and *haul* on the board. Review the definition of a vowel digraph. Have children say each word aloud and have a volunteer circle the vowel digraph in each. Then, ask children to suggest other words with the same digraphs.

Practice and Apply

Sound to Symbol Read the directions to pages 197 and 198. Have children identify each picture name. Remind children that on page 198 they need to both circle the digraph and write it to finish the word. Then, encourage them to trace the entire word.

Writing On page 197, encourage children to say each word in the bubbles before they write the word next to the appropriate picture.

Reading You may wish to use *Once Upon a Time,* MCP Phonics and Reading Super Skills Library 2, Level B, to review reading words with vowel digraphs in the context of a story.

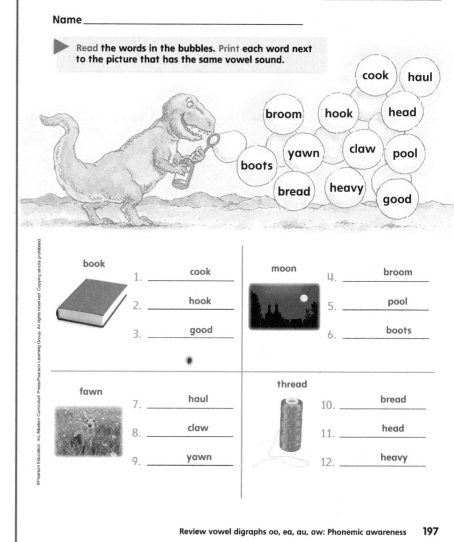

Name_____

▶ Read the words in the bubbles. Print each word next to the picture that has the same vowel sound.

cook   haul   broom   hook   head   yawn   claw   pool   boots   bread   heavy   good

book
1. ___ cook
2. ___ hook
3. ___ good

moon
4. ___ broom
5. ___ pool
6. ___ boots

fawn
7. ___ haul
8. ___ claw
9. ___ yawn

thread
10. ___ bread
11. ___ head
12. ___ heavy

Review vowel digraphs oo, ea, au, aw: Phonemic awareness   **197**

ESL/ELL ENGLISH LANGUAGE LEARNERS

Materials: Phonics Word Cards, Set 2, 149–176

Confirm English language learners' knowledge of the vowel digraphs *oo, ea, au,* and *aw.*

- Display several Phonics Word Cards that represent each sound. Pronounce the words and have children repeat them.
- Make the sounds of *oo.* Read aloud the words in the bubbles on page 197.
- Read each word again. Invite children to clap when they hear words with the sounds of *oo.*
- Repeat the same procedure with the remaining digraphs. Then, have children say all the words in the bubbles.

VISUAL/KINESTHETIC LEARNERS

Materials: index cards, marker

On cards, write an equal number of words with *au, aw, oo,* and *ea* digraphs so that each child receives one word. Children try to find classmates with the same digraph and then arrange their cards in alphabetical order in the shortest amount of time.

▶ Say the name of each picture. Circle the letters that stand for the vowel sound in the picture's name. Then, print the letters to finish its name. Trace the whole word.

1. (aw) / oo / ea — s **aw**

2. aw / (ea) / oo — br **ea** d

3. aw / oo / (ea) — f **ea** ther

4. ea / au / (oo) — sp **oo** n

5. oo / (ea) / aw — thr **ea** d

6. au / ea / (oo) — p **oo** l

7. (oo) / au / ea — w **oo** d

8. (aw) / oo / ea — str **aw**

9. ea / (aw) / oo — f **aw** n

10. ea / oo / (au) — l **au** ndry

11. (aw) / ea / oo — cl **aw** s

12. oo / (ea) / aw — h **ea** d

198   Review vowel digraphs oo, ea, au, aw

HOME With your child, make lists of words that rhyme with *saw* and *pool*. Then, check the spelling.

CURRICULUM CONNECTIONS

SPELLING
Have children answer each question with the correct spelling word. Then, reverse the order of both parts of each question, having children spell the words.
1. If *c-o-o-k* is *cook*, what is *b-o-o-k?*
2. If *b-r-e-a-d* is *bread*, what is *h-e-a-d?*
3. If *b-r-o-o-d* is *brood*, what is *f-o-o-d?*
4. If *c-l-a-w* is *claw*, what is *d-r-a-w?*
5. If *P-a-u-l* is *Paul*, what is *h-a-u-l?*

WRITING
Have children read the words in the bubbles on page 197. Invite them to each choose one set of answer words and write a silly sentence or two-line rhyme using the words and perhaps the name of the picture. For example: *That steak is so big it will break the plate* or *Get the apron off the hook and cook with a book.*

TECHNOLOGY **AstroWord** Vowel Digraphs & Diphthongs

AUDITORY LEARNERS
Have children sit in a circle. Say a sentence containing words with vowel digraph sounds such as *My dog's claw got caught in my sweater and pulled a thread loose.* Have each player whisper it to the next person until everyone has heard it. Compare what the last person hears with the original sentence.

CHALLENGE
Have children add to each list of answer words on page 197. Then, ask them to each choose one list, write a tongue twister with the words in it, and teach the tongue twister to a classmate.

EXTRA SUPPORT/INTERVENTION
Materials: Phonics Word Cards, Set 2: Vowel Digraph Words (149–176)
Set word cards in a specific classroom location. Have sets of partners take turns sorting and reading the cards by vowel digraph group. Children can then reshuffle them and read the words in random order. See Daily Phonics Practice, pages 256–257.

Integrating Phonics and Reading

Guided Reading
Have children read the title, *Once Upon a Time.* Ask them to name stories that begin with these words.
First Reading Ask children which story the younger girl wanted to hear.
Second Reading Write the words *good, food,* and *saw* on the board. Have children find the words, read the sentence, and then use the word in an original sentence.
Comprehension
Ask children the following questions:
• Why was the younger girl unhappy? *Recall/ Understanding Character*
• Why do you think the older girl kept changing the story? *Reflective Analysis/Personal Response*
ESL/ELL English Language Learners
Read the title to children. Explain that the phrase "once upon a time" is the way that many stories from long ago begin.

Phonics and Reading / Phonics and Writing

Vowel Digraphs oo, ea, au, aw

Skill Focus

Children will

★ read words that contain the vowel digraphs *oo*, *ea*, *au*, and *aw* in context.

★ write words with vowel digraphs to finish sentences.

★ build words with vowel digraphs.

Teach

Phonemic Awareness: Phoneme Isolation
Say the following words aloud, one at a time: *look, tool, spread, Paul, shawl*. Have children repeat each word and then say the vowel sound they hear in the middle of each one. Remind children that each vowel sound they named is a vowel digraph.

Sound to Symbol Write *book, cool, bread, haul,* and *crawl* on the board. Point to each word and have children say it in unison. Then, have volunteers go to the board, choose a word, say it, and circle the vowel digraph.

Read Words in Sentences Write these sentences on the board.

* **I saw a dinosaur at the museum.**
* **Its head looked huge!**

Have children read the sentences, identify the words that contain vowel digraphs, and underline the digraphs. (*saw, dinosaur, head, looked*)

Practice and Apply

Phonics and Reading Read the story with children. Have them identify words with vowel digraphs.

Critical Thinking In discussing Talk About It, children should recognize that the plants died because of the cold, and the animals had no plants to eat, so they died too.

Reading Use *Dinosaur Days,* MCP Phonics and Reading Super Skills Library 2, Level B, to give children additional practice reading words with vowel digraphs.

Phonics and Writing For page 200, explain that each word children make must be a real word. Tell them that only two of the three tiles for each item will make real words.

Name _____

Phonics & Reading Read the article. Print a word with **oo, ea, au,** or **aw** from the article on the lines below to finish each sentence.

Where Are the Dinosaurs?

Long ago, the heavy feet of dinosaurs shook the earth. Then, something awful happened. These awesome animals died. What really happened?

Some scientists think a meteor or comet hit the earth, causing great fires. Dust and ash blocked the sun's light and changed the weather. Warm places became cool. Plants and animals died because of the cold. The dinosaurs could not find food.

Other scientists have taught that the dinosaurs did not disappear, but became other animals as the world changed. If this is true, then they are still with us!

1. The _____heavy_____ feet of dinosaurs once _____shook_____ the earth.

2. A comet may have hit the earth, _____causing_____ great fires.

3. These _____awesome_____ animals have all died.

 TALK About It Why couldn't the dinosaurs find food?

Digraphs oo, ea, au, aw: Critical thinking **199**

FOCUS ON ALL LEARNERS

ESL/ELL ENGLISH LANGUAGE LEARNERS
Confirm that English language learners can recognize and read words containing vowel digraphs.

* With children's books closed, read aloud "Where Are the Dinosaurs?" on page 199 to create background knowledge.

* Invite children to open their books. Have volunteers take turns reading story sentences aloud.

* Have children work in pairs to highlight words in the story that contain vowel digraphs.

* Then, read aloud item 1. Have a volunteer reread the related part of the article. Have children suggest words to complete the sentence. Continue in the same manner with the remaining items.

KINESTHETIC LEARNERS **GROUPS**

Materials: index cards, marker

Make cards for the vowel digraphs *oo, ea, au,* and *aw,* and tape them to the board. Have volunteers take turns secretly choosing a word from page 199 that is spelled with one of the digraphs. Using the matching digraph card, the player should add one letter at a time that comes before or after the digraph until the others can find and spell the whole word from the story.

Building Words

Phonics & Writing

Use a vowel digraph to complete the words on the tiles. On the lines, write each real word you make.

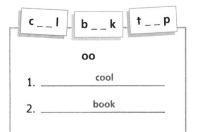

c _ _ l   b _ _ k   t _ _ p

oo

1. _____ cool
2. _____ book

y _ _ n   w _ _ d   h _ _ k

aw

3. _____ yawn
4. _____ hawk

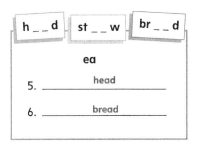

h _ _ d   st _ _ w   br _ _ d

ea

5. _____ head
6. _____ bread

p _ _ se   m _ _ t   h _ _ l

au

7. _____ pause
8. _____ haul

 Write a sentence for one of the words you made.

_____

_____

 HOME With your child, make a word search puzzle using four of the words he or she made.

CURRICULUM CONNECTIONS

SPELLING

You may wish to posttest the vowel digraph spelling words at this time.

1. **book**   I need to find a dinosaur **book**.
2. **draw**   I want to **draw** *Apatosaurus*.
3. **haul**   I had to **haul** home the ten books I found.
4. **head**   Now, my **head** is filled with facts!
5. **food**   Dinosaurs ate plants or hunted for **food**.

READING

Bring in a recent newspaper science article. Tell children that each news writer tries to answer the questions *who?, what?, when?, where?, why?,* and *how?* Write these question words on the board. Read the article aloud, having children identify information that answers the questions.

 **TECHNOLOGY** **AstroWord** Vowel Digraphs & Diphthongs

---

AUDITORY/VISUAL LEARNERS GROUPS

Write these words in two columns on the board: *weather, laundry, cool, wood, awful; shook, food, head, paw, haul.* Have children read them aloud. Ask volunteers to draw lines to connect words with the same vowel digraph sound.

CHALLENGE

Challenge children to write poems about the disappearance of the dinosaurs. Suggest that children use the facts in the story and their own ideas as they write their poems. When they have finished, invite them to share their poems with classmates.

EXTRA SUPPORT/INTERVENTION

Materials: drawing paper; crayons or markers

Write each of the following words on separate sheets of drawing paper: *claw, book, head, paws, heavy, look, jaw, haul, stood, read, dinosaur, food.* Each child should write a sentence for one word and illustrate it. Children can share their sentences and pictures with one another. See Daily Phonics Practice, pages 256–257.

Integrating Phonics and Reading

Guided Reading

Have children read the title and look at the illustration. Ask children who they think drew the illustration.

First Reading Ask children where the illustration on the cover came from.

Second Reading Have children name the twins and list other words in the story with the same vowel digraphs.

Comprehension

After reading, ask children the following questions:

- What were some of the things the twins did with dinosaurs? *Recall/Summarize*
- What would you have named this book? Explain. *Reflective Analysis/Personal Response*

ESL/ELL English Language Learners

To understand Paul and Dawn's transition from youngster to adult, help children look through the pages noting the pictures and text that indicate they are growing and changing.

Take-Home Book

Review Vowel Digraphs

Skill Focus

Children will

★ read words that contain vowel digraphs in the context of a story.

★ review selected high-frequency words in the context of a story.

★ reread for fluency.

Teach

Build Background

- Remind children that the title of this unit is "Dinosaur Days." Ask children to share some of the information they have learned in this unit about dinosaurs.

- Write the word *dinosaur* on the board and have children read it aloud. Have children discuss what they think the earth was like when dinosaurs lived.

Phonemic Awareness: Phoneme Isolation
Say the word *dinosaur*, dividing the word into syllables as you say it: *di-no-saur.* Ask children to repeat the vowel sound they hear in the last syllable. Circle the *au* and remind them that this is an example of a vowel digraph. Review the other vowel digraphs: *oo, ea, aw.* Ask volunteers to give an example of a word for each digraph.

Practice and Apply

Read the Book Have children put the Take-Home Book together. Encourage them to look through the book and discuss the pictures. Read the story together. Discuss whether children were surprised by the ending.

Sound to Symbol Have children take turns reading parts of the book. Ask children to identify words with vowel digraphs. Invite volunteers to write the words on the board, circling the digraphs.

Review High-Frequency Words Write the words *ever, near,* and *some* on the board. Have children spell and say them, blending the sounds.

Reread for Fluency Have children reread the book to increase their fluency and comprehension. Remind them to take the books home to read with family members.

Name _____

Where Is My Mother?

The sun shone on a huge egg. The egg shook and began to crack. Soon, a head looked out. "Hmmm," the baby dinosaur thought, "Where is my mother?" He crawled out of the egg and looked around.

Now, dinosaur was huge. One day he lifted his head, and a smile spread on his face. "Oh my, you are my mother, and you were near me all the time." They paused to snuggle and nibble some branches.

Review vowel digraphs: Take-home book   **201**

FOCUS ON ALL LEARNERS

ESL/ELL ENGLISH LANGUAGE LEARNERS

Materials: chart paper, highlighters, markers

Review with English language learners words that contain vowel digraphs.

- Make a four-column chart on chart paper. Head the columns *oo, ea, au, aw.* Then, help children put together their Take-Home Books.

- Have children work with partners to look through the story for words that contain vowel digraphs. Have them highlight the words as they find them.

- Review orally the words children find. Then, have volunteers write them on the chart under the appropriate heading.

VISUAL/KINESTHETIC LEARNERS

Materials: one index card per child

Cut a rectangle from the center of each card, creating "word frames." As you say each of these words, have children locate them in their books and place their frames around them: *dinosaur, because, head, crawled, looked, jaws, saw, shook, soon, spread, booming, pausing, paused.*

Dinosaur looked up, but because he was so small, he saw only grass and strange trees. As he grew, he saw that the trees looked bigger, and the grass looked smaller. Still, he could not find his mother.

2

FOLD

The strange trees looked very tall now, and they made booming noises. Dinosaur wondered if he would ever find his mother. With his jaws, he ate plants without pausing, and he grew and grew.

3

SCIENCE

Ask children to make a list of other animals whose babies are hatched from eggs. Then, have them draw posters titled "It All Started With an Egg" showing several of these animals. Have children label the animals they draw.

WRITING

Ask children what they think happened after the baby dinosaur found its mother. Brainstorm ideas. Then, have children write a fifth page for the story that tells what happened next. Encourage children to draw a picture too.

READING

Explain that even in a book of fiction, some events might have really happened. Draw a two-column chart and label it *Real* and *Not Real*. Have children suggest details from the story that fall into one or the other of the categories. List them on the chart. For example, *Real: A baby dinosaur hatches from its shell. Not Real: Dinosaurs don't talk.*

TECHNOLOGY   **AstroWord** Vowel Digraphs & Diphthongs

AUDITORY/VISUAL LEARNERS   *INDIVIDUAL*

Materials: audiocassette tape, cassette player

Have a volunteer read the book aloud and record it on tape, possibly including sound effects. Other children can take turns listening to the tape and reading along silently.

CHALLENGE

Invite children to write a four-sentence summary of the story. Explain that a summary tells the main idea of the story but that it is shorter than the original story. Suggest that children write one sentence for each page of the story.

EXTRA SUPPORT/INTERVENTION

Before children read, and as they preview the pictures on each page, have them point to and read the words they recognize. Call attention to each word with a vowel digraph. Then, have children point to any words that are unfamiliar. Use context and phonics clues to help children read the words. See Daily Phonics Practice, pages 256–257.

Diphthongs ou, ow

Skill Focus

Children will

★ define a diphthong.

★ read and write words with the diphthongs *ou* and *ow*.

★ Recognize and read high-frequency words.

ESL/ELL English language learners whose native languages identify one sound per letter may experience difficulty understanding that a vowel plus a consonant can make a separate sound.

Teach

Phonemic Awareness: Phoneme Categorization Say the following words: *clown, home, house.* Repeat the words and have children identify which words have the same vowel sound. (*clown, house*)

Sound to Symbol Write the words *clown* and *house* on the board. Point to each word as you say it aloud. Have children repeat the words. Ask them whether the vowel sound they hear is short or long. (*neither*) Circle *ow* and *ou* and explain that they are diphthongs, two letters that are blended together to make one sound. Write the words *town* and *mouse* on the board. Have volunteers say each word and circle the diphthong.

Practice and Apply

Sound to Symbol Read the rhyme on page 203 and have children repeat it. Invite children to name the words with the same vowel sound as in *ouch*.

Read the rule on page 203. Call on various children to explain what a diphthong is. Then, read the directions and have children identify the picture names.

Writing Read the directions on page 204. Have volunteers restate them in their own words. Remind children both to circle the word and to write it on the line. Children will have the opportunity to read the high-frequency words *edge* and *beyond.*

Critical Thinking In discussing Talk About It, be sure children recognize that the person states he or she lives near a farm.

Reading Use *Wilbert Took a Walk,* MCP Phonics and Reading Super Skills Library 2, Level B, to provide practice in reading words that have diphthongs.

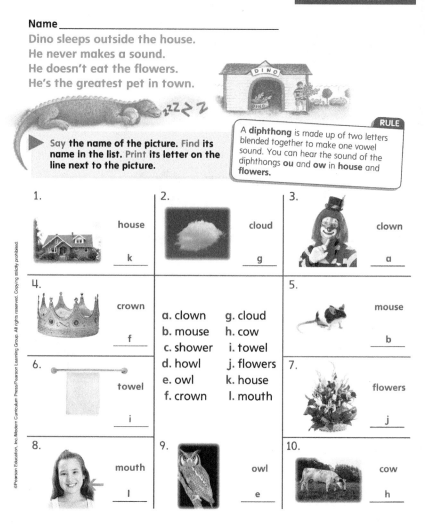

Name_____

Dino sleeps outside the house.
He never makes a sound.
He doesn't eat the flowers.
He's the greatest pet in town.

Say **the name of the picture. Find its name in the list. Print its letter on the line next to the picture.**

RULE
A **diphthong** is made up of two letters blended together to make one vowel sound. You can hear the sound of the diphthongs **ou** and **ow** in **house** and **flowers.**

1. house — k
2. cloud — g
3. clown — a
4. crown — f
5. mouse — b
6. towel — i
7. flowers — j
8. mouth — l
9. owl — e
10. cow — h

a. clown   g. cloud
b. mouse   h. cow
c. shower   i. towel
d. howl   j. flowers
e. owl   k. house
f. crown   l. mouth

Diphthongs ou, ow   **203**

FOCUS ON ALL LEARNERS

ESL/ELL ENGLISH LANGUAGE LEARNERS

Introduce new words with diphthongs *ow* and *ou*.

• Tell children that many words make the sounds of *ou* and *ow* and review these sounds.

• Have children look at and name the picture clue for item 1 on page 203. Correct pronunciation or prompt other answers, as appropriate.

• For items 2–10, continue naming, or having children name, each picture clue aloud.

• In small groups, repeat items 1–3, guiding children to find the names of the picture clues on the list. Have children complete the page in pairs. Confirm responses together.

VISUAL LEARNERS GROUPS

Materials: Phonics Word Cards, Set 2: Diphthong words (177–187); paper bag

Place the cards in the bag and invite children to take turns drawing a card from the bag and making up a sentence using both words on the card.

Read each sentence. Circle the **ou** or **ow** word in the sentence. Print it on the line.

1. I live on the edge of a small (town.)   town

2. My (house) is near a farm.   house

3. I spend a lot of time (outdoors.)   outdoors

4. From my yard, I can see (cows) and horses.   cows

5. In the summer, I watch the farmer (plow) his field.   plow

6. His tractor makes a (loud) noise.   loud

7. At night, I hear many different (sounds)   sounds

8. I can hear (owls) calling.   owls

9. I like to watch the (clouds) beyond the hills.   clouds

10. In the fall, the (flowers) on the hill bloom.   flowers

11. Today, I saw a flock of birds flying (south.)   south

12. They sense that winter is (about) to start.   about

TALK About It! Where does the person telling the story live?

HOME Ask your child to read the story to you.

CURRICULUM CONNECTIONS

SPELLING

Use the sample sentences below as you pretest the diphthong spelling words for this unit.

1. **house**   I share my **house** with my family.
2. **owl**   The **owl** hooted in the oak tree.
3. **spoil**   Some food will **spoil** if it is not kept cold.
4. **boy**   Did that **boy** draw this picture?
5. **grew**   I **grew** two inches this year.

READING

Talk with children about the *setting* of a story. Ask what the setting is for the illustration on page 203. (*a backyard*) The sentences on page 204 tell a story. Ask children when and where it takes place. (*It is the end of fall and the place is just outside a small town in a farming area.*) Have children identify the settings of some of their favorite books and stories.

 **TECHNOLOGY**   **AstroWord**   Vowel Digraphs & Diphthongs

---

AUDITORY/KINESTHETIC LEARNERS

Print *ow* on the board. Dictate the *ow* words from page 203 and call on children to add and erase letters as needed to spell each word. Repeat the activity with the *ou* words.

CHALLENGE

Materials: audiocassette tape, cassette player

Have children dictate on tape a story about where they would like to live. Have them use these words as they describe the town, neighborhood, or city: *town, house, outdoors, loud, sounds, clouds, flowers, about.*

EXTRA SUPPORT/INTERVENTION

Before children work on page 204 independently, read the sentences aloud and have children raise their hands when they hear a word with the *ou* or *ow* diphthong. Then, have them finish the page on their own. See Daily Phonics Practice, page 257.

Integrating Phonics and Reading

Guided Reading

After reading the title and looking at the cover, ask children to name some interesting places they have visited while walking.

First Reading Have children use the text and illustrations to explain what happened on Wilbert's walk.

Second Reading On the board, write *out, clouds,* and *down.* Have children find these words in the story and pronounce them.

Comprehension

Ask children the following questions:

- What are some of the things that happened to Wilbert as he walked? *Recall/Using Picture Clues*
- Is this story real or make-believe? How do you know? *Inference/Make Judgments*

ESL/ELL **English Language Learners**

Point out the words *fall down* and *slow down* on pages 9 and 13. Help children to model the meanings of these words.

204

Diphthongs ou, ow

Skill Focus

Children will

★ read and write words with the diphthongs *ou* and *ow*.

★ distinguish between the long *o* sound of *ow* and the diphthong *ow*.

ESL/ELL If you notice oral hesitation among English language learners whose native languages identify one sound per letter, provide additional oral practice.

Teach

Phonemic Awareness: Phoneme Categorization Say the following words, emphasizing the vowel sounds: *cow, house, home.* Say the words again and have children tell you which two words have the same vowel sound. *(cow, house)* Repeat the procedure with the words *row, plow, own. (row, own)*

Sound to Symbol Write the words *cow* and *house* on the board. Have children say the words and identify the vowel sound in each. Circle *ow* and *ou* and remind children that these are vowel diphthongs. Ask a volunteer to explain what a diphthong is. Then, write *row* and *own* on the board. Have children say the words and identify the vowel sound. *(long o)* Explain that *ow* can also stand for the sound of long *o*. Encourage children to name other words in which *ow* has the sound of long *o*.

Practice and Apply

Sound to Symbol Before children begin working on page 205, have them read chorally the words in the box. Then, read the directions and complete item 1 together. Read the rule at the top of page 206 and then read the directions. Remind children to say each word on page 206 so they can distinguish between the two sounds of *ow* before they make *x*'s for their answers. At the bottom of page 206, remind children to first circle the *ow* word and then mark an *x* in the appropriate column.

Reading You may wish to use *Squirrels,* MCP Phonics and Reading Super Skills Library 2, Level B, to reinforce reading words with diphthongs in the context of a story.

Name _____

▶ Find a word in the box that answers each riddle. Print it on the line.

owl	flower	house	plow
cow	cloud	clown	ground

1. I am in the sky.
   Sometimes I bring you rain.
   What am I?

   _____cloud_____

2. I wear a funny suit.
   I do many tricks.
   I can make you smile.
   What am I?

   _____clown_____

3. I am in the garden.
   I am very colorful.
   I may grow in your yard, too.

   _____flower_____

4. You can plant seeds in me.
   The farmer must plow me.
   What am I?

   _____ground_____

5. I am wide awake in the dark.
   I hoot and have big eyes.
   What am I?

   _____owl_____

6. You can see me at the farm.
   I eat green grass.
   I give you good milk.
   What am I?

   _____cow_____

7. You can live in me.
   I will keep you warm and cozy.
   What am I?

   _____house_____

8. The farmer uses me.
   I help him make his garden.
   What am I?

   _____plow_____

Diphthongs ou, ow   **205**

FOCUS ON ALL LEARNERS

ESL/ELL ENGLISH LANGUAGE LEARNERS

Materials: 20 index cards, marker

Confirm English language learners' familiarity with the two sounds of *ow*.

• Read the words at the top of page 206. Ask children to say *o* whenever they hear the sound of long vowel *o*, and to say *ow* when they hear the diphthong.

• Have them work in pairs to complete the first part of the page, taking turns saying the words.

• Have children work in small groups to read the sentences at the bottom of the page, then circle the *ow* word and put an *x* in the column that tells the sound the diphthong makes.

• Invite volunteers to read aloud their answers.

AUDITORY/KINESTHETIC LEARNERS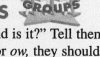

Invite children to play a game of "Which sound is it?" Tell them that if you say a word with the diphthong *ou* or *ow*, they should open their mouth; if they hear the vowel pair *ow* with the long *o* sound, they touch their noses. Use words such as *round, grown, house, mouth, brown, snow, outside, known, owner, power.*

▶ Print an X beside each word in which **ow** stands for the long **o** sound.

> **RULE**
> Remember, **ow** can stand for the long **o** sound, as in **snow**, or it can make a sound of its own, as in **clown**.

1. ＿＿ how　　2. _X_ snow　　3. _X_ own　　4. ＿＿ town

5. ＿＿ crowd　6. ＿＿ now　　7. _X_ bowl　　8. _X_ grow

9. _X_ low　　10. ＿＿ plow　11. ＿＿ power　12. ＿＿ owl

13. _X_ slow　14. _X_ flow　15. _X_ know　16. _X_ show

17. ＿＿ brown　18. _X_ crow　19. ＿＿ crown　20. ＿＿ down

21. ＿＿ towel　22. _X_ glow　23. _X_ throw　24. ＿＿ shower

25. ＿＿ cow　　26. _X_ blow　27. _X_ arrow　28. ＿＿ tower

▶ Circle the **ow** word in each sentence. Print an X in the correct column to show which sound **ow** makes.

	long vowel	diphthong
29. The circus came to our (town.)	＿＿	x
30. We went to the (show) last night.	x	＿＿
31. We sat in the very first (row.)	x	＿＿
32. The star was a funny (clown.)	＿＿	x
33. He made the (crowd) laugh.	＿＿	x

Help your child make cards for words 1–10 and sort them according to the **ow** sound.

CURRICULUM CONNECTIONS

SPELLING
Ask children to match the incomplete words with the diphthongs to write their spelling words. Provide children with copies of the words to study on their own.

1.　s p _ _ l　　oy　　(*spoil*)
2.　_ _ l　　　oi　　(*owl*)
3.　g r _ _　　ou　　(*grew*)
4.　b _ _　　　ow　　(*boy*)
5.　h _ _ s e　　ew　　(*house*)

ART
Invite children to draw or paint pictures of circus clowns. Have them add sentences that tell what clowns do that is funny, using these words in their descriptions if possible: *clown, crowd, now, show.*

AstroWord　Vowel Digraphs & Diphthongs

AUDITORY/VISUAL LEARNERS　GROUPS
Have children make a word ladder of *ow* words, substituting the first and last consonant sounds to make new words. (For example: *how, cow, low, slow, frown, brown, crow*) Then, have them read the words, noting when the *ow* letters make the diphthong *ow* or the long *o* sound.

CHALLENGE
Have children work in pairs to use words from the pages to create sentences with several *ou* and *ow* words. Model an example such as *I know there is a cow in the house with a flower on her crown.* Encourage children to use some *ou* and *ow* words not on the pages.

EXTRA SUPPORT/INTERVENTION
Materials: Phonics Word Cards, Set 2: Long *o* and Diphthong words (1–6, 177–187)

Have children practice each group of words separately. Then, mix the cards together, having children read the words, identify the vowel sounds, and use the words in sentences. See **Daily Phonics Practice, page 257.**

Integrating Phonics and Reading

Guided Reading
To prepare for reading the story, have children discuss what they know about squirrels. Include physical descriptions, food, and actions.
First Reading Have children tell about where the boy found squirrels.
Second Reading Invite children to find five words with the diphthongs *ou* and *ow*.

Comprehension
Ask children the following questions:

- Why do you think the bird and the squirrel in the tree did not look at the boy? *Inference/ Picture Clues*

- Do you agree that the best squirrels were the clouds in the air? *Reflective Analysis/ Personal Response*

ESL/ELL English Language Learners
Some children may not be able to identify the frog on page 14 or the snail on page 15. Write the names on the board focusing children's attention on the drawings of these animals.

Diphthongs oi, oy

Skill Focus

Children will

★ read words with the diphthongs *oi* and *oy*.

★ write words with *oi* and *oy*.

ESL/ELL English language learners whose native languages have a separate sound for each vowel may have a tendency to add an additional syllable when pronouncing words.

Teach

Phonemic Awareness: Phoneme Isolation
Say the following words, emphasizing the medial vowel sound in each: *noise, toys*. Repeat the words naturally and have children say them after you. Ask children to say the sound they hear in the middle of both words.

Sound to Symbol Write *noise* and *toys* on the board. Point to each word and have children say it aloud. Underline the *oi* and the *oy*. Explain that *oi* and *oy* are diphthongs. Ask a volunteer to explain what a diphthong is and to identify other diphthongs they have learned. (*ou, ow*)

Write this sentence on the board: *Roy points at the shiny coin.* Read the sentence aloud with children. Have volunteers name the words that contain diphthongs, identify the sound, and underline the letters that stand for the sound. (*Roy, points, coin*)

Practice and Apply

Sound to Symbol Discuss the rule at the top of page 207. Then, read the directions. Have children identify the picture names before they complete the activity.

Writing Read the directions to page 208. Using colored chalk, demonstrate on the board how children are to mark their answers. You may want to read the story to children before they begin the page. Circulate through the room to be sure children understand what to do. Remind them to look back at the story to help them answer the questions.

Critical Thinking Discuss Talk About It. Ask children what they might like to buy at a museum store.

Reading Use *The Tale of Cowboy Roy,* MCP Phonics and Reading Super Skills Library 2, Level B, to reinforce the sounds of *oi* and *oy*.

Picture-Text Match

Name _____

▶ Circle **the name of each picture.**

> **RULE**
> The diphthongs **oi** and **oy** usually stand for the same sound. You can hear that sound in **coin** and **boy**.

1. bow / (boil) / bill

2. (boy) / bag / toy

3. corn / coil / (coins)

4. sail / sell / (soil)

5. oak / (oil) / out

6. toil / tail / (toys)

7. paint / (point) / pail

8. (noise) / nail / nose

9. fame / (foil) / fawn

▶ Finish **each sentence with a word from the box.**

Box: enjoy / toy / coins

10. I have saved a few dollars and some ____coins____.

11. I will buy a ____toy____ robot kit.

12. I will ____enjoy____ putting it together.

Diphthongs oi, oy: Words in context   **207**

FOCUS ON ALL LEARNERS

ESL/ELL **ENGLISH LANGUAGE LEARNERS**

Create an opportunity to reinforce orally the meanings of words with the sound of *oi/oy*, despite written differences.

• Read aloud the directions on page 207. Use the name of each picture clue in a sentence, followed by the answer choices. ("The pot will *boil* on the stove." bow, boil, bill) Have children circle the word choice that has the same sound.

• Have children take turns pronouncing orally their answers to confirm correctness.

AUDITORY/VISUAL LEARNERS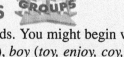

Compile lists of rhyming *oi* and *oy* words. You might begin with the words *soil* (boil, foil, coil, spoil, oil), *boy* (toy, enjoy, coy, annoy, joy, Roy), and *join* (coin). Invite children to add a column of other diphthong *oi* and *oy* words also.

▶ Read the story. Use a red crayon to circle each *oi* word.
Use a blue crayon to draw a box around each *oy* word.

Uncle Roy's Surprise

Uncle (Roy) asked [Troy] and his sister [Joyce] to (join) him on a surprise trip! [Joyce] knew where Uncle (Roy) was taking them, but she did not tell. She did not want to (annoy) Uncle (Roy) or (spoil) the surprise.

[Troy] was (overjoyed) when they got to the museum. Both [Troy] and [Joyce] (enjoyed) seeing the dinosaurs. [Troy] liked *Tyrannosaurus rex,* the king of the meat-eaters, best of all. He could almost hear the (noisy) roars of its (voice.)

Uncle (Roy) told [Troy] and [Joyce] that they could choose a (toy) at the museum's shop. They felt so (joyful) [Troy's] (choice) was a model of *Tyrannosaurus rex.* He was a very lucky [boy!]

▶ Use the words you marked to answer the questions.

1. How did Troy feel when they got to the museum? _____ overjoyed

2. What was Troy's sister's name? _____ Joyce

3. How did Troy think the dinosaur's roars may have sounded? _____ noisy

4. What could Troy and Joyce choose? _____ toy

 TALK about it
What other things could they have seen at the museum?

 HOME Have your child make up his or her own story using some of the words he or she circled or boxed.

208 Diphthongs oi, oy: Critical thinking

CURRICULUM CONNECTIONS

SPELLING

Display the spelling words *owl, grew, house, boy,* and *spoil.* Ask children to write them on paper in alphabetical order. Have partners check each other's spelling and order and then quiz each other orally on the words.

WRITING

Invite children to write about something they enjoy doing. Encourage them to use at least two of these words: *toy, noise, enjoy, join, joy, choice, coins,* and *boy.* When they have finished, encourage them to read their papers to partners.

MATH

Have children survey their classmates to see what their favorite dinosaurs are. Have them make a list of the different dinosaurs, tallying their choices. Then, have them chart the choices in a bar graph, showing the favorite by the tallest column and the least favorite by the shortest.

 TECHNOLOGY **AstroWord** Vowel Digraphs & Diphthongs

AUDITORY/KINESTHETIC LEARNERS GROUPS

Play a version of "Simon Says." Tell children that if a direction includes an *oi* or *oy* sound, they should follow the instruction: *Simon says, point to your nose.* But if you say *Simon says, pull on your nose,* children do nothing. Commands with *oi* and *oy* might include: *Jump for joy; Cry like a spoiled baby; Be a toy robot; Make a squeaking noise.*

CHALLENGE

Provide children with books about dinosaurs and ask them to write a paragraph about their favorite dinosaur. Challenge children to use as many words with *oi* or *oy* as they can. Allow them to use pages 207 and 208 to help them.

EXTRA SUPPORT/INTERVENTION

Materials: Phonics Word Cards, Set 2: Diphthong words (188–202)

Pair children with fluent readers and have them practice reading the words together and using each word in a sentence. See Daily Phonics Practice, page 257.

Integrating Phonics and Reading

Guided Reading
Share the illustration on page 3 with children. Then, ask them to predict what might happen between these two characters in the story.

First Reading Using the pictures and text, have children name some of the things Cowboy Roy could do.

Second Reading Invite children to find words with *oi* or *oy* and read the sentences that contain those words.

Comprehension
Ask children the following questions:

• Do you think Cowboy Roy was able to do all the things he said he could do? Why or Why not? *Personal Response/Reflective Analysis*

• At the end of the story, what was the snake able to say he could do? *Recall/Picture Clues*

ESL/ELL English Language Learners
Explain to children what a *cowboy* is and help them to explore what his job might entail. Point out that *cowboy* is a compound word.

Diphthongs oi, oy

Skill Focus

Children will

★ read words with the diphthongs *oi* and *oy*.

★ write words with *oi* and *oy* to finish sentences.

★ recognize and read high-frequency words.

Teach

Phonemic Awareness: Phoneme Substitution Say the word *oil* and have children say it after you. Then, ask children to add a *b* before *oil* to make a new word. (*boil*) Repeat the procedure with *c*, *f*, *s*, and *br*. (*coil, foil, soil, broil*)

Sound to Symbol Write *oil* and *broil* on the board. Have children say the words and identify the diphthong. (*oi*) Then, write the words *toy, boy,* and *enjoy* on the board. Say the words aloud and have children repeat them. Have volunteers identify the vowel sound and circle the diphthong in each word. (*oy*) Remind children that *oi* and *oy* are diphthongs because they represent vowel sounds that are blended together.

Write the following phrases on the board and have children read them, then identify and circle the diphthongs: *boiled peas; noisy children; choice of toys; join the fans.*

Practice and Apply

Blend Phonemes With children, pronounce the words in the boxes on pages 209 and 210 before they complete the pages. Encourage children to say each word, blending the phonemes together.

Writing Read the directions to the activities. For page 209 and the top of page 210, tell children to read the sentence with their answer. For the bottom of page 210, remind children that they should think about the question before they answer *yes* or *no*. Children will have the opportunity to read the high-frequency words *pours* and *listen*.

Critical Thinking As you discuss Talk About It with children, have them explain their answers.

Reading Use *The Royal Goose,* MCP Phonics and Reading Super Skills Library 2, Level B, to read words with the diphthongs *oi* and *oy*.

Name _____

▶ **Find** the word in the box that will finish each sentence. **Print** it on the line.

spoil	Joy
oil	choice
joins	Floyd's
boy	enjoy
toys	noise

1. Floyd is a hungry _____boy_____.

2. He does not want to play with his _____toys_____.

3. He would like to _____enjoy_____ a bowl of popcorn.

4. _____Floyd's_____ friend Joy wants popcorn, too.

5. Popcorn won't _____spoil_____ their dinner.

6. Joy _____joins_____ Floyd in the kitchen.

7. Floyd pours some _____oil_____ in a pot.

8. _____Joy_____ tells him to be careful.

9. The children listen for a popping _____noise_____.

10. Did Floyd and Joy make a good _____choice_____?

TALK About It Do you think they made a good choice? Why?

Diphthongs oi, oy: High-frequency words, critical thinking   **209**

FOCUS ON ALL LEARNERS

ESL/ELL ENGLISH LANGUAGE LEARNERS

Create an opportunity to reinforce orally the meanings of words with the sound of *oi* and *oy*.

• Read aloud the word list on page 209. Preview the context of the story. Then, have children orally volunteer a word to finish each sentence.

• After confirming each word choice, have children write the word as they spell it aloud. Continue the process with items 1–7 on page 210.

• Read aloud items 8–15 on page 210. Have children answer *yes* or *no* as they circle their responses.

AUDITORY/KINESTHETIC LEARNERS

Tell children to listen carefully as you read aloud the following groups of words. Have them stand up when they hear a word with the sound of the *oi* or *oy* diphthong: *nosy, nose, noise; jaw, jay, joy; point, post, part; noise, meat, most; join, tow, toy; owl, oil, owe.*

▶ **Find the word in the box that will finish each sentence. Print it on the line.**

1. ___Joyce___ is glad the circus is in town.

2. She loves the ___noise___ of the crowd.

3. The clown rides in a ___toy___ cart.

4. She smiles and ___points___ at the funny clown.

5. She sees a ___boy___ standing up on a horse.

6. Nothing can ___spoil___ the day for Joyce.

7. Joyce always ___enjoys___ a day at the circus.

> spoil
> enjoys
> toy
> Joyce
> noise
> points
> boy

▶ **Circle yes or no to answer each question.**

8. Is a penny a coin? **(Yes)** No

9. Is joy being very sad? Yes **(No)**

10. Can you play with a toy? **(Yes)** No

11. Is oil used in a car? **(Yes)** No

12. Is a point the same as paint? Yes **(No)**

13. Can you boil water? **(Yes)** No

14. Can you make a choice? **(Yes)** No

15. Is a loud noise quiet? Yes **(No)**

 With your child, take turns using the *oi* and *oy* words in new sentences.

210 Diphthongs *oi, oy*

CURRICULUM CONNECTIONS

SPELLING

Ask children to call out the spelling word that answers each riddle below and then "write" each word in the air as they recite the letters.

1. It begins like *grass;* rhymes with *drew.* (grew)

2. It begins like *berry;* rhymes with *toy.* (boy)

3. It begins like *on;* rhymes with *towel.* (owl)

4. It begins like *hen;* rhymes with *mouse.* (house)

5. It begins like *spell;* rhymes with *broil.* (spoil)

SOCIAL STUDIES

Display examples of the coins in use in the United States today. Gather library books that focus on the history and minting of coins. Encourage children to find out about coins from other times and places. You may wish to display coins you own from other countries.

TECHNOLOGY **AstroWord** Vowel Digraphs & Diphthongs

VISUAL LEARNERS PARTNERS

Print *oi* and *oy* words on the board, using blank spaces for the vowels of the diphthongs. Have partners work together to copy the words, filling in the correct vowels and checking the dictionary for words they are unsure of.

CHALLENGE

Challenge children to use *oi* and *oy* words to write their own *yes* and *no* questions. Review the questions they answered on page 210. Then, have them write their own questions on chart paper and read them aloud to the class. Have the class answer *yes* or *no.*

EXTRA SUPPORT/INTERVENTION

Materials: mural paper, markers

Invite children to make an *oi* and *oy* "pictionary" mural. Have each child choose one *oi* or *oy* word, write a sentence using the word, and draw a picture to illustrate the sentence. Display the mural on a classroom wall. See Daily Phonics Practice, page 257.

Integrating Phonics and Reading

Guided Reading

Have children read the title and look through the story to determine who the characters in the story are.

First Reading Ask children how the goose got into the castle.

Second Reading Have children find the *oi* and *oy* words in the story. Challenge them to find an equal number of long *o* words.

Comprehension

After reading, ask children the following questions:

• Why did the king and queen think that there was something wrong with the prince? *Inference/Cause and Effect*

• Why do you think the vet knew what was wrong with the boy when no one else did? *Reflective Analysis/Prior Knowledge*

ESL/ELL English Language Learners
Read the title and look at the picture. Ask children what the word *royal* means. You might point out the crown on the goose's head, if necessary.

Diphthong ew

Skill Focus

Children will

★ read words with the diphthong *ew*.

★ write words with *ew* to finish sentences.

★ recognize and read high-frequency words.

ESL/ELL Native Spanish speakers are familiar with diphthongs formed by two vowels, but they are not familiar with diphthongs formed by a vowel and a consonant. Provide practice with words containing these sounds.

Teach

Phonological Awareness: Rhyme Explain that you are going to say some groups of words. Children are to tell you which words rhyme in each group.

- chew, crew, crow
- new, know, stew
- Stan, knew, mew

Sound to Symbol Write *chew, new,* and *stew* on the board. Point to each one as children say it aloud. Ask children how the words are alike. (*They rhyme and they end in* ew.) Circle *ew* in each word. Explain that the diphthong *ew* makes the sound they hear at the end of *chew, new,* and *stew.* Remind children that in a diphthong the sounds of two letters blend together. Then, write *ew* on the board. Invite volunteers to add a letter or letters before *ew* to make additional words.

Practice and Apply

Blend Phonemes Read the rule on page 211. Have several children restate it in their own words. Then, invite children to read the words in the box, blending phonemes. For page 212, suggest that they try each of the three words in the sentence before they circle their choice.

Writing For page 211, you may want to have children raise their hands if they have difficulty reading any of the words in the sentences. Remind them that each word in the box will be used only once. As children work on page 212, they will read the high-frequency word *loved.*

Critical Thinking Encourage children to use information in the story to explain their answer to the Talk About It question.

Reading Use *The Kite That Flew Away,* MCP Phonics and Reading Super Skills Library 2, Level B, to practice reading words with the diphthong *ew.*

211

Name _____

> Find **the word in the box that will finish each sentence.** Print **it on the line.**

RULE
The diphthong **ew** stands for the long **u** sound. You can hear the long **u** sound in **new** and **few.**

1. I have a _____new_____ pack of sugarless gum.

2. I put a _____few_____ pieces into my mouth.

3. I began to _____chew_____ the gum.

4. Then, I _____blew_____ a giant bubble.

5. That bubble grew and _____grew_____.

6. Suddenly, I _____knew_____ I was in trouble.

7. The bubble broke, and pieces _____flew_____ everywhere.

8. I _____threw_____ the pieces of chewed gum away.

9. I think I will have a warm bowl of _____stew_____ instead.

| grew |
| blew |
| chew |
| flew |
| stew |
| new |
| threw |
| knew |
| few |

> Print **the missing letters for a word that** rhymes **with each word. Trace the whole word.**

10. few

  st **ew**

11. crew

  thr **ew**

12. grew

  fl **ew**

FOCUS ON ALL LEARNERS

ESL/ELL ENGLISH LANGUAGE LEARNERS

This reading comprehension activity focuses on selecting words containing the diphthong *ew* in context.

- Summarize the story for English language learners before they begin page 212.

- Focus children's comprehension by paraphrasing each sentence, such as: *Someone wanted a pet. Drew, blew, knew—which is a person's name?* If children are unsure, tell them that the correct answer is the short version of the name *Andrew.* Reinforce correct responses or prompt miscues.

- Complete the activity as a class. Correct misconceptions based upon the context.

VISUAL/KINESTHETIC LEARNERS GROUPS

Invite children to role-play the action described on page 211. As you or a volunteer reads aloud the eight sentences, have the children pantomime the action. Then, have children use the *ew* words from the sentences to describe what happened in their own words.

▶ Circle **the word that will finish each sentence.**

1. (**Drew**, Blew, Knew) wanted a pet.

2. He went to a pet shop called (crew, dew, **Flew**) the Coop.

3. He saw puppies (**chewing**, stewing, mewing) on toy bones.

4. Baby birds (**flew**, stew, knew) around their cages.

5. They (few, **threw**, grew) seeds on the floor.

6. Drew really wanted a (mew, stew, **new**) kitten.

7. He saw a (chew, **few**, grew) kittens.

8. One (**chewed**, threw, grew) its food.

9. Another kitten saw him and (flew, **mewed**, chewed).

10. Drew (grew, dew, **knew**) he wanted that kitten.

11. Drew named his kitten (**Mews**, Stews, Dews) because it always mewed.

12. That kitten (new, **grew**, chew) bigger every day.

13. Mews liked it when Drew (few, **threw**, mew) a toy to him.

14. He liked to (**chew**, new, stew) on Drew's shoelaces.

15. Mews tried to hide under the (screws, grew, **newspaper**).

16. From the window he watched birds as they (**flew**, crew, dew).

17. When the wind (**blew**, drew, stew), Mews chased fallen leaves.

18. He licked drops of morning (mew, **dew**, chew).

19. Before Drew (threw, few, **knew**) it, Mews was his friend.

20. Drew really loved his (stew, **new**, flew) pet.

 What do you think Drew liked best about Mews?

 With your child, take turns reading sentences from the story.

212 Diphthong ew: High-frequency words, critical thinking

CURRICULUM CONNECTIONS

SPELLING

You may wish to use the context sentences below as you posttest the spelling words.

1. **owl**   The **owl** hooted in the oak tree.
2. **grew**   A tree **grew** in my backyard.
3. **boy**   That **boy** lives next door to me.
4. **house**   Our **house** is painted red.
5. **spoil**   Eating snacks may **spoil** your dinner.

SOCIAL STUDIES

Invite children to practice being reporters for the school newspaper. Have them write news stories about something that happened recently or will happen at school. Point out the word *new* hidden in *news*. Explain that news stories are about current events.

 AstroWord Vowel Digraphs & Diphthongs

AUDITORY/VISUAL LEARNERS PARTNERS

Materials: Phonics Word Cards, Set 2: Diphthong words (203–207)

Have partners take turns choosing a card, saying the word on one side of the card and using it in a sentence. Then, the other child does the same with the word on the reverse of the card.

CHALLENGE

Invite children to write poems using rhyming words with *ew.* Ask them to begin by brainstorming a list of words and ideas. When children have finished, have them illustrate their poems and read them to classmates.

EXTRA SUPPORT/INTERVENTION

Write the letters *thr, fl, st, kn, gr, bl, f,* and *n* in the margin next to an outline of an eight-rung ladder. Then, have children take turns adding *ew* to one of these beginning sounds to make a new word for each rung in the ladder. **See Daily Phonics Practice, page 257.**

Integrating Phonics and Reading

Guided Reading

Have children read the title. Ask them how it is possible for a kite to fly away. You may also wish to use the activity under English Language Learners below.

First Reading Have children explain how the kite flew away.

Second Reading Invite children to find and list the words with the diphthong *ew.*

Comprehension

After reading, ask children the following questions:

• Why couldn't anyone catch the kite? *Inference/ Draw Conclusions*

• Why did the kite fall? *Recall/Cause and Effect*

ESL/ELL English Language Learners

In preparation for reading the story, discuss flying kites. Ask children if they have ever made a kite or flown a kite. Have them share their experiences.

Phonics and Spelling / Phonics and Writing

Vowel Pairs, Vowel Digraphs, and Diphthongs

Skill Focus

Children will

★ spell and write words with vowel pairs, vowel digraphs, and diphthongs.

★ write a free-verse poem using words with vowel pairs, vowel digraphs, and diphthongs.

Teach

Phonics and Spelling Review with children that a *vowel pair* is two vowels that come together to make a long vowel sound such as *ai* in *pail*, *oe* in *toe*, *oa* in *boat*, *ay* in *pay*, *ee* in *jeep*, *ea* in *beads*, or *ie* in *pie*. A *vowel digraph* is two letters that come together to make a short sound or a special sound such as *ea* in *head*, *au* in *pause*, *aw* in *claw*, or *oo* in *pool* or *book*. A *diphthong* is two letters blended together to make one sound such as *oi* in *point*, *oy* in *boy*, *ew* in *mew*, *ou* in *loud*, or *ow* in *now*.

Make three-columns on the board: *Vowel Pair, Vowel Digraph, Diphthong.* Have children sort these words by writing them in the correct column: *goat, seed, head, cow, oil, look, blew, boy, frown, haul, hawk, few, cloud, tie, day.*

Practice and Apply

Phonics and Spelling Read the directions on page 213. Have children name the pictures. Suggest they read aloud the words in the box to hear the vowel sounds before they write the words on the page. Remind them to circle the letters that stand for the vowel sound.

Phonics and Writing Before children write a free-verse poem about a dinosaur, read the words in the box. Have children suggest other words that can be used to describe a dinosaur. Write the words on the board so that children may refer to them. Remind children that a free-verse poem does not rhyme.

Reading Use *Molly's Broccoli,* MCP Phonics and Reading Super Skills Library 2, Level B, to review reading words with vowel pairs, vowel digraphs, and diphthongs.

213

Spelling

Name _____

Phonics & Spelling Say and spell the words in the box. Name each picture and write each word whose name has the same vowel sound. Then, circle the letters that stand for the vowel sound.

owl	rain	seed	wealth	lie	tray
coat	cool	draw	boy	food	house
pie	spoil	hoe	bean	haul	head

1. boat
c(o a)t
h(o e)

2. cloud
(o w)l
h(o u)s e

3. coins
b(o y)
s p(o i)l

4. peach
s(e e)d
b(e a)n

5. pail
r(a i)n
t r(a y)

6. fawn
d r(a w)
h(a u)l

7. tooth
c(o o)l
f(o o)d

8. bread
w(e a)l t h
h(e a)d

9. tie
l(i e)
p(i e)

Review vowel pairs, digraphs, diphthongs   **213**

FOCUS ON ALL LEARNERS

ESL/ELL ENGLISH LANGUAGE LEARNERS

Review the letter combinations in this unit orally with children, focusing on the letters used to make each sound.

• Write on the board each word from the box on page 213.

• Model pronunciation; have children read the words chorally.

• Ask volunteers to underline on the board the vowel combinations they see in each word. Confirm accuracy.

• Name each picture clue on page 213 for children. Complete item 1 together, having children say, spell aloud, then write two words whose names have the same vowel sound.

• Complete the activity as a group. Check for correctness.

KINESTHETIC/VISUAL LEARNERS

Materials: index cards, marker

Write these words on the cards: *brain, day, seed, peach, boat, town, pie, toe, book, head, haul, draw, tooth, cloud, cow, coin, boy, grew.* Have children sort the words into three piles: vowel pairs, vowel digraphs, and diphthongs.

Writing

When you write a **free-verse poem**, you can use colorful words to describe something or tell how you feel. Rhyming words are not used in a free-verse poem. The writer says a lot in a few words.

▶ Write a free-verse poem about dinosaurs. Use some of the words in the box. Share your poem with the class.

look	tail	noise	claw	tie
ready	meat	found	toe	few
day	eat	green	die	new

Use colorful words to tell about dinosaurs.

_____

_____

_____

_____

Do not use rhyming words.

_____

_____

_____

_____

Invite your child to read his or her poem aloud to family members.

CURRICULUM CONNECTIONS

SPELLING

Cumulative Posttest

The Unit 6 spelling words can be posttested now.

1. **food**   **Food** is what we eat to help us grow.
2. **grew**   Our tree **grew** to be very tall.
3. **tie**   I will **tie** a knot in the rope.
4. **pie**   Mom's cherry **pie** is tasty.
5. **draw**   I like to **draw** birds.
6. **boy**   That **boy** is my brother.
7. **spoil**   Please do not **spoil** Meg's surprise.
8. **haul**   I **haul** my horse in a trailer.
9. **hoe**   I will **hoe** the garden and plant beans.
10. **boat**   The **boat** is tied to the dock.
11. **head**   I cut my **head** when I fell.
12. **bean**   My **bean** plant is growing tall.
13. **seed**   Did you swallow the **seed**?
14. **book**   Is that a library **book**?
15. **owl**   The **owl** hunts for food at night.
16. **house**   My family lives in a yellow **house**.
17. **tray**   I will bring Mom her lunch on a **tray**.
18. **rain**   I carry an umbrella in the **rain**.

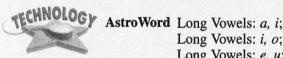

AstroWord Long Vowels: *a, i*;
Long Vowels: *i, o*;
Long Vowels: *e, u*;
Vowel Digraphs &
Diphthongs

AUDITORY/VISUAL LEARNERS GROUPS

Display and read examples of entries in children's dictionaries. Have children each choose one spelling word, write it in a sentence, and illustrate the sentence. Gather children's work into a pictionary of words with vowel pairs, vowel digraphs, and diphthongs.

CHALLENGE

Encourage children to write another poem about a dinosaur or another large animal, only this time the poem should be a rhyming one. Have children brainstorm a list of rhyming words to use. Upon completion, suggest children illustrate their poem. Challenge them to include words with vowel pairs, vowel digraphs, and diphthongs.

EXTRA SUPPORT/INTERVENTION

Materials: index cards

Write the words in the boxes on pages 213 and 214 on index cards. Have children practice reading and spelling the words. Encourage them to create a sentence for each word. See Daily Phonics Practice, pages 255–257.

Integrating Phonics and Reading

Guided Reading

Read the title and ask children to describe how the girl may be feeling.

First Reading Have children review some of the things Molly says she will do instead of eating broccoli.

Second Reading On the board, title three columns: *vowel pairs; vowel digraphs; diphthongs*. Then, have children find words from the story and list them below the appropriate heading.

Comprehension

After reading ask the following questions:

• Who likes broccoli in Molly's house? *Recall/ Summarize*

• Do you agree with the way Molly solved her problem about eating the broccoli? Explain. *Reflective Analysis/Personal Response*

ESL/ELL English Language Learners

Some children may not understand the vocabulary in the thought balloons. Reread the story and explain the humor in Molly's thoughts.

Take-Home Book

Review Vowel Pairs, Vowel Digraphs, and Diphthongs

Skill Focus

Children will

★ read words with vowel pairs, vowel digraphs, and diphthongs in the context of a story.

★ review selected high-frequency words in the context of a story.

★ reread for fluency.

Teach
Build Background

• Remind children that the title of this unit is "Dinosaur Days" and that they have been reading about dinosaurs throughout the unit. Discuss with children what they have learned about them.

• Ask children if they like riddles and to explain why. Tell children that they are going to be reading riddles about dinosaurs.

Phonemic Awareness: Phoneme Categorization Title three columns on the board: *Vowel Pairs, Digraphs,* and *Diphthongs.* Then, write and say these words aloud: *clown, clean, sound hawk, gray, feet, too, haul,* and *joy.* Ask volunteers to write each word under the correct title. Then, have volunteers say the vowel sound and underline the letters that stand for that sound. (*Vowel Pairs: clean, gray, feet; Digraphs: hawk, too, haul; Diphthongs: clown, sound, joy*)

Practice and Apply

Read the Book Offer help to children as they put their book together. Encourage them to to preview the book and then read it together.

Sound to Symbol Have children take turns reading the riddles aloud. Ask children to identify the words that contain vowel pairs (*sleep, train, playing, tree*); digraphs (*dinosaur, noon, goofy*); and diphthongs (*how, down, outer, boys, enjoy, house*). Invite volunteers to write the words on the board, spelling and saying them aloud.

Review High-Frequency Words Write the words *loved* and *should* on the board. Have children spell the words and say them, blending the sounds.

Reread for Fluency Have children reread the book to increase their fluency and comprehension. Remind them to take the books home to share with their families.

215

Best-Loved Dinosaur Riddles

Name

---FOLD---

1. What do you call dinosaur fossils that sleep until noon?

1. lazy-bones

⓵

6. What do you call a goofy dinosaur?

7. On what side of a dinosaur's house should he plant a tree?

6. a silly-osaurus   7. on the outside

④

FOCUS ON ALL LEARNERS

ESL/ELL ENGLISH LANGUAGE LEARNERS

Activate children's awareness of the target vowel sounds by assigning English language learners specific tasks to complete.

• Have volunteers read the riddles one at a time to the group. Have other children respond with the answers. Have children try to explain the jokes; clarify, as needed, for comprehension.

• Have children circle words in the story that contain the target vowel combinations, then copy them onto chart paper to reinforce writing.

• Have English language learners read the lists chorally.

AUDITORY/VISUAL LEARNERS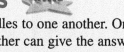

Ask partners to practice telling the riddles to one another. One partner can ask the question, and the other can give the answer. When children know the riddles by heart, encourage interested partners to perform their riddles for another class.

2. How did the dinosaur find the missing train?

3. What do you call a triceratops that fell down?

2. He followed the tracks!   3. A dino-sore

②

------FOLD------

4. What do dinosaurs drink from in outer space?

5. Why do the boys and girls enjoy playing with the dinosaur?

4. flying saucers   5. It is tons of fun.

③

✂

216   Review vowel pairs, digraphs, diphthongs: Take-home book

---

CURRICULUM CONNECTIONS

LITERATURE

Ask children what other large animals besides dinosaurs are featured in literature. (Examples are *bears, hippos, elephants, whales,* and *dragons.*) Encourage them to gather books about such animals. Using these books as examples, discuss why children might enjoy reading about large, monstrous animals like dinosaurs.

WRITING

Invite children to think of their favorite riddles that involve people or animals. (You might have riddle books on hand as sources.) Have children rewrite riddles using dinosaurs as the characters.

ART

Point out the illustration of the "silly-osaurus" on page 4 of the Take-Home Book. Invite children to name their own special dinosaur and illustrate it. For example, children might create an "icy-saurus" or a "pretty-saurus." Have children share their illustrated dinosaurs with the class.

 **AstroWord** Long Vowels: *a, i*; Long Vowels: *i, o*; Long Vowels: *e, u*; Vowel Digraphs & Diphthongs

---

KINESTHETIC LEARNERS

Materials: index cards, marker

Make cards for these words from the book: *house, outer, dinosaur, goofy, tree, house, train, sleep, noon, down, boys, enjoy, playing,* and *how.* Have children read the words aloud from the cards. Then, have them use their books and match each card to its location in the riddles.

CHALLENGE

Invite children to find their favorite books about dinosaurs or favorite riddle books in the classroom book corner, the library, or at home. Invite children to read favorite excerpts to their classmates.

EXTRA SUPPORT/INTERVENTION

Read *Best-Loved Dinosaur Riddles* aloud, inviting children to study the pictures and guess the answers before you read them. Then, have them turn their books upside down and read each answer with you. See *Daily Phonics Practice,* pages 255–257.

216

Unit Checkup

Review Vowel Pairs, Vowel Digraphs, and Diphthongs

Skill Focus

Children will

★ read and write words with vowel pairs, vowel digraphs, and diphthongs.

★ write words that contain vowel pairs, vowel digraphs, or diphthongs to complete sentences.

▶ Teach

Phonemic Awareness: Phoneme Substitution Tell children that you are going to say a word. They are to replace the beginning sound with another sound to make a new word. Use these words, one at a time: *tail, bay, seed, seal, toe, tie, boat, took, soon, head, cause, draw, mouse, town, boil, toy,* and *crew.*

Sound to Symbol Write the above words on the board. Have children say each word. Invite volunteers to circle the vowel pair, the vowel digraph, or the diphthong and create an oral sentence for each word. Review the definition of vowel pair, vowel digraph, and diphthong. Make three columns on the board and have children write the words in the appropriate column.

▶ Practice and Apply

Assess Skills Read the directions on page 217. Then, have children take turns reading the answer choices. Remind children to circle the answer and to write it on the line. After children have completed page 217, read the directions to page 218. You might want to go over the pronunciation of *tyrannosaurus* and *allosaurus.* Remind children to sound out any other words they are not sure how to pronounce. Encourage them to reread each sentence with their answer choice to see if it makes sense.

217

Name _____

▶ Circle the word that will finish each sentence. Then, print it on the line.

1. A baby deer is a _____fawn_____. seal (fawn) feather

2. Green _____beans_____ are good to eat. (beans) baits bowls

3. A place where you can see animals is a _____zoo_____. (zoo) zipper hook

4. Dried grass that horses eat is _____hay_____. seed (hay) day

5. A small animal with a long tail is a _____mouse_____. men mitt (mouse)

6. Something you row is a _____boat_____. (boat) beach boy

7. You walk on your two _____feet_____. (feet) foot flat

8. One animal that gives milk is a _____cow_____. cloud crow (cow)

9. Something that was never used is _____new_____. grew (new) draw

10. A dish under a cup is a _____saucer_____. train faucet (saucer)

Vowel pairs, digraphs, diphthongs: Assessment   **217**

FOCUS ON ALL LEARNERS

ESL/ELL ENGLISH LANGUAGE LEARNERS

Practice reading words using the target vowel combinations in context by having English language learners choose the missing words to complete sentences.

• Copy item 1 on page 217 onto the board. Ask children to read along silently in their books as you read the sentence aloud.

• Write the three answer choices on the board. Underline the vowel combinations in each and have a volunteer model their sounds.

• Ask children which word best completes the sentence. Read each choice aloud, modeling how the completed sentence would sound.

• Model circling the answer, then writing it on the line. Complete the remainder of the page as a class. Model aloud the directions for page 218; pair children to complete the page.

VISUAL LEARNERS   GROUPS

Invite volunteers to spell words on the board that contain vowel combinations studied in this unit. Have them leave out the vowel pair, vowel digraph, and diphthong letters. Other children can guess what the words are, asking for hints to the words' meanings if necessary.

217

ASSESS UNDERSTANDING OF UNIT SKILLS

▶ Fill in the bubble in front of the word that will finish each sentence.

1. Dinosaurs ___ their eggs in nests. ● laid ○ paid

2. The mother ___ around the eggs. ● coiled ○ boiled

3. Many dinosaurs ___ huge. ○ saw ● grew

4. The giant tyrannosaurus ate ___. ○ meet ● meat

5. It had a long claw on each ___. ● toe ○ foe

6. It had a large ___. ○ bread ● head

7. It caught animals in its strong ___. ● jaws ○ hauls

8. The allosaurus had very sharp ___. ● teeth ○ seeds

9. It had bony spikes on its ___. ○ sail ● tail

10. No dinosaurs are alive ___. ● now ○ cow

11. They ___ long ago. ● died ○ lied

12. We can only guess what they ___ like. ● looked ○ playing

218   Vowel pairs, digraphs, diphthongs: Assessment

STUDENT PROGRESS ASSESSMENT

You may wish to review the observational notes you made as children worked through the activities in the unit. These notes can help you evaluate the progress children made in the unit.

PORTFOLIO ASSESSMENT

Review the written materials children have collected in their portfolios. Conduct interviews with children to discuss their work and progress since the beginning of this unit. As you review children's work, evaluate how well they use phonics skills.

DAILY PHONICS PRACTICE

For children who need additional practice with the skills in this unit, see Daily Phonics Practice on pages 255–257.

PHONICS POSTTEST

To assess children's mastery of the skills in this unit, use the posttest on pages 179g–179h.

AUDITORY/KINESTHETIC LEARNERS

Ask children to stand in a straight line going across the room. Have them take a step forward if word pairs you say have the same vowel sound and a step backward if they don't. Use word pairs such as: *boat, bowl; beach, boy; train, day; cloud, cow;* and *grew, draw.*

CHALLENGE

Challenge children to learn a new dinosaur fact from an encyclopedia or library book—something they didn't learn as they studied the unit. Record their new information on chart paper and have children circle the vowel pairs, diphthongs, and vowel digraphs in the facts.

EXTRA SUPPORT/INTERVENTION

Preview or review the sentences on pages 217 and 218 before or after children complete the checkup. Have children find words in the sentences and in the word choices that have matching vowel sounds and/or spellings. See Daily Phonics Practice, pages 255–257.

Teacher Notes

UNIT 7

Prefixes, Synonyms, Antonyms, Homonyms

THEME: MAKE IT, BAKE IT

CONTENTS

TEACHING PLANS

Student Performance Objectives

In Unit 7, children will be introduced to the prefixes *re-*, *un-*, and *dis-*, and to synonyms, antonyms, and homonyms within the context of the theme "Make It, Bake It." By the conclusion of the unit, children will be able to

▶ Recognize the prefixes *re-*, *un-*, and *dis-* and add them to base words

▶ Distinguish among the prefixes and add them to base words

▶ Identify synonyms, antonyms, and homonyms

▶ Apply these skills in decoding and in using words in context

Assessment Options

In Unit 7, assess children's ability to read and write words with prefixes and words that are synonyms, antonyms, and homonyms. Use the Unit Pretest and Posttest for formal assessment. For ongoing assessment, you may wish to use children's work on the Review pages, Take-Home Books, and Unit Checkups. You may also want to encourage children to evaluate their own work and to participate in setting goals for their own learning.

ESL/ELL Some of your English language learners may require additional assessment strategies to meet their special language needs. Take note of pronunciation difficulties as they occur, but assess performance based on children's ability to distinguish specific sounds when pronounced by a native speaker.

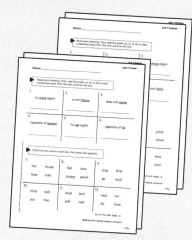

FORMAL ASSESSMENT

Use the Unit 7 Pretest on pages 219e–219f to help assess a child's knowledge at the beginning of the unit and to plan instruction.

ESL/ELL Before administering the Pretest, preview the underlined word clues and answer choices on page 219e so that children are familiar with them. Say the name of each word as children say it along with you. Reinforce the meaning of any confusing direction words, such as *opposite* and *again*.

Use the Unit 7 Posttest on pages 219g–219h to help assess mastery of unit objectives and to plan for reteaching, if necessary.

ESL/ELL Some children may understand a concept but have difficulty comprehending directions. Read directions aloud to the group and model how to complete the test.

INFORMAL ASSESSMENT

Use the Review pages, Unit Checkup, and Take-Home Book in the student book to provide an effective means of evaluating children's performance.

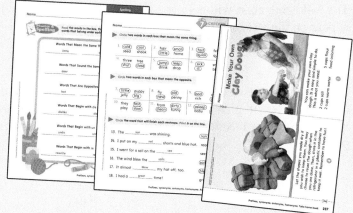

Unit 7 Skills	Review pages	Checkups	Take-Home Books
Prefixes	227–228, 235–236	239–240	237–238
Synonyms	235–236	239–240	237–238
Antonyms	235–236	239–240	237–238
Homonyms	235–236	239–240	237–238

STUDENT PROGRESS CHECKLIST

Use the checklist on page 219i to record children's progress. You may want to cut the sections apart to place each child's checklist in his or her portfolio.

PORTFOLIO ASSESSMENT

This logo appears throughout the teaching plans. It signals opportunities for collecting children's work for individual portfolios. You may also want to include the Pretest and Posttest, the Review pages, the Unit Checkup, Phonics & Reading, Phonics & Spelling, and Phonics & Writing pages.

219c

Pretest and Posttest

DIRECTIONS

To help you assess children's progress in learning Unit 7 skills, tests are available on pages 219e–219h.

Administer the Pretest before children begin the unit. The results of the Pretest will help you identify each child's strengths and needs in advance, allowing you to structure lesson plans to meet individual needs. Administer the Posttest to assess children's overall mastery of skills taught in the unit and to identify specific areas that will require reteaching.

ESL/ELL Note that the objective of both the Unit 7 Pretest and Posttest is reading and writing words with prefixes and words that are synonyms, antonyms, and homonyms. To ensure that vocabulary recognition is not a distraction, show pictures that illustrate the meaning of each word tested. Reinforce with frequent sight recognition and reading opportunities throughout the unit.

PERFORMANCE ASSESSMENT PROFILE

The following chart will help you identify specific skills as they appear on the tests and enable you to identify and record specific information about an individual's or the class's performance on the tests.

Depending on the results of each test, refer to the Reteaching column for lesson-plan pages where you can find activities that will be useful for meeting individual needs or for daily phonics practice.

Answer Keys

Unit 7 Pretest, page 219e (BLM 43)

1. rewind	7. hot, cold
2. unhappy	8. fast, slow
3. disagree	9. stop, go
4. disappear	10. thick, thin
5. reuse	11. loud, soft
6. untie	12. near, far

Unit 7 Pretest, page 219f (BLM 44)

13. noisy, loud, quiet	19. week
14. ill, sick, well	20. pair
15. simple, easy, hard	21. made
16. giggle, laugh, cry	22. red
17. close, shut, open	23. pale
18. start, begin, finish	24. tail

Unit 7 Posttest, page 219g (BLM 45)

1. unload	7. old, new
2. dismount	8. high, low
3. rewrap	9. open, close
4. disloyal	10. wet, dry
5. recheck	11. long, short
6. unlikely	12. easy, hard

Unit 7 Posttest, page 219h (BLM 46)

13. large, huge, tiny	19. toe
14. trash, junk, treasure	20. pain
15. mean, cruel, kind	21. heal
16. bother, annoy, amuse	22. so
17. friend, pal, enemy	23. aunt
18. quick, fast, slow	24. sent

Performance Assessment Profile

Skill	Pretest Questions	Posttest Questions	Reteaching	
			Focus on All Learners	**Daily Phonics Practice**
Prefixes	1–6	1–6	221–228, 235–238	258
Synonyms	13–18	13–18	229–230, 235–238	258–259
Antonyms	7–18	7–18	231–232, 235–238	258–259
Homonyms	19–24	19–24	233–238	258–259

Name _____

> Read each meaning. Then, add the prefix *un*, *re*, or *dis* to each underlined word. Print the new word on the line.

1. to <u>wind</u> again	2. is not <u>happy</u>	3. does not <u>agree</u>
_____	_____	_____
4. opposite of <u>appear</u>	5. to <u>use</u> again	6. opposite of <u>tie</u>
_____	_____	_____

> Circle the two words in each box that mean the opposite.

7. hot house blue cold	8. fast slow puppy pencil	9. stop little go duck
10. thick wall zoo thin	11. loud bird soft nest	12. near run far chair

Go to the next page. →

BLM 43 Unit 7 Pretest: Prefixes, antonyms

Name_____

> Circle the word in each row that means the same as the first word.
> Underline the word that means the opposite of the first word.

13.	**noisy**	sound	quiet	quick	loud
14.	**ill**	sick	funny	well	cold
15.	**simple**	enjoy	hard	easy	taste
16.	**giggle**	tear	laugh	joke	cry
17.	**close**	open	closet	shut	key
18.	**start**	race	here	begin	finish

> Fill in the bubble beside the word that will finish each sentence.

19. Last _____ a friend came for a visit.
    ○ weed ○ week ○ weak

20. We worked together to make a _____ of kites.
    ○ pair ○ pear ○ pare

21. We _____ them from colored paper.
    ○ maid ○ mad ○ made

22. Jon's kite was bright _____.
    ○ red ○ read ○ reed

23. My kite was _____ green.
    ○ pail ○ pal ○ pale

24. I added a _____ made of cloth.
    ○ tall ○ tail ○ tale

Possible score on Unit 7 Pretest is 24. Number correct _____

BLM 44 Unit 7 Pretest: Synonyms, antonyms, homonyms

Name _____

> Read each meaning. Then, add the prefix *un, re,* or *dis* to each underlined word. Print the new word on the line.

1. opposite of <u>load</u> _____	2. opposite of <u>mount</u> _____	3. to <u>wrap</u> again _____
4. is not <u>loyal</u> _____	5. to <u>check</u> again _____	6. is not <u>likely</u> _____

> Circle the two words in each box that mean the opposite.

7. luck old cat new	8. swim ski high low	9. close jump open clown
10. white wet door dry	11. puppy long new short	12. rock easy hard knot

Go to the next page. →

Name_____

 Circle the word in each row that means the same as the first word. Underline the word that means the opposite of the first word.

13. **large**   elephant   tiny   huge   many

14. **trash**   junk   paper   reuse   treasure

15. **mean**   kind   cruel   happy   bully

16. **bother**   learn   sister   annoy   amuse

17. **friend**   pal   home   enemy   parent

18. **quick**   tired   slow   last   fast

Fill in the bubble beside the word that will finish each sentence.

19. In August I broke my _____.
    ◯ toe   ◯ tow   ◯ two

20. I was in a lot of _____.
    ◯ pane   ◯ pan   ◯ pain

21. I had to stay in bed so that it could _____.
    ◯ heat   ◯ heal   ◯ heel

22. I was _____ bored!
    ◯ so   ◯ sew   ◯ sow

23. My _____ learned about my accident.
    ◯ ant   ◯ aim   ◯ aunt

24. So, she _____ me a present.
    ◯ cent   ◯ seat   ◯ sent

Possible score on Unit 7 Posttest is 24. Number correct _____

BLM 46 Unit 7 Posttest: Synonyms, antonyms, homonyms

219h

Student Progress Checklist

Make as many copies as needed to use for a class list. For individual portfolio use, cut apart each child's section. As indicated by the code, color in boxes next to skills satisfactorily assessed and insert an *X* by those requiring reteaching. Marked boxes can later be colored in to indicate mastery.

Student Progress Checklist

Code: ■ Satisfactory   ☒ Needs Reteaching

Student: _____	Skills	Comments / Learning Goals
_____ Pretest Score: _____ Posttest Score: _____	☐ Prefixes ☐ Synonyms ☐ Antonyms ☐ Homonyms	
Student: _____ _____ Pretest Score: _____ Posttest Score: _____	Skills ☐ Prefixes ☐ Synonyms ☐ Antonyms ☐ Homonyms	Comments / Learning Goals
Student: _____ _____ Pretest Score: _____ Posttest Score: _____	Skills ☐ Prefixes ☐ Synonyms ☐ Antonyms ☐ Homonyms	Comments / Learning Goals
Student: _____ _____ Pretest Score: _____ Posttest Score: _____	Skills ☐ Prefixes ☐ Synonyms ☐ Antonyms ☐ Homonyms	Comments / Learning Goals

BLM 47 Unit 7 Checklist

ESL/ELL English Language Learners

Throughout Unit 7 there are opportunities to assess English language learners' ability to read and write words with prefixes and words that are synonyms, antonyms, and homonyms. Some of your English language learners may require additional assessment strategies to meet their special language needs. Take note of difficulties with pronunciations as they occur, but assess performance based on children's ability to distinguish specific sounds when pronounced by a native speaker.

Lesson 102, pages 221–222 Native speakers of Spanish likely are familiar with prefixes, including *re-*. Provide frequent oral opportunities for speakers of other languages to distinguish the prefix and its meaning from the base word.

Lesson 103, pages 223–224 Native speakers of Spanish likely are familiar with prefixes, including *re-*. Provide opportunities for speakers of other languages to form, pronounce, and use words with prefixes.

Lesson 104, pages 225–226 The prefix *des-* in Spanish often has the same meaning as *dis-* or *un-* in English.

Lesson 105, pages 227–228 Prefix is a concept that most English language learners will pick up quickly. Reinforce meanings and provide opportunities for children to hear and say *re-*, *un-*, and *dis-*, making the correct long or short vowel sounds.

Lesson 108, pages 233–234 Native speakers of Spanish may be familiar with homonyms in their native language, due to similar pronunciation of *b* and *v;* soft *c, s,* and *z;* soft *g* and *j;* *ll* and *y;* and the silent *h.* Emphasize homonyms in context. Have children memorize the different spellings of word pairs.

Lesson 109, pages 235–236 A strong emphasis on spelling may be inappropriate for English language learners who have not reached an intermediate level of proficiency. Allow children to use invented spelling and the phonics skills they are building upon as a foundation for future spelling success.

Lesson 110, pages 237–238 Although English language learners may experience these concepts in their home languages, the sounds and spellings of English are new. Provide frequent opportunities for children to hear and use words in personally meaningful contexts.

Lesson 111, pages 239–240 Since English language learners may be familiar with these concepts in their native languages, provide specific instruction for problem areas of pronunciation.

Spelling Connections

INTRODUCTION

The Unit Word List is a comprehensive list of spelling words drawn from this unit. The words are grouped by the structural elements presented in the unit. To incorporate spelling into your phonics program, use the activity in the Curriculum Connections section of each teaching plan.

ESL/ELL It is recommended that English language learners reach the intermediate level of English proficiency before focusing on spelling. Introduce the words and their meanings through pictures or realia.

The spelling lessons utilize the following approach.

1. Administer a pretest of the list words that have not yet been introduced. Dictation sentences are provided.

2. Provide practice.

3. Reassess. Dictation sentences are provided.

A final review that covers the structural elements of Unit 7 is provided on page 235.

DIRECTIONS

Make a copy of Blackline Master 48 for each child. After administering the Spelling pretest, give children a copy of the word list.

Children can work with a partner to practice spelling the words orally. They can also create letter cards to use to form the words on the list. You may want to challenge children to make new words by substituting other prefixes, synonyms, antonyms, or homonyms. Children can write words of their own on My Own Word List (see Blackline Master 48).

Have children store their list words in the envelopes in the backs of their books. You may want to suggest that students keep a spelling notebook, listing words with similar patterns. Another idea is to build Word Walls with children and display them in the classroom. Each section of the wall can focus on words with a single phonics element. The walls will become a good resource for spelling when children are writing.

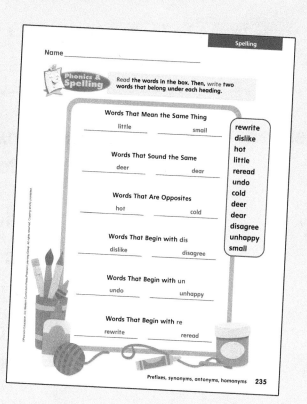

Name _____

Phonics & Spelling

Read the words in the box. Then, write two words that belong under each heading.

Words That Mean the Same Thing
little   small

Words That Sound the Same
deer   dear

Words That Are Opposites
hot   cold

Words That Begin with dis
dislike   disagree

Words That Begin with un
undo   unhappy

Words That Begin with re
rewrite   reread

rewrite
dislike
hot
little
reread
undo
cold
deer
dear
disagree
unhappy
small

Prefixes, synonyms, antonyms, homonyms   **235**

Unit Word List

Prefixes
rewrite
unhappy
dislike
reread
undo
disagree

Homonyms, Synonyms, Antonyms
dear
deer
little
small
hot
cold

Name _____

Unit 7 WORD LIST

Words with Prefixes

rewrite

unhappy

dislike

reread

undo

disagree

Homonyms, Synonyms, Antonyms

dear

deer

little

small

hot

cold

My Own Word List

My Own Word List

Phonics Games, Activities, and Technology

The following collection of ideas offers a variety of opportunities to reinforce phonics skills while actively engaging children. The games, activities, and technology suggestions can easily be adapted to meet the needs of your group of learners. They vary in approach so as to consider children's different learning styles.

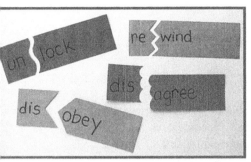

PREFIX PUZZLES

Distribute sentence strips, markers, and scissors. Then, have children write words containing prefixes on sentence strips. They should leave space between the prefix and the base word. Show them how to make a distinctive cut to separate the prefix from the base word to create a puzzle. Have small groups of children combine their puzzle pieces. Then, suggest each group work together to assemble the words. After each word is formed, have them read and define it and then use it in a sentence.

PREFIX BINGO

Provide children with blank bingo game boards and beans or other small markers. Have children fill the board by randomly writing the prefixes *re-*, *un-*, and *dis-* in the spaces. To play, call out a word containing one of these prefixes and have children repeat it. Have them cover the prefix heard in the word with one of the markers. Play until someone has bingo.

Variation: Instead of writing prefixes, give children a list of words containing prefixes to write on their boards. Then, as you define each word (for example, *unwrap* could be defined as "the opposite of *wrap*"), children can cover the word on their board.

WORD-HUNT GAME

Give each child graph paper with one-inch squares. Demonstrate how to make a word-search puzzle by writing one letter in each block to form words containing prefixes. Words may be written across, down, or diagonally. You may want to limit the words to three or four. Then, have children fill the rest of the blocks with random letters. Have children exchange puzzles with a partner and search for the hidden words.

Variation: You may wish to provide children with a list of words beginning with the prefixes *un-*, *re-*, and *dis-* to use in their puzzles. Before children construct their puzzles, have them read, define, and use each word in a sentence that illustrates its meaning.

ESL/ELL English language learners who are just becoming familiar with the Roman alphabet or with writing print horizontally from left to right may experience difficulty with this activity. To simplify, use the Unit 7 Word List and have children create puzzles based only on left-to-right reading. Children can select words from their lists and darken the frame of the graph-paper boxes to indicate how many letters each word has. Have children work in pairs, with the clue-giver providing oral descriptive clues to the puzzle-solving partner.

GRAPHIC DEFINITIONS

Have children write antonym pairs in a way that illustrates their meaning. For example, the word *fat* can be written with large, round letters while the word *thin* can be written with narrow, thin letters. Other antonym pairs might include *tall, short; smile, frown; mountain, valley; square, round;* and *little, big.*

ESL/ELL To simplify this activity for English language learners, provide the visual framework of the puzzle and the first words. Children answer by writing the second word in the pair following the style of the visual clue. Provide models before allowing children to work together.

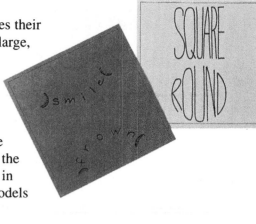

SYNONYM MATCH-UP

Give pairs of children tagboard (cut into 6-inch by 12-inch pieces), markers, yarn, scissors, and tape. Have them construct their own synonym match-up games by writing words in a column on the left side of the tagboard. On the right side, have them write synonyms for these words in random order. After each word in the left-hand column, children can attach a length of colored yarn with tape. Have partners exchange puzzles with another pair. Have children solve the puzzles by using the yarn to connect the synonym pairs. You may want to write synonym pairs on the chalkboard for children to use as ideas and to copy.

Variation: This game can be modified to reinforce antonyms and homonyms by writing these word pairs instead of synonyms.

HOMONYM RIDDLES

Write the following homonym pairs on the board: *hare, hair; not, knot; pair, pear; bare, bear; plain, plane; fair, fare; right, write; heard, herd.* Have children fold sheets of paper to make eight boxes. Then, ask these riddles and have children write the homonym pair that answers each riddle.

1. What do you call the fur of a rabbit? (hare hair)
2. What do you call an untied piece of string? (not knot)
3. What do you call two pieces of a yellow fruit? (pear pair)
4. What do you call a hairless grizzly? (bare bear)
5. What do you call a jet that is not fancy? (plain plane)
6. What do you call a reasonable price for a bus ticket? (fair fare)
7. What do you call correct penmanship? (right write)
8. What do you call listening to a group of cows? (heard herd)

"OHS" GAME

Provide children with three index cards and have them write the letters *O*, *H*, and *S* on the cards. Explain that the *O* stands for words that are opposites, *H* for words that are homonyms, and *S* for words that are synonyms. Then, say pairs of words such as *kind, nice; knight, night;* and *new, old* and have children display the card that identifies how the words in each pair are related.

HOMONYM CHALLENGE

Share examples such as *I can see the sea* or *I felt weak all last week,* in which pairs of homonyms are used in the same sentence. Then, ask children to select several other homonym pairs from a Word Wall or a list on the chalkboard and use them to write and illustrate their own sentences.

SIX-MINUTE PREFIX RACE

Divide children into small groups. Hold up a card with the prefix *un-* and have each group work together as a team for a two-minute race to write as many words as they can that begin with the prefix. Repeat this procedure with cards for the prefixes *re-* and *dis-*. Bring the groups together and have each group share its words. Then, compile the lists and add them to a classroom Word Wall.

WRITING THE RIGHT WORD

Write these sentences on the chalkboard and explain that each sentence contains a homonym that is used incorrectly. Have children identify the error and write the correct word.

1. The whether was hot and dry. (weather)
2. My ant sent me a lovely birthday gift. (aunt)
3. I maid my bed. (made)
4. We road our bikes to school. (rode)
5. That shoe hurts my heal. (heel)
6. What time does the son set? (sun)
7. Are these pants on sail? (sale)
8. I need a new pair of blew jeans. (blue)

HOMONYM DOMINOES

Assign children partners and have them use Blackline Master 49 to play a game of homonym dominoes. Before playing, review the words on the dominoes with children. Then, have them cut along the dashed lines to separate the dominoes. Have partners combine their sets and turn all the pictures face down. Then, have each child select five dominoes. The first child to play displays a domino. The other child continues the chain by matching a homonym to one of the words on display. If the child does not have a domino that matches, he or she must continue to select from the face-down dominoes until a match is made. The game continues until one player is out of dominoes.

SPIN A "NYM"

Create a spinner by drawing lines to divide a large paper plate or a tagboard circle into sixteen sections. In the center, fasten a partially opened paper clip or a strip of tagboard with a metal brad. In each space, write the following words: *near, cold, upper, fast, many, summer, empty, sink, night, tale, sun, cent, here, first, good, laugh.* Have pairs of children take turns spinning the spinner and then give a synonym, an antonym, or a homonym for the word they have spun.

TECHNOLOGY

The following software products reinforce children's understanding of a variety of phonics skills.

Reading Blaster™ Ages 6–9
Interactive lessons help students understand word relationships, how to gather information to draw conclusions, and how to use prefixes, suffixes, antonyms, and synonyms. Software includes 9 levels of reading content and 7 reading activities with multiple skill levels.

** Sunburst Technology
    1900 South Batavia Ave.
    Geneva, IL 60134
    (800) 321-7511
    www.sunburst.com

Beginning Reading 1-2
As children interact with two different stories, they learn to read with repeating and rhyming words and picture clues. An audio guidance feature focuses on phonics skills. With Create-a-Story, children are invited to make up a story of their own using the new words they've learned.

** School Zone
    1819 Industrial Drive
    Grand Haven, MI 49417
    www.schoolzone.com

Name _____

week	pale

beet	rode

heel	made

meat	so

tow	bare

son	pain

blew	two

to	deer

sea	pair

tale	sun

wait	knight

cent	weak

dear	heal

pane	see

sew	hare

maid	hear

here	beat

night	sale

road	toe

hair	tail

pear	weight

pail	sent

sail	blue

bear	meet

BLM 49 Unit 7 Activity

Home Connections

The Home Connections features of this program are intended to involve families in their children's learning and application of phonics skills. Three effective opportunities to make connections between home and school include the following.

- **HOME LETTER**
- **HOME NOTES**
- **TAKE-HOME BOOKS**

HOME LETTER

The letter to be sent home at the beginning of Unit 7 informs family members that children will be learning to read and write words containing prefixes as well as words that are synonyms, antonyms, and homonyms, within the context of the unit theme, "Make It, Bake It." Two activities designed to reinforce these words are suggested. The first activity suggests rereading the article on page 219, and discussing the crafts that children are familiar with. Then, they find words in the article to which the prefixes *re-* and *un-* can be added. In the second activity, family members are encouraged to look for words in a recipe to which the prefixes *un-*, *re-*, and *dis-* can be added. Both activities support the child's learning to read and write words with prefixes. The letter, available in both English and Spanish, also suggests books relating to the theme of arts and crafts that family members can enjoy reading together.

HOME NOTES

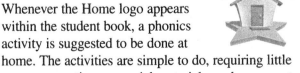

Whenever the Home logo appears within the student book, a phonics activity is suggested to be done at home. The activities are simple to do, requiring little or no preparation or special materials, and are meant to reinforce the targeted phonics skills.

Home Notes in Spanish are also available for both teachers and parents to download and use from our website, www.PlaidPhonics.com.

TAKE-HOME BOOKS

Within the student book, are Take-Home Books that can be cut out and assembled. The story language in each book reinforces the targeted phonics skills. The books can then be taken home and shared with family members. In Unit 7, one Take-Home Book is available, focusing on words containing prefixes as well as words that are synonyms, antonyms, and homonyms, within the unit theme, "Make It, Bake It."

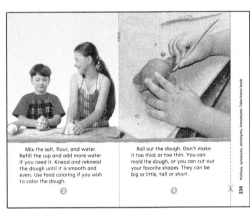

Prefixes, Synonyms, Antonyms, Homonyms

Skill Focus

Assess Prior Knowledge

To assess children's prior knowledge of prefixes, synonyms, antonyms, and homonyms, use the pretest on pages 219e–219f.

Unit Focus

Build Background

- Write the unit theme "Make It, Bake It" on the board. Discuss the theme and invite students to share examples of things they can make or bake.

- Have children look at the picture on the page. Explain that the mola was made by a Cuña Indian woman. Children will be reading about how the molas are made.

- You might want to use a map to point out Panama in Central America so that children can see where the Cuña Indians live. With children, read the text and discuss the information about the molas.

Introduce the Unit Skills

- Have children reread the text. Write the words *stretches* and *reaches* on the board. Explain that words with almost the same meanings are called *synonyms*.

- Write the word *on* on the board. Ask children what word in the second paragraph means the opposite of *on*. (*off*) Explain that words that are opposites are called *antonyms*.

- Write the word *uncover* on the board and have children find it in the story. Circle *un* and explain that *un* is a *prefix*.

- Remind children that the Cuña Indian women sew. Write *sew* on the board. Ask children to spell another word that sounds the same as *sew*. (*so*) Tell children that *sew* and *so* are *homonyms*.

Critical Thinking When children discuss Talk About It, have them explain their choice for a design.

Read Aloud

Prefixes, Synonyms, Antonyms, Homonyms
Theme: Make It, Bake It

Molas: Colors on Colors

A red and black bird stretches its wings. A pink, green, and yellow tree reaches to an orange sun. This design is part of a mola made by a Cuña Indian woman.

The Cuña Indians live on the San Blas Islands off the coast of Panama in Central America. They are known for their beautiful molas.

The molas are made by sewing colorful layers of cloth together. A design is cut into each layer to uncover each color. Many designs show animals and plants that live on the islands. Some people display their molas as pictures.

TALK About It What design would you choose for a mola?

THEME FOCUS

MOLA ART

Children can make a mola design with sheets of colored paper. Have them cut out a design and glue it to another paper. Then, instruct them to cut around the design but to leave a border around the design. Explain that they should then place it on another sheet of paper. They should continue following the same process with other shapes until they have put together a picture that they like.

VISIT A MUSEUM

Plan a field trip to a nearby art museum. Arrange for a child-centered tour that includes exhibits of three-dimensional art forms. Art and children's museums often offer opportunities for hands-on craft experiences.

BRING AN ARTIST TO CLASS

Invite a local artist, such as a potter, photographer, quilter, painter, or cake decorator, to display samples of his or her work and demonstrate how they were created. You may also be able to schedule an on-site visit so children can experience the artist's studio or workplace environment.

Dear Family,

In this unit about making things, your child will learn about prefixes (word parts that begin words), synonyms (words with similar meanings), homonyms (words that sound alike), and antonyms (words with opposite meanings). As your child becomes familiar with these forms, you might try these activities together.

▶ With your child, reread the article "Molas: Colors on Colors" on page 219. Talk about the crafts you and your child are familiar with. Then, find words in the article to which the prefixes re and un can be added, such as unstretches or remade.

▶ Read the directions for a recipe. Together, look for words to which the prefixes **re**, **un**, and **dis** can be added to make new words—for example: reheat, unwrap, discover.

To make mashed potatoes, place peeled potatoes in a pot with water. Cover the pot and cook on low heat. When done, add milk, salt and pepper, and mash the potatoes. Serve hot with butter.

You and your child might enjoy reading these books together.

Easy Origami
By Dokuohtei Nakano

The Button Box
by Margarette S. Reid

Sincerely,

_____

Estimada familia:

En esta unidad, que trata sobre la construcción de cosas, su hijo/a aprenderá diferentes tipos de palabras, incluyendo prefijos (la parte con la que comienza una palabra), sinónimos (palabras con significados semejantes), homónimos (palabras con el mismo sonido) y antónimos (palabras con significados opuestos). A medida que su hijo/a se vaya familiarizando con estas formas, pueden hacer las siguientes actividades juntos.

▶ Lean de nuevo con su hijo/a el artículo titulado "Molas: Colors on Colors" ("Molas: colores sobre colores") en la página 219. Hablen sobre las artesanías que ustedes y su hijo/a conocen. Después, busquen palabras en el artículo a las que se les pueden añadir los prefijos **re** y **un**, como unstretches o remade.

▶ Lean las instrucciones de una receta. Busquen juntos palabras a las que se les pueden añadir los prefijos **re**, **un** y **dis** para formar nuevas palabras, como por ejemplo: reheat, unwrap, discover.

▶ Ustedes y su hijo/a disfrutarán leyendo estos libros juntos.

Easy Origami de Dokuohtei Nakano
The Button Box de Margarette S. Reid

Sinceramente,

_____

(220) Unit 7 • Introduction

HOME CONNECTIONS

- The Home Letter on page 220 will help involve family members in the phonics skills children study in this unit. Have children take the page home and encourage them to ask family members to complete the activities with them.

- Suggest that children look for the books listed on the letter when they go to the library.

LEARNING CENTER ACTIVITIES

MATH CENTER

Provide a variety of pre-cut shapes along with additional construction paper, scissors, and glue. Display examples of different artists' use of shape and pattern in books of artwork or as illustrations in picture books. Children can use cut- and torn-paper shapes to create abstract patterns or realistic images of their own.

ART CENTER

Supply special origami paper or other lightweight paper squares for children to use for folding a simple origami bird or other animal or shape. Refer to an origami book and model the basic folds and directions before placing materials in the art center. Then, in the center, post step-by-step instructions with illustrations or samples for children to follow. You might also provide books with easy-to-follow origami directions so that interested children can progress on their own.

SOCIAL STUDIES CENTER

Have children cut out samples of visual art or crafts from magazines. Examples might include illustrations, advertising scenes or layouts, pleasing-to-the-eye food items, product logos, charts, and maps, as well as photos of three-dimensional works of art or craft items. Invite children to make collages of their favorite items. Discuss different occupations that relate to art, including those that involve functional, commercial, and fine art. You might also have children note the contributions of artists to their phonics books or other school materials.

BULLETIN BOARD

On a bulletin board entitled "Look at Us Create!" highlight the process of creating by displaying photographs or self-portraits of classroom artists at work. You may wish to have children add descriptive captions and then point out prefixes or brainstorm synonyms, antonyms, or homonyms for words in their captions.

Prefixes re- and un-

Skill Focus

Children will

★ form new words by adding the prefixes *re-* and *un-* to base words.

★ write words with the prefixes *re-* and *un-* to finish sentences.

★ recognize and read high-frequency words.

ESL/ELL Native speakers of Spanish likely are familiar with prefixes, including *re-*. Provide frequent oral opportunities for speakers of other languages to distinguish the prefix and its meaning from the base word.

Teach

Introduce Prefixes *re-* and *un-* Say the words *tie* and *retie,* segmenting *retie* into its two syllables: *re-tie.* Ask children to tell how the words are alike and different. (Tie *is part of both words. The second word begins with* re-.) Then, write these sentences on the board.

- **I will tie my shoes and then I will retie them.**

- **I will cover this book and then I will uncover it.**

Have volunteers read the sentences and model their meaning. Then, circle *re-* and *un-* and explain that these are prefixes, a syllable that can be added to the beginning of a base word and changes the meaning of words. Explain that when *re-* is added to a base word, it means to do something *again.* For example, *retie* means to tie *again.* The prefix *un-* means the opposite of an action or *not.* For example, *uncover* means *not* covered or the opposite of *cover.*

Practice and Apply

Sound to Symbol Read the rhyme at the top of page 221. Have volunteers identify the words with prefixes, write the words on the board, circle the prefixes and underline the base words. (*recycle, reglue, reuse*)

Writing Read the rules on pages 221 and 222. Remind children to add *re-* or *un-* to each word as they complete the exercises on these pages. Children will have the opportunity to read the high-frequency words *favorite* and *probably.*

Critical Thinking In discussing Talk About It, have children define *redo* before they answer the question.

Reading Use *Wrong Way Robot,* MCP Phonics and Reading Super Skills Library 1, Level B, to provide practice in reading and understanding words with prefixes.

Name_____

Don't throw out old puppets.
Recycle them instead!
Just reglue the hair and eyes,
And then reuse the head.

▶ Add **re** to the word beside each sentence. Use **the new words to** finish the sentences.

> **RULE**
> The prefix **re** usually means **do again.** Add **re** to the base word **glue** to make **reglue.**
> **Reglue** the hair and eyes.

1. Every day I do things that I have to _____redo_____. | do |

2. When I get up, I _____remake_____ my bed. | make |

3. I _____rebrush_____ my teeth after I eat. | brush |

4. I _____repack_____ my backpack before school. | pack |

5. I _____retie_____ my shoes. | tie |

6. When my camera needs film, I _____reload_____ it. | load |

7. I read and _____reread_____ my favorite books. | read |

8. I write and _____rewrite_____ my stories. | write |

9. Every night I _____rewind_____ my alarm clock. | wind |

TALK About It What things do you redo every day?

Prefix re-: High-frequency words, critical thinking   **221**

FOCUS ON ALL LEARNERS

ESL/ELL ENGLISH LANGUAGE LEARNERS

Materials: construction paper strips in two colors

Reinforce English language learners' pronunciation and recognition of words with the prefixes *re-* and *un-*.

- On one strip of colored paper, print *re-*. On the other, print *un-*.

- On strips of the same color as the appropriate prefix, print verbs from the boxes on pages 221–222. Have volunteers read each of the verbs aloud. Model pronunciation, if necessary. Have children repeat.

- Have children read one verb at a time aloud. Link the *re-* card to the verb and have children repeat.

- Follow the same procedure with the prefix *un-*.

VISUAL/KINESTHETIC LEARNERS   GROUPS

Materials: index cards, marker

On the cards, print base words to which *re-* or *un-* may be added, such as *lock, paint, tie, happy, fold,* and *pack.* Have volunteers choose cards and pantomime the base words. Discuss which prefix(es) could be added. Invite children to demonstrate ways the new words might be acted out.

▶ Add **un** to the word beside each sentence. Use **the new words to** finish the sentences.

> **RULE**
> The prefix **un** means the opposite of the original word. Add **un** to the base word **lock** to make **unlock**.
> The key **unlocks** the door.

1. Every day we do things and ____undo____ them. | **do** |

2. We dress and ____undress____. | **dress** |

3. We button and ____unbutton____ our clothes. | **button** |

4. We tie our shoes and then ____untie____ them. | **tie** |

5. We lock and ____unlock____ doors. | **lock** |

6. We buckle our seat belts and ____unbuckle____ them. | **buckle** |

7. We wrap up our lunches and then ____unwrap____ them. | **wrap** |

8. We pack our backpacks and ____unpack____ them. | **pack** |

9. We load film in a camera and later ____unload____ it. | **load** |

10. I am not ____unhappy____ about all this undoing. | **happy** |

11. It just seems a little ____unusual____ to me. | **usual** |

12. It's probably ____unlikely____ things will ever change. | **likely** |

With your child, take turns making up new sentences for the *un-* words.

222   Prefix un-: High-frequency words

CURRICULUM CONNECTIONS

SPELLING

Use the following dictation sentences to pretest the unit spelling words with prefixes.

1. **rewrite**   I need to **rewrite** my words.
2. **unhappy**   I am **unhappy** when it rains.
3. **undo**   I must **undo** everything I just did!
4. **disagree**   When we play games, I often **disagree** with my brother.
5. **reread**   I like to **reread** good books.
6. **dislike**   I **dislike** my early bedtime.

SOCIAL STUDIES

Talk about reasons for having recycling programs. Discuss resources, such as oil and trees, that cannot be replaced or take a long time to replace. List items your community recycles. Have partners make posters (on recycled paper) with pictures and text that encourage recycling at home and school.

TECHNOLOGY   **AstroWord** Prefixes

AUDITORY LEARNERS GROUPS

Materials: index cards, marker

Write the answer words from pages 221 and 222 on cards. Lay them face up and have children ask each other riddles based on the words. For example: *I do this to my shoe before I take it off.* (untie)

CHALLENGE

Have children work in pairs to brainstorm three lists of base words: words that take only *un-*, words that take only *re-*, and words that take both. Have partners compare lists with other pairs of children and make a master list for the class.

EXTRA SUPPORT/INTERVENTION

Have children add *re-* or *un-* to base words from pages 221–222 that you list on the board. Ask them to print the new words on paper. Have them write sentences for three of the words with prefixes. See Daily Phonics Practice, page 258.

Integrating Phonics and Reading

Guided Reading

Have children look through the story and predict what it will be about. You may also wish to use the English Language Learners activity below.
First Reading Ask children what Katy wanted to do.
Second Reading Have children use these words to tell about the story: *untied, unrolled, unpacked, unhooked, unfold, retry.*

Comprehension

After reading, ask children the following questions:

- What were some of the things that the robot did wrong? *Recall/Summarize*
- Do you think Katy will make a good scientist when she grows up? Why or why not? *Reflective Analysis/Personal Response*

ESL/ELL English Language Learners

Read the title and look at the picture. Ask children what words that begin with *re-* tell what the girl might have to do with her robot. (*redo, remake*)

Prefixes re- and un-

Skill Focus

Children will

★ form new words by adding the prefixes *re-* and *un-* to base words.

★ write words with the prefixes *re-* and *un-* to finish sentences.

★ write words with the prefixes *re-* and *un-* to describe pictures.

ESL/ELL Native speakers of Spanish likely are familiar with prefixes, including *re-*. Provide opportunities for speakers of other languages to form, pronounce, and use words with prefixes.

Teach

Introduce Prefixes *re-* and *un-* Invite children to pantomime packing, unpacking, and repacking a backpack. Then, write the words *pack, unpack,* and *repack* on the board. Have children explain how the words are alike and different. (*They all contain the base word* pack, *but* unpack *and* repack *have prefixes.*) Underline the prefix *un-*. Review that *un-* means the opposite of the base word or *not*. Then, underline *re-*. Review that *re-* means to do an action *again*.

Make two columns on the board, the first headed *not*, the second *again*. Then, have children write these words in the appropriate column and underline the prefix: *unhappy, reopen, retry, unwrap.*

Practice and Apply

Writing Read both sets of directions on page 223. Have children restate them in their own words. Then, have a volunteer complete item 1 aloud and explain the answer. Encourage children to reread each sentence with their word choice. For page 224, read the directions. Remind children to use the picture clues to help them as they write their answer.

Reading You may wish to use *Starfishers to the Rescue,* MCP Phonics and Reading Word Study Skills Library, Level B, to review and reinforce reading words with prefixes.

223

Name _____

▶ Add **re** or **un** to the word beside each sentence. Use **the** new word to finish the sentence.

1. Last night my baby sister _____ unpacked _____ my backpack. | packed |

2. She tried to _____ redo _____ my homework with her crayon. | do |

3. I had to _____ rewrite _____ my story. | write |

4. Now, I _____ recheck _____ my backpack every night. | check |

5. I am very _____ unhappy _____ about it. | happy |

6. My things are _____ unsafe _____ around my sister. | safe |

▶ Print one word that means the same as each pair of words.

7. not cooked _____ uncooked
8. not safe _____ unsafe
9. not able _____ unable
10. not kind _____ unkind

11. spell again _____ respell
12. use again _____ reuse
13. play again _____ replay
14. tell again _____ retell

Prefixes re-, un-　**223**

FOCUS ON ALL LEARNERS

ESL/ELL ENGLISH LANGUAGE LEARNERS

Assess children's ability to say and write prefixes.

• Read aloud and pantomime, if necessary, what children are to do on page 223.

• Ask a volunteer to read aloud item 1. Assist with the pronunciation. Ask the group to look at the picture for a clue and decide whether the correct word is *unpacked* or *repacked*. Review what each choice means and have a volunteer answer aloud. Have children write the correct answer.

• Complete through item 6 orally, reading items one at a time as the group tries words with *re-* and *un-*.

• Review the prefixes for *not* and *again* orally; have children work in small groups to complete items 7–14. Review answers aloud.

AUDITORY/KINESTHETIC LEARNERS

Materials: blank game spinner, marker

Write a selection of these base words on the spinner: *read, tie, build, happy, play, pack, buckle, lock, fill, heat, write, wind, tell, use, safe.* Have children take turns making new words by adding *un-* or *re-* to the words they spin. Children should say the new word aloud and use it in a sentence.

► Add the prefix **un** or **re** to each underlined word. Print the new word on the line.

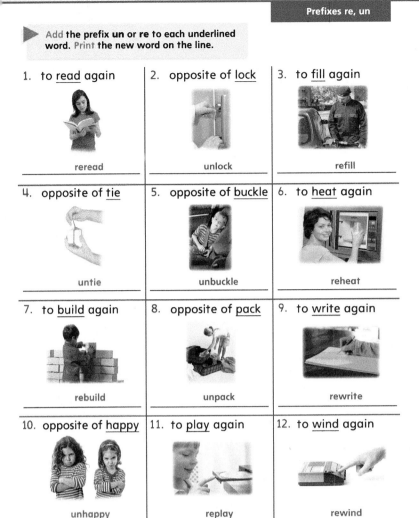

1. to <u>read</u> again	2. opposite of <u>lock</u>	3. to <u>fill</u> again
reread	unlock	refill
4. opposite of <u>tie</u>	5. opposite of <u>buckle</u>	6. to <u>heat</u> again
untie	unbuckle	reheat
7. to <u>build</u> again	8. opposite of <u>pack</u>	9. to <u>write</u> again
rebuild	unpack	rewrite
10. opposite of <u>happy</u>	11. to <u>play</u> again	12. to <u>wind</u> again
unhappy	replay	rewind

HOME Write prefixes (*re-, un-*) and base words on separate cards. Match them to make new words.

224 Prefixes re-, un-; Base words

CURRICULUM CONNECTIONS

SPELLING

Have volunteers spell the base words *write, happy, like, read, do,* and *agree* on the board. Then, dictate the spelling words one at a time and have children recite the correct spellings by adding prefixes to the base words shown. Spelling words are *rewrite, unhappy, dislike, reread, undo,* and *disagree.* Copy and distribute the first half of the Unit 7 spelling list. Children can use the words for home study.

READING

Talk with children about the reading strategy called *rereading.* Discuss how rereading a selection can help them better understand a difficult article. Read aloud a paragraph or two from a science or social studies book. Model the strategy of rereading. Ask children to give examples of when they might want to reread a certain passage.

TECHNOLOGY AstroWord Prefixes

VISUAL/KINESTHETIC LEARNERS GROUPS

Materials: index cards, marker

On the cards, write two sets of base words that either *re-, un-,* or both prefixes can be added to. Place one set face down in front of each of two class teams. In relay style, players choose a word and write it on the board, adding *re-, un-,* or both. Award points for each correctly spelled word that makes sense.

CHALLENGE

Ask children to make a list of materials that can be recycled and give their ideas about how some of these materials can be reused to help the environment.

EXTRA SUPPORT/INTERVENTION

Write these sentences on the chalkboard and have children circle the prefixes and bases in words with *re-* and *un-: Dad will reheat supper; Mom will refill the gas tank; I will rewrite my report; Can you rewind my watch?; The baby is unhappy; Uncooked meat is unsafe.* See Daily Phonics Practice, page 258.

Integrating Phonics and Reading

Guided Reading

Have children read the title and study the picture. Ask who or what they think the *Starfish* is.
First Reading Help children to review the first four chapters by using the chapter headings.
Second Reading Have children find these words in Chapter 4: *unstrapped, rejoin, unexpected.* Encourage them to create two sentences for each word—one with the prefix, the other without.

Comprehension

After reading, ask children these questions:
• With news of the upcoming earthquake, what plan did the people on the *Starfish* make? *Recall/Summarize*
• Why are the Starfishers safe from the *tsunami*? *Critical Thinking/Cause and Effect*

ESL/ELL English Language Learners
Talk about the words rescue, scientists, and *tsunami.* Explain to and model for children the meanings of these words, as necessary.

Prefix dis-

Skill Focus

Children will

★ form new words by adding the prefix *dis-* to base words.

★ write words with the prefix *dis-* to finish sentences.

★ recognize and read high-frequency words.

ESL/ELL The prefix *des-* in Spanish often has the same meaning as *dis-* or *un-* in English.

Teach

Introduce the Prefix *dis-* Ask children to raise their right hand if they agree with this statement or raise their left hand if they disagree: *Our classroom is very large.* Count the "votes" for each and then write the words *agree* and *disagree* on the board with the appropriate number of votes beside each. Ask how the two words are alike. (*The base word is* agree.) Underline *dis-*. Ask what *disagree* means. (*not agree*) Explain that *dis-* is a prefix that means "not" or "the opposite of."

Write these sentences on the board.

- **Please connect the train cars.**
- **I like cold weather.**

Have volunteers read the sentences. Suggest they add *dis-* to the underlined words. Ask them how the meaning of the sentence changed.

Practice and Apply

Writing Read the rule on page 225. Have volunteers use the words *order* and *disorder* in sentences. Then, read the directions to both pages. Remind children to reread the sentence after they write their answer to make sure it makes sense. Children will have the opportunity to read the high-frequency word *again*.

Critical Thinking In discussing Talk About It, encourage children to explain both what the boy thought happened to his shoe and what actually happened.

Reading You may wish to use *Starfishers to the Rescue*, MCP Phonics and Reading Word Study Skills Library, Level B, to reinforce reading words with prefixes in the context of a story. You may wish to discuss small sections of the book at a time.

Name _____

▶ Add **dis** to the word beside each sentence. Use the new words to finish the sentences.

> **RULE**
> The prefix **dis** also means the opposite of the original word. Add **dis** to the base word **order** to make **disorder**.

1. My shoe _____disappeared_____ again. | appeared |

2. I _____disliked_____ that it was missing. | liked |

3. "Why did you _____disobey_____ me, Wags?" | obey |

4. "You know I'm _____displeased_____ when you take my things." | pleased |

5. "That was a _____disloyal_____ thing to do." | loyal |

6. "Wags, you are a _____disgrace_____." | grace |

7. Wags barked to _____disagree_____. | agree |

8. He pulled my shoe out of my _____disorderly_____ toy chest. | orderly |

TALK About It What did the boy think happened to his shoe?

Prefix dis-: High-frequency words, critical thinking   **225**

FOCUS ON ALL LEARNERS

ESL/ELL ENGLISH LANGUAGE LEARNERS

Materials: index cards, markers

Assess English language learners' ability to use pages 225–226 to use the prefix *dis-* correctly and explain its meaning.

- Ask a volunteer to read item 1 on page 225 aloud; assist with pronunciation.

- Ask a child to change *appeared* in the box at the end of the sentence to *disappeared,* using *dis-*. Confirm correct responses. Model writing *disappeared* on the board.

- Complete the activity orally, asking volunteers to read items one at a time as the group provides an oral response for each verb; confirm orally before children write the words on their papers.

- Complete page 226 as a group. Have children work together to complete items 1–3; review as a group. Encourage children to complete items 4–6 on their own; confirm answers aloud.

VISUAL/KINESTHETIC LEARNERS

Materials: art paper, magazines, glue

Have children cut out (or draw) pictures of things they like and dislike and glue them on paper. Ask them to take turns finishing these sentences with partners: *I like this because _____; I dislike this because _____.*

▶ Fill in the bubble beside the word that will finish each sentence. Write the word on the line.

1.	Mr. Fixit will ___disconnect___ the telephone before fixing it.	○ discolor ● disconnect
2.	The rider will ___dismount___ and let her horse rest.	● dismount ○ distaste
3.	Meg and Peg are twin sisters, but they ___disagree___ about many things.	● disagree ○ disappear
4.	The puppy ___disobeyed___ its owner and ran outside with her hat.	○ dishonest ● disobeyed
5.	John loves green beans, but he ___dislikes___ eggplant.	● dislikes ○ disgrace
6.	Kirk made the dirt appear, so he had to make it ___disappear___.	● disappear ○ distrust

HOME With your child, take turns making up sentences for the unused *dis-* words on this page.

226 Prefix dis-

CURRICULUM CONNECTIONS

SPELLING

Have partners take turns dictating the spelling words *rewrite, unhappy, dislike, reread, undo,* and *disagree* to each other at the board. Children can check the words together, rewriting any misspelled words three times.

WRITING

On chart paper, write "A Disagreeable Day." Read the title and ask children for things that might make a day disagreeable or unpleasant. Encourage them to use words with the prefix *dis-* in their ideas. List responses on the chart. For example: *My dog disappeared; I disobeyed Mom and she yelled;* and *I disliked my dinner.* Ask children to use some of the ideas or others of their own to write a short story about a disagreeable day.

TECHNOLOGY **AstroWord** Prefixes

AUDITORY LEARNERS GROUPS

Say the base words *obey, agree, orderly, trust,* and *appear.* Have children add the prefix *dis-* to each word and say the new words. Ask volunteers to tell what the new words mean and use them in sentences.

CHALLENGE

Write the words *disagree, disobey, dislike, disappear, dismount,* and *disconnect* on the board. Have sets of partners choose one word each to act out with gestures and dialogue. Dialogue should not include the chosen word.

EXTRA SUPPORT/INTERVENTION

Invite children to become Ollie Opposite, a character who disagrees with everyone. Say a sentence containing a base word. Have Ollie repeat the sentence but add the prefix *dis-* to the base word. Use sentences such as *I like ice cream* or *I always agree with you.* See Daily Phonics Practice, page 258.

Integrating Phonics and Reading

Guided Reading
Have children turn to the Glossary on page 64. Go over the words with them and discuss unfamiliar terms.
First Reading Ask children to explain who had to be rescued and why.
Second Reading Have children find the words *disagreed* (p. 32) and *disappear* (p. 56). Have them read the original sentence and then reread the sentence without the prefix *dis-.* Ask how the meaning changed.

Comprehension
After reading, ask children the following questions:
• Why was one of the Hawaiian Islands in danger? *Recall/Cause and Effect*
• Why did Ana want to go along to the island? *Inference/Draw Conclusions*
ESL/ELL **English Language Learners**
Help children to understand the meaning of *transport* and why it was needed in the story.

Review Prefixes re-, un-, dis-

Skill Focus

Children will

★ form new words by adding the prefixes *re-, un-,* and *dis-* to base words.

★ read and write words with the prefixes *re-, un-,* and *dis-*.

ESL/ELL Prefix is a concept that most English language learners will pick up quickly. Reinforce meanings and provide opportunities for children to hear and say *re, un,* and *dis,* making the correct long or short vowel sounds.

Teach

Review Prefixes *re-, un-, dis-* Say these words and have children identify the base word and prefix in each: *unwrap, repack, disappear, disobey, redo, unhappy.* Review that when *re-* is added to a base word, it means to do something *again.* For example, *repack* means to pack *again.* The prefix *un-* means the opposite of an action or *not.* For example, *unhappy* means *not* happy or the opposite of *happy.* The prefix *dis-,* when added to a base word, means the opposite of the word. For example, *disobey* means the opposite of *obey.*

Write these phrases on the board: *replay the tape, dislike the song, unlock the case.* Point to each phrase and have children read it aloud. Have volunteers identify the word with the prefix, circle the prefix, and explain what the word means. Then, have another volunteer read the phrase without the prefix and explain how the meaning changes.

Practice and Apply

Writing Explain that children will be forming words with prefixes. Read the directions to each section on pages 227–228. Remind children that the words they make must be real words because each prefix does not work with each word. Suggest they say the words to themselves to see if they sound correct.

Reading Use *The Lost and Found Game,* MCP Phonics and Reading Word Study Skills Library, Level B, to review prefixes with children. You may wish to discuss small sections of the book at a time.

Name _____

▶ Add **un, dis,** or **re** to each base word to make a new word. Print the word on the line.

un or dis		re or dis	
1. _dis_ agree 2. _un_ happy		7. _dis_ able 8. _re_ writes	
3. _dis_ obey 4. _un_ easy		9. _re_ new 10. _dis_ like	
5. _un_ lucky 6. _dis_ please		11. _re_ pay 12. _dis_ loyal	

▶ Add **un, dis,** or **re** to each underlined word to change the meaning of the sentence. Print the new word on the line.

13. Grandpa was <u>pleased</u> about the plans for his party. — displeased

14. He said he felt <u>easy</u> about getting gifts. — uneasy

15. Sadly, Sue <u>wrapped</u> the present she had made. — unwrapped

16. Then, Jake said they would <u>obey</u> Grandpa just once. — disobey

17. With a grin, Sue <u>wrapped</u> the gift. — rewrapped

18. She <u>tied</u> the bow. — retied

19. Grandpa was not <u>happy</u> with his party after all. — unhappy

Review prefixes re-, un-, dis-: Words in context **227**

FOCUS ON ALL LEARNERS

ESL/ELL ENGLISH LANGUAGE LEARNERS

Engage English language learners in reading and using the prefixes *re-, un-,* and *dis-* in context and in writing.

• Complete items 1–12 on page 227 orally as a group. Review misconceptions.

• For items 13–19, have children take turns reading aloud to the group the sentences on their page. Instruct children which words to underline; then, review choices for prefixes orally.

• Have children take turns reading their revised sentences to each other in pairs or in small groups.

AUDITORY LEARNERS

Say sentences with base words to which *dis-* or *un-* can be added, such as *I trust big animals; I agreed with my brother; I am able to go to school.* Have children say the opposite of each by adding prefixes to the base words.

▶ Draw a line **from the prefix to a base word to make a new word. Write** the word on the line.

un — write
dis — happy
re — obey

1. __unhappy__
2. __disobey__
3. __rewrite__

dis — easy
re — agree
un — pay

4. __disagree__
5. __repay__
6. __uneasy__

▶ Add **re, un,** or **dis** to the base word to make a word that will finish the sentence. Write the new word on the line.

7.	Amber will __rewrap / unwrap__ the gift.	wrap
8.	Alex and Max __disagree__.	agree
9.	Rita will __rebuild__ the house.	build
10.	Taro is never __unkind__ to animals.	kind
11.	Look! The ice is still __unsafe__.	safe
12.	My baby sister __dislikes__ rice.	likes
13.	The magician made the bird __disappear__.	appear

HOME Have your child use the new words in the boxes at the top of the page in sentences.

CURRICULUM CONNECTIONS

SPELLING

At this time, you may wish to posttest the first group of spelling words for this unit.

1. **dislike**   I **dislike** very cold weather.
2. **undo**   Can you **undo** a mean remark?
3. **rewrite**   **Rewrite** this sentence neatly.
4. **unhappy**   I am **unhappy** with this color.
5. **disagree**   I **disagree** with that opinion.
6. **reread**   I will **reread** to find the answer.

WRITING

Invite children to tell about times they received nice surprises. Ask them to write a thank-you note to a person who provided a surprise. Encourage them to include words with prefixes.

LANGUAGE

Have children add *dis-* or *un-* to these words: *appear, honest, able, agree, safe, like, fair, happy, kind, easy, sure, obey, pleased.* Invite children to say pairs of sentences such as: *I was sure I knew my spelling words. Now, I am unsure.*

TECHNOLOGY   **AstroWord** Prefixes

Integrating Phonics and Reading

Guided Reading
Have children read the titles of the first three chapters and look at the pictures. Ask them if they have ever gone to a rummage or garage sale.
First Reading Ask children what problem the children on the baseball team had.
Second Reading Have children explain the meaning of *rejoin* and *rewrote* and tell how the words are used in Chapter 3.
Comprehension
After reading Chapters 1–3, ask children the following questions:
* What is a rummage sale and why did the children decide to have one? *Recall/Cause and Effect*
* Why did the children decide to make a sign about the sale? *Inference/Draw Conclusions*
ESL/ELL English Language Learners
Help children understand what the phrase *Lost and Found* means. You may want to revisit the title's meaning after children finish the book.

VISUAL/KINESTHETIC LEARNERS GROUPS

Materials: art or construction paper, markers

Cut out round "stepping stones" and divide them between two teams. Mark start and finish lines on the floor. Team members write *re-, un-,* and *dis-* words on the "stones" and hand them to a team "stepper," who lays them down stone-to-stone, trying to reach the finish line first. Have children remove any nonsense or misspelled words as they are placed.

CHALLENGE

Ask children to talk about exciting discoveries they have made at home or at school. Then, have them write poems or stories inspired by their discoveries. Challenge them to use at least one word for each of the prefixes *re-, un-,* and *dis-.*

EXTRA SUPPORT/INTERVENTION

Read and discuss the sentences on page 227 together. As words are chosen to change the sentence meanings, have volunteers explain the developing premise in their own words. See Daily Phonics Practice, page 258.

Synonyms

Skill Focus

Children will

★ define *synonym*.

★ identify synonyms for given words.

★ write synonyms in the context of a letter.

Teach

Introduce Synonyms Say the following sentence: *I see a large dog.* Talk with children about what they imagined when you said the sentence. Ask children if they can think of another word to describe a large dog. (*Possible answers: big, huge*) Explain that words that have the same or almost the same meaning are called *synonyms*.

Say these word pairs and ask children what they notice about each pair: *little, small; happy, glad; shout, yell.* (*The words in each pair mean the same or almost the same thing.*) Ask children what words that have the same meaning are called. (*synonyms*)

Then, write these sentences on the board, underlining the words shown.

- **I made a drawing of the sea.**
- **There were small boats sailing on big waves.**
- **My friend and I watched from the land.**

With children read the sentences. Encourage volunteers to replace each underlined word with its synonym. Rewrite the sentences with the new words.

Practice and Apply

Writing Have children read the *synonym* rule on page 229 and apply it to the words *gifts* and *presents*. Make sure children understand the directions on pages 229 and 230. Invite volunteers to state the directions in their own words.

Critical Thinking After children have completed page 230, have them read the new version of the letter. Be sure children recognize that Peggy wrote to Pablo to thank him for the gifts he gave her at her birthday party.

Reading Use *Soccer Sue*, MCP Phonics and Reading Word Study Skills Library, Level B, to provide practice in identifying and using synonyms.

229

Name _____

The gifts and presents are wrapped.
It's easy and simple to do.
Little and small, big and large,
Here's a box for you!

> **Print each word from the box beside a word that means the same thing.**

> **RULE**
> **Synonyms** are words that have the same or almost the same meaning. **Gifts** and **presents** mean the same thing.

1. big ___large___   2. small ___little___

3. happy ___glad___   4. quick ___fast___

5. sick ___ill___   6. jump ___leap___

> glad
> ill
> leap
> fast
> little
> large

> **Circle the word in each row that means the same as the first word.**

7. jolly	sad	big	(happy)	jump
8. junk	gems	(trash)	list	top
9. pile	(heap)	near	rest	stop
10. sleep	awake	(nap)	paint	read
11. sick	(ill)	quick	lazy	glad
12. quick	step	slow	pony	(fast)
13. sound	sad	(noise)	find	happy
14. large	(huge)	many	tiny	blue
15. close	move	let	(shut)	see

Synonyms   **229**

FOCUS ON ALL LEARNERS

ESL/ELL ENGLISH LANGUAGE LEARNERS

Have children experience letter writing by asking them to pretend that they are completing a letter. Allow children to personalize and sign the letter themselves.

- Copy the letter onto a sheet of stationery, leaving space for the two names. Photocopy for each child and distribute. Summarize the contents of the letter on page 230.

- Read the directions aloud to the group; together, review the word list in the box on page 230.

- Ask children to complete the letters on their own, using synonyms for the words that appear beneath the lines. Review answers.

- Allow children to "mail" corrected letters to their addresses.

VISUAL/KINESTHETIC LEARNERS

Materials: index cards, markers

Write pairs of synonyms on separate cards. Partners can arrange them face down in rows and take turns turning over two cards at a time to find and remove matching sets. The player with the most matches wins.

▶ Finish **Peggy's letter.** Print a word from the box that means the same thing as the word below each line.

friend	kind	big
gifts	laugh	little
noise	happy	enjoy
fast	races	
hope	easy	

May 10

Dear Pablo,

I'm _____**happy**_____ that you came to my party.
        glad

It was _____**kind**_____ of you to bring _____**gifts**_____.
     nice   *presents*

The _____**big**_____ book looks _____**easy**_____ to read.
    large   *simple*

I will _____**enjoy**_____ reading it. When I wind up the
     like

_____**little**_____ robot, it _____**races**_____ _____**fast**_____
  small   *runs*   *quickly*

and makes a funny _____**noise**_____. It makes me
             sound

_____**laugh**_____ to watch it. Thank you very much.
  giggle

I _____**hope**_____ to see you soon.
   wish

            Your _____**friend**_____,
                    pal

            Peggy

TALK *About It!* Why did Peggy write to Pablo?

HOME Ask your child to read Peggy's letter to you.

230 Synonyms

CURRICULUM CONNECTIONS

SPELLING

You may wish to pretest the synonym, antonym, and homonym spelling words at this time.

1. **dear**   My puppy is **dear** to me.
2. **deer**   A **deer** lives in the forest.
3. **cold**   I like **cold** milk.
4. **hot**   I like to drink **hot** chocolate.
5. **little**   My **little** brother is six.
6. **small**   My socks are too **small**.

WRITING

Ask children to write invitations for a party. Have them begin their invitations with *Dear,* tell when and where the party will be, and why they want the person to come. Help children circle words that have synonyms.

LANGUAGE

Reread the rhyme on page 229 and ask what words describe the sizes of the boxes in the illustration. (*little, small, big, large*) Discuss other words that might describe the boxes. Tell children that describing words are called adjectives. Have them brainstorm adjectives that might describe such things as a painting, your classroom, a present, or the playground.

AUDITORY LEARNERS   GROUPS

Form two teams. Say words from pages 229–230. Have children take turns naming a synonym and, if answering correctly, putting the team's *X* or *O* in a tic-tac-toe grid drawn on the board. Three in a row wins.

CHALLENGE

Materials: thesaurus

Introduce the thesaurus as an alphabetically arranged book of synonyms. Invite children to find at least three words from pages 229 and 230 that have entries in a thesaurus and list the synonyms they find.

EXTRA SUPPORT/INTERVENTION

Have children dictate a group story, using words from the box on page 230. Invite children to read the story and then cross out and insert synonyms where they can. Read the reworded story together. See Daily Phonics Practice, pages 258–259.

Integrating Phonics and Reading

Guided Reading

Have children look at the cover, read the title, and preview the illustrations. Ask what they think the book will be about.

First Reading Invite children to describe the main character and tell why she is called Soccer Sue.

Second Reading Reread selected sentences and have children suggest a synonym for a particular word. For example:

- Then, a man with a <u>nice</u> smile began to talk. (*kind*)

Comprehension

Ask children the following questions:

- Why did Sue want to quit soccer? ***Recall/ Cause and Effect***
- How did Sue feel at the end of the story? ***Reflective Analysis/Personal Response***

ESL/ELL **English Language Learners**

Review Chapters 1 and 2. Discuss what soccer is, the equipment that is needed, and how it is played.

Antonyms

Skill Focus

Children will

★ define *antonym*.

★ identify antonyms for given words.

★ write antonyms.

Teach

Introduce Antonyms Say this sentence aloud: *The big dog barked at the little dog.* Repeat the sentence and ask children which two words in the sentence have the opposite meaning. (*big, little*) Explain that words that are opposite, or nearly opposite, in meaning are called *antonyms*.

Write these word groups on the board.

- **over   under   easy**
- **many   slow   few**
- **stop   awake   start**

Invite volunteers to read a group of words and then circle the two words that are antonyms. Encourage others to think of sentences using the two antonyms in each group.

Practice and Apply

Sound to Symbol Read the rhyme at the top of page 231. Have children repeat it as a group. Ask them to identify the words in the rhyme that are opposite in meaning. (*hot, cold; rain, shine; day, night; summer, winter*) Then, write one word from each pair on the board. Have volunteers write the word that is an antonym beside the original word. Ask children what an antonym for *best* might be. (*worst*)

Writing Review the antonym rule on page 231. Have children tell why *hot* and *cold* fit the definition. Read aloud the directions for both pages and identify the pictures on page 232. You may wish to read through the lists of words on both pages before children begin to write.

Reading Use *Giants Alive*, MCP Phonics and Reading Word Study Skills Library, Level B, to provide practice in identifying and using antonyms.

Name _____

Hot or cold, rain or shine,
My dog likes the backyard best.
Day or night, summer or winter,
He needs a place to rest.

▶ Find **a** word in the box that means the opposite of each word. Print **its** letter on the line.

RULE

Antonyms are words that are opposite or almost opposite in meaning. **Hot** and **cold** mean the opposite of each other.

a. old	b. wet	c. start	d. full	e. slow
f. last	g. down	h. hot	i. good	j. short
k. out	l. well	m. few	n. winter	o. long
p. far	q. lower	r. shallow	s. shut	t. awake
u. thick	v. wide	w. white	x. hard	

1. **b** dry   2. **g** up   3. **n** summer   4. **o** short

5. **p** near   6. **e** fast   7. **j** tall   8. **i** bad

9. **h** cold   10. **u** thin   11. **l** sick   12. **m** many

13. **c** stop   14. **q** upper   15. **f** first   16. **r** deep

17. **a** new   18. **d** empty   19. **s** open   20. **k** in

21. **t** asleep 22. **x** easy   23. **w** black   24. **v** narrow

---

FOCUS ON ALL LEARNERS

ESL/ELL ENGLISH LANGUAGE LEARNERS

Determine English language learners' ability to pair antonyms.

- Select words from pages 231–232 and write them on red sentence strips; write their antonyms on green strips.

- Hang the strips in two vertical columns from a wall or on a bulletin board.

- Set the timer for a reasonable amount of time; encourage children to work together to "beat the clock," pairing antonyms next to each other. Review children's pairings.

- Have children work in small groups to complete page 231. Point out that they should write the letters, not the words, in the box.

AUDITORY/VISUAL LEARNERS

Have children draw two five-step ladders on paper. Have children go up one ladder and down the other, writing an antonym for each of the following words you say: *cold* (*hot*), *first* (*last*), *dry* (*wet*), *shallow* (*deep*), *night* (*day*), *near* (*far*), *stop* (*go*), *soft* (*hard*), *laugh* (*cry*), *out* (*in*). Responses may vary.

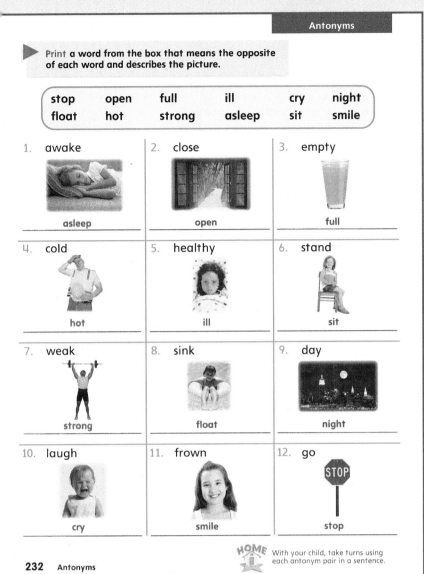

Antonyms

▶ Print a word from the box that means the opposite of each word and describes the picture.

stop	open	full	ill	cry	night
float	hot	strong	asleep	sit	smile

1. awake — asleep
2. close — open
3. empty — full
4. cold — hot
5. healthy — ill
6. stand — sit
7. weak — strong
8. sink — float
9. day — night
10. laugh — cry
11. frown — smile
12. go — stop

232 Antonyms

 With your child, take turns using each antonym pair in a sentence.

CURRICULUM CONNECTIONS

SPELLING

Give each child six pieces of note paper. Have them write one spelling word on each paper as you give these clues.

1. One is an animal and one begins a letter. (*deer, dear*)
2. They mean the same as tiny. (*little, small*)
3. They name opposite temperatures. (*hot, cold*)

Check and correct the spellings together, noting the meanings of deer and *dear*. Then, have children cut apart the letters and respell the words. Be sure children have copies of the spelling list to practice on their own.

WRITING

Reread the rhyme on page 231 and review the antonym pairs. Write this rhyme frame on the board and have children substitute other pairs to create their own versions of the poem.

_____ or _____, _____ or _____,

My dog likes the backyard best.

_____ or _____, _____ or _____,

He needs a place to rest.

VISUAL/KINESTHETIC LEARNERS *INDIVIDUAL*

Have children copy the following words on paper and cut them into word cards: *hurt, harm, well, sick, happy, jolly, unhappy, sad, quick, fast, slow, poky, close, shut, open, unlock.* Ask children to make as many different synonym and antonym pairs as they can and record each pair on paper.

CHALLENGE

Materials: a thesaurus listing both synonyms and antonyms

Explain that a thesaurus often has antonyms as well as synonyms for words. Encourage children to find additional antonyms for several of the words on pages 231 and 232, using the thesaurus. Then, have them write a sentence for each new antonym.

EXTRA SUPPORT/INTERVENTION

Materials: index cards, markers

Invite children to make five word-card pairs for antonyms on pages 231 and 232, and then work with partners to mix their cards together and match the word pairs. See Daily Phonics Practice, pages 258–259.

Integrating Phonics and Reading

Guided Reading
Have children read the title and look through the story to name the animals they will be learning about.
First Reading Invite children to describe some of the biggest animals.
Second Reading Have children find and name antonyms for these words in the story: *big, taller, over, long, end, old, stand, run, over, warm, high, fast, closes.*

Comprehension
Ask children the following questions:
• Why is it difficult for the giraffe to get a drink of water? *Recall/Cause and Effect*
• Which animal did you find the most interesting? Explain. *Reflective Analysis/Personal Response*

ESL/ELL English Language Learners
Some of the words in the book may be difficult for children to understand. Review the words in the glossary on page 32, modeling meanings as needed.

232

Homonyms

Skill Focus

Children will

★ define *homonym*.

★ identify homonyms for given words.

★ write homonyms to finish sentences.

ESL/ELL Native speakers of Spanish may be familiar with homonyms in their native language, due to similar pronunciation of *b* and *v*; soft *c*, *s*, and *z*; soft *g* and *j*; *ll* and *y*; and the silent *h*. Emphasize homonyms in context. Have children memorize the different spellings of word pairs.

Teach

Introduce Homonyms Encourage children to listen carefully as you say these sentences.

- **Can you see the blue sea?**
- **All week I felt weak.**
- **I rode my new bike on the road.**

Read the sentences again and ask what children notice about them. (*Each sentence has two words that sound the same.*) Have them identify the words. (*see, sea; week, weak; rode, road*)

Practice and Apply

Have a volunteer read the rhyme at the top of page 233. Have children reread it together. Encourage them to point to *sea* and *see*. Ask what they notice about the two words. (*They sound the same but are spelled differently and have different meanings.*) Tell children that words like *sea* and *see* are called *homonyms*. Then, ask children to find other homonym pairs in the poem. (*sew, so; blue, blew*)

Writing Read the homonym rule on page 233 and have children apply it to *blue* and *blew*. Read the directions for each section on pages 233 and 234. After children have completed the pages, encourage them to use several of the homonym pairs in original sentences that show their meanings.

Reading You may wish to use *Hootie Joins In*, MCP Phonics and Reading Word Study Skills Library, Level B, to provide practice in reading and recognizing homonyms.

Homonyms

Name _____

Grandma will sew a blue-green quilt
So everyone can see,
How the wind blew the boats about
On a stormy day at sea.

▶ Find **a word in the box that sounds the same as each word below. Print the word on the line.**

> **RULE**
> **Homonyms** are words that sound alike but have different spellings and meanings. **Blue** and **blew** are homonyms.

tail	here	to	road	pail	heal
blue	week	cent	sail	maid	sea

1. heel ___heal___   2. see ___sea___   3. rode ___road___

4. sent ___cent___   5. tale ___tail___   6. blew ___blue___

7. weak ___week___   8. pale ___pail___   9. hear ___here___

10. two ___to___   11. sale ___sail___   12. made ___maid___

▶ Circle **the word that will finish each sentence. Print it on the line.**

13. Maggie ___rode___ her horse into the woods.   road (rode)

14. Her puppy wagged its ___tail___ and ran along.   (tail) tale

15. They saw a ___deer___ hidden behind a tree.   dear (deer)

16. Maggie watched the ___sun___ set in the west.   son (sun)

Homonyms   **233**

FOCUS ON ALL LEARNERS

ESL/ELL ENGLISH LANGUAGE LEARNERS

Have English language learners practice saying and writing the homonyms identified in this lesson.

- Copy the words from the box on page 234 onto chart paper in one column. Read each aloud; have children pronounce after you.

- Have children read items 1–15 aloud; correct pronunciation, as needed.

- Name one item chorally. Match it to a word on the chart; have a volunteer write the homonym next to its mate on the chart.

- Have children copy the homonym from the word box onto their papers to identify the homonyms. Review words aloud, having children spell each word to emphasize written distinctions.

AUDITORY/VISUAL LEARNERS

Invite partners to write original story titles that include pairs of homonyms, such as "The Knight Who Was Afraid of the Night." Encourage children to refer to their pages if they need ideas for words.

▶ Find a word in the box that sounds the same as each word below. **Print** it on the line.

rose	meat	blew	too	pane
tow	tale	week	four	wait
beet	bare	sea	dear	sew

1. weight ___wait___
2. rows ___rose___
3. weak ___week___
4. bear ___bare___
5. blue ___blew___
6. beat ___beet___
7. deer ___dear___
8. two ___too___
9. for ___four___
10. pain ___pane___
11. see ___sea___
12. meet ___meat___
13. so ___sew___
14. tail ___tale___
15. toe ___tow___

▶ Use words from the box and the activity above to **finish** the sentences.

16. Pete bought a new kite last ___week___.

17. He could not ___wait___ to try it out.

18. He could ___see___ his friends playing outside.

19. He pulled on his ___blue___ jeans in a hurry.

20. He wanted to fly his kite ___too___.

 Help your child write each homonym on a card or paper and then match them.

234 Homonyms: Words in context

CURRICULUM CONNECTIONS

SPELLING

To assess children's mastery of the second half of the unit spelling list, you may posttest these spelling words at this time.

1. **little**   The **little** bird sang a song.
2. **hot**   My oatmeal is **hot**.
3. **cold**   I put on a coat when I am **cold**.
4. **small**   My shoes are a size too **small**.
5. **deer**   I saw a **deer** at the petting zoo.
6. **dear**   This necklace is **dear** to me.

WRITING

Invite children to use homonym pairs to write riddles. Model an example such as *What is a story and what is something a dog can wag? (a tale and a tail)* Have children write riddles on one side of their paper and answers on the other side and then share them with each other.

KINESTHETIC LEARNERS GROUPS

Materials: index cards, paper bag, marker

Make word cards for homonym pairs such as *choose, chews; ate, eight; sun, son; weigh, way; great, grate; sail, sale;* and *plain, plane.* Put one of each pair in the bag and display the others. Children take turns choosing a word from the bag, finding its homonym, and using the words in sentences.

CHALLENGE

Ask the riddle *Why did the sailor put his glasses in the ocean? (So he could "sea.")* Invite children to use homonym pairs to create their own riddles with double meanings.

EXTRA SUPPORT/INTERVENTION

Materials: chart paper, marker

Write these word pairs on chart paper and have children supply the missing letters and read the homonyms: *pain, pa_e; sent, _ent; sail, s_l; week, we_k; see, se_; blue, bl__; deer, de_r; tale, ta_l.* Model sentences for each of the spellings and invite children to provide others. See Daily Phonics Practice, pages 258–259.

Integrating Phonics and Reading

Guided Reading
Have children read the title. Ask them to explain who they think Hootie is.
First Reading Ask children why Hootie could not sleep at the beginning of the story.
Second Reading Have children locate the homonyms *hoo* and *who* and explain why this pair of words is important to the story.

Comprehension
Ask children the following questions:
- Why did Hootie have a problem when he moved near the birds? *Recall/Cause and Effect*
- How did Hootie finally make the birds happy? *Recall/Cause and Effect*

ESL/ELL English Language Learners
Many verbs in this story may be unfamiliar to English language learners. When possible, model these verbs, such as *glared, chirped, poked,* and *flocked.*

Lesson 109
Pages 235–236

Phonics and Spelling / Phonics and Writing

Review Prefixes, Synonyms, Antonyms, and Homonyms

Skill Focus

Children will

★ spell and write synonyms, antonyms, homonyms, and words with prefixes.

★ write a set of instructions using synonyms, antonyms, homonyms, and words with prefixes.

ESL/ELL A strong emphasis on spelling may be inappropriate for English language learners who have not reached an intermediate level of proficiency. Allow children to use invented spelling and the phonics skills they are building upon as a foundation for future spelling success.

Teach

Phonics and Spelling Review the following:

- *Synonyms* are words with the same, or nearly the same, meaning.
- *Antonyms* are words that are opposite in meaning.
- *Homonyms* are words that sound alike but have different spellings and different meanings.
- *Prefixes* are added to the beginning of words to make new words.

Then, write these words on the board: *repack, untie, sun, son, disappear, untrue, huge, giant, blew, blue, present, gift, stop, go.* Have children say the words and determine which words belong together and why.

Practice and Apply

Phonics and Spelling Read the directions for page 235. With children, say the words in the box so that children can hear the sounds before they categorize the words.

Phonics and Writing Before children begin writing the instructions, have them brainstorm a list of their favorite sandwiches. Write their suggestions on the board. Discuss what is needed for each kind of sandwich. Remind children that they need to include in order all the steps for making the sandwich when they write the instructions.

Reading Use *Making Lily Laugh,* MCP Phonics and Reading Word Study Skills Library, Level B, to review synonyms, antonyms, homonyms, and words with prefixes.

235

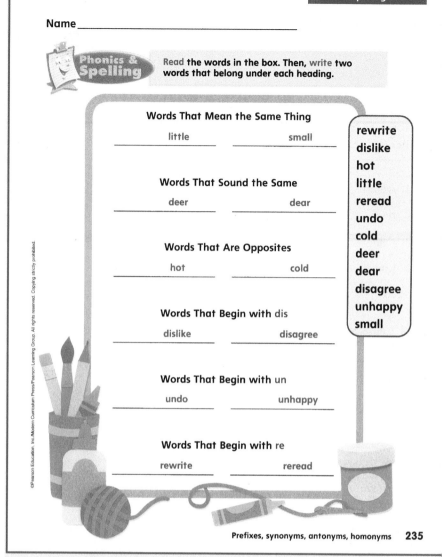

Spelling

Name_____

Phonics & Spelling Read the words in the box. Then, write two words that belong under each heading.

Words That Mean the Same Thing
little   small

Words That Sound the Same
deer   dear

Words That Are Opposites
hot   cold

Words That Begin with dis
dislike   disagree

Words That Begin with un
undo   unhappy

Words That Begin with re
rewrite   reread

rewrite
dislike
hot
little
reread
undo
cold
deer
dear
disagree
unhappy
small

Prefixes, synonyms, antonyms, homonyms   **235**

FOCUS ON ALL LEARNERS

ESL/ELL ENGLISH LANGUAGE LEARNERS

Confirm English language learners' ability to identify by sight and sound the concepts in this lesson.

- Re-create the outline of page 235 on an overhead transparency and display.
- Starting with the first heading, confirm with children what we call words that mean the same thing. Write *synonyms* to the right of the first heading.
- Have volunteers name examples aloud, having the rest of the group agree or disagree. Review misconceptions.
- Continue the process for homonyms, antonyms, and the prefixes *un-, dis-,* and *re-.*
- Have children work in pairs to sequence the words in the Word List under the headings on page 235. Review orally.

AUDITORY/VISUAL LEARNERS

Materials: large cutout of a tree; pear-shaped cutouts

Display the "Pair Tree" on a wall. Invite children to write pairs of homonyms on pear-shapes and attach them to the tree. Challenge children to include any homonym triples they can think of. (*pear, pair, pare; to, too, two; so, sew, sow*)

A **set of instructions** are written to tell how to make or do something. The writer tells what the instructions are for, and lists the materials that are needed. Then, the steps needed to follow the directions are written in order and numbered.

▶ Write **a set of instructions** telling how to make your favorite sandwich. Use some of the words in the box to help you.

unwrap	recover	two	to	top
bottom	dislike	slice	piece	reuse

Tell what the instructions are for.	_____
	_____
List what is needed.	_____
	_____
	_____
Tell the steps in order and number them.	_____
	_____
	_____
	_____
	_____
	_____

With your child, create another *set of instructions* for making or doing something.

236 Prefixes, synonyms, antonyms, homonyms

CURRICULUM CONNECTIONS

SPELLING

Cumulative Posttest

Use the list and sentences below to test children's mastery of the Unit 7 spelling words.

1. **unhappy** I am **unhappy** when I am sick.
2. **disagree** I **disagree** with my sister when she tells me what to do.
3. **reread** Will you **reread** that sentence?
4. **dislike** I **dislike** being thirsty.
5. **rewrite** I will **rewrite** my messy homework.
6. **small** That **small** book is mine.
7. **little** My kitten is **little**.
8. **dear** My grandmother always calls me "**dear**."
9. **deer** **Deer** get into my father's garden.
10. **undo** Can you **undo** the latch on the gate?
11. **hot** I like to swim in **hot** weather.
12. **cold** I like to ice-skate in **cold** weather.

AUDITORY/KINESTHETIC LEARNERS GROUPS

Materials: beanbag

Children pass a beanbag or other small object around a circle as you chant *Round and round the circle this way. Spell the spelling word I say.* Then, say a word from the unit spelling list. The player with the beanbag says the first letter of the word and successive children add the next letters.

CHALLENGE

Invite children to make paintings to fit these titles: *Happiness, Discovery, The Unusual, Hot and Cold,* and *Unhappiness.* Have children explain how their paintings illustrate the titles.

EXTRA SUPPORT/INTERVENTION

Materials: Phonics Word Cards, Set 2, 227–256

Hand out one card to each child. The child says the word on the card and then says a word that is a synonym, antonym, or homonym. Other children identify which it is. See Daily Phonics Practice, pages 258–259.

Integrating Phonics and Reading

Guided Reading

Direct children's attention to the cover and ask them to predict what kind of problem the characters have.

First Reading Ask what problem Roy had at the beginning of the story.

Second Reading Have children find the words *appearance, assume,* and *effect* in the glossary. Then, have them use a prefix with *appearance,* identify a synonym for *assume,* and an antonym for *effect.*

Comprehension

Ask children the following questions:

• What was Piggler and why didn't it work? *Recall/Cause and Effect*

• Why do you think the giggling pig made Lily laugh? *Reflective Analysis/Personal Response*

ESL/ELL **English Language Learners**

Children may benefit from acting out the various verbs used in the story. Help children distinguish words, such as *laugh, giggle, smile; laugh, cry.*

<u>Take-Home Book</u>

Review Prefixes, Synonyms, Antonyms, and Homonyms

Skill Focus

Children will

★ read synonyms, antonyms, homonyms, and words with prefixes in the context of a story.

★ reread for fluency.

ESL/ELL Although English language learners may experience these concepts in their home languages, the sounds and spellings of English are new. Provide frequent opportunities for children to hear and use words in personally meaningful contexts.

►Teach
Build Background

• Review with children that the theme of this unit is "Make It, Bake It." Ask them to name arts and crafts they have been doing recently. Have them explain which have been their favorite activities.

• Ask children how many of them have worked with clay. Explain that they will learn how to make a clay dough from flour, salt, and water.

Review Skills: Categorization Review the meanings of prefixes, synonyms, antonyms, and homonyms. Then, say the categories and ask children to tell which words belong in that group.

• **Words with prefixes:** *play, replay, rewrite*

• **Synonyms:** *little, huge, small*

• **Antonyms:** *tall, short, thin*

• **Homonyms:** *pail, bucket, pale*

►Practice and Apply
Read the Book Guide children as they put together the Take-Home Books. Have them preview their book and then read the book together. Discuss what they learned about making clay dough.

Sound to Symbol Have volunteers read the book. Then, invite children to identify words with prefixes (*refill, reknead, reuse*), synonyms (*easy, simple; smooth, even*), antonyms (*thick, thin; big, little; tall, short; wet, dry*), and homonyms (*need, knead; too, to*).

Reread for Fluency Have children reread the book to increase their fluency and comprehension. Remind them to take the books home to share with their families.

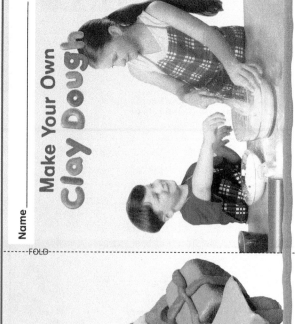

Name _____

Make Your Own Clay Dough

You can make your own clay dough. It is easy and simple to do. This is what you need:

2 cups salt   5 cups flour
2 cups warm water   food coloring

1

Let the shapes you made dry if you wish to keep them. You may choose to reuse the dough when you are done. Then, store it in the refrigerator in a plastic container to keep it wet. Remember to have fun!

4

Prefixes, synonyms, antonyms, homonyms: Take-home book   **237**

FOCUS ON ALL LEARNERS

ESL/ELL **ENGLISH LANGUAGE LEARNERS**
Introduce the *Make Your Own Clay Dough* book, and preview the words *to, too; easy, simple; wet, dry; reuse, refill, reknead; need, knead; smooth, even.*

• Encourage children to look at the photographs and talk about them. Ask: *What are the children doing? How are they using the clay dough?*

• Confirm that children recognize the synonyms, antonyms, prefixes, and homonyms in the story and can clearly pronounce them.

• Create a list on the board of the target words they name.

AUDITORY/KINESTHETIC LEARNERS

Materials: measuring cup, mixing bowl with cover, spoon, salt box, pitcher, flour bag or canister, rolling pin, plastic knife, cookie cutters

Have volunteers use the props to retell and act out the directions as explained in *Make Your Own Clay Dough.*

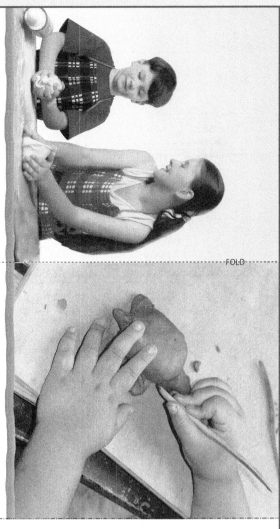

Mix the salt, flour, and water. Refill the cup and add more water if you need it. Knead and reknead the dough until it is smooth and even. Use food coloring if you wish to color the dough.

Roll out the dough. Don't make it too thick or too thin. You can mold the dough, or you can cut out your favorite shapes. They can be big or little, tall or short.

238 Prefixes, synonyms, antonyms, homonyms: Take-home book

READING

Write these directions on the board and have children number them in correct order. Discuss the importance of following recipes in the correct sequence.

__ Knead the dough. (*3*)

__ Add more water if you need it. (*2*)

__ Roll out the dough. (*4*)

__ Cut the dough into shapes. (*5*)

__ Mix the salt, flour, and water. (*1*)

__ Let the shapes dry. (*6*)

WRITING

Have children make lists of things they can form from clay dough. Begin by suggesting animals, seasonal ornaments, stars, and even the letters of their names. Have them draw pictures of what the items would look like.

ART

Provide materials for making clay dough to small groups of children. After the dough is made, have children mold it into shapes they choose. You may also want to provide shaping materials such as cookie cutters, garlic presses (to make "hair"), and plastic knives for cutting. When the shapes have dried, children can paint their creations.

VISUAL/KINESTHETIC LEARNERS GROUPS

Materials: ingredients and utensils for making dough as listed in *Make Your Own Clay Dough*

As volunteers take turns reading aloud pages in the Take-Home Book, have others work together to follow the directions and make the clay dough. School aides, upper-grade students, or parents may be able to help with this activity.

CHALLENGE

Ask each child to think of something he or she can make or do well, such as taking care of a hamster, packing a lunch, feeding a dog, baking brownies, cleaning a room, or playing soccer. Then, have children write directions for doing these things and illustrate the steps. Challenge them to include synonyms, antonyms, homonyms, and words with the prefixes *re-*, *un-*, and *dis-*.

EXTRA SUPPORT/INTERVENTION

Before children read the words, have them "read" the pictures, explaining what is happening on each page. Then, help them practice any unfamiliar words as they read the text. See Daily Phonics Practice, pages 258–259.

Lesson 111 — Pages 239–240

Unit Checkup

Review Prefixes, Synonyms, Antonyms, and Homonyms

Skill Focus

Children will

★ read and identify synonyms, antonyms, homonyms, and words with prefixes.

★ write synonyms, antonyms, homonyms, and words with prefixes.

★ complete sentences using homonyms.

ESL/ELL Since English language learners may be familiar with these concepts in their native languages, provide specific instruction for problem areas of pronunciation.

Teach

Review Skills Ask volunteers to review the definitions of synonyms, antonyms, and homonyms. Then, write this verse on the board.

> The old man made a tiny new boat,
> Set in a small bottle of blue.
> He knew the big stores would sell it,
> For only a dollar or two.

Read the verse aloud and then have children repeat it. Have children find the synonyms (*tiny, small*), and antonyms (*old, new; small, big*), and homonyms (*new, knew*).

Then, write the prefixes *re-*, *un-*, and *dis-* on the board. Have children add a prefix to these words and use them in a sentence: *work, do, safe, tie, like*.

Practice and Apply

Assess Skills With children, read each set of directions on pages 239–240, and have children restate them. After they have completed the pages, have children discuss what they learned about prefixes, synonyms, antonyms, and homonyms.

Name _____

▶ Circle **two words in each box that mean the same thing.**

1. (cold) (cool) / seed shook
2. hair (small) / (little) home
3. (fast) fell / (quick) queen
4. three tree / (shut) (close)
5. (jump) (leap) / drink drop
6. (sick) snow / (ill) blow

▶ Circle **two words in each box that mean the opposite.**

7. (little) puppy / jelly (big)
8. fly (old) / (new) penny
9. (bad) candy / rich (good)
10. they (fast) / play (slow)
11. from (dirty) / (clean) funny
12. (asleep) play / baby (awake)

▶ Circle **the word that will finish each sentence. Print it on the line.**

13. The ____sun____ was shining.   (sun)   son
14. I put on my ____red____ shorts and blue hat.   read   (red)
15. I went for a sail on the ____sea____.   see   (sea)
16. The wind blew the ____sails____.   (sails) sales
17. It almost ____blew____ my hat off, too.   (blew) blue
18. I had a ____great____ time!   grate (great)

Prefixes, synonyms, antonyms, homonyms: Assessment **239**

FOCUS ON ALL LEARNERS

ESL/ELL ENGLISH LANGUAGE LEARNERS

Materials: cassette recorder or guest speaker

Since English language learners may become dependent upon the speech patterns of a single speaker, provide another speaker of English.

• Invite a speaker to provide a different voice using a natural rate of speech to record the directions, item numbers, and answer choices for items 1–12 on page 239 and 1–6 on page 240.

• Tell children that they will hear another voice read the items aloud. They should complete the questions independently, when possible.

• Play the recording, pausing after each item and providing verbal cues and support, as needed. Monitor comprehension difficulties. Review responses as a group.

AUDITORY/VISUAL LEARNERS

Write *large* on the board and have a child name a synonym, antonym, or homonym for it. Write the word next to *large* and ask for a synonym, antonym, or homonym for the new word. Continue the word chain as far as possible. Start other word chains with the words *steel, thick, unhappy, knew, lovely, unwrap,* and *colorful.*

Fill in the bubble beside the word that names or describes each picture.

1.
○ tale
○ tell
● tail

2.
● heel
○ hail
○ heal

3.
○ day
● deer
○ dear

4.
○ rode
○ rod
● road

5.
● sun
○ son
○ soon

6.
○ knows
● nose
○ now

Read the words. Fill in the bubble next to the word that has the same meaning.

7. opposite of wrap
● unwrap
○ rewrap

8. to play again
● replay
○ display

9. opposite of mount
● dismount
○ remount

10. opposite of appear
○ reappear
● disappear

11. spell again
○ dispell
● respell

12. to tie again
○ untie
● retie

13. opposite of like
● dislike
○ relike

14. opposite of do
○ redo
● undo

15. to pack again
● repack
○ unpack

240 Prefixes, synonyms, antonyms, homonyms: Assessment

ASSESS UNDERSTANDING OF UNIT SKILLS

STUDENT PROGRESS ASSESSMENT

You may wish to review the observational notes you made as children worked through the activities in the unit. These notes can help you evaluate the progress children have made.

PORTFOLIO ASSESSMENT

Review the written materials children have collected in their portfolios. Conduct interviews with children to discuss their work and progress since the beginning of this unit. As you review children's work, evaluate how well they use the phonics skills they have practiced.

DAILY PHONICS PRACTICE

For children who need additional practice with the skills in this unit. See Daily Phonics Practice, pages 258–259.

PHONICS POSTTEST

To assess children's mastery of skills in this unit, use the posttest on pages 219g–219h.

VISUAL/KINESTHETIC LEARNERS

Materials: three shoe boxes, index cards, marker

Write a synonym, antonym, or homonym pair from the student pages on each card and stack cards face down. Write *Sound the Same, Mean the Same,* and *Opposites* on the three boxes. Children choose cards, read them, and place them in the matching boxes.

CHALLENGE

Materials: Phonics Word Cards, Set 2: Synonyms, Antonyms, Homonyms (227–256)

Invite children to work with partners to find as many synonym, antonym, and homonym pairs as they can on the cards. Ask them to list each pair. You might have them add other words that mean the opposite or the same as the antonyms or synonyms on the cards.

EXTRA SUPPORT/INTERVENTION

Read aloud the words in the items on pages 239 and 240 with children before they begin. Include the sentences on page 239. See Daily Phonics Practice, pages 258–259.

Teacher Notes

Teacher Notes

Daily Phonics Practice

Contents

Initial Consonants

◆ Group children according to their first or last names. For example, *All of you whose last names begin with* b *as in book, stand next to the bookshelf.*

◆ Ask volunteers to act out a key word for each consonant (except *x*), for example, *b—bat, c—catch, d—dance, f—fall,* and so on.

◆ Have children sort objects or pictures into groups of things whose names have the same beginning sounds (for example, *pen, pencil, paper*). Children can then place an alphabet card for that letter with the group.

◆ Have children play a game of "I Spy." Invite them to take turns giving clues to objects in the room whose names begin with consonant letters. For example, *I spy something you can open and close that begins with the sound of* d. (*door, drawer*)

◆ Let children make up tongue twisters with common consonants, such as "Peter Piper picked a peck of pickled peppers."

◆ Display an alphabet strip or alphabet cards. Write a word such as *log* on the board and pronounce it, pointing to the initial consonant. Invite volunteers to name rhyming words (*dog, fog, hog, jog*) and point to the letter whose sound begins that word.

◆ Have children take turns making up riddles about words beginning with given letters. For example, *I swim in water. People try to catch me. My name begins with* f. *What am I?* (*fish*)

◆ Say pairs of words and ask the class to say *Yes!* if the beginning sounds match and *No!* if they don't. Some examples are *yard, barn; map, men; get, game.*

◆ Play "Beat the Clock." Draw a clock face on the board, using these consonants instead of numbers: *l, d, p, h, m, b, n, t, r, k, s, f.* Ask children to beat the clock by starting at twelve o'clock and saying words that begin with the sound each letter represents.

◆ Have children take turns making word ladders by changing the initial consonants of words. Demonstrate, for example, by changing *fan* into *pan.*

◆ Have children play "I'm Going on a Trip." Say, for example, *I'm going on a trip, and I'm bringing a gift and a game. What will you bring?* Children respond with a word that has the same beginning sound as the words you say. (*goat, gum, goose*)

Final Consonants

◆ Divide the class into two groups, "Beginnings" and "Endings." Say two words. The Beginnings stand up if the beginning sounds are the same, and the Endings stand up if the ending sounds are the same. Occasionally, say words with the same initial and final sounds (*man, men*) so that both groups stand.

◆ Have children take turns making word ladders by changing the final consonants of words. Demonstrate, for example, by changing *pen* into *pet.*

- Have children sort objects or pictures into groups of things whose names have the same ending sounds (for example, *book, clock, chalk*). Children can then place an alphabet card for that letter with the group.

- Have children play a game of "I Spy." Invite them to take turns giving clues to objects in the room. For example, *I spy something you can write with. It ends with the sound of* l. (*pencil*)

- Say pairs of words and ask the class to say *Yes!* if the ending sounds match and *No!* if they don't. Some examples are *tall, bell; pan, dot; good, lid.*

- Have children help you create lists of words that begin with different consonants, such as *c, h, l,* and *t.* Then, name a final consonant. Have children find words in the list that end with that consonant and read the words aloud.

UNIT 1 LESSONS 4–7

Medial Consonants

- Say a letter and four words, asking children to raise their hands each time they hear the sound of that letter in the middle of a word. Use words such as the following: *n—fallen, penny, finish, nothing; m—calm, summer, money, family.*

- Ask children to listen for a repeated middle sound as you say phrases such as *mellow yellow melons.* Invite volunteers to name the letter that stands for that sound.

- Distribute several consonant letter cards to children. Tell them to listen to the words you say and to hold up their card if they have the consonant that stands for the middle sound in the word. Say, for example, *dinner, ladder, collar, hammer, rabbit, seven.*

- Display picture cards for *balloon, ladder, wagon, apple, camel, mittens,* and *tiger.* Let pairs of children take turns naming each picture and the letter that stands for the middle sound in its name.

Daily Phonics Practice

UNIT 2 LESSONS 8–11, 15, 21–23

Short Vowels a, i

- Ask children to stand up when they hear a word with short *a.* Then, say three words, one of which has the short *a* sound, for example, *bet, bat, bit; hat, hit, hot.* Repeat for short *i.*

- Have small groups work together to make collages of pictures of objects whose names have the short *a* and *i* sounds. Help children label each picture with its name.

- Write the word *bag* on the board. Invite a volunteer to erase the *a* and substitute it with an *i.* Have children read the new word. (*big*) Repeat with other words, but make sure new words are real words.

- Have children play a game of "I Spy." Invite them to take turns giving clues to objects in the room. For example, *I spy something that holds things and has the short* a *sound.* (*bag*)

◆ Pass out word cards for short vowel words. Ask children with short *a* word cards to come to the front of the classroom. Have the entire class read the short *a* words aloud. Repeat for words with short *i*.

◆ Let two volunteers play "Ping-Pong Rhymes." Player 1 names a short *a* or *i* word, and Player 2 gives a rhyming word. Children then reverse roles.

◆ Play a word scramble game. Write a three-letter short *a* or *i* word on the board with the letters in random order. Ask children to write the word in the correct order. For example, *igp* becomes *pig*.

◆ Have children take turns making up riddles about words containing short *a* or *i*. For example, *I am something you can do in water. My name has the short* i *sound.* (*swim*)

◆ Let pairs of children play "Concentration," using picture cards for words with short vowel sounds and alphabet cards. Each child turns over a picture card and an alphabet card. The object is to match the vowel sound in the picture name with the letter (for example, *cap* and *a*).

UNIT 2 LESSONS 12–13, 15–19, 21–23

Short Vowels u, o, e

◆ Ask children to stand up when they hear a word with short *u*. Then, say three words, one of which has the short *u* sound: for example, *beg, bog, bug; not, nut, net.* Repeat for short *o* and *e*.

◆ Have children take turns making word ladders by changing the medial vowel letter in words. Demonstrate, for example, by changing *bud* into *bed*.

◆ Distribute the following letter cards to nine children: *t, b, s, n, d, g, u, u, u.* Ask the children to arrange themselves so that the letters form short *u* words. (*tub, but, sun, dug, bus, bug, sub, bun*) Repeat for short *o* and *e* words.

◆ Have small groups work together to make collages of pictures of objects whose names have the short *u, o,* and *e* sounds. Help children label each picture with its name.

◆ Have children play a game of "I Spy." Invite them to take turns giving clues to objects in the room. For example, *I spy something that tells time and has the short* o *sound.* (*clock*)

◆ Distribute word cards for short vowel words. Ask children with short *u* word cards to come to the front of the classroom. Have the entire class read the short *u* words aloud. Repeat for words with short *o* and *e*.

◆ Let two volunteers play "Ping-Pong Rhymes." Player 1 names a short *u, o,* or *e* word, and Player 2 gives a rhyming word. Children then reverse roles.

◆ Ask a volunteer to name a short *u* word. Play "Duck, Duck, Goose" and ask "goose" to name another short *u* word. Continue playing for several rounds. Repeat for short *o* and *e*.

◆ Have children take turns making up riddles about words containing short *u, o,* or *e*. For example, *I am something you can do and frogs can do, too. My name has the short* o *sound.* (*hop*)

◆ Let pairs of children play "Concentration," using picture cards for words with short vowel sounds and alphabet cards. Each child turns over a picture card and an alphabet card. The object is to match the vowel sound in the picture name with the letter (for example, *cup* and *u*).

Daily Phonics Practice

Long Vowels a, i

◆ Ask children to wave their hands when they hear a word with long vowel *a*. Then, say three words, one of which has the long *a* sound: for example, *like, lake, leak,* or *pale, pile, pole*. Repeat for long *i*.

◆ Print the vowels *a* and *i* on the board. Ask a volunteer to select a vowel and then say and write a word that has the long sound for that vowel. Then, ask for a rhyming word.

◆ Let pairs of children play "Concentration," using picture cards for words with long vowel sounds. The object is to match pictures whose names rhyme.

◆ Invite children to participate in a scavenger hunt for long *a* words. Allow them ten minutes to search the classroom for objects whose names have the long *a* sound (for example, *game, table, tape, paper, plate*). Print their words on the board. Repeat for long *i*.

◆ Shuffle picture cards for long vowel words and show them one at a time. Ask children to name the vowel sound in each picture's name. Then, have children group the cards according to vowel sounds.

◆ Let children play "Go Fish" with word cards for long vowel words. The object is to match words with the same long vowel sound.

◆ Have children play a game of "Change It." Write these words on the board: *cap, kit, rip, mad, can, dim*. Ask children to add *e* to the end of each word and read the new word they make.

◆ Have children play "I'm Going on a Trip." Say, for example, *I'm going on a trip, and I'm bringing skates and a game. What will you bring?* Children respond with a word that has the same long vowel sound as the words you say. (*cake, grapes, plane*)

◆ On the board, draw a tic-tac-toe grid and write a long *a* or long *i* word in each section. Let two children take turns reading a word aloud, erasing it, and replacing it with an *X* or *O*. The first one to get three *X*'s or *O*'s in a row is the winner.

◆ Let two teams play "Chalkboard Baseball." Draw a baseball diamond on the board and print *a* in the middle. Batters advance by naming long *a* words, with an incorrect word being an out. After three outs, the second team takes over. Repeat for long *i*.

Long Vowels u, o

◆ Shuffle picture cards for long vowel words and show them one at a time. Ask children to name the vowel sound in each picture's name. Then, have children group the cards according to vowel sounds.

◆ Print the vowels *u* and *o* on the board. Ask a volunteer to select a vowel and then say and write a word that has the long sound for that vowel. Then, ask for a rhyming word.

◆ Have children play a game of "Change It." Write these words on the board: *cut, tub, hop, cub, rob, not*. Ask children to add *e* to the end of each word and read the new word they make.

- Let children play "Go Fish" with word cards for long vowel words. The object is to match words with the same long vowel sound.

- On the board or on a sheet of paper, draw a tic-tac-toe grid and write a long *u* or long *o* word in each box. Let two children take turns reading a word aloud and marking it with an *X* or *O*. The first one to get three *X*'s or *O*'s in a row is the winner.

UNIT 3 LESSONS 32–33, 35–37

Long Vowel e

- Draw the outline of a tree on a large piece of oak tag. Provide newspapers and magazines. Ask children to find and cut out words with the long *e* sound and attach them on the tree.

- Write ten words on the board, six of which have the long *e* sound. Have volunteers circle the long *e* words.

- Have children play "I'm Going on a Trip." Say, for example, *I'm going on a trip, and I'm bringing beets and beans. What will you bring?* Children respond with a word that has the long *e* sound. (*geese, cream, sheep*)

- Invite children to play a rhyming game with long *e* words. Say each of these words, one at a time, and ask children to name as many rhyming words as they can: *feet, cheap, clean, dream, cheek, bee.*

- Invite children to play "Shop for Sheep." Cut out and number the outlines of ten sheep. On the back of each, write a long *e* word. To "buy" a sheep, children say, I'd like to buy sheep number 3, and then read the word on that sheep.

Daily Phonics Practice

UNIT 4 LESSONS 38, 44, 52, 53, 65

Compound Words

- Print compound word equations on the board, such as *base + ball* = _____. Invite volunteers to "add" the words together to make compound words.

- Print compound words on strips of paper, read the words, and then cut the strips apart between the two smaller words. Let children read the smaller words, then put them together, and read the compound word.

- Print compound words on tagboard squares and arrange them on the floor in a hopscotch pattern. Let children take turns tossing a beanbag onto the squares. Have them read the word the beanbag lands on and tell what two words make up the compound word.

- Print the two parts of compound words on separate cards and place the cards face up. Have groups of children combine two cards to make a compound word and write the word on the board.

- Distribute the cards from the above activity randomly. Let children match their cards with others to form compound words. Together, pairs read aloud the compound word they have formed.

Daily Phonics Practice

- Let pairs of children play "Ping-Pong Compounds." Player 1 suggests the first part of a compound word, such as rain, and Player 2 responds with the second part, such as coat or bow.

- Give two teams a list of compound words. Teams take turns reading a word to each other and making up sentences that tell what the word means. For example: *Toothbrush. A toothbrush is a brush for teeth.*

- Invite small groups to create rebus equations for compound words and challenge other groups to solve them.

- Have children play a game of "I Spy." Invite them to take turns giving clues to objects in the classroom whose names are compound words. For example, *I spy something you paint with. (paintbrush)*

- Encourage pairs of children to write riddles for which the answers are compound words. Children should include clues for each smaller word in the compound. For example: *My first part is a home; my second is a ship. What am I? (houseboat)*

UNIT 4 LESSONS 39, 44, 52, 53, 65

One- and Two-Syllable Words

- Invite volunteers to name as many animals as they can whose names contain two syllables, such as *camel, zebra, hippo, tiger,* and so on. Have the rest of the class repeat each name and clap out the syllables.

- Call on volunteers to say their names or write them on the board. Challenge others to tell how many syllables are in each name.

- Read aloud a list of words—such as *rabbit, music, cabin, pie, face, visit, pail, monkey, milk, robot*—and ask children to clap their hands for each syllable they hear.

- Have children play a game of "I Spy." Invite them to take turns giving clues to objects in the classroom whose names have two syllables. For example, *I spy something you cut with. (scissors)*

- Label two bags 1 and 2. Spread word cards for one- and two-syllable words next to the bags. Invite two volunteers to "bag" as many words as they can in ten seconds by telling how many syllables a word has and putting it in the correct bag.

- Let teams of children play the "syllable race" game. A member of each team comes to the board. Read aloud a one- or two-syllable word. The first child to write the correct number of syllables in the word scores that number of points for his or her team.

UNIT 4 LESSONS 40, 44, 52, 53, 64, 65

Words Ending in le

- Ask each child to fold a sheet of paper into fourths and draw in each section a picture of a word that ends with a consonant + *le*, such as *table, rattle, apple,* and *fiddle.* Have children trade papers and identify each other's drawings.

- Say an *le* word, such as *wiggle,* and ask children to name a rhyming word. (*jiggle, squiggle*)

- Distribute flashcards for *le* words. Have pairs of children take turns showing each other one side of a card. The partner writes his or her word and divides it into syllables. Have children create sentences for each word pair.

- Write *le* words on the board, such as *saddle, little, apple, candle, table,* and *eagle*. Make up a riddle for each word; for example, *This goes on a horse's back.* Call on volunteers to choose a word that answers the riddle. (*saddle*)

UNIT 4 LESSONS 41, 42, 44, 52, 53, 64, 65

Hard and Soft c and g

- Divide the class into two groups, "cats" and "mice." Tell the cats to make whiskers with their fingers when they hear a hard c word and the mice to make ears with their fingers when they hear a soft *c* word. Say words such as these: *city, come, fence, cut, center.*

- Divide the class into two groups, "Hard Sounds" and "Soft Sounds." Ask children to raise their hands when they hear their sound in these words: *cent, giant, garden, page, city, huge, gift, cork, dance.*

- Shuffle word cards for words with hard and soft *c* and *g* sounds. Invite pairs of children to sort the words according to the sound for *c* and *g*.

- Make up riddles for words with hard and soft *c* and *g* sounds. Give clues that include the sound. For example, *This animal with a long neck has a soft* g *sound in its name.* (*giraffe*)

UNIT 4 LESSONS 45–49, 52, 53, 65

Blends with r, l, s; Final Blends

- Prepare flashcards for words with a target blend and place them in a grab bag. Have children take turns drawing a card from the bag, reading the word, and using it in a sentence.

- Print initial (or final) blends on index cards and give one to each child. Then, say a series of words with those blends. Ask children to raise their cards when they hear a word with their blend and repeat the word.

- Play the "Ice-Cream Cone" game. Draw seven cones on the board and label each *br, cr, dr, fr, gr, pr,* and *tr.* Invite volunteers to name a word that begins with each blend. Each child then draws a scoop of ice cream on the correct cone and prints the word in it.

- Have children work in small groups to make up tongue twisters for words with blends. Some examples are *blue bug, black bug; Fred's flags fly free.*

- Have children work in pairs to write hink-pink riddles that use blends. For example: *What color never lies?* (*true blue*) You may wish to provide a few hink-pinks to get children started: *stuck truck; clown frown; brain drain.*

- Invite pairs of children to play "Ping-Pong Blends." Give the players a word with a beginning blend. They then alternate naming words that begin with that blend until one partner can't think of a word.

- Print words with blends on index cards. Invite children to play "Give Me a Clue." A child takes a card and gives a clue to the word. If no one can guess, the child gives another clue, and so on, until someone guesses correctly.

Daily Phonics Practice

♦ Invite children to play a rhyming game. Say a word and tell children that you are thinking of a rhyming word that begins with a particular consonant blend. For example, *This word rhymes with* cake *and begins with* sn. (*snake*)

♦ Ask children to create shopping lists using words with blends. A sample list might include *grapes, skim milk, bread,* and *cream.*

♦ Have children play "I'm Going on a Trip." Say, for example, *I'm going on a trip, and I'm bringing bread. What will you bring?* Children respond with a word that has the same initial blend as the word you say. (*brush, bricks, broom*)

UNIT 4 LESSONS 50–53, 65

y as a Vowel

♦ Write *long e* and *long i* on two strips. Let volunteers hold up each strip. Distribute cards for words with *y* as a vowel. Call on children to read their words aloud and stand behind the child holding the name for the sound of *y* in the word.

♦ Place cards on which you have written *y = long e* and *y = long i* on the chalkboard ledge. Divide the class into two teams. Then, read words such as *fly, rainy, baby, cry, jelly,* and *by.* The first player to pick up the correct card for the *y* sound scores a point.

♦ Use a different color chalk to print each of these words on the board: *yes, baby, my.* Then, say the words *you, try, cry, silly, yell, lady, fly, yet,* and *funny,* and ask volunteers to print them in the correct color under the word with the same *y* sound.

♦ Have children form three groups. Assign one the consonant *y* sound, one the long *e* sound, and the third the long *i* sound. Have groups stand when they hear their sound in these words: *shy, cherry, yellow, you, my, lucky, story, spry, party, young, cry.*

♦ Shuffle word cards for words with *y* as a consonant and *y* with the long *e* and long *i* sounds. Invite pairs of children to sort the words according to the sound for *y.*

UNIT 4 LESSONS 54–57, 59, 63–65

Consonant Digraphs sh, th, wh, ch, ck, kn, wr

♦ Encourage children to make up tongue twisters for consonant digraphs, such as "She sells seashells by the seashore."

♦ Shuffle word cards for words with consonant digraphs. Invite pairs of children to sort the words according to their digraphs.

♦ Ask children to create shopping lists using words with consonant digraphs. A sample list might include *cheese, peaches, chicken,* and *wheat.*

♦ Print the consonant digraphs *sh, th, wh, ch, kn,* and *wr* on the chalkboard. Hold up picture cards for words beginning with those digraphs. Have children name the picture and identify the consonant letters that stand for the beginning sound in the picture name.

♦ Let children play charades by pantomiming words that contain digraphs, such as *shark, think, whale, chimp, kick, knock,* and *write.* Invite teams to guess the words and identify the digraphs.

◆ Give each child a strip of paper and ask them to write a word that begins with *sh*, *th*, *wh*, or *ch*. Help children tape the strips together to make a digraph chain.

◆ Let pairs of children play "Concentration," using picture or word cards for words with consonant digraphs. The object is to match pictures or words with the same digraphs.

◆ Play "Beat the Clock." Draw a clock face on the board, using digraphs instead of numbers. Ask children to beat the clock by starting at twelve o'clock and saying words that begin with that digraph.

◆ Make up riddles for words with consonant digraphs. Give clues that include the digraph. For example, *This sharp thing on a rose stem has* th *in its name.* (*thorn*)

◆ Let children play twenty questions for words with digraphs. Lead the first game yourself and then let the child who guesses correctly lead the next game.

UNIT 4 LESSONS 60–65

r-Controlled Vowels ar, or, ir, er, ur

◆ Have children take turns making up riddles for words with *r*-controlled vowels. For example, *I'm the opposite of* near. (*far*)

◆ Place word cards for words with *r*-controlled vowels in a grab bag. Have children take turns drawing a card from the bag, reading the word, and using it in a sentence.

◆ Print the letters *b*, *f*, *h*, *m*, *p*, *s*, and *t* on separate cards. On the board, print *ar*, *er*, *ir*, *or*, *ur*. Show one consonant card at a time, and invite children to name as many *r*-controlled vowel words as they can that begin with that consonant. Print their suggestions on the board.

◆ Let children play twenty questions for words with *r*-controlled vowels. Lead the first game yourself and then let the child who guesses correctly lead the next game.

◆ Have children form five teams and assign each team an *r*-controlled vowel. Give teams five minutes in which to record as many words as they can think of with their *r*-controlled vowel.

◆ Draw a racetrack on the board, divided into spaces. Say *car*. Two players take turns naming words that rhyme with *car*. Correct rhyming words move the player ahead one space; incorrect words move the player back one space. Repeat for other *r*-controlled vowel words.

◆ Shuffle word cards for words with *r*-controlled vowels. Invite pairs of children to sort the words according to the *r*-controlled vowels.

◆ Let children play a game of "Mystery Cards," using picture cards for words with *r*-controlled vowels. One child chooses a card and describes the picture without naming it. The class then guesses the picture name and identifies the *r*-controlled vowel.

◆ Have children form five groups and assign each group an *r*-controlled vowel. Say several words with *r*-controlled vowels and have groups identify which words have their *r*-controlled vowel. Encourage children to write their words.

◆ Have children take turns making word ladders by changing the initial and final consonants and vowel letters in words with *r*-controlled vowels. Demonstrate, for example, with *barn*, *bark*; *park*, *pork*.

♦ Separate the class into two teams. A child from each team writes a sentence containing a word with an *r*-controlled vowel on the board. Teammates then add other *r*-controlled words to the sentence. A team scores a point for using the five *r*-controlled vowels, such as *That bird has purple feathers and sings in the cornfield on the farm.*

Daily Phonics Practice

UNIT 5 LESSONS 66–69, 80–82

Contractions

♦ Pronounce several words, such as *fast, didn't, table, he's, can't,* and *we'll.* Ask children to raise their hands when they hear a contraction. As contractions are identified, ask what two words were put together to form the contraction.

♦ Write ten contractions on the board and ask volunteers to write the two words that make up each one.

♦ Have pairs of children take turns showing the side of flashcards with two words and naming the contraction and then showing the contraction and naming the words from which it is formed.

♦ Let children play "Concentration," using cards for pairs of words and their matching contractions. Players turn over two cards at a time, trying to match words and contractions.

♦ Print contractions on tagboard squares and arrange them on the floor in a hopscotch pattern. Let children take turns tossing a beanbag onto the squares. Have them read the word the beanbag lands on and tell what two words form the contraction.

♦ Cut out large construction-paper circles and cut them in half. On one half, write two words from which a contraction can be formed and on the other half write the contraction. Distribute the half circles. Let children find the person with the matching half of their circle.

♦ On the board, write in one column words that can be contracted and in a second column write their contractions in random order. Have children take turns drawing lines to match words and contractions.

♦ Make several tic-tac-toe grids with contractions printed in the boxes. Using one color marker, Player 1 writes the two words that form one of the contractions. Player 2 does the same, using a different color marker. The game continues until one child has won.

♦ Have children form two teams. Display a flashcard for a contraction. A player from each team writes on the board the words that form the contraction. Award one point for a correct answer.

♦ On the board, print contraction equations, such as *I + will* = _____. Call on volunteers to write the contractions that solve the equations.

UNIT 5 LESSONS 70, 74, 78–82

Plural Endings -s, -es

♦ Invite children to take turns pantomiming animals while the class guesses what animals they are. Challenge children to write on the board the plural forms of the animal names.

- Tell children that you will show them pictures and hold up one finger for a word that names one and two fingers for a word that names more than one. Have children name each picture, using the singular or the plural form depending on the number of fingers.

- On large cards, print a variety of singular nouns and the endings -s and -es. Invite pairs of children to make plural words. One child takes a word card, and the other takes a card with -s or -es. They then hold the cards together to form the plural.

- On the board, print words such as *puff, peach, fox, bug, toy, bird*, and *lunch*. Give each child two index cards, one with -s on it and the other with -es. Point to each word and ask children to hold up the card that shows which ending they would add to make it plural.

- Have children form six groups, one each for words ending in -ss, -x, -z, -ch, -sh, and -y. Encourage children to write several words with the assigned ending. Then, have groups exchange words and write the plural forms of the words they receive.

UNIT 5 LESSONS 71–74, 80–82

Inflectional Endings -ing, -ed

- Have children add -ing to these verbs and use them in sentences: *fish, cook, clean, add, help, play, show, need, roll, look*. Repeat for -ed.

- On the board, write pairs of verbs, such as *calling, called; talking, talked*. Call on volunteers to tell which verbs tell an action that is happening and which tell an action that happened in the past.

- Print the endings -ing and -ed on the board. Then, draw a train with an engine and twelve cars. Print words on every other car: *walk, stop, skate, clean, hope, save*. Ask volunteers to load the train by adding an ending to a word and printing the new word in the next car.

- Draw two ladders on the board, labeled -ing and -ed. Invite children to take turns climbing a ladder by writing a word with the appropriate ending on a rung of the ladder.

- Print the words *smile, chase, bake, hope*, and *like* on strips of paper and the endings -ing and -ed five times each on chart paper. Ask volunteers to choose a word, cut off the e, and tape it in front of -ing or -ed to make a new word.

- On the board, write *Rabbit Running, Lion Leaping*, and the endings -ing and -ed. Say several base words. Have volunteers add one of the endings listed to the base words and write them on the board under *Rabbit* if the final consonant is doubled and under *Lion* if it is not.

UNIT 5 LESSONS 75–77, 80–82

Suffixes -ful, -less, -ness, -ly

- Shuffle flashcards for words with suffixes. Have children choose a card, read the word aloud, tell its meaning, and use it in a sentence.

- Review the meanings of the suffixes. Print these phrases on the board: *full of thanks, without rest, being sick, in a sad way*. Ask children to name a word with a suffix that means the same as each phrase. (*thankful, restless, sickness, sadly*)

- Let small groups of children play "Suffix Concentration." For each group, make a set of cards having pairs of words with the same suffix. The object is to match words with the same suffixes.

◆ Have children form small groups. For each group, prepare a set of cards with base words and suffixes. Invite children to make as many words as they can in a given time by combining base words and suffixes.

◆ On the board, print suffix equations, such as *sweet + ness = _____*. Call on volunteers to write the words that solve the equations.

◆ Let pairs of children play a suffix guessing game. One partner writes a word with a suffix, such as joyful, and then gives the other a clue for the word. For example, I'm thinking of a word that means full of joy.

UNIT 5 LESSONS 77–78, 80–82

Suffixes -er, -est

◆ Provide objects in groups of three, such as sticks of different lengths or blocks of different sizes. Have children place each set of objects in ascending order on the chalkboard ledge. Help them label the objects (for example, *long, longer, longest*).

◆ Ask children to draw pictures of three things that vary in one quality. Let them exchange pictures and label each other's pictures with words that compare.

◆ Let children play a guessing game. The leader says something like *I am thinking of an animal that is bigger than a mouse and smaller than a dog. What is it?* (cat, squirrel)

◆ Have children form groups of three, and assign a word to each group, such as *big, hot, fast, rich, dark.* Each group is to make up three sentences, using the base word and the suffixes *-er* and *-est*.

Daily Phonics Practice

UNIT
6

UNIT 6 LESSONS 83–87, 99–101

Vowel Pairs ai, ay, ee, ea, ie, oe, oa

◆ Let children work in pairs to look through magazines or catalogs to find pictures of things whose names have vowel pairs. Children can use the pictures to create collages. Help them label each picture.

◆ Challenge children to make up hink-pink riddles by using words with vowel pairs. Offer this example: *What do you call a day off from school?* (a play day)

◆ On index cards, print words having vowel pairs. Put the cards in a paper bag. Invite children to take turns drawing three cards from the bag and making up a sentence using all three words.

◆ Have children work in pairs or small groups to write rhymes using words with vowel pairs that stand for the long *a, e, i,* and *o* sounds.

◆ Print the vowel pairs _ai_, _ay_, _ee_, _ea_, _ie_, _oe_, and _oa_ on the board, with blanks as shown. Challenge volunteers to make as many words as they can from each pair by filling in different consonants.

◆ Have children sit or stand in a circle. Say a vowel pair, such as "long *a* spelled *ay*," and toss a beanbag to one player. That child says and spells a word with that pattern and tosses the beanbag to another player.

◆ Create vowel pair cards and place them on the chalkboard ledge. Then, write the following incomplete words on the board: *r__n, d__, tr__, m__l, t__, t__, b__t*. Invite volunteers to hold up vowel pair cards in the blanks to make words.

◆ Play "Beat the Clock." Draw a clock face on the board, using vowel pairs instead of numbers. Ask children to beat the clock by starting at twelve o'clock and saying words that contain that vowel pair.

◆ Write *ran* on the board and ask children to add a letter to make a new word with a long *a* vowel sound. (*rain*) Follow a similar procedure with other words: *bed* (*bead*), *got* (*goat*), *fed* (*feed*).

◆ Have children form four teams. On the board, draw four ladders, labeled *long a, long e, long i,* and *long o*. Invite team members to take turns writing words with their vowel sound in the rungs of their ladders.

UNIT 6 LESSONS 88–93, 99–101

Vowel Digraphs oo, ea, au, aw

◆ Provide children with a large foot or boot cut from construction paper. Challenge them to print on each as many *oo* words in five minutes as they can that have the corresponding sound of *oo*.

◆ Provide each child with either a spoon (or a balloon) or a book. Write these words on the board: *noon, pool, wood, boot, spoon, hood, shook, stool*. As you point to a word, ask children to say it and hold up their object if it matches the sound of *oo*.

◆ Print these words on the board: *hop, fan, led, hot, had, hunt, red*. Challenge children to make new words by changing each vowel to the digraph *oo, ea, au,* or *aw*. Have children write their new words on the board and circle the digraphs.

◆ Print sets of words on the board, one of which does not belong, for example, *bread, head, speak; stool, stood, took*. Ask pairs of children to say the words to each other and decide which word in each set does not belong.

◆ Have children form four teams. Assign each team a vowel digraph. Give teams five minutes to record as many words as they can think of with their digraph. Award one point for each correct word.

◆ Let two volunteers play "Ping-Pong Rhymes." Player 1 names a word with a vowel digraph (*saw*), and Player 2 gives a rhyming word (*claw*). Children then reverse roles.

◆ Let children play a game of "Mystery Cards," using picture cards for words with vowel digraphs. One child chooses a card and describes the picture without naming it. The class then guesses the picture name and identifies the vowel digraph.

◆ Have children take turns making up riddles about words containing vowel digraphs. For example, *I am something cats have on their feet. My name has* aw. (*claws*)

◆ Print the vowel digraphs _oo_, _ea_, _au_, and _aw_ on the board, with blanks as shown. Challenge volunteers to make as many words as they can from each pair by filling in different consonants.

◆ Make word cards for *bead, fool, head, spoon, wood, speak,* and *real.* Hide the cards around the classroom and assign one team of students the vowel digraph *ea* and the other, *oo.* Send students on a treasure hunt to look for words with their vowel digraph.

◆ Give clues to riddles that can be answered with hink pinks, including the vowel sound in the clue. For example: "*oo* as in *school*—a closet for a cleaning tool." (*broom room*)

UNIT 6 LESSONS 94–101

Diphthongs ou, ow, oi, oy, ew

◆ On index cards, print several words with diphthongs, such as *boil, joyful, mouse, cow,* and *chew.* Invite volunteers to draw a card, look at it, and pantomime the word for the class to guess.

◆ Have children form five teams. Assign each team a diphthong. Give teams five minutes to record as many words as they can think of with their diphthong. Award one point for each correct word.

◆ Make word cards for *clown, mouth, house, mouse, flower, plow, about,* and *down.* Hide the cards around the classroom and assign one team of students the diphthong *ou* and the other, *ow.* Send them on a treasure hunt to look for words with their diphthong.

◆ Write words with the diphthongs *ou, ow, oi, oy,* and *ew* on index cards (two for each diphthong). Let children play "Concentration," trying to match words with the same diphthong.

◆ Have children take turns making up riddles about words with diphthongs. For example, *I make people laugh at the circus. What am I?* (*clown*)

◆ Print these words on the board: *fee, too, clod.* Challenge children to make new words by changing the vowels into the diphthong *ou, ow, oi, oy,* or *ew.* Have children write their new words on the board and circle the diphthongs.

◆ Play "Beat the Clock." Draw a clock face on the board, using diphthongs instead of numbers. Ask children to beat the clock by starting at twelve o'clock and saying words that contain that diphthong.

◆ Invite children to play a version of "Simon Says." Give them actions to perform, such as these for the diphthongs *ow, ou,* and *oy*—sit down, turn around, smile with joy. If they do not hear a word with the /ou/ sound, they stand still.

◆ On index cards, print scrambled words with diphthongs, such as *wolp* (*plow*), *oty* (*toy*), and *wne* (*new*). Invite volunteers to pick a card, unscramble the word, say it, and print it on the board.

◆ Print *ou, ow, oi, oy,* and *ew* on the board. Invite children to play "Mystery Cards." Shuffle picture cards for words with diphthongs. Have volunteers pick a card, say the vowel sound in the picture name, and describe the picture without naming it. Challenge the class to guess the picture name and identify the diphthong.

Daily Phonics Practice

Prefixes re-, un-, dis-

◆ In one column on the board, print words with prefixes, such as *unclean, reread*, and *dislike*. In a second column, print their meanings randomly: *not like, read again, not clean*. Invite volunteers to draw lines to match words with their meanings.

◆ Say sentences with base words in them and ask children to say the opposite by repeating the sentences, but adding *un-* or *dis-* to the base words. For example: *I like ice cream. I dislike ice cream.*

◆ Have children form three groups and assign each group a prefix. Ask groups to list words that begin with their prefix. Then, invite them to use the words in sentences that describe things they do.

◆ Challenge groups of children to look through a dictionary to find six words that begin with the prefixes *re-, un-*, and *dis-*. Have children share their words with the class.

◆ On the board, write words to which more than one prefix can be added, such as *lock* (*relock, unlock*) and *able* (*disable, unable*). Ask volunteers to name the new words that can be made and tell what they mean.

◆ Have children form three groups and assign each group a prefix. Print these words on the board: *known, read, cover, do, lucky, make, glue, like*. Have teams tell whether their prefixes can be added to any of the words, say the new words, and write them on the board.

◆ Write these words on paper strips: *wrap, fold, load, please, fair, use*. Print the prefixes *re-, un-*, and *dis-* on the board. Let volunteers choose a word and match it with a prefix to make a new word.

◆ Let pairs of children play a guessing game. One writes a word with the prefix *re-, un-*, or *dis-*, such as *unkind*, and gives the partner a clue, such as *I'm thinking of a word that means "not kind."* The partner tries to guess the word. They then reverse roles.

◆ Encourage pairs of children to make up riddles for which the answers are words with prefixes. For example: *When you get birthday presents wrapped in paper, you do this to them.* (*unwrap*)

◆ Write the following mixed-up base words and prefixes on the board: *replease, disfair, unnew*. Invite pairs of children to divide each mixed-up word and then match the base word to the correct prefix.

Synonyms, Antonyms, Homonyms

◆ Write the following words on index cards and distribute them to ten children: *pull, tug, sad, unhappy, sick, ill, tired, sleepy, cold, chilly*. Have children read their words and pair up with those whose words have almost the same meaning.

◆ Follow the same procedure as above for words with opposite meanings: *hot, cold, low, high, light, dark, old, new, dry, wet*.

Daily Phonics Practice

- Give a group of children a list of words, such as *wet, thin, tall*, and *big*. The leader says the first word on the list. The others race to name a word that has almost the same meaning. The first to answer takes the list and serves as leader.

- Repeat the above activity for antonyms, with children providing words with opposite meanings from the ones on the list.

- Prepare sets of cards for synonyms and let children play "Synonym Concentration." Players turn over two cards at a time, trying to match words with almost the same meaning.

- Prepare sets of cards for antonyms and let children play "Antonym Concentration," matching words with opposite meanings.

- Say a word, such as *happy*, and call on a volunteer to name a synonym. (*glad*) Invite that child to say another word and ask for a synonym. Continue until several children have had a turn. Repeat for antonyms.

- Write scrambled words on the board. Call on volunteers to unscramble and write each word and then write its homonym: for example, *pira—pair, pear*, or *pare; hree—here, hear*.

- Write the headings *Synonyms, Antonyms*, and *Homonyms* on the board and have children form three teams. Hold up a word card. Team members then write a synonym, antonym, or homonym for the word under the correct heading. Award a point for each correct answer.

- Write sets of homonyms on the board, such as *pare, pair*, and *pear*. Then, ask sets of questions that can be answered with one of the homonyms. For example: *What means "to peel"? (pare) What is two of something? (pair) What is a kind of fruit? (pear)*

Teacher Notes

Teacher Notes

Teacher Notes